# COUNSELING
# A Comprehensive Profession

**Samuel T. Gladding**

University of Alabama at Birmingham

MERRILL PUBLISHING COMPANY
A Bell & Howell Information Company
Columbus   Toronto   London   Melbourne

*To Thomas M. Elmore, who first instructed me in the art and science of counseling, and patiently taught me by example how to make the process personal*

Cover: Henry Moore sculpture, *Large Oval with Points, 1970.* Columbus Museum of Art, Ohio. Gift to the Columbus Museum of Art from Lazarus, in commemoration of its 125th anniversary, the Hattie W. and Robert Lazarus Fund of The Columbus Foundation, Charles Y. and Frances N. Lazarus, Robert, Jr. and Mary K. Lazarus, Rose L. Shinbach, and Howard D. and Babette L. Sirak

Published by
Merrill Publishing Company
A Bell & Howell Information Company
Columbus, Ohio 43216

This book was set in Bookman.

Administrative Editor: Vicki Knight
Production Coordinator: Constantina Geldis
Art Coordinator: Patrick L. Welch
Cover Designer: Cathy Watterson

Library of Congress Catalog Card Number: 87–62715
International Standard Book Number: 0–675–20697–9
Printed in the United States of America
3 4 5 6 7 8 9—92 91 90

# PREFACE

The profession of counseling has changed dramatically since its inception. The initial emphasis of counselors was on vocational guidance, but each generation has focused on distinct human problems and concerns. Now counseling can truly be considered comprehensive. As such, counseling covers both preventive and remedial services spanning a wide range of people and specializations. Most texts that beginning counseling students read do not reflect the dynamic growth, scope, and development of the profession in a readable and understandable way. The texts often suffer from being brief, overly detailed, or limited in coverage, such as dealing only with general theories or a particular type of counseling. For that reason this book has been written.

The purpose of *Counseling: A Comprehensive Profession* is to introduce you to the broad spectrum of counseling—its history, theories, process, professional issues, and major specialties. The emphasis in this text is on the personhood of the counselor as well as the various approaches to counseling. Effective counseling can never be done in a cookbook fashion. As with the other helping disciplines, counseling must be personalized.

The book is divided into two main parts. The first is a 10-chapter overview. It includes a history of the profession, an examination of personal and professional qualities of effective counselors, and an exploration of psychodynamic, affective, cognitive, and behavioral counseling theories. It also looks at common aspects of the counseling process, regardless of theory, and emphasizes the importance of ethical and legal issues in counseling.

The second part centers on counseling as a speciality. These 10 chapters focus on consultation, group counseling, school and college counseling, marriage and family counseling, rehabilitation and mental health counseling, career counseling, counseling in a multicultural society, creative arts in counseling, evaluation and research in counseling, and psychological tests in counseling. As in the first part, these chapters expose the reader to classic and recent literature and focus on pragmatic aspects of counseling derived from theory. At the end of each chapter, students are challenged through a set of classroom activities to more thoroughly integrate ideas in the text with their own experiences.

A common theme in this work is that counseling has come of age. That theme is represented best in organizations such as the American Association for Counseling and Development and Division 17 (Counseling Psychology) of the American Psychological Association. Counseling is separate from clinical psychology, social work, psychiatry, and other helping professions in both its background and its emphasis. No one profession "owns" the helping process, though there are unique qualities about each profession just as there are special personal qualities needed to become a helper. It is important that counselors know what distinguishes and unites them with other helpers. This hard-core knowledge enables them to form a stronger identity and function more efficiently.

This text is the result of almost 3 years of writing and research and over 17 years of practice as a professional counselor. The project was outlined at Fairfield University in Connecticut, and the manuscript itself was written in Birmingham, Alabama. Numerous individuals have contributed to its development and growth, including Drs. Thomas M. Elmore and Wesley D. Hood at Wake Forest University and W. Larry Osborne at the University of North Carolina at Greensboro, who were all instrumental in teaching me the fundamentals of counseling and inspiring me to enter the profession; Dr. James S. Davidson, my department chair at the University of Alabama at Birmingham, for giving me writing time away from other teaching duties and for taking the photographs in this book; Dr. C. W. Yonce for his careful, constructive, and thorough critiques of the first drafts of this work; and to UAB graduate students, especially Jennifer Dorris and Marianne Dreyspring, who contributed suggestions and materials to this work. My clients in public and private counseling settings have taught me much over the years, and I am also indebted to professional colleagues at the Rockingham County Mental Health Center (North Carolina) and at James P. Cotton & Associates (Birmingham) for their contributions to my thoughts and practice.

Finally, I wish to acknowledge the contribution of the following outside readers of this manuscript: Susan Sears, Ohio State University; Paul W. Power, University of Maryland; Stephen S. Feit, Idaho State University; Alice Lawler, University of Texas at Austin; Jonell Kirby, West Virginia College of Graduate Studies; Susan Spooner, University of Northern Colorado; Angelo Boy, University of New Hampshire; Hal Adams, University of Iowa; Holly A. Stadler, University of Missouri at Kansas City; Dwight Auvenshine, University of Kentucky; and Thomas Elmore, Wake Forest University. They had excellent ideas on how to improve the manuscript, and their feedback made my job more exciting. I owe a special debt to Vicki Knight, administrative editor of the college division at Merrill Publishing, for encouraging me to complete this project on time and giving me excellent guidance and direction in my writing. In addition, my wife, Claire, has been graciously understanding, sensitive, and supportive of me through this entire process, especially during revisions and during her pregnancy with our son, Benjamin. Her patience and humor have helped brighten my days and made writing more of a joy.

*Samuel T. Gladding*

# CONTENTS

Photo by James S. Davidson III.

# CHAPTER 1

# History and Systems of Counseling

*There is a quietness that comes*
*in the awareness of presenting names*
*and recalling places*
*in the history of persons*
*who come seeking help.*
*Confusion and direction are a part of the process*
*where in trying to sort out tracks*
*that parallel into life*
*a person's past is traveled.*
*Counseling is a complex riddle*
*where the mind's lines are joined*
*with scrambling and precision*
*to make sense out of nonsense,*
*a tedious process*
*like piecing fragments of puzzle together*
*until a picture is formed.*[1]

[1]Gladding, 1978, p. 148. Copyright AACD. Reprinted with permission. No further reproduction authorized without written permission of AACD.

Counseling is distinguished from other mental health disciplines by both its history and its present emphases. Such helping professions as psychiatry and clinical psychology concentrate primarily on the treatment of severe emotional disorders. Social work deals primarily with the social and legal aspects of assisting others. In contrast, counseling focuses on the prevention of serious mental health problems through education and short-term treatment. Counselors work with persons, groups, families, and systems that are experiencing situational and developmental problems. Counseling's emphasis on prevention, education, and growth make it attractive to those seeking to make healthy transitions and to live productively (Cole & Sarnoff, 1980).

Counseling has not always been as encompassing and respected a profession. It has evolved over the years. Many people, unaware of that evolution, associate all counseling with schools or equate the word *guidance* with *counseling.* A consequence is that old ideas are often mistaken as innovations. C. H. Patterson, a pioneer in counseling, once observed that some writers in counseling journals seem "ignorant of the history of the counseling profession . . . [and thus] go over the same ground covered in publications of the 1950s and 1960s" (Goodyear & Watkins, 1983, p. 594). A similar criticism could be made of the general public. Therefore, it is important to examine the history of counseling here—a counselor informed about the evolution of the profession is more likely to make real contributions to the field.

There have always been "counselors"—people who would listen to others and help resolve difficulties. Before the 1900s, most counseling was in the form of advice or of supplying information. As a profession, counseling is quite new (Aubrey, 1977, 1982). In the United States, it developed out of a humanitarian concern to improve the lives of those adversely affected by the Industrial Revolution of the mid to late 1800s (Aubrey, 1983). The social-reform movement of the time triggered the development of school guidance and related counseling activities, such as the promotion of vocational theory (Parsons, 1909). The spread of mass public education, the emergence of psychometrics, and various changes in population makeup also influenced the growth of counseling as a profession (Aubrey, 1977; Goodyear, 1984). The overall base of counseling was and is interdisciplinary in nature (Glanz, 1974).

This chapter will introduce you to the events and circumstances that shaped modern counseling. By understanding the past, you may better appreciate present and future trends of the profession.

## DEFINITION OF COUNSELING

The word *counseling* is used in various ways. One hears of "carpet counselors," "color coordination counselors," "pest control counselors," "financial counselors," and so on. These "counselors" are most often glorified salespersons. They are to counseling what "furniture doctors" are to medicine (see Figure 1.1, p. 6). The meaning of the word *counseling* as a profession is relatively new (Belkin, 1975). It grew out of the guidance movement and in opposition to traditional psychotherapy. To explain what counseling is, these two concepts must be defined.

### Guidance

*Guidance* is a concept that "in the counseling profession has gone the way of 'consumption' in medicine" (Tyler, 1986, p. 153). An early distinction was that guidance focused on helping individuals make important choices, whereas counseling focused on helping individuals make changes. Much of the early work in guidance occurred in schools, where an adult would help a student make important decisions, such as choosing a vocation. That relationship was between unequals—teacher and pupil—and was beneficial in helping a less-experienced person find direction in life. Similarly, children have long received "guidance" from parents, ministers, scout leaders, and coaches and in the process have gained an understanding of themselves and their world (Shertzer & Stone,

"Essentially, what I hear you saying is, you've resolved your sugar/saccharin conflict, but you're still not secure with your role as a decaf drinker."

**FIGURE 1.1**

*Source:* Millard, J. (1987, May 6). *Chronicle of Higher Education, 33,* p. 49. Used with permission.

1981). This type of guidance will never become passé, because no matter what the age or stage of life, a person often needs help in making choices. Yet, such guidance is only one part of the overall service provided by professional counseling.

## Psychotherapy

*Psychotherapy* (*therapy* for short) differs significantly from counseling. Traditional psychotherapy might be described as follows (Pietrofesa, Hoffman, & Splete, 1984, pp. 6–7):

☐ Deals with the more serious problems of mental illness

☐ Emphasizes the past more than the present

☐ Emphasizes insight more than change

☐ Requires the therapist to hide rather than reveal values and feelings

☐ Requires the therapist to take the role of an expert rather than a sharing partner with the client

Psychiatrists and clinical psychologists have generally used the term to describe their work (Nugent, 1981).

Trotzer and Trotzer (1986) point out that the differences between counseling and therapy are mostly in the perception of the person providing the service. Psychotherapy most often refers to a long-term relationship (i.e., 20 to 40 sessions over a period of six months to two years) that focuses on reconstructive change. Counseling, on the other hand, "tends to be short-term, averaging 8 to 12 sessions spread out over several months" (p. 268) and to be focused on the resolution of problems. Counseling is also most often provided in an out-patient setting, whereas therapy is provided in both in-patient and out-patient settings. Some experts (Baruth & Huber, 1985; Brammer & Shostrom, 1982; Patterson, 1973) hold that there is considerable overlap in the work of counselors and psychotherapists (see Figure 1.2). They point out that some theories used in counseling are commonly referred to as therapies. Throughout this book, we will emphasize an approach of counselor and client working together even though some of the theories examined in detail are often labeled therapies and employed in a psychotherapeutic manner.

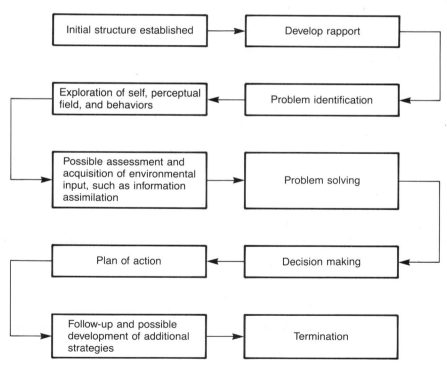

**FIGURE 1.2**  The work of counselors and that of psychotherapists have similar processes.

*Source:* From *Counseling: An Introduction* (p. 8) by J. J. Pietrofesa, A. Hoffman, H. H. Splete, 1984, Boston: Houghton Mifflin. Copyright 1982 by Houghton Mifflin. Reprinted by permission.

### Counseling

Both the American Association for Counseling and Development (AACD) and Division 17 (Counseling Psychology) of the American Psychological Association (APA) have defined counseling on numerous occasions. Their definitions contain a number of points in common, some of which follow:

☐ *Counseling is a profession.* Practitioners should complete a prescribed course of study, leading eventually to a masters or a doctorate. Counselors are members of organizations that set professional and ethical standards, and promote licensing by states and certification by national associations (Wittmer & Loesch, 1986). The processes of certification and licensure and the adherence to ethical codes assure the public that the counselor meets minimal educational and professional standards. Counselors should possess personal qualities of maturity, empathy, and warmth. Overall, counseling is active and differs considerably from just listening to problems.

☐ *Counseling deals with personal, social, vocational, and educational concerns.* Counselors work only in areas they are competent to handle. Problems dealt with depend on the counselor's background and education but may include those related to schools, colleges, mental health centers, hospitals, nursing homes, employment centers, correctional institutions, and rehabilitation settings.

☐ *Counseling is conducted with those considered within the "normal range" of functioning.* Clients have adjustment, developmental, or situational concerns, and their problems require short-term intervention. Clients are not considered "sick" but "stuck." Sometimes they just need information, but they are usually looking for a way to clarify and use the information they already possess.

☐ *Counseling is theory-based and takes place in a structured setting.* Counselors draw from a number of affective, behavioral, and cognitive theories and work in a structured environment with various individuals, groups, families, and systems.

☐ *Counseling is a process in which clients learn how to make decisions and formulate new ways of behaving, feeling, and thinking* (Smaby & Tamminen, 1978). Counselors focus on the goals their clients wish to achieve. Clients explore their present level of functioning and the changes that must be made to achieve personal objectives. Thus, counseling involves both choice and change, evolving through such distinct stages as exploration, goal setting, and action (Egan, 1986).

☐ *Counseling encompasses various subspecialties.* These include school counseling, marriage and family counseling, mental health counseling, rehabilitation counseling, and career counseling. Each has specific educational and experiential requirements for practitioners.

By combining these points, we can define counseling more precisely. *Counseling* is a relatively short-term, interpersonal, theory-based, professional activity guided by ethical and legal standards that focuses on helping persons who are basically psychologically healthy to resolve developmental and situational problems. The activity itself is a process that evolves through distinct stages. Personal, social, vocational, and educational matters are all areas of concern, and therefore the profession comprises a number of subspecialties. A practitioner must complete a required course of study on either the masters or doctoral level to be licensed or certified as a professional counselor.

## HISTORY OF COUNSELING

Most of the pioneers in the early guidance movement, which evolved into the profession of counseling, were social reformers. They saw needs in American society and took steps to fulfill those needs. Initially, these pioneers were involved primarily in educational/vocational guidance, child study, legal reform, and psychometrics. There was no recognized discipline of counseling during this early period—"no mention of counseling was made in the professional literature until 1931" (Aubrey, 1983). The *guidance movement* focused on teaching children and young adults about themselves, others, and the world of work. It was built on specific information and lessons, such as moral instruction and interpersonal relations (Nugent, 1981). Classroom teachers and administrators were the main practitioners.

One way to chart the evolution of counseling is to trace the important events and personal influences through the decades of the twentieth century. Keep in mind that the development of professional counseling, like the activity itself, was a process. Thus, some names and events will not fit neatly into a rigid chronology.

### 1900–1909

Three men are generally recognized as the prominent leaders of this period—Jesse B. Davis, Frank Parsons, and Clifford Beers.

Davis was the first person to set up a systematized guidance program in the public schools (Aubrey, 1977). As superintendent of the Grand Rapids (Michigan) school system, he suggested in 1907 that classroom teachers of English composition teach their students a lesson in guidance once a week, the purpose of which was to build character and prevent problems. Davis, influenced by such progressive American educators as Horace Mann and John Dewey, believed that proper guidance would help cure the ills of American society (Aubrey, 1977). What Davis and other progressive educators advocated was not counseling in the modern sense but a forerunner of counseling, school guidance.

The work of Frank Parsons in Boston was similar to that of Davis in its focus on growth and prevention, but the influence of Parsons was greater. Parsons, often called the Father of Guidance, is best known for having founded Boston's Vocational Bureau in 1908. The establishment of the bureau represented a major step in the institutionalization of vocational guidance. Parsons worked with young people who were in the process of making career decisions. He theorized that choosing a vocation was a matter of relating three factors—a knowledge of work, a knowledge of self, and a matching of the two (Crites, 1980). Parsons devised a number of procedures to help his clients learn more about themselves and the world of work. His book *Choosing a Vocation* (1909), published one year after his death, was quite influential, especially in Boston. For example, the superintendent of the Boston Schools, Stratton Brooks, designated 117 elementary and secondary teachers as "vocational counselors" (Nugent, 1981). The "Boston example" soon spread to other major cities as school personnel recognized the need for vocational planning. By 1910, 35 cities were attempting to emulate Boston (Lee, 1966).

Clifford Beers, a former Yale student, was hospitalized for mental illness several times during his life. He found conditions in mental institutions deplorable and exposed them in a very popular book, *A Mind that Found Itself* (1908). Beers advocated better mental-health facilities and reform in the treatment of the mentally ill. His work had an especially powerful influence on the fields of psychiatry and psychology. "Many of these people referred to what they were doing as counseling" (Hansen, Stevic, & Warner, 1986, p. 8). The influence of Beers was the impetus for the start of the mental health movement in the United States, and his work was a forerunner of mental health counseling.

### 1910s

Two important events had a profound impact on the development of counseling during this decade. The first was the founding in 1913 of the National Vocational Guidance Association (NVGA), which began publishing a bulletin in 1915 (Goodyear, 1984). In 1921, the *National Vocational Guidance Bulletin* began publication on a regular basis. It evolved in later years to become the *National Vocational Guidance Magazine* (1924–33), *Occupations, The Vocational Guidance Magazine* (1933–44), *Occupations, The Vocational Guidance Journal* (1944–52), *Personnel and Guidance Journal* (1952–84), and finally the *Journal of Counseling and Development* (1984). The importance of NVGA is that it established an association and a literature with which professionals could identify, uniting the guidance movement for the very first time.

World War I was the second important event. The U.S. Army, in order to screen its personnel, commissioned the development of numerous psychological instruments, among them the Army Alpha and Army Beta intelligence tests. Several of the Army's screening devices were employed in civilian populations after the war, and psychometrics became a popular movement.

Aubrey (1977) has observed that because the vocational guidance movement developed without an explicit philosophy, it quickly embraced psychometrics to gain a legitimate foundation in psychology. Reliance on psychometrics had both positive and negative effects. On the positive side, it gave vocational guidance specialists a stronger and more "scientific" identity. On the negative side, it distracted many of those specialists from developments in other behavioral sciences, such as sociology, biology, and anthropology.

### 1920s

The Roaring Twenties were relatively quiet for the developing guidance profession. This was a period of consolidation. Education courses for counselors, which had begun at Harvard in 1911, almost exclusively emphasized vocational guidance during the 1920s. The dominant influences on the emerging profession were the progressive theories of education and the federal government's use of guidance services with war veterans.

A notable event in the guidance movement was the certification of counselors in both Boston and New York in the mid-1920s (Lee, 1966; Nugent, 1981). Another important event was the development of the first standards for the preparation and evaluation of occupational materials (Lee, 1966). An indirect influence was the publication by Edward Strong of the Strong Vocational Interest Inventory (SVII) in 1928. Although the publication of this instrument did not have an immediate impact on the field, it set the stage for future directions.

Overall, the decade saw the guidance movement gain acceptance within American society. It was also a decade in which the narrow emphasis of the movement on vocational interests began to be challenged. Counselors were broadening their focus to include issues of personality and development.

### 1930s

The 1930s were not as quiet as the 1920s, in part because of the Great Depression (Ohlsen, 1983). A highlight of the decade was the development of the first theory of counseling, by E. G. Williamson and his colleagues at the University of Minnesota. Williamson took Frank Parsons' theory, modified it, and employed the modification in working with students. His emphasis on a directive, counselor-centered approach came to be known as the "Minnesota point of view." That approach dominated counseling for the next two decades. decades.

Another major occurrence was the broadening of counseling beyond narrow, occupational concerns. The seeds for this broadening were sown in the 1920s when Edward Thorndike and other psychologists began to challenge the vocational orientation of the guidance movement (Lee, 1966). The work of John Brewer completed that change in emphasis. Brewer saw "education as guidance" and published a book by that title in 1932. He proposed that every teacher be a counselor and that guidance be incorporated into the school curriculum as a subject. Brewer advocated that all of education should focus on preparing students to live outside of the school environment. His emphasis made counselors see vocational decisions as just one part of guidance responsibilities.

The 1930s also saw an increased involvement by the U.S. government in counseling, especially in the establishment of the U.S. Employment Service. This agency published the first edition of the *Dictionary of Occupational Titles* (DOT) in 1939. The DOT, which became a major source of career information for guidance specialists working with students and the unemployed, described known occupations in the United States and coded them according to job titles.

### 1940s

Three major events of the 1940s radically shaped the practice of counseling: the theory of Carl Rogers, World War II, and the involvement of government in counseling following the war.

Carl Rogers rose to prominence in 1942 with the publication of his book *Counseling and Psychotherapy,* which challenged the counselor-centered approach of Williamson as well as major tenets of Freudian psychoanalysis. Rogers placed the emphasis on the client and advocated what was described as a "nondirective" approach to working with clients. His ideas were both widely accepted and harshly criticized. Rogers advocated giving to clients the responsibility for their own growth. He thought that if clients had an opportunity to be accepted and listened to by a counselor, then they would begin to know themselves better and become more congruent (genuine). He described the role of the counselor as being nonjudgmental and accepting. In this role, the counselor served as a mirror, reflecting the verbal and emotional manifestations of the client.

Aubrey (1977, p. 292) has written that before Rogers the literature in guidance and counseling

> was of a very practical nature and dealt with such topics as testing, cumulative records, orientation procedures, vocations, placement functions, and so on. In addition, this early literature dealt extensively with the goals and purpose of guidance. With Rogers, a sudden change occurred and there was a new emphasis on the techniques and methods of counseling, research, and refinement of counseling technique, selection, and training of future counselors, and the goals and objectives of counseling. Guidance, for all intents and purposes, would suddenly disappear as a major consideration in the bulk of the literature and be replaced by a decade or more of concentration on counseling.

The so-called Rogers revolution had a major impact on both counseling and psychology. Each still identifies Rogers as a central figure in its professional history.

With the advent of World War II, a request was made by the U.S. government for counselors and psychologists to help in the selection and training of specialists for the military and for industry (Ohlsen, 1983). The war also brought about a new way of looking at vocations for men and women. That so many women worked outside the home during the war made a lasting impact. Traditional occupational sex roles began to be questioned, and greater emphasis was placed on personal freedom than ever before.

After the war, the U.S. Veterans Administration (VA) funded the training of counselors and psychologists through the granting of stipends and paid internships for those engaged in graduate study. The VA also "rewrote specifications for vocational counselors and coined the term 'counseling psychologist'" (Nugent, 1981, p. 25). Monies made available through the VA and the GI bill (benefits for veterans) influenced teaching professionals in graduate education to define their curriculum offerings more precisely. Counseling psychology, as a profession, began to move further away from its historical alliance with vocational guidance.

## 1950s

"If one decade in history had to be singled out for the most profound impact on counselors, it would be the 1950s" (Aubrey, 1977, p. 292). Indeed, the 1950s produced at least four major events that dramatically changed the history of counseling: the establishment of the American Personnel and Guidance Association (APGA), the establishment of Division 17 (Counseling Psychology) within the American Psychological Association (APA), the National Defense Education Act (NDEA), and the introduction of new guidance and counseling theories.

**APGA.** The American Personnel and Guidance Association (APGA) grew out of the American Council of Guidance and Personnel Associations (ACGPA), a loose confederation of organizations "concerned with educational and vocational guidance and other personnel activities" (Harold, 1985, p. 4). It operated from 1935 to 1951. The major drawback of ACGPA was its lack of power to commit its members to any course of action. APGA was formed in 1952 with the purpose of more formally organizing those groups interested in guidance, counseling, and personnel matters. Its original four divisions were the American College Personnel Association (Division 1), the National Association of Guidance Supervisors and Counselor Trainers (Division 2), NVGA (Division 3), and the Student Personnel Association for Teacher Education (Division 4) (Harold, 1985). Super (1955) argues that during its early history APGA was merely an interest group and not a professional organization, because it did not originate or enforce standards for membership.

**Division 17.** In 1952 the Division of Counseling Psychology (Division 17) of the American Psychological Association was formally established. The formation of the division required the dropping of the term *guidance* from what had formerly been the Counseling and Guidance Division of APA. Part of the impetus for the division's formation came from the Veterans Administration, but the main impetus came from members of APA who were interested in working with a more "normal" population than that seen by clinical psychologists (Whiteley, 1984). Once created, Division 17 became more fully defined. Super (1955), for instance, distinguished between counseling psychology and clinical psychology, holding that counseling psychology was more concerned with normal human growth and development than was clinical psychology and that counseling psychology was influenced in its approach by both vocational counseling and humanistic psychotherapy. Despite the work of Super, counseling psychology has had a difficult time establishing a clear identity within APA (Whiteley, 1984). Yet the existence of the division has had a major impact on the growth and development of counseling as a profession.

**NDEA.**  A third major event in the 1950s was the passage in 1958 of the National Defense Education Act (NDEA), which was enacted following the Soviet Union's launching of *Sputnik I.* The act's primary purpose was to identify scientifically and academically talented students and promote their development. The act provided funds for upgrading school counseling programs through Title V-A. It also established counseling and guidance institutes and provided funds and stipends to train counselors through Title V-B. NDEA was extended to include elementary counseling in 1964 (Nugent, 1981). By 1965 the number of school counselors had exceeded 30,000 (Armour, 1969).

**New Theories.**  The last major event during this decade was the refinement of new guidance and counseling theories. Before 1950, debates among counselors centered on whether directive or nondirective counseling was best. During the 1950s, debate gradually shifted away from exclusive focus on these two positions. Behavioral theories, like Joseph Wolpe's systematic desensitization, began to gain influence. Cognitive theories also made an appearance, as witnessed by the growth during the decade of Albert Ellis's Rational Emotive Therapy and Eric Berne's Transactional Analysis. Learning theory, self-concept theory, Donald Super's work in career development, and advances in developmental psychology also made an impact (Aubrey, 1977). By the end of the decade, the number and complexity of theories associated with counseling had grown considerably.

## 1960s

The initial focus of the 1960s was on counseling as a developmental profession. Gilbert Wrenn set the tone for the decade in his widely influential book *The Counselor in a Changing World* (1962). His emphasis, reinforced by such other prominent professionals as Leona Tyler and Donald Blocher, was on working with others to resolve developmental needs. Wrenn's book had influence throughout the 1960s, though its impact was moderated by such events as the Vietnam War and the Civil Rights movement, as well as by the growth of competing points of view.

One powerful influence to emerge during the decade was humanistic counseling theories of Dugald Arbuckle, Abraham Maslow, and Sidney Jourard. Also important was the phenomenal growth of the group movement. The emphasis of counseling shifted from a one-on-one encounter to small group interaction. Behavioral counseling emerged as even more important with the appearance of John Krumboltz's *Revolution in Counseling* (1966), in which he promoted learning (beyond insight) as the root of change. Thus, the developmental focus with which the decade had began had become sidetracked. As Aubrey (1977) notes, "The cornucopia of competing counseling methodologies presented to counselors reached an all-time high in the late 1960s" (p. 293).

Two other noteworthy trends occurred during this decade. One was begun by the passage of the 1963 Community Mental Health Centers Act, which authorized the establishment of community mental health centers. These centers opened up opportunities for the employment of counselors outside educational settings. A second trend was the beginning of more professionalism within APGA and the continued professional movement with Division 17 of APA. In 1961, APGA published a "sound code of ethics for counselors" (Nugent, 1981, p. 28). Also during the 1960s, Loughary, Stripling, and Fitzgerald (1965) edited an APGA report that summarized role definitions and training standards for school counselors. Division 17, which had further clarified the definition of a counseling psychologist at the 1964 Greyston Conference, began in 1969 the publication of a professional journal, *The Counseling Psychologist.*

### 1970s

The 1970s saw the emergence of several trends. Among the more important were the rapid growth of counseling outside educational settings, the formation of helping-skills programs, the beginning of licensure for counselors, and the further development of APGA as a professional organization for counselors.

***Counseling Diversification.*** The rapid growth of counseling outside educational settings started in the decade when mental-health centers and community agencies began to employ counselors. Before this time almost all counselors had been employed in educational settings, usually public schools. But the demand for school counselors decreased in the 1970s as the economy underwent several recessions and the number of school-age children began to decline. The rate of growth for school counselors was 1–3 percent each year from 1970 through the mid-1980s, compared to an increase of 6–10 percent during the 1960s (Shertzer & Stone, 1981). In addition, the number of counselor-education programs increased from 327 in 1964 to about 475 by 1980 (Hollis & Wantz, 1980). This dramatic rise in the number of counselor-education programs meant that there were more counselors competing for the jobs available (Stienhauser, 1985).

The diversification of counseling caused specialized training to be offered in counselor-education programs. It also meant the development of new concepts of counseling. For example, Lewis and Lewis (1977) coined the term *community counselor* for a new type of counselor, who could function in multidimensional roles regardless of employment setting. Many community counseling programs were established, and counselors became more common in such agencies as mental health clinics, hospices, employee assistance programs, and substance abuse centers. Equally as striking, and more dramatic in growth, was the formation of the American Mental Health Counselor Association (AMHCA) within APGA. Founded in 1976, AMHCA quickly became one of the largest divisions within APGA and united mental health counselors into a professional organization in which they could better define their roles and goals.

***Helping-Skills Programs.***   The 1970s saw the development of helping-skills programs, which concentrated on relationship and communication skills. Begun by Truax and Carkhuff (1967) and Ivey (1971), they tended to be programs that would actually teach basic counseling skills to professional and nonprofessionals alike. The emphasis was humanistic. It was assumed that there were certain fundamental skills that must be mastered to establish satisfactory personal interaction. A bonus for counselors who received this type of training was that they could teach it to others rather easily. Thus, one way counselors could now consult was to teach some of their skills to others, mainly teachers and paraprofessionals. In many ways, this trend was a new version of Brewer's concept of education as guidance.

***State Licensure.***   By the mid-1970s, state boards of examiners of psychologists had become more restrictive. Some of their restrictions, such as barring graduates of counseling programs in education departments from taking the psychology licensure exam, caused considerable tension, not only between APA and APGA but also within the APA membership itself (Ohlsen, 1983). The result was a move by APGA toward state and national licensure for counselors. By 1987, 25 states had passed either counselor licensure laws or certification laws.

***A Strong APGA.*** During the 1970s, the APGA emerged as an even stronger professional organization. Several changes altered its image and function, one of which was the building of its own headquarters in Alexandria, Virginia. APGA also began to question its professional identification. "Guidance" and "personnel" seemed outmoded in defining the organization's emphases.

In 1973, the Association of Counselor Educators and Supervisors (ACES), a division of APGA, outlined the standards for a masters degree in counseling. In 1977, ACES approved guidelines for doctoral preparation in counseling (Stripling, 1978). During the decade, the membership of the organization increased to almost 40,000, and three new divisions were chartered: the Association for Religious and Value Issues in Counseling (ARVIC), the Association for Specialists in Group Work (ASGW), and the Association for Humanistic Education and Development (AHEAD).

### 1980s

In 1983, APGA changed its name to the American Association for Counseling and Development (AACD), a name that aptly reflected the organization's emphases. By 1987, AACD had a membership of over 55,000. It was composed of the following divisions and organizational affiliates:

☐ American College Personnel Association (ACPA)

☐ American Mental Health Counselors Association (AMHCA)

☐ American Rehabilitation Counseling Association (ARCA)

☐ American School Counselor Association (ASCA)

☐ Association for Adult Development and Aging (AADA)

☐ Association for Counselor Education and Supervision (ACES)

☐ Association for Humanistic Education and Development (AHEAD)

☐ Association for Measurement and Evaluation in Counseling and Development (AMECD)

☐ Association for Multicultural Counseling and Development (AMCD)

☐ Association for Religious and Value Issues in Counseling (ARVIC)

☐ Association for Specialists in Group Work (ASGW)
☐ Military Educators and Counselors Association (MECA)
☐ National Career Development Association (NCDA)
☐ National Employment Counselor Association (NECA)
☐ Public Offender Counselors Association (POCA)

## SYSTEMS OF COUNSELING

A review of the history of counseling would not be complete without examining the systems to which counselors adhere. A *system* is a unified and organized set of ideas, principles, and behaviors. Systems associated with counseling are concerned with diagnosis, theory, ethics, and law. Counselors have both borrowed and created systems that fit the profession. Indeed, the strength of counseling ultimately depends on a continuation of that process. We will briefly look at problems associated with systems, especially in the most important areas of counseling, diagnosis and theory. Ethical and legal aspects of counseling will be dealt with in Chapter 10.

### Unsystematic Beginnings

That counseling is not governed by one dominant theoretical or diagnostic system is hardly surprising considering its historical development. In many respects, the history of counseling parallels that of psychology, which evolved from various disciplines. Like psychology, counseling has passed through a number of stages, some of which have tended to regenerate themselves, such as the emphasis on humanistic education in both the 1930s and 1970s and the emphasis on authoritarian and vertical counseling relationships in the 1940s and 1980s (Watkins & Goodyear, 1984). As far back as the late 1940s, the lack of a system for counseling was noted. Robert Mathewson (1949, p. 73) observed that counseling was in "a search for a system . . . to win free from inadequate frames borrowed from traditional philosophy and education, from psychology, from political formulations underlying democratic government, from the concepts of physical science, etc."

Until the late 1940s, counseling used a variety of systems. Because the profession was without an organizational base, different factions defined what they did according to the system that suited them best. Some counseling professionals recognized the need for a unifying systematic approach to their discipline, but the unplanned growth of the movement proved an obstacle.

Leo Goldman, while editor of the *Personnel and Guidance Journal*, promoted the first major exploration for a unifying system of counseling (1974). Before Goldman, such counseling pioneers as Ralph Berdie (1972) had proposed that counseling should cast off its "borrowed procedures, theories, and methods from a variety of disciplines" (p. 451) and define itself more fully. Berdie suggested counselors become "applied behavioral scientists." But it was Goldman who devoted an entire issue of his journal to the innovative Cube concept (Figure 1.3).

The *Cube*, presented as a systematic way of organizing counseling services, was a radical idea and the cause of much discussion. In a thought-provoking article introducing the Cube, Clyde Parker noted (1974, p. 350), "For too long we have allowed the profession to be directed by what is new and different rather than by any systematic exploration of the alternative modes available. Using the Cube as a guide, we can see that our efforts might range from individual, direct, therapeutic interventions to attempts at creating a more humane institutional environment by effective use of the media."

The Cube model describes three dimensions of counselor intervention—the target, the purpose, and the method (Morrill, Oetting, & Hurst, 1974). Although the model generated a tremendous

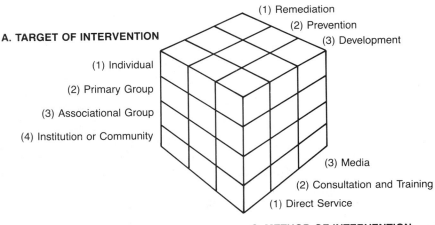

**FIGURE 1.3**   The Cube.

*Source:* From "Dimensions of Counselor Functioning" by W. H. Morrill, E. R. Oetting, & J. C. Hurst, 1974, *Personnel and Guidance Journal, 52,* p. 355. Copyright 1972 by Morrill, Oetting, and Hurst. Reprinted by permission.

amount of research in its presentation of 36 potential areas of counseling, the Cube's overall impact on counseling was relatively small. A main reason was the tremendous number of competing ideas. Also, the Cube did not address theory directly.

### Recent Developments

Other attempts to develop systems unique to counselors can be seen in the helping-skills programs of Carkhuff and Ivey and in the classification system for clients' problems created by Celotta and Telasi-Golubcow (1982). The problem with these approaches is their limited scope. For instance, the main helping skills are not unique to counseling; rather, they are applicable in any area of human relations. The system of classification and treatment by Celotta and Telasi-Golubcow is more geared to counseling. Clients' problems are classified along a continuum from behavioral specific to general systems (Figure 1.4). The authors suggest that counselors orient their initial approach with clients at Level 5 (behavior problems), shifting emphasis as clients disclose their problems. The more specific the problems and the shorter their duration, the quicker counselors can help. When problems are conceptualized as part of the system, a referral is made. Although this model gives counselors appropriate guidelines to follow, it lacks a thorough conceptualization of the mission of counseling.

Several other systematic perspectives on counseling have also been introduced. Corey, for instance, presents nine primary theories employed in counseling and psychotherapy, delineates their similarities and differences, and shows how counselors can draw from all or some of them in formulating a style of counseling (1986). His model is rich in information and shows how systematic integration of theories is a difficult process. In a similar integrative way, Baruth and Huber (1985) have organized basic counseling and psychotherapy approaches according to the main orientation of theories, such as cognitive, affective, or behavioral. One of their premises is that counselors should work from a theoretical orientation but with a systematic synthesis of other therapeutic positions. They label their approach the "pragmatic therapeutic position" (p. 9). Their view is well thought out. By knowing what theories are available and how they may best be used, counselors are able to be effective in their work; the system requires counselors to gain a knowledge of theory and applicability simultaneously. Although both of these approaches are good, they represent syntheses rather than innovations in counseling systems.

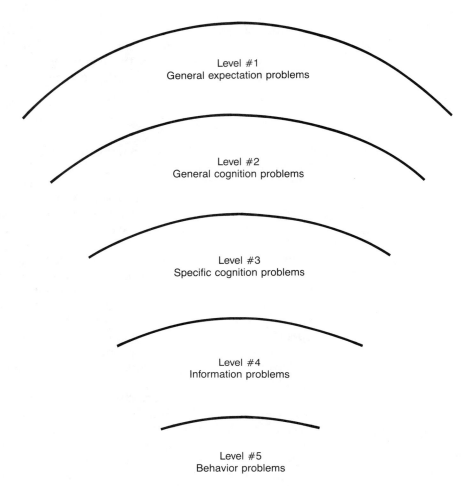

**FIGURE 1.4**  A continuum of clients' problems.

*Source:* From "A Problem Taxonomy for Classifying Clients' Problems" by B. Celotta & H. Telasi-Golubcow, 1982, *Personnel and Guidance Journal, 61,* p. 74. Copyright AACD. Reprinted with permission. No further reproduction authorized without further permission of AACD.

## Present Systems

Counseling has developed dramatically during this century, but it still lacks a clear systems base. It is like a person who mounted a horse and rode off in all directions (Ungersma, 1961). At present, counselors primarily rely on well-developed counseling theories, such as those covered in this text. For diagnosis, most counselors use the third edition of the *Diagnostic and Statistical Manual of*

*Mental Disorders* (DSM-III) (American Psychiatric Association, 1980). This is a comprehensive but controversial manual (Schacht, 1985). The DSM-III is appropriate for some counseling approaches and a general knowledge of it is valuable, if not critical, for counselors who frequently work with other helping professionals (Seligman, 1983, 1986).

The systems deficiency may be alleviated somewhat in the future if AACD and Division 17 within APA achieve stronger professional identities and if counseling focuses more on its own interests. Barclay (1983) advocates that counselors become better informed about theories of counseling and about counseling's history. Kuhn (1969) points out that shifts in thinking take place over time, as inquirers find present systems inadequate to explain existing data. There is hope that a unifying system may develop in counseling as the profession matures through research and experience. There are some indications that such a development may be about to occur (Newton & Caple, 1985).

## SUMMARY

This chapter presents a survey of counseling. Counseling, as distinguished from guidance and traditional psychotherapy, is concerned with the developmental and situational difficulties of otherwise well-functioning persons. It is a short-term, theory-based approach to the resolution of problem areas, and it focuses on personal, social, vocational, and education concerns. Counselors work in a variety of settings and adhere to professional, legal, and ethical standards as defined by the organizations with which they are affiliated and the states in which they reside.

An examination of the history of counseling shows that the profession has an interdisciplinary base. Its history began in the vocational guidance movement. Counseling also has a base in psychometrics and psychology. The involvement of the government in counseling during and after World War I, the Great Depression, World War II, and the *Sputnik* era has had a major impact on the development of counseling. Such innovators as Frank Parsons, Clifford Beers, Jesse Davis, John Brewer, E. G. Williamson, Carl Rogers, Gilbert Wrenn, John Krumboltz, Alan Ivey, and Leo Goldman have shaped the development of the profession.

Counseling has never developed a unifying systems approach. Until that occurs, AACD and its divisional affiliates, along with Division 17 of APA, will continue to refine the standards for the education of counselors. We address these standards in Chapter 2.

## CLASSROOM ACTIVITIES

1. How do you distinguish between the terms *counseling, psychotherapy,* and *guidance?* In groups of three, choose a spokesperson to argue that the terms are similar and another spokesperson to argue that the terms are distinctive. The third person should give feedback to both persons about what was said.
2. What decade do you consider to be the most important for the development of counseling? Is there a decade you consider least important? Be sure to give reasons for your position.
3. What is your understanding of counseling now that you have read this chapter? Discuss how counseling is similar to or different from what you expected. Be explicit.
4. From the innovators mentioned in this chapter, or from a list suggested by your instructor, investigate in more detail the life and influence of a historical figure in counseling. Share your information with the class as a whole.
5. Invite a professional counselor into your classroom to speak on his or her observations about how counseling has changed over the decades. Ask what system(s) unite counseling. How does this person's experience compare with what you have learned in this chapter?

## REFERENCES

American Psychiatric Association (1980). *Diagnostic and statistical manual of mental disorders* (3rd ed.). Washington, DC: Author.

Armour, D. J. (1969). *The American counselor.* New York: Russell Sage.

Aubrey, R. F. (1977). Historical development of guidance and counseling and implications for the future. *Personnel and Guidance Journal, 55,* 288–295.

Aubrey, R. F. (1982). A house divided: Guidance and counseling in twentieth century America. *Personnel and Guidance Journal, 60,* 198–204.

Aubrey, R. F. (1983). The odyssey of counseling and images of the future. *Personnel and Guidance Journal, 61,* 78–82.

Barclay, J. R. (1983). Searching for a new paradigm in counseling. *Personnel and Guidance Journal, 62,* 2.

Baruth, L. G., & Huber, C. H. (1985). *Counseling and psychotherapy: Theoretical analyses and skills applications.* Columbus, OH: Merrill.

Belkin, G. S. (1975). *Practical counseling in the schools.* Dubuque, IA: William C. Brown.

Berdie, R. F. (1972). The 1980 counselor: Applied behavioral scientist. *Personnel and Guidance Journal, 50,* 451–456.

Brammer, L. M., & Shostrom, E. L. (1982). *Therapeutic psychology.* Englewood Cliffs, NJ: Prentice Hall.

Brewer, J. M. (1932). *Education as guidance.* New York: Macmillan.

Celotta, B., & Telasi-Golubcow, H. (1982). A problem taxonomy for classifying clients' problems. *Personnel and Guidance Journal, 61,* 73–76.

Cole, H. P., & Sarnoff, D. (1980). Creativity and counseling. *Personnel and Guidance Journal, 59,* 140–146.

Corey, G. (1986). *Theory and practice of counseling and psychotherapy* (3rd ed.). Monterey, CA: Brooks/Cole.

Crites, J. O. (1981). *Career counseling: Models, methods, and materials.* New York: McGraw-Hill.

Egan, G. (1986). *The skilled helper* (3rd. ed.). Monterey, CA: Brooks/Cole.

Gladding, S. T. (1978). In the midst of the puzzles and counseling journey. *Personnel and Guidance Journal, 57,* 148.

Glanz, E. G. (1974). *Guidance foundations, principles and techniques.* Boston: Allyn & Bacon.

Goldman, L. (1974). Introduction: How this issue came to be. *Personnel and Guidance Journal, 52,* 346.

Goodyear, R. K. (1984). On our journal's evolution: Historical developments, transitions, and future directions. *Journal of Counseling and Development, 63,* 3–9.

Goodyear, R. K., & Watkins, C.E., Jr. (1983). C. H. Patterson: The counselor's counselor. *Personnel and Guidance Journal, 61,* 592–597.

Hansen, J. C., Stevic, R. R., & Warner, R. W. (1986). *Counseling: Theory and process* (4th ed.). Boston: Allyn & Bacon.

Harold, M. (1985). Council's history examined after 50 years. *Guidepost, 27* (10), 4.

Hollis, J. W., & Wantz, R. A. (1980). *Counselor preparation.* Muncie, IN: Accelerated Development.

Ivey, A. E. (1971). *Microcounseling: Innovations in interviewing training.* Springfield, IL: Thomas.

Krumboltz, J. D. (Ed.) (1966). *Revolution in counseling.* Boston: Houghton Mifflin.

Kuhn, T. S. (1969). *The structure of scientific revolutions.* Chicago: University of Chicago Press.

Lee, J. M. (1966). Issues and emphases in guidance: A historical perspective. In J. M. Lee & N. J. Pallone (Eds.), *Readings in guidance and counseling.* New York: Sheed & Ward.

Lewis, J., & Lewis, M. (1977). *Community counseling: A human services approach.* New York: Wiley.

Loughary, J. W., Stripling, R. O., & Fitzgerald, P. W. (Eds.) (1965). *Counseling: A growing profession.* Washington, DC: American Personnel and Guidance Association.

Mathewson, R. H. (1949). *Guidance policy and practice.* New York: Harper.

Morrill, W. H., Oetting, E. R., & Hurst, J. C. (1974). Dimensions of counselor functioning. *Personnel and Guidance Journal, 52,* 354–359.

Newton, F. B., & Caple, R. B. (1985). Once the world was flat: Introduction and overview. *Journal of Counseling and Development, 64,* 163–164.

Nugent, F. A. (1981). *Professional counseling.* Monterey, CA: Brooks/Cole.

Ohlsen, M. M. (1983). *Introduction to counseling.* Itasca, IL: Peacock.

Parker, C. A. (1974). The new scope of counseling. *Personnel and Guidance Journal, 52,* 348–350.

Parsons, F. (1909). *Choosing a vocation.* Boston: Houghton Mifflin.

Patterson, C. H. (1973). *Theories of counseling and psychotherapy.* New York: Harper & Row.

Pietrofesa, J. J., Hoffman, A., & Splete, H. H. (1984). *Counseling: An introduction.* Boston: Houghton Mifflin.

Rogers, C. R. (1942). *Counseling and psychotherapy.* Boston: Houghton Mifflin.

Schacht, T. E. (1985). DSM-III and the politics of truth. *American Psychologist, 40,* 513–521.

Seligman, L. (1983). An introduction to the new DSM-III. *Personnel and Guidance Journal, 61,* 601–605.

Seligman, L. (1986). *Diagnosis and treatment planning in counseling.* New York: Human Sciences Press.

Shertzer, B., & Stone, S. C. (1981). *Fundamentals of guidance.* Boston: Houghton Mifflin.

Smaby, M. H., & Tamminen, A. W. (1978). Counseling for decisions. *Personnel and Guidance Journal, 57,* 106–110.

Steinhauser, L. (1985). A new PhD's search for work: A case study. *Journal of Counseling and Development, 63,* 300–303.

Stripling, R. O. (1978). ACES guidelines for doctoral preparation in counselor education. *Counselor Education and Supervision, 17,* 163–166.

Super, D. E. (1955). Transition: From vocational guidance to counseling psychology. *Journal of Counseling Psychology, 2,* 3–9.

Trotzer, J.P., & Trotzer, T. B. (1986). *Marriage and family.* Muncie, IN: Accelerated Development.

Truax, C. B., & Carkhuff, R. R. (1967). *Toward effective counseling and psychotherapy: Training and practice.* Chicago: Aldine.

Tyler, L. E. (1986). Farewell to guidance. *Journal of Counseling and Human Service Professions, 1,* 152–155.

Ungersma, A. J. (1961). *The search for meaning.* Philadelphia: Westminister.

Watkins, C.E., Jr., & Goodyear, R. K. (1984). C. H. Patterson: Reflections on client-centered therapy. *Counselor Education and Supervision, 23,* 178–186.

Whiteley, J. M. (1984). Counseling psychology: A historical perspective. *The Counseling Psychologist, 12,* 2–109.

Wittmer, J. P., & Loesch, L. C. (1986). Professional orientation. In M. D. Lewis, R. L. Hayes, & J. A. Lewis (Eds.), *The counseling profession* (pp. 301–330). Itasca, IL: F. E. Peacock.

Wrenn, C. G. (1962). *The counselor in a changing world.* Washington, DC: American Personnel and Guidance Association.

Photo by James S. Davidson III.

# CHAPTER 2

# The Effective Counselor: Personal, Theoretical, and Educational Factors

*In the midst of a day*
*that has brought only grey skies, hard rain,*
*and two cups of lukewarm coffee,*
*You come to me with Disney World wishes*
*Waiting for me to change into:*
*a Houdini figure with Daniel Boone's style*
*Prince Charming's grace and Abe Lincoln's wisdom*
*Who with magic words, a wand,*
*frontier spirit, a white horse, and perhaps a smile*
*Can cure all troubles in a flash.*
*But reality sits in a green-cushioned chair—*
*lightning has struck a nearby tree,*
*Yesterday ended another month,*
*I'm uncomfortable sometimes in silence,*
*And unlike fantasy figures*
*I can't always be*
*what you see in your mind.*[1]

---

**P**eople become counselors for many reasons. Some reasons, like some of the people involved, are healthier than others. A small percentage of entry-level students decide to pursue a career in counseling because of the potential for advancement and recognition or because of the need for self-therapy (Pietrofesa, Hoffman, & Splete, 1984). Others choose a career in counseling because of unsatisfied needs for intimacy, acceptance, or nurturance (Patterson & Eisenberg, 1983). But most students seek to become counselors for broader and more alturistic reasons. Regardless of whether one chooses the field for a career or not, studying the theories and techniques associated with counseling can be helpful. As Cavanagh (1982) points out, by studying counseling one may gain insight into one's own life, obtain knowledge and skill in relating to others, and come to realize how the counseling process works.

The effectiveness of counseling depends on numerous variables, including the background, education, skill, and experience of the counselor. The process itself usually has some kind of effect: if not beneficial, then most likely harmful (Bergin, 1980; Carkhuff, 1969; Ellis, 1984; Mays & Franks, 1980). In this chapter we will explore the personal, theoretical, and educational factors that influence the counselor and examine the nature of the counseling process itself.

## PERSONAL CHARACTERISTICS

There are a number of personal characteristics associated with being an effective counselor. According to Cormier and Cormier (1985), "the most effective helper is one who has successfully integrated the personal and scientific parts of himself or herself— in other words, who has achieved a balance of interpersonal and technical competence" (pp. 11–12). They list six qualities of effective counselors:

☐ *Intellectual competence*  Counselors must have a thorough knowledge of many theories, as well as the desire and ability to learn.

☐ *Energy*  Counseling is emotionally draining and physically demanding. Counselors must have the ability to be active in their sessions.

☐ *Flexibility*  Effective counselors are not tied to one specific theory or set of methods. Instead, they adapt what they do to meet the needs of their clients.

☐ *Support*  The counselor supports the client in making his or her own decisions, helps engender hope and power, and avoids trying to rescue the client.

☐ *Goodwill*  The nature of goodwill encompasses such qualities as the counselor's desire to work on behalf of the client in a constructive way that ethically promotes client independence.

☐ *Self-awareness*  This quality includes knowledge of one's self, including attitudes and feelings about self and the ability to recognize how and what factors affect those attitudes and feelings.

According to Holland (1977a), specific personality types are attracted to certain work environments and correspond best with those environments. The environment in which a counselor works is primarily a social and problem-oriented one. It calls for skill in interpersonal relationships and for creativity. The more aligned the personality of the counselor is to the environmental setting, the more effective and satisfied that counselor will be.

Wiggins and Weslander (1979) found empirical support for Holland's hypothesis. They studied the personality traits and rated the job performance of 320 counselors in four states. In general, those counselors rated "highly effective" scored highest on the social and artistic scales of the Vocational Preference Inventory (Holland, 1977b). Counselors rated as "ineffective" in general scored highest on the realistic and conventional scales of that test. Other factors, such as sex, age, and level of education, were not found to be significant in predicting effectiveness. The results of this research indicate that the personality of the counselor is related to effectiveness in the profession. But the relationship is extremely complex—persons of many different personality types manage to find places within the broad field of counseling and to make significant contributions to the profession and to their clients.

There are several other personality-related factors that strongly influence counselor effectiveness, including stability, harmony, constancy, and purpose within the counselor's life. The effectiveness of counseling is related to the personal "togetherness" of the counselor (Carkhuff & Berenson, 1967). Counselors experience the same difficulties as everyone else. They must deal with aging, illness, death, marriage, parenting, careers, and a host of other common situations. The critical issue is not whether they will face personal problems, but how they will deal with them (Corey, Corey, & Callanan, 1984). Some strategies for dealing with problems are healthier than others, such as trying to remain objective, accepting and confronting the situation, and asserting one's wishes. Counselors who develop healthy personal lives are more likely to be effective on a professional level because they can concentrate on their clients' problems rather than on their own.

To maintain a healthy approach, successful counselors use preventive measures to avoid *burnout*, i.e., becoming emotionally and/or physically drained to the point that they cannot perform their functions meaningfully. No one can forever function adequately if he or she never steps out of the professional role. Counselors must develop interests outside of counseling and avoid taking their work home, either mentally or physically. A number of researchers (Boy & Pine, 1980; Pines & Aronson, 1981; Savicki & Cooley, 1982; Watkins, 1983) suggest ways counselors can avoid or treat burnout. Among their suggestions are:

☐ Associating with healthy individuals
☐ Working with committed colleagues and with organizations that have a sense of mission
☐ Being reasonably committed to a theory of counseling
☐ Using stress-reduction exercises
☐ Modifying environmental stressors
☐ Engaging in self-assessment
☐ Periodically examining and clarifying counseling roles, expectations, and beliefs
☐ Obtaining personal therapy

☐ Setting aside free and private time

☐ Maintaining an attitude of detached concern when working with clients

☐ Retaining an attitude of hope

Also influencing the effectiveness of counselors is the range of characteristics they display to others. Rogers (1961) thinks that the personhood of counselors is more important than their techniques. He lists three essential characteristics for them to display—congruence (genuineness), positive regard, and empathy. He considers empathy the most important of these three.

Cavanagh (1982) also stresses the importance of the person in counseling. He cites research that indicates effective counseling is more dependent on the personality of the counselor than on the counselor's knowledge or skills. His point is not that knowledge and skills are unimportant but that education will not change the basic characteristics of a person. Successful counselors display certain core qualities, such as self-knowledge, competence, good psychological health, trustworthiness, honesty, strength, warmth, patience, and sensitivity. Corey, Corey, and Callanan (1984) also list a set of ideal traits of effective counselors, including goodwill, the ability to be present for others, a recognition of one's own personal power, a willingness to be vulnerable and take risks, self-respect and self-appreciation, a willingness to serve as a model for clients, and a growth orientation. Both lists are well made. Effective counselors, on a personal level, have a vision of where they are going in life. They are growing as persons and are helping others do the same.

In summing up previous research about the personalities and interests of counselors, Auvenshine and Noffsinger (1984, p. 151) report that:

> Counselors as a group generally share strong interests in social service, scientific, literary, and persuasive activities. They are more interested in working with people than with data or things. Effective counselors must be emotionally mature, stable, and objective. They must have self-awareness and be secure in that awareness, incorporating their own strengths and weaknesses realistically. They express strong needs for affiliation and nurturance. They are generally perceived by others as being outgoing, friendly, patient, sensitive, compassionate, and practical.

No person possesses all of the qualities of a "perfect" counselor, but because of temperament, background, and experience, some are better suited to become counselors than others. Those whose personal attributes match the demands of the profession are more likely to be personally and professionally satisfied with the role of counselor.

## THE THEORETICAL APPROACH

Only recently have there been numerous theoretical approaches to counseling. When professional counseling began to emerge in the late 1940s and early 1950s there were only two major theoretical orientations—Williamson's clinical-counseling (directive) approach and Rogers's client-centered (nondirective) approach. Psychoanalysis was accepted as a general background for all counselors (Nugent, 1981). Such a limited choice of theoretical models made the process of becoming a counselor less complicated than now, but no less intense. Today, as then, an effective counselor decides which theory or theories and methods to use on the basis of educational background, philosophy, and the needs of clients. Not all approaches are appropriate for all counselors or clients, but a theoretical base is necessary for every effective counselor.

### Importance of Theory

Theory is the underpinning of good counseling. Without theory as a guide, a counselor operates in darkness. Brammer and Shostrom (1977, p. 28) stress the practical value of good theory to the counselor:

> Theory helps to explain what happens in a counseling relationship and assists the counselor in predicting, evaluating, and improving results. Theory provides a framework for making scientific observations about counseling. Theorizing encourages the coherence of ideas about counseling and the production of new ideas. Hence, counseling theory can be very practical by helping to make sense out of the counselor's observations.

Boy and Pine (1983) elaborate on the practical value of theory by suggesting that theory is the *why* behind the *how* of counselor roles—theory provides a framework within which counselors can operate. Those guided by theory can more completely meet the demands of their roles, because they have reasons for what they do. Boy and Pine point out six functions of theory that make counseling practical:

☐ Theory helps counselors find unity and relatedness within the diversity of existence.

☐ Theory compels counselors to examine relationships they would otherwise overlook.

☐ Theory gives counselors operational guidelines by which to work and helps them in evaluating their development as professionals.

☐ Theory helps counselors focus on relevant data and tells them what to look for.

☐ Theory helps counselors assist clients in the effective modification of their behavior.

☐ Theory helps counselors evaluate both old and new approaches to the process of counseling. It is the base from which new counseling approaches are constructed.

### Eclectic Counseling

Many professional counselors are *eclectic* in their use of theory and techniques. An eclectic approach is the reported emphasis of some 25 percent of counselor-education programs nationwide (Hollis & Wantz, 1986). Counselors who embrace this approach use various theories to match the needs of various clients. An eclectic approach can be hazardous to the counseling process if the counselor is not thoroughly familiar with all the theories involved.

The approach of undereducated counselors is sometimes sarcastically referred to as "electric"—they try any and all methods that "turn them on." The problem with an "electric" orientation (an unsystematic eclectic approach) is that the counselor can do more harm than good if there is no understanding about what is contributing to the ultimate goal of helping the client.

Cavanagh (1982) proposes a "healthy" eclectic approach to counseling that requires the counselor to have: (1) a sound knowledge and understanding of the counseling theories used; (2) a basic integrative philosophy of human behavior, one that brings together disparate parts of differing theories into a meaningful collage; and (3) a flexible means of fitting the approach to the client, not vice versa. Counselors who follow Cavanagh's model may operate effectively with an eclectic approach. The critical variables in being a "healthy" eclectic counselor are both a mastery of theory and an acute sensitivity to knowing what approach to use when, where, and how (Harman, 1977).

### The Basis of Theory

Ohlsen (1982) implicitly agrees with Cavanagh about healthy eclecticism. He points out that most counseling theories have been developed by exceptional practitioners who have formulated theories on the basis of experience and observation. Yet most theorists are somewhat tentative about their positions, realizing that no one theory will fit all situations. Indeed, one theory may not be adequate for the same client over an extended period. Thus, counselors must choose their theoretical positions carefully and regularly reassess them.

Some theoretical models are more comprehensive than others, and effective counselors are aware of which theories are most comprehensive and for what reasons. Hansen, Stevic, & Warner (1986) list five requirements of a good theory. An effective theoretical position is:

☐ *Clear, easily understood, and communicable*  It is coherent and not contradictory.

☐ *Comprehensive*  It encompasses explanations for a wide variety of phenomena.

☐ *Explicit and heuristic*  An effective theory generates research because of its design.

☐ *Specific in relating means to desired outcomes*  Good theory has within it a way of achieving a desired end product.

☐ *Useful to its intended practitioners*  It provides guidelines for research and practice.

In addition to these five qualities, a good theory for a given counselor is one that matches the counselor's own personal philosophy of helping. Shertzer and Stone (1974) suggest that a counseling theory must fit a counselor like a suit of clothes fits a person. Some theories, like some suits of clothes, need tailoring—an effective counselor realizes the importance of alterations. A counselor should learn a wide variety of counseling theories and know how to apply each without violating its internal consistency (Auvenshine & Noffsinger, 1984). If the counselor departs from the theory, he or she must have good reasons for doing so. Theories are always translated into appropriate counseling behaviors and are used as a way of producing and evaluating a client's progress.

## EDUCATIONAL QUALITIES

Few people have the ability to work effectively as counselors without formal education in human development and counseling (Kurpius, 1986). The level of education needed is directly related to the level at which one works. There are three levels of helping relationships—nonprofessional, paraprofessional, and professional. Each level of this hierarchy assumes that the helper has acquired the helping skills necessary for the task (Figure 2.1).

Nonprofessional helpers may be friends, colleagues, untrained volunteers, or supervisors who try to be helpful to those in need but who possess various degrees of wisdom and skill. Paraprofessional helpers are usually human-service workers who have received some formal training in human relations skills but who work as part of a

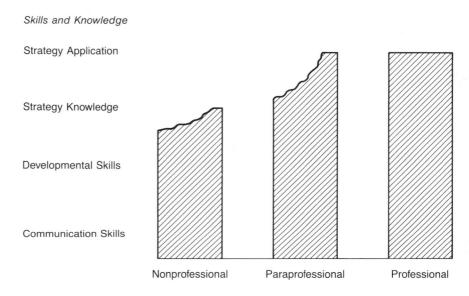

**FIGURE 2.1** The three levels of helping relationships and the skills and knowledge required for each.

*Source:* From EFFECTIVE HELPING, by Barbara F. Okun. Copyright © 1987, 1982, 1976 by Wadsworth, Inc. Reprinted by permission from Brooks/Cole Publishing Company, Monterey, California 93950.

team instead of as individuals. The types of occupations filled by people on this level include mental health technicians, child care workers, probation personnel, and youth counselors. Professional helpers are specially educated to provide assistance, such as psychiatrists, psychologists, and counselors.

## *Professional Helping Specialties*

Each professional specialty has its own educational and practice requirements. Psychiatrists earn a medical degree and complete a residency in psychiatry. They must pass both national and state examinations in order to practice. Psychologists may earn a doctor of philosophy degree (Ph.D.), a doctor of education degree (Ed.D.), or a doctor of psychology degree (Psy.D.). Their coursework and internships may be concentrated in clinical, counseling, or school-related areas. All states license psychologists, but the requirements for licensure differ from state to state. Most clinically oriented psychologists attain listing in the *National Register of Health Service Providers,* which has uniform standards for inclusion.

Professional counselors obtain either a masters degree or a doctorate in counselor education and complete internships in such specialty areas as rehabilitation counseling, school counseling, agency counseling, career counseling, and marriage and the family counseling. They are usually certified by the National Board of Certified Counselors (see Chapter 10 for requirements) or licensed to practice by individual states or both.

The words *licensure* and *certification* have specific meanings. Fretz and Mills (1980, p. 7) define licensure as "the statutory process by which an agency of government, usually a state, grants permission to a person meeting predetermined qualifications to engage in a given occupation and/or use a particular title and to perform specified functions." Certification, on the other hand, is either a professional, statutory, or nonstatutory process "by which an agency or association grants recognition to an individual for having met certain predetermined professional qualifications. Stated succinctly, certification . . . is a 'limited license'—that is, the protection of title only" (p. 7). Neither licensure nor certification ensures in and of itself that a professional helper will be effective, but these processes are first steps in the process of promoting quality by assuring that practitioners who define themselves by a title actually meet the qualifications implied by such a designation.

### Two Counseling Emphases

Within the profession of counseling, there are two areas of emphasis—counseling psychology and counselor education. Elmore (1984) maintains the two emphases have common roots and share many concerns. Gladding (1985), on the other hand, sees counselor education as a separate emerging profession. Hollis and Wantz (1986) summarize the accreditation criteria for both counseling psychology programs and counselor education programs.

An accredited counseling psychology program is one that has met the standards drawn up by the American Psychological Association in cooperation with the Division of Counseling Psychology (Division 17). These programs are valued because they assure both students and prospective employers that at least minimum skills necessary to practice psychology as a profession have been achieved. Graduates of accredited programs thus have an advantage in obtaining employment and licensure. Not every program that applies for accreditation obtains this recognition, but those that do have met the following standards (Hollis & Wantz, 1986, p. 82):

☐ Professional psychology programs generally are located in universities or schools of professional psychology that offer doctoral training and are approved by one of the six regional accreditation bodies recognized by the Council on Post-Secondary Accreditation (COPA).

☐ Program must be clearly identified and labeled as a psychology program and must be a recognizable, coherent organization entity.

☐ Faculty must be well qualified and must have clear authority and primary responsibility for all aspects of the program.

☐ The plan of study must be integrated and organized with assurance of breadth of exposure to the field of psychology including a curriculum with equivalency of at least 3 academic years of full-time resident graduate study. The course work must include scientific and professional ethics and standards, research design and methodology, statistics and psychological measurement, biological bases of behavior, cognitive-affective bases of behavior, social bases of behavior, individual behavior, and courses in specialty areas.

☐ Supervised practicum, internship, and field or laboratory training must be included. The minimum practicum experience is 300 hours, of which at least 200 hours are in direct service experience and 50 hours of formally scheduled supervision. Internship must be full-time for 1 year or the equivalent with an experience of at least 1500 hours.*

An accredited program in counselor education is one recognized at either the masters or doctoral level. The accrediting body for counselor education programs is the Council for Accreditation of Counseling and Related Educational Programs (CACREP). This independent body evolved from the efforts of the Association for Counselor Education and Supervision (ACES) and the American Association for Counseling and Development (AACD) to establish standards and guidelines for counseling independently of the National Council for Accreditation of Teacher Education (NCATE). On the masters level, CACREP accredits programs in community/ agency counseling, school counseling, and student personnel services in higher education. Graduates from accredited masters programs have an advantage in obtaining admittance to accredited counselor education doctoral programs, meeting the educational requirements for counselor licensure/certification, and obtaining employment as a counselor. The following standards must be met (Hollis & Wantz, 1986, pp. 84–85):

☐ The program must have objectives that were developed by the faculty in the institution of higher education where offered. The institution must provide a graduate program in counselor education with opportunity for full-time study throughout the academic year.

☐ The program of study includes a core of courses with content applicable to the following areas: human growth and development, social and cultural foundations, helping relationships, groups, consultation, lifestyle and career development, appraisal of the individual, research and evaluation, and professional orientation.

☐ The program must provide specialized studies necessary for practice in different work settings so that each student may gain skills needed to work effectively in the professional setting where the student plans to practice.

☐ Specific counseling practica have sufficient duration and continuity to assure optimum professional development as evidenced through such outcome measures as evaluation ratings by program and site supervisors, assessments by employers, current and former students, and by other performance indicators and qualitative evaluation methods.

☐ Ordinarily, practica will be one quarter time of a work week extended over a minimum of one academic term. Variations should be described and justified in the self-study.

☐ Specific internships have sufficient duration and continuity to assure optimum professional development as evidenced through such outcome measures as evaluation ratings by program and site supervisors, assessments by employers, current and former students, and by other performance indicators and qualitative evaluation methods. It is desirable that the internship be a paid experience.

☐ Ordinarily, internships will be full-time of a work week extended over a minimum of one academic term or half-time of a work week extended over two academic terms. Variations should be described and justified in the self-study.

☐ Research facilities must be available within the counselor preparation institution to faculty and students.*

Doctoral studies criteria are different. CACREP standards for counselor education programs that offer the Ph.D. or Ed.D. are (Hollis & Wantz, 1986, pp. 85–86):

---

*Reprinted from *Counselor Preparation 1986–1989.* Copyright 1986 by Accelerated Development Inc. Reprinted by permission.

☐ The doctoral program consists of a minimum of 4 academic years of graduate preparation, including the entry program and a year of internship. A minimum of 1 academic year of full-time graduate study beyond the entry program is required.

☐ Supervised experiences include the completion of at least 1 academic year (36 weeks) of full-time internship.

☐ Competencies in statistics, research design, and other research methodology are to be obtained by all students.

☐ In addition to the core areas of preparation, students are to gain a depth of knowledge and skills in one or more areas such as learning theory, career guidance, research, testing, or evaluation.

☐ Beyond course work and seminars students are to be provided opportunities to participate in conferences, workshops, special training programs, and other professional activities that will assist in bridging the gap between the campus and the professional world.*

Graduates of CACREP accredited doctoral programs have more career opportunities because of their background and, like their counterparts in counseling psychology, have acquired more prestige. A growing number of graduate schools are applying for either APA or CACREP accredited counseling programs because of the benefits and recognition for both themselves and their students.

### Education in Other Counseling Specialty Areas

Within the field of counselor education, new specialties are emerging. Nejedlo, Arredondo, and Benjamin (1985) outline the knowledge bases and skills for counselors working with the following populations or situations: adults, athletes, business/industry, schools (elementary, middle, secondary, postsecondary), gerontology, marriage and family, mental health, private practice, and spiritual. The emphasis is on personal and professional renewal, as well as program renewal. According to these authors, there must be a renewed emphasis on core knowledge within counseling as well as within specialties and they stress core knowledge in the area shown in Figure 2.2

Finally, remember that one's education as a counselor is never finished. There are always new theories and research reports to read and evaluate. Counselors who stop reading professional publi-

---

*Reprinted from *Counselor Preparation 1986–1989.* Copyright 1986 by Accelerated Development Inc. Reprinted by permission.

**FIGURE 2.2**   Core knowledge bases for all counselors.

| | |
|---|---|
| ☐ the helping relationship | ☐ individual assessment |
| ☐ counseling theory | ☐ individual potential |
| ☐ transpersonal counseling | ☐ life span development |
| ☐ change theory | ☐ lifelong learning |
| ☐ learning theory/styles | ☐ developmental programming |
| ☐ group counseling | ☐ substance abuse |
| ☐ family systems theory | ☐ prevention |
| ☐ referral process | ☐ societal trends |
| ☐ life style and career | ☐ social/cultural foundations |
|    development | ☐ cultural pluralities |
| ☐ world of work | ☐ human rights |
| ☐ domestic and world politics | ☐ sexual equality |
| ☐ domestic and world | ☐ moral issues |
|    economics | ☐ ethics |
| ☐ political process | ☐ systems management |
| ☐ professional orientation | ☐ technological systems |
| ☐ personality theory | ☐ resource management |
| ☐ abnormal behavior | ☐ grant writing |
| ☐ physical disabilities | ☐ evaluation |
| ☐ human behavior | ☐ research |
| ☐ holistic health | |

*Source:* From *Imagine: A Visionary Model for the Counselors of Tomorrow* (p. 6) by R. J. Nejedlo, P. Arredondo, L. Benjamin, 1985, DeKalb, IL: George's Printing. Reprinted by permission of Robert J. Nejedlo.

cations or attending in-service workshops and conventions quickly find their skills and abilities dated. Part I of Section A of the AACD Ethical Standards states that counselors should make "continuous efforts to improve professional practices, teaching, service, and research" (see Appendix A for AACD Ethical Standards). Engaging in "continuous efforts" of this type may be expensive in terms of time and money, but the cost of not keeping up professionally (i.e., becoming incompetent or outdated) is much higher.

## SUMMARY

The qualities necessary to become an effective counselor will continue to evolve as specialty areas in counseling increase in number. Yet there will always be some basic qualities on personal, theoretical, and educational levels that must be achieved.

The core personality of the counselor is crucial. Persons feel more comfortable working in one counseling environment rather than another because of interests, disposition, and abilities. The majority of effective counselors have social and artistic interests (as measured by Holland's Vocational Preference Inventory) and enjoy working with people in a variety of ways. They are generally characterized as warm, friendly, open, sensitive, patient, and creative in helping others. They are consistently working on their own mental health and strive to avoid becoming burned out and ineffective.

Effective counselors are also aware of the importance of good theory to sound practice. They know that theory is the *why* behind the *how* of technique and that nothing is more practical than mastering major theoretical approaches to counseling. Effective counselors are not unsystematic and capricious in using theories, and many of them practice a "healthy" eclectic way of working. They also interpret theories in accordance with the setting in which they are located and in accordance with their own personalities.

Effective counselors most likely have gone through an accredited counseling program or its equivalent on either a doctoral or masters level. They have also achieved the skills and experience necessary to work in counseling specialty areas and have obtained licensure or certification or both. Effective counselors, regardless of specialty, keep their knowledge up to date by participating in continuing education programs.

## CLASSROOM ACTIVITIES

1. Research indicates that some personality types are more suited to be counselors than others. Suppose you do not possess the ideal personality for this profession. What are some ways you could compensate for a deficiency? Do you think John Holland's typology is right? In groups of three, discuss your reaction to the qualities of personality associated with effective counseling.

2. Review the personal, theoretical, and educational qualities ideal counselors possess. Discuss how you think these qualities might differ if you were counseling outside of the United States, such as in India, Germany, Egypt, or Peru. Share your opinions with the class as a whole.

3. Do you think the accreditation standards of Division 17 and CACREP are more similar than different? What specifically makes you think so? In groups of four discuss which standards you prefer and your rationale.

4. If you were going to research the question of counselor effectiveness, what questions would you want answered? Pick an area of counselor effectiveness not covered in this chapter and conduct a brief review of the literature. Report your results to the class.

5. Investigate the licensure and certification laws in your state for psychiatrists, psychologists, social workers, and counselors. Compare how the requirements are similar and dissimilar. How do the standards for counselors compare with those of other helping professionals?

# REFERENCES

Auvenshine, D., & Noffsinger, A. L. (1984). *Counseling: An introduction for the health and human services.* Baltimore: University Park Press.

Bergin, A. E. (1980). Negative effects revisited: A reply. *Professional Psychology, 11,* 93–100.

Boy, A. V., & Pine, G. J. (1980). Avoiding counselor burnout through role renewal. *Personnel and Guidance Journal, 59,* 161–163.

Boy, A. V., & Pine, G. J. (1983). Counseling: Fundamentals of theoretical renewal. *Counseling and Values, 27,* 248–255.

Brammer, L. M., & Shostrom, E. L. (1977). *Therapeutic psychology: Fundamentals of counseling and psychotherapy* (3rd ed.). Englewood Cliffs, NJ: Prentice-Hall.

Carkhuff, R. R. (1969). *Helping and human relations* (Vol. I & II). New York: Holt, Rinehart & Winston.

Carkhuff, R. R., & Berenson, B. G. (1967). *Beyond counseling and psychotherapy.* New York: Holt, Rinehart & Winston.

Cavanagh, M. E. (1982). *The counseling experience.* Monterey, CA: Brooks/Cole.

Corey, G., Corey, M. S., & Callanan, P. (1984). *Issues & ethics in the helping profession* (2nd ed.). Monterey, CA: Brooks/Cole.

Cormier, W. H., & Cormier, L. S. (1985). *Interviewing strategies for helpers* (2nd ed.). Monterey, CA: Brooks/Cole.

Ellis, A. (1984). Must most psychotherapists remain as incompetent as they are now? In J. Hariman (Ed.), *Does psychotherapy really help people?* Springfield, IL: Thomas.

Elmore, T. M. (1984). Counselor education & counseling psychology: A house divided? *ACES Newsletter, 44,* 4, 6.

Fretz, B. R., & Mills, D. H. (1980). *Licensing and certification of psychologists and counselors.* San Francisco: Jossey-Bass.

Gladding, S. T. (1973). Reality sits in a green-cushioned chair. *Personnel and Guidance Journal, 54,* 222.

Gladding, S. T. (1985). History and systems of counseling: A course whose time has come. *Counselor Education and Supervision, 24,* 325–331.

Hansen, J. C., Stevic, R. R., & Warner, R. W. (1986). *Counseling: Theory and process* (4th ed.). Boston: Allyn & Bacon.

Harman, R. L. (1977). Beyond techniques. *Counselor Education and Supervision, 17,* 157–158.

Holland, J. (1977a). *The self-directed search.* Palo Alto, CA: Consulting Psychologists Press.

Holland, J. L. (1977b). *The vocational preference inventory.* Palo Alto, CA: Consulting Psychologists Press.

Hollis, J. W., & Wantz, R. A. (1986). *Counselor preparation 1986–1989.* Muncie, IN: Accelerated Development.

Kurpius, D. J. (1986). The helping relationship. In M. D. Lewis, R. L. Hayes, & J. A. Lewis (Eds.), *The counseling profession* (pp. 96–129). Itasca, IL: Peacock.

Mays, D. T., & Franks, C. M. (1980). Getting worse: Psychotherapy or no treatment— The jury should still be out. *Professional Psychology, 11,* 78–92.

Nejedlo, R. J., Arredondo, P., & Benjamin, L. (1985). *Imagine: A visionary model for the counselors of tomorrow.* DeKalb, IL: George's Printing.

Nugent, F. A. (1981). *Professional counseling.* Monterey, CA: Brooks/Cole.

Okun, B. (1982). *Effective helping* (2nd ed.). Monterey, CA: Brooks/Cole.

Patterson, L. E., & Eisenberg, S. (1983). *The counseling process.* Boston: Houghton Mifflin.

Pietrofesa, J. J., Hoffman, A., & Splete, H. H. (1984). *Counseling: An introduction*

(2nd ed.). Boston: Houghton Mifflin.

Pines, A., & Aronson, E. (1981). *Burnout: From tedium to personal growth.* New York: Free Press.

Rogers, C. R. (1961). *On becoming a person.* Boston: Houghton Mifflin.

Savicki, V., & Cooley, E. J. (1982). Implications of burnout research and theory for counselor educators. *Personnel and Guidance Journal, 60,* 415–419.

Shertzer, B., & Stone, S. C. (1974). *Fundamentals of counseling.* Boston: Houghton Mifflin.

Watkins, C. E., Jr. (1983). Burnout in counseling practice: Some potential professional and personal hazards of becoming a counselor. *Personnel and Guidance Journal, 61,* 304–308.

Wiggins, J., & Weslander, D. (1979). Personality characteristics of counselors rated as effective or ineffective. *Journal of Vocational Behavior, 15,* 175–185.

Photo by James S. Davidson III.

CHAPTER **3**

# The Theory and Practice of Individual Counseling: Psychoanalytic Approaches

*I know how the pressure can build sometimes*
*In your own metallic tea-kettle world,*
*Sporadically you whistle to me,*
*At other times you explode!*
*Somewhere beneath that noisy facade*
*(In silence or stillness perhaps)*
*Feelings might flow with quickness and strength,*
*Like the Dan or the Shenandoah,*
*But now they incessantly boil in your mind*
*Steam-filling dark shadows and choking conversation.*[1]

Counseling, by definition, is a process that involves interpersonal relationships (Patterson, 1985). Frequently, it is conducted on an individual level where an atmosphere of trust is fostered between counselor and client that ensures communication, exploration, change, and growth. In counseling, a client gains the benefit of immediate feedback from the counselor about behaviors, feelings, and plans. Overall, the amount of growth and change that takes place in any type of counseling depends on these four variables:

the counselor

the client

the setting

the theoretical orientation

We have already examined some of the more universal qualities of an effective counselor. Certain characteristics seem to distinguish these counselors, including a good understanding of self and others, an awareness of the importance of counseling theory, and a sound educational background. The goals and personalities of clients and counselors have a powerful impact on each other and on the counseling process itself. The setting in which counseling is conducted is also critical; counselors respond to client needs in different ways in different settings, such as schools, rehabilitation agencies, and mental health centers. The focus of this chapter, as well as the next three, will be on theoretical orientation, specifically, theoretical orientations of counselors in individual situations.

## THEORY INTO PRACTICE

With over 200 approaches to individual counseling in use, counselors have a wide variety of theories from which to choose (Corsini, 1981; Herink, 1980). Effective counselors scrutinize the theories they employ for proven effectiveness and for a match to personal beliefs about the nature of people and change. Most counseling approaches fall within four broad categories:

psychoanalytic

cognitive

affective

behavioral

We will examine certain well documented theories under each of these headings. For each theory, we will first look at the background of the principal founder or founders. As Corsini (1984) says, "There appears to be a concordance between the personality of a psychotherapy innovator and the system he or she has developed" (p. 10). Then, each theory will be examined in these terms:

view of human nature

role of the counselor

goals

techniques

An evaluation of strengths and limitations will end the examination. As you study each theory, ask yourself which would be comfortable for you to use. Speculate about how you might use each approach and with what types of clients.

In this chapter, Freudian (classical) psychoanalytic theory will be covered because of its dominance in a variety of counseling approaches (Corsini, 1984). Adlerian theory will also be covered because of its close historical link to classical psychoanalysis and its importance in counseling. Before delving into either theory, however, we will briefly examine the wide impact psychoanalytic theories have had overall on counseling.

### Psychoanalytic Theories

From a historical point of view alone, psychoanalytic theories are important. They were among the first to gain recognition and acceptance by the general public. Sigmund Freud is the person most often associated with these approaches, and it was the genius of

Freud that created the original ideas associated with psychoanalysis. Many prominent theorists of counseling (e.g., Alfred Adler, Albert Ellis, Rollo May, and Fritz Perls) were directly influenced by Freud's concepts, either through association with Freud himself or through use of his ideas. Other theorists (e.g., Carl Rogers and B. F. Skinner) have developed theories in direct opposition to Freud's ideas. Still other theorists (e.g., Carl Jung, Anna Freud, Erik Erikson, Harry Stack Sullivan, Karen Horney, and Heinz Kohut) have used modified Freudian concepts in developing their own theories. Sigmund Freud and psychoanalysis permeate counseling literature. To be uninformed about psychoanalysis and its concepts is to be an undereducated counselor.

## CLASSICAL PSYCHOANALYTIC THEORY

### Freud

The life of Sigmund Freud has been the focus of many books. His official biographer, Ernest Jones, wrote a definitive three-volume work (1953, 1955, 1957) on the life of Freud and the development of his ideas.

Sigmund Freud was born at Freiburg, Austria, in 1856, the first son of his father's second marriage. He was given special privileges by his mother, who had higher hopes for Sigmund than she did for the five daughters and two sons born after him. In 1860, Freud's father moved the family to Vienna, and there Freud spent most of the remainder of his life.

Freud, an excellent student, was limited in his occupational choices because of his financial limitations and Jewish background. Deciding to pursue medicine, he entered the University of Vienna in 1873 and received his medical degree in 1881, mastering research methods as well as the normal coursework. He married Martha Bernays in 1886, and fathered six children, the youngest of whom, Anna, became famous in her own right as a child psychoanalyst.

Freud supported his family through his private practice in psychiatry, working primarily with hysterics. Initially, he used hypnosis as his main form of treatment, a technique he had mastered in France under the tutelage of neurologist Jean Charcot. Freud discovered that much of his success depended on the relationship he developed during the treatment process rather than on the hypnosis itself, leading him to explore how he might use that relationship in combination with hypnosis.

Freud had been impressed during medical school with Joseph Breuer's cathartic method of treating hysterics, in which Breuer had his patients relive painful experiences and work through emotional events suppressed for years. Breuer's method employed the use of hypnosis, but Freud added a new twist to it by pressing his hand on patients' foreheads whenever they would begin to verbally block out materials. In the process of touching the forehead, Freud assured his patients they could remember long-forgotten important events and thoughts. This method Freud called free association. Freud used free association to explore the unconscious minds of his patients, and the material uncovered in the process became the stuff of interpretation and analysis. Thus, "psychoanalysis" was born. His work with others, as well as four years of self-analysis, gave him new insight into the nature of persons, and he began to stress the importance of the unconscious in the understanding of personality.

Many of his colleagues, and later the general public, were outraged by Freud's emphasis on the importance of sexuality and aggression in the etiology of personality. Nevertheless, his ideas attracted a number of followers, and in 1902 he formally organized in his home what became known in 1908 as the Viennese Psychoanalytic Society. This group acquired international prominence when Freud and some of his followers accepted an invitation in 1908 to lecture at Clark University in the United States. Despite the displacements of wars and a number of personal and professional setbacks, Freud and the theory of psychoanalysis continued to grow and develop. The establishment of professional journals and international congresses devoted to the theory, as well as the prolific and heuristic writing of Freud himself, has assured the prominence of psychoanalysis in history. Freud died in London in 1939, a refugee from the Nazi occupation of Austria.

### View of Human Nature

An understanding of Freud is essential if one is to understand why various counseling approaches have developed as they have. His theory, generally referred to as psychoanalysis, evolved throughout Freud's lifetime, but many of the main tenets of it were set down in his books *The Interpretation of Dreams* (1900/1955), *New Introductory Lectures on Psychoanalysis* (1923/1933), and *The Ego and the Id* (1923/1947).

Freud's view of human nature is dynamic; that is, he believes there is the transformation and exchange of energy within one's personality (Hall, 1954). Much of what Freud described, however, is metaphorically written because a majority of the hypotheses he proposed could not be proven scientifically at the time (Hergenhahn, 1984). Nevertheless, it was Freud's hope that his theories would eventually be empirically verified, and he developed techniques of working with his patients that were based on this premise.

For Freud, human nature is explained in terms of a conscious mind, a preconscious mind, and an unconscious mind. The *conscious* mind is attuned to events in the present, to an awareness of the outside world. The *preconscious* mind is an area between the conscious and unconscious minds and contains aspects of both. Within the preconscious are hidden memories or forgotten experiences that can be remembered if a person is given the proper cues.

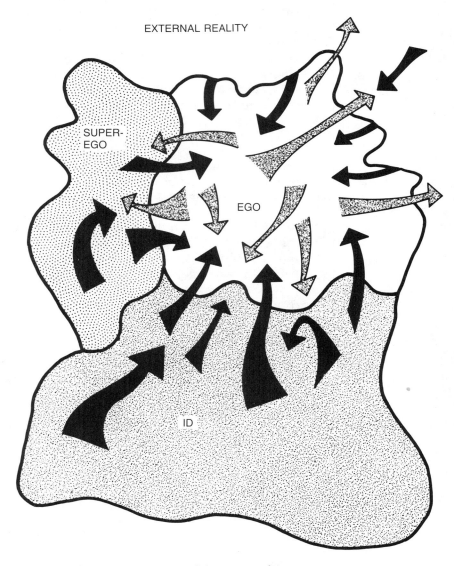

**FIGURE 3.1**  The three parts of the personality.

Source: *From Abnormal Psychology: Current Perspectives* (3rd ed.), Richard R. Bootzin (coordinating author). Copyright © 1980 by Random House, New York, NY. Reprinted by permission of Random House.

For example, a person may recall another person's name after a long separation if enough reminders are generated. Finally, beneath the preconscious mind is the *unconscious* mind, the most powerful and least understood part of the personality.

***Id, Ego, and Superego.*** The personality, according to Freud, consists of three parts—id, ego, and superego (Figure 3.1). The id and the superego are confined to the unconscious; while the ego operates primarily in the conscious as well as in the preconscious and unconscious. The *id* comprises the basic inherited givens of the personality and is present from birth. It is amoral, impulsive, and irrational and works according to the *pleasure principle.* The id pursues what it wants, because it cannot tolerate tension. The id operates through drives, instincts, and images (e.g., dreaming, hallucinating, and fantasizing)—a thought process known as the *primary process.* Although primary-process thinking may bring temporary relief, it is ultimately not satisfying. Thus, the id discharges energy to the ego, which is another way of obtaining what it wants.

If left on its own and empowered, the id would probably destroy a person or cause trouble by acting on the primitive aggressive and sexual drives it harbors. Those who have not grown beyond letting their ids serve as a guide for action lack insight into the consequences of what they are doing.

The id contains basic life energy, collectively known as *eros,* and also basic death instincts, known as *thanatos.* At first Freud associated eros with sexuality, but later he modified this idea, describing all life-preserving instincts as eros and the psychic energy that went with them as *libido.* That each person has some sort of death wish was the result of Freud's observing the destructiveness of World War I and his belief that since humans are composed of inorganic matter they ultimately have a desire to return to this state of being. The premise of thanatos was never fully developed, but Freud thought that any acts of aggression or foolishly dangerous behaviors, such as taking unnecessary risks, were displays of thanatos.

To keep the person from being either too self-indulgent or too morally restrained, the *ego* moderates the wishes and desires of the id and superego. The ego is the second system to develop, after the id and before the superego. Initially, the ego keeps the id from getting out of control. It is often called "the executive of the mind" when it is fully developed because of the way it functions to keep the desires of the id and superego in check while realistically helping the person to interact with the outside world. The ego works according to the *reality principle,* reality being what exists (Hall,

1954). As such, the ego devises ways to achieve appropriate goals, obtain energy for activities from the id (the source of all energy), and keep the person in harmony with the environment. The ego's way of thinking is known as the *secondary process.* This process is nothing more than rationally thinking through situations that develop. A strong ego is essential to healthy functioning.

The *superego,* in contrast to the id, is the moral branch of the mind, operating according to what is ideal. The superego, arising from moral teachings of a child's parents, strives for perfection. Consequently, the superego is said to function according to the *moral principle.* It rewards those who follow parental and societal dictates and do what they have been taught through a mechanism called the *ego ideal.* For example, children who have been taught by their parents that neatness is a virtue will feel good when they keep a neat room. On the other hand, those who act against what they have been taught are punished through the part of the superego called the *conscience,* which induces guilt. The superego locks a person into rather rigid moral patterns if given free reign (Leak and Christopher, 1982). Since the goal is perfection, the superego sometimes forces people into restrained action or no action when they face a dilemma.

***Developmental Stages.*** In addition to the three levels of personality, psychoanalysis is built on what Freud referred to as psychosexual developmental stages. Counselors who work psychoanalytically should understand at which stage a client is functioning because the stages are directly linked to the plan of treatment. Each of the four main stages concerns a zone of pleasure that is dominant at a particular time. In the first stage, the *oral stage,* the mouth is the chief pleasure zone. Children under the age of one are in this stage and obtain basic gratification from sucking and biting. In the second stage, the *anal stage,* children of age one to two delight in either withholding or eliminating feces during toilet training. This stage involves the first really significant conflict between the child's internal instincts and external demands.

In the third stage, the *phallic stage,* children of ages three through five attempt to resolve their sexual identities. The chief zones of pleasure are the sex organs, and members of both sexes must work through their sexual desires in a conflict of feelings known as the *Oedipus complex.* Freud thought that the conflict was clearer and was more completely resolved in boys than girls. Initially, both boys and girls are attracted to their mother because she is the source of great pleasure. They both see their father as a rival for the mother's love and attention. Feelings about the mother change, however, as boys and girls discover their own sexual identities.

For a boy, there is a desire to possess the mother sexually. Yet there is a fear that if he makes his wishes known, the father, who is bigger and stronger, will become angry and castrate him. A boy assumes that his penis is the source of conflict between him and his father and that girls, because they lack a penis, have been castrated. Although the boy may feel hostile toward the father, he represses his desire for his mother and eventually comes to identify with the father, thus gaining vicarious satisfaction through father/mother interactions.

The Oedipus complex for the girl, sometimes called the Electra complex, is less clearly resolved. A young girl comes to notice that she does not have a penis and that boys do. Freud says she blames her mother for the lack of this valued organ and envies her father for possessing one ("penis envy"). Thus, she has both negative and positive feelings toward each parent and is sexually ambivalent at the end of the stage. She takes some consolation from her ability to have babies, since boys cannot; it may be especially gratifying to her to have male children.

The wishes of young boys and girls are not manifested directly during the phallic stage. Rather, they are disguised in the form of dreams, fantasy, and play. Nevertheless, the wishes are real and if not resolved will lead to future intrapersonal and interpersonal difficulties. Freud thought the basic ingredients of the adult personality had formed by the end of the phallic stage.

After the phallic stage, between ages 6 and 12, is a quiet period known as *latency.* It is a time when there is little manifest interest in sexuality. Instead, energy is focused on peer activities and personal mastery of cognitive learning and physical skills. Around puberty the last of the psychosexual phases occurs, the *genital stage.* If all has gone well previously, each gender takes more interest in the other and normal heterosexual patterns of interaction appear. If there have been unresolved difficulties in any of the first three stages (collectively known as the pregenital stages), the person may have difficulty adjusting to the adult responsibilities that begin at the genital stage. Freud believed that two difficulties could arise in the pregenital stages—excessive frustration or overindulgence. In such cases, the person would become "fixated" (or arrested) at that level of development and would become overly dependent in the use of so-called defense mechanisms.

**Defense Mechanisms.** *Ego defense mechanisms* are what protect a person from being overwhelmed by anxiety, through adaptation to situations or through distortion or denial of events. Defense mechanisms are normal and operate on an unconscious level. Anna Freud (1936) and other ego psychologists later elaborated on Freud's ideas about defense mechanisms. Among the main defense mechanisms are the following:

☐ *Repression* The mechanism by which the ego involuntarily excludes from consciousness any unwanted or painful thoughts, feelings, memories, or impulses. Repression is the most basic defense mechanism, the one on which others are built. The ego must use energy to keep excluded areas from consciousness, but sometimes the repressed thoughts "slip out" in dreams or verbal expressions. Repression is considered the "cornerstone or foundation-stone of psychoanalysis" (Nye, 1981, p. 29).

☐ *Projection* The mechanism by which a person attributes an unwanted emotion or characteristic to someone else in an effort to deny that the emotion or characteristic is a part of one's self. For example, a man may say that his boss is mad at him instead of that he is mad at his boss.

☐ *Reaction Formation* The mechanism by which anxiety-producing thoughts, feelings, or impulses are repressed and their opposites expressed. For example, a hostess at a party may shower a disliked guest with attention. Reaction formation is often detected because of the intensity in which the opposite emotion is expressed.

☐ *Displacement* The mechanism by which energy is channeled away from one object to an alternative, that is, to a safe target. For instance, a person who has had a hard day at the office may come home and kick the dog. A positive form of displacement is known as *sublimation,* in which a drive that cannot be expressed directly is channeled into constructive activities. For example, those who for some reason are unable to express themselves sexually may take care of children. Freud thought sublimation was a major means of building civilization.

☐ *Regression* The mechanism by which a person returns to an earlier stage of development. For example, a child when placed under stress may begin to wet the bed. Virtually all people regress if placed under enough pressure.

☐ *Rationalization* The mechanism by which a person finds reasonable explanations for unreasonable or unacceptable behaviors in order to make them sound logical and acceptable. For example, a client might say: "I did it because everyone else was" or "I really didn't think it was going to be worth the time I'd have to spend, so I didn't do it."

☐ *Denial*  The mechanism by which an unpleasant or traumatic event or situation is not acknowledged consciously. Denial protects people from having to face painful experiences. For instance, a couple may deny they are having marital problems when both are aware that the relationship is deteriorating. Denial may initially help a person cope with certain situations, such as war, but if perpetuated it ultimately becomes destructive.

☐ *Identification*  The mechanism by which a person incorporates the qualities of another. Identification serves the purposes of removing any fear a person might have of another and of giving a person new behavioral skills. Thus, a child might identify with a feared parent. Identification, like sublimation, differs from other defense mechanisms in that it can help a person realistically solve problems (Hansen, Stevic, & Warner, 1986).

Overall, Freud's view of human nature stresses conflict between conscious and unconscious forces (Arlow, 1984). The theory is deterministic in nature, holding that a person's adult personality is formed through resolving the gender-specific stages of childhood. If a person has a traumatic childhood and fails to resolve a stage, the person will need to work through this unresolved stage later in life.

### Role of the Counselor

Professionals who practice classical psychoanalysis function in the role of expert. They encourage their clients to talk about whatever comes to mind, especially about childhood experiences. To create an atmosphere in which the client feels free to express difficult thoughts, psychoanalysts, after a few face-to-face sessions, will often have the client lie down on a couch while the analyst remains out of view (usually seated behind the client's head). The analyst's role is to let the clients gain insight by reliving and working through the unresolved past experiences that come into focus during the sessions. The development of transference is encouraged to help clients deal realistically with unconscious material. Unlike some other approaches, the psychoanalytic counselor interprets for the client. Overall, the counselor employs both active and passive techniques. Psychological assessment instruments, especially projective tests, are often employed. Psychoanalytic counselors also use diagnostic labels to help themselves classify clients and develop appropriate treatment plans for them.

### Goals

The goals of psychoanalysis, which vary according to the client, focus mainly on personal adjustment, usually including a reorganization of internal forces within the person. A primary goal in most cases is to help the client become more aware of the unconscious aspects of his or her personality. The unconscious includes repressed memories and wishes too painful or threatening to have been dealt with initially. But repressing thoughts does not stop them from having influence; repression just makes identifying those thoughts more difficult. Psychoanalysis strives to help clients gain insight into themselves.

A second major goal, often tied to the first, is to assist a client in working through a developmental stage not previously resolved. If accomplished, clients become unstuck and able to live more productively. Working through unresolved developmental stages may require a major reconstruction of the personality. As a consequence, psychoanalysis is often a long, intense, and expensive process (Nye, 1981).

A final goal of psychoanalysis is helping clients cope with the demands of the society in which they live. Unhappy people, according to this theory, are not in tune with themselves or society. Psychoanalysis stresses environmental adjustment, especially in the areas of work and intimacy. The focus is on strengthening the ego so that one's perceptions and plans will be more realistically oriented.

### Techniques

Freudian techniques are most often applied within a specific setting, such as the office of a private counselor or the interview room of a hospital. Among the most prominent of these techniques are free association, dream analysis, analysis of transference, analysis of resistance, and interpretation. Each technique will be examined separately, though in practice they must be considered integrated.

***Free Association.*** Repressed material in the unconscious is always seeking release. On a daily basis, this material may be expressed in the form of jokes of a sexual or an aggressive nature, or through so-called Freudian slips—slips of the tongue, such as

"I loathe you" instead of "I love you." In psychoanalysis, the client is encouraged to relax and freely recall early childhood memories or emotional experiences. During this *free association,* the client abandons the normal way of censoring thoughts by consciously repressing them and instead says whatever comes to mind, even if the thoughts seem silly, irrational, suggestive, or painful. In this way, the id is requested to speak and the ego remains silent (Freud, 1936). Thus, unconscious material enters the conscious mind, and there the counselor deals with it interpretively.

At times, clients resist free association by blocking their thoughts or denying their importance or both. Psychoanalysts make the most of these moments by attempting to help the client work through the resistance. Often such resistance is concerned with significant earlier unresolved relationships. Regardless, the counselor assures the client that even seemingly trivial thoughts or feelings are important, and many times such assurance is enough to overcome the resistance.

**Dream Analysis.**   Clients report dreams to the counselor on a regular basis. Freud believed that dreams are a main avenue to understanding the unconscious, even calling dreams "the royal road to the unconscious." He thought dreams were an attempt to fulfill a childhood wish or to express unacknowledged sexual desires. He insisted on getting at the nature of dreams through breaking them down into parts and treating them in as much detail as possible (Capuzzi & Black, 1986).

In *dream analysis,* the client is encouraged to dream and remember his or her dreams. Not everything in the dream is considered important. The counselor is especially sensitive to two aspects of any dream, the *manifest* content (obvious and apparent meaning) and the *latent* content (hidden but true meaning) (Jones, 1979). The analyst helps interpret both aspects. Some dream symbols are obvious, such as hostility being expressed as death or an accident (Nye, 1981). Other symbols are vague and thus difficult to interpret. Freud's method is considered the first "scientific" approach to the study of dreams.

**Analysis of Transference.**   Through *transference*, a client is able to work through difficult emotional experiences with others, such as parents, by displacing those emotions onto the counselor. The analyst encourages this transference and interprets for the client the positive or negative feelings expressed. The very release of these feelings is therapeutic as an emotional catharsis. But the real value of these experiences comes in the client's gaining self-knowledge through the counselor's analysis of the transference. Those who experience transference and understand what is happening are then freed to move on to another developmental stage (Singer, 1970).

**Analysis of Resistance.**   Sometimes clients initially make progress while undergoing psychoanalysis and then slow down or stop. Their *resistance* to the therapeutic process may take many forms, such as missing appointments, being late for appointments, not paying fees, persisting in transference, blocking thoughts during free association, or refusing to recall dreams or early memories. When resistance occurs in any form, it is vital that the counselor deal with it immediately. An analysis of resistance by the counselor can help a client gain insight into the resistance as well as other behavior. If resistance is not dealt with, the therapeutic process will probably come to a halt.

**Interpretation.**   Another technique employed by counselors who work from a psychoanalytic orientation is *interpretation*. Interpretation should be considered as a part of the other four techniques examined and as complementary to them. It is the process whereby the counselor helps the client understand the meaning of past and present personal events. Interpretation encompasses explanations and analysis of a client's thoughts, feelings, and actions. Counselors must carefully time employment of such interpretation. If it comes too soon in the relationship, it can drive the client away. On the other hand, if it is not employed at all or is infrequently used, the client may fail to develop insight. Only when the client is ready can interpretation make a significant impact on the client's growth and development.

### Evaluation

Classical psychoanalysis has several strengths:

☐ The approach emphasizes the importance of sexuality and the unconscious in human behavior. Before this theory, sexuality, especially childhood sexuality, was denied, and little attention was paid to unconscious forces. Now, many theories acknowledge both the importance of the person as a sexual being and the power of the unconscious mind.

☐ The approach lends itself to empirical studies. It is heuristic. Freud's proposals have generated a tremendous amount of research since the early 1900s. Much of the research supporting the theory is reported in the form of case histories and reactions in such professional journals as the *American Psychoanalytic Association Journal*, the *International Journal of*

*Psychoanalysis,* and *Psychoanalytic Review.* A good deal of the research attacking the theory is reported as empirical studies in other reputable journals. The theory itself challenges researchers to develop sophisticated methods of inquiry so that studies about it can be made more comparable.

☐ The approach provides a base of support for a number of diagnostic instruments. Many psychological tests, such as the Thematic Apperception Test or the Rorschach Ink Blots, are rooted in psychoanalytic theory. Many other tests used by counselors are outgrowths of this theory or reactions to it.

☐ The approach has great complexity, a reflection of the complexity of human nature. Counselors of any theoretical persuasion can gain a greater appreciation of human development and various associated problems through understanding psychoanalysis (Corey, 1986).

☐ The approach has grown and developed through the years. Nye (1981) reports that there are some 10,000 practicing classical psychoanalysts in the United States. There are undoubtedly many other professionals who engage in a modified form of psychoanalysis, such as ego psychology or object relations. Psychoanalysis continues to evolve.

☐ The approach appears to be effective for those who suffer from a wide variety of disorders, including hysteria, narcissism, obsessive-compulsive reactions, character disorders, anxiety, phobias, and sexual difficulties (Arlow, 1984).

☐ The approach stresses the importance of developmental stages. This emphasis has influenced a significant amount of investigation since Freud's time, especially the work of Erikson (1963) and Levinson (1978). This type of knowledge is invaluable when proposing an individual treatment plan.

Despite the strengths of psychoanalysis, most modern professional counselors do not use the approach. The reasons are many, but among them are the following:

☐ The approach is quite time consuming and expensive. A person who undergoes psychoanalysis is usually seen three to five times a week over a period of many years (Arlow, 1984; Nye, 1981).

☐ The approach does not seem to lend itself to working with older clients. Many psychoanalysts will not see any client over the age of 50.

☐ The approach has been claimed almost exclusively by psychiatry. Counselors without a medical degree have a difficult time receiving extensive training in psychoanalysis (Turkington, 1985). In many ways psychoanalysis has become a closed system. Analysts with a medical degree belong to the largest and most prestigious psychoanalytic society, the American Psychoanalytic Association. Other helping professionals hold membership in organizations such as the American Academy of Psychoanalysis and the National Psychological Association for Psychoanalysis (Arlow, 1984).

☐ The approach is based on many concepts that are not easily communicated or understood. The id, ego, and superego, for instance, of the person might be represented in more easily understood ways. A general rule of thumb in working with clients is to employ the least technical terminology and methods possible. Furthermore, counseling for various reasons mainly focuses on health, whereas the tradition of psychoanalysis and its terminology is one that has concentrated mostly on pathology.

☐ The approach is deterministic in nature. Freud thought that there were certain limitations a person encounters just because of gender. This controversial side of the theory, especially as it affects women, has subsided because of the influence of ego psychology and the interpretation of Freud by women scholars (Winkler, 1986). Yet, the appropriateness of psychoanalysis for females continues to be questioned.

☐ The approach does not lend itself to the needs of most individuals who seek professional counseling. The psychodynamic model has become associated more with those who have major adjustment difficulties or who want or need to explore the unconscious. Yet, many individuals who seek help from counselors have less-disruptive developmental disorders.

## ADLERIAN COUNSELING

### Adler

Alfred Adler was born in 1870 at Penzig, Austria, a suburb of Vienna. He was the second of six children in a middle-class Jewish family. Adler shared a close relationship with his mother until his younger brother was born, when, feeling abandoned, he sought the support of his father.

Adler was a sickly child and was injured often. He was run over in the street, suffered from rickets, and almost died of pneumonia at age 5. At age 3, he witnessed the death of a younger brother. It is little wonder that Adler was later attracted to the profession of medicine.

To make up for his physical limitations, Adler spent a great deal of his childhood outside playing with other children, and he went out of his way to cultivate their friendship. He was not a good student at first, and he did so poorly in mathematics at the secondary level that his teacher suggested his father take him out of school and apprentice him to a shoemaker. Adler studied to overcome this deficiency and eventually became skilled in math.

In 1895, he graduated in medicine from the University of Vienna. His first practice was as an ophthalmologist, but his interests turned first to neurology and finally to psychiatry. As a practicing psychiatrist, Adler was invited to join Freud's Vienna Psychoanalytic Society, where he quickly gained prominence. Adler always thought of himself as a colleague rather than a disciple of Freud. He early disagreed with Freud's theoretical approach, especially Freud's emphasis on sexuality. Adler developed a theoretical orientation less deterministic than Freud's and much more hopeful. He stressed the importance of subjective feelings rather than biological drives as the primary motivating force of life. Because of the differences with Freud, Adler resigned as president of the society in 1910 and, with about a third of the society's members, established the rival Society of Individual Psychology.

During World War I, Adler served as a physician in the Austrian army, and after the war he was very instrumental in setting up child guidance clinics in the Vienna schools. Adler worked to refine his theory and spoke widely in Europe and the United States. He fled Hitler's rise to power and in 1932 was appointed to a position in medical psychology at the Long Island College of Medicine. Adler died of a heart attack in 1937 while on a lecture tour in Aberdeen, Scotland. He was survived by his wife, two daughters, and a son.

Although Adler was a popular speaker and the author of over 300 published papers and books, he has not generally received credit for many of the concepts he formulated. Such terms as *inferiority complex, social interest, empathy,* and *life-style* originated with Adler and were quickly absorbed by other scholars as well as the public. His theory waned in popularity during the 1940s and 1950s, but it was revitalized during the 1960s.

### *View of Human Nature*

Adler thought people are motivated mainly by social interests. His theory holds that conscious aspects of behavior, rather than the unconscious, are central to the development of personality. A major tenet is that people strive to become successful (i.e., the best they can be); therefore, their behavior is goal directed and purposeful. Underlying this tenet is Adler's belief that each person strives for growth and has a need for wholeness. Thus, there is a tendency for them to try to fulfill their own unique potential, a process he called "striving for perfection," or completeness (Adler, 1964). There is also a tendency for each person initially to feel inferior to others. If this feeling is not overcome, the person develops an *inferiority complex.* On the other hand, a person who overcompensates for feelings of inferiority develops a *superiority complex.*

Adler believed that people are as influenced by future (*teleological*) goals as by past causes. His theory places considerable emphasis on *birth order,* in that those who share ordinal birth positions (e.g., firstborns) may have more in common with one another than siblings from the same family (Dreikurs, 1950). Five ordinal positions are emphasized in Adlerian literature on the *family constellation:* firstborns, secondborns, middle children, youngest children, and the only child (Dreikurs, 1957, 1964; Sweeney, 1981):

☐ *Firstborns*   These are initially the "reigning monarchs" of a family, because at first they receive undivided attention from parents. Firstborns are socialized to conform, achieve, behave, and please. They take responsibility when parents are absent and often act as parent substitutes in large families. All firstborns experience the loss of their unique position in the family when a second child is born. The experience of being "dethroned" may either cause them to become resentful or help them understand better the significance of power and authority.

☐ *Secondborns*   This position is an enviable one, according to Adler, but one that is not without drawbacks. Secondborns never have to worry about the issues of power and authority the way firstborns do, because they are born into a family atmosphere in which they will never be dethroned. Usually, these individuals are more outgoing, carefree, creative, and less concerned with rules than firstborns. They frequently pursue roles not taken by firstborns, and are more than likely to be just the opposite of their older sibling.

☐ *Middle children*   These individuals often feel "squeezed in" and treated unfairly. They do not develop the close, personal types of alliances that an oldest or a youngest child develop. But because of their position, middle children learn a great deal about family politics and the art of negotiation. These skills can prove useful to them in manipulating events to get what they want and in picking areas where they can be successful.

☐ *Youngest children*   The youngest in the family has both difficulties and opportunities different from his or her siblings. Youngest children receive a great deal of attention from others, who are likely to cater to their needs. These children may become charmers, but they may also have difficulty breaking out of the role of being the baby or the family pet. Thus, they face the danger of becoming spoiled. At the same time, youngest children may make great strides in achieving because of the role models provided for them by older siblings.

☐ *Only children*   Any child born seven or more years apart from siblings is psychologically an only child. These children, as a group, are never dethroned and are at an advantage, like oldest children, in receiving a great deal of attention. Thus, they may mature early and become high achievers. They may also develop rich imaginations because of the amount of time they spend alone. Major disadvantages of this position are that only children may become pampered, selfish, and not well socialized.

In addition to birth order, the family environment is very important to a person's development, particularly in the first five years of life. Adlerian theory stresses that each person creates a *style of life* by the age of five, primarily through interacting with other family members. A negative family atmosphere might be authoritarian, rejective, suppressive, materialistic, overprotective, or pitying (Dreikurs, 1964). One's perception of the family atmosphere, rather than any events themselves, however, is crucial in the development of a style of life (Adler, 1964). Thus, individuals behave as if the world were a certain way and are guided by their *fictions*, that is, there subjective evaluations of themselves and their environments. Five basic mistakes caused by these fictions are (Mosak, 1984, p. 78):

☐ *Overgeneralizing*   Viewing everything as the same.

☐ *False or impossible goals of security*   Trying to please everyone.

☐ *Misperceptions of life and life's demands*   Believing one never gets any breaks.

☐ *Minimization or denial of one's worth*   Thinking that one will never amount to anything.

☐ *Faulty values*   Believing in the necessity of being first no matter what needs to be done to get there.

In contrast to these mistakes, a healthy style of life focuses on three main tasks—society, work, and sexuality. Adler places strong emphasis on the person's developing social interests and thus contributing to *society*. His theory also holds that *work* is essential for human survival and that we must learn to be interdependent. Furthermore, a person must define his or her *sexuality* in regard to self and others, in a spirit of cooperation rather than competition. There are two other challenges of life Adler also mentioned without fully developing—spirituality and coping with self (Dreikurs & Mosak, 1966). We will not elaborate on these but only state that facing any life task takes *courage*—a willingness to take risks without knowing what the consequences may be.

### Role of the Counselor

Adlerian counselors function primarily as diagnosticians, teachers, and models in the equalitarian relationships they establish with their clients. They try to assess the reasons clients are oriented to a certain way of thinking and behaving. The counselor makes an assessment by gathering information on the family constellation and on a client's earliest memories. The counselor then shares interpretations, impressions, opinions, and feelings with the client and concentrates on promoting the therapeutic relationship. The client is encouraged to examine and change a faulty life-style by developing social interests. Adlerians are frequently active in sharing hunches or guesses with clients, and are often directive in assigning clients "homework," such as to act "as if" the client were the person the client wants to be. Adlerian counselors employ a variety of techniques, some of which are borrowed from other approaches—since Adler was not specific in detailing how counselors should operate when using his theory. As a general rule, Adlerian counselors make little use of assessment techniques, such as psychological tests, but they usually employ life history questionnaires to gather data. They generally avoid the types of diagnoses found in the DSM-III but use their own language to describe the dynamics they encounter within a person, such as "discouraged."

### Goals

The goals of Adlerian counseling revolve around helping people develop healthy life-styles. This may mean educating them to what such a life-style is, as well as helping them overcome feelings of inferiority. One of the major goals of Adlerian counseling is to encourage clients to cultivate social interests. A faulty style of life is self-centered and based on mistaken goals and incorrect assumptions associated with feelings of inferiority. These feelings might stem from being born with a physical or mental defect, from being pampered by parents, or from being neglected. The feelings must be corrected and inappropriate forms of behavior stopped. To do so, the counselor assumes the role of a teacher as well an interpreter of events. Adlerian counseling deals with the whole person.

The client is ultimately in charge of deciding whether to pursue social or self-interests, but Adlerian counselors stress four goals of the therapeutic process (Dreikurs, 1967):

Establishment of a counseling relationship

Analysis of client life-style

Development of client insight

Behavior change

We will examine each of these goals in connection with the techniques that accompany it.

### *Techniques*

The establishment of a counseling relationship is crucial if the other three goals of Adlerian counseling are to be achieved and there are certain techniques that help enhance this process. Adlerian counselors try to develop a warm, supportive, empathic, friendly, and equalitarian relationship with other clients. Counseling is seen as a collaborative effort. Adlerian counselors actively listen and try to help their clients define specific goals and discover what prevents the achievement of those goals. A counselor also may focus on the strengths of the client. A counselor may employ confrontation at times, pointing out client inconsistencies. The primary objective of the counselor is to maintain a flexible interaction process and in so doing stress client responsibility (Dinkmeyer, Dinkmeyer, & Sperry, 1987).

After a relationship has been established, the counselor concentrates on an analysis of the client's life-style, including examination of the client's family constellation, early memories, dreams, and priorities. As previously noted, the family constellation and the atmosphere in which children grow greatly influence both a person's self-perception and a person's perceptions of others. No two children are born into the same environment, but a child's ordinal position and assessment of the family atmosphere have a major impact on development and behavior. Often a client is able to gain insight by recalling early memories, especially events before the age of 10. Adler (1958) contended that a person remembers childhood events that are consistent with his or her present view of self, others, and the world in general. Thus, Adlerian counselors look both for themes and for specific details within these early recollections (Watkins, 1985). Figures from the past are treated as prototypes rather than specific individuals—they may represent a client's attitude toward power, weakness, men, women, or almost anything else. Recent, as well as past, dreams are also a part of life-style analysis. Adlerian theory holds that dreams are a possible rehearsal for future courses of action. Recurrent dreams are especially important. A look at the client's priorities is also helpful in understanding the client's style of life. A client may persist in one predominant life-style, such as always trying to please, unless challenged to change.

Counselors next try to help clients develop insight, especially by asking open-ended questions and making interpretations. Open-ended questions allow clients the opportunity to explore patterns in their lives that have previously gone unnoticed. Interpretation often takes the form of intuitive guesses. The ability to empathize is especially important in this process, for the counselor must be able to feel what it is like to be the client before zeroing in on the reasons for the client's present behaviors. At other times, interpretations are based on the counselor's general knowledge of ordinal position and family constellation. True to the equalitarian spirit of the process, clients are never forced to accept the counselor's point of view.

To accomplish the last goal of the Adlerian counseling process, behavioral change, specific techniques are used. Change is encouraged through:

☐ *Confrontation*   The process by which the counselor challenges a client to consider his or her own private logic. When clients examine this logic, they often realize they can change it and their behavior.

☐ *Asking "The Question"*   The process by which the counselor asks, "What would be different if you were well?" Clients are often asked "The Question" during the initial interview, but it is appropriate to ask at any time.

☐ *Encouragement*   Encouragement implies faith in a person (Dinkmeyer & Losoncy, 1980; Dreikurs, 1964). Counselors encourage their clients by stating their belief that behavior change is possible.

☐ *Acting "as if"*   The process by which a client is instructed to act "as if" the client were the person he or she wanted to be, the person the client sees in dreams, for instance (Gold, 1979).

☐ *Spitting in the client's soup*   The process by which a counselor points out certain behavior to the client and in so doing ruins the payoff for that behavior. For example, a mother who always acts superior to her daughter by showing the daughter up may continue to do so after the behavior is pointed out, but the reward for doing so is now gone.

☐ *Catching oneself* The process by which clients learn to become aware of any self-destructive behaviors or thoughts. At first, the counselor may help in the process, but eventually this responsibility is taken over by clients.

☐ *Task setting* The process by which a client initially sets short-range, attainable goals and then eventually works up to long-term, realistic objectives. Once a client makes behavioral changes and realizes some control over life, the counseling ends.

### *Evaluation*

The Adlerian approach to counseling has a number of strengths:

☐ The approach fosters an equalitarian atmosphere through the positive techniques the counselors promote. Rapport and commitment are enhanced by these processes, and the chances for change are increased. The encouragement and support of the counselor is a valued commodity. Adlerian counselors approach their clients with an educational orientation and take an optimistic outlook on life.

☐ The approach is versatile. "Adlerian theorists have developed counseling models for working with children, adolescents, parents, entire families, teacher groups, and other segments of society" (Purkey & Schmidt, 1987, p. 115). Four typical faulty goals of adolescents—power, attention, revenge, and inadequacy—and proposed counseling strategies to deal with the manifestations of each have been described by Kelly and Sweeney (1979). Dinkmeyer and his associates have been especially active in adapting Adlerian theory to parent and children groups (Dinkmeyer, 1982a, b; Dinkmeyer & McKay, 1976, 1983; Dinkmeyer, McKay, & Dinkmeyer, Jr., 1980). Lowe (1982) has made Adlerian theory applicable to adults and family units.

☐ The approach is useful in the treatment of a variety of DMS-III disorders, including conduct disorders, antisocial disorders, anxiety disorders of childhood and adolescence, some affective disorders, and personality disorders (Seligman, 1986).

☐ The approach has contributed to other helping theories and to the public's knowledge and understanding of human interactions. Many of Adler's ideas have been integrated into other approaches to counseling. Such concepts as freedom, phenomenology, interpretation of events, life scripts, growth, and personal responsibility are found in existential, Gestalt, rational-emotive, transactional analysis, person-centered therapy, and reality counseling or therapy. Adlerian terms have also become a part of the public's vocabulary, such as *inferiority complex*.

On the other hand, the Adlerian approach is not without its limitations:

☐ The approach lacks a firm supportive research base. There are relatively few empirical studies that clearly outline its effectiveness (Wallace, 1986). More investigations are needed if the theory is to develop systematically. Journals devoted to the Adlerian viewpoint, such as the *Journal of Individual Psychology*, may rectify this situation.

☐ The approach is vague in many of its terms and concepts. Corey (1986) notes that Adler placed emphasis on practice and teaching instead of on theoretical definitions and organization. Although a number of prominent educators, such as Dreikurs, Mosak, Dinkmeyer, and Sweeney, have attempted to clarify the Adlerian approach, some of its ideas remain unclear. Adler was especially nebulous about "how" to work with clients.

☐ The approach may be too narrow. Adler, who called his approach individual psychology, stressed social cooperation and interest. His view is considered by some critics to be neglectful of other dimensions of life (Prochaska, 1984).

## SUMMARY

In this chapter two importance theories of individual counseling have been emphasized. Classical psychoanalysis is considered by many practitioners to be the "grandparent" of all modern theories of helping. Although the ideas of the founder of psychoanalysis, Sigmund Freud, are controversial, his thoughts about human nature and the helping process are comprehensive. They have been elaborated on and refined since his death in 1939, and classical psychoanalysis is still a widely practiced approach.

Alfred Adler's theory has been less controversial over the years. Adlerian theory has been clarified since Adler's death in 1937, and these refinements have made this approach not only more understandable but also more popular, especially in educational environments.

These theories differ in a number of ways. Psychoanalysis is biologically based and stresses causality, psychosexual development, the dynamics of the mind, and instincts. Adlerian theory, on the other hand, is socially based, interpersonal, and subjective and emphasizes the future, holism, equalitarianism, and the importance of choice. Both theories focus on the importance of childhood, the working through of real or perceived unresolved situations, and behavioral goals.

Psychoanalysis is not used by many professionals who identify themselves as counselors because of its cost in time and money and because few counselors receive the training needed to master the approach. The approach is also not applicable for the client populations many counselors serve. The Adlerian approach to counseling, however, is widely practiced in school and institutional settings. Its popularity can be attributed to its hopefulness and the employability of its techniques in multiple settings.

## CLASSROOM ACTIVITIES

1. Discuss with another classmate which of the two theories presented in this chapter you find most attractive. State your reasons and listen to his or hers. Speculate about how each of these approaches might be used in the following settings: a mental hospital, a public secondary school, a rehabilitation center, and a community agency.
2. Brainstorm as many examples of defense mechanisms as you can. Share your examples with a classmate and then with the class as a whole.
3. As a class, divide into five groups according to Adler's description of the five ordinal positions in a family—firstborns, secondborns, middle children, youngest children, and only children. Appoint a scribe in each group to take notes. Then discuss with other group members your perceptions of

being a child in that position. After the discussions, have each group scribe report back to the group as a whole.
4. Divide into groups of three, rotating the roles of counselor, client, and observer. Try to implement some of the specific ways you think a psychoanalytic or Adlerian counselor would act in working with clients who have the following problems: depression, anxiety, poor self-identity, and phobias. After each role play, discuss what each person observed and learned.
5. What specific aspects of psychoanalysis and Adlerian theory do you think should be researched first? Why? Write your responses down and share them with the class as a whole. Rank the class's list according to importance.

## REFERENCES

Adler, A. (1958). *What life should mean to you.* New York: Capricorn.

Adler, A. (1964). *Social interest: A challenge to mankind.* New York: Capricorn.

Arlow, J. A. (1984). Psychoanalysis. In R. J. Corsini (Ed.), *Current psychotherapies* (3rd ed., pp. 14–55). Itasca, IL: Peacock.

Capuzzi, D., & Black, D. K. (1986). The history of dream analysis and the helping relationship: A synopsis for practitioners. *Journal of Humanistic Education and Development, 24,* 82–97.

Corey, G. (1986). *Theory and practice of counseling and psychotherapy* (3rd ed.). Monterey, CA: Brooks/Cole.

Corsini, R. J. (Ed.). (1981). *Handbook of innovative psychotherapies.* New York: Wiley.

Corsini, R. J. (1984). Introduction. In R. J. Corsini (Ed.), *Current psychotherapies* (3rd ed., pp. 1–13). Itasca, IL: Peacock.

Dinkmeyer, D. (1982a). *Developing understanding of self and others (DUSO D-1).* Circle Pine, MN: American Guidance Service.

Dinkmeyer, D. (1982b). *Developing understanding of self and others (DUSO D-2).* Circle Pine, MN: American Guidance Service.

Dinkmeyer, D., Dinkmeyer, D., Jr., & Sperry, L. (1987). *Adlerian counseling and psychotherapy* (2nd ed.). Columbus, OH: Merrill.

Dinkmeyer, D., & Losoncy, L. E. (1980). *The encouragement book: Becoming a positive person.* Englewood Cliffs, NJ: Prentice-Hall.

Dinkmeyer, D., & McKay, G. D. (1976). *Systematic training for effective parenting (STEP).* Circle Pine, MN: American Guidance Service.

Dinkmeyer, D., & McKay, G. D. (1983). *Systematic training for effective parenting/ Teen (STEP/Teen).* Circle Pine, MN: American Guidance Service.

Dinkmeyer, D., McKay, G. D., & Dinkmeyer, D., Jr. (1980). *Systematic training for effective teaching (STET).* Circle Pine, MN: American Guidance Service.

Dreikurs, R. R. (1950). *Fundamentals of Adlerian psychology.* Chicago: Alfred Adler Institute.

Dreikurs, R. R., with Soltz, V. (1964). *Children: The challenge.* New York: Hawthorne.

Dreikurs, R. R. (1967). *Psychodynamics, psychotherapy, and counseling.* Chicago: Alfred Adler Institute.

Dreikurs, R. R., & Mosak, H. H. (1966). The tasks of life I: Adler's three tasks. *Individual Psychologist, 4,* 18–22.

Erikson, E. H. (1963). *Childhood and society.* New York: Norton.

Freud, A. (1936). *The ego and the mechanisms of defense.* New York: International Universities Press.

Freud, S. (1923/1933). *New introductory lectures on psychoanalysis.* New York: Norton.

Freud, S. (1923/1947). *The Ego and the Id.* London: Hogarth Press.

Freud, S. (1900/1955). *The interpretation of dreams.* London: Hogarth Press.

Gladding, S. T. (1974). Tea-kettle song. *The School Counselor, 21,* 209.

Gold, L. (1979). Adler's theory of dreams: An holistic approach to interpretation. In B. B. Wolman (Ed.), *Handbook of dreams: Research, theories, and applications.* New York: Litton.

Hall, C. S. (1954). *A primer of Freudian psychology.* New York: The American Library.

Hansen, J. C., Stevic, R. R., & Warren, R. W., Jr. (1986). *Counseling: Theory and process* (4th ed.). Boston: Allyn & Bacon.

Hergenhahn, B. R. (1984). *An introduction to theories of personality.* Englewood Cliffs, NJ: Prentice-Hall.

Herink, R. (Ed.). (1980). *The psychotherapy handbook.* New York: New American Library.

Jones, E. (1953). *The life and work of Sigmund Freud* (Vol. 1). New York: Basic Books.

Jones, E. (1955). *The life and work of Sigmund Freud* (Vol. 2). New York: Basic Books.

Jones, E. (1957). *The life and work of Sigmund Freud* (Vol. 3). New York: Basic Books.

Jones, R. M. (1979). Freudian and post-Freudian theories of dreams. In B. B. Wolman (Ed.), *Handbook of dreams: Research, theories, and applications.* New York, Litton.

Kelly, E. W., Jr., & Sweeney, T. J. (1979). Typical faulty goals of adolescents: A base for counseling. *The School Counselor, 26,* 236–246.

Leak, G. K., & Christopher, S. B. (1982). Freudian psychoanalysis and sociobiology. *American Psychologist, 37,* 313–322.

Levinson, D. (1978). *The seasons of a man's life.* New York: Knopf.

Lowe, R. N. (1982). Adlerian/Dreikursian family counseling. In A. M. Horne & M. M. Ohlsen (Eds.), *Family counseling and therapy* (pp. 329–359). Itasca, IL: Peacock.

Mosak, H. H. (1984). Adlerian psychotherapy. In R. J. Corsini (Ed.), *Current psychotherapies* (3rd ed., pp. 56–107). Itasca, IL: Peacock.

Nye, R. D. (1981). *Three psychologies: Perspectives from Freud, Skinner, and Rogers* (2nd ed.). Monterey, CA: Brooks/Cole.

Patterson, C. H. (1985). *The therapeutic relationship.* Monterey, CA: Brooks/Cole.

Prochaska, J. O. (1984). *Systems of psychotherapy: A transtheoretical analysis* (2nd ed.). Homewood, IL: Dorsey Press.

Purkey, W. W., & Schmidt, J. J. (1987). *The inviting relationship.* Englewood Cliffs, NJ: Prentice-Hall.

Seligman, L. (1986). *Diagnosis and treatment planning in counseling.* New York: Human Sciences Press.

Singer, E. (1970). *Key concepts in psychotherapy* (2nd ed.). New York: Basic Books.

Sweeney, T. J. (1981). *Adlerian counseling: Proven concepts and strategies* (2nd ed.). Muncie, IN: Accelerated Development.

Turkington, C. (1985). Analysts sued for barring non-MDs. *APA Monitor, 16* (5), 2.

Wallace, W. A. (1986). *Theories of counseling and psychotherapy.* Boston: Allyn & Bacon.

Watkins, C. E., Jr. (1985). Early recollections as a projective technique in counseling: An Adlerian view. *AMHCA Journal, 7,* 32–40.

Winkler, K. J. (1986). Scholars prescribe Freud's "talking cure" for problems. *Chronicle of Higher Education, 33* (8), 4–6.

Photo by James S. Davidson III.

# The Theory and Practice of Individual Counseling: Affective Approaches

*I feel at times that I'm wasting my mind*
  *as we wade through your thoughts and emotions.*
*With my skills I could be in a world-renowned clinic*
  *with a plush, private office, soft padded chairs,*
  *and a sharp secretary at my command.*
*Instead of here in a pink cinderblock room*
  *where it leaks when it rains*
  *and the noise seeps under the door like water.*
*But in leaving, you pause for a moment*
  *as your voice spills out in a whisper:*
  *"Thanks for being here when I hurt."*
*With those words my fantasies end, as reality,*
  *like a wellspring begins filling me*
  *with life-giving knowledge, as it cascades through my mind,*
*That in meeting you, when you're flooded with pain,*
  *I discover myself.*[1]

---

[1]Gladding, 1975, p. 746. Copyright AACD. Reprinted with permission. No further reproduction authorized without permission of AACD.

**A**mong the most prominent affective theories are the ones covered in this chapter—person-centered counseling, existential counseling, and Gestalt therapy. According to Cormier and Hackney (1987), the most used of these approaches is person-centered counseling, followed by Gestalt therapy and then existential counseling.

These affective theories have basic characteristics in common. First, they all focus on the primacy of affect as a cause of and/or contributor to the development of certain human actions and reactions (Zajonc, 1984). Second, they stress helping clients cope with or change their emotions as a premise for making other life alterations. Third, all emphasize human phenomenology and how a person's views of the environment affect behavior. Fourth, the theories are characterized by the relationship between counselor and client, which has been described as a "person-to-person climate" (Baruth & Huber, 1985, p. 24). Finally, affective theories are humanistic in their orientations, focusing on the unique growth and development within each individual.

A problem shared by all affective theories is a vagueness in describing the techniques employed. Of the approaches covered in this chapter, existential counseling is especially weak in this area, whereas Gestalt therapy is strongest. Prominent professionals associated with affective theories include Carl Rogers, Angelo Boy, Gerald Pine, Rollo May, Victor Frankl, Irvin Yalom, Sidney Jourard, Fritz Perls, Laura Perls, William Passons, Irma Lee Shepherd, and Joen Fagan. Although there is some overlap and similarity, each of these approaches differs in its emphases.

## PERSON-CENTERED COUNSELING

### Carl Rogers

Carl Rogers, the individual most identified with person-centered counseling, was born in 1902 at Oak Park, Illinois, a suburb of Chicago. He was the fourth of six children in his family. His parents, who were fundamentalist Christians, discouraged Rogers from forming friendships outside of the family because of the bad influence others might have on him. Rogers (1980) describes his childhood as solitary, with "no close friend and only superficial personal contact" (p. 29). When he was 12, his family moved to a farm outside of Chicago, and there he developed a strong interest in science and reading. Among his early scientific experiments was an investigation of a species of moth. The teenaged Rogers read everything he could get his hands on, including encyclopedias and dictionaries.

Rogers describes himself as being socially inept in high school. A major turning point occurred when he enrolled at the University of Wisconsin in 1919 to study agriculture. There he became involved with a YMCA group and began to develop good friendships. He also started dating and began to become more trusting of others. A major event for Rogers was a six-month trip he took in 1922 as one of 10 American students to attend the World Student Christian Federation conference in Peking, China. The trip exposed Rogers to people of other cultures and religions, and he broke away from the domination of his parents. He also changed his major to history, with the goal of eventually becoming a minister. After graduation in 1924, Rogers enrolled in New York's Union Theological Seminary, but two years later he became discouraged with the prospect of becoming a minister. He transferred to Teachers College, Columbia University, where he studied clinical and educational psychology, receiving an M.A. degree in 1928 and a Ph.D. in 1931.

After completing his studies, Rogers took a position with the Society for the Prevention of Cruelty to Children in Rochester, New York. His 12-year tenure with this agency greatly influenced his later theory of counseling. Rogers found that the psychoanalytic approach to working with troubled individuals, which was dominant in this work setting, was time-consuming and often ineffective. Insight alone produced little change, but clients with whom Rogers formed an open and permissive relationship did seem to improve. Rogers left Rochester in 1940 to accept a professorship at Ohio State University. Two years later, his ideas on counseling were published in his first book on theory, *Counseling and Psychotherapy* (1942). He refined and revised the ideas through extensive research in the 1950s and 1960s at the Universities of Chicago and Wisconsin. It was at Wisconsin that Rogers first examined the effectiveness of his approach with diagnosed schizophrenics in a hospital setting. In 1964, Rogers became a resident fellow at the Western Behavioral Sciences Institute; in 1968, he helped establish the Center for the Study of Persons at La Jolla, California. Among his books are *Client-Centered Therapy* (1951), *On Becoming a Person* (1961), *Freedom to Learn* (1969), and *A Way of Being* (1980). Rogers always considered his theory to be ever evolving, going beyond the boundaries of individual counseling to become relevant in groups, family counseling, and international relations. He died in 1987.

### View of Human Nature

Implicit in person-centered counseling is this view of human nature: people are essentially good (Rogers, 1961). Humans are characteristically "positive, forward-moving, constructive, realistic, and trustworthy" (Rogers, 1957, p. 199). Each person is aware, inner-directed, and moving toward self-actualization from infancy on. Rogers (1959) held that human infants possess the following traits:

☐ Whatever an infant perceives is that infant's reality. An infant's perception is an internal process of which no one else can be aware.

☐ All infants are born with a self-actualizing tendency that is satisfied through goal-directed behavior.

☐ An infant's interaction with the environment is an organized whole, and everything an infant does is interrelated.

☐ The experiences of an infant may be seen as positive or negative according to whether the experiences enhance the actualization tendency.

☐ Infants maintain experiences that are actualizing and avoid those that are not.

For Rogers, *self-actualization* is the most prevalent and motivating drive of existence and encompasses actions that influence the total person. "The organism has one basic tendency and striving—to actualize, maintain, and enhance the experiencing organism" (Rogers, 1951, p. 487). It is the belief of person-centered theorists that each person is capable of finding a personal meaning and purpose in life.

Rogers views the individual from a phenomenological perspective: what is important is the person's perception of reality rather than an event itself (Rogers, 1955). This way of seeing the person is similar to that of Adler. The concept of *self* is another that Rogers and Adler share, except that for Rogers this concept is so central to his theory that his ideas are often referred to as *self theory.* The self is an outgrowth of what a person experiences, and an awareness of self helps a person differentiate him- or herself from others (Nye, 1981). For a healthy self to emerge, a person needs *positive regard,* such as love, warmth, care, respect, and acceptance.

Often in childhood, as well as later in life, a person is given *conditional regard* by parents and others. Feelings of worth develop if the person behaves in certain ways, because conditional accep- tance teaches the person to feel valued only when conforming to others' wishes. Thus, a person may have to deny or distort a perception when someone on whom the person depends for approval sees a situation differently. An individual who is caught is such a dilemma becomes aware of incongruities between self-perception and experience. If a person does not do as others wish, he or she will not be accepted and valued. Yet if a person conforms, he or she opens up a gap between the *ideal self* the person is striving to become and the *real self* that the person is. The further the ideal self is from the real self, the more alienated and maladjusted a person becomes.

### Role of the Counselor

The role of the counselor is a *holistic* one. The counselor sets up and promotes a climate in which the client is free to explore all aspects of self (Rogers, 1951, 1980). This atmosphere focuses on the counselor/client relationship, which Rogers describes as one with a special "I-Thou" personal quality. The counselor is aware of the verbal and nonverbal language of the client, and the counselor reflects back what he or she is hearing or observing (Braaten, 1986). Neither the client nor the counselor knows what direction the sessions will take or what goals will emerge in the process. Yet, the counselor trusts the client to develop an agenda on which the client wishes to work. The counselor's job is to *facilitate* rather than direct.

Person-centered counselors make limited use of psychological tests. Testing is usually only done at the request of the client. The counselor then focuses with the client on the meaning of the test for that client rather than on test scores. One innovative test often used in evaluating clients is the *Q sort technique* (Hergenhahn, 1984). This procedure has three steps. First, the client is given 100 cards, each of which contains a self-descriptive sentence, such as "I am intelligent" or "I despise myself." Next, the client is asked to place the cards in nine piles from "most like me" to "least like me."

After this self-sort, the client sorts the cards again by placing them according to how he or she would ideally like to be. The final step of the process is correlating the degree of similarity between the two sorts before, during, and after counseling.

The use of diagnosis is eschewed because diagnosis is philosophically incompatible with the objectives of the approach. Diagnosis categorizes people and implies each person is not unique. Diagnosis also puts the counselor in charge, because once a diagnosis is made a treatment plan follows.

### Goals

The goals of person-centered counseling are concerned with the client as a person, not on his or her problem. Rogers (1977) emphasizes that people need to be assisted in learning how to cope with situations. One of the main ways this can be accomplished is by helping a client become a fully functioning individual who has no need to apply defense mechanisms to everyday experiences. Such a person becomes increasingly willing to change and grow. As such, the person is more open to experience, more trusting of self-perception, and engaged in self-exploration and evaluation (Rogers, 1961). Further, a fully functioning person develops a greater acceptance of self and others and becomes a better decision maker in the here and now. Ultimately, a client is helped to identify, use, and integrate his or her own resources and potential (Boy & Pine, 1963).

Rogers (1961) held that as a result of person-centered counseling clients should become: "more realistic in their self-perceptions; more confident and self-directing; more positively valued by themselves; less likely to repress aspects of their experiences; more mature, socialized, and adaptive in their behavior; less upset by stress and quicker to recover from it; and more like the healthy integrated well-functioning person in their personality structures" (p. 375).

### Techniques

Person-centered techniques have evolved through the years. Hart (1970) identifies three periods of this evolution, each of which has stressed different techniques:

1. *Nondirective Period* (1940–50)   During this period, person-centered counselors emphasized forming a relationship with clients by creating a permissive and noninterventive atmosphere. The main techniques used were acceptance and clarification.

2. *Reflective Period* (1950–57) This seven-year span was characterized by counselors' placing their greatest emphasis on creating a nonthreatening relationship. The main techniques employed were responding to clients' feelings and reflecting back to clients underlying affect.

3. *Experiential Period* (1957–80) This period began when Rogers (1957) issued his statement on the "necessary and sufficient conditions" of counseling: empathy, positive regard (acceptance), and congruence (genuineness) (Gelso & Carter, 1985). *Empathy* is the ability of the counselor to feel with clients and convey this understanding back to them. As Rogers (1975) noted: "The research keeps piling up and it points strongly to the conclusion that a high degree of empathy in a relationship is possibly the most potent and certainly one of the most potent factors in bringing about change and learning" (p. 3). *Positive regard,* also known as acceptance, is a deep and genuine caring for the client as a person, that is, a "prizing" of the person just for being (Rogers, 1961, 1980). *Congruence,* or genuineness, is the condition of being "transparent" in the therapeutic relationship by giving up roles and facades (Rogers, 1980). This period helped make person-centered counseling more active and well-defined.

Since 1980, person-centered counselors have tried a number of other techniques such as limited self-disclosure of feelings, thoughts, and values (Corey, 1986). The person-centered approach keeps being refined, but in general there seems to be a movement away from a focus on technique to a greater emphasis on the counselor's attitudes and flexibility (Boy & Pine, 1982; Gelso & Carter, 1985).

The most common way a counselor helps any type of client is through establishing a relationship. Rogers (1967) believed that "significant positive personality change does not occur except in a relationship" (p. 73). He listed six necessary and sufficient conditions for a *counseling relationship* (p. 73):

☐ Two persons are in psychological contact.

☐ The first person, the client, is in a state of incongruence and is vulnerable or anxious.

☐ The second person, the counselor, is congruent, or integrated in the relationship.

☐ The counselor experiences unconditional positive regard for the client.

☐ The counselor experiences an empathic understanding of the client's internal frame of reference and attempts to communicate this experience to the client.

☐ There is at least a minimal degree of communication to the client of the counselor's understanding and unconditional positive regard.

Rogers (1959) viewed the necessary and sufficient conditions of counseling as existing on a continuum. Except for the first condition, the conditions do not exist on an all-or-nothing basis.

Methods that help promote the counselor/client relationship include, but are not limited to, the following: active and passive listening, accurate reflection of thoughts and feelings, clarification, summarization, confrontation, and general or open-ended leads (Poppen & Thompson, 1974). All of these techniques have been incorporated into other counseling approaches and into systematic human relations training courses. We will examine them in later chapters on the counseling process. Overall, person-centered counseling places a minimum emphasis on formal techniques and a maximum focus on the therapeutic relationship.

### Evaluation

Person-centered counseling can be evaluated from many perspectives. Some of the strengths of this theory are:

☐ The approach has evolved over the years. Rogers (1980) considered the person-centered approach to be applicable to solving a wide range of human problems, including institutional changes, labor-management relationships, leadership development, and international diplomacy. He summed up his view of the approach in this way: "I am no longer talking simply about psychotherapy, but about a point of view, a philosophy, an approach to life, a way of being, which fits any situation in which growth—of a person, a group, or a community—is part of the goal" (Rogers, 1980, p. ix).

☐ The approach has generated a great amount of research. Person-centered theory stresses objective, quantitative methods, as well as subjective, qualitative procedures, in understanding human behavior. In the 1950s and 1960s when Rogers was employed in academic settings, he and his students produced a wealth of studies verifying the effectiveness of his theory. Person-centered counseling was one of the first theories to have researchers set up systematic evaluation of hypotheses.

☐ The approach is effective. Among other findings are that person-centered counseling helps improve psychological adjustment, learning, and frustration tolerance and helps decrease defensiveness (Grummon, 1972). It is appropriate in treating mild-to-moderate anxiety states, adjustment disorders, and conditions not attributable to mental disorders, such as uncomplicated bereavement or interpersonal relations (Seligman, 1986).

☐ The approach focuses on the open relationship established by counselors and clients and the short-term nature of the process. Rogers' theory more than most emphasizes the importance of an accepting counselor-client relationship. Specific dimensions of the relationship have been examined for their impact on the total process of counseling (Carkhuff, 1969a, b).

☐ The approach takes a relatively short time to learn initially and with its emphasis on mastering listening skills is a basis for training many paraprofessional helpers.

☐ The approach has a positive view of human nature. Person-centered counseling revolutionized the field of helping when it was first introduced because its approach was so different from the more pessimistic and deterministic views of the day. One of the strongest reasons why people change is the belief that they can change. Person-centered counselors are strong believers in such a process.

The limitations of the theory are also noteworthy:

☐ The approach initially provided few instructions for counselors on how to establish relationships with clients and bring about change. The work of Carkhuff (1969a, b) and Gazda (1973) in making person-centered goals more specific has helped rectify this deficiency. Still, person-centered theory is sometimes viewed as an approach without clearly defined terms or techniques (Nye, 1981).

☐ The approach depends on bright, insightful, and hard-working clients for its best results. Thus, it has limited applicability and is seldom employed with the severely handicapped or with young children (Thompson & Rudolph, 1983).

☐ The approach ignores diagnosis, the unconscious, and innately generated sexual and aggressive drives. Many critics think the approach is overly optimistic. Even though Rogers compiled a great deal of data supporting his point of view, much of that research is attacked as being simplistic and based on self-reports (Hergenhahn, 1984).

☐ The approach deals only with surface issues and does not challenge the client to explore deeper areas. The argument here is that only deep change is lasting and since person-centered counseling is short-term, it cannot make a permanent impact on the person.

## EXISTENTIAL COUNSELING

The existential approach to counseling is unique in its diversity because there is no unanimity among existentialists about how to formulate a theory to accompany their ideas of helping others. Existentialism is represented in the writings of several prominent American theorists associated with counseling, such as Sidney Jourard, Victor Frankl, Abraham Maslow, Irvin Yalom, Rollo May, and Clark Moustakas. Its philosophical roots, though, are European. The bedrock of existentialism is found in the writings of Sören Kierkegaard, Fëdor Dostoevski, Jean-Paul Sartre, Albert Camus, Edmund Husserl, Friedrich Nietzsche, Martin Buber, and Martin Heidegger.

All existentialists have some beliefs in common, such as the importance of anxiety, values, freedom, and responsibility as well as an emphasis on finding meaning. But existentialists differ widely in their emphases. For example, Dostoevski stresses the importance of consciousness, Kierkegaard concentrates on human anxiety and dread, and Buber focuses on the treatment of persons and our relationships with them in an "it" or "thou" relationship. Rollo May (1961) and Victor Frankl (1962) are probably the best-known theorists of existential counseling, and it is on them and their ideas that we shall concentrate our attention.

### Rollo May

Rollo May was born in 1909 in Ada, Ohio. Like Alfred Adler, May was the second child of six children. Unlike Adler, May was the oldest son in his family. His father, who worked for the YMCA, encouraged Rollo to learn self-discipline through the sport of swimming. May, despite a close relationship with his father, saw himself as a loner during his childhood.

In 1930, May graduated in English from Oberlin College and then accepted a position teaching English at Anatolia College in Greece. During two of his summer vacations in Greece, May traveled to Vienna and enrolled in seminars conducted by Alfred Adler. As a result, May became interested in psychoanalysis. In 1933, he returned to the United States to enter the Union Theological Seminary. There he was strongly influenced by Paul Tillich, an existential theologian. After a brief career as a Congregational minister, May decided to pursue a degree in clinical psychology from Columbia University. Tuberculosis interrupted his studies. He struggled with the illness for almost two years, during which time he was strongly impressed with the writings of the Danish existentialist Sören Kierkegaard. Upon recovery, May completed his doctorate at Columbia in 1949 and joined the faculty of the William Allanson White Institute in New York City. He subsequently lectured at some of America's most distinguished universities, including Yale and Harvard.

### Victor Frankl

Victor Frankl was born in 1905 at Vienna, Austria. He received a medical degree in 1930 and a Ph.D. in 1949 from the University of Vienna. Frankl established the Youth Advisement Centers in Vienna and directed them for a 10-year period (1928–38). He also held several hospital appointments in Vienna between 1930 and 1942. During part of World War II (1942–45), he was imprisoned in Nazi concentration camps at Auschwitz and Dachau, where his parents, a brother, and his wife died. Although Frankl was a student of Freud's, he became interested in existentialism in the 1930s through reading such philosophers as Heidegger, Scheler, and Legan. He began formulating his ideas about an existentialist approach to counseling before his death camp experiences, having used the term *logotherapy* as early as 1938 (*logo*, which denotes finding meaning, is derived from Greek). The impact of the concentration camps crystalized Frankl's thoughts about the meaning of life and suffering, and it was partly his determination to share his beliefs that kept him alive.

In 1947, he joined the faculty of the University of Vienna; he later became associated with the United States International University in San Diego, California. He has lectured widely at many of America's most prestigious universities and has written extensively. His best-known books are *Man's Search for Meaning* (1962, a revision of *From Death-Camp to Existentialism*, 1946) and *The Will to Meaning* (1969). It is sometimes said that he is the founder of the third school of Viennese psychotherapy, logotherapy, with Freud's psychoanalytic theory being the first and Adler's individual psychology being second.

### View of Human Nature

As a group, existentialists believe people form their lives by the choices they make. Even in the worst of situations, such as the Nazi death camps, there is an opportunity to make important life and death decisions, such as whether to struggle to stay alive (Frankl, 1969). Existentialists focus on this freedom of choice and the action that goes with it. They view people as the authors of their lives; how much one restricts his or her life depends on personal decisions.

They contend that a person is responsible for any choice made and that some choices are healthier and more meaningful than others. According to Frankl (1962), the "meaning of life always changes, but . . . it never ceases to be" (p. 113). We can discover life's meaning in three ways:

☐ By doing a deed, that is by achieving or accomplishing something.

☐ By experiencing a value, such as a work of nature, culture, or love.

☐ By suffering, that is by finding a proper attitude toward unalterable fate.

Existentialists believe that psychopathology is a failure to make meaningful choices and to maximize one's potential (McIllroy, 1979).

Choices may be avoided and potentials not realized because of the anxiety that is involved in action. Anxiety is often associated with paralysis, but May (1977) argues that normal anxiety may be healthy and motivational and can help people change. Thus, existentialism focuses on the meaning of anxiety in human life. The emphasis within this framework is on the inner person and how authentic individuals search for values in life. By being aware of feelings and the finite nature of human existence, a person comes to make healthy and life-enhancing choices.

### Role of the Counselor

There are no uniform roles that all existential counselors follow. Every client situation they encounter is considered unique. Basically, counselors concentrate on being authentic with their clients and entering into deep and personal relationships with them. It is not unusual for a counselor to share personal experiences with a client in order to deepen the counseling relationship and help the client realize a shared humanness and struggle. Buhler and Allen (1972) suggest that existential counselors focus on person-to-person relationships that emphasize mutuality, wholeness, and growth. The counselor serves as a model in the relationship for how to achieve individual potential and make decisions. The counselor concentrates on helping the client experience subjective feelings, gain clearer self-understanding, and move toward the establishment of a new way of being in the world.

Existential counselors do not use psychological tests, nor do they make diagnoses in accordance with the DSM-III. Both of these procedures would be antithetical to the thrust of this approach. It is interesting to note, however, that some psychological instruments (such as the Purpose in Life test) are based on existential premises and that anxiety is dealt with on several levels in the DSM-III.

## Goals

The goals of existentialists include helping clients realize the importance of responsibility, awareness, freedom, and potential. Existentialists hope that during the course of counseling, clients will take more responsibility for their lives than they have previously. "The aim of therapy is that the patient experience his existence as real" (May, Angel, & Ellenberger, 1958, p. 85). Through such a process, the client is freed from being an observer of events to becoming a shaper of meaningful personal activity.

A client becomes more responsible partly because of the relationship built with the counselor. In the relationship, a client becomes more aware of personal freedom. Thus, a major goal of counseling is for clients to shift from an outward to an inward frame of reference. No longer will activities depend on the judgment of others; rather, activities will be evaluated by clients first. Further goals of counseling include making the client more aware of his or her existence, calling attention to the client's uniqueness, helping the client improve in encounters with others, and assisting the client in establishing a will to meaning and a direction in life (Cunningham & Peters, 1973).

## Techniques

The existential approach has fewer techniques available than almost any other model. Frankl (1967) wrote that "approaching human beings merely in terms of techniques necessarily implies manipulating them" (p. 139). According to Corey (1982), "Few techniques flow from this approach, because it stresses understanding first and technique second" (p. 242). Kemp (1976) has emphasized that the counselor's readiness to work with a client is of the uppermost importance and that no person can be understood by a rational approach alone. Counselors must be open and inquiring within the sessions. They must also accept the truth unique to each individual and be able and willing to work with ambiguity.

Thus, the most effective and powerful technique existential counselors have is the relationship with the client. Ideally, the counselor transcends his or her own needs and focuses on the client (Wallace, 1986). In the process, the counselor is open and self-revealing in an attempt to help the client become more in touch with personal feelings and experiences. The emphasis in the relationship is on authenticity, honesty, and spontaneity.

Existential counselors also make use of confrontation. Clients are confronted with the idea that everyone is responsible for his or her own life. Existential counselors borrow some techniques from other models, such as imagery exercises, awareness exercises, and goal setting activities. An example of a situation in which these borrowed techniques are used is when a counselor leads a client through a typical day in the client's life five years in the future. In such a process, a client is able to see the meaning in life more clearly by experiencing what choices are being made now.

## *Evaluation*

As with other approaches, there are a number of strengths in the existential approach to counseling:

☐ The approach emphasizes the uniqueness of each individual. It is a very humanistic approach to working with others (Yalom, 1980).

☐ The approach recognizes that anxiety is not necessarily a negative condition. Anxiety is a part of human life and can motivate some individuals to make healthy and productive decisions.

☐ The approach opens the door for counselors to a tremendous amount of philosophy and literature that is both informative and enlightening about human nature. The philosophical base of existentialism has the potential to support a systematic counseling theory.

The limitations of the existential approach are noted especially by professionals who embrace more structured approaches. We will focus on several of these apparent deficiencies:

☐ The approach has not produced a fully developed model of counseling. Professionals who stress developmental stages of counseling are particularly vehement in this criticism of the approach.

☐ The approach lacks educational and training programs. Each practitioner is unique. Although uniqueness is valued, it prohibits the systematic teaching of the theory. Wallace (1986) wonders if May's existential approach, for instance, will last.

☐ The approach is difficult to implement because of its subjective nature. Existentialism lacks the type of methodology and validation processes prevalent in most other approaches. In short, it lacks the uniformity that beginning counselors can readily understand.

☐ The approach is closer to existential philosophy than it is to other theories of counseling. This distinctiveness limits its usefulness.

## GESTALT THERAPY

Gestalt therapy is associated with Gestalt psychology, a school of thought that stresses perception of completeness and wholeness. The term *gestalt* means whole figure. Gestalt psychology and therapy arose as a reaction to the reductionist emphasis in other schools of psychology and counseling, such as psychoanalysis and behaviorism. Thus Gestalt theory emphasizes how people function as total units. The approach was popularized in the 1960s by Fritz Perls, who focused on helping individuals become more in touch with the many aspects of their personhood. Laura Perls (Fritz's wife) and Paul Goodman helped Perls develop and refine his original ideas. A number of other theorists, including Joen Fagan and Irma Lee Shepherd (1970), developed the model further, but it is on the work of Perls that the therapy rests.

### Fritz Perls

Friederick Salomon Perls was born in 1893 in Berlin into a middle-class Jewish family. He had a younger and an older sister. His parents fought bitterly and Perls disliked his older sister, yet he remembered his childhood as happy. He loved to read and was a top student in grade school. In secondary school, Perls encountered difficulty because of a conservative learning environment and because of his own rebellious spirit. He failed the seventh grade twice and as an adolescent had difficulty obeying authorities. Nevertheless, he not only completed his secondary education—once placed in a more liberal environment—but also was awarded a medical degree from Frederich Wilhelm University in 1920. His schooling was interrupted by World War I, during which he served as a medic with the German army.

Perls trained as a psychoanalyst in both Vienna and Berlin. Wilhelm Reich and Karen Horney each had a part in Perls' analysis.

Later, he took a position at the Institute for Brain Injured Soldiers in Frankfort. It was there that Perls became associated with Kurt Goldstein, from whom he learned to view humans as complete entities instead of as made of separate parts.

In 1933, Perls fled Nazi Germany and found a position as a psychoanalyst in Johannesburg, South Africa. He and his wife, Laura Posner Perls, built a strong practice there, as they had previously done in Germany. In 1936, Perls attended an International Psychoanalytic Congress in Czechoslovakia, where he met Freud. A brief interchange with Freud left Perls feeling humiliated. Thereafter, Perls, who had been humiliated frequently by his father, dedicated himself to proving Freud and psychoanalysis wrong.

Perls immigrated to the United States in 1946. Although his ideas were initially not readily accepted, he gained prominence through his book *Gestalt Therapy* (1951), through his establishment of the Gestalt Institutes, and through his lectures and workshops at the Esalen Institute in Big Sur, California. Perls was an actor at heart and loved to parade his ideas before the public. Laura Perls, long separated from Fritz, continued to be supportive of her husband until his death in 1970. Perls recounts many of the more personal moments of his life in the autobiographical *In and Out of the Garbage Pail* (1972).

### View of Human Nature

Gestaltists believe that human beings work for wholeness and completeness in life. Each person has a self-actualizing tendency that emerges through personal interaction with the environment and the beginning of self-awareness. Self-actualization is centered in the present; it "is the process of being what one is and not a process of striving to become" (Kempler, 1973, p. 262). The Gestalt view of human nature is one that places trust on the inner wisdom of people, much as person-centered counseling does. Each person seeks to live integratively and productively, striving to coordinate the various parts of the person into a healthy, unified whole. From a Gestalt perspective, a person is more than a sum of parts (Perls, 1969).

The Gestalt view is antideterministic: each person is able to change and become responsible. Individuals are thus actors in the events around them, not just reactors to events. Overall, the Gestalt point of view takes a position that is existential, experiential, and phenomenological: the now is what really matters; one discovers different aspects of oneself through experience, not through talk; and one's own assessment and interpretation of one's life at a given moment in time is what is most important.

A trouble for many individuals, according to Gestalt theory, is an overdependency on intellectual experience (Simkin, 1975). Such an emphasis diminishes the importance of emotions and the senses, limiting a person's ability to respond to various situations. Another problem numerous people face is the inability to identify and resolve "unfinished business"—earlier thoughts, feelings, and reactions that still affect personal functioning and interfere with living life in the present. The most frequent unfinished business in life is not forgiving one's parents for their mistakes. Gestaltists do not attribute either of these difficulties to any unconscious forces within persons. Rather, the focus is on awareness: every person operates on some conscious level, from being very aware to being very unaware.

Healthy individuals are those who are most aware. Such people realize that body signs, such as headaches or stomach pains, may indicate a need to change behavior. They are also aware of personal limitations. For instance, in conflicts with others, one may be able to resolve the situation or one may just have to dismiss it. A healthy person avoids complicating such situations through embellishment with fantasy. Instead, the person focuses "sharply on one need (the figure) at a time while relegating other needs to the background. When the need is met—or the Gestalt is closed or completed—it is relegated to the background and a new need comes into focus (becomes the figure)" (Thompson & Rudolph, 1983, p. 66). Such functioning requires that a person recognize internal needs and learn how to manipulate those needs and the environment (Perls, 1976).

According to Gestaltists, a person may experience difficulty in several ways. First, a person may lose contact with the environment and the resources in it. Second, a person may become overinvolved with the environment and thus out of touch with the self. Third, a person may fail to put aside unfinished business, that is unfulfilled needs, uncompleted situations, or unexpressed feelings. Fourth, a person may become fragmented, or scattered in many directions. Fifth, a person may experience what Perls labeled the conflict between the "topdog" (what one thinks one should do) and the "underdog" (what one wants to do). Finally, a person may have difficulty in handling the dichotomies of life, such as love/hate, masculinity/femininity, and pleasure/pain.

### Role of the Counselor

The role of the Gestalt counselor is to create an atmosphere that will promote the exploration by a client of what is needed in order to grow. The counselor provides such an atmosphere by being intensely and personally involved with clients and by being honest. Polster and Polster (1973) stress that counselors must be exciting and energetic and also fully human. Involvement occurs in the now, which is a continuing process (Perls, 1969). The now experience often involves having the counselor help a client focus on the blocking of energy and the experience of using that energy in positive and adaptive ways (Zinker, 1978). The now also entails the counselor's helping the client recognize patterns in the client's life (Fagan, 1970).

There are rules that Gestalt counselors follow in helping clients become more aware of the now (Levitsky & Perls, 1970). Among these are:

☐ *The principle of now*  Always using the present tense.

☐ *I and Thou*  Always addressing someone directly instead of talking about him or her to the counselor.

☐ *The use of I*  Substituting the use of *I* for *it*, especially when talking about the body.

☐ *The use of an awareness continuum*  Focusing on how and what rather than on why.

☐ *The conversion of questions*  Asking clients to convert questions into statements.

Gestalt counselors do not make use of standardized assessment instruments, such as psychological tests, nor do they diagnose their clients according to classification standards provided in the DSM-III.

### Goals

The goals of Gestalt therapy are well defined. They include an emphasis on the here and now, a recognition of the immediacy of experience, a focus on nonverbal as well as verbal expression, and a focus on the concept that life includes the making of choices (Fagan and Shepherd, 1970). The Gestalt approach concentrates on helping a client resolve the past in order to become integrated. This goal includes the completion of mentally growing up. It emphasizes the coalescence of the emotional, cognitive, and behavioral aspects of the person. A primary focus of Gestalt therapy is the acceptance of polarities within the person (Gelso & Carter, 1985). As a group, Gestalt therapists stress action, pushing their clients to experience feelings and behaviors. They stress the meaning of the word *now*. Perls (1970) has developed a formula that expresses the essence of this word: "Now = experience = awareness = reality. The past is no more and the future not yet. Only the now exists" (p. 14).

In order to be mature in the now, a person often must shed neurotic tendencies. Perls (1970) identifies five layers of neurosis that potentially interfere with one's being authentically in touch with oneself: the phony, the phobic, the impasse, the implosive, and the explosive. The first, the phony layer, consists of pretending to be something that one is not. At this level, there is a lot of game playing and fantasy enactment—trying to act as if one were something one is not. When a person becomes more aware of the games he or she is playing, he or she can be more honest, open, and in touch with unpleasantness and pain.

The second layer, the phobic, is an attempt to avoid recognizing aspects of self the person would prefer to deny. People who experience this layer of awareness are afraid that if they acknowledge who they are and present it to others, they will be rejected. Below this layer is the impasse layer, where individuals wonder how they are going to make it in the environment. There is no sense of direction at this level, and the person is adrift in a sea of helplessness and dread.

The fourth and fifth layers, the implosive and explosive, are often grouped together. At those layers, a person frequently feels vulnerable to feelings. Yet, as he or she peels back the layers of defensiveness built up over the years, he or she becomes alive in an explosion of joy, sorrow, or pain that leads to being authentic. When a person reaches this point, the now can be experienced most fully.

### Techniques

Some of the most innovative counseling techniques ever developed are found in Gestalt therapy. These techniques take two forms— exercises and experiments. Exercises are ready-made techniques, such as frustration actions, fantasy, role playing, and psychodrama (Covin, 1977). These exercises are employed to evoke a certain response from the client, such as anger or exploration. Experiments, on the other hand, are activities that grow out of the interaction between counselor and client. Experiments are not planned, and what is learned is often a surprise to both the client and the counselor. Many of the techniques of Gestalt therapy take the form of these unplanned experiments (Zinker, 1978). However, we will concentrate on those that are exercise oriented.

One common exercise Gestaltists use is *dream work*. Perls describes dreams as "messages" that represent the person's place at a certain time (Bernard, 1986). Unlike in psychoanalysis, Gestalt counselors do not interpret. Rather, clients present dreams and are then directed to experience what it is like to be each part of the dream—a type of dramatized free association. In this way, a client can get more in touch with the multiple aspects of the self. The person with repetitive dreams is encouraged to realize that unfinished business is being brought into awareness and that there is need to take care of the message delivered.

Another effective technique is the *empty chair.* A client talks to the various parts of the personality, such as a dominant side and a passive side. An empty chair is the focus. A client may simply talk to the chair as a representative of one part of the self, or the client may switch from chair to chair and have each chair represent a different part. In this dialogue, both rational and irrational parts of the client come into focus; the client not only sees these sides but also becomes able to deal with the dichotomies within the self. This method is not recommended for the severely emotionally disturbed (Bernard, 1986).

One of the most powerful Gestalt exercises is confrontation. Counselors point out to clients incongruent behaviors and feelings, such as a client's smiling when admitting to nervousness. Truly nervous people do not smile. Confrontation involves counselors asking clients *what* and *how* questions. *Why* questions are avoided because they lead to intellectualization.

A counselor may purposely frustrate a client at times in order to help the client move beyond present states of denial (Harman, 1975). The counselor hopes that the client makes valuable interpretations when confronted. Techniques that center on working in the here and now focus on helping break out of old habits and become more in touch with the self.

Some other powerful Gestalt exercises that are individually oriented are used primarily, though not exclusively, in groups. Four of the most prominent are:

☐ *Making the rounds*   Used in a group context this exercise is employed when the counselor feels a particular theme or feeling expressed by a client should be faced by every person in the group. The client may say, for instance, "I can't stand anyone." The client is then instructed to say this sentence to each person in the group, adding some remarks about each group member. The rounds exercise is very flexible and may include nonverbal and positive feelings too. By participating in it, clients become more aware than before of inner feelings.

☐ *I take responsibility*   Consists of the client's making statements about perceptions and closing each statement with the phrase "and I take responsibility for it." It helps clients integrate and own perceptions and behaviors.

☐ *Exaggeration*   Consists of clients' accentuating unwitting movement or gestures. In doing so, the inner meanings of these behaviors become more apparent.

☐ *May I feed you a sentence*   Consists of the counselor, who is aware that implicit attitudes or messages are implied in what the client is saying, asks if the client will say a certain sentence given by the counselor that makes the client's thoughts explicit. If the counselor is correct about the underlying message, the client will gain insight as the sentence is repeated.

### Evaluation

Gestalt therapy has a number of strengths:

☐ The approach emphasizes helping people incorporate and accept all aspects of life. An individual cannot be understood outside the context of the whole person choosing to act on the environment in the present (Passons, 1975).

☐ The approach helps a client focus on resolving areas of unfinished business. When a client is able to make these resolutions, life can be lived more productively.

☐ The approach places primary emphasis on doing rather than talking. Activity helps individuals experience what the process of change is all about and make more rapid progress.

☐ The approach is flexible and not limited to a few techniques. Any activity that helps clients become more integrative can be employed in Gestalt therapy.

☐ The approach is appropriate for certain affective disorders, anxiety states, somatoform disorders, adjustment disorders, and such DSM-III diagnoses as occupational problem and interpersonal problem (Seligman, 1986). In short, Gestalt therapy is versatile.

Even though there are some major strengths and advantages to Gestalt therapy, it also has limitations:

☐ The approach lacks a strong theoretical base. Some critics view Gestalt counseling as all experience and technique and "gimmicky" (Corey, 1986). They maintain it is antitheoretical. In support of that position, they cite Perls, "Lose your mind and come to your senses."

☐ The approach deals strictly with the *now* and *how* of experience (Perls, 1969). This two-pronged principle does not allow for passive insight and change, with which some clients feel most comfortable.

☐ The approach eschews diagnosis and testing. There are some individuals who need to be screened before experiencing such an intense method of counseling. Although Gestalt therapists screen their clients for appropriateness, some critics argue the process needs to be more uniform and thorough.

☐ The approach is too concerned with individual development and is criticized for its self-centeredness. The focus is totally on feeling and concentrated on personal discovery. Although many counseling theories are centered on individual development, Gestalt therapy is seen as being extreme in this regard.

## SUMMARY

Of the three affective approaches explored, the person-centered approach is the most popular. It is one of the easiest theories to learn on a surface level. That Rogerian techniques have been more concretely defined has added to the attractiveness of this theory. Gestalt therapy has also continued to generate strong interests. Although the Gestalt approach is criticized for being heavy on technique and light on theory, it produces major change in many clients. Existential counseling has just the opposite problem: it is steeped in philosophy but short on technique. Yet existential counseling continues to attract adherents because of its focus on the meaning of life.

As a group, affective approaches do not make much use of psychological tests, formal diagnoses, or rigid techniques. A trademark of these approaches is that they tailor what they do to the needs of the client. Counselors assess those needs by establishing strong relationships with clients. Existential counseling is the most nondirective of these theories, whereas Gestalt therapy is most directive. All of the theories share the belief that clients are capable of change, integration, and positive growth. Person-centered theory has the strongest support from research data. Existential counseling is often thought of as more of a philosophy than a counseling approach and has practically no research data to back it up.

## CLASSROOM ACTIVITIES

1. Compare and contrast how you understand a practitioner from each of the three affective approaches would work with the following types of clients: an alcoholic, a school-phobic child, a spouse abuser, an unemployed drifter. How are the approaches similar and different?

2. Read *A Way of Being* (1980) by Carl Rogers. Then discuss in small groups how Rogers' theory was influenced by his own personal development and how person-centered theory could be applied to educational, political, industrial, medical, recreational, and managerial settings of which you are

aware. Be as specific as you can in translating the theory to these settings. Discuss your views with the class as a whole.

3. How do you think counselors from affective approaches would handle reluctant clients, such as a child sent to the counselor or a prisoner whose sentence requires counseling? Discuss your ideas in dyads and then share them with the class as a whole.

4. Rollo May held that the best counselors are those who have been "wounded," that is, gone through suffering and healing themselves. In small groups, discuss what experiences counselors might best use to help them understand themselves and their clients better. What are the advantages of having experienced a situation similar to your clients'? What are the disadvantages?

5. There are approximately 50 Gestalt institutes in the United States. With the help of your instructor or librarian, locate as many of them as you can and find out what types of training programs they offer. If possible, interview a professional who practices Gestalt and ask how he or she would compare the approach to a person-centered one.

## REFERENCES

Baruth, L. G., & Huber, C. H. (1985). *Counseling and psychotherapy: Theoretical analyses and skills applications.* Columbus, OH: Merrill.

Bernard, J. M. (1986). Laura Perls: From ground to figure. *Journal of Counseling and Development, 64,* 367–373.

Boy, A. V., & Pine, G. J. (1963). *Client-centered counseling in the secondary school.* Boston: Houghton Mifflin.

Boy, A. V., & Pine, G. J. (1982). *Client-centered counseling: A renewal.* Boston: Allyn & Bacon.

Braaten, L. J. (1986). Thirty years with Rogers's necessary and sufficient conditions of therapeutic personality change. *Person-Centered Review, 1,* 37–49.

Buhler, C., & Allen, M. (1972). *Introduction to humanistic psychology.* Monterey, CA: Brooks/Cole.

Carkhuff, R. R. (1969a). *Helping and human relations* (Vol. 1). New York: Holt, Rinehart & Winston.

Carkhuff, R. R. (1969b). *Helping and human relations* (Vol. 2). New York: Holt, Rinehart & Winston.

Corey, G. (1982). *Theory and practice of counseling and psychotherapy* (2nd ed.). Monterey, CA: Brooks/Cole.

Corey, G. (1986). *Theory and practice of counseling and psychotherapy* (3rd ed.). Monterey, CA: Brooks/Cole.

Cormier, L. S., & Hackney, H. (1987). *The professional counselor: A process guide to helping.* Englewood Cliffs, NJ: Prentice-Hall.

Covin, A. B. (1977). Using Gestalt psychodrama experiments in rehabilitation counseling. *Personnel and Guidance Journal, 56,* 143–147.

Cunningham, L. M., & Peters, H. J. (1973). *Counseling theories.* Columbus, OH: Merrill.

Fagan, J. (1970). The task of the therapist. In J. Fagan & I. L. Shepherd (Eds.), *Gestalt therapy now.* Palo Alto, CA: Science and Behavior Books.

Fagan, J., & Shepherd, I. L. (1970). Theory of Gestalt therapy. In J. Fagan & I. L. Shepherd (Eds.), *Gestalt therapy now.* Palo Alto, CA: Science and Behavior Books.

Frankl, V. (1962). *Man's search for meaning: An introduction to logotherapy.* New York: Washington Square Press.

Frankl, V. (1969). *Psychotherapy and existentialism: Selected papers on logotherapy.* New York: Simon & Schuster.

Frankl, V. (1969). *The will to meaning: Foundations and applications of logotherapy.* New York: New American Library.

Gazda, G. M. (1973). *Human relations development: A manual for education.* Boston: Allyn & Bacon.

Gelso, C. J., & Carter, J. A. (1985). The relationship in counseling and psychotherapy: components, consequences, and theoretical antecedents. *The Counseling Psychologist, 13,* 155–243.

Gladding, S. T. (1975). Here and now. *Personnel and Guidance Journal, 53,* 746.

Grummon, D. L. (1972). Client-centered therapy. In B. Stefflre & W. H. Grant (Eds.), *Theories of counseling* (2nd ed.). New York: McGraw- Hill.

Harman, R. L. (1975). A Gestalt point of view on facilitating growth in counseling. *Personnel and Guidance Journal, 53,* 363–366.

Hart, J. (1970). The development of client-centered therapy. In J. T. Hart & T. M. Tomlinson (Eds.), *New directions in client-centered therapy.* Boston: Houghton Mifflin.

Hergenhahn, B. R. (1984). *An introduction to theories of personality.* Englewood Cliffs, NJ: Prentice-Hall.

Kemp, C. G. (1976). Existential counseling. In G. S. Belkin (Ed.), *Counseling directions in theory and practice.* Dubuque, IA: Kendall/Hunt.

Kempler, W. (1973). Gestalt therapy. In R. Corsini (Ed.), *Current psychotherapies* (pp. 251–286). Itasca, IL: Peacock.

Levitsky, A., & Perls, F. S. (1970). The rules and games of Gestalt therapy. In J. Fagan & I. L. Shepherd (Eds.), *Gestalt therapy now* (pp. 140–149). Palo Alto, CA: Science and Behavior Books.

May, R. (Ed.). (1961). *Existential psychology.* New York: Random House.

May, R. (1977). *The meaning of anxiety* (rev. ed.). New York: Norton.

May, R., Angel, E., & Ellenberger, H. (Eds.). (1958). *Existence.* New York: Simon & Schuster.

McIllroy, J. H. (1979). Career as life-style: An existential view. *Personnel and Guidance Journal, 57,* 351–354.

Nye, R. D. (1981). *Three psychologies* (2nd ed.). Monterey, CA: Brooks/Cole.

Passons, W. R. (1975). *Gestalt approaches to counseling.* New York: Holt, Rinehart & Winston.

Perls, F. (1969). *Gestalt therapy verbatim.* Lafayette, CA: Real People Press.

Perls, F. (1970). Four lectures. In J. Fagan & I. L. Shepherd (Eds.), *Gestalt therapy now.* Palo Alto, CA: Science and Behavior Books.

Perls, F. (1972). *In and out of the garbage pail* New York: Bantam Books.

Perls, F. (1976). *The Gestalt approaches and eye witnesses to therapy.* New York: Bantam Books.

Polster, E., & Polster, M. (1973). *Gestalt therapy integrated: Contours of theory and practice.* New York: Brunner/Mazel.

Poppen, W. A., & Thompson, C. L. (1974). *School counseling: Theories and concepts.* Lincoln, NE: Professional Educators Publications.

Rogers, C. R. (1942). *Counseling and psychotherapy.* Boston: Houghton Mifflin.

Rogers, C. R. (1951). *Client-centered therapy.* Boston: Houghton Mifflin.

Rogers, C. R. (1955). Persons or science? A philosophical question. *American Psychologist, 10,* 267–278.

Rogers, C. R. (1957). The necessary and sufficient conditions of therapeutic personality change. *Journal of Consulting Psychology, 21,* 95–103.

Rogers, C. R. (1959). A theory of therapy, personality, and interpersonal relationships, as developed in the client-centered framework. In S. Koch (Ed.), *Psychology: A study of science* (Vol. 3, pp. 184–256). New York: McGraw-Hill.

Rogers, C. R. (1961). *On becoming a person.* Boston: Houghton Mifflin.

Rogers, C. R. (1967). The conditions of change from a client-centered viewpoint. In B. Berenson & R. Carkhuff (Eds.), *Sources of gain in counseling and psychotherapy.* New York: Holt, Rinehart & Winston.

Rogers, C. R. (1969). *Freedom to learn.* Columbus, OH: Merrill.

Rogers, C. R. (1975). Empathic: An unappreciated way of being. *The Counseling Psychologist, 5,* 2–10.

Rogers, C. R. (1980). *A way of being.* Boston: Houghton Mifflin.

Seligman, L. (1986). *Diagnosis and treatment planning in counseling.* New York: Human Sciences Press.

Simkin, J. S. (1975). An introduction to Gestalt therapy. In F. D. Stephenson (Ed.), *Gestalt therapy primer.* Springfield, IL: Thomas.

Thompson, C. L., & Rudolph, L. B. (1983). *Counseling children.* Monterey, CA: Brooks/Cole.

Wallace, W. A. (1986). *Theories of counseling and psychotherapy.* Boston: Allyn & Bacon.

Yalom, I. D. (1980). *Existential psychotherapy.* New York: Basic Books.

Zajonc, R. (1984). On the primacy of affect. *American Psychologist, 39,* 117–123.

Zinker, J. (1978). *Creative process in Gestalt therapy.* New York: Random House.

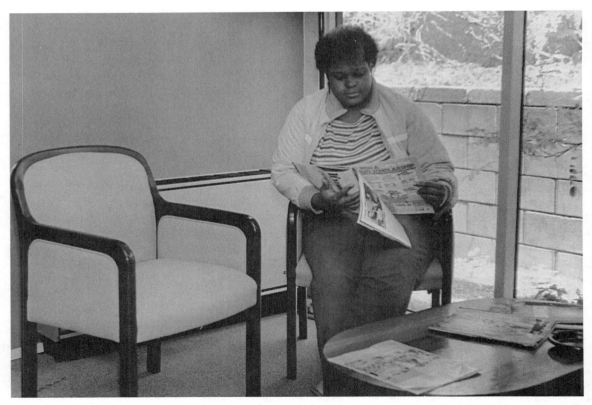

Photo by James S. Davidson III.

# The Theory and Practice of Individual Counseling: Cognitive Approaches

*She works in a world I have never known*
*Full of rainbow pills and lilac candles*
*Woven together with simple time-stitches*
*A pattern of color in a gray fabric factory*
*Where she spends her days*
    *spinning threads*
       *that go to Chicago by night.*
*Once with a little girl smile and a giggle*
*She flew to Atlanta in her mind,*
*Opening the door to instant adventures*
    *far from her present fatigue,*
*That was a journey we shared*
    *arranging her thoughts in a patchwork pattern*
    *until the designs and desires came together. . . .* [1]

C ognitive theories of counseling focus on thinking. Most cognitive theorists would agree in substance with Proverbs 23:7, that "as he thinketh in his heart, so is he." They might also agree with Shakespeare's Hamlet, who says, "There's nothing either good or bad but thinking makes it so."

Cognitive theorists believe that thoughts influence feelings and behaviors. If a person changes a way of thinking, feelings and behaviors will be modified as a result. These theories are successful in working with clients who are average to above-average in intelligence, who have moderate to high levels of functional distress, who are able to identify thoughts and feelings, who are not psychotic or disabled by present problems, who are willing and able to complete systematic homework assignments, who possess a repertoire of behavioral skills and responses, and who process information on a visual and auditory level (Cormier & Hackney, 1987). Cognitive approaches are also frequently used in working with clients who have inhibited functioning, such as depression.

There is considerable activity among counselors to unite these theories with behavioral theories into a cognitive-behavioral approach, as exemplified in the cognitive behavior modification of Don Meichenbaum (1977) and the cognitive therapy of Aaron Beck (1976). Nevertheless, some theories remain primarily cognitive in nature whereas others remain primarily behavioral. In this chapter two prominent cognitive theories are examined—Albert Ellis's rational-emotive therapy (RET) and Eric Berne's transactional analysis (TA).

## RATIONAL-EMOTIVE THERAPY

### Albert Ellis

The founder of rational-emotive therapy (RET), Albert Ellis, is described by Weinrach (1980) as "abrasive, impatient, and lacking in some of the basic social graces that my mother spent hours indoctrinating me with" but also "brilliant, sensitive, perceptive, humorous, and stimulating" (p. 152). Ellis's fit into both of these descriptions is partially the result of his life history.

Albert Ellis was born in 1913 at Pittsburgh, Pennsylvania, into a Jewish family. His parents eventually had a daughter and another son. Early in his life, Ellis's family moved to New York City, where he has spent most of his life. Ellis describes his father in positive and neutral terms, though the elder Ellis was absent from home a great deal. From his father, Ellis believes he acquired his intelligence, drive, and persistence (Newhorn, 1978). His mother was quite independent for her time, often idiosyncratic in her behavior, happy, and nonsmothering.

At five, Ellis almost died from tonsillitis; he later suffered from acute nephritis and diabetes (Morris & Kanitz, 1975). Ellis thought most members of his family were "pretty crazy," and by age seven he was largely on his own (Weinrach, 1980). The divorce of his parents when he was 12 caused him to give up plans to be a Hebrew teacher, and he became instead a self-described "probabilistic atheist," someone who does not believe that God exists but would accept empirical evidence to the contrary.

Ellis's dream as an adolescent was to become a writer. He planned to make enough money to retire early in life and then devote his time to writing. In 1934, he graduated in business from the City College of New York, and he worked in the business world until the mid-1940s. When not working, he wrote fiction. When his literary efforts proved unsuccessful, he decided to study psychology. From Columbia University, Ellis received a master's degree in 1943 and a Ph.D. in 1947 in clinical psychology.

Ellis's wish to become a psychoanalytic clinical psychologist was at first frustrated because institutions that specialized in such training only admitted medical professionals. He finally succeeded in obtaining analysis from the Karen Horney group and practiced classic psychoanalysis in the early 1950s. Ellis, dissatisfied with that approach, began in 1955 the practice of his own theory, rational-emotive therapy (RET), which was primarily a cognitive theory in the beginning. Its main tenets were first published in his *Reason and Emotion in Psychotherapy* (1962). RET has since broadened its base considerably and now includes behavioral and emotional concepts.

Two nonprofit institutes have been established by Ellis to promote RET: The Institute for Rational Living, a scientific and educational foundation established in 1959; and the Institute for Rational-Emotive Therapy, an institution for professional training and clinical services established in 1968. Ellis, a prolific writer, has produced over 500 articles, some 50 books, and numerous films and tapes. Each week, he sees as many as 80 clients for individual sessions and conducts up to eight group sessions. Annually, he gives about 200 workshops and talks. Yet Ellis does not consider himself a compulsive worker, because he does not have to work and he does not have to prove himself (Weinrach, 1980). He relaxes by reading, listening to music, and socializing.

Ellis has been married twice. He is a nationally known counselor and sex therapist and has received a number of professional awards, including Humanist of the Year by the American Humanist Association. He does not see any conflict between religion and RET, and points to John Powell's book, *Fully Human, Fully Alive* (1976), as a way RET and religious teachings can be combined.

## *View of Human Nature*

RET assumes that people are both "inherently rational and irrational, sensible and crazy" (Weinrach, 1980, p. 154). According to Ellis (1979), this duality is biologically inherent, and it is perpetuated unless a new way of thinking is learned. Irrational thinking may include the invention of upsetting and disturbing thoughts. Ellis (1962) lists 11 common irrational beliefs that can be quite disturbing. These fallacies, which have been used in formulating various tests, have been correlated "with various kinds of emotional disturbance" (Ellis, 1984, p. 266). They are the following:

- ☐ It is absolutely essential to be loved or approved of by every significant person in one's life.
- ☐ To be worthwhile, a person must be competent, adequate, and achieving in everything attempted.
- ☐ Some people are wicked, bad, and villainous and therefore should be blamed or punished.
- ☐ It is terrible and a catastrophe whenever events do not occur as one hopes.
- ☐ Unhappiness is the result of outside events, and therefore a person has no control over such despair.
- ☐ Something potentially dangerous or harmful should be cause for great concern and should always be kept in mind.

- ☐ Running away from difficulties and responsibilities is easier than facing them.
- ☐ A person must depend on others and must have someone stronger on whom to rely.
- ☐ The past determines one's present behavior and thus cannot be changed.
- ☐ A person should be upset by the problems and difficulties of others.
- ☐ There is always a right answer to every problem, and a failure to find this answer is a catastrophe.

Although Ellis (1973) does not deal with the developmental stages of individuals, he thinks that children are more vulnerable to outside influences and irrational thinking than are adults. By nature, he believes, human beings are gullible and highly suggestible and thus easily disturbed. Overall, people have within themselves the means to control their thoughts, feelings, and actions, but they must first realize what they are telling themselves, i.e., their "self-talk," in order to gain command of their lives (Ellis, 1962). This is a matter of personal conscious awareness. The unconscious mind is not included in Ellis's conception of human nature.

Ellis believes it is a mistake for people to evaluate or rate themselves beyond the idea that everyone is a fallible human being. He especially discourages the use of any form of the verb *to be* (e.g., is, was, am, has been, being) to describe a person. He reasons that human problems do not come from the id, as Freud envisioned, or from the "what if," but rather from the "is." The verb "to be" makes it difficult to separate the person from his or her actions. Therefore, Ellis advocates that individuals speak and think of their behavior as separate from their personhood; for example: "I act badly" rather than "I am bad" (Ellis & Harper, 1975). By avoiding such a use of the verb *to be*, a more rational thought process is fostered and a person gains the freedom to change—the focus is directed to altering specific behaviors instead of overhauling the personality.

### Role of the Counselor

In the RET approach, counselors are active and direct. They are instructors, teaching and correcting the client's cognitions. Ellis (1980) identifies several characteristics highly desirable for RET counselors. They need to be bright, knowledgeable, empathetic, persistent, scientific, interested in helping others, and users themselves of RET.

The main assessment conducted by RET counselors is the evaluation of a client's thinking. Some formal tests are used to measure rational/irrational thinking, but the evaluation process is primarily accomplished in counselor/client sessions. As a rule, RET practitioners do not rely heavily on the diagnostic categories found in the DSM-III.

## Goals

The primary goals of RET focus on helping people realize that they can live more rational and productive lives. Ellis's approach is heavily influenced by Stoic philosophy, and he is fond of quoting a first century Stoic, Epictetus, who wrote, "Men feel disturbed not by things, but by the views which they take of them." Often individuals disturb themselves by changing wishes and desires into demands. Ellis points out that when a person uses such words as *must, should, ought, have to,* and *need,* the person is making demands of wishes and thinking irrationally. Many individuals think that wishes must or should occur and that if a wish remains unfulfilled the result is a catastrophe. RET helps clients stop making such demands and becoming upset through "catastrophizing." Clients in RET may express some negative feelings, but a major goal is to help clients avoid having more of an emotional response to an event than is warranted. Ellis frequently uses puns and other humorous devices to help his clients see how irrational thinking develops and how silly the consequences of such thinking are. He cautions clients not to "should on themselves" and advises them to avoid "musterbation." He has even composed a number of rational songs to help remind himself and others to think rationally. For example, Ellis (1980) has penned the following to the tune of the Whiffenpoof song:

> I cannot have all of my wishes filled—
> Whine, whine, whine!
> I cannot have every frustration stilled—
> Whine, whine, whine!
> Life really owes me the things that I miss,
> Fate has to grant me eternal bliss!
> And if I must settle for less than this—
> Whine, whine whine![2]

[2]SOURCE: From *Rational Humorous Songs: A Garland of Rational Songs* by Albert Ellis, 1980, New York: Institute for Rational Emotive Therapy. Copyright 1980 by Institute for Rational Emotive Therapy. Reprinted by permission.

Another goal of RET is to assist people in changing any self-defeating habits of thought or behavior. One way this is accomplished is through teaching clients the so-called ABCs of RET. *A* stands for the activating experience; *B* represents how the person thinks about the experience; and *C* is the emotional reaction to *B* (Figure 5.1). Many clients believe that an experience directly causes feelings—a "cognitive bypass." Left out in this conceptualization is the thought process that leads to the development of emotions. For example, a person may lose a job or an opportunity and assert that the experience has caused depression. RET helps such a person learn how to recognize his or her own "emotional anatomy" and how feelings are attached to thoughts.

Thoughts about experiences may be characterized in four ways—positive, negative, neutral, or mixed. A positive thought leads to positive feelings, and so on. For example, if a host at a party reminds a man that he has had too much to drink, he may think about the care and concern shown by the host in his behalf and thus have positive feelings. Or this person may have negative feelings about this same event because he thinks that the host is being critical of him, has no right to do so, and therefore should not comment about his behavior. Neutral thoughts include simply noting the host's actions and moving on to another thought. Mixed thoughts are when the person has both negative and positive thoughts at once. The resulting feeling is ambivalence.

Overall, RET encourages clients to be more tolerant of themselves and others and to achieve personal goals. These goals are accomplished partly through having people learn to think rationally in order to change self-defeating behavior and through helping clients learn new ways of acting. Ellis has devised a number of homework assignments, such as "shame attack" exercises. These exercises usually include an activity that is harmless but dreaded, such as introducing oneself to a stranger or asking for a glass of water in a restaurant. By participating in such exercises, a client learns the ABCs of RET on a personal level and comes to realize more fully that the world does not stop if a mistake is made or a want remains unfulfilled. A client also learns that others are "fallible human beings" and need not be perfect. Finally, a client learns that

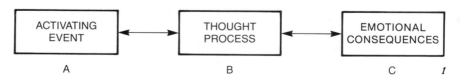

**FIGURE 5.1** The ABCs of RET.

goals may be achieved without "catastrophizing," "awfulizing," or "terriblizing" about personal situations.

### Techniques

RET encompasses a number of diverse techniques. Two of the primary ones are teaching and disputing. Before changes can be made, clients have to learn the basic ideas of RET and how thoughts are linked with emotions and behaviors. As a process, RET is highly didactic and very directive. In the first couple of sessions, counselors teach their clients the anatomy of an emotion—that feelings are a result of thoughts and not events and that self-talk influences emotions. It is critical that the client master the ability to dispute irrational thoughts.

Disputing thoughts and beliefs takes one of three forms— cognitive, imaginal, and behavioral. The process is most effective when all three forms are used (Walen, DiGiuseppe, & Wessler, 1980). *Cognitive disputation* involves the use of direct questions, logical reasoning, and persuasion. Direct questions may challenge the client to prove that his or her response is logical. Sometimes these inquiries involve the use of the word *why*, which is seldom used in counseling because of the way it puts most people on the defensive and closes off exploration. Examples of questions in cognitive disputation include "Why must you?" and "Why must that be so?" During these inquiries, clients learn to distinguish between rational and irrational thoughts and learn the superiority of rational thoughts.

*Imaginal disputation* depends on the client's ability to imagine and employs a technique known as *rational-emotive imagery* (REI) (Maultsby, 1984). REI may be used in one of two ways. First, the client may be asked to imagine a situation where he or she is likely to become upset. The client examines his or her self-talk during that imagined situation. Then the counselor asks the client to envision the same situation but this time to be more moderate in his or her self-talk. Second, the counselor asks a client to imagine a situation in which the client feels or behaves differently from some real instance. The client is then instructed to examine the self-talk used in this imagined situation. REI takes practice. It may work both with clients who have vivid imaginations and, with practice, with those who do not.

The *emotional control card* (ECC) is a device that helps clients reinforce and expand the practice of REI (Sklare, Taylor, & Hyland, 1985). Four emotionally debilitating categories (anger, self-criticism, anxiety, and depression) are listed on the wallet-sized ECC (Ellis, 1986). Under each category is a list of inappropriate or self-destructive feelings and a parallel list of appropriate or nondefeating feelings (Figure 5.2). In a potentially troubling situation, a client may refer to the card and change the quality of feelings about that situation. At the next session with the counselor, the client discusses the use of the card in cognitively restructuring thoughts to make them rational.

*Behavioral disputation* involves behaving in a way that is the opposite of the client's usual way. Sometimes behavioral disputation may take the form of bibliotherapy, in which the client reads a self-

| Inappropriate or Self-Destructive Feelings | Appropriate or Nondefeating Feelings |
|---|---|
| *Anger* <br> Feelings of resentment, anger, madness, fury, rage | *Irritation* <br> Feelings of (mild or intense) irritation, displeasure, annoyance, frustration; anger at people's acts but not at their persons |
| *Self-criticism* <br> Feelings of humiliation, shame, embarrassment, inadequacy; discounting self as a person | *Criticism of one's behavior* <br> Feelings of (mild or intense) regret, sorrow, displeasure, doubt; criticism of one's behavior but not of one's total self |
| *Anxiety* <br> Feelings of anxiety, nervousness, hypertension, panic, helplessness, horror | *Concern* <br> Feelings of (mild or intense) concern, caution, vigilance; tension about one's performance but not about one's self |
| *Depression* <br> Feelings of depression, worthlessness, undeservingness, guilt, self-downing | *Sadness* <br> Feelings of (mild or intense) sadness, sorrow, regret, discontentment, displeasure; feeling that one is a person who has performed badly but is not a bad person |

**FIGURE 5.2**  Emotional control card (revised version).

help book (a number of books for all ages are distributed by the Institute for Rational-Emotive Therapy). At other times behavioral disputation includes role playing and the completion of a homework assignment in which a client actually does activities previously thought impossible to do. The client brings the completed assignment to the RET counselor at the next counseling session and evaluates it with the counselor's help.

Two other powerful techniques include confrontation and encouragement. As previously noted, RET counselors explicitly encourage clients to abandon thought processes that are not working and to try RET. Sometimes, the RET counselor will challenge a client who claims to be thinking rationally but in truth is not. At other times, the counselor encourages a client to continue working from a RET base even when discouraged. Confrontation need not be done in the manner Ellis uses: vigorously confronting and attacking the client's beliefs (Johnson, 1980). Instead, a counselor may be empathetic and insistent at the same time

One interesting variation on RET is *rational behavior therapy* (RBT), which was formulated by Maxie Maultsby (1971, 1973, 1975, 1984). RBT emphasizes cognitive change in a more behavioral way than originally conceptualized by Ellis. It involves checking the activating event as if one were a camera in order to be sure of objectivity. Disputation of a person's self-talk takes the form of a debate based on five rules for rational behavior. Rational behavior:

☐ Affirms objective reality
☐ Protects the self
☐ Accomplishes personal goals most quickly
☐ Discourages unwanted trouble with others
☐ Prevents significant emotional conflict.

In RBT, clients regularly complete a homework assignment in the form of a *rational self-analysis* (RSA), in which they write down significant events in their lives and their thoughts and feelings associated with those events. The beliefs of the person are then evaluated for their degree of rationality and changed in accordance with the rules of rational behavior. This method of assessing a client's thoughts is useful in maintaining a record of client progress. The RSA method consist of six steps. These steps of rational self-analysis are:

☐ *Step 1*   A listing of facts and events as initially seen by the client.
☐ *Step 2*   A review of the self-talk associated with the events in question.

☐ *Step 3*   A listing of the emotional consequences of that self-talk.

☐ *Step 4*   A so-called camera check of the events in question to check for objectivity.

☐ *Step 5*   A rational debate of the self-talk using the rules for rational behavior.

☐ *Step 6*   A listing of the client's emotional goals for the future.

Many of the concepts of rational behavior therapy, such as homework assignments and rational emotive imagery, are now included as a part of RET. Nevertheless, RBT remains distinct from several other variations of RET.

### Evaluation

RET has a number of strengths:

☐ The approach is clear, easily learned, and effective. Most clients have few problems in understanding the principles or terminology of RET. Roush (1984) reports that RET is effective with many different types of individuals, including adolescents. Seligman (1986) notes that it is appropriate for the treatment of affective disorders, anxiety disorders, and adjustment disorders. Ellis (1977) provides research data on the effectiveness of RET with different types of clients in specific settings.

☐ The approach can easily be combined with behavioral techniques to help clients experience more fully what they are learning. Maultsby's rational behavior therapy is a good example of this type of combination. Ellis is sometimes referred to as a forerunner of the cognitive-behavioral counseling approaches.

☐ The approach is relatively short-term, usually lasting from 10 to 50 sessions. Clients may continue to use the approach in their lives on a self-help basis. The economical and efficiency aspects of RET are impressive.

☐ The approach has an impressive amount of literature and research available for clients and counselors. Few other theories have developed as much bibliotherapeutic material. Ellis is a prolific writer and researcher, as are many other RET practitioners. Ellis's two nonprofit institutes are constantly engaged in empirical studies on the use of RET with a wide variety of clients.

☐ The approach has continued to evolve over the years as techniques have been refined. An example of the way RET has evolved is found in noting the difference between "inelegant" and "elegant" RET. Inelegant RET, which was developed first, focuses on the activating event and the distortions clients usually have about these events (Ellis, 1977, 1979). It does not give clients any coping strategies for dealing with situations in which the perception of an event matches reality. Instead, clients are encouraged to assure themselves that they will do better in the future or that they are good persons. Elegant RET, on the other hand, concentrates on the beliefs of clients and focuses on their taking responsibility for their own feelings and not blaming others. Clients realize in the process that success in everything is not essential and that catastrophe is not the result of every unfulfilled want.

The limitations of this approach are few but significant:

☐ The approach cannot be used effectively with individuals who have severe thought disorders, such as schizophrenics, and it is not productive with people who are severely mentally impaired. A person who is bright benefits most from this approach.

☐ The approach may be too closely associated with its founder, Albert Ellis. Many individuals have difficulty separating the theory from the eccentricities of Ellis. Although Johnson (1980) urges counselors to adapt the theory and techniques of RET to their own personalities and styles of counseling, some counselors still eschew the approach because of its connection with Ellis.

☐ The approach is limited if its practitioners do not combine its early cognitive base with more behavioral and emotive techniques. Ellis (Weinrach, 1980) says that RET has always been a diverse approach, and he advocates its use in various settings. The theory is now much broader than when it was originally formulated, but many counselors still concentrate on the cognitive side of RET, limiting its usefulness.

## TRANSACTIONAL ANALYSIS

### Eric Berne

A second major cognitive theory is transactional analysis (TA), which was formulated by Eric Berne in the early 1960s. The theory rose to prominence through the publication of two best-selling books, *Games People Play* (1964) by Eric Berne and *I'm OK—You're*

*OK* (1967) by Thomas Harris. Berne was fearful that the popularity of these books would undermine the seriousness of his work. Instead, popularity made the theory more attractive.

Eric Berne was born in 1910 in Montreal, Canada, where his father was a doctor and his mother was a writer and editor. Eric was five years older than his only sibling, a sister. Berne was close to his father, who died at the age of 38, when Eric was nine years old. Berne followed in his father's footsteps, earning a medical degree from McGill University in 1935. He then completed a psychiatric residency at Yale, set up a private practice in Connecticut and New York, became a U.S. citizen, and married. During World War II, he served as an army psychiatrist in Utah, where he started practicing group therapy.

After the war, he settled in Carmel, California, where he separated from his wife and completed his first book, *The Mind in Action*, a critical survey of psychiatry and psychoanalysis. He also resumed the psychoanalytic training he had started before the war. A part of that training was his analysis, which was supervised by Erik Erikson, who insisted Berne not remarry until after the analysis was finished. Berne did as directed but remarried in 1949, and became the father of two children, as he had in his first marriage. He built a study in his house away from the noise of the children and in 1950 began setting a demanding schedule for himself that included consultations and practice in Carmel, San Francisco, and Monterey. His only break occurred on Friday night when he played poker at his house.

In 1956 Berne was turned down for membership in the Psychoanalytic Institute. This rejection proved to be a turning point in his life. He reacted by disassociating himself with psychoanalysis and devoting his time to the development of transactional analysis, which has a psychoanalytic flavor. Dusay (1977) describes the formulation of TA as proceeding through four phases. In the first phase (1955–62), Berne developed the concept of ego states. His ideas were influenced by his clients' descriptions of behaving as a child, as a parent, and as an adult (the three ego states). In the second phase (1962–66), Berne concentrated on ideas about transactions and games. It was during this time that the International Transactional Analysis Association was created (1964) and that Berne published the popular *Games People Play*. In the third phase (1966–70), emphasis was placed on the reasons some individuals choose to play certain games in life. In the fourth phase (from 1970), emphasis was placed on action and energy distribution.

Berne was involved in the first three phases of this development. After a second divorce in 1964, he spent a great deal of time writing. At one time, he was working on the manuscripts of six books, as well as editing the *Transactional Analysis Bulletin*. He also gave numerous lectures and seminars. Berne's third marriage was short-lived; he died of a heart attack in 1970 at the age of 60.

### *View of Human Nature*

Transactional analysis is an optimistic theory. Its basic assumption is that people can change despite any unfortunate events of the past. TA is antideterministic in believing that people have choices in their lives—what was decided can be redecided at a later date. As James and Jongeward (1970) emphasize, "Transactional analysis is a rational approach to understanding behavior and is based on the assumption that all individuals can learn to trust themselves, think for themselves, make their own decisions, and express their feelings" (p. 12).

TA focuses on four major methods of understanding and predicting human behavior:

☐ *Structural analysis*   Understanding what is happening within the individual.

☐ *Transactional analysis*   Describing what happens between two or more people.

☐ *Game analysis*   Understanding transactions between individuals that lead to bad feelings.

☐ *Script analysis*   Understanding the life plan that an individual is following.

**Structural Analysis.**   In structural analysis, each person is considered to have three functional *ego states*—Child, Parent, and Adult.

Berne (1964) defines an ego state as "a consistent pattern of feeling and experience directly related to a corresponding consistent pattern of behavior" (p. 364). He notes that the findings of Wilder Penfield and his associates (1952, 1954) offer support for this definition. Penfield, a neurosurgeon, found that an electrode applied to different parts of the brain evokes memories and feelings long forgotten by the person. The implication of this research is that the brain functions like a tape recorder to preserve complete experiences in sequence in a form recognizable as ego states.

The first ego state to develop is the *Child*, which is that part of the personality characterized by childlike behaviors and feelings. Childlike behavior might be described as inquisitive, affectionate, selfish, mean, playful, whiny, and manipulative. The Child ego state consists of three subdivisions—the Natural (Free) Child, the Adaptive Child, and the Little Professor. The *Natural Child* is the part of the person that is spontaneous, impulsive, feeling oriented, and often self-centered and pleasure loving. The *Adaptive Child* is the compliant part of the personality that has yielded to the wishes and demands of parental figures. These adaptations of natural impulses occur in response to traumas, experiences, and training. Often the adaptive child uses such phrases as "I have to," "I'm supposed to," and "I should." The *Little Professor*, replete with unschooled wisdom, is creative, intuitive, and responsive to nonverbal messages.

The *Parent* ego state incorporates the attitudes and behaviors of parental figures—the dos, shoulds, and oughts. Outwardly, these messages are expressed through prejudice, criticism, and nurturing behavior. Parental messages are present throughout a person's life. A response to any thoughtful question that occurs within 10 seconds usually comes from the parent ego state. The parent ego state consists of two subdivisions—the Nurturing Parent and the Critical Parent. The *Nurturing Parent* is the part of the person that comforts, praises, and aids others. The *Critical Parent* is that part of the person that finds fault, displays prejudices, disapproves, and prevents others from feeling good about themselves. These two parts of the Parent are recognized through such nonverbal behaviors as pointing a finger at someone and through such verbal statements as "that's too bad, but don't worry."

The *Adult* ego state is not subdivided or related to a person's age. It is the objective, thinking, data-gathering part of the person. The adult ego state tests reality, much as the ego does in Freud's system. The Adult is rational and organized. In some ways it functions like a computer, expressing itself through such phrases as "I understand" and "I'm going to."

Sometimes, the different ego states operate simultaneously. For example, a young woman may observe an attractive man and go through the following self-dialogue: "He is really good looking and well spoken [Adult], but he's probably stuck up [Critical Parent], although I've heard he's very sensitive [Nurturing Parent]. I wonder how I could attract him [Little Professor]. I get real excited just thinking of him [Natural Child], yet I have to be in early on weekday nights because of my job [Adaptive Child]."

A major focus of transactional analysis is determining which ego state(s) a person is using. Although TA does not favor any ego state over another, the theory stresses the importance of being able to balance responses when necessary and appropriate. Those who constantly exhibit just one ego state do not function as well as those who are more flexible. One way of assessing the ego state(s) a person uses most is through the use of an egogram (Dusay and Dusay, 1979). The egogram of a person who responds mostly from the adult ego state is shown in Figure 5.3.

***Transactional Analysis.*** The second way of understanding and predicting human behavior involves the diagramming of ego state transactions. The diagramming of transactional analysis is interpersonal, in contrast to the intrapersonal diagramming of structural analysis. Transactions may occur on one of three levels—complementary, crossed, or ulterior.

In a *complementary transaction*, both persons are operating either from the same ego state (e.g., child-to-child, adult-to-adult) or from complementary ego states (e.g., parent-to-child, adult-to-

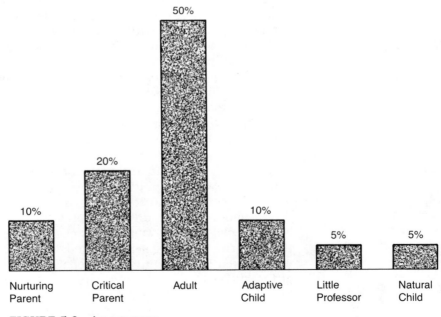

**FIGURE 5.3** An egogram.

parent). Responses are predictable and appropriate. For example, an adult-to-adult transaction might be:

**P1:**   What time is it?

**P2:**   It is 7 o'clock.

A child-to-child transaction would involve more playfulness. For example:

**P1:**   Let's go play with Billy.

**P2:**   Yea! We could have lots of fun with him!

A parent-to-parent transaction, however, would be more nurturing or critical, as in the following:

**P1:**   You never do anything right.

**P2:**   That's because you're always finding fault with my work.

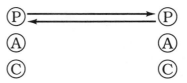

In a *crossed transaction,* an inappropriate ego state is activated, producing an unexpected response. Crossed transactions hurt. When they occur, persons tend to withdraw from each other or switch topics. An example of a crossed transaction is when a person, who is operating from a child ego state and hoping for a complementary parent ego state response, receives instead a comment from the other person's adult ego state:

**P1:**   Can you help me carry these bags? They must weigh a ton.

**P2:** Those bags weigh approximately twenty pounds and you are capable of carrying them.

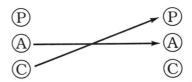

An *ulterior transaction* is one in which two ego states operate simultaneously and one message disguises the other. Ulterior transactions appear to be complementary and socially acceptable even though they are not. For example, at the end of a date one person may say to the other: "Do you want to come in and see my etchings?" On the surface this question might seem to be coming from the adult ego state. In reality it is coming from the child ego state: "Want to come in and have some fun together?"

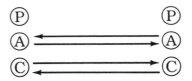

***Game Analysis.*** Games are ulteriorly motivated transactions that appear complementary on the surface but end in bad feelings. People play games to structure time, to achieve recognition, to make others predictable, and often to prevent intimacy. Since intimacy involves risks, games keep people safe from exposing their thoughts and feelings. Games, which have a predictable end, are categorized as first degree, second degree, and third degree.

First degree games are played in social circles with anyone who is willing to participate. They generally lead to mild upsets. An example of a first degree game is Seducto, which can initially be exciting and fun. In this game, a male and female enjoy an evening flirting with each other until one turns the other down and both leave feeling slightly uncomfortable. A second degree game occurs when the players go after bigger stakes, usually in more intimate circles, and end up with bad feelings. An example of a second degree game is Uproar, in which two persons get angrier and angrier until one or both of them gets very upset by being called a name or being put down. A third degree game usually involves tissue damage, and the players end up in jail, the hospital, or the morgue. An example of this game is Cops and Robbers, in which people dare those in authority to catch them and yet leave clues about where they can be cornered. At each game level, there is more danger of permanent damage. Very few games have a positive or neutral outcome (Berne,

1964). The list of possible games is almost endless once one realizes what a game is and is able to persuade others to play it. In the long run, those who play games are losers.

**Script Analysis.** Berne believed that everyone makes a *life script*, or life plan, early in childhood, by the age of five. These scripts, which determine how one interacts with others, are based on interpretations of external events. Positive messages given to a child function as permissions and do not limit people in any way. Negative messages, or *injunctions*, are more powerful and may become the basis for destructive scripts. Many parental injunctions begin with "don't"—"Don't succeed," "Don't grow," "Don't be that way." Unless a person makes a conscious attempt to overcome such injunctions, the result may be a miserable life.

A life script involves the ability to get *strokes*, (i.e., verbal or physical recognition) for certain behaviors. Most people's life scripts revolve around the giving and receiving of strokes. Berne points out that negative strokes (punishments) are better than no strokes at all (being ignored). Strokes result in the collection of either good or bad feelings, known as *stamps.* When individuals collect enough stamps, they cash them in on behaviors. For example, a teenager may collect enough bad feelings from failing grades to justify quitting school or enough good feelings from studying hard to attend a party. Healthy people give and receive positive strokes most often.

Common negative script patterns are these:

☐ *Never scripts*  A person never gets to do what he or she wants because the parent forbids it (e.g., "Marriage is bad; never get married").

☐ *Until scripts*  A person must wait until a certain time to do something before he or she can have a reward (e.g., "You cannot play until you have all your work done").

☐ *Always scripts*  A person tells him- or herself that it is necessary to continue doing the same thing (e.g., "You should always continue at any job once started").

☐ *After scripts*  A person expects difficulty after a certain event (e.g., "After age 40 life is downhill").

☐ *Open-ended scripts*  A person does not know what he or she is supposed to do after a given time (e.g., "Be active while you're young").

There are also miniscripts within people's lives that focus on the minute-by-minute occurrences. Some of the most common of them are: Be Perfect, Be Strong, Hurry Up, Try Hard, Please

Someone. These five messages, called *drivers*, allow people to escape their life scripts—but the escape is only temporary.

The ideal life script in TA terms is informed by the position I'm OK, You're OK (a "get on with" position) (Harris, 1967). People may operate from three other positions, however. I'm OK, You're not OK (a "get-away-from" position); I'm not OK, You're OK (a "get-nowhere-with" position); and I'm not OK, You're not OK (a "get-rid-of" position). Figure 5.4 shows these positions.

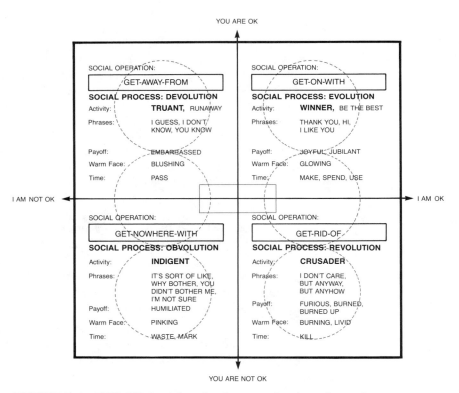

**FIGURE 5.4** THE OK Corral is the diagram for classifying the outcomes of the events in your life: *get-on-with, get-away-from, get-nowhere-with,* or *get-rid-of.* You can choose how you want a situation to come out before the end of it. Not all events can end in a get-on-with. You cannot get-on-with everybody and everything. Healthy people use each one of the four ways.

*Source:* F. H. Ernst, Jr. Copyright by F. H. Ernst. Reprinted by permission.

Everyone operates from each of these four positions at various times, but well functioning individuals learn to recognize an unhealthy position and modify thoughts and behaviors accordingly. Berne held that life scripts can be rewritten if a person becomes more conscious of what he or she is thinking and makes concerted efforts to change.

### Role of the Counselor

TA treatment assigns the counselor the initial role of being a teacher. The counselor first must explain to the client the language and concepts of TA, a new way of thinking about self. After this is accomplished, the counselor contracts with the client for specific changes and helps the person achieve those changes.

TA counselors do not rely heavily on formal psychological tests, although a counselor does assess client functioning. Assessment is usually done through an egogram or another less formal method. The purpose is to determine how a client is spending time and from which ego states that client is operating. Diagnosis based on DSM-III categories is not stressed.

### Goals

Primary goals in TA focus on helping clients transform themselves from "frogs" into "princes and princesses." It is not enough that persons learn to adjust, as in psychoanalysis. Instead, the emphasis is on the attainment of health and autonomy. Counselors help their clients to: identify and restore distorted or damaged ego states, develop the capacity to use all ego states, utilize the Adult ego state with its reasoning powers, alter inappropriate life scripts, and adopt a position of I'm OK, You're OK (Berne, 1966).

In becoming autonomous, clients exhibit more awareness, intimacy, and spontaneity, become free of games, and eliminate self-defeating scripts. They become more in touch with their past but at the same time are freed from previous negative influences. A major emphasis of TA is on learning about the self in order to decide who one wishes to become (Goulding & Goulding, 1979).

### Techniques

TA has initiated several good techniques in helping clients reach their goals. Among the most common of these are structural analysis, transactional analysis, game analysis, and script analysis. Others include:

☐ *Treatment contract*   Consists of a specific, concrete contract that emphasizes agreed-upon responsibilities for both counselors and clients (Dusay & Dusay, 1984). The contract lets each know when counseling goals have been reached. Some behavioral approaches also use a treatment contract.

☐ *Interrogation*   Involves speaking to a client's Adult ego state until the counselor receives an adult response. The technique can be very confrontational. If not used properly, interrogation will be ineffective and supply only historical material.

☐ *Specification*   Consists of the identification of the ego state that initiated a transaction. Specification takes place from the Adult ego state of both the client and counselor.

☐ *Confrontation*   Involves the counselor pointing out inconsistencies in the client's behavior or speech. The TA use of this technique varies little from its use in other theories.

☐ *Explanation*   Occurs on an Adult-to-Adult ego state level as the counselor teaches the client about some aspect of TA.

☐ *Illustration*   Serves to enlighten the client or elaborate on a point. An illustration is a story that is often humorous and as such speaks to both the Child and the Adult ego states of the client.

☐ *Confirmation*   Used when previously modified behavior occurs again and the counselor points this out to the client. Only when the client has a firmly established Adult ego state can this technique be effective.

☐ *Interpretation*   Involves the counselor's explaining to the Child ego state of the client the reasons for the client's behavior. This technique is mainly a psychodynamic procedure and is used only when the client has an effectively functioning Adult ego state.

☐ *Crystallization*   Consists of an Adult-to-Adult transaction in which the client comes to an awareness that individual game playing may be given up if so desired. Thus, the client is free to do as he or she chooses and the TA process is virtually complete.

Almost all of the techniques in TA involve some combination of questioning, confrontation, and dialogue. Among the most frequently asked questions of TA counselors are:

What are the nicest and worst things your parents ever said to you?

What is your earliest memory?

What is the family story about your birth?

What is your favorite fairy tale, story, or song?

How would you describe your mother and father?

How long do you expect to live?

To be most effective, a TA counselor must always be careful to assess the ego strengths of individual clients. A client is usually capable of making new decisions about life once he or she discovers different aspects of the self.

TA is presently divided into three main schools of treatment—the Classical School, the Cathexis School, and the Redecision School (Barnes, 1977). All of these schools use contracts as their primary method of intervention and have the achievement of autonomy as their final goal of treatment.

## *Evaluation*

TA has a number of strengths:

☐ The approach uses terms that are easily understood and clearly defined.

☐ The approach is easily and effectively combined with other more action-oriented counseling theories. The use of TA and Gestalt therapy together has been especially powerful (James & Jongeward, 1971).

☐ The approach puts the responsibility of change on the client. Individuals can choose to change or remain the same.

☐ The approach is goal directed. The contractual nature of the counseling process makes it possible for both counselors and clients to know when treatment should be terminated.

TA is not without limitations, however.

☐ The approach has been criticized for its primary cognitive orientation. To understand is only the beginning of change. TA promotes understanding. But unless the approach is used with another more action-oriented theory, TA is limited in its effectiveness.

☐ The approach is also criticized for its simplicity, structure, and popularity. TA is so widely known that there are some people who use the terminology but do not practice the theory. These individuals intellectualize their problems but take few actions to modify them.

☐ The approach does not place emphasis on the authenticity of the counselor (Corey, 1986). In the counseling process, the counselor is seen as an equal with the client. Unlike a Rogerian approach, however, little attention is paid to the person of the counselor in the counseling process.

## SUMMARY

Two of the most prominent cognitive theories of counseling are RET and TA. They clearly have much in common. For instance, both agree that if people gain insight into their thinking processes, they can change. Thinking influences feeling and behavior. Both approaches also stress that counseling is a learning process and that counselors often operate in the role of teacher. The theories further emphasize the importance of clients' work outside of formal therapeutic sessions. Both theories are very structured and require clients to learn new vocabularies, as well as restructure their thoughts. There are training centers for individuals interested in learning skills in either approach and professional journals devoted to each theory.

Although these theories have much in common, they are also quite different. For instance, RET incorporates many more techniques than does TA. However, TA counselors will often combine their theory with other approaches, such as Gestalt, in order to make it more active and strong. RET and its offshoots have fewer new terms for the client to learn, and RET practitioners often have their clients working in advanced stages of counseling before TA counselors do. Yet, TA has a much more complex view of human nature than RET, although the research data base of TA is not as strong.

Both RET and TA are continuing to develop. They are both in the process of demonstrating their appropriateness in a number of settings and with a variety of client problems.

## CLASSROOM ACTIVITIES

1. Pair up with another student and discuss which of the two theories presented in this chapter you find most attractive. Support your view with specifics from the approaches.
2. Do a rational self-analysis (RSA) on a situation that is real in your life. Have another student go over the results with you. What

did you learn from doing this exercise that you could pass on to a client that you ask to complete an RSA?
3. In groups of three, role play how you think an RET or a TA counselor would act in helping individuals with the following concerns—procrastination, interpersonal conflict, stress, adjustment to a new living

situation, and grief. One student should take the role of the client, one the counselor, and the other the observer. After the role play is over, the observer should give feedback to the counselor. The counselor and client should also explain how they experienced the process. Then switch roles until everyone has had a chance to be in each role.

4. Keep a list of the number and types of "games" you find yourself playing for a

week. Try to notice any patterns that emerge. Share your findings with fellow classmates in an open class discussion.

5. Which do you find most attractive: affective theories or cognitive theories? State your reasons as specifically as possible. What support does recent professional literature offer on the effectiveness of the theories you chose? Do a search of the literature for articles written in the last three years on the theories you chose.

## REFERENCES

Barnes, G. (1977). Introduction. In G. Barnes (Ed.), *Transactional analysis after Eric Berne: Teachings and practices of three TA schools* (pp. 3–31). New York: Harper's College Press.

Beck, A. T. (1976). *Cognitive therapy and emotional disorders.* New York: International Universities Press.

Berne, E. (1964). *Games people play.* New York: Grove Press.

Berne, E. (1966). *Principles of group treatment.* New York: Oxford University Press.

Corey, G. (1986). *Theory and practice of counseling and psychotherapy* (3rd ed.). Monterey, CA: Brooks/Cole.

Cormier, L. S., & Hackney, H. (1987). *The professional counselor: A process guide to helping.* Englewood Cliffs, NJ: Prentice-Hall.

Dusay, J. M. (1977). The evolution of transactional analysis. In G. Barnes (Ed.), *Transactional analysis after Eric Berne: Teachings and practices of three TA schools* (pp. 32–52). New York: Harper & Row.

Dusay, J., & Dusay, K. M. (1979). Transactional analysis. In R. Corsini (Ed.), *Current psychotherapies* (2nd ed.). Itasca, IL: Peacock.

Dusay, J. M., & Dusay, K. M. (1984). Transactional analysis. In R. Corsini (Ed.), *Current psychotherapies* (3rd ed.). Itasca, IL: Peacock.

Ellis, A. (1962). *Reason and emotion in psychotherapy.* New York: Lyle Stuart.

Ellis, A. (1973). Rational-emotive therapy. In R. Corsini (Ed.), *Current psychotherapies* (pp. 167–206). Itasca, IL: Peacock.

Ellis, A. (1977). The basic clinical theory of rational-emotive therapy. In A. Ellis and R. Grieger (Eds.), *Handbook of rational-emotive therapy* (pp. 3–34). New York: Springer.

Ellis, A. (1979). Rational-emotive therapy. In R. Corsini (Ed.), *Current psychotherapies* (2nd ed., pp. 185–229). Itasca, IL: Peacock.

Ellis, A. (1980). Foreword. In S. R. Walen, R. DiGiuseppe, & R. L. Wessler, *A practitioner's guide to rational-emotive therapy* (pp. vii–xii). New York: Oxford University Press.

Ellis, A. (1984). Rational-emotive therapy (RET) and pastoral counseling: A reply to Richard Wessler. *Personnel and Guidance Journal, 62,* 266–267.

Ellis, A. (1986). An emotional control card for inappropriate and appropriate emotions in using rational-emotive imagery. *Journal of Counseling and Development, 65,* 205–206.

Ellis, A., & Harper, R. A. (1975). *A new guide to rational living*. North Hollywood, CA: Wilshire.

Gladding, S. T. (1974). Patchwork. *Personnel and Guidance Journal, 53*, 39.

Goulding, M., & Goulding, R. (1979). *Changing lives through redecision therapy*. New York: Brunner/Mazel.

Harris, T. (1967). *I'm OK—You're OK*. New York: Harper & Row.

James, M., & Jongeward, D. (1971). *Born to win: Transactional analysis with Gestalt experiments*. Reading, MA: Addison-Wesley.

Johnson, N. (1980). Must the RET therapist be like Albert Ellis? *Personnel and Guidance Journal, 59*, 49–51.

Maultsby, M. C., Jr. (1971). *Handbook of rational self-counseling*. Lexington, KY: University of Kentucky Medical Center.

Maultsby, M. C., Jr. (1973). *More personal happiness through rational self-counseling*. Lexington, KY: University of Kentucky Medical Center.

Maultsby, M. C., Jr. (1975). *Help yourself to happiness*. New York: Institute for Rational Living.

Maultsby, M. C., Jr. (1984). *Rational behavior therapy*. Englewood Cliffs, NJ: Prentice-Hall.

Meichenbaum, D. (1977). *Cognitive behavior modification: An integrative approach*. New York: Plenum.

Morris, K. T., & Kanitz, M. (1975). *Rational-emotive therapy*. Boston: Houghton Mifflin.

Newhorn, P. (1978). Albert Ellis. *Human behavior, 7*, 30–35.

Penfield, W. (1952). Memory mechanisms. *Archives of Neurology & Psychiatry, 67*, 178–198.

Penfield, W., & Jasper, H. (1954). *Epilepsy and the functional anatomy of the human brain*. Boston: Little, Brown.

Powell, J. (1976). *Fully human, fully alive*. Niles, IL: Argos.

Roush, D. W. (1984). Rational-emotive therapy and youth: Some new techniques for counselors. *Personnel and Guidance Journal, 62*, 414–417.

Seligman, L. (1986). *Diagnosis and treatment planning in counseling*. New York: Human Sciences Press.

Sklare, G., Taylor, J., & Hyland, S. (1985). An emotional control card for rational-emotive imagery. *Journal of Counseling and Development, 64*, 145–146.

Walen, S. R., DiGiuseppe, R., & Wessler, R. L. (1980). *A practitioner's guide to RET*. New York: Oxford University Press.

Weinrach, S. G. (1980). Unconventional therapist: Albert Ellis. *Personnel and Guidance Journal, 59*, 152–160.

Photo by James S. Davidson III.

# The Theory and Practice of Individual Counseling: Behavioral Approaches

*At times I envy the bandaid man*
    *who cleaned my cuts when I was young*
*While painting me as "mercurochrome clown"*
    *before he patched my pain with adhesive.*
*That was security to know he cared and would be around*
    *to fix, when possible, all the hurts of childhood*
    *that come in growing to be man.*
*His job, I think, was easier than mine*
    *for in counseling I can't always see*
    *your past wounds, scars, and might-have-beens.*
*If I could, on days like today,*
    *I might like the old man I remember*
    *try with gentleness to cover them.*
*For you sit beside me with tears in your eyes*
    *and I know how slowly it takes words to heal.*[1]

---

[1]Gladding, 1975, p. 520. Copyright AACD. Reprinted with permission. No further reproduction authorized without written permission of AACD.

**B**ehavioral theories of counseling focus on a broad range of client behaviors. Often, a person has difficulties because of a deficit or an excess of behavior. Counselors who take a behavioral approach seek to help clients either learn new, appropriate ways of acting or modify or eliminate excessive actions. In all cases, adaptive behaviors replace those that were maladaptive and the counselor functions as a learning specialist for the client (Krumboltz, 1966). Behavioral counseling approaches are especially popular in institutional settings, such as mental hospitals or sheltered workshops. They are the approaches of choice in working with clients who have such specific problems as an eating disorder, substance abuse, and psychosexual dysfunction. Behavioral approaches are also useful in addressing anxiety, stress, assertiveness, parenting, and social interaction (Seligman, 1986; Thoresen & Coates, 1980).

## OVERVIEW OF BEHAVIORAL APPROACHES

The term *behavioral* encompasses a wide range of ideas, practices, and theories. On one end of the behavioral continuum are the so-called radical behaviorists, such as B. F. Skinner (1974), who focus predominantly on learning principles and avoid examining any "mentalistic" concepts, such as thoughts. On the other end of the continuum are researchers, such as Donald Meichenbaum (1977) and Aaron Beck (1976), who emphasize the importance of mental processes (e.g., perceptions) in human behavior and view thoughts as a type of behavior. The present trend in behavioral counseling recognizes "that behavior and perception play a reciprocal role in the process of change" (Barclay, 1980, p. 457).

In its infancy (early 1900s through 1930s), behaviorism was concerned almost entirely with outward observations and was promoted as a scientific approach to the study of human life, primarily through the efforts of John B. Watson (1925). It was Watson, through his work with a child called Little Albert, who demonstrated that human emotions are learned and can be generalized (Watson & Raynor, 1920). After World War I, the ideas of behaviorists were explored by such researchers as Mary Cover Jones (1924), who demonstrated how counterconditioning can be employed to help children overcome phobic reactions.

After World War II, behaviorism achieved more prominence. Clinical psychology promoted the idea that therapists could be scientific practitioners. Also attracting national attention was the work of such researchers as B. F. Skinner (1953) in operant conditioning, Joseph Wolpe (1958) in respondent (i.e., classical) conditioning, Hans Eysenck (1960) in the treatment of abnormal behavior, and Albert Bandura (Bandura & Walters, 1963) in the effects of vicarious learning. During the 1950s, the term *behavior therapy* was introduced as a way of describing behavioral approaches to resolving client problems (Yates, 1970).

John Krumboltz (1966) is credited with popularizing behaviorism in counseling. Krumboltz drew upon Bandura's earlier work and in so doing revolutionized the counseling profession (Hosford, 1980). The ideas of Krumboltz, as well as behaviorism in general, gained widespread acceptance in the 1970s. By the 1980s, behavioral approaches had generally split into three main theories—respondent learning, operant conditioning, and social modeling. Counselors who employ a behavioral approach often integrate aspects of each of these theories. William Glasser's Reality Therapy is also considered a behavioral approach, though its differences from other behavioral approaches are considerable.

Cormier and Hackney (1987) note that clients who appear to have the most success with behavioral counseling are those who are:

☐ Predominantly goal-oriented and have a need for achievement and results.

☐ Action-oriented with a need to be doing something.

☐ Interested in changing either a discrete response or a limited number of behaviors.

## THREE MAIN BEHAVIORAL THEORIES

The three main behavioral counseling theories developed both in isolation and in dialogue with one another. The first of these, *respondent learning* (or classical conditioning) was formulated by Ivan Pavlov in Russia near the turn of the century and then popularized in the United States by John B. Watson (1913). The second, *operant conditioning*, was formulated by B. F. Skinner, who drew on the ideas of classical conditioning, but thought individuals were more active in the learning process than this theory allowed. The third theory, *social modeling*, is best seen in the work of its initial proponent, Albert Bandura, who thinks that most learning is a result of copying or imitating.

### B. F. Skinner

One of the dominant figures in behaviorism is B(urrhus) F(rederick) Skinner, who was born in Susquehanna, Pennsylvania, in 1904. He was the oldest of two sons, but his younger brother died at age 16. Skinner's father, a wealthy attorney, wanted his son to become an attorney, but Skinner showed skills in other areas, such as an early facility with mechanical devices, including the making of roller-skate scooters, blow guns, model airplanes, and a flotation system to separate green from ripe elderberries (Skinner, 1967). These inventions were precursors to such later devices as the infant Air Crib and the Skinner Box. The young Skinner was also interested in animal behavior and at a country fair was highly impressed by a troupe of performing pigeons. He later used pigeons to demonstrate aspects of his theory by teaching them to do a variety of tasks.

Although mechanically adept, Skinner was never a good athlete. He enjoyed music, however, and played the saxophone in a jazz band. His home environment was warm, comfortable, and stable, imbued with the virtues of small-town, middle-class America at the turn of the century (Skinner, 1976). His parents did not use corporal punishment.

Skinner wanted to be a writer. He majored in English literature at Hamilton College, where he earned Phi Beta Kappa honors and graduated in 1926. Back home, he set about the task of writing, having been encouraged in his efforts by Robert Frost. After a year, he moved to New York's Greenwich Village to live among writers and benefit from a stimulating environment. There he discovered the works of Ivan Pavlov and John B. Watson, as well as those of Bertrand Russell and Francis Bacon. Soon, he gave up writing ambitions to become a psychologist, though he had never taken a psychology course in college. He was accepted for graduate study in psychology at Harvard, where he was awarded a master's degree in 1930 and a Ph.D. in 1931. After another five years of postdoctoral training, he joined the faculty of the University of Minnesota in 1936, the same year he married Yvonne Blue.

Skinner's first book, *The Behavior of Organisms* (1938), was followed by other major works, and Skinner rapidly developed a national reputation. He left Minnesota for the University of Indiana in 1945, where he chaired the department of psychology until he returned to Harvard in 1948. At Indiana, he wrote perhaps his most influential book, *Walden Two* (1948), which in simple terms describes a utopian society functioning without punishment and according to the principles of learning. The writing itself was a remarkable experience for Skinner—intensively done with much emotion (Elms, 1981).

At Harvard, Skinner continued to be a prolific writer. His best book on theory, *Science and Human Behavior* (1953), describes how learning principles can be applied in all areas of society. *Beyond Freedom and Dignity* (1971), also influential, outlined the steps necessary for civilization to survive and flourish. In the early 1980s, Skinner wrote about how behavioral principles could be applied to problems of the aged (Skinner & Vaughan, 1983). Overall, Skinner can be classified as a behavioral determinist, because of his emphasis on learning as the primary determinant of human actions.

### View of Human Nature

Despite the great diversity of thought among behaviorists, certain characteristics can be identified as basic to the approach. Rimm and Cunningham (1985) list these:

- ☐ Behaviorists as a group concentrate on behavioral processes, that is, processes closely associated with overt behavior.
- ☐ Behaviorists concentrate on the here and now as opposed to the then and there of behavior.
- ☐ Behaviorists assume that all behavior is learned, whether it be adaptive or maladaptive.
- ☐ Behaviorists believe learning can be effective in changing maladaptive behavior.
- ☐ Behaviorists focus on setting well-defined therapy goals for clients.

☐ Behaviorists reject the idea that human personality is composed of traits.

☐ Behaviorists stress the importance of obtaining empirical evidence and scientific support for any techniques used.

In general, behaviorists believe learning—and thus development—occurs in one of three main ways—respondent learning, operant conditioning, and social modeling. These ways are used by all organisms, though only human learning is addressed here.

**Respondent Learning.** The person or organism need not be an active participant in order to learn, according to this theory. Rather, learning occurs through the association of two stimuli. The best-known example of this is Pavlov's famous experiments with his laboratory dogs. Pavlov found that when a dog's hunger was paired with the sound of a bell before the dog was fed, the dog would associate the bell with the food reward and begin to salivate in response to the bell, before the food was served. In this case, the bell, initially a *neutral stimulus*, became a *conditioned* (learned) *stimulus* because of its association with an *unconditioned* (natural) *stimulus*, the food. The dog's salivating to the sound of the bell became a *conditioned* (learned) *response*, as opposed to the *unconditioned response* of naturally salivating when presented with food.

In a similar way, many human emotions, such as phobias, arise because of paired associations. For example, a person may have an accident after eating a certain food. The association of the food with the accident, even though the two are unrelated, may result in that person's eventual fear or avoidance of the food. Clients often associate feelings with certain events, and vice versa. The sound of music, the smell of certain odors, the sight of certain colors, and the touch of a stranger are experiences that individuals may react to emotionally because of respondent learning. People need not be actively involved with environmental forces for learning to occur. Once learned, these associations can be unlearned, with new ones taking their place, a process known as *counterconditioning*.

**Operant Conditioning.** According to the theory of operant conditioning, for learning to occur it is essential that a person be involved as an active participant with the environment. Operant conditioning focuses primarily on how individuals operate in the environment. In general, the idea is that a person is rewarded or punished for actions and thus learns to discriminate which behaviors bring rewards and which do not. The person is then likely to increase behavior that is rewarded and decrease behavior that is either punished or not reinforced. For example, one will often repeat behavior that brings recognition, financial gain, or satisfaction of physical needs. Skinner's (1953) basic premise—the foundation on which operant conditioning is built—is that when a certain behavior is followed closely by a *reinforcer* (a reward), the chances are increased for that behavior to occur again in similar or identical circumstances. In other words, the consequences of a behavior determine whether that behavior will be learned or repeated.

***Social Modeling.*** Driving a car, using the correct fork at a dinner party, and reacting appropriately to a new client are often learned through observations. Learning through observation and imitation is called social modeling. Bandura (1977) theorizes that almost all important learning takes place through social modeling. The advantages of such learning are many, but chief among them are a saving of time, energy, and effort in the acquiring of new skills. Learning through social modeling "also emphasizes the self-regulation of behavior and thus deemphasizes the importance of external reinforcers. . . . Learning may occur independently of reinforcement" (Hergenhahn, 1984, p. 234). In a later section of this chapter we will focus on what conditions are most effective in promoting such learning.

### Role of the Counselor

A counselor may take one of several roles depending on the behavioral orientation and the client's goals, but generally a counselor who takes a behavioral approach is very active in counseling sessions. The client learns, unlearns, or relearns specific ways of behaving. In that process, the counselor functions as teacher, director, and expert (Corey, 1986). A directive role is especially prominent if the counselor adheres to a theory of either respondent learning or operant conditioning. When the counselor adheres to a theory of social modeling, he or she may seem to be less active, but in such cases, the counselor directly teaches by serving as a model for the client or finding appropriate models for the client to imitate (Bandura, 1971, 1977).

Counselors using a behavioral approach differ widely as to the use of psychological tests and diagnoses. Most employ some form of assessment device(s) with their clients, but usually these instruments measure behavior and action. Rarely do counselors use paper-and-pencil personality tests. For diagnosis, clients are described according to behaviors they display, many of which are listed in the DSM-III.

## Goals

The goals of the behaviorist are similar to those of many other counselors. Basically, the counselor wants to help clients make good adjustments to life circumstances and achieve personal and professional objectives. Thus, the focus is on modifying or eliminating the maladaptive behavior the client displays, while at the same time helping the client acquire healthy, constructive ways of acting. Just to eliminate a behavior is not enough; unproductive actions must be replaced with productive ways of responding. A major step in the behavioral approach is for the counselor and client to reach mutually agreed-upon goals. Blackham and Silberman (1971) suggest four specific steps counselors and clients should take in this process:

☐ *Define the problem*   If a problem is to be solved, it must be stated concretely. Thus, a client is asked to specify when, where, how, and with whom the problem arises. The counselor may benefit from actually observing the problem behavior, but that is not absolutely necessary.

☐ *Take a developmental history*   It is useful for both client and counselor to have some knowledge about how the client has handled past circumstances and whether the presenting problem might be organically based.

☐ *Establish specific goals*   Behavioral counselors help clients break down goals into small, achievable units. Counselors also set up learning experiences for clients to develop any needed skills (Krumboltz & Thoresen, 1976). For example, if a woman wishes to complete college, she must first select and then pass courses during a school's initial term. This may require that she learn new study habits and ways of interrelating with others, such as with roommates.

☐ *Determine the best methods for change*   There are usually several behavioral methods that could help a client reach desired goals. If one method does not work, it may be modified or a new one may be tried. Continuous assessment of the effectiveness of methods is critical.

In general, behavioral counselors specialize in assisting clients in learning how to set up and achieve specific goals and subgoals.

Counselors are concrete, objective, and collaborative in their work (Krumboltz, 1966).

### Techniques

Behavioral counselors have at their disposal some of the best-researched and most effective counseling techniques available. A sample of the most widely employed techniques will be covered in this section, but because the literature is so rich the reader is urged to consult professional publications that describe these and other techniques in more detail.

**General Behavioral Techniques.** General behavioral techniques are applicable to all of the three behavioral theories, though a given technique may be more applicable to one of the theories at a given time or in a specific circumstance.

*Reinforcement.* Reinforcers are those events that when following a behavior increase the probability of the behavior recurring. A reinforcer may be either positive or negative. A *positive reinforcer* is valued and considered pleasurable by the person affected. There are no universal positive reinforcers, but some events and objects frequently serve in this capacity, such as social recognition, money, and food. A *negative reinforcer* is an aversive stimulus whose removal is contingent upon performance of a desired action—the removal of the aversive stimulus is reinforcing for the person involved. For example, a mother nags her daughter until the daughter washes the dishes. The nagging could be viewed as a negative reinforcer, especially if peace is valued by the daughter. In behavioral counseling, positive reinforcers are used more frequently than negative ones. In some situations, praise from the counselor when the client completes an action is a positive reinforcer.

A reinforcer may also be either primary or secondary. A *primary reinforcer* is one that is valued intrinsically, such as food. A *secondary reinforcer* acquires its value through being associated with a primary reinforcer, such as some kind of token (e.g., money). Clients are the best experts on what activities or items are most reinforcing for them.

*Schedules of reinforcement.* When a behavior is first being learned, it should be reinforced every time it occurs, that is, by *continuous reinforcement.* After a behavior is established, however, it should be reinforced less frequently, that is, by *intermittent reinforcement.* Schedules of reinforcement operate according to either the number of responses (ratio) or the length of time (interval) between reinforcers. Both ratio and interval schedules are either fixed or variable. If a counselor knows what type of schedule is most preferred by a client, the reinforcers can be set up accordingly.

**Shaping.** Behavior learned gradually in steps through successive approximation is known as *shaping.* When clients are learning new skills, counselors may assist by helping break down behavior into manageable units. Shaping occurs when a person actually practices a behavior or when a person imagines doing more of a task than previously (i.e., focused imagery).

**Extinction.** *Extinction* is the elimination of a behavior because of a withdrawal of the reinforcement for it. Few individuals will continue doing something that is not rewarding. For example, when a client is no longer reinforced for talking about a certain subject, the client will quit bringing it up. Talk about the subject has disappeared and is said to be extinct.

**Punishment.** Punishment involves the presentation of a negative reinforcer to a situation or the removal of a positive reinforcer from a situation in order to suppress or eliminate a behavior. A counselor may punish a client with a critical statement, such as, "I knew you couldn't do it." In a similar way, a teacher may punish a child with removal from the classroom, keeping the child isolated for a few minutes (i.e., time out).

**Specific Behavioral Techniques.** Specific behavioral techniques are refined behavioral methods that combine general techniques in precise ways. They are generally respondent or operant approaches to working with clients.

*Self-monitoring.* Self-monitoring occurs when clients learn to modify their own behaviors. It involves two related processes, self-observation and self-recording (Goldiamond, 1976). The first process requires that a person notice particular behaviors he or she does; the second focuses on the recording of these behaviors. Self-monitoring interferes with learned habits by having the client count the occurrences of specific behaviors that are normally done without thought. Such self-monitoring increases the client's awareness of behaviors and assures that the client is more conscious of when and how certain actions occur. This knowledge is a preliminary step to change.

*Environmental planning.* This procedure involves a client's setting up a part of the environment to promote or limit certain behaviors (Krasner & Ullmann, 1973). For example, if a client associates painful memories with a certain place, a daily schedule is planned to avoid that setting. Likewise, to control a situation and therefore promote desirable interaction, a client may arrange a room or chairs in a certain way.

***Systematic desensitization.*** This technique is designed to help clients overcome anxiety in particular situations. A client is asked to describe the situation that causes anxiety and then is requested to rank this situation and related events on a hierarchical scale, from aspects of it that cause the client no concern (0) to those that are most troublesome (100). The higher up the scale, the more anxious the client becomes. To help avoid anxiety and face the situation, the counselor teaches the client to relax physically. Then the hierarchy is reviewed, starting with low anxiety items, until the client feels anxiety, in which case the client is helped to relax again. The idea is that a person cannot feel anxious and physically relaxed at the same time, a phenomenon called *reciprocal inhibition* (Wolpe, 1958).

***Implosive therapy and flooding.*** *Implosive therapy* was first introduced by Thomas Stampfl in 1961. It involves a desensitization to a situation by having a client imagine an anxiety-producing situation that may have dire consequences. The client is not taught to relax first (as in systematic desensitization). This technique should not be used by beginning counselors. *Flooding* is less traumatic than implosive therapy. In flooding, an anxiety-producing scene is imagined, but one without dire consequences, as in implosive therapy.

***Aversive techniques.*** Although most behaviorists recommend that positive techniques be employed first, sometimes it is necessary to use aversive techniques, such as punishment. Such techniques are useful when one behavior must be eliminated before another can be taught. Among aversive techniques are:

☐ *Time out* A technique in which a client is separated from the opportunity to receive positive reinforcement. It is a mild aversive technique that requires careful monitoring and is most effective when employed for short periods of time, such as five minutes. An example of time out is separating a child from classmates when the child misbehaves.

☐ *Overcorrection* A technique in which a client first restores the environment to its natural state and then makes it "better than normal." For example, children who throw food in the lunch room might be required to clean up their mess and wax the floor!

□ *Covert sensitization* A technique in which undesired behavior is eliminated by associating it with unpleasantness. It is used in treating clients who have problems with smoking, obesity, substance abuse, and sexual deviation. Covert sensitization is a verbal technique in which unpleasant scenes are paired with scenes of deviant behavior (Corey, 1982, p. 151).

Aversive stimuli are usually not effective in the long run for three reasons: their emotional effects soon dissipate, they may interfere with the learning of desired behaviors, and they may encourage the client to try to escape, which when successful becomes a positive reinforcer. Further, ethical and legal concerns are associated with all aversive techniques. Before any of them are administered, counselors should obtain written permission from their clients.

***Modeling.*** Modeling is a technique that involves mental as well as physical activity. Synonyms for modeling include observational learning, imitation, social learning, and vicarious learning. Perry and Furukawa (1980) refer to modeling as a process "in which the behavior of an individual or a group, the model, acts as a stimulus for similar thoughts, attitudes, or behavior on the part of another individual who observes the model's performance" (p. 131).

There are more advantages than disadvantages to the employment of modeling in counseling. For instance, it is economical in time and money, easily administered, directed toward positive behavioral change, visually appealing, and of little or no risk to clients. Bandura (1969) found that models closest to the observer's age, gender, race, and attitude have the greatest effect. Live models, symbolic models (i.e., those on films and videos), and multiple models (i.e., groups of people) are equally effective in producing desired behavior change. In addition, covert models (i.e., a client imagines a model performing a desired activity) are also quite effective (Cautela, 1976). Often, modeling is combined with specific cognitive techniques, such as imagery or self-talk, to produce a more powerful effect than when this technique is used alone.

***Assertiveness Training.*** The major tenet of *assertiveness training* is that a person should be free to express thoughts and feelings appropriately without feeling undue anxiety (Alberti & Emmons, 1982). The technique consists of counterconditioning anxiety and reinforcing assertiveness. A client is taught that everyone has the right (not the obligation) of self-expression. The client then learns the differences among aggressive, passive, and assertive actions.

A client tells the counselor at the beginning what the objectives are, such as to be able to speak out at a public meeting. The counselor then gives the client feedback—both positive and negative—about present behavior. The next steps of the process involve the modeling of the desired behavior and the client's role playing of the behavior just seen. The counselor then reinforces the behavior and helps shape the client's actions. Finally, the client is given homework assignments to be completed between sessions (Bellack & Hersen, 1977). Assertive behaviors should be shaped gradually in order to keep the client encouraged and on track. The objective of assertiveness training is for individuals to feel good about behaviors and not be aggressive or manipulative of others.

### Cognitive Behavioral Techniques

Some of the most exciting new techniques in counseling have been originated by cognitive behaviorists during the last few years. Among the most effective of these techniques are stress inoculation and thought stopping:

☐ *Stress inoculation* This is a preventive technique, like medical inoculation, where individuals are taught sets of coping skills to help them handle stressful events. The process has three phases. First, the client is helped to achieve an understanding of the nature of stress and coping. Second, the client is taught specific coping skills and is reinforced for using the ones the client already possesses. The final phase emphasizes client practice—coping skills are used in clinical settings and in real situations. Overall, stress inoculation involves focusing on what lies ahead, grouping stressful events into manageable doses, thinking of ways to handle small stressful events, and practicing coping skills (Meichenbaum, 1985).

☐ *Thought stopping* This is a technique that helps a client who ruminates about the past or has irrational thoughts stop such a self-defeating process and live more productively. A counselor initially asks the client to think in the self-defeating manner. In the midst of such thoughts, the counselor suddenly yells, "Stop." The yelling of the word interrupts the thought process and makes it impossible to continue. There are several components of the thought-stopping process (Cormier & Cormier, 1979). Basically, the technique teaches the client to progress from outside control to inner control of negative thought patterns. The technique also helps a client replace self-defeating thoughts with assertive, positive, or neutral ones.

## Evaluation

There are numerous strengths of a behavioral approach. Among them are:

☐ The approach deals directly with symptoms. Since most clients seek help because of specific problems, counselors who work directly with symptoms are often able to assist clients immediately. Further, behavioral counseling is an appropriate approach to use in attention-deficit disorders, conduct disorders, eating disorders, substance-abuse disorders, psychosexual dysfunction, impulse control disorders, and phobic disorders (Seligman, 1986).

☐ The approach is focused on the here and now. A client does not have to examine the past to obtain help in the present. Thus, a behavioral approach is economical in both time and money.

☐ The approach has an abundance of available techniques that counselors can use. Thoresen and Coates (1980) chart how behavioral techniques, as reported by Krumboltz and Thoresen (1969, 1976), more than doubled in less than a decade (Table 6.1). Furthermore, Groden and Cautela (1981) have shown how behavioral techniques may be employed by counselors in numerous settings. There are also many behaviorally oriented counseling journals, such as the *Journal of Applied Behavior Analysis.*

☐ The approach is based on learning theory, which is a well-formulated and documented way to acquire new behaviors (Krumboltz & Thoresen, 1969, 1976).

☐ The approach is used by counselors who are organized into the Association for the Advancement of Behavior Therapy (AABT), which has published ethical guidelines for its members (Azrin, Stuart, Risely, & Stolz, 1977). The AABT promotes the practice and edification of behavioral counseling methods, while simultaneously trying to protect the public from unscrupulous practitioners.

☐ The approach has exceptionally good research on how behavioral techniques affect the process of counseling. Novice counselors may follow one of the many research designs. A common denominator among all behavioral approaches is a commitment to objectivity and evaluation (Corey, 1986).

There are also several major limitations to a behavioral approach:

**TABLE 6.1** Available techniques for behavioral approaches, 1969 and 1976, as reported by Krumboltz & Thoresen (1969, 1976).

| Behavioral Techniques, 1969 | Behavioral Techniques, 1976 |
|---|---|
| Aversive conditioning | Aversive counterconditioning |
| Contracts | Contracts |
| Guided practice | Cognitive restructuring |
| Instruction | Covert reinforcement |
| Modeling | Covert sensitization |
| Programmed materials | Differential feedback |
| Punishment | Extinction |
| Reinforcement | Flooding (implosion) |
| Role-playing | Focused imagery |
| Simulation | Guided practice |
| Systematic desensitization |    (behavioral rehearsal) |
| Token systems | "Homework" assignments |
| | Information-giving |
| | Instruction |
| | Intermittent reinforcement |
| | Paradoxical intention |
| | Positive reinforcement |
| | Programmed (reading) materials |
| | Reinforcement of incompatible |
| |    alternatives |
| | Relaxation |
| | Role-playing |
| | Satiation |
| | Self-instruction |
| | Self-monitoring |
| | Self-punishment |
| | Self-reinforcement |
| | Shaping |
| | Simulation |
| | Stimulus control |
| | Systematic desensitization |
| | Thought stopping |
| | Time out |
| | Token systems |

*Source:* From THE BEHAVIOR THERAPIST, Carl E. Thoresen, editor. Copyright © 1980 by Wadsworth, Inc. Reprinted by permission of Brooks/Cole Publishing Company, Pacific Grove, California 93950.

☐ The approach does not deal with the total person, just explicit behavior. Critics contend that many behaviorists, such as Skinner, have taken the person out of personality and replaced it with an emphasis on laws that govern actions in specific environments. This emphasis may be too simple in explaining complex human interaction (Hergenhahn, 1984).

☐ The approach is sometimes applied mechanically. Goldstein (1973) notes that "the most common error of neophyte behavior therapists is to start employing techniques too quickly" (p. 221). Even though most behaviorists are careful to establish rapport with their clients and to make counseling a collaborative effort, the fact that behaviorists did not initially stress the counselor/client relationship has hurt the approach's image.

☐ The approach has been best demonstrated under controlled conditions that are difficult to replicate in normal counseling situations. Implicit in that criticism is an uneasiness that much of learning theory has been formulated using lower animal forms, such as rats and pigeons. Thus, many counselors worry if a behavioral approach will work for human clients, who operate in less than ideal environments.

☐ The approach includes techniques that may be ahead of the theory (Thoresen & Coates, 1980). There is a proliferation of new methods being generated by behavioral counselors, yet the theory that should underlie these methods has not kept pace.

☐ The approach ignores the client's past history and unconscious forces. Although this approach may work quite well with someone who clearly has a behavioral concern, those who wish to resolve past issues or deal with insight from the unconscious may not be helped.

☐ The approach does not consider developmental stages (Sprinthrall, 1971). Skinner (1974) notes that a child's world "develops," but he and many other behaviorists think that developmental stages do little to explain overt behavior. Instead, they contend that the acquisition of learning has universal characteristics.

## REALITY THERAPY

Reality therapy is a behavioral approach with a phenomenological base and an existential heart. It is more than just a compromise among the main behavioral theories. Reality therapy stresses that a person's inner world is most influential in determining which behaviors the person chooses. It is action oriented, concrete, didactic, directive, behavioral and cognitive, and it emphasizes the fulfillment of individual psychological needs.

### William Glasser

William Glasser, the originator of reality therapy, was born in Cleveland, Ohio, in 1925, the third and youngest child in a closely knit family. He describes his childhood as happy and uneventful but, as is true with his theory, he does not emphasize the past. In school, he played in the band and developed a strong interest in sports. After graduating at 19 from the Case Institute of Technology with a degree in chemical engineering, he began graduate work in clinical psychology. He finished work for a master's degree in 1948, but his doctoral dissertation was rejected. He then entered medical school at Western Reserve University, graduating with a medical degree in 1953. Glasser next moved with his wife, Naomi Judith Silver, to California for a psychiatric residency at UCLA, which he completed in 1957. Although he had hoped to establish a private psychiatric practice, he soon found that referrals were slow in coming because of his open resistance to traditional psychoanalytic treatment. Thus, he took a position as head psychiatrist at the Ventura School for Girls, a state operated facility for juvenile delinquents.

At Ventura in the 1960s, Glasser began to formalize his approach to counseling. As a resident, his doubts on the effectiveness of classical psychoanalysis had been supported by one of his faculty supervisors, G. L. Harrington. Harrington helped Glasser develop some of the basic tenets of reality therapy. Glasser's first book, *Mental Health or Mental Illness?* (1961), contained many of the ideas that were later more formally expressed in *Reality Therapy: A New Approach to Psychiatry* (1965). Glasser (1965) developed reality therapy because he thought "conventional psychiatry wastes too much time arguing over how many diagnoses can dance at the end of a case history" (p. 49). He found that by using the basic principles of reality therapy, he was able to cut recidivism at the Ventura school to only 20 percent.

Shortly after the publication of *Reality Therapy*, Glasser founded the Institute of Reality Therapy in Canoga Park, California. At the institute, he has done some of his most creative work. He applied reality therapy to school settings in *Schools Without Failure* (1969) and to the areas of identity in *The Identity Society* (1972). In *Positive Addiction* (1976) he asserted that individuals can become stronger instead of weaker from so-called addictive habits. Two examples of habits that improve physical and mental health are jogging and meditation.

Since 1981, Glasser has linked his original ideas with control theory, which holds that individuals act to control the world around them. Two of Glasser's more recent books, *Stations of the Mind* (1981) and *Take Effective Control of Your Life* (1984), reflect that theoretical stance and also emphasize how the brain influences our inner perceptions.

### *View of Human Nature*

Reality therapy does not include a comprehensive theory of human development, yet it offers it practitioners a focused view of important aspects of human life. Glasser and Zunin (1979) believe there is a health or growth force within everyone. This force is manifested on two levels, the physical and the psychological. There is the need to obtain such life necessities as food, water, and shelter. There is also the need to obtain identity, especially a meaningful and successful sense of self. "Basically people want to be content and enjoy a success identity, to show responsible behavior and to have meaningful interpersonal relationships" (p. 315). The building of a successful identity is premised on resolving physiological needs.

Problems arise when people are either not taught to take responsibility for behavior or refuse to accept that responsibility. Glasser (1965) contends that "we all have the same needs but we vary in our ability to fulfill them" (p. 9). These needs are: (1) the need to love and be loved, and (2) the need to feel we are worthwhile to ourselves and others. Each person establishes an identity in life regardless of whether needs are met. But those whose needs are met achieve a "success identity," whereas those whose needs are not met establish a "failure identity."

Although reality therapy does not adhere to a comprehensive developmental model of human development, Glasser (1965, 1969, 1981) believes that human learning is a life-long process. For instance, he thinks that even infants develop specific needs, such as love, which for them "may be a dry diaper, a soft nipple, or a toss in the air followed by a hug or kiss" (Glasser, 1981, p. 41). Furthermore, he thinks there are two critical periods in children's lives. In the first, between ages two and five, children learn early socialization skills (such as how to relate to their parents, siblings, and friends) and they begin to deal with frustrations and disappointments. In this period, children especially need the love, acceptance, guidance, and involvement of their parents. If that is not forthcoming, a child may begin to establish a failure identity. In the second critical period, between ages five and ten, children are involved with school and are gaining both knowledge and a self-concept. Many children establish a failure identity during this period because of socialization difficulties or learning problems (Glasser, 1969).

Glasser's view of human nature also focuses on consciousness. Human beings operate on a conscious level; they are not driven by unconscious forces or instincts (Glasser, 1965). Individuals may not always be aware of reasons for what they do, but this unawareness is more similar to Freud's preconscious than to his unconscious. Glasser stresses the importance of the present in human interactions: everyone has a personal history but one's actions are based now on the needs one perceives. The link between perception and behavior is important in explaining a person's action. As Glasser (1981) observes, behavior is the control of perceptions (BCP).

### Role of the Counselor

The counselor serves primarily as a teacher and model, accepting of the client in a warm and involved way. The counselor focuses on behaviors of the client in an active, direct, practical, didactive, and cognitive manner (Corey, 1986). Counselor/client interaction emphasizes the behaviors that the client would like to change and the ways to go about making desired changes a reality. There is no attempt to test, diagnose, interpret, or otherwise analyze client actions. Reality therapists do not concentrate on early childhood experiences, client insights, aspects of the unconscious, or mental illness and blame.

### Goals

The primary goal of reality therapy is to assist the client in becoming psychologically strong and rational, that is, autonomous and responsible for behaviors that affect self and others (Corey, 1986; Wallace, 1986). Glasser (1981) contends that to help people, "we must help them gain strength to do worthwhile things with their lives and at the same time become warmly involved with the people they need" (p. 48).

Another goal is to get individuals to take responsibility for their behaviors. Responsible behavior allows individuals to take charge of actions, obtain goals, and not interfere with others.

Responsible behavior leads to the formation of a success identity, which enables clients to live more productive and harmonious lives.

A further goal is to help the client clarify what he or she wants in life. It is vital for a person to be aware of life goals if the person is to act responsibly. In assessing goals, reality therapists help the client examine personal assets as well as environmental supports and hindrances. It is the responsibility of the client to choose behaviors that fulfill personal needs. Glasser (1976) lists six criteria on which to judge whether a person is choosing a suitable and healthy behavior:

☐ The behavior is noncompetitive

☐ The behavior is easily completed without a lot of mental effort

☐ The behavior is done or can be done by oneself

☐ The behavior has value for the person

☐ The client believes that improvements in life-style will result if he or she practices the behavior

☐ The person can practice the behavior without being self-critical

Another goal is to help the client formulate a realistic plan to achieve personal needs and wishes. Poor mental health is sometimes the result of a person's not knowing how to achieve what he or she has planned. Glasser advocates that plans be as specific and concrete as possible. Once a plan is formulated, alternative behaviors, decisions, and outcomes are examined, and often a contract is written. The focus is on helping individuals become more responsible and realize that no single plan is absolute.

An additional goal of reality therapy is to have the counselor become involved with the client in a meaningful relationship (Glasser, 1980, 1981). This relationship is based on understanding, acceptance, empathy, and a willingness by the counselor to express faith in the ability of the client to change. The counselor helps the client establish boundaries for his or her behavior, but is not critical if the client is unable to complete a behavior. Often, to facilitate the development of the relationship, the counselor will risk disclosing personal information to the client.

Another goal of reality therapy is to focus on behavior and the present. Glasser believes that behavior is interrelated with cognition and affect, and that a change in behavior also brings about change in the other two (Glasser & Zunin, 1979). He emphasizes present activities because they are controlled by the client—the client has no control over the past.

Finally, reality therapy aims to eliminate punishment and excuses from the client's life. Often, a client will use the excuse that he or she cannot carry out a plan because of punishment for failure by either the counselor or people in the outside environment. Reality therapy helps the client formulate a new plan if the old one does not work. The emphasis is on planning, revision, and eventual success rather than on setbacks. The entire procedure is one that empowers the client and enables the client to be more productive.

### Techniques

Reality therapy relies heavily on teaching as a primary technique. Glasser (1965) states that "the specialized learning situation . . . is made up of three separate but interwoven procedures" (p. 21). First, there is involvement between counselor and client in which the client begins to face reality and to see how a behavior is unrealistic. Second, the counselor rejects the unrealistic behavior of the client without rejecting the client as a person. Finally, the counselor teaches the client better ways to fulfill needs within the confines of reality.

There are eight basic steps to reality therapy on which all techniques are based:

1. Establishing a relationship
2. Focusing on present behavior
3. Evaluating by the client of his or her behavior
4. Developing a contract or plan of action
5. Getting a commitment from the client
6. Not accepting excuses
7. Allowing reasonable consequences, but refusing to use punishment
8. Refusing to give up on the client

These steps are not a recipe for successful counseling, but guidelines for helping. They are sequential, so counselors know where to begin their work.

The initial process of establishing a relationship with the client is probably the most crucial procedure in reality therapy. If the client and counselor fail to establish rapport, progress is impossible. Such a relationship is ongoing rather than a one-time event. When an initial relationship is established, the second step of the sequence begins, focusing on present behavior. Like the behaviorists, gestaltists, and rational behavior therapists, reality therapists are not very interested in the past. They stress the present because current behavior is most amenable to client control. Further, if this behavior is changed, then thoughts and feelings are also modified.

Next, the client is asked to evaluate how responsible personal behavior is. Irresponsible behavior contributes to a client's identity as a failure because the behavior often alienates the client from significant others. If a client recognizes a behavior as irresponsible, the client is motivated to change. If there is no recognition, the therapeutic process will break down. It is crucial that the client, not the counselor, does the evaluation.

After evaluation, a client focuses on making a plan for changing irresponsible behavior. The plan stresses actions that the client will take, not behaviors that he or she will eliminate. Further, the plan may be formalized in a written contract in which responsible alternatives are spelled out. The client is then requested to make a commitment to the plan of actions. In this procedure, the counselor makes it clear that no excuses will be accepted for a client's not carrying out the plan of action; neither will the counselor blame or punish. In essence, responsibility is placed entirely on the client. If the client fails to accomplish the plan, Glasser thinks the client should suffer the natural or reasonable consequences of that failure (Evans, 1982). He also stresses (Glasser, 1965, 1980) that the counselor should not give up on the client, if the client fails to accomplish a goal. Instead, the counselor stubbornly and tenaciously hangs in with the client to make a new plan or revise an old one. Most clients are used to being put down or abandoned when goals are not achieved. Glasser's approach gives the client an opportunity to alter that cycle of failure.

Basically, reality therapy uses action-oriented techniques. Corey (1982) and Wallace (1986) note that some of the more effective and active techniques of this approach are role playing, using humor, confrontation, formulation of specific plans, role modeling, defining limits, and involvement. We have already mentioned the importance of involvement, planning, defining limits, and modeling, so here we will elaborate a bit more on the use of humor, confrontation, and role playing.

Humor is an appropriate technique in reality therapy, if it is used sparingly. Most clients do not see difficult situations as funny, yet if a counselor times a remark just right, the client may come to see some silliness in the behavior in question. The ability to laugh at oneself promotes the ability to change, because the situation is seen from a new perspective. In no case should humor be used as a sarcastic putdown in counseling. When employed in such a manner, it is likely to deteriorate the counselor/client relationship and adversely affect the course of counseling.

Confrontation mainly involves the counselor's asking the client about a behavior; it is a way of helping the client accept responsibility for his or her actions. As such, confrontation is not that different from the confrontation of other approaches. Similarly, role playing in reality therapy is like that employed in other counseling approaches. However, the purpose of role playing in reality therapy is to help the client bring the past or future into the present and assess how life will be different when he or she starts behaving differently. Role plays are almost always followed by counselor feedback sessions.

### Evaluation

Reality therapy has a number of strengths:

☐ The approach can be applied to many different populations. It is especially appropriate in the treatment of conduct disorders, substance-abuse disorders, impulse-control disorders, personality disorders, and antisocial behavior. It can be employed in individual counseling with children, adolescents, adults, and the aged. It is also appropriately employed in group, marriage, and family counseling. The approach has such versatility that it is helpful in almost any setting that emphasizes mental health and adjustment, such as hospitals, mental health clinics, schools, prisons, rehabilitation centers, and crisis centers (Seligman, 1986).

☐ The approach is concrete. Both counselor and client are able to assess how much progress is being made and in what areas, especially if a contract is drawn up that is goal specific. If a client is doing well in modifying one behavior and not another, increased attention can be given to the underdeveloped area.

☐ The approach emphasizes the short term. Reality therapy is usually limited to a relatively few sessions which focus on behavior in the present and future. Clients work with conscious and verifiable objectives that can be achieved quickly.

☐ The approach has a national training center. The Institute for Reality Therapy seeks to promote a uniform educational experience among practitioners who employ this theory, as well as the publication of professional literature.

☐ The approach promotes responsibility and freedom within individuals without blame or criticism or an attempt to restructure the entire personality. Many individuals simply need help with certain behaviors, and reality therapy takes care of this need.

Reality therapy also has limitations:

☐ The approach emphasizes the here and now of behavior so much that it ignores other concepts, such as the unconscious and personal history. Sometimes, a person may be informed by the unconscious, such as by dreams. In other cases, a person may need to relive and resolve past traumas. Reality therapy makes little allowance for the unconscious or personal history.

☐ The approach holds that all forms of mental illness are attempts to deal with external events (Glasser, 1984). Mental illness does not happen to us, Glasser believes; a person chooses mental illness in order to help control his or her world. Glasser ignores biology as a factor in mental illness, a stance considered by some critics to be naive and irresponsible.

☐ The approach is too simple. Reality therapy has few theoretical constructs, though with its tie to control theory it is becoming more sophisticated. Still, Glasser does not deal with the full complexity of human life, such as developmental stages. His theory lacks comprehensiveness.

☐ The approach may be too value-laden and moralistic. Glasser (1972) has disavowed that reality therapy was intended to function in this way. The counselor who practices reality therapy does not judge a client's behavior; the client judges the behavior. The role of the counselor is to support the client in a personal exploration of values. Still, an overzealous practitioner could easily impose values on a client. Thus, this criticism is aimed at a potential difficulty rather than the theory as advocated by its founder.

☐ The approach is used by some counselors who are insufficiently involved with their clients, settle for general goals, force a plan, or proceed too quickly to commitment (Wubbolding, 1975). The point has some validity, but with proper supervision and national certification such mistakes should not occur frequently.

Finally, Corey (1982) notes that reality therapy has changed its approach since the early 1960s despite an initial denial by Glasser (1976). Acceptance is more emphasized now than previously, and the integration of control theory as the bedrock of the approach has made the focus of the theory different from before. These changes should be emphasized more if reality therapy is to be thoroughly understood.

## INTEGRATION OF INDIVIDUAL THEORIES

At the beginning of the chapters on theories, the idea of a healthy eclectic approach to counseling was introduced. It is hoped that in examining the various approaches to counseling, you have thought of ways to integrate some of the theories and techniques into your own future practice.

Two prominent approaches have attempted such an integration. One was developed by Zander Ponzo (1976). It is his contention that in the first phase of counseling—awareness—Rogerian and Gestalt methods can be used in order to establish a good relationship with clients. An existential approach would be appropriate at this stage also. In phase two of his view of counseling—cognitive reorganization—Ponzo draws heavily upon the more cognitive theories of TA and RET in order to help his clients change maladaptive or nonproductive thinking. Finally, in his phase three of counseling—behavior change—Ponzo utilizes the behavioral approaches to counseling. Clients are helped to act differently and more productively.

A second and more encompassing approach is offered by Arnold Lazarus (1967, 1971, 1976), who initially defined his approach as "technical eclecticism." According to Lazarus, a client's personality is organized by seven modes of functioning: ongoing behaviors, affective processes, sensations, images, cognitions, interpersonal relationships, and biological functions. Collectively, these modes are grouped under the acronym BASIC ID. Treatment focuses on influencing each of these modes, but the choice of what systematic approach to use with a client depends on where the client is experiencing the most difficulty. Human modes are interactional, Lazarus believes, and there is a "firing order" by which one mode influences another. The goal of treatment, then, is multifaceted and involves influencing the behavior of the entire person by selectively working in one or two primary areas.

Ponzo's and Lazarus's methods of trying to achieve a healthy eclecticism are not the only ways this can be done. It is vital for each counselor to discover what systematic approaches work best for him or her. The two systems just mentioned are good models on which to base one's own thinking about the integration of counseling approaches. Both Ponzo and Lazarus understand human nature and their theories of counseling well and are therefore able to be effective. They also appear to have knowledge about themselves and their clients. All of these factors are crucial to master if one is to use individual counseling theories appropriately. To help you gain a clearer picture of the various counseling approaches, and to stimulate your thinking about integrative and systematic approaches to counseling, Table 6.2 is provided for your examination.

**TABLE 6.2** Summation of counseling approaches.

| Approach | Psychoanalysis | Adlerian Counseling | Person-centered Counseling | Existential Counseling |
|---|---|---|---|---|
| Major Theorists | Sigmund Freud<br>Ann Freud<br>Heinz Kohut | Alfred Adler<br>Rudolph Driekurs<br>Don Dinkmeyer | Carl Rogers<br>Angelo Boy<br>Gerald Pine | Rollo May<br>Victor Frankl<br>Abraham Maslow<br>Irvin Yalom<br>Sidney Jourard |
| View of Human Nature | Emphasis on early childhood and psychosexual stages of development; importance of unconscious and ego defense mechanisms; focus on biological deterministic aspects of behavior | Emphasis on social interest as a primary motivator; focus on birth order, family constellation, style of life, and teleological (future) goals as major influences of personal growth and development | Emphasis on humans as basically good, positive, forward-moving and trustworthy; phenomenological view of self; person is self-directed and growth oriented if provided with the right conditions | Belief in human freedom and choice of life-style; focus on meaning of anxiety, meaning of life, and relevance of individual experience |
| Role of the Counselor | Counselor as expert; encourages transference and exploration of the unconscious; use of interpretation | Counselor in equalitarian relationship with client; models, teaches, and assesses client's situation; shares hunches; assigns homework; encourages | Stresses holism, I-thou quality; counselor facilitates, focuses on uniqueness of client; counselor is the technique; emphasis on personal warmth, empathy, acceptance, concreteness, and genuineness | Emphasis on counselor authenticity and understanding of client as unique; stress on personal relationship, modeling, and sharing of experiences |
| Goals | Make the unconscious conscious; work through unresolved developmental stages; help the client learn to cope and adjust; reconstruction of personality | Cultivate social interests; correct faulty assumptions and mistaken goals; develop client insight; bring about behavioral change through acting as if | Self-exploration; openness to self, others; self-directed and realistic; more accepting of self, others, and environment; focus on the here and now | Helps clients realize their responsibility, awareness, freedom, and potential; shift from outward frame of reference |

| Gestalt Therapy | Rational-Emotive Therapy | Transactional Analysis | Behavioral Counseling | Reality Therapy |
|---|---|---|---|---|
| Fritz Perls<br>Laura Perls<br>Irma Lee Shepherd<br>Joen Fagan | Albert Ellis<br>Maxie Maultsby | Eric Berne<br>Carl Steiner<br>Thomas Harris<br>Graham Barnes | John B. Watson<br>B. F. Skinner<br>Joseph Wolpe<br>Albert Bandura<br>John Krumboltz | William Glasser |
| Emphasis on importance of wholeness and completeness in human life; stress on inner wisdom of person and importance of affect; phenomenological and antideterministic; stresses change | Humans are both inherently rational and irrational; biological duality; humans can disturb themselves by what they think; children are most vulnerable; mistake for people to use form of the verb *to be* to describe themselves. | Optimistic that people can change; each individual is composed of three interacting ego states of parent, adult, child; stresses importance of intrapersonal integration and analysis of transactions, games, time, and scripts for individual health and growth | All human behaviors are learned; old behaviors can be extinguished and new behaviors established; respondent learning, operant conditioning, and social modeling the three primary ways of learning | Health or growth force in all individuals; problems occur when people don't take responsibility for behavior; learning is a life-long process; people need to love and be loved and feel worthwhile and successful, act to control the world around them for various purposes |
| Counselor must be authentic, exciting, and energetic; emphasis on the now; helps client resolve unfinished business; counselor stresses verbal and nonverbal messages, congruence; use of *I* for *it* | Active, direct counselor teaches, confronts, corrects; counselor concentrates on A-B-Cs of self-talk. | Counselor as teacher; contracts with client for change; instructs in language of TA | Counselor as teacher, director, and expert; active in sessions; assists client in clarifying goals and modifying behaviors | Counselor as teacher and model; focus on establishing a relationship with client; counselor is active, direct, practical, didactic |
| Emphasis on immediacy of experience; making choices in the now; resolving the past, becoming congruent; growing up mentally; shedding neuroses | Help clients live more rational and productive lives, stop thinking irrationally; stresses elimination of oughts, shoulds, musts, i.e. making wants into demands; elimination of self-defeating habits; tolerance and acceptance of self and others | Transformation; attainment of health and autonomy; becoming more aware, game free, intimate, and OK | Help clients make good adjustment, modify maladaptive behavior, learning productive responses; establish and achieve specific concrete goals and subgoals | Assist individuals to become psychologically strong and rational, take responsibility, clarify goals, formulate a realistic plan, focus on behavior and the present, eliminate punishment and excuses |

| Approach | Psychoanalysis | Adlerian Counseling | Person-centered Counseling | Existential Counseling |
|---|---|---|---|---|
| **Techniques** | Free association; dream analysis; analysis of transference; analysis of resistance; interpretation | Use of empathy, support, warmth, collaboration; stress on client strengths and responsibility through confrontation; examination of client's memories, dreams, and priorities; focus on interpretation, asking The Question, spitting in the client's soup, catching oneself, and task setting | Acceptance, clarification; reflection of feeling; use of empathy, positive regard, congruence, self-disclosure; active/passive listening; open-ended questions/statements; summarization | Counselor openness and inquiringness; acceptance of client uniqueness; emphasis on relationship; working with ambiguity; confrontation; borrowing of other active techniques that work, such as imagery or awareness exercises |
| **Strengths** | Emphasis on importance of sexuality and unconscious in human behavior; supportive of diagnostic instruments; multidimensional; continued evolution effective in select cases; focus on developmental stages of human life, especially childhood | Encouragement and support of counselor in an equalitarian relationship; versatility; useful in specific disorders; contribution of ideas to the public and professional vocabulary, e.g., inferiority complex | Openness and evolution of theory; applicable to a wide range of human problems; effectiveness with specific disorders, e.g., adjustment disorders; short-term treatment; effectiveness with paraprofessionals; positive view of human nature | Humanistic emphasis; focus on anxiety as a motivator; use of philosophy and literature to inform/direct |
| **Limitations** | Time-consuming and expensive; a closed system of practice, limited mainly to psychiatry; focus on pathology; deterministic; not efficient method for less-disturbed individuals | Lack of a firm research base; vagueness of concepts/terms and the how of counseling; narrowness of approach | Lack of concreteness; works best with verbal, bright clients; ignores unconscious and innate drives; deals with surface issues | Not fully developed; lack of training approaches to learning theory; subjective, lacks uniformity; more philosophical and less functional than other theories; avoids diagnoses and testing |

**TABLE 6.2** *(continued)*

| Gestalt Therapy | Rational-Emotive Therapy | Transactional Analysis | Behavioral Counseling | Reality Therapy |
|---|---|---|---|---|
| Use of exercises and experiments; exercises include frustration actions, fantasy, role playing, and psychodrama; experiments grow out of client/counselor interaction; use of dream work, empty chair, confrontation, making the rounds, exaggeration, and I take responsibility | Counselor uses teaching and disputing; clients learn the anatomy of an emotion; imagery, persuasion, logical reasoning, reminder devices, homework assignments, bibliotherapy, shame attacks, and rational self-analyses | Emphasis on treatment contracts, specific and concrete; use of techniques such as interrogation, specification, confrontation, illustration, and crystallization; concentration on early memories/stories; often combined with Gestalt techniques for action | Use of reinforcement—positive/negative, primary/secondary, continuous/intermittent; shaping, extinction, self-monitoring, punishment, environmental planning, systematic densensitization, implosion, flooding, time out, overcorrection, imitation, stress inoculation, thought stopping | Teaching, focusing, evaluating; helping client make a plan and commit to it; not blaming, not giving up on client, role playing, using humor, confronting, role modeling; defining limits; involvement with client; feedback |
| Helps individual incorporate all parts of life, resolve past; stresses doing and being active; appropriate for certain affective disorders | Direct, clear, effective, and easily learned, combines well with other theories; treatment is short-term; centralized training centers; theory continues to evolve | Easily understood and clearly defined terminology; easy to combine with other theories; puts responsibility on client for choosing; goal directed | Focus on symptoms; focus on here and now; abundance of available procedures; based on learning theory; well-organized practitioners; effective for certain disorders; well researched; continually growing in sophistication; can be combined with other theories, especially cognitive | Applicable to many different populations; effective with certain disorders; concreteness; short-term; centralized training center; promotes responsibility and freedom without blaming; stresses here and now; integrates control theory |
| Lack of a strong theoretical base; gimmicky; does not allow for passive learning; eschews testing/diagnosis; self-centeredness of approach | Not applicable to all clients, especially those who are mentally impaired; associated with unconventional theorist Albert Ellis; still viewed as primarily cognitive | Cognitive orientation limiting; simplicity and popularity dilute effectiveness; lack of emphasis on qualities of the counselor | Doesn't deal with total person, just behaviors; may be applied mechanically; sometimes difficult to replicate in actual counseling conditions; techniques getting ahead of theory; ignores past history and the unconscious; doesn't consider developmental stages | Ignores unconscious, personal history, mental illness; theoretically simplistic; may become value ladened unless supervised appropriately; ignores its own history of evolution |

## SUMMARY

The most prominent behavioral theories of counseling have been covered in this chapter. It is clear that many of them have much in common, yet each is also unique. The basic premise of all these approaches is that if a person changes behavior, changes in thinking and feeling will follow. The behaviorists, as well as Glasser, stress that behavior change comes first.

Basically, counselors who work from a behavioral perspective focus on present actions and perceptions that clients wish to learn, unlearn, or modify. Counselors are concrete and goal directed, but work in collaboration with their clients. Often, contracts are established between counselor and client to identify when the goals of counseling have been reached. In behavioral counseling, a clinician can work from a respondent, operant, or social modeling theoretical base.

All of these theories, as well as the ones examined in previous chapters, are effective in both broad and selective ways. For some clients, a specific theoretical orientation at a select time is best. To maximize time and effort, effective counselors constantly evaluate the impact of an approach and review the professional literature on what theories work best with what type of client in what circumstances. Which theoretical orientation counselors choose depends on the personality of the counselor, the personality of the client, and the setting, as well as on other variables unique to a particular situation. All of the theories in this chapter, and those in previous ones, have strengths and limitations. They may be selectively integrated or employed separately.

In closing, it is critical to emphasize how important it is to explore each theory in depth. Such exploration continues well after a course of study has been completed. Counseling is a process that is ever expanding and changing.

## CLASSROOM ACTIVITIES

1. Which of the behavioral theories do you find most attractive? State the reasons for your decision with other class members. Which theories do you anticipate using? Find several research articles that support the effectiveness of these theories and share the summaries of them with the class.
2. In 1956 there was a debate between Carl Rogers and B. F. Skinner: Skinner took the position that the environment is the sole determiner of behavior; Rogers proposed that human behavior is determined by self-concept. Read recent articles and books by both men and if possible listen to the tape of the debate. How do you think they would debate now? Stage a simulated debate between these two theorists in which several class members act as spokespersons for each side. Then discuss how it feels to argue as a Skinnerian or Rogerian.

3. How would you compare the main behavioral theories with Glasser's reality therapy? Are they all really the same? If not, what makes them different? List similarities and differences among the approaches and discuss your ideas with other class members.

4. What do you think of the integration of individual theories into a composite or eclectic approach? Investigate recent attempts to formulate a healthy eclecticism.

Discuss in small groups the strengths and limitations of working in such a way.

5. What are some activities you can do after your formal education is complete in order to keep abreast of developments in counseling theory and to keep your counseling skills up-to-date? Survey practicing counselors to find out how they stay current. Discuss your findings with fellow classmates.

# REFERENCES

Alberti, R. E., & Emmons, M. L. (1982). *Your perfect right: A guide to assertive behavior* (4th ed.). San Luis Obispo, CA: Impact.

Azrin, N. H., Stuart, R. B., Risely, T. R., & Stolz, S. (1977). Ethical issues for human services. *AABT Newsletter, 4,* 11.

Bandura, A. (1969). *Principles of behavior modification.* New York: Holt, Rinehart & Winston.

Bandura, A. (1971). Psychotherapy based upon modeling principles. In A. E. Bergin & S. L. Garfield (Eds.), *Handbook of psychotherapy and behavior change.* New York: Wiley.

Bandura, A. (1977). *Social learning theory.* Englewood Cliffs, NJ: Prentice-Hall.

Bandura, A., & Walters, R. H. (1963). *Social learning and personality development.* New York: Rinehart & Winston.

Barclay, J. R. (1980). The revolution in counseling: Some editorial comments. *Personnel and Guidance Journal, 58,* 457.

Beck, A. (1976). *Cognitive therapy and the emotional disorders.* New York: International Universities Press.

Bellack, A. S. & Hersen, M. (1977). *Behavior modification: An introductory textbook.* Baltimore: Williams & Wilkins.

Blackham, G J., & Silberman, A. (1971). *Modification of child behavior.* Belmont, CA: Wadsworth.

Cautela, J. R. (1976). The present status of covert modeling. *Journal of Behavior Therapy and Experimental Psychiatry, 6,* 323–326.

Corey, G. (1982). *Theory and practice of counseling and psychotherapy* (2nd ed.). Monterey, CA: Brooks/Cole.

Corey, G. (1986). *Theory and practice of counseling and psychotherapy* (3rd ed.). Monterey, CA: Brooks/Cole.

Cormier, L. S., & Hackney, H. (1987). *The professional counselor.* Englewood Cliffs, NJ: Prentice-Hall.

Cormier, W. H., & Cormier, L. S. (1979). *Interviewing strategies for helpers: A guide to assessment, treatment, and evaluation.* Monterey, CA: Brooks/Cole.

Elms, A. C. (1981). Skinner's dark year and *Walden Two. American Psychologist, 36,* 470–479.

Evans, D. (1982). What are you doing? An interview with William Glasser. *Personnel and Guidance Journal, 60,* 460–464.

Eysenck, H. J. (1960). *Behavior therapy and the neuroses.* New York: Pergamon.

Gladding, S. T. (1975). The bandaid man. *Personnel and Guidance Journal, 53,* 520.

Glasser, W. (1965). *Reality therapy: A new approach to psychiatry.* New York: Harper & Row.

Glasser, W. (1969). *Schools without failure.* New York: Harper & Row.

Glasser, W. (1972). *The identity society.* New York: Harper & Row.

Glasser, W. (1976). *Positive addiction.* New York: Harper & Row.

Glasser, W. (1980). Reality therapy: An explanation of the steps of reality therapy. In W. Glasser (Ed.), *What are you doing? How people are helped through reality therapy.* New York: Harper & Row.

Glasser, W. (1981). *Stations of the mind.* New York: Harper & Row.

Glasser, W. (1984). *Take effective control of your life.* New York: Harper & Row.

Glasser, W., & Zunin, L. M. (1979). Reality therapy. In R. Corsini (Ed.), *Current psychotherapies* (2nd ed.). Itasca, IL: Peacock.

Goldiamond, I. (1976). Self-reinforcement. *Journal of Applied Behavior Analysis, 9,* 509–514.

Goldstein, A. (1973). Behavior therapy. In R. Corsini (Ed.), *Current psychotherapies* (pp. 207–249). Itasca, IL: Peacock.

Groden, G., & Cautela, J. R. (1981). Behavior therapy: A survey of procedures for counselors. *Personnel and Guidance Journal, 60,* 175–179.

Hergenhahn, B. R. (1984). *An introduction to theories of personality* (2nd ed.). Englewood Cliffs, NJ: Prentice-Hall.

Hosford, R. E. (1980). The Cubberley conference and the evolution of observational learning strategies. *Personnel and Guidance Journal, 58,* 467–472.

Jones, M. C. (1924). The elimination of children's fears. *Journal of Experimental Psychology, 7,* 383–390.

Krasner, L., & Ullmann, L. P. (1973). *Behavior influence and personality: The social matrix of human action.* New York: Holt, Rinehart & Winston.

Krumboltz, J. D. (1966). Behavioral goals of counseling. *Journal of Counseling Psychology, 13,* 153–159.

Krumboltz, J. D., & Thoresen, C. E. (1969). *Behavioral counseling.* New York: Holt, Rinehart & Winston.

Krumboltz, J. D., & Thoresen, C. E. (1976). *Counseling methods.* New York: Holt, Rinehart & Winston.

Lazarus, A. A. (1967). In support of technical eclecticism. *Psychological Reports, 21,* 415–416.

Lazarus, A. A. (1971). *Behavior therapy and beyond.* New York: McGraw-Hill.

Lazarus, A. A. (1976). *Multimodel behavior therapy.* New York: Springer.

Meichenbaum, D. H. (1977). *Cognitive-behavior modification.* New York: Plenum.

Meichenbaum, D. H. (1985). Cognitive-behavioral therapies. In S. J. Lynn & J. P. Garske (Eds.), *Contemporary psychotherapies: Models and methods* (pp. 261–286). Columbus, OH: Merrill.

Perry, M. A., & Furukawa, M. J. (1980). Modeling methods. In F. H. Kanfer & A. P. Goldstein (Eds.), *Helping people change* (pp. 131–171). New York: Pergamon Press.

Ponzo, Z. (1976). Integrating techniques from five counseling theories. *Personnel and Guidance Journal, 54,* 415–419.

Rimm, D. C., & Cunningham, H. M. (1985). Behavior therapies. In S. J. Lynn & J. P. Garske (Eds.), *Contemporary psychotherapies: Models and methods* (pp. 221–259). Columbus, OH: Merrill.

Seligman, L. (1986). *Diagnosis and treatment planning in counseling.* New York: Human Sciences Press.

Skinner, B. F. (1938). *The behavior of organisms: An experimental analysis.* Englewood Cliffs, NJ: Prentice-Hall.

Skinner, B. F. (1948). *Walden two.* New York: Macmillan.

Skinner, B. F. (1953). *Science and human behavior.* New York: Macmillan.

Skinner, B. F. (1967). Autobiography. In E. G. Boring & G. Lindzey (Eds.), *A history of psychology in autobiography,* (Vol. 5, pp. 387–413). New York: Appleton-Century-Crofts.

Skinner, B. F. (1974). *About behaviorism.* New York: Knopf.

Skinner, B. F. (1976). *Particulars of my life.* New York: McGraw-Hill.

Skinner, B. F., & Vaughan, M. E. (1983). *Enjoy old age.* New York: Norton.

Sprinthall, N. A. (1971). A program for psychological education: Some preliminary issues. *Journal of School Psychology, 9,* 373–382.

Thoresen, C. E., & Coates, T. J. (1980). What does it mean to be a behavior therapist? In C. E. Thoresen (Ed.). *The behavior therapist* (pp. 1–41). Monterey, CA: Brooks/Cole.

Wallace, W. A. (1986). *Theories of counseling and psychotherapy.* Boston: Allyn & Bacon.

Watson, J. B. (1913). Psychology as a behaviorist views it. *Psychological Review, 20,* 158–177.

Watson, J. B. (1925). *Behaviorism.* New York: Norton.

Watson, J. B., & Raynor, R. (1920). Conditioned emotional reactions. *Journal of Experimental Psychology, 3,* 1–14.

Wolpe, J. (1958). *Psychotherapy by reciprocal inhibition building.* Stanford, CA: Stanford University Press.

Wubbolding, R. E. (1975). Practicing reality therapy. *Personnel and Guidance Journal, 53,* 164–165.

Yates, A. J. (1970). *Behavior therapy.* New York: Wiley.

Photo by James S. Davidson III.

CHAPTER **7**

# Building a Counseling Relationship

*Your words splash heavily upon my mind*
*    like early cold October rain*
*        falling on my roof at dusk.*
*The patterns change like an Autumn storm*
*    from violently rumbling thundering sounds*
*        to clear, soft steady streams of expression.*
*Through it all I look at you*
*    soaked in past fears and turmoil;*
*Then patiently I watch with you in the darkness*
*    for the breaking of black clouds*
*        that linger in your turbulent mind*
*And the dawning of your smile*
*    that comes in the light of new beginnings.*[1]

[1]Gladding, 1975, p. 149. Copyright AACD. Reprinted with permission. No further reproduction authorized without written permission of AACD.

Counseling is a process that develops in definable stages with recognizable transitions. The first stage in the process involves building a relationship. It focuses on engaging clients to explore issues that directly affect them. There are two struggles that go on at this time (Napier & Whitaker, 1978). One is the *battle for structure,* which involves issues of administrative control (e.g., scheduling, fees, participation in sessions). The other is the *battle for initiative,* which concerns motivation for change and client responsibility. It is essential that counselors "win" the first battle and that clients "win" the second. If there are failures at these points, the counseling effort will be prematurely terminated and both the counselor and client may feel worse for the experience.

There are other factors that also influence the progress and direction of counseling, such as the physical setting, the background of the client, the skill of the counselor, and the quality of the relationship established. In this chapter, we will explore these factors, the nature of the first interview, and the exploration stage of counseling. Carkhuff (1969) and Ivey (1971, 1983) have demonstrated that some counseling responses cut across theoretical lines in helping build a client/counselor relationship. But, as Patterson (1985a) says, effective counselors base their behaviors on sound and proven theories.

# FACTORS THAT INFLUENCE THE COUNSELING PROCESS

## Structure

Clients and counselors sometimes have different perceptions about the purpose and nature of counseling. Clients often do not know what to expect from the process or how they should act (Riordan, Matheny & Harris, 1978). This uncertainty can inhibit the counseling process unless some structure is provided (Ritchie, 1986). "Structure in counseling is defined as a joint understanding between the counselor and client regarding the characteristics, conditions, procedures, and parameters of counseling" (Day & Sparacio, 1980, p. 246). It helps to clarify the relationship between the counselor and the client, give it direction, protect the rights, roles, and obligations of both counselors and clients, and ensure the success of counseling (Brammer & Shostrom, 1977; Day & Sparacio, 1980).

Structure is provided throughout all the stages of counseling, but it is especially important at the beginning. Dorn (1984) states that "clients usually seek counseling because they are in a static behavior state" (p. 342). The client feels out of control. In order to help clients gain new directions in their lives, counselors provide constructive guidelines. Their decisions on how to establish this structure are based on their theoretical orientation to counseling, the personalities of their clients, and the major problem areas with which they will deal. Too much structure can be just as detrimental as not enough (Patterson & Eisenberg, 1983). Thus, counselors need to stay flexible and negotiate the nature of the structure with their clients on an ongoing basis (Day & Sparacio, 1980).

The importance of structure is most obvious when a client arrives for counseling with unrealistic expectations (Patterson & Eisenberg, 1983). A counselor needs to move quickly to establish structure at such times. One way this may be done is for the counselor to inform the client about the counseling process and the counselor through the use of a professional disclosure statement (Gill, 1982). Such a statement defines the counselor's philosophy of human nature, as well as the purposes, expectations, responsibilities, methods, and ethics of counseling.

Practical guidelines are part of building the structure. These include time limits (such as a 50-minute session), action limits (for the prevention of destructive behavior), role limits (what will be expected of each participant), and procedural limits (in which the client is given the responsibility to work on specific goals or needs)

(Brammer & Shostrom, 1977; Goodyear & Bradley, 1980; Kelly & Stone, 1982). Guidelines also provide information on fee schedules and other important concerns of clients. In general, a structure promotes the development of counseling by providing a framework in which the process can take place. "It is therapeutic in and of itself" (Day & Sparacio, 1980, p. 246).

### *Initiative*

Initiative can be thought of as the motivation to change. Ritchie (1986) notes that most counselors and counseling theories assume that clients will be cooperative. Indeed, many clients come to counseling on a voluntary or self-referred basis. They experience tension and concern about themselves or others, but they are willing to work hard in counseling sessions (Patterson & Eisenberg, 1983). However, other clients are more reserved about participating in counseling. Vriend and Dyer (1973) have estimated that the majority of clients who visit counselors are reluctant to some degree. When counselors meet reluctant counselees, they often do not know what to do with them, much less how to do it. Many counselors end up blaming themselves or their clients if counseling is not successful (West, 1975). Such recriminations need not occur if counselors understand the dynamics involved in working with these difficult clients. Part of this understanding involves a counselor's imagining the role of an involuntary client and asking how it would feel coming for counseling (Ritchie, 1986). A role reversal exercise of this type can promote counselor empathy in dealing with reluctant and resistant clients.

A *reluctant client* is one who has been referred by a third party and is frequently "unmotivated to seek help" (Ritchie, 1986, p. 516). Many school children and court-referred clients are good examples. They do not wish to be in counseling, let alone to talk about themselves. Many reluctant clients terminate counseling prematurely and report dissatisfaction with the process (Paradise & Wilder, 1979).

The term *resistant client* refers to a person in counseling who is unwilling to change (Ritchie, 1986). Such an individual may have actively sought counseling but does not wish to go through the pain that change demands. Instead, the client clings to the certainty of present behavior, even when counterproductive and dysfunctional. Resistant clients include those who refuse to make decisions, who are superficial in dealing with problems, or who do not take any action to resolve a problem area, such as practicing a homework technique assigned by the counselor.

There are several ways counselors can help clients win the battle for initiative and thus achieve success in counseling. One way is to anticipate the anger, frustration, and defensiveness that some clients display (Ritchie, 1986). Counselors who realize that a percentage of their clients are reluctant or resistant are much more able to work with these individuals. A second way is to show acceptance, patience, and understanding. Such nonjudgmental attitudes promote trust in the relationship.

A third way is for counselors to use persuasion (Kerr, Claiborn, & Dixon, 1982; Senour, 1982). All counselors have some influence on clients, and vice versa (Dorn, 1984; Strong, 1982). How a counselor responds to the client, directly or indirectly, can make a significant difference in whether the client takes the initiative in working to produce change. Roloff and Miller (1980) mention two direct persuasion techniques employed in counseling: the "foot in the door" and the "door in the face." In the first technique, the counselor asks the client to comply with a minor request and then later follows with a larger request. In the second technique, the counselor asks the client to do a seemingly impossible task and then follows by requesting the client to do a more reasonable task.

A final way a counselor can assist the client in gaining the initiative is through confrontation. The counselor simply points out to the client exactly what the client is doing. The client then takes responsibility for doing something different, especially if what he or she has been doing has not been working.

## The Physical Setting

Counseling can occur almost anywhere, but some physical settings help promote the process better than others. Benjamin (1981) and Shertzer and Stone (1980) address external conditions involved in counseling. Among the most important factors that will help or hurt the process is the place in which the counseling occurs. Most counseling will occur in a room though Benjamin (1981) relates the story of conducting counseling in a tent. He says there is no universal quality that a room should have "except it should not be overwhelming, noisy, or distracting" (p. 3). Shertzer and Stone (1980) implicitly agree: "the room should be comfortable and attractive" (p. 252). There are certain features of a counseling office that will improve its general appearance and probably facilitate counseling by not distracting the client. These features include soft lighting, quiet colors, an absence of clutter, and harmonious, comfortable furniture. Clients usually adjust to the belongings of the room regardless.

The distance between counselor and client—the spatial features of the environment, or proxemics—can also affect the relationship. Individuals differ about the level of comfort experienced in interactions with others. The comfort level is influenced by cultural background, gender, and the nature of the relationship, among other things (Shertzer & Stone, 1980; Sielski, 1979). A distance of 30 to 39 inches has been found to be the average range of comfort between most counselors and clients of both genders (Haase, 1970). This optimum distance may vary because of the room size and furniture arrangement of the counselor's office (Haase & DiMattia, 1976).

How the furniture is arranged depends on the counselor. Some counselors prefer to sit behind a desk during sessions, but most do not. Pietrofesa, Hoffman, and Splete (1984) note that a desk can be a physical and symbolic barrier against the development of a close relationship. Benjamin (1981) suggests that counselors include two chairs and a nearby table in the setting. The chairs should be set at a 90 degree angle from one another, so that clients can look either at their counselors or straight ahead. The table can be used for many purposes, such as a place for a box of tissues. Benjamin's ideas are strictly his own; each counselor must find a physical arrangement that is comfortable for him or her.

Both Benjamin (1981) and Shertzer and Stone (1980) agree that regardless of the arrangement within the room, counselors should not be interrupted when conducting sessions. All phone calls should be held. If necessary, counselors should put Do Not Disturb signs on the door to keep others from entering. Auditory and visual privacy is mandated by professional codes of ethics and assures maximum client self-disclosure.

## Client Qualities

Counseling relationships start with first impressions. The way in which counselor and client perceive each other is vital to the establishment of a productive relationship. Warnath (1977) points out that "clients come in all shapes and sizes, personality characteristics, and degrees of attractiveness" (p. 85). Some clients are more likely to be successful in counseling than others. The most successful candidates for traditional approaches tend to be YAVIS—*y*oung, *a*ttractive, *v*erbal, *i*ntelligent, and *s*uccessful (Schofield, 1964). Less successful candidates are seen as HOUNDs—*h*omely, *o*ld, *u*nintelligent, *n*onverbal, and *d*isadvantaged—or DUDs—*d*umb, *u*nintelligent, and *d*isadvantaged (Allen, 1977). These acronyms are cruel (Lichtenberg, 1986), but counselors are influenced by the appearance and sophistication of the people with whom they work (Cormier & Cormier, 1985). According to Brown (1970) counselors most enjoy working with clients they think have the potential to change.

Ponzo (1985) notes that a number of stereotypes have been built around the physical attractiveness of individuals. The physically attractive are perceived as healthiest. Thus, the way in which counselors interact with clients may be influenced by physical factors. Goldstein (1973), for instance, found that clients who were seen by their counselors as most attractive talked more and were more spontaneous when compared to other clients. Therefore, aging clients and those with physical handicaps may face invisible but powerful barriers in certain counseling situations. Ponzo (1985) suggests that counselors become aware of the importance of physical attractiveness in their own lives and monitor their behavioral reactions when working with attractive clients. Otherwise, stereotypes and unfounded assumptions may "lead to self-fulfilling prophecies" (p. 485).

The nonverbal behaviors of clients are very important, too. Clients constantly send counselors unspoken messages about how they think or feel. Mehrabian (1971) and his associates found that expressed like and dislike between individuals could be explained as follows (p. 43):

> Total liking equals 7% verbal liking plus 38% vocal liking plus 55% facial liking. Thus the impact of facial expression is greatest, then the impact of the tone of voice (or vocal expression), and finally that of the words. If the facial expression is inconsistent with the words, the degree of liking conveyed by the facial expression will dominate and determine the impact of the total message.

Thus, a client who reports that all is going well but looks down at the ground and frowns while doing so is probably indicating just the opposite. Therefore, a client's body gestures—such as eye contact, facial expression, and vocal quality—must be considered as important in a counseling relationship. It is also crucial to consider the cultural background of the person whose body language is being evaluated and to interpret nonverbal messages cautiously (Gazda, Asbury, Balzer, Childers, & Walters, 1977; Sielski, 1979).

### Counselor Qualities

The personal and professional qualities of counselors are very important in facilitating any helping relationship, such as individual counseling. Okun (1982) notes that "it is hard to separate the helper's personality characteristics from his or her levels and styles of functioning, as both are interrelated" (p. 34). Okun (1982) lists five important characteristics she believes helpers on any level should possess: self-awareness, honesty, congruence, ability to communicate, and knowledge.

Counselors who continually develop their self-awareness skills are in touch with their values, thoughts, and feelings. They are more likely than not to have a clear perception of their own and their clients' needs and accurately assess both. Such awareness can help them in being more honest with themselves and others. They are able to be more congruent and build trust simultaneously. Counselors who possess this type of knowledge are most likely to communicate clearly and accurately.

Three other characteristics that make counselors initially more influential are: perceived expertness, attractiveness, and trustworthiness (Strong, 1968). Expertness is the degree to which a counselor is perceived as knowledgeable and informed about his or her specialty. Counselors who display certificates and diplomas in their offices are usually perceived as more credible than those who do not and as a result are likely to be effective (Loesch, 1984; Siegal & Sell, 1978). Clients want to work with counselors who appear to know the profession well.

Attractiveness is a function of perceived similarity between a client and counselor. Counselors can make themselves more attractive by speaking in clear, simple sentences unencumbered by jargon and by appropriate self-disclosure. The manner in which a counselor greets the client and maintains eye contact can also increase the attractiveness rating. Counselors who use nonverbal cues in responding to clients, such as head nodding and eye contact, are seen as more attractive than those who do not (Claiborn, 1979; LaCross, 1975). The attire of the counselor also makes a difference (Hubble & Gelso, 1978).

Trustworthiness is related to the sincerity and consistency of the counselor. It is a function of the counselor's not having a personal axe to grind; that is, the counselor's needs are not gratified at the expense of the client. "There is and can be no such thing as instant intimacy" (Patterson, 1985b, p. 124). It is through patterns of behavior that demonstrate care and concern that trustworthiness and intimacy are generated. Most clients are neither completely distrusting nor given to blind trust. But, as Fong and Cox (1983) note, many clients will test the trustworthiness of the counselor by requesting information, telling a secret, asking a favor, inconveniencing the counselor, self-deprecation, or questioning the motives and dedication of the counselor. It is essential, therefore, that the counselor respond to the question of trust, rather than to the verbal content, in order to facilitate the counseling relationship. Many beginning counselors make the mistake of dealing with surface issues instead of real concerns.

## TYPES OF INITIAL INTERVIEWS

The counseling process begins with the initial session. Levine (1983) points out that many authorities in the profession have observed that "the goals of counseling change over time and change according to the intimacy and effectiveness of the counseling relationship" (p. 431). How much change happens, or whether there is a second session, is usually determined by the results of the first session.

### Client vs. Counselor Initiated Interviews

Benjamin (1981) distinguishes between two types of first interviews: those initiated by clients and those initiated by counselors. When the initial interview is requested by a client, the counselor is often unsure of the client's purpose. This uncertainty may create anxiety in the counselor. However, Benjamin (1981) recommends that counselors work to overcome these feelings by listening as hard as possible to what the client has to say. He cautions against using any type of formula with which to begin the session. The helping interview is more of an art than a science, and every counselor must work out a style based on "experience, stimulation, and reflection" (p. 11). Benjamin also advises that initially the counselor should not inquire about any problem the client may have, because the client may not have a problem in the traditional sense of the word and may just be seeking information. When the first session is requested by the counselor, Benjamin (1981) believes the counselor should immediately state the reason for wanting to see the client. Otherwise, the client is kept guessing and tension is created.

Patterson and Eisenberg (1983) think that all clients enter counseling with some anxiety and resistance. Benjamin (1981) hypothesizes that most counselors are also "a bit frightened and uncertain" (p. 11) upon conducting the first interview. The feelings that clients and counselors have may result in the acting out of behaviors, such as seduction or aggression (Watkins, 1983). Counselors can prevent such occurrences, through the exchange of information with clients. Manthei (1983) advocates that presentations by counselors about themselves and how they function be multimodal—visual, auditory, written, spoken, descriptive, and so on. This type of procedure ensures the likelihood that clients will make more meaningful choices and participate more fully in the counseling process.

Hackney and Cormier (1979) point out that the initial counseling interview can be used in two ways. The first way is as an intake interview to collect needed information about the client. The second way is as the beginning of a relationship. Either way is appropriate, and there are certain tasks common to both, though the skills emphasized in the two ways differ.

### Information-oriented First Interview

If the purpose of the first interview is to gather information, the structure of the session will be counselor focused since the counselor wants the client to talk about certain subject matters. The counselor will predominantly respond to the client through the use of probes, accents, closed questions, and requests for clarification (Hackney & Cormier, 1979). These responses are aimed at eliciting facts.

The *probe* is a question that usually begins with *who, what, where,* or *how.* It requires more than a one or two word response; for example: "What do you plan to do about getting a job?" Few probes ever begin with the word *why.* The reason is that *why* usually connotes disapproval and places a client on the defensive (Benjamin, 1981).

An *accent* is the highlighting by the counselor of the last few words of the client. For example:

**Client:** The situation I'm in now is driving me crazy!

**Counselor:** Driving you crazy?

A *closed question* is one that requires a specific and limited response, such as a *yes* or *no.* It often begins with the words *is, do,* or *are* (Galvin & Ivey, 1981):

**Counselor:** Do you enjoy meeting other people?

**Client:** Yes.

The closed question is quite effective in eliciting a good deal of information in a short period of time. But it does not encourage elaboration that might also be helpful.

In contrast to the closed question is the *open question,* which typically begins with such words as *what, how,* or *could* and allows the client more time to talk. The major difference between a closed and open question "is whether or not the question encourages more client talk" (Galvin & Ivey, 1981, p. 539).

Finally, a *request for clarification* is a response used to be sure the counselor understands what the client is saying. These requests require the client to repeat or elaborate on material just covered. For example, a counselor might say: "Please help me understand this relationship" or "I don't see the connection here."

There are a number of facts that counselors will wish to obtain in an information-oriented first interview. The assumption of counselors who work in this way is that this information may be used as a part of a psychological, vocational, or psychosocial assessment. Counselors who are employed by medical, mental health, correctional, rehabilitation, and social agencies are especially prone to conduct these types of interviews. Hackney and Cormier (1979) have outlined some of the data counselors gather in such initial sessions (Figure 7.1).

### Relationship-oriented First Interview

Interviews that focus on feelings or relationship dynamics differ markedly from information-oriented first sessions in that the concentration is more on the feelings of the client. Common counselor responses include: restatement, reflection of feelings, summarizing feelings, request for clarification, and acknowledgment of nonverbal behavior (Hackney & Cormier, 1979).

A *restatement* is a simple mirror response to a client that lets the client know the counselor is actively listening. Used by itself, it is relatively sterile and ineffective:

**Client:** I am not sure if I'll ever find a suitable mate. My job keeps me on the road and isolated.

**Counselor:** You don't know if you will ever find a spouse because of the nature of your job.

*Reflection of feeling* is similar to a restatement, except it deals with verbal and nonverbal expression. Reflections may be on several levels; some convey more empathy than others. An example is a counselor who responds this way to a client who is silently sobbing over the loss of a parent: "You're still really feeling the pain."

*Summarizing feelings* is the paraphrasing by the counselor of a number of feelings that have been conveyed. For example, a counselor might say to a client: "John, if I understand you correctly, you are feeling depressed over the death of your father and discouraged that your friends have not helped you work through your grief. In addition, you feel your work is boring and that your wife is emotionally distant from you."

The last two types of statements differ from the *acknowledgment of nonverbal behavior*. In such, the counselor may say to a client: "I notice that your arms are folded across your chest and you're looking at the floor." This type of response does not interpret the meaning of the behavior.

**FIGURE 7.1**   An information-oriented first interview.

---

I. Identifying Data
   A. Client's name, address, telephone number through which client can be reached. This information is important in the event the counselor needs to contact the client between sessions. The client's address also gives some hint about the conditions under which the client lives (e.g., large apartment complex, student dormitory, private home, etc.).
   B. Age, sex, marital status, occupation (or school class and year). Again, this is information that can be important. It lets you know when the client is still legally a minor, and provides a basis for understanding information that will come out in later sessions.
II. Presenting problems, both primary and secondary
   It is best when these are presented in exactly the way the client reported them. If the problem has behavioral components, these should be recorded as well. Questions that help reveal this type of information include:
   A. How much does the problem interfere with the client's everyday functioning?
   B. How does the problem manifest itself? What are the thoughts, feelings, etc., that are associated with it? What observable behavior is associated with it?
   C. How often does the problem arise? How long has the problem existed?
   D. Can the client identify a pattern of events that surround the problem? When does it occur? With whom? What happens before and after its occurrence?
   E. What caused the client to decide to enter counseling at this time?
III. Client's current life setting
   How does the client spend a typical day or week? What social and religious activities, recreational activities, etc., are present? What is the nature of the client's vocational and/or educational situation?
IV. Family History
   A. Father's and mother's ages, occupations, descriptions of their personalities, relationships of each to the other and each to the client and other siblings.
   B. Names, ages, and order of brothers and sisters; relationship between client and siblings.
   C. Is there any history of mental disturbance in the family?
   D. Descriptions of family stability, including number of jobs held, number of family moves, etc. (This information provides insights in later sessions when issues related to client stability and/or relationships emerge.)

---

## BEGINNING THE INITIAL INTERVIEW

There is no one place to begin an initial interview, but many experts recommend that counselors start by trying to make their clients feel comfortable (Hackney & Cormier, 1979; Pietrofesa, Hoffman, & Splete, 1984; Shertzer & Stone, 1980). This means that counselors set aside their own agendas and focus in on the person of the client. Shertzer and Stone (1980) designate this type of behavior as *rapport*. Rapport is established and maintained by counselors who are

**FIGURE 7.1** *(continued)*

V. Personal History
   A. Medical history: any unusual or relevant illness or injury from prenatal period to present.
   B. Educational history: academic progress through grade school, high school, and post-high school. This includes extracurricular interests and relationships with peers.
   C. Military service record.
   D. Vocational history: Where has the client worked, at what types of jobs, for what duration, and what were the relationships with fellow workers?
   E. Sexual and marital history: Where did the client receive sexual information? What was the client's dating history? Any engagements and/or marriages? Other serious emotional involvements prior to the present? Reasons that previous relationships terminated? What was the courtship like with present spouse? What were the reasons (spouse's characteristics, personal thoughts) that led to marriage? What has been the relationship with spouse since marriage? Are there any children?
   F. What experience has the client had with counseling, and what were the client's reactions?
   G. What are the client's personal goals in life?
VI. Description of the client during the interview
   Here you might want to indicate the client's physical appearance, including dress, posture, gestures, facial expressions, voice quality, tensions: how the client seemed to relate to you in the session: client's readiness of response, motivation, warmth, distance, passivity, etc. Did there appear to be any perceptual or sensory functions that intruded upon the interaction? (Document with your observations.) What was the general level of information, vocabulary, judgment, abstraction abilities displayed by the client? What was the stream of thought, regularity, and rate of talking? Were the client's remarks logical? Connected to one another?
VII. Summary and recommendations
   In this section you will want to acknowledge any connections that appear to exist between the client's statement of a problem and other information collected in this session. What type of counselor do you think would best fit this client? If you are to be this client's counselor, which of your characteristics might be particularly helpful? Which might be particularly unhelpful? How realistic are the client's goals for counseling? How long do you think counseling might continue?

*Source:* Harold Hackney/L. Sherilyn Cormier, COUNSELING STRATEGIES AND OBJECTIVES, 2/E © 1979, pp. 53–55. Reprinted by permission of Prentice-Hall, Inc., Englewood Cliffs, New Jersey.

genuinely interested in and accepting of the individuals with whom they work. Ivey (1983) states that the two "most important micro-skills for rapport building are basic attending behavior and client observation skills" (p. 228). A counselor needs to tune in to what the client is thinking and feeling and how the client is behaving. Establishing and maintaining rapport is vital for the disclosure of information and the ultimate success of counseling. One way rapport is initiated by counselors is through inviting clients to focus on reasons for seeking help. Appropriate beginning inquiries are such general questions as "What brings you to see me?" and "What would you like to talk about?" (Pietrofesa, Hoffman, & Splete, 1984). These types of unstructured invitations are open-ended and allow clients to take the initiative (Hackney & Cormier, 1979). In such situations clients are most likely to talk about priority topics.

The amount of talking clients engage in and the insight and benefits derived from the initial interview can be enhanced by the counselor through appropriately conveying empathy, encouragement, support, caring, attentiveness, acceptance, and genuineness. Of all of these qualities, empathy is the most important.

### Empathy

Rogers (1961) describes empathy as the counselor's ability to "enter the client's phenomenal world—to experience the client's world as if it were your own without ever losing the 'as if' quality" (p. 284). Empathy involves two specific skills, perception and communication (Patterson & Eisenberg, 1983). A counselor who can accurately perceive what it is like to be the client but cannot communicate that experience is a limited helper. The ability to communicate clearly plays a vital role in any counseling relationship (Okun, 1982).

In the initial interview, it is critical that counselors be able to convey primary empathy (Patterson & Eisenberg, 1983). *Primary empathy* is the ability by the counselor to respond in such a way that it is apparent to both client and counselor that the counselor has understood the client's major themes. Primary empathy is conveyed through nonverbal communication and various verbal responses. *Advanced empathy* (see chapter 8) "is a process of helping a client explore themes, issues, and emotions new to his or her awareness" (Patterson & Eisenberg, 1983, p. 51). The use of this second level of empathy is usually inappropriate for an initial interview because it examines too much material too quickly. In either case, empathy may be fostered by attentiveness—the amount of verbal and nonverbal behavior shown to the client.

### Verbal and Nonverbal Behavior

Verbal behaviors include those communications that show a desire to comprehend or discuss what is important to the client (Cormier & Cormier, 1985). These behaviors, which include probing, requesting clarification, restatement, and summarizing feelings, indicate that the counselor is focusing in on the person of the client. Equally important are the counselor's nonverbal behaviors. Mehrabian (1970) found that physically attending behaviors on the part of the counselor—such as smiling, leaning forward, eye contact, gesturing, and head nodding—are very effective nonverbal ways of conveying to clients that the counselor is interested in and open to them.

Egan (1986) summarizes five nonverbal skills involved in initial attending. They are best remembered through the use of the acronym *SOLER*. The S is a reminder to face the client squarely, which can be understood literally or metaphorically, depending on the situation. The important thing is that the counselor shows involvement and interest in the client. The O is a reminder to adopt an open posture, one that is free from crossed arms and legs and shows nondefensiveness. The L reminds the counselor to lean toward the client. Leaning too far and being too close to the client may be frightening, but leaning too far away from the client indicates uninterest. The counselor needs to find a middle distance that is comfortable for both parties. The E represents eye contact. Good eye contact with most clients is a sign that the counselor is attuned to the client. For other clients, less eye contact will be appropriate. The R is a reminder to the counselor to relax. A counselor needs to be comfortable.

Okun (1982) lists supportive verbal and nonverbal helping behaviors that counselors display throughout counseling (Table 7.1). As you examine these behaviors, ask yourself how you could initially demonstrate each of these qualities.

### Nonhelpful Interview Behavior

In building a relationship, counselors must realize what they should not do as well as what they should do. Otherwise, nonhelpful behaviors may be included in their counseling repertoire. Patterson and Eisenberg (1983) list four major ways that usually block counselor/client communication and thus are generally avoided: advice giving, lecturing, excessive questioning, and storytelling.

*Advice giving* is the most controversial of these four behaviors. Knowles (1979) found that 70 to 90 percent of all responses by volunteer helpers on a crisis line consisted of giving advice. When a counselor does the same, especially in the first session, the advice may in effect be denying a client the chance to work through personal thoughts and feelings about a subject and thus curtail the ultimate ability of the client to make difficult decisions. Thus, a response meant to be helpful ends up hurtful by disempowering the client.

**TABLE 7.1** Supportive helping behaviors.

| Verbal | Nonverbal |
| --- | --- |
| uses understandable words | tone of voice similar to helpee's |
| reflects back and clarifies helpee's statements | maintains good eye contact |
| appropriately interprets | occasional head nodding |
| summarizes for helpee | facial animation |
| responds to primary message | occasional smiling |
| uses verbal reinforcers (for example, "mm-mm," "I see," "Yes") | occasional hand gesturing |
| | close physical proximity to helpee |
| | moderate rate of speech |
| calls helpee by first name or "you" | body leans toward helpee |
| appropriately gives information | occasional touching |
| answers questions about self | |
| uses humor occasionally to reduce tension | |
| is nonjudgmental | |
| adds greater understanding to helpee's statement | |
| phrases interpretations tentatively so as to elicit genuine feedback from helpee | |

*Source:* From EFFECTIVE HELPING, Barbara F. Okun. Copyright © 1987, 1982, 1976 by Wadsworth, Inc. Reprinted by permission from Brooks/Cole Publishing Company, Pacific Grove, California 93950.

Sack (1985) suggests that advice giving need not always be destructive. He notes that there are emergency situations (as in crisis counseling) where for the immediate welfare and safety of the client some direct action must be taken, including the giving of advice. He cautions counselors, however, to listen carefully to make sure whether the client is in fact asking for advice or simply being reflective through self-questions. There is a big difference in "What should I do?" and "I wonder what I should do?" In addition, Sack advocates the responses developed by Carkhuff (1969) as ways counselors can respond to direct requests for advice. Counselors, in this model, respond through one of seven ways: respect, empathy, genuineness, concreteness, self-disclosure, confrontation, and immediacy. The conclusion of Sack (1985) is that counselors must examine their roles in counseling in order to "free themselves of the limitations and pitfalls of giving advice and move toward employing a variety of responses that can more appropriately address their clients' needs" (p. 131).

*Lecturing*, or preaching, is "really a disguised form of advice giving" (Patterson & Eisenberg, 1983, p. 46). It sets up a power struggle between the counselor and client that neither can win. Patterson and Eisenberg suggest that counselors are probably lecturing when they say more than three consecutive sentences in a row to their clients. Instead of lecturing, counselors can be effective by following the client's lead (Evans, Hearn, Uhlemann, & Ivey, 1984).

*Excessive questioning* is a common mistake of many counselors. In such a situation, the client feels as though he or she is being interrogated instead of counseled. The client has little chance for taking the initiative and may become quite guarded. Counseling relationships are more productive when counselors avoid asking more than two questions in a row and when they keep the questions they ask open instead of closed.

*Storytelling* is the final nonhelpful behavior. Its use has been explored by Patterson and Eisenberg (1983). There are a few prominent professionals who can use stories to benefit clients. Milton Erickson is one. Most counselors, however, should stay away from storytelling because the story usually focuses attention on the counselor instead of the client and does not help the client resolve problems.

Other nonhelpful verbal and nonverbal behaviors are listed by Okun (1982). Some of these, such as yawning, clearly show uninterest in the counselor for the client. Others, such as advice giving, appear to be helpful only when the counselor is interested and involved. As you examine this list, think of when you last experienced the behaviors mentioned (see Table 7.2).

## EXPLORATION AND THE IDENTIFICATION OF GOALS

In the final part of building a counseling relationship, the counselor helps the client explore specific areas and begin to identify goals the client wants to achieve. Hill (1975) emphasizes that establishing goals is crucial in providing direction. Egan (1986) observes that exploration and ultimately the identification of goals often occurs when a client is given the opportunity to talk about situations—to tell personal stories. The counselor reinforces the client's focus on self by providing the client structure, by actively listening (hearing both content and feelings), and by helping the client identify and clarify goals.

Rule (1982) states that goals "are the energizing fabric of daily living" but are often elusive (p. 195). He describes some goals as unfocused, unrealistic, and uncoordinated. *Unfocused goals* are

**TABLE 7.2**   Nonhelping behaviors.

| Verbal | Nonverbal |
|---|---|
| advice giving | looking away from helpee |
| preaching | sitting far apart or turned away |
| placating | from helpee |
| blaming | sneering |
| cajoling | frowning |
| exhorting | scowling |
| extensive probing and questioning, | tight mouth |
| especially "why" questions | shaking pointed finger |
| directing, demanding | distracting gestures |
| patronizing attitude | yawning |
| overinterpretation | closing eyes |
| using words helpee doesn't | unpleasant tone of voice |
| understand | rate of speech too slow or too fast |
| straying from topic | |
| intellectualizing | |
| overanalyzing | |
| talking about self too much | |

*Source:* From EFFECTIVE HELPING, by Barbara F. Okun. Copyright © 1987, 1982, 1976 by Wadsworth, Inc. Reprinted by permission from Brooks/Cole Publishing Company, Pacific Grove, California 93950.

those not identified, too broad, or not prioritized. Sometimes counselors and clients may leave unfocused goals alone, because the time and expense of "chasing" them is not as productive as changing unwanted behaviors. In most cases, however, it is helpful to identify a client's goals, place them into a workable form, and decide which goals to pursue first.

*Unrealistic goals,* as defined by either counselor or client, are such goals as happiness, perfection, progress, being number one, and self-actualization. They have merit but are not easily attainable for long periods. For example, the client who is happy about being promoted will soon have to settle into the duties of the new job and the reality of future job progress. Unrealistic goals may best be dealt with by putting them in the context of broader life goals and having the client devise exploratory and homework strategies for dealing with those goals.

*Uncoordinated goals,* according to Rule (1982), are generally divided "into two groups: those probably really uncoordinated and those seemingly uncoordinated" (p. 196). In the first group are goals that may be incompatible with one another or with the personality of the client. A person who seeks counseling but really does not wish to work on changing is an example of an individual with incompatible goals. These clients are often labeled as resistant. In the second group, Rule places the goals of clients who appear to have uncoordinated goals but really do not. These individuals may be afraid to take personal responsibility and engage any helper in a "yes . . . but" dialogue.

Dyer and Vriend (1977) emphasize that there are seven specific criteria for judging effective goals in counseling. These are:

☐ *Goals are mutually agreed on by client and counselor* Without mutuality neither party will invest much energy in working on the goals.

☐ *Goals are specific* If goals are too broad, they will never be met.

☐ *Goals are relevant to self-defeating behavior* There are many possible goals for clients to work on but only those that are relevant to helping change self-defeating action should be pursued.

☐ *Goals are achievement and success oriented* Counseling goals need to be realistic and have intrinsic as well as extrinsic payoffs for clients.

☐ *Goals are quantifiable and measurable* It is important that both client and counselor know when goals are achieved. When goals are defined quantitatively, achievement is most easily recognized.

☐ *Goals are behavioral and observable* This criterion relates to the one before it: an effective goal is one that can be seen when achieved.

☐ *Goals are understandable and can be restated clearly* It is vital that client and counselor communicate clearly about goals. One way to assess how well this process is achieved is through restating goals in one's own words.

Egan (1986) cautions that in the exploratory and goal-setting stage of counseling, several problems may occur which inhibit the building of a solid client/counselor relationship. The most notable of these difficulties are: moving too fast, moving too slow, fear of intensity, client rambling, and excessive time and energy devoted to probing the past. Counselors who are forewarned about such potential problems are in a much better position to address them effectively. It is vital that counselors work with clients to build a mutually satisfying relationship from the very first. When this process occurs, a more active working stage of counseling begins.

## SUMMARY

Building a relationship, the first stage in counseling, is a continuous process. It begins by having the counselor "win" the battle for structure and the client "win" the battle for initiative. In such situations, both parties are winners. The client wins by becoming more informed about the nature of counseling and what to expect. The counselor wins by creating an atmosphere in which the client is comfortable and not hesitant to share thoughts and feelings.

Counseling may occur in any setting, but some circumstances are more likely than others to promote its development. Counselors need to be aware of the physical setting in which this experience takes place. Clients may well adjust to any room in which counseling is conducted. Yet there are certain qualities about an environment, such as the seating arrangement, that make counseling more conducive. Other less apparent qualities also affect the building of a relationship. For example, the perception of clients and counselors of one another is very important. Attractive clients who are young, verbal, intelligent, and social may be treated in a much more positive way than clients who are older, less intelligent, and seemingly unmotivated. Clients are likely to work best with counselors perceived as trustworthy, attractive, and knowledgeable.

Regardless of the external circumstances and the initial perceptions, a counselor who attends to the verbal and nonverbal expressions of a client is more likely to establish rapport. The relationship may be further enhanced by the counselor's conveying of empathy and other helpful skills, such as restatement and reflection, that cut across counseling theory. When counselors are most attuned to their own values and feelings, they are able to be even more effective. The initial counseling interview can be counselor or client initiated and can center on the gathering of information or on relationship dynamics. In any of these situations, it is vital for the counselor to explore with the client the reasons for and possibilities of counseling. Such disclosures can encourage clients to define goals and facilitate the setting of mutually agreed upon agenda in counseling. When this step is accomplished, the work of reaching goals occurs.

## CLASSROOM ACTIVITIES

1. Imagine that you are about to conduct your first counseling session in an environment of your own choosing. How would you furnish this setting and how would you spend your first 10 minutes with an ideal client?

Make notes and drawings of this experience and share it with another class member.

2. What type of people most appeal to you? Which ones do you have the most difficulty with? Role play, in groups of three, a 15

minute session with an imagined difficult client for you. Notice your verbal and non-verbal behaviors. Give your client and observer feedback on what you noticed about yourself and then listen to their feedback on what they observed.

3. What are some things you can do to make yourself more attractive (likeable) to your client? Share your list with fellow classmates in an open discussion. Does your combined list of behaviors differ from Okun's list? How? Which items do you consider most crucial for you as a counselor to achieve if you are to be effective?

4. Discuss in groups of four some strategies

you could employ to help an unrealistic client become more realistic about counseling. In your discussion, have each member of the group play a different type of unrealistic client. Notice how your responses differ in particular situations.

5. What are your feelings about being a counselor now that you have some idea about what the first stage of this process is like? Discuss your feelings and the thoughts behind them with other members of the class. Do they differ substantially from what they were at the beginning of the course? How?

# REFERENCES

Allen, G. (1977). *Understanding psychotherapy: Comparative perspectives.* Champaign, IL: Research Press.

Benjamin, A. (1981). *The helping interview* (3rd ed.). Boston: Houghton Mifflin.

Brammer, L. M., & Shostrom, E. L. (1977). *Therapeutic psychology* (3rd ed.). Englewood Cliffs, NJ: Prentice-Hall.

Brown, R. D. (1970). Experienced and inexperienced counselors' first impressions of clients and case outcomes: Are first impressions lasting? *Journal of Counseling Psychology, 17,* 550–558.

Carkhuff, R. R. (1969). *Helping and human relations.* New York: Holt, Rinehart & Winston.

Claiborn, C. D. (1979). Counselor verbal intervention, non-verbal behavior and social power. *Journal of Counseling Psychology, 26,* 378–383.

Cormier, W. H., & Cormier, L. S. (1985). *Interviewing strategies for helpers* (2nd ed.). Monterey, CA: Brooks/Cole.

Day, R. W., & Sparacio, R. T. (1980). Structuring the counseling process. *Personnel and Guidance Journal, 59,* 246–249.

Dorn, F. J. (1984). The social influence model: A social psychological approach to counseling. *Personnel and Guidance Journal, 62,* 342–345.

Dyer, W. W., & Vriend, J. (1977). A goal-setting checklist for counselors. *Personnel and Guidance Journal, 55,* 469–471.

Egan, G. (1986). *The skilled helper* (3rd ed.). Monterey, CA: Brooks/Cole.

Evans, D. R., Hearn, M. T., Uhlemann, M. R., & Ivey, A. E. (1984). *Essential interviewing.* Monterey, CA: Brooks/Cole.

Fong, M. L., & Cox, B. G. (1983). Trust as an underlying dynamic in the counseling process: How clients test trust. *Personnel and Guidance Journal, 62,* 163–166.

Galvin, M., & Ivey, A. E. (1981). Researching one's own interviewing style: Does your theory of choice match your actual practice? *Personnel and Guidance Journal, 59,* 536–542.

Gazda, G. M., Asbury, F. R., Balzer, F. J., Childers, W. C., & Walters, R. (1977). *Human relations development: A manual for educators.* Boston: Allyn & Bacon.

Gill, S. J. (1982). Professional disclosure and consumer protection in counseling. *Personnel and Guidance Journal, 60,* 443–446.

Gladding, S. T. (1975). Autumn storm. *Personnel and Guidance Journal, 54,* 149.

Goldstein, A. P. (1973). *Structural learning therapy: Toward a psychotherapy for the poor.* New York: Academic Press.

Goodyear, R. K., & Bradley, F. O. (1980). The helping process as contractual. *Personnel and Guidance Journal, 58,* 512–515.

Haase, R. F. (1970). The relationship of sex and instructional set to the regulation of interpersonal interaction distance in a counseling analogue. *Journal of Counseling Psychology, 17,* 233–236.

Haase, F. R., & DiMattia, D. J. (1976). Spatial environments and verbal conditioning in a quasi-counseling interview. *Journal of Counseling Psychology, 23,* 414–421.

Hackney, H., & Cormier, L. S. (1979). *Counseling strategies and objectives* (2nd ed.). Englewood Cliffs, NJ: Prentice-Hall.

Hill, C. (1975). A process approach for establishing counseling goals and outcomes. *Personnel and Guidance Journal, 53,* 571–576.

Hubble, M. A., & Gelso, C. J. (1978). Effects of counselor attire in an initial interview. *Journal of Counseling Psychology, 25,* 581–584.

Ivey, A. E. (1971). *Microcounseling.* Springfield, IL: Thomas.

Ivey, A. E. (1983). *Intentional interviewing and counseling.* Monterey, CA: Brooks/Cole.

Kelly, K. R., & Stone, G. L. (1982). Effects of time limits on the interview behavior of type A and B persons within a brief counseling analog. *Journal of Counseling Psychology, 29,* 454–459.

Kerr, B. A., Claiborn, C. D., & Dixon, D. N. (1982). Training counselors in persuasion. *Counselor Education and Supervision, 22,* 138–147.

Knowles, D. (1979). On the tendency of volunteer helpers to give advice. *Journal of Counseling Psychology, 26,* 352–354.

LaCross, M. B. (1975). Non-verbal behavior and perceived counselor attractiveness and persuasiveness. *Journal of Counseling Psychology, 22,* 563–566.

Levine, E. (1983). A training model that stresses the dynamic dimensions of counseling. *Personnel and Guidance Journal, 61,* 431–433.

Lichtenberg, J. W. (1986). Counseling research: Irrelevant or ignored? *Journal of Counseling and Development, 64,* 365–366.

Loesch, L. (1984). Professional credentialing in counseling—1984. *Counseling and Human Development, 17,* 1–11.

Manthei, R. J. (1983). Client choice of therapist or therapy. *Personnel and Guidance Journal, 61,* 334–340.

Mehrabian, A. (1970). Some determinants of affiliation and conformity. *Psychological Reports, 27,* 19–29.

Mehrabian, A. (1971). *Silent messages.* Belmont, CA: Wadsworth.

Napier, A., & Whitaker, C. (1978). *The family crucible.* New York: Harper & Row.

Okun, B. F. (1982). *Effective helping* (2nd ed.). Monterey, CA: Brooks/Cole.

Paradise, L. V., & Wilder, D. H. (1979). The relationship between client reluctance and counseling effectiveness. *Counselor Education and Supervision, 19,* 35–41.

Patterson, C. H. (1985a). New light for counseling theory. *Journal of Counseling and Development, 63,* 349–350.

Patterson, C. H. (1985b). *The therapeutic relationship.* Monterey, CA: Brooks/Cole.

Patterson, L. E., & Eisenberg, S. (1983). *The counseling process* (3rd ed.). Boston: Houghton Mifflin.

Pietrofesa, J. J., Hoffman, A., & Splete, H. H. (1984). *Counseling: An introduction* (2nd ed.). Boston: Houghton Mifflin.

Ponzo, Z. (1985). The counselor and physical attractiveness. *Journal of Counseling and Development, 63*, 482–485.

Ritchie, M. H. (1986). Counseling the involuntary client. *Journal of Counseling and Development, 64*, 516–518.

Riordan, R., Matheny, K., & Harris, C. (1978). Helping counselors minimize client resistance. *Counselor Education and Supervision, 18*, 6–13.

Rogers, C. R. (1961). *On becoming a person.* Boston: Houghton Mifflin.

Roloff, M. E., & Miller, G. R. (Eds.). (1980). *Persuasion: New directions in theory and research.* Beverly Hills, CA: Sage.

Rule, W. R. (1982). Pursuing the horizon: Striving for elusive goals. *Personnel and Guidance Journal, 61*, 195–197.

Sack, R. T. (1985). On giving advice. *AMHCA Journal, 7*, 127–132.

Schofield, W. (1964). *Psychotherapy: The purchase of friendship.* Englewood Cliffs, NJ: Prentice-Hall.

Senour, M. N. (1982). How counselors influence clients. *Personnel and Guidance Journal, 60*, 345–349.

Shertzer, B., & Stone, S. C. (1980). *Fundamentals of counseling* (3rd ed.). Boston: Houghton Mifflin.

Siegal, J. C., & Sell, J. M. (1978). Effects of objective evidence of expertness and non-verbal behavior on client perceived expertness. *Journal of Counseling Psychology, 25*, 188–192.

Sielski, L. M. (1979). Understanding body language. *Personnel and Guidance Journal, 57*, 238–242.

Strong, S. R. (1968). Counseling: An interpersonal influence process. *Journal of Counseling Psychology, 15*, 215–224.

Strong, S. R. (1982). Emerging integrations of clinical and social psychology: A clinician's perspective. In G. Weary and H. Mirels (Eds.), *Integrations of clinical and social psychology* (pp. 181–213). New York: Oxford Press.

Vriend, J., & Dyer, W. W. (1973). Counseling the reluctant client. *Journal of Counseling Psychology, 20*, 240–246.

Warnath, C. F. (1977). Relationship and growth theories and agency counseling. *Counselor Education and Supervision, 17*, 84–91.

Watkins, C.E., Jr. (1983). Counselor acting out in the counseling situation: An exploratory analysis. *Personnel and Guidance Journal, 61*, 417–423.

West, M. (1975). Building a relationship with the unmotivated client. *Psychotherapy: Theory, Research and Practice, 12*, 48–51.

Photo by James S. Davidson III.

# CHAPTER 8

# *Working in a Counseling Relationship*

*I listen and you tell me how*
  *the feelings rage and toss within you.*
*A mother died, a child deserted,*
  *and you, that child, have not forgotten*
  *what it is to be alone.*
*I nod my head as your words continue*
  *rich in anger from early memories,*
*Feelings that you tap with care*
  *after years of shaky storage.*
*As you drink their bitter flavor,*
  *which you declined to taste at seven,*
*I wince in my mind while watching you*
  *open your life to the dark overflow*
  *of pain that has grown strong with age.*[1]

---

[1]Gladding, 1977, p. 50. Copyright AACD. Reprinted with permission. No further reproduction authorized without written permission of AACD.

T he successful outcome of any counseling effort depends on a working alliance between counselor and client (Gelso & Carter, 1985). The building of this relationship is a developmental process and involves the exploration by both counselor and client of the situation that has motivated the client to seek help. Carkhuff and Anthony (1979) refer to the two processes that should occur at this time as the *involvement* and *exploration* phases of helping (see Chapter 7). After these phases have been completed, the counselor works with the client to move into the *understanding* and *action* phases. Initially, the client's concerns may be stated broadly and in general terms; as the counseling process continues, specific objectives are refined.

Clients arrive in counseling with certain areas of their lives open or understood and other areas hidden or suppressed. The so-called Johari window, shown in Figure 8.1, is a conceptual device that may be used to represent the way most individuals enter the counseling relationship (Luft, 1970).

The objectives of the first two phases of counseling are to help the client relax enough to tell his or her story and to discover information from areas of the self about which the client is blind, or has no knowledge (see Figure 8.1). Once a better understanding of these areas is obtained (either verbally or nonverbally), the client decides on an informed basis how to proceed. The client extends the dimensions of the area of free activity while shrinking the dimensions of the more restrictive areas (Figure 8.2).

It may appear that the counseling process—as described in this book and as represented in the Johari window—is linear, but

|  | Known to Self | Not Known to Self |
|---|---|---|
| **Known to Others** | I.<br><br>Area of Free Activity | III.<br><br>Blind Area—Blind to self, seen by others |
| **Not Known to Others** | II.<br>Avoided or Hidden Area—Self hidden from others | IV.<br><br>Area of Unknown Activity |

**FIGURE 8.1**   The Johari window of the client.

*Source:* From *Of Human Interaction* by Joseph Luft (Palo Alto, CA: National Press Books, 1969). By permission of Joseph Luft.

this is not the case. Steps overlap considerably (Egan, 1986), and some techniques that are employed in the involvement and exploration phases are also used in the understanding and action phases. Yet, new and different skills are regularly incorporated. Thus counseling requires constant sensitivity to the status of the relationship at any given time and alertness to new needs and demands as they develop.

In this chapter, we will explore the skills commonly associated with the understanding and action phases of counseling, while keeping other processes in mind. The understanding and action

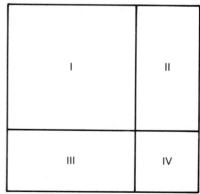

**FIGURE 8.2**   Johari window as modified through the relationship with the counselor.

*Source:* From *Of Human Interaction* by Joseph Luft (Palo Alto, CA: National Press Books, 1969). By permission of Joseph Luft.

phases involve the employment of a number of counselor skills, including: changing perceptions, leading, multifocused responding, accurate empathy, self-disclosure, immediacy, confrontation, contracting, and rehearsal. In addition to the specific skills involved, clients and counselors must work through any transference or countertransference issues that arise out of earlier situations or present circumstances (Gelso & Carter, 1985). There is, of course, a constant need to uncover and appropriately use "real" aspects of the counselor/client relationship.

## COUNSELOR SKILLS IN THE UNDERSTANDING AND ACTION PHASES

### Changing Perceptions

Clients often come to counseling as a last resort: the perception is that the situation is not only serious but hopeless (Watzlawick, 1983). "People think their perceptions and interpretations are accurate. When they communicate their view of reality to others, it is commonly accepted as factual" (Cavanagh, 1982, p. 30). There exists what Cormier and Cormier (1985) describe as *functional fixity,* or "seeing things in only one way or from one perspective or being fixated on the idea that this particular situation or attribute is *the* issue" (p. 418).

For example, a middle-aged man may say that he is concerned about taking care of his elderly mother. He realizes that personal attention to this task will take him away from his family and put a strain on them and him. Further, he is aware that his energy will be drained from his business and he might not receive the promotion he wants. He is torn between caring for two families and himself and sees his situation as an either/or problem. Appropriate and realistic counseling objectives would be: to find community and family resources the man could use to help take care of his mother, his family, and himself; to find out what he needs to do in order to relieve himself of sole responsibility in this case; and to find concrete ways he can increase his work efficiency but not his stress. The focus on taking care of self and others, as well as using community and family resources, gives the man a different perception of his situation and may help him deal with it in a realistic and healthy manner.

Counselors can help most clients change distorted or unrealistic objectives by offering them the opportunity to explore thoughts and desires within a safe, accepting, and nonjudgmental environment. Goals may be refined or altered using cognitive, behavioral, or cognitive-behavioral strategies, such as by redefining the problem, altering behavior in certain situations, or by both perceiving the problem in a more manageable way and acting accordingly (Okun, 1982).

One of the most common ways perceptions change is through *reframing*, which involves offering the client another probable viewpoint of why an event might have happened. For instance, the rude behavior of a person may be explained as the result of pressure experienced in trying to complete a task rather than dislike for the rudely treated person. Reframing is used in family counseling to help the family change its focus from one member to the whole family as the source of the problem. In cases of individuals, Cormier and Cormier (1985) point out that reframing can reduce resistance and mobilize the client's energy to do something differently by changing his or her perception of the problem. Reframing also may help the client become more aware of situational factors associated with behavior. The client's explanation of troublesome areas shifts from a simplistic attribution of traits—such as "I'm a bum"—to a more complex and accurate view—such as "I have some days when things don't go very well and I feel worthless" (Ellis, 1971).

## *Leading*

To change client perceptions requires a high degree of persuasive skill and some direction from the counselor. Such input is known as a *lead*. The term *leading* was coined by Francis Robinson (1950) to describe certain deliberate behaviors counselors engage in for the benefit of their clients. Leads vary in length, and some are more appropriate at one stage of counseling than another. Robinson initially used the analogy of a football quarterback and receiver to describe a lead. A good quarterback anticipates where the receiver will be on the field and throws the ball to that spot. The same is true of a counselor and a client. The counselor anticipates where the client is and where the client is likely to go. The counselor then responds accordingly. If the counselor misjudges the client and either leads too far (i.e., is too persuasive or direct) or not far enough (i.e., is too uninvolved and nondirect), the counseling relationship will suffer.

Patterson and Eisenberg (1982) list a number of leads counselors can use with their clients (Figure 8.3). Some, such as silence, acceptance, and paraphrasing, are most appropriate at the beginning of the counseling process. Others, such as persuasion, are more directive and more appropriate in the understanding and action phases of counseling.

| | |
|---|---|
| **Least leading response** | |
| Silence | When the counselor makes no verbal response at all, the client will ordinarily feel some pressure to continue and will choose how to continue with minimum input from the counselor. |
| Acceptance | The counselor simply acknowledges the client's previous statement with a response such as "Yes" or "Uhuh." The client is verbally encouraged to continue, but without content stimulus from the counselor. |
| Restatement (paraphrase) | The counselor restates the client's verbalization, including both content and affect, using nearly the same wording. The client is prompted to re-examine what has been said. |
| Clarification | The counselor states the meaning of the client's statement in his or her own words, seeking to clarify the client's meaning. Sometimes elements of several of the client's statements are brought into a single response. The counselor's ability to perceive accurately and communicate correctly is important, and the client must test the "fit" of the counselor's lead. |
| Approval (affirmation) | The counselor affirms the correctness of information or encourages the client's efforts at self-determination. "That's good new information," or "You seem to be gaining more control." The client may follow up with further exploration as he or she sees fit. |
| General leads | The counselor directs the client to talk more about a specific subject with statements such as "Tell me what you mean," or "Please say some more about that." The client is expected to follow the counselor's suggestion. |
| Interpretation | The counselor uses psychodiagnostic principles to suggest sources of the client's stress or explanations for the client's motivation and behavior. The counselor's statements are presented as hypotheses, and the client is confronted with potentially new ways of seeing self. |
| Rejection (persuasion) | The counselor tries to reverse the client's behavior or perceptions by actively advising different behavior or suggesting different interpretations of life events than those presented by the client. |
| Reassurance | The counselor states that, in his or her *judgment,* the client's concern is not unusual and that people with similar problems have succeeded in overcoming them. The client may feel that the reassurance is supportive but may also feel that his or her problem is discounted by the counselor as unimportant. |
| Introducing new information or a new idea | The counselor moves away from the client's last statement and prompts the client to consider new material. |
| **Most leading response** | |

**FIGURE 8.3** Continuum of leads.

Source: From *The Counseling Process* (3rd ed.), by Lewis E. Patterson and Sheldon Eisenberg.

The type of lead a counselor gives is in part determined by the theoretical approach he or she embraces and the current phase of counseling. Minimal leads are best used in the building phase of a relationship because they are low-risk. Maximum leads, on the other hand, are more challenging and should be employed only after a solid relationship has been established.

### Multifocused Responding

Counselors can further enhance their effectiveness by remembering that individuals perceive in different ways. Some clients experience the world visually: they "see" what is happening. Others are primarily auditory: they "hear" the world around them. Still others are kinesthetically oriented: they "feel" the situations as though physically in touch with them. Ivey (1983) and Lazarus (1981) think that tuning into the client's major modes of perceiving and learning is crucial to helping cause change. Because many clients have multiple ways of knowing the world, counselors should vary their responses and incorporate words that reflect an understanding of the clients' worlds. For example, the counselor might say to a multimodal person, "I see your point and hear your concern. I feel that you are really upset."

Baruth and Huber (1985) also point out the importance of a counselor's responding in the client's own language. They distinguish between the predominantly affective, behavioral, and cognitive nature of speech. Affective responses focus on a client's feelings, behavioral responses focus on actions, and cognitive responses focus on thoughts. Thus, a counselor who is working with an affectively oriented individual will select words accordingly. Table 8.1 shows some of the most common of these words as identified by Cormier and Cormier (1985).

### Accurate Empathy

There is near-universal agreement among practitioners and theorists that the use of empathy is one of the most vital elements in counseling and that it transcends counseling stages (Fiedler, 1950; Gladstein, 1983; Hackney, 1978; Rogers, 1975; Truax & Mitchell, 1971). In chapter 7, two types of empathy were briefly noted.

The basic type has been called primary empathy. The second level is known as advanced empathy (Carkhuff, 1969). Accurate empathy on both levels is achieved when the counselor sees the

**TABLE 8.1** Commonly used affect words.

| Level of Intensity | Category of Feeling | | | | | | |
|---|---|---|---|---|---|---|---|
| | Happiness | Sadness | Fear | Uncertainty | Anger | Strength, Potency | Weakness, Inadequacy |
| Strong | Excited<br>Thrilled<br>Delighted<br>Overjoyed<br>Ecstatic<br>Elated<br>Jubilant | Despairing<br>Hopeless<br>Depressed<br>Crushed<br>Miserable<br>Abandoned<br>Defeated<br>Desolate | Panicked<br>Terrified<br>Afraid<br>Frightened<br>Scared<br>Overwhelmed | Bewildered<br>Disoriented<br>Mistrustful<br>Confused | Outraged<br>Hostile<br>Furious<br>Angry<br>Harsh<br>Hateful<br>Mean<br>Vindictive | Powerful<br>Authoritative<br>Forceful<br>Potent | Ashamed<br>Powerless<br>Vulnerable<br>Cowardly<br>Exhausted<br>Impotent |
| Moderate | "Up"<br>Good<br>Happy<br>Optimistic<br>Cheerful<br>Enthusiastic<br>Joyful<br>"Turned on" | Dejected<br>Dismayed<br>Disillusioned<br>Lonely<br>Bad<br>Unhappy<br>Pessimistic<br>Sad<br>Hurt<br>Lost | Worried<br>Shaky<br>Tense<br>Anxious<br>Threatened<br>Agitated | Doubtful<br>Mixed up<br>Insecure<br>Skeptical<br>Puzzled | Aggravated<br>Irritated<br>Offended<br>Mad<br>Frustrated<br>Resentful<br>"Sore"<br>Upset<br>Impatient<br>Obstinate | Tough<br>Important<br>Confident<br>Fearless<br>Energetic<br>Brave<br>Courageous<br>Daring<br>Assured<br>Adequate<br>Self-confident<br>Skillful | Embarrassed<br>Useless<br>Demoralized<br>Helpless<br>Worn out<br>Inept<br>Incapable<br>Incompetent<br>Inadequate<br>Shaken |
| Weak | Pleased<br>Glad<br>Content<br>Relaxed<br>Satisfied<br>Calm | "Down"<br>Discouraged<br>Disappointed<br>"Blue"<br>Alone<br>Left out | Jittery<br>Jumpy<br>Nervous<br>Uncomfortable<br>Uptight<br>Uneasy<br>Defensive<br>Apprehensive<br>Hesitant<br>Edgy | Unsure<br>Surprised<br>Uncertain<br>Undecided<br>Bothered | Perturbed<br>Annoyed<br>Grouchy<br>Hassled<br>Bothered<br>Disagreeable | Determined<br>Firm<br>Able<br>Strong | Frail<br>Meek<br>Unable<br>Weak |

client's world from the latter's point of view and is able to communicate this understanding back (Egan, 1986).

Primary accurate empathy involves communicating basic understanding of what the client is feeling and of the experiences and behaviors underlying these feelings. It helps in the establishment of the counseling relationship, in data gathering, and in problem clarification. For example, a client might say, "I'm really feeling like I can't do anything for myself." The counselor replies, "You're feeling helpless." Advanced accurate empathy reflects not only what the client stated but also what he or she implied or stated incompletely.

For example, in advanced accurate empathy a counselor notes that a client says, "and I hope everything will work out" while looking off into space. The counselor responds, "For if it doesn't you're not sure what you will do next."

Empathy, like other counseling skills, involves three elements: (1) awareness, (2) technology (know-how), and (3) assertiveness (Egan, 1986). There are several levels of responses counselors can make that reflect different aspects of empathy. A scale formulated by Carkhuff (1969), called Empathic Understanding in Interpersonal Process, is a measure of these levels. It is composed of five levels, each of which either adds to or subtracts from the meaning and feeling tone of a client's statement.

The specific levels of empathy are described by Carkhuff (1969) as follows:

*Level 1* The verbal and behavioral expresssions of the helper either do not attend to or detract significantly from the verbal and behavioral expressions of the helpee(s). . . .

*Level 2* While the helper responds to the expressed feelings of the helpee(s), he (or she) does so in such a way that he (or she) subtracts noticeable affect from the communications of the helpee.

*Level 3* The expressions of the helper in response to the expressions of the helpee(s) are essentially interchangeable. . . .

*Level 4* The responses of the helper add noticeably to the expressions of the helpee(s) in such a way as to express feelings a level deeper than the helpee was able to express himself (or herself).

*Level 5* The helper's responses add significantly to the feeling and meaning of the expressions of the helpee(s) in such a way as to accurately express feeling levels below what the helpee . . . was able to express. . . .

Responses at the first two levels are not considered empathic, and in fact, inhibit the creation of an empathic environment. For example, if a client reveals that he or she is heartbroken over the loss of a lover, a counselor operating on either of the first two levels might reply, "Well, you want your former love to be happy, don't you?" Such a response misses the pain that the client is feeling.

It is only at level 3 on the Carkhuff scale that a counselor's response is rated as "interchangeable" with that of a client. The cartoon in Figure 8.4 depicts the essence of such an interchange. On levels 4 and 5, the counselor either "adds noticeably" or "adds significantly" to what the client has said. It is this ability to go beyond what the client says that distinguishes counseling from conversation or other less-helpful forms of behavior (Carkhuff,

**FIGURE 8.4**

*Source:* Cartoon by Nels Goud, 1983, *Personnel and Guidance Journal, 61,* p. 635. Copyright AACD. Reprinted with permission. No further reproduction authorized without written permission of AACD.

1972). An example of a higher level empathy response is seen in the following interchange:

> **Client:** I have been running around from activity to activity until I am so tired I feel like I could drop.
>
> **Counselor:** Your life has been a merry-go-round of activity and you'd like to slow it down before you collapse. You'd like to be more in charge of your own life.

Means (1973) elaborates on levels 4 and 5 and shows how counselors can add noticeably and significantly to the client's perception of: an emotional experience, an environmental stimulus, a behavior pattern, a self-evaluation, a self-expectation, and beliefs about self. Client statements are extremely varied, and counselors must therefore be flexible in responding to them (Hackney, 1978). Whether a response by the counselor is one containing accurate empathy or not is determined by the reaction of the client (Turock, 1978). Regardless, in the understanding and action phases of counseling, it is important that counselors integrate the two levels of empathy they use in responding to those seeking help.

### Self-Disclosure

Self-disclosure is a term that originated with Sidney Jourard (1958). It refers to making oneself known to another person by revealing personal information. Self-disclosure is necessary on the part of clients for successful counseling to occur (Hansen, Stevic, & Warner,

1986). Clients are more likely to trust counselors who disclose personal information (up to a point) and are prone to make reciprocal disclosures if the client/counselor relationship is strong (Curtis, 1981). Counselors employ self-disclosure on a formal basis at the initial interview by giving clients written statements about the counselor and the counseling process. They also use self-disclosure spontaneously in counseling sessions to reveal personal facts to a client, especially during the understanding and action phases. This latter use of self-disclosure is important in facilitating client movement.

Egan (1986) says that counselor self-disclosure serves two principal functions: modeling and developing a new perspective. A client learns to be more open by observing the counselor being open. Self-disclosure on the part of counselors can also help clients see that counselors are not free of problems or devoid of feelings (Hackney & Cormier, 1979). Thus, in hearing about different aspects of the counselor's personal life, a client may examine other aspects of his or her own life, such as stubbornness or fear, and realize that some difficulties or experiences are universal and manageable. Egan (1986) stresses that self-disclosure should be selective and focused, should not add to the client's problems, and should not be used too often. The process is not linear, and more self-disclosure is not necessarily better.

Kline (1986) observes that clients perceive self-disclosure as risky and may be hesitant to take such a risk. Hesitancy may take the form of: refusing to discuss issues, changing the subject, being silent, and excessive talking. He suggests that counselors can help clients overcome these fears not only by modeling self-disclosure but also by inviting clients to do the same. A counselor may also explore any negative feelings a client has about the process, contract with the client to talk about a certain subject area, and confront the client with an avoidance of a specific issue.

### Immediacy

"Immediacy involves a counselor's understanding and communicating of what is going on between the counselor and client within the helping relationship, particularly the client's feelings, impressions, and expectations, as well as the wants of the counselor" (Turock, 1980, p. 169). There are basically two kinds of immediacy: relationship immediacy and here-and-now immediacy (Egan, 1986). *Relationship immediacy* involves the counselor's ability to discuss with the client the quality of their relationship, whether it is strained, boring, or productive. *Here-and-now immediacy* is the discussion of any given transaction as it is happening. For example, a client may wish to know what the counselor thinks of him or her for revealing or concealing a certain fact. The counselor explores how the client is feeling or thinking in the moment.

Egan (1986) believes that immediacy requires more courage or assertiveness than almost any other interpersonal communication skill. Turock (1980) lists three fears many counselors have in regard to immediacy. First, the counselor may be afraid that the client will misinterpret the counselor's message. The response of immediacy requires a counselor to make a tentative guess or interpretation of what the client is thinking or feeling, and a wrong guess can cause the counselor to lose credibility in the eyes of the client. A second fear associated with immediacy is that it may produce an unexpected outcome. Many counseling skills, such as reflection, have predictable outcomes; immediacy does not. Its use may break down a familiar pattern between the counselor and client. In the process, their relationship may suffer. Finally, immediacy may influence a client's decision to terminate, because he or she can no longer control or manipulate the relationship. Some clients play games, such as "Ain't it awful," and expect their counselors to respond accordingly (Berne, 1964). When the client receives an unexpected payoff, he or she may decide not to stay in the relationship.

Egan (1982) states that immediacy is best used in the following situations:

> In a directionless relationship
>
> Where there is tension
>
> Where there is a question of trust
>
> When there is considerable social distance between counselor and client
>
> Where there is client dependency
>
> Where there is counterdependency
>
> When there is an attraction between counselor and client

### Confrontation

Confrontation, like immediacy, is often misunderstood. Uninformed counselors think confrontation involves an attack on their clients (Baruth & Huber, 1985; Egan, 1986). Instead, it is an invitation. It challenges a client to examine, modify, and/or control an aspect of behavior. "It helps people see more clearly what is happening, what the consequences are, and how they can assume responsibility for taking action to change in ways that can lead to a more effective life and better and fairer relationships with others" (Tamminen &

Smaby, 1981, p. 42). A good, responsible, caring, and appropriate confrontation produces growth and encourages an honest examination of oneself. Sometimes, it may actually be detrimental to the client if the counselor fails to confront. Avoiding such a confrontation of the client's behavior is known as the "MUM effect" (Rosen & Tesser, 1970) and results in the counselor's being less effective than he or she otherwise would be.

There are certain boundaries to confrontation (Leaman, 1978). The counselor needs to be sure that the relationship with the client is strong enough to sustain a confrontation. The counselor also must time a confrontation appropriately and remain true to the motives that have led to the act of confronting (Cavanagh, 1982). It is more productive in the long run to confront a client's strengths than a client's weaknesses (Berenson & Mitchell, 1974). The counselor should challenge the client to use resources the client is failing to employ. Regardless of whether confrontation involves strengths or weaknesses, counselors use a *you said/but look* structure to implement this process (Hackney & Cormier, 1979). The first part of such a confrontation is the *you said* part; for example: "You said you wanted to get out more and meet people." In the second portion, the *but look* part, the discrepancy or contradiction in the client's words and actions is highlighted. For example, in connection with a client's wanting to meet more people but instead staying home and looking at television, the counselor might say: "But you are now watching television four to six hours a night."

## Contracting

There are two aspects of contracting: one focuses on the processes involved in reaching a goal; the other concentrates on the final outcome. Egan (1982) observes that in goal setting, the counselor operates from a theoretical base that directs his or her actions. The client may have to learn to change ways of thinking, feeling, and behaving in order to obtain goals. That counselors and clients engage in contractual behavior is a natural occurrence. Goodyear and Bradley (1980) point out that all interpersonal relationships are contractual, but some are more explicit than others. Since the median number of counseling sessions may be as few as five to six (Lorion, 1974), it is useful and timesaving for counselors and clients to work on goals through a contract system. Such a system lets both parties participate in determining direction in counseling and in evaluating change.

There are other advantages to the use of contracts in counseling. Thomas and Ezell (1972) list several. First, a contract provides a written record of what goals the counselor and client have agreed to pursue and the course of action to be taken. Second, the formal nature of a contract and its time limits may act as motivators for a client who tends to procrastinate. Third, if the contract is broken down into definable sections, a client may get a clear feeling that problems can be solved. Fourth, a contract puts the responsibility for any change on the client and thus serves as motivation. Finally, the contract system assures that clients will return to counseling on a more regular basis than would otherwise be the case by specifically outlining the number of sessions to be held.

There are several approaches to setting up contracts. Goodyear and Bradley (1980) offer several recommendations for promoting maximum effectiveness:

- [ ] It is essential that counselors indicate to their clients that the purpose of counseling is to work. It is important to begin with a statement such as "On what would you like to work?" rather than "What would you like to talk about?"

- [ ] It is vital that the contract for counseling be for change in regard to the client instead of a person not present. The counselor can act as a consultant when the client wishes to examine the behavior of another person, such as a child who throws temper tantrums, but work of this type is limited.

- [ ] The counselor must insist on setting up contracts that avoid the inclusion of client "con words." These are words, such as *try*, that are not specific and that usually result in the client's failing to achieve a goal.

- [ ] The counselor must be wary of client goals that include "shoulds." Statements of this type are often based on a desire to please someone else. For instance, a client who sets an initial goal that includes the statement "I should please my spouse more" may do so only temporarily because in the long run the goal does not please the client. A way to avoid contract goals that include "shoulds" is to ask what the client really wants.

- [ ] Concreteness in defining specifically what clients want to achieve through counseling is also vital. There is a great deal of difference in those clients who state that they wish to be "happy" and those who explain that they want to "lose 10 pounds" or "talk to at least three new people a day." The latter goals are much preferred.

- [ ] The counselor must insist that contracts focus on change. Clients may wish to understand the reasons why they do something, but insight alone rarely produces action. Therefore, counselors must emphasize contracts that promote change in a client's behaviors, thoughts, or feelings.

Even though contracts are an important part of helping clients define, understand, and work on specific aspects of their lives, a contract system is not without its disdvantages. Okun (1982) stresses that contracts need to be open for renegotiation by both parties. This process is often time-consuming and personally taxing. Thomas and Ezell (1972) list several other weaknesses of a contract system in counseling. First, a counselor cannot hold a client to a contract. The agreement has no external rewards or punishments the counselor can use to force the client to fulfill the agreement. Second, some client problems may not lend themselves to the contract system. For example, the client who wants to make new friends may contract to visit places where there is good opportunity to encounter the types of people with whom he or she wishes to be associated, but there is no way a contract can assure that the client will make new friends. Third, such a way of dealing with problems focuses on outward behavior. Even if the contract is fulfilled successfully, the client may not have achieved insight or altered perception. Finally, the initial appeal of a contract is limited. Clients who are motivated to change and who may find the idea fresh and appealing may become bored with such a system in time.

In determining how formal to make the contract with a client, a counselor must consider the background of the client, the client's motivational levels, the nature of the presenting problems, and what resources are available to the client to assure the successful completion of the contract. Goodyear and Bradley (1980) suggest that the counselor ask how the client might sabotage the contract. This question helps make the client more aware of any resistance he or she harbors to fulfillment of the agreement.

### Rehearsal

Once a contract is set up, the counselors can help the client maximize the chances of fulfilling it by getting the client to rehearse or practice designated behavior. The old adage that practice makes perfect is as true for clients who wish to reach a goal as it is for athletes. There are two ways clients can rehearse: overtly and covertly (Cormier & Cormier, 1985). Overt rehearsal requires the client to verbalize or act out what he or she is going to do. For example, if a woman is going to ask a man out for a date, she will want to rehearse what she is going to say and how she is going to act before she actually encounters a man. Covert rehearsal is imagining or reflecting on the desired goal. For example, if a student has a speech to give, she can first imagine the conditions under which she will perform and then reflect about how to organize the subject matter to be presented. Imagining the situation beforehand can alleviate unnecessary anxiety and help the student perform better.

Sometimes a client needs coaching by the counselor in the rehearsal period. The coaching may take the form of the counselor's providing temporary aids to help the client remember what to do next (Bandura, 1976). It may simply involve giving feedback on what the client is thinking or doing. Feedback helps the client recognize and correct any problem areas (Geis & Chapman, 1971), as long as it is not overdone. Counselors can also assign clients homework to help them practice the skills learned in the counseling sessions and to help them generalize such skills to all areas of their lives. Shelton and Levy (1981) suggest that homework has numerous benefits, including heightened awareness and increased efficiency of treatment. Cognitive and behavioral counselors especially like homework assignments, but almost all counselors of whatever orientation support this form of helping clients help themselves.

## TRANSFERENCE AND COUNTERTRANSFERENCE

The emphasis in this chapter, as in the previous one, has been on counselor skills that help promote development during the counseling process. These skills are essential if the counselor is to avoid so-called circular counseling, in which the same ground is covered over and over again. There is an equally important aspect of counseling, however, that influences the quality of the outcome: the relationship between counselor and client. The ability of the counselor and client to work effectively with each other is largely influenced by the relationship they develop. Counseling can be an intensely emotional experience (Cormier & Cormier, 1985). In a few instances, counselors and clients genuinely dislike each other or have incompatible personalities (Cavanagh, 1982; Patterson & Eisenberg, 1982). Usually, however, counselors and clients can and must work through transference and/or countertransference phenomena that result from the emotions they feel and express to one another. While some counseling theories emphasize transference and countertransference more than others, these two concepts occur to some extent in almost all counseling relationships.

### Transference

*Transference* is the projection by the client of past or present feelings, attitudes, or desires onto the counselor (Brammer &

Shostrom, 1977). The concept, from the literature of psychoanalysis, originally emphasized the transference of earlier life emotions. Today, however, the phenomenon is "not restricted to psychoanalytic therapy" (Corey, Corey, & Callanan, 1984) and may be based on current experiences.

All counselors have what Gelso and Carter (1985) describe as a "transference pull," that is, an image generated through the use of personality and a particular theoretical approach. A client reacts to the image of the counselor in terms of the client's own personal background and current conditions. The way the counselor sits, speaks, gestures, or looks may trigger a reaction from the client. An example of such an occurrence is a client's saying to a counselor, "You sound just like my mother." The statement in and of itself may be observational. But if the client starts behaving as if the counselor were the client's mother, transference has occurred.

Five patterns of transference behavior frequently appear in counseling. The client may perceive the counselor as: (1) ideal, (2) seer, (3) nurturer, (4) frustrator, or (5) nonentity (Watkins, 1983, p. 207). The counselor may at first enjoy transference phenomena that hold him or her in a positive light. Such enjoyment soon wears thin. In order to overcome any of the effects associated with these types of transference experiences, Watkins (1983) advocates the specific approaches shown in Table 8.2.

Cavanagh (1982) notes that transference can be either direct or indirect. Direct transference is well represented in the example of the client's thinking of the counselor as mother. Indirect transference is harder to recognize. It is usually revealed in client statements or actions that are not obviously directly related to the counselor (e.g., "Talk is cheap and ineffective" or "I think counseling is the experience I've always wanted"). Regardless of its degree of directness, transference is either negative or positive. Negative transference, although painful to handle initially, must be worked though. It has a more direct impact on the quality of the counseling relationship. Positive transference, especially a mild form, may not be readily acknowledged because it appears at first to add something to the relationship (Watkins, 1983). Indirect or mild forms of positive transference are least harmful to the work of the counselor and client.

Cavanagh (1982) holds that both negative and positive transference are forms of resistance. As long as the client keeps the attention of the counselor on transference issues, little progress is made in setting goals or achieving goals. To resolve transference issues, the counselor may deal with them directly and in an interpersonal manner rather than in an analytical manner. For example, if the client complains that all counselors care about is

**TABLE 8.2** Conceptualizing and intervening in transference patterns.

| Transference Pattern | Client Attitudes/Behaviors | Counselor Experience | Intervention Approach |
|---|---|---|---|
| Counselor as ideal | Profuse complimenting, agreements<br>Bragging about counselor to others<br>Imitating counselor's behaviors<br>Wearing similar clothing<br>Hungering for counselor's presence<br>General idealization | Pride, satisfaction, strength<br>Feelings of being all-competent<br>Tension, anxiety, confusion<br>Frustration, anger | Focus on: client's expectations, effects of these expectations<br>intra-punitive expressions<br>trend toward self-negation<br>tendency to give up oneself |
| Counselor as seer | Ascribes omniscience, power to counselor<br>Views counselor as "the expert"<br>Requests answers, solutions<br>Solicitation of advice | Feelings of being all-knowing<br>Expertness, "God-complex"<br>Self-doubt, questioning of self<br>Self-disillusionment<br>Sense of incompetence | Focus on: client's need for advice<br>lack of decision<br>lack of self-trust<br>opening up of options |
| Counselor as nurturer | Profuse emotion, crying<br>Dependence and helplessness<br>Indecision, solicitation of advice<br>Desire of physical touch, to be held<br>Sense of fragility | Feeling of sorrow, sympathy<br>Urge to soothe, coddle, touch<br>Experiences of frustration, ineptitude<br>Depression and despair<br>Depletion | Focus on: clients' need for dependence<br>feeling of independence<br>unwillingness to take responsibility for self<br>behavioral-attitudinal alternatives |
| Counselor as frustrator | Defensive, cautious, guarded<br>Suspicious and distrustful<br>"Enter-exit" phenomenon<br>Testing of counselor | Uneasiness, on edge, tension<br>"Walking on eggshells" experience<br>Increased monitoring of responses<br>Withdrawal and unavailability<br>Dislike for client<br>Feelings of hostility, hate | Focus on: trust building,<br>relationship enhancement<br>purpose of transference pattern<br>consequences of trusting others<br>reworking of early experience |
| Counselor as nonentity | "Topic shifting," lack of focus<br>Volubility, thought pressure<br>Desultory, aimless meanderings | Overwhelmed, subdued<br>Taken aback<br>Feelings of being used, discounted<br>Lack of recognition<br>Sense of being a "nonperson"<br>Feelings of resentment, frustration<br>Experience of uselessness | Focus on: establishing contact<br>getting behind the client's verbal barrier<br>effects of quietness-reflection on client<br>distancing effects of the transference |

*Source:* From "Countertransference: Its Impact on the Counseling Situation" by C. E. Watkins, Jr., 1985, *Journal of Counseling and Development, 63,* p. 208. Copyright AACD. Reprinted with permission. No further reproduction authorized without further permission of AACD.

being admired, the counselor can respond: "I agree that some counselors may have this need and it is not very helpful. On the other hand, we have been focusing in on your goals. Let's go back to those goals and if the needs of counselors, as you observe them, become relevant to your goals we will explore that issue."

Corey, Corey, and Callanan (1984) see a therapeutic value in working through transference. They believe that the counselor/client relationship will improve once the client has resolved distorted perceptions about the counselor. The improved relationship will be mainfested in the client's having more trust and confidence in the counselor, if the situation is handled sensitively. Further, by resolving feelings of transference, a client may gain insight into the past and thus become free to act differently in the present and future.

### Countertransference

*Countertransference* refers to the counselor's projected emotional reaction to or behavior toward the client (Hansen, Stevic, & Warner, 1986). It can destroy the counselor's ability to be objective. Unless resolved adequately, it can be detrimental to the counseling relationship.

Kernberg (1975) observes that there are two major approaches to the problem of conceptualizing countertransference. In the first, which is known as the classic approach, countertransference is seen negatively and is viewed as the direct or indirect unconscious reaction of the counselor to the client. The second perspective, the total approach, sees countertransference as more positive. From this perspective countertransference is a diagnostic tool for understanding aspects of the client's unconscious motivations. A third approach, which originated in the 1970s and was described by Blanck and Blanck (1979), conceives countertransference as possessing both positive and negative aspects. Watkins (1985) sees this third approach as more realistic than the first two.

Countertransference may be manifested in a number of ways (Corey, Corey, & Callanan, 1984): a constant desire by the counselor to please the client; identifying with the problems of the client so much the counselor loses objectivity; the development of sexual or romantic feelings toward the client; compulsive advice giving; and a desire to develop a social relationship with the client.

Watkins (1985) thinks that countertransference can be expressed in a myriad of ways. However, he views four forms of countertransference as particularly noteworthy: (1) overprotection, (2) benign, (3) rejecting, and (4) hostile. The first two forms of countertransference described by Watkins are examples of overidentification, in which the counselor loses his or her ability to remain emotionally distant from the client. The last two forms are examples of disidentification, in which the counselor becomes emotionally removed from the client. Disidentification may express itself in counselor behavior that is aloof, nonempathetic, hostile, cold, or antagonistic.

It is vital that counselors work through any negative or nonproductive countertransference. Otherwise, the progress of the client will lessen and both counselor and client will be hurt in the process (Brammer & Shostrom, 1977; Cavanagh, 1982; Watkins, 1985). It is also important that a counselor recognize that he or she is experiencing countertransference feelings (Watkins, 1985). Once aware of such feelings, a counselor needs to discover the reasons behind them (Brammer & Shostrom, 1977). Some consistent way of monitoring this self-understanding is critical, and one way this may be done is to undergo supervision. Counselors, like clients, have blind spots, hidden areas, and aspects of their lives that are unknown to them. Working in a supervisory relationship with another counselor, monitoring one's own audio and video tapes of counseling sessions, and self- analysis are excellent ways to address countertransference.

## THE REAL RELATIONSHIP

The emphasis of this chapter has been on the skills and interpersonal qualities that contribute to a working alliance between a counselor and client that ultimately result in client self-understanding and the achievement of goals. The use of leads, different levels of empathy, confrontation, encouragement, contracts, and the recognition of and working through transference and countertransference all contribute to the counseling process. In concluding this chapter, however, there is one other quality on which we must focus. This is what Gelso and Carter (1985) call the "real relationship." The real relationship begins as a two-way experience between counselor and client from their first encounter. The counselor is real by being genuine (owning his or her thoughts and feelings), by trying to facilitate genuineness in the client, and by attempting to see and understand the client in a realistic manner. The client also contributes to the realness of the relationship by attempting to be genuine and to perceive the situation realistically.

The real relationship that exists in counseling has been written about mostly from the viewpoint of the counselor and has been misunderstood, according to Gelso and Carter. Therefore, they propose five propositions about the nature of this relationship. First, the real relationship is a positive element that exists from the very beginning of counseling. Second, the importance of a real relationship is tied to the counselor's theoretical orientation but is atheoretical for the client. Third, every theoretical orientation must attend to the real relationship. Fourth, the real relationship increases and deepens during the counseling process. Finally, counselor and client have different expectations and actualizations of the real relationship. Nevertheless, they believe the real relationship is at the heart of successful counseling.

While the work of Gelso and Carter is still too new to evaluate thoroughly, their emphasis on the "real" dimension of a counselor/client relationship should be recognized and appreciated. Growth is fostered in the security that it is acceptable and desirable to be oneself and to act accordingly. Clients are usually trapped in stereotypes of what they should be and how they should act. If a client experiences the counselor's acceptance of the self, the client is more likely to change. Likewise, a counselor is more likely to grow within a real relationship with a client. "Realness," although not precisely defined at present, appears to be an important part of counseling.

## SUMMARY

The two phases of counseling emphasized in this chapter have been understanding and action. They occur after a client and counselor have established a relationship and explored possible goals toward which to work. Both of these processes are facilitated by mutual interaction on the part of the individuals involved. The counselor can help the client through the appropriate use of leads, challenges to perception, multifocused responding, accurate empathy, self-disclosure, immediacy, confrontation, contracts, and rehearsal. These skills are focused on the client, but they are also helpful to the counselor's gaining self-insight.

Client and counselor must work through transference and countertransference, respectively. We have emphasized in this chapter that all counseling perspectives have elements of these two dimensions of a counseling relationship. Some clients and counselors will encounter less transference and countertransference than others, but it is important that each person recognize when he or she is engaged in such modes of communication. The more in touch people are with these ways of relating, the less damage they are likely to do in their relationships with significant others and the more self-insight they are likely to achieve. A successful resolution of these issues promotes realness, and at the base of growth and goal attainment is the ability to experience the world from a realistic perspective.

## CLASSROOM ACTIVITIES

1.  Discuss in groups of three the probable employment of the counseling skills that you have learned in this text. For example, how do you think you will know when to be silent and when to confront?
2.  In the present and previous chapters, the use of persuasion has been mentioned as an appropriate counselor skill. Role play in groups of three the following situations where persuasion might be employed: (1) a small boy who is afraid of all dogs; (2) a student who has high test anxiety; (3) an old person who is shy; and (4) a marriage partner who will not fight fairly with his or her spouse. Do you experience persuasion differently in these situations? Discuss your feelings with the class as a whole.
3.  In groups of four, in which two people role play a counselor and client and two observe, enact situations where the counselor demonstrates that he or she knows how to display the different levels of empathy. After the counselor has demonstrated mastery of these skills, he or she should receive feedback from the client and the observers about their impressions of each enactment.
4.  Practice confrontation and immediacy skills in the same groups as were formed for activity 3. Discuss among yourselves and then with the class as a whole the differences and similarities between these two counseling skills.
5.  Transference and countertransference are still hotly debated issues. Divide the class into two teams with one team taking the position that these two phenomena occur in counseling and one team taking the position that only "real" relationships are manifested between counselors and clients. Select a three-member panel from the class to judge the debate and give the class feedback on the points made by each side.

## REFERENCES

Bandura, A. (1976). Effecting change through participant modeling. In J. D. Krumboltz & C. E. Thoresen (Eds.), *Counseling methods* (pp. 248–265). New York: Holt, Rinehart & Winston.

Baruth, L. G., & Huber, C. H. (1985). *Counseling and psychotherapy.* Columbus, OH: Merrill.

Berensen, B. G., & Mitchell, K. M. (1974). *Confrontation: For better or worse.* Amherst, MA: Human Resource Development Press.

Berne, E. (1964). *Games people play.* New York: Grove Press.

Blanck, G., & Blanck, R. (1979). *Ego psychology II: Psychoanalytic developmental psychology.* New York: Columbia University Press.

Brammer, L. M., & Shostrom, E. L. (1977). *Therapeutic psychology* (3rd ed.). Englewood Cliffs, NJ: Prentice-Hall.

Carkhuff, R. R. (1969). *Helping and human relations: Selection and training* (Vol. 1). New York: Holt, Rinehart & Winston.

Carkhuff, R. R. (1972). *The art of helping.* Amherst, MA: Human Resource Development Press.

Carkhuff, R. R., & Anthony, W. A. (1979). *The skills of helping.* Amherst, MA: Human Resource Development Press.

Cavanagh, M. E. (1982). *The counseling experience.* Monterey, CA: Brooks/Cole.

Corey, G., Corey, M. S., & Callanan, P. (1984). *Issues & ethics in the helping professions* (2nd ed.). Monterey, CA: Brooks/Cole.

Cormier, W. H., & Cormier, L. S. (1985). *Interviewing strategies for helpers.* Monterey, CA: Brooks/Cole.

Curtis, J. M. (1981). Indications and contraindications in the use of therapist's self-disclosure. *Psychological Reports, 49,* 499–507.

Egan, G. (1982). *The skilled helper* (2nd ed.). Monterey, CA: Brooks/Cole.

Egan, G. (1986). *The skilled helper* (3rd ed.). Monterey, CA: Brooks/Cole.

Ellis, A. (1971). *Growth through reason.* Palo Alto, CA: Science and Behavior Books.

Fiedler, F. (1950). The concept of the ideal therapeutic relationship. *Journal of Consulting Psychology, 45,* 659–666.

Geis, G. L., & Chapman, R. (1971). Knowledge of results and other possible reinforcers in self-instructional systems. *Educational Technology, 11,* 38–50.

Gelso, C. J., & Carter, J. A. (1985). The relationship in counseling and psychotherapy: Components, consequences, and theoretical antecedents. *The Counseling Psychologist, 13,* 155–243.

Gladding, S. T. (1977). Memory traces. *North Carolina Personnel and Guidance Journal, 6,* 50–51.

Gladstein, G. A. (1983). Understanding empathy: Integrating counseling, developmental, and social psychology perspectives. *Journal of Counseling Psychology, 30,* 467–482.

Goodyear, R. K., & Bradley, F. O. (1980). The helping process as contractual. *Personnel and Guidance Journal, 58,* 512–515.

Hackney, H. (1978). The evolution of empathy. *Personnel and Guidance Journal, 57,* 35–38.

Hackney, H., & Cormier, L. S. (1979). *Counseling strategies and objectives* (2nd ed.). Englewood Cliffs, NJ: Prentice-Hall.

Hansen, J. C., Stevic, R. R., & Warner, R. W., Jr. (1986). *Counseling: Theory and process* (4th ed). Boston: Allyn & Bacon.

Ivey, A. E. (1983). *Intentional interviewing and counseling.* Monterey, CA: Brooks/Cole.

Jourard, S. M. (1958). *Personal adjustment: An approach through the study of healthy personality.* New York: Macmillan.

Kernberg, O. *Borderline conditions and pathological narcissism.* New York: Jason Aronson.

Kline, W. B. (1986). The risks of client self-disclosure. *AMHCA Journal, 8,* 94–99.

Lazarus, A. A. (1981). *The practice of multimodal therapy.* New York: McGraw-Hill.

Leaman, D. R. (1978). Confrontation in counseling. *Personnel and Guidance Journal, 56,* 630–633.

Lorion, R. P. (1974). Patient and therapist variables in the treatment of low-income patients. *Psychological Bulletin, 81,* 344–354.

Luft, J. (1970). *Group process: An introduction to group dynamics.* Palo Alto, CA: National Press Books.

Means, B. L. (1973). Levels of empathic response. *Personnel and Guidance Journal, 52,* 23–28.

Okun, B. F. (1982). *Effective helping* (2nd ed.). Monterey, CA: Brooks/Cole.

Patterson, L. E., & Eisenberg, S. (1982). *The counseling process* (3rd ed.). Boston: Houghton Mifflin.

Robinson, F. P. (1950). *Principles and procedures of student counseling.* New York: Harper & Brothers.

Rogers, C. R. (1975). Empathic: An unappreciated way of being. *The Counseling Psychologist, 5,* 2–10.

Rosen, S., & Tesser, A. (1970). On the reluctance to communicate undesirable information: The MUM effect. *Sociometry, 33,* 253–263.

Shelton, J. L., & Levy, R. L. (1981). *Behavioral assignments and treatment compliance.* Champaign, IL: Research Press.

Tamminen, A. W., & Smaby, M. H. (1981). Helping counselors learn to confront. *Personnel and Guidance Journal, 60,* 41–45.

Thomas, G. P., & Ezell, B. (1972). The contract as counseling technique. *Personnel and Guidance Journal, 51,* 27–31.

Truax, C., & Mitchell, K. (1971). Research on certain therapist interpersonal skills in relation to process and outcome. In A. E. Bergin and S. L. Garfield (Eds.), *Handbook of psychotherapy and behavior change: An empirical analysis.* New York: Wiley.

Turock, A. (1978). Effective challenging through additive empathy. *Personnel and Guidance Journal, 57,* 144–149.

Turock, A. (1980). Immediacy in counseling: Recognizing clients' unspoken messages. *Personnel and Guidance Journal, 59,* 168–172.

Watkins, C. E., Jr. (1983). Transference phenomena in the counseling situation. *Personnel and Guidance Journal, 62,* 206–210.

Watkins, C. E., Jr. (1985). Countertransference: Its impact on the counseling situation. *Journal of Counseling and Development, 63,* 356–359.

Watzlawick, P. (1983). *The situation is hopeless, but not serious.* New York: Norton.

Photo by James S. Davidson III.

# CHAPTER 9

# Termination of Counseling Relationships

*Active as I am in sessions*
*going with you to the marrow of emotions*
*our shared journey has an end.*
*Tonight, as you hesitantly leave my office*
*to the early darkness of Winter days*
*and the coldness of December nights,*
*you do so on your own.*
*Yet, this season of crystallized rain*
*changes, if however slowly,*
*and our time and words together*
*can be a memory from which may grow*
*a new seed of life within you,*
*Not without knowledge of past years' traumas*
*but rather in the sobering realization*
*that in being heard a chance is created*
*to fill a time with different feelings,*
*And savor them in the silent hours*
*when you stand by yourself alone.*[1]

[1]Gladding, 1977, p. 51. Copyright AACD. Reprinted with permission. No. further reproduction authorized without written permission of AACD.

**T**ermination is probably the least researched and most neglected aspect of counseling. Many theorists and counselors assume that termination will occur naturally, leaving both client and counselor pleased and satisfied with the results. Goodyear (1981) states that "it is almost as though we operate from a myth that termination is a process from which the counselor remains aloof and to which the client alone is responsive" (p. 347). But the termination of a counseling relationship is a two-way process that is often complex and potentially difficult. It may well produce strong and mixed feelings on the part of both the counselor (Goodyear, 1981) and the client (London, 1982) and is often inadequately handled (Ward, 1984).

In this chapter, we will address the concept of termination as a multidimensional process that can take any of several forms. Specifically, we will examine the general function of termination, as well as termination of individual sessions, termination of counseling relationships, termination strategies, resistance to termination, premature termination, counselor-initiated termination, and the importance of terminating a relationship on a positive note. The related areas of follow-up, referral, and recycling in counseling will also be covered.

## FUNCTION OF TERMINATION

Directly addressing the process of termination has been historically avoided for several reasons. Two of the most prominent ones are suggested by Ward (1984). First, termination is associated with loss—a traditionally taboo subject in all parts of society. Counseling emphasizes growth and development rather than loss and ending. Second, termination is not directly related to the host of microskills, such as reflection and accurate feedback, that are emphasized in facilitating counseling relationships (Ivey, 1983). It is not a process usually highlighted in counselor education. But the significance of termination has begun to emerge because of societal trends, such as the aging of the American population, the wide acceptance of the concept of stages in life (Sheehy, 1976), and an increased attention to death as a part of the life span (Kubler-Ross, 1969).

Termination serves several important functions, the most obvious of which is signaling that something is finished. Life is a series of hellos and good-byes (Goldberg, 1975; Maholick & Turner, 1979). Hellos begin at birth and good-byes end at death. Between birth and death, individuals enter into and leave a succession of experiences, including jobs, relationships, and life stages. Growth and adjustment depend on an ability to make the most of these experiences and learn from them. To begin something new, a former experience must be completed and resolved (Perls, 1969). Termination is the opportunity to end a learning experience properly. Yet in counseling, termination "is more than an act signifying the end of therapy"; it is also a motivator (Yalom, 1975, p. 365).

Both client and counselor are motivated by knowing that the counseling experience is limited in time. The awareness is similar to that of a young person realizing he or she cannot remain a promising youth forever. Such a realization often spurs one on to hard work while there is still time to do something significant. Some counselors, such as those associated with Strategic Family Therapy, purposefully limit the number of counseling sessions so that clients and counselors will be more aware of time constraints and make the most of the sessions. Munro and Bach (1975) found that limiting time is effective in individual counseling, too.

Another function of termination has to do with its use in maintaining changes already achieved and in generalizing the problem-solving skills acquired (Dixon & Glover, 1984). Successful counseling results in significant changes in the way the client thinks, feels, or acts. These changes are rehearsed in counseling, but must be practiced in the real world. Termination provides an opportunity for such practice. The client can always go back to the counselor for any needed follow-up, but termination is the natural point for the practice of independence to begin. It is a potentially empowering experience for the client.

## ISSUES OF TERMINATION

### *Termination of Individual Sessions*

Termination is an issue during individual counseling sessions. Initial counseling sessions should have clearly defined time limits (Pietrofesa, Hoffman, & Splete, 1984; Hackney & Cormier, 1979). The range of 45 to 50 minutes is generally considered proper. It usually takes a counselor 5 to 10 minutes to adjust to the client and the client's concerns. Thus, counseling sessions that terminate too quickly may be as unproductive as ones that last too long.

Benjamin (1981) proposes two important factors in closing an interview. First, both client and counselor should be aware that the session is ending. Second, no new material should be introduced or discussed during this ending. If new material is introduced by the client, the counselor needs to work to make it the anticipated focus of the next session. On rare occasions, the counselor will have to deal with the new material on an emergency basis.

There are several ways a counselor can close an interview effectively. One is simply to make a brief statement indicating that time is up (Benjamin, 1981; Hackney & Cormier, 1979). For example: "It looks like our time is up for today." The simpler the statement the better. If a client is discussing a number of subjects in an open-ended manner near the end of a session, the counselor should remind the client that there are only 5 to 10 minutes left. The client can then focus attention on important matters. As an alternative or in addition to the direct statement, the counselor can use nonverbal gestures to indicate that the session is ending. These include looking at one's watch or standing up (Pietrofesa, Hoffman, & Splete, 1984). Nonverbal gestures are probably best used with verbal indicators. Each reinforces the other.

Toward the end of the interview it is usually helpful to summarize what has happened in the session, and this may be initiated by either the counselor or the client (Hansen, Stevic, & Warner, 1986). A good summary ties together the main points of the session and "should be brief, to the point, and without interpretation" (Hackney & Cormier, 1979, p. 57). If done mutually, a summary allows counselor and client to realize what each got out of the session and provides a means of clearing up any misunderstandings.

An important part of terminating any individual session is setting up the next appointment (Hansen, Stevic, & Warner, 1986). Most problems are resolved over time, and both client and counselor need to know when they will meet again to continue the work in progress.

### *Termination of a Counseling Relationship*

Counseling relationships vary in length and purpose. It is vital to the health and well-being of everyone that the subject of termination be brought up early so that counselor and client can make the most of their time together (Cavanagh, 1982). Individuals need time to prepare for the end of a meaningful relationship, such as that shared by a counselor and client. There may be some sadness even if the relationship ends in a positive way. Thus, termination should not necessarily be presented as the zenith of the counseling experience. Hackney and Cormier (1979) stress that it is better to play down the importance of termination rather than to play it up.

The counselor and client must agree on when termination of the relationship is appropriate and will be helpful. Generally, they will give each other verbal messages about a readiness to terminate. For example, a client may say, "I really think I've made a lot of progress over the past few months"; or a counselor may state, "You appear to be well on your way to no longer needing my services." Statements of this type suggest the beginning of the end of the counseling relationship. They usually imply a recognition of growth or resolution. At other times, a number of different behaviors may signal the end of the relationship. These include a decrease in the intensity of work between counselor and client, the use of more humor or intellectualizing, and less denial, withdrawal, anger, mourning, or dependence (Corey, Corey, Callanan, & Russell, 1982; McGee, Schuman, & Racusen, 1972; Shulman, 1979).

Hackney and Cormier (1979) believe that in a relationship which has lasted more than three months, the final three to four weeks should be spent discussing the impact of termination. Shulman (1979) suggests that as a general rule-of-thumb, one-sixth of the time spent in a counseling relationship be devoted to the topic.

Maholick and Turner (1979) suggest specific areas of concern when deciding whether to terminate counseling. These include:

- [ ] An examination of whether the client's initial problem or symptoms have been reduced or eliminated.
- [ ] A determination of whether the stress-producing feelings that led to counseling have been eliminated.
- [ ] An assessment of the client's coping ability and degree of understanding of self and others.
- [ ] A determination of whether the client can relate better to others and is able to love and be loved.

☐ An examination of whether the client has acquired abilities to plan and work productively.

☐ An evaluation of whether the client can better play and enjoy life.

These areas are not equally as important for all clients, but it is essential that before termination of counseling clients feel confident to live effectively without this relationship (Ward, 1984).

There are at least two other ways to facilitate the ending of a counselor/client relationship in addition to those already discussed. One involves the use of fading. Dixon and Glover (1984) define *fading* as "a gradual decrease in the unnatural structures developed to create desired changes" (p. 165). A desired goal of all counseling is to help clients become less dependent on the counselor and the counseling sessions and more dependent on themselves and the positive reinforcement of natural contingencies. In order to promote fading, counseling sessions can be spaced further apart or simply shortened (Cormier & Cormier, 1985).

Another way to promote termination is to help clients develop more successful problem-solving skills (Dixon & Glover, 1984). Clients, like everyone else, are constantly faced with problems. If the counselor can help the client learn more effective ways to cope with these difficulties, the client will no longer need the counseling relationship. This is a process of generalization from counseling experience to life. At its best, this process includes an emphasis on education and prevention, as well as on decision-making skills for crisis situations.

### Resistance to Termination

Resistance to termination may come from either the counselor or client. Patterson and Eisenberg (1983) note that resistance is especially likely when the counseling relationship has been of long duration or has involved a high level of intimacy. Other factors that may promote resistance include the pain of earlier losses, loneliness, unresolved grief, need gratification, fear of rejection, and fear of having to be self-reliant. Some of these factors are more prevalent with clients, whereas others are more likely to characterize the experience of counselors.

**Client Resistance.** Resistance to termination is expressed by clients in many ways. Two easily recognizable ways are asking for more time at the end of a session and asking for more appointments once a goal has been reached. Another more troublesome way a client resists is the development of new problems, such as depression or anxiety, that were not a part of the client's original concerns. The manifestation of these "symptoms" makes termination more difficult, and in such situations a client may convince the counselor that only this counselor can be of help. Thus, the counselor may feel obligated to continue working with the person for either personal or ethical reasons.

Lerner and Lerner (1983) believe that client resistance is often the result of a fear of change. If clients come to experience and value a counseling relationship, they may fear that they cannot function well without it. Clients who have grown up in unstable or chaotic environments, involving alcoholism or divorce for instance, may be especially prone to hold on to the stability found in counseling and to the relationship developed with the counselor. It is vital that the counselor recognize the special needs of these individuals and the difficulties they have in coping with loneliness and intimacy (Loewenstein, 1979; Weiss, 1973). It is even more critical that the counselor take steps to help such clients help themselves by exploring with them the advantages of working in other therapeutic settings, such as in support groups. For such clients, counseling is potentially addictive, and if they are to function in healthy ways, they must find alternative sources of support.

***Counselor Resistance.*** Some counselors are reluctant to say goodbye at the appropriate time. Clients who have special or unusual needs or those who are very productive may be especially attractive to counselors. Goodyear (1981, p. 348) lists eight conditions under which termination may be especially difficult for counselors:

1. When termination signals the end of a significant relationship.
2. When termination arouses the counselor's anxieties about the client's ability to function independently.
3. When termination arouses guilt in the counselor about not having been more effective with the client.
4. When the counselor's professional self-concept is threatened by the client who leaves abruptly and angrily.
5. When termination signals the end of a learning experience for the counselor (e.g., the counselor may have been relying on the client to learn more about the dynamics of a disorder or about a particular subculture).
6. When termination signals the end of a particularly exciting experience of living vicariously through the adventures of the client.
7. When termination becomes a symbolic recapitulation of other (especially unresolved) farewells in the counselor's life.
8. When termination arouses in the counselor conflicts about his or her own individuation.

It is important that counselors recognize any difficulties in letting go of certain clients. A counselor may seek consultation from colleagues in dealing with this problem or may want to undergo counseling to resolve the problem. The latter option is especially valuable if the counselor has a personal history of detachment, isolation, and excessive fear of intimacy. Kovacs (1965, 1976) reports that many persons who enter the helping professions possess just such characteristics.

### Premature Termination

The question of whether a client terminates counseling prematurely is not one that can be measured by the number of sessions the client has completed. Rather, premature termination has to do with how well the client has achieved the personal goals established in the beginning and how well the client is functioning generally (Ward, 1984).

Baruth and Huber (1985) note that there are some clients who show little, if any, commitment or motivation to change their present circumstances and request that counseling be terminated after the very first session. Other clients express this desire after realizing the work necessary for change. Still others make this wish known more indirectly by missing or being late for appointments. Regardless of how clients express a wish for premature termination, it is likely to trigger thoughts and feelings within the counselor that must be dealt with. Hansen, Warner, and Smith (1980) suggest that the topic of premature termination be discussed openly between a counselor and client if the client expresses a desire to terminate before specified goals have been met or even if the counselor suspects that premature termination may occur. With discussion, the thoughts and feelings of both the client and counselor can be examined and a premature ending can often be prevented.

Sometimes, a client just fails to keep an appointment and does not call to reschedule. In such cases, the counselor should make an attempt to get in touch with the client and, if finding that the client wishes to quit, should set up an exit interview. Ward (1984) says that there are four possible benefits from such an interview:

☐ An exit interview may help the client resolve any negative feelings resulting from the counseling experience itself.

☐ An exit interview serves as a way to invite the client to continue in counseling, if the client so wishes.

☐ Another form of treatment or a different counselor can be considered if the client so desires.

☐ An exit interview increases the chances that the next time the client needs help, he or she will seek counseling.

Cavanagh (1982) holds that in premature termination, counselors often make one of two mistakes. One is to blame either the counselor or the client for what is happening. A counselor is more likely to blame the client, but in either case someone is berated and the problem is compounded. It may be more productive for the counselor to think of the situation as one in which no one is at fault. A second mistake on the part of the counselor is to act in a cavalier way about the situation. An example of a cavalier attitude is the counselor who says, "It is too bad this client has chosen not to continue counseling, but I've got others." Instead of making either mistake, Cavanagh recommends that counselors find out why a client terminated prematurely. Possible reasons include:

☐ To see if the counselor really cares

☐ To try to elicit positive feelings from the counselor

☐ To punish or try to hurt the counselor

☐ To eliminate anxiety

☐ To show the counselor that the client has found a cure elsewhere

☐ To express to the counselor that the client does not feel understood

Cavanagh believes counselors need to understand that regardless of what they do as counselors, some clients are going to terminate counseling prematurely. Such a realization allows counselors to feel they do not have to be perfect. It also enables them to acknowledge that no matter how talented and skillful a counselor is, some clients will find another counselor more helpful.

Not all people who seek counseling are equally ready to work in such a relationship, and the readiness level may vary as the relationship continues. It may be that some clients need to terminate prematurely for good reasons. Such action on the client's part does not necessarily reflect on the counselor's competence. Counselors can control only a limited number of variables in a counseling relationship.

### Counselor-Initiated Termination

The opposite of premature termination is counselor-initiated termination. A counselor sometimes needs to end relationships with some or all clients. The reasons include illness, working through countertransference, relocation to another area, an extended trip, or the realization that the client's needs could be better served by someone else. These are what Cavanagh (1982) classifies as "good reasons" for the counselor to terminate.

There are also poor reasons, which include a counselor's feelings of anger, boredom, or anxiety. If a counselor ends a relationship because of such feelings, the client may feel rejected and even worse than in the beginning. It is one thing for a person to handle rejection from peers; it is another for that same person to handle rejection from a counselor. Cavanagh notes that although a counselor may have some negative feelings about a client, it is possible to acknowledge and work through those feelings without behaving in an extreme or detrimental way.

Both London (1982) and Seligman (1984) present models for helping clients deal with the temporary absence of the counselor. They stress that clients and counselors should prepare as far in advance as possible for temporary termination by openly discussing the impending event and working through any strong feelings about the issue of separation. A client may actually benefit from counselor-initiated termination by realizing that the counselor is human and replaceable, by understanding that a person has choices about how to deal with interpersonal relationships, by exploring previous feelings and major life decisions, and by learning more clearly that new behaviors carry over into other life experiences (London, 1982). There may also be a refocusing during the termination process that helps clients see more clearly the issues on which to work.

Seligman (1984) recommends a more structured way of preparing clients for counselor-initiated termination than does London, but both models can be effective. It is important in any situation of this kind to make sure a client has the names and numbers of at least a couple of counselors to contact in case of an emergency during the counselor's absence.

### Ending on a Positive Note

The process of termination, like counseling itself, involves a series of "checkpoints" whereby counselors and clients can evaluate the progress they are making and determine their readiness to move on to another stage (Maholick & Turner, 1979). It is important that termination be mutually agreed upon, if at all possible, so that all involved can move on in ways deemed most productive. This is not always possible. Patterson and Eisenberg (1983, pp. 115–117) give eight guidelines for ending an intense counseling relationship in a positive way. They suggest that the counselor do the following.

☐ "Be clearly aware of the client's needs and wants." At the end of a counseling relationship, the client may need time to talk to the counselor about the impending termination. This may require a few sessions to complete.

☐ "Be clearly aware of your own needs and wants." Counseling is not a one-way street, and counselors who take care of others without taking care of themselves will most likely experience difficulty in terminating relationships. It is vital that a counselor acknowledges personal feelings and needs about a counseling relationship before it ends.

☐ "Be aware of your previous experiences with separation and your inner reaction to these experiences." The feelings generated from one intense relationship may be similar to those which occur in another. A counselor should be emotionally self-aware in order to avoid countertransference and be genuine in relationships.

☐ "Invite the client to share how he or she feels about ending the experience." This guideline is similar to the first, but it focuses on the emotions, not the thoughts, of the client. Clients need to express themselves as completely as possible if closure is to be of maximum benefit.

☐ "Share honestly with the client how you feel about the counseling experience." This is another aspect of the counselor's being real in the relationship. Part of this sharing includes revealing to the client what you, as a counselor, have learned from this particular counseling experience.

☐ "Review the major events of the counseling experience and bring the review into the present." The focus of this process is to help a client see where he or she is now as compared to the beginning of counseling and realize more fully the growth that has been accomplished. The procedure includes a review of significant past moments and turning points in the relationship with a focus on personalizing the summary of the relationship experience.

☐ "Supportively acknowledge the changes the client has made." At this point the counselor lets the client know that he or she recognizes the progress that has been achieved and actively encourages the client to maintain it.

☐ "Invite the client to keep up to date on what is happening in his or her life." Counseling relationships eventually end, but the caring and concern the counselor has for the client are not automatically terminated at the final session. Clients need to know that the counselor continues to be interested in what is happening in their lives. Updating can be accomplished in part through follow-up sessions.

## ISSUES RELATED TO TERMINATION

### *Follow-up*

"Follow-up entails checking to see how the helpee is doing, with respect to whatever the problem was, sometime after termination has occurred" (Okun, 1982, p. 195). Follow-up is a step many counselors neglect, yet it is important because it reinforces the gains clients have made in counseling and helps both counselor and client reevaluate the experience. It also emphasizes the genuine care and concern the counselor has for the client. Such follow-up can be conducted on either a short-term or long-term basis (Baruth & Huber, 1985; Cormier & Cormier, 1985). Short-term follow-up is usually conducted three to six months after a counseling relationship terminates. Long-term follow-up is conducted at least six months after termination.

Follow-up may take many forms but there are four main ways it is usually conducted (Cormier & Cormier, 1985). The first is to invite the client in for a session to discuss any progress the client has continued to make in achieving desired goals. A second way is through a telephone call to the client. A call allows the client to report to the counselor, though there is only verbal interaction. A third way is for the counselor to send the client a letter asking about the client's current status. A fourth and more impersonal way of doing a follow-up is for the counselor to mail the client a questionnaire dealing with current levels of functioning. Many public agencies use this type of follow-up as a way of showing accountability. Such procedures do not preclude the use of more personal follow-up procedures by individual counselors. Although time-consuming, a personal follow-up is probably the most effective way of evaluating past counseling experiences. It helps assure clients that they are cared about as individuals and are more than just statistics.

Sometimes, regardless of the type of follow-up used, it is helpful if the client monitors his or her own progress through the use of graphs or charts. Then, when relating information to the counselor the client can do so in a more concrete and objective way. If counselor and client agree at the end of the last session on a follow-up time, this type of self-monitoring may be especially meaningful and may provide the client concrete proof of progress and clearer insight into current needs.

## *Referral and Recycling*

Counselors are not able to help everyone who seeks assistance. When a counselor realizes that a situation is unproductive, it is important to know whether to terminate the relationship or make a referral. A *referral* basically is arranging other assistance for a client when the initial arrangement is not or cannot be helpful (Okun, 1982). There are many reasons for referring, some of which are:

☐ The client has a problem the counselor does not know how to handle.

☐ The counselor is inexperienced in a particular area (e.g., substance abuse or mental illness) and does not have the necessary skill to help the client.

☐ The counselor knows of a nearby expert who would be more helpful to the client.

☐ The counselor and client have incompatible personalities (Goldstein, 1971).

☐ The relationship between counselor and client is stuck in an initial phase of counseling.

Referrals involve a how and a when. The how of making a referral has to do with knowing how to call on a helping resource and how to handle the client in order to maximize the chances that he or she will follow through in the referral process. A client may resist a referral if the client feels rejected by the counselor. Patterson and Eisenberg (1983) suggest that a counselor spend at least one session with the client in preparation for the referral. There are some clients for whom it will be necessary to spend several sessions. The when of making a referral involves timing. The longer a client works with a counselor, the more reluctant the client may be to see someone else. Thus, timing is crucial. If a counselor suspects an impasse with a certain client, the counselor should refer that client as soon as possible. On the other hand, if the counselor has worked with the client for a while, the counselor should be sensitive in giving the client enough time to get used to the idea of working with someone else.

Recycling is an alternative when the counselor thinks the counseling process has not yet worked but can be made to do so. *Recycling* is basically the reexamination of all phases of the therapeutic process (Baruth & Huber, 1985). It may be that goals were not properly defined or an inappropriate strategy was chosen. Whatever the case, by reexamining the counseling process, counselor and client can decide how or if to revise and reinvest in the counseling process. Counseling, like other experiences, is not always successful on the first attempt. Recycling gives both counselor and client a second chance to achieve what each wants—positive change.

## SUMMARY

Termination is an important but often neglected and misunderstood phase of counseling. The subjects of loss and ending are usually given less emphasis in counseling than those of growth and development. Thus, the subject of termination is often either ignored or just taken for granted. Yet successful termination is vital to the health and well-being of both counselor and client. It is a phase of counseling that can determine the success of all previous phases and, therefore, must be handled with skill. Otherwise, everyone in the counseling relationship will become stuck in reviewing data or in areas that may be of little use. Termination has the function of providing the client a chance to try new behaviors and of serving as a motivator.

In this chapter we have emphasized the procedures involved in conducting the termination of an individual counseling session, as well as the extended counseling relationship. Both clients and counselors must be prepared for these endings. One way to facilitate this preparation is through the use of structure, such as time frames and both verbal and nonverbal signals. Clients need to learn problem-solving skills before a counseling relationship is over so that they can depend on themselves rather than their counselors when they face difficult life situations. Nevertheless, it is important that a client be given permission to contact the counselor if needed again. An open policy does much to alleviate anxiety.

There are times when either counselor, client, or both are resistant to termination of the relationship. Many times this resistance is related to unresolved feelings of grief and separation. When a client has such feelings, the client may choose to terminate the relationship prematurely. A counselor may also initiate termination but usually does so for good reasons. Regardless of who initiates termination, it is vital that all involved know what is happening and prepare accordingly. If possible, it is best to end counseling on a positive note. Once termination is completed, it is helpful to conduct some type of follow-up within a year. Sometimes referrals or recycling procedures are indicated in order to ensure that the client receives the type of help needed.

## CLASSROOM ACTIVITIES

1. In dyads, discuss the most significant termination experiences of your life, such as death of a loved one, graduation, or life stages. Evaluate with your partner the positive things you learned from these experiences as well as the pain you felt.
2. In groups of five, take turns role playing different forms of counselor/client resistance to termination at the end of a session. Have one person play the part of the counselor, one person the part of the client, two persons the parts of alter egos for counselor and client, and one person the part of an observer/evaluator. After everyone has had a chance to play the counselor, discuss with one another the feelings you had related to resistance in yourself and others, and what strategies seemed to work best in overcoming resistance.
3. Write down ways you think you can tell if a counselor or client is ready to end a relationship. Then silently enact two or more of your behaviors in front of your classmates and let them describe what you are doing and how they would react to it.
4. As a class, divide into two teams and debate the issue of whether counseling relationships must end on a positive note. Pay special attention to the benefits that a client or counselor might derive from terminating counseling on a negative note.
5. What are your feelings about recycling? In groups of four discuss what you think and feel about this procedure. Also, role play how you would refer a difficult client to another professional.

## REFERENCES

Baruth, L. G., & Huber, C. H. (1985). *Counseling and psychotherapy.* Columbus, OH: Merrill.

Benjamin, A. (1981). *The helping interview* (3rd ed.). Boston: Houghton Mifflin.

Cavanagh, M. E. (1982). *The counseling experience.* Monterey, CA: Brooks/Cole.

Corey, G., Corey, M. S., Callanan, P. J., & Russell, J. M. (1982). *Group techniques.* Monterey, CA: Brooks/Cole.

Cormier, W. H., & Cormier, L. S. (1985). *Interviewing strategies for helpers* (2nd ed.). Monterey, CA: Brooks/Cole.

Dixon, D. N., & Glover, J. A. (1984). *Counseling: A problem-solving approach.* New York: Wiley.

Gladding, S. T. (1977). Memory traces. *North Carolina Personnel and Guidance Journal, 6,* 50–51.

Goldberg, C. (1975). Termination—A meaningful pseudodilemma in psychotherapy. *Psychotherapy: Theory, Research, and Practice. 12,* 341–343.

Goldstein, A. (1971). *Psychotherapeutic attraction.* New York: Pergamon.

Goodyear, R. K. (1981). Termination as a loss experience for the counselor. *Personnel and Guidance Journal, 59,* 349–350.

Hackney, H. & Cormier, L. S. (1979). *Counseling strategies and objectives* (2nd ed.). Englewood Cliffs, NJ: Prentice-Hall.

Hansen, J. C., Stevic, R. R., & Warner, R. W., Jr. (1986). *Counseling: Theory and process* (4th ed.). Boston: Allyn & Bacon.

Hansen, J., Warner, R., & Smith, E. (1980). *Group counseling: Theory and process* (2nd ed.). Chicago: Rand McNally.

Ivey, A. E. (1983). *Intentional interviewing and counseling.* Monterey, CA: Brooks/Cole.

Kovacs, A. L. (1965). The intimate relationship: a therapeutic paradox. *Psychotherapy: Theory, Research, and Practice, 2,* 97–103.

Kovacs, A. L. (1976). The emotional hazards of teaching psychotherapy. *Psychotherapy: Theory, Research, and Practice, 13,* 321–334.

Kubler-Ross, E. (1969). *On death and dying.* New York: Macmillan.

Lerner, S., & Lerner, H. (1983). A systematic approach to resistance: Theoretical and technical considerations. *American Journal of Psychotherapy, 37,* 387–399.

London, M. (1982). How do you say good-bye after you've said hello? *Personnel and Guidance Journal, 60,* 412–414.

Loewenstein, S. F. (1979). Helping family members cope with divorce. In S. Eisenberg & L. E. Patterson (Eds.), *Helping clients with special concerns.* Boston: Houghton Mifflin.

Maholick, L. T., & Turner, D. W. (1979). Termination: That difficult farewell. *American Journal of Psychotherapy, 33,* 583–591.

McGee, T. F., Schuman, B. N., & Racusen, F. (1972). Termination in group psychotherapy. *American Journal of Psychotherapy, 26,* 521–532.

Munro, J. N., & Bach, T. R. (1975). Effect of time-limited counseling on client change. *Journal of Counseling Psychology, 22,* 395–398.

Okun, B. F. (1982). *Effective helping* (2nd ed.). Monterey, CA: Brooks/Cole.

Patterson, L. E., & Eisenberg, S. (1983). *The counseling process* (3rd ed.). Boston: Houghton Mifflin.

Perls, F. S. (1969). *Gestalt therapy verbation.* Lafayette, CA: Real People Press.

Pietrofesa, J. J., Hoffman, A., & Splete, H. H. (1984). *Counseling: An introduction* (2nd ed.). Boston: Houghton Mifflin.

Seligman, L. (1984). Temporary termination. *Journal of Counseling and Development, 63,* 43–44.

Sheehy, G. (1976). *Passages: Predictable crises of adult life.* New York: Bantam.

Shulman, L. (1979). *The skills of helping individuals and groups.* Itasca, IL: Peacock.

Ward, D. E. (1984). Termination of individual counseling: Concepts and strategies. *Journal of Counseling and Development, 63,* 21–25.

Weiss, R. S. (Ed.). (1973). *Loneliness.* Cambridge, MA: M.I.T. Press.

Yalom, I. D. (1975). *The theory and practice of group psychotherapy* (2nd ed.). New York: Basic Books.

# CHAPTER 10

# Ethical and Legal
# Aspects of Counseling

*In the cool grey dawn of early September,*
*I place the final suitcase into my Mustang*
*And silently say "good-bye"*
   *to the quiet beauty of North Carolina.*
*Hesitantly, I head for the blue ocean-lined coast*
   *of Connecticut.*
*Bound for a new position and the unknown.*
*Traveling with me are a sheltie named "Eli"*
   *and the still fresh memories of our last counseling session.*
*You, who wrestled so long with fears*
   *that I kiddingly started calling you "Jacob,"*
   *are as much a part of me as my luggage.*
*Moving in life is bittersweet—*
*Like giving up friends and fears.*
*The taste is like smooth, orange, Fall persimmons,*
   *deceptively delicious but tart.*[1]

---

[1]Gladding, 1984, p. 146. Copyright AACD. Reprinted with permission. No further reproduction authorized without written permission of AACD.

ounseling is not a value-free activity. "Values are the core of
the counseling relationship" (Hansen, Stevic, & Warner,
1986, p. 547). On the basis of the values held by counselors
and clients directions are taken and decisions made. Counseling is
also "a moral enterprise requiring responsibleness; that is, action . . . based on careful, reflective thought about which response
is professionally right in a particular situation" (Tennyson & Strom,
1986, p. 298). Counselors are guided in their thoughts and actions
by values, by professional and personal ethics, and by legal procedures and precedents. Thus, it is impossible to apply a cookbook
approach to counseling, because both clients and counselors are
unique in regard to their life histories, psychological needs, and
values (DePauw, 1986).

Counselors who are not clear about their personal values,
ethics, and legal responsibilities, as well as those of clients, could
cause harm despite best intentions (Huber & Baruth, 1987; Ladd,
1971). Therefore, it is vital for counselors to become knowledgeable
about professional guidelines for working with others. In this
chapter, we will explore the ethical standards and legal constraints
and mandates under which counselors operate. Each affects the
other.

## DEFINITIONS: ETHICS, MORALITY, AND LAW

Ethics involves "making decisions of a moral nature about people
and their interaction in society" (Kitchener, 1986, p. 306). The

terms *ethics* and *morality* are often used synonymously, and in many ways they overlap. Van Hoose and Kottler (1985) point out that both terms deal with "what is good and bad or the study of human conduct and values" (p. 2). Yet the terms also have different meanings.

"Ethics is generally defined as a philosophical discipline that is concerned with human conduct and moral decision making" (Van Hoose & Kottler, 1985, p. 3). It is normative in nature and focuses on principles and standards that govern relationships between individuals, such as in counseling. *Morality*, on the other hand, involves judgment or evaluation of action. It is associated with the employment of such words as *good, bad, right, wrong, ought,* and *should* (Brandt, 1959).

Hummel, Talbutt, and Alexander (1985) define *law* as the precise codification of governing standards that are established to ensure legal and moral justice. Law is created by legislation, court decision, and tradition, as in English common law (Remley, 1985). The law does not dictate what is ethical in a given situation, but rather what is legal. Sometimes, what is legal at a given time— matters of race, age, or sex, for example—is considered unethical or immoral by some significant segment of society. In such conflicts between the legal and the ethical/moral systems of a society, a resolution is usually worked out in the courts. Although laws are more objective and specific than most ethical or moral codes, they are often changed in response to challenges by individuals and groups.

## MAKING ETHICAL DECISIONS

Professional counselors who are members of such groups as the American Association for Counseling and Development (AACD) and the American Psychological Association (APA) are concerned with ethics and values, but some counselors are better informed or attuned to these issues than are others. Patterson (1971) has observed that the professional identity of the counselor is related to his or her knowledge and practice of ethics. Some counselors operate from personal ethical standards without regard to the ethical guidelines developed by AACD or APA. Such counselors usually function well until faced with a dilemma "for which there is no apparent good or best solution" (Swanson, 1983b, p. 57). At such times, ethical issues arise. The formal ethical standards of professional groups do not often offer specific directions about what counselors should do in given situations (Rosenbaum, 1982). But they do provide guidelines for resolving ethical dilemmas. Counselors may experience conflict in determining what conduct should be in regard to two or more constituencies, such as a client, an organization, or the profession (Hayman & Covert, 1986). And even after decisions are made and executed, the actions taken may not erase all vestiges of conflict (Kitchener, 1986). Nevertheless, making ethical decisions is an integral part of being a counselor.

Some ways of resolving conflicts are more productive and ethical than others, and counselors need to be aware of these. That many counselors are not well informed about such matters is illustrated in a study conducted in western New York state by Hayman & Covert (1986). These researchers found five types of ethical dilemmas most prevalent among the university counselors they surveyed: confidentiality, role conflict, counselor competence, conflicts with employer or institution, and degree of dangerousness. The situational dilemmas that involved danger were the least difficult to resolve; those that dealt with counselor competence and confidentiality were the most difficult. The surprising finding of this study, however, was that less than one-third of the 54 respondents indicated they relied on published professional guidelines in resolving ethical dilemmas. Instead, most used "common sense." A strategy based solely on common sense is probably one of the least-productive ways of dealing with ethical concerns. Professionally it may be unethical—at best unwise—to use such a strategy exclusively.

A division within AACD—the Association for Religious and Values Issues in Counseling (ARVIC)—is especially concerned with values and ethics among counseling professionals (Bartlett, Lee, & Doyle, 1985). This division, which deals with ethical concerns regularly, addressed such issues as counseling the aged, values education, and feminism long before these issues were concerns among most counselors. In addition to the vanguard work on ethics and values accomplished by ARVIC through committees and its journal, *Counseling and Values,* both APA and AACD have developed associational and speciality codes of ethics, and each organization contains an active ethics committee.

### Development of Ethical Codes

APA led the way in developing a code of ethics and has been continuously involved in updating and revising this document (Welfel & Lipsitz, 1983a). APA (1981a, b) publishes a general code of ethics, *Ethical Principles of Psychologists,* as well as *Speciality Guidelines for the Delivery of Services by Counseling Psychologists.* In addition, APA (1982) prints a casebook for the providers of psychological services in order to assist them in determining when and how psychological services should be delivered. When APA members violate the professional ethics code, appropriate action, which may include dismissal from APA membership, is taken.

It was on the original APA code of ethics that AACD (then the American Personnel and Guidance Association, or APGA) based its first standards (Allen, 1986). The initial AACD Code of Ethics was approved in 1961 (Callis, Pope, & DePauw, 1982) and has been revised periodically since (e.g., 1974 and 1981). AACD also produces an *Ethical Standards Casebook* (Callis, Pope, & DePauw, 1982). In addition to the AACD ethical standards, six AACD divisions have adopted their own standards (Allen, 1986). The American Association of Marriage and Family Therapists (AAMFT) has also developed a code of ethics for professionals involved in couple and family counseling.

## Reasons for Ethical Codes

Ethical standards exist for many reasons. Generally, they "are designed to provide some guidelines for the professional behavior of members" of organizations such as AACD and APA (Swanson, 1983, p. 53). Van Hoose and Kottler (1985) offer three reasons for the existence of codes of ethics for professionals:

- ☐ Ethical standards protect the profession from government. They allow the profession to regulate itself and to function autonomously instead of being controlled by legislation.
- ☐ Ethical standards help in controlling internal disagreements and bickering, thus promoting stability within the profession.
- ☐ Ethical standards protect practitioners from the public, especially in regard to malpractice suits. If professionals behave according to ethical guidelines, the behavior is judged to be in compliance with accepted standards (Talbutt, 1981).

In addition, ethical standards provide some protection for clients from charlatans and incompetent counselors (Swanson, 1983b). Clients can use codes of ethics, as counselors do, as a guide in evaluating questionable treatment.

## Unethical Behavior

Unethical behavior can take many forms. Levenson (1986) and Swanson (1983b) list some of the most prevalent unethical behaviors:

Violation of confidentiality

Exceeding one's level of professional competence

Negligent practice

Claiming expertise one does not possess

Imposing one's values on a client

Creating dependency in a client

Sexual activity with a client

Certain conflicts of interest

Questionable financial arrangements, such as charging excessive fees

Improper advertising

Yet the temptations common to people everywhere exist for counselors. They include "physical intimacy, the titillation of gossip, or the opportunity (if the gamble pays off) to advance one's career" (Welfel & Lipsitz, 1983a, p. 328).

Some forms of unethical behavior are obvious and willful, whereas others are more subtle and unintentional. In any case, the harmful outcome is the same. The ethical standards casebooks published by AACD and APA both contain examples in which counselors are presented with questionable ethical situations and are asked to decide what an ethical response would be. Each situation involves a standard of the ethical code, and responses are rated according to how closely they are in line with that standard. There are many counseling situations in which the proper behavior is not obvious (Huber & Baruth, 1987). It is therefore crucial for counselors to consult casebooks, colleagues, and professional codes of ethics when they are in doubt about what to do in a given situation.

## Professional Codes of Ethics

A *professional code of ethics* is a set of standards of conduct "based upon an agreed-on set of values" by which professionals in a given occupation, such as counseling or psychology, voluntarily abide (Hansen, Stevic, & Warner, 1986, p. 528). Such a code is one of the major signs that a profession has developed into a mature discipline (Stadler, 1986). Professionals are characterized by a claim to specialized knowledge and a code of ethics (Friedson, 1973).

In AACD, APA, and AAMFT, ethical standards are arranged under topical sectional headings. (See appendices A, B, and C for AACD, APA, & AAMFT ethical standards, respectively). In the AACD code, there are eight major sections of ethical standards. These sections contain the type of material found in many ethical codes. The first section is general and deals with the professional responsibilities counselors have to clients, colleagues, and work setting. It also addresses professional qualifications, fees, and personal rights. The second section covers material connected with the counseling relationship, including confidentiality, imminent danger, record keeping, and referral. In the third section, issues connected with measurement and evaluation are covered. These include the purpose for testing, the setting and justification for the selection of test instruments, test standardization and interpretation. The fourth section covers research and publication. It provides guidelines for conducting research that protects the rights of participants and for the publication of research reports and other documents.

The fifth section deals with consultation, giving guidelines for professional conduct. Issues related to private practice are covered in the sixth section. The seventh section deals with personnel administration, recognizing that most counselors are employed in public or quasi-public institutions. It addresses such issues as in-service training and the responsibilities a counselor has to an employer. The final section addresses preparation standards. It focuses on the responsibility graduate education programs in counseling have in regard to their students. For example, graduate programs are responsible for conducting programs in accordance with current relevant guidelines of AACD.

## Limitations of Ethical Codes

Remley (1985) notes that ethical standards are general and idealistic in nature, seldom answering specific questions. Furthermore, he points out that such standards do not address the area of "foreseeable professional dilemmas" (Remley, 1985, p. 181). Rather, they provide guidelines, based on experiences and values, of how counselors should behave. In many ways, ethical standards represent the collected wisdom of a profession at a particular point in time.

A number of specific limitations exists in any code of ethical standards. Among the ones most frequently listed are (Beymer, 1971; Corey, Corey, & Callanan, 1984; Mabe & Rollin, 1986; Talbutt, 1981):

☐ Some issues cannot be resolved by a code of ethics.

☐ There are difficulties in enforcing ethical codes.

☐ There are sometimes conflicts within the standards delineated by the code.

☐ There are legal and ethical issues that codes do not cover.

☐ Ethical codes are historical documents, and what may be acceptable practice at one time may be considered unethical later.

☐ There are sometimes conflicts between ethical and legal codes.

☐ Ethical codes do not address cross-cultural issues.

☐ Ethical codes do not address *every* possible situation.

☐ There is often difficulty in bringing the interest of all parties involved in an ethical dispute together systematically.

☐ Ethical codes are not proactive documents in helping counselors decide what to do in new situations.

Thus ethical codes are useful in many ways, but they do have their limitations. Counselors need to be aware that they will not always find the guidance they want when consulting these documents. In fact, counselors may sometimes become more confused, especially if they belong to two or more professional counseling organizations that have different codes of ethics. Nevertheless, whenever an ethical issue arises in counseling, the counselor should first consult ethical standards to see whether the situation is addressed.

### Conflicts Within Ethical Codes

The adoption of ethical codes and the emphasis on them have come with the increased professionalism of counseling (Stude & McKelvey, 1979). But the presence of such standards poses a potential dilemma for many counselors, for three reasons. First, as Stadler (1986) points out, in order to act ethically counselors must be aware of ethical codes and be able to differentiate an ethical dilemma from other types of dilemmas, a differentiation that is not always easy. A person may take a stand on a controversial issue (e.g., homosexuality) that he or she seemingly supports with ethical principles but that in reality is supported only by personal beliefs or biases.

Second, there are often different ethical principles in a code, such as AACD's, that offer conflicting guidelines about what to do in a given situation (Stadler, 1986). An example is the potential conflict over providing a client confidentiality and acting in the client's best interest. A client may reveal an attempt to harass someone else or to harm himself or herself. In such a situation, the counselor who keeps this information confidential may actually act against the best interests of the client and the community in which the client resides.

Third, conflicts may occur when counselors belong to two or more professional organizations whose codes of ethics differ, such as the codes of APA and AACD. Such counselors may become involved in situations in which the ethical action is unclear. Mabe and Rollin

(1986) note, for instance, that APA's code of ethics has only six paragraphs dealing with assessment, whereas AACD's ethical standards are much more elaborate. If a professional belongs to both organizations and is dealing with assessment instruments, which code of ethics should be followed?

## GUIDELINES FOR ACTING ETHICALLY

Stadler (1986) says that "four ethical principles relate to the activities and ethical choices of counselors: beneficence (doing good and preventing harm), nonmaleficence (not inflicting harm), autonomy (respecting freedom of choice and self-determination), and justice (fairness)" (p. 291). All of these principles involve conscious decision making by counselors throughout the counseling process.

Swanson (1983b) also lists four guidelines he deems important in assessing whether counselors are acting in ethically responsible ways. The first is personal and professional honesty. Counselors need to operate openly with themselves and those with whom they work. Hidden agendas or unacknowledged feelings both hinder relationships and place counselors on shaky ethical grounds. A second guideline is acting in the best interest of clients. This ideal is easier to discuss than to achieve. A counselor may impose personal values on clients at times and ignore what the client really wants (Gladding & Hood, 1974). At other times, a counselor may fail to recognize an emergency and too readily accept the idea that the best interest of the client is served by doing nothing.

A third guideline is that counselors act without malice or personal gain. Some clients are difficult to like or deal with, and it is with these individuals that counselors must be especially careful. A final guideline is whether counselors can justify an action "as the best judgment of what should be done based upon the current state of the profession" (Swanson, 1983b, p. 59). In order to make such a decision, counselors must keep up with current trends by reading the professional literature, attending in-service workshops and conventions, and becoming actively involved in local, state and national counseling activities.

### Ethics in Specific Counseling Situations

Ethical behavior is greatly influenced by the prevalent attitudes in the setting in which one works and by those held by one's colleagues. Ladd (1971) observes that "most organizations that employ counselors are organized not collegially or professionally, as is in part the case with universities and hospitals, but hierarchically. In a hierarchical organization the administrator or executive decides which prerogatives are administrative and which are professional" (p. 262). Counselors should always attempt to check thoroughly the general polices and principles of an institution before accepting employment, because employment in a specific setting implies that the counselor agrees with its policies and principles. When counselors find themselves in situations that misuse their services and do not act in the best interests of their clients, they must act either to change the institution through educational or persuasive means or find other employment.

The potential for major ethical crises between a counselor and his or her employer exists in many school settings. Boy and Pine's (1968) observation that school counselors are often used as tools for school administrators is still true in some places. Huey (1986) stresses that in school counseling settings, where there is the possibility of conflict between a counselor's loyalty to the employer and the client, "the counselor should always attempt to find a resolution that protects the rights of the client; the ethical responsibility is to the client first and the school second" (p. 321).

Another counseling situation in which ethical crises are common is marriage and family counseling (Corey, Corey, & Callanan, 1984; Huber & Baruth, 1987). The reason is that the counselor is treating a number of individuals together as a system, and it is unlikely that all members of the system have the same goals (Wilcoxon, 1986). Added to this difficulty is that APA ethical guidelines are designed for individual situations (Margolin, 1982), whereas AACD's ethical standards are geared to individual and group counseling. Only the ethical code of AAMFT addresses situations involving couples and families. Since many counselors are not associated with AAMFT, they are unaware of these standards and base their decisions on ethical guidelines that may be inappropriate. An ethically mandated solution to this dilemma is for counselors not to work with couples and families if they have no expertise in marriage and family counseling.

Other settings or situations in which there are significant potential ethical dilemmas are: counseling the elderly (Fitting, 1986), genetic counseling (Witmer, Wedl, & Black, 1986), cross-cultural counseling (Ibrahim & Arredondo, 1986), and counseling research (Robinson & Gross, 1986). In this last area, there are four main ethical issues that must be resolved: "(a) informed consent, (b) coercion and deception, (c) confidentiality and privacy, and (d) reporting the results" (Robinson & Gross, 1986, p. 331).

### *Promoting Ethical Decision Making in Counselors*

Welfel and Lipsitz (1983a) note that even though there is a heightened awareness among professionals of the need to promote the study and practice of ethics in counseling and psychotherapy, few courses dealing with ethics "enable students to be more aware of ethical issues" (p. 326).

Van Hoose and Paradise (1979) conceptualize the ethical behavior of counselors in terms of a five-stage developmental continuum of reasoning. These stages are:

1. *Punishment orientation*   At this stage, the counselor believes external social standards are the basis for judging behavior. If clients or counselors violate a societal rule, they should be punished.

2. *Institutional orientation*   Counselors who operate at this stage believe in and abide by the rules of the institutions for which they work. They do not question the rules put in place by the institution's authorities and base their decisions upon the rules.

3. *Societal orientation*   This stage of ethical reasoning is characterized by basing decisions on societal standards. If there is a question of whether the needs of society or an individual should come first, the needs of society are always given priority.

4. *Individual orientation*   The needs of the individual are given top priority at this stage. Counselors are aware of societal needs and are concerned about the law, but they focus on what is best for the individual.

5. *Principle (conscience) orientation*   In this last stage of ethical reasoning, concern for the individual is primary and ethical decisions are based on internalized ethical standards and not on external considerations.

As Welfel and Lipsitz (1983b) point out, the work of Van Hoose and Paradise is especially important because it "is the first conceptual model in the literature that attempts to explain how counselors reason about ethical issues" (p. 36). It is heuristic in nature and can form the basis for empirical studies into the promotion of ethical behavior.

Several models (Gumaer & Scott, 1985; Kitchener, 1986; Pelsma & Borgers, 1986) have been proposed for educating counselors in ethical decision making. The one by Gumaer and Scott (1985) is a method for training group workers based on the ethical guidelines of the Association for Specialists in Group Work (ASGW). (See appendix D for ASGW ethical guidelines.) It uses case vignettes and Carkhuff's three-goal model of helping: self-exploration, self-understanding, and action. Kitchener (1986) proposes an integrated model of goals and components for an ethics education curriculum based on research on the psychological processes underlying moral behavior and on current thinking in the area of applied ethics. She includes in her curriculum "a sensitizing of counselors to ethical issues, improving their abilities to make ethical judgments, encouraging responsible ethical actions, and tolerating the ambiguity of ethical decision making" (Kitchener, 1986, p. 306). Her model and the one proposed by Pelsma and Borgers are both process-oriented and assume that counselors will not learn to make ethical decisions by just practice on their own. Pelsma and Borgers especially emphasize the how as opposed to the what of ethics, that is, how to reason ethically in a field such as counseling that is constantly changing. Their emphasis on process and reasoning rather than on answers and solutions has important implications for ethics education.

## THE LAW AND COUNSELING

The profession of counseling is governed not only by ethical standards but by legal ones as well. *Legal* refers to "law or the state of being lawful," and *law* refers to "a body of rules recognized by a state or community as binding on its members" (Shertzer & Stone, 1980, p. 386). Contrary to popular opinion, "law is not cut and dried, definite and certain, or clear and precise" (Van Hoose & Kottler, 1985, p. 44). Rather, law is always seeking compromise between individuals and parties. It offers few definite answers, and there are always notable exceptions to any legal precedent. There is "no general body of law covering the helping professions" (Van Hoose & Kottler, 1985, p. 45). But there are a number of court decisions and statutes that influence legal opinion in regard to counseling.

Stude and McKelvey (1979) observe that the law is "generally supportive or neutral" (p. 454) toward professional codes of ethics and toward counseling in general. The law supports licensure or certification of counselors as a means of ensuring that those who enter the profession attain at least minimal standards. It also supports the general "confidentiality of statements and records provided by clients during therapy" (p. 454). In addition, the law is neutral "in that it allows the profession to police itself and govern counselors' relations with their clients and fellow counselors" (p. 454). Stude and McKelvey (1979) note that the only time the law "overrides" a professional code of ethics is when it is necessary "to protect the public health, safety, and welfare" (p. 454). The situations in which this necessity is most likely to occur have to do with confidentiality, when disclosure of information is necessary to prevent harm.

## Legal Recognition of Counseling

Swanson (1983a) points out that counseling gained professional recognition and acceptance in part through the legal system. As recently as 1960, counseling did not have a strong enough identity as a profession to be recognized legally. In that year a judge ruled in the case of *Bogust v. Iverson* that a counselor with a doctoral degree could not be held liable for the suicide of one of his clients because counselors were "mere teachers" who received training in a department of education.

It was not until 1971, in an *Iowa Law Review Note*, that counselors were legally recognized as professionals who provided personal as well as vocational and educational counseling. The profession was even more clearly defined in *Weldon v. Virginia State Board of Psychologists Examiners* in 1974, in which the judgment rendered was that counseling was a profession distinct from psychology. The U.S. House of Representatives further refined the definition of counseling and recognized the profession in H.R. 3270 (94th Congress, 1976) by stating that counseling is "the process through which a trained counselor assists an individual or group to make satisfactory and responsible decisions concerning personal, educational and career development."

Swanson (1983a) notes that state laws regulating counseling, such as the first one passed in Virginia in 1976, "saw counseling as a generic profession" (p. 29) with specialties, such as career counseling. Further impetus for defining counseling as a profession came with the adoption and implementation of minimum preparation standards, such as those adopted by the Council for the Accreditation of Counseling and Related Education Programs (CACREP) in the late 1970s.

## Professional Credentialing

With the recognition of counseling as a separate professional entity, there developed the need for regulation through credentialing procedures. There are basically four types of professional credentials, two of which, certification and licensure, have considerable prestige. In the past, most credentials were awarded by the states, but now certification is often the function of a professional organization. The four types of credentialing procedures from lowest to highest (Swanson, 1983a) are as follows.

☐ *Inspection*   This is the process in which "a state agency periodically examines the activities of a profession's practitioners to ascertain whether they are practicing the profession in a fashion consistent with the public safety, health, and welfare" (Swanson, 1983a, p. 28). Many state agencies that employ counselors, such as mental health centers, are subject to having their personnel and their programs inspected on a regular basis. Such an inspection may include a review of case notes on treatment during a specific period, a review of agency procedures, and even personal interviews.

☐ *Registration*   This plan requires the practitioners of a profession, such as counseling, to submit information to the state concerning the nature of their practice. Usually a professional organization, such as a state division of AACD, will assume the responsibility for setting standards necessary to qualify as a registrant and for maintaining a list of names of those who voluntarily meet those standards. This method has been employed in North Carolina as a way to gain legal recognition for counselors in that state, using the title "registered practicing counselor" (Locke, 1984).

☐ *Certification*   This type of recognition occurs when a state board or department issues a certificate to an individual in a specialty, such as counseling. Certification basically implies that the person has met the minimum skills necessary to engage in that profession and has no known character defects that would interfere with such a practice. Many times states require candidates for certification to pass a competency test and submit letters of reference before a certificate will be issued. School counselors were among the first counselors to be certified. On the national level, some counselor organizations, such as the National Board of Certified Counselors (NBCC), practice certification procedures. A counselor who wishes to be NBCC certified must prove to have studied specific counseling-related courses, such as human growth and development, groups, and appraisal, before being allowed to sit for the national exam. (See Figure 10.1.)

☐ *Licensure*   This, the highest form of credentialing, is often called "title protection." It differs in purpose from certification but requires similar procedures in terms of education and testing for competence (Shimberg, 1981). Once licensure requirements are established, individuals cannot practice a profession legally without obtaining a license. Licensure is almost

## What is the National Board for Certified Counselors?

The NBCC is a non-profit, independent organization whose purposes are to establish and monitor a national counselor certification process, to identify to professionals and the public those counselors who have obtained the voluntary certification, and to maintain a register of certified counselors. NBCC was created in 1982 as a result of the efforts of the American Association for Counseling and Development (AACD) in promoting professional credentialing standards for counselors.

NBCC grants two different professional certifications — National Certified Counselor and National Certified Career Counselor. Counselors who meet NBCC's standards and obtain certification are also required to maintain and renew certification through continuing education. Through its certification programs, NBCC provides a national standard in the counseling profession that can be used as a measure of professionalism.

## What Does National Certified Counselor Mean?

Counselors certified by the NBCC are authorized to identify themselves as "NCCs" — National Certified Counselors. These counselors meet the generic professional standards established by the NBCC and agree to abide by the NBCC Code of Ethics in professional practice. NCCs work in a variety of educational and social service settings such as schools, private practice, mental health agencies, correctional facilities, community agencies, rehabilitation agencies, and business and industry. NCCs are trained to assist persons with a variety of needs — aging, vocational development, adolescence, family and marriage concerns, to name just a few. Individual NCCs may limit practice to special areas of interest or expertise (e.g. career development, ethnic groups, etc.) or age group (adolescents, older adults, etc.). In addition to being certified by NBCC, some NCCs are licensed by their state or hold a specialty certification such as mental health, career, or rehabilitation counseling.

## How Does a Counselor Become a National Certified Counselor?

Candidates for NCC must meet both the minimum education and professional counseling experience requirements established by NBCC. NCCs hold a master's degree or doctorate in counseling or a closely related field from a regionally accredited university. NCCs have at least two years professional counseling experience and must document supervised experience. All NCCs must pass a written counselor certification examination. NCCs are certified for a period of five years. In order to renew certification the NCC must participate in approved continuing education activities. This continuing education requirement is meant to ensure that NCCs stay current in the counseling field.

## What Does National Certified Career Counselor Mean?

Career development specialists certified by the NBCC are authorized to identify themselves as "NCCCs" — National Certified Career Counselors. These counselors meet the professional career counseling standards established by NBCC and agree to abide by the NBCC Code of Ethics in professional practice. The NCCC credential means that the career counselor has achieved the highest certification in the career development field. NCCCs help people make decisions and plans related to life/career directions. Among the many strategies and techniques used by the NCCCs are assisting in developing individualized career plans; administering and interpreting tests to assess abilities; conducting individual and group sessions to help clarify life/career goals; and teaching job hunting skills and assisting in the development of resumes. You should ask the NCCC you are considering for a detailed explanation of services he/she offers.

## How Does a Career Counselor Become Certified by NBCC?

National Certified Career Counselors must hold the National Certified Counselor credential before they may become certified in the career

specialty. Candidates for NCCC must meet both minimum education and professional career counseling experience requirements established by NBCC. NCCCs hold a master's degree or doctorate in counseling or a closely related field from a regionally accredited university. The NCCC's graduate coursework must include lifestyle and career development, tests and measurements, and a career counseling practicum/internship. NCCCs have at least three years professional career counseling experience and must document a supervised experience. The candidate for NCCC must pass the NBCC Career Counseling Specialty Examination.

## What Are the NBCC Ethical Standards for Practice?

All NCCs and NCCCs agree to abide by the NBCC Code of Ethics in practice. The NBCC Code of Ethics states that National Certified Counselors only offer services for which they are professionally qualified, respect the integrity and promote the welfare of the client, and commit themselves to establishing appropriate fees.

You may wish to ask the NCC you are considering for a copy of the NBCC Code of Ethics as well as asking for a detailed explanation of services offered and your financial and time commitments.

## How Many Counselors Are Certified by NBCC?

Over 16,000 counselors have successfully completed the NBCC certification process and approximately 1,000 of these NCCs also hold the career counseling specialty certification.

## How Can I Find a National Certified Counselor or Certified Career Counselor?

The National Board for Certified Counselors publishes a national register of NCCs and listings of NCCCs. Consumers may write to NBCC for a free list of National Certified Counselors or National Certified Career Counselors in their geographic area.

**FIGURE 10.1**  National Board of Certified Counselors standards.

exclusively a state-governed process, and those states that have licensure have established boards to oversee the issuing of licenses. In general, the licensing of counselors has gained momentum in the 1980s in a way that parallels the growth in the licensing of psychologists in the 1960s and 1970s. There is no national licensing for counselors.

### Legal Aspects of the Counseling Relationship

Counselors must follow specific legal guidelines in working with certain populations. For example, P.L. 94-142 (the Education for All Handicapped Children Act of 1975) provides that schools must make provisions for the free, appropriate public education for all children in the least-restrictive environment possible. A part of this process is the development of an individual education plan (IEP) for each child, as well as the provision for due-process procedures and the identification of and record-keeping on every handicapped child (Humes, 1978). School counselors who work with handicapped children have specific tasks to complete under the terms of this act. In a similar way, counselors have a legal obligation under all child-abuse laws to report suspected cases of child abuse to proper authorities, usually specific personnel in a state social welfare office. Furthermore, the legal obligations of counselors are well defined under the Family Educational Rights and Privacy Act of 1974, known as the Buckley amendment. This statute gives students access to certain records kept on them by educational institutions.

Counselors have considerable trouble in situations where the law is not clear or where there is a conflict between the law and professional counseling ethics. Such situations often involve confidentiality. Corey, Corey, and Callanan (1984) note that confidentiality is an important obligation of counselors. The concept originated in ethical codes to safeguard client's rights. But there are limitations to confidentiality. Denkowski and Denkowski (1982) contend that counselors should inform clients of potential situations in which confidentiality may have to be broken.

A landmark court case that reflects the importance of limiting confidentiality is *Tarasoff v. Board of Regents of the University of California*, which was decided in 1976. In this case, a student, Prosenjit Poddar, who was a voluntary outpatient at the student health services on the Berkeley campus of the University of California, informed the psychologist who was counseling him that he intended to kill his former girlfriend, Tatiana Tarasoff, when she arrived back on campus. The psychologist notified the campus police, who detained and questioned the student about his proposed activities. The student, who denied any intention of killing Tarasoff, acted rationally and was released. Poddar refused further treatment by the psychologist, and no other steps were taken to deter him from his intended action. Two months later, he killed Tarasoff. Her parents sued the Regents of the University of California for failing to notify the intended victim of a threat against her. The California Supreme Court ruled in their favor, holding in effect that a therapist has a duty to protect the public that overrides any obligation to maintain client confidentiality.

Thus, there is a limit to how much confidentiality a counselor can or should maintain. When it appears that a client is dangerous to him- or herself or to others, the laws of most states specify that this information must be reported. Knapp and Vandecreek (1982) note, however, that there are variations in state laws and reporting such information is often difficult. They suggest when there is the risk of client violence, a counselor should try to defuse the danger, while also satisfying any legal duty. They recommend consulting with professional colleagues who have expertise in working with violent individuals and also documenting the steps taken.

### Civil and Criminal Liability

The Tarasoff case raises the problem of counselor liability and malpractice. Basically, liability issues in counseling are concerned with whether counselors have caused harm to clients (Wittmer & Loesch, 1986). The concept of liability is directly connected with malpractice. Hummel, Talbutt, and Alexander (1985) define *malpractice* in counseling "as harm to a client resulting from professional negligence, with negligence defined as the departure from acceptable professional standards" (p. 70). Although there are relatively few counselor malpractice lawsuits, professional counselors need to make sure they protect themselves from such possibilities. Two ways to do this are to follow one's professional code of ethics and to follow normal practice standards (Hopkins & Anderson, 1985).

Liability can be classified under two main headings: civil and criminal. Civil liability "means that one can be sued for acting wrongly toward another or for failing to act when there was a recognized duty to do so" (Hopkins & Anderson, 1985, p. 21). Criminal liability, on the other hand, involves a counselor's working with a client in a way the law does not allow (Burgum & Anderson, 1975).

The concept of civil liability rests on the concept of *tort*, "a wrong that legal action is designed to set right" (Hopkins &

Anderson, 1985, p. 21). The legal wrong can be against a person, property, or even against someone's reputation and may be unintentional or direct. Hopkins and Anderson (1985) list five situations where counselors are most likely to face civil liability suits for malpractice: (1) malpractice in particular situations (birth control, abortion, prescribing and administering drugs, treatment), (2) illegal search, (3) defamation, (4) invasion of privacy, and (5) breach of contract. Three situations in which counselors risk criminal liability are: (1) accessory to a crime; (2) civil disobedience; and (3) contributing to the delinquency of a minor (Burgum & Anderson, 1975; Hopkins & Anderson, 1985).

### Client Rights and Records

Clients have a number of legal as well as ethical rights in counseling, but clients frequently do not know about those rights. One of the first tasks of counselors is to inform clients of their rights. Hansen, Stevic, and Warner (1986) point out that there are two main types of client rights—implied and explicit. Both relate to due process. *Implied rights* are linked to substantive due process. When a rule is made that arbitrarily limits an individual, he or she has been denied substantive due process. On the other hand, an individual's procedural due process has been violated when an explicit rule has been broken. In either case, a client has a right to know what recourse he or she has when one of these two types of rights is violated. Legally, the issue of rights is clearer in dealing with adults than with children. Remley (1985) notes "that children under the age of majority do not have the capacity or right to make decisions for themselves" (p. 182). Nevertheless, children have rights and are legally protected from any arbitrary professional actions.

The records of all clients are legally protected, except under special circumstances. For example, there are some instances, such as those provided by the Buckley amendment, in which an individual has the right legally to inspect his or her record. There are also some cases cited by Hummel, Talbutt, and Alexander (1985) in which third parties have access to student information without the consent of the student or parent. In the vast majority of cases, counselors are legally required to protect clients of all ages by keeping records under lock and key and not disclosing any information about a client without that client's written permission. It is vital for counselors to check the legal codes of their states for exact guidelines. In no case, however, should confidential information about a client be given on the telephone, and counselors are ethically and legally bound to ensure that a client's rights are protected by not discussing counseling cases in public.

## SUMMARY

Counselors are like other professionals in having established codes of ethics to guide them in the practice of helping others. The ethical standards of AACD, APA, and AAMFT are three of the main documents counselors consult when they face ethical dilemmas. In addition, six AACD divisions have their own ethical codes and counseling psychologists also have theirs. Nevertheless, acting ethically is not always easy, comfortable, or clear.

In making an ethical decision, counselors rely on personal values as well as ethical standards and legal precedents. They also consult with professional colleagues. It is imperative that counselors become well-informed in the area of ethics, for the sake of their well-being and that of their clients. It is not enough that counselors have an academic knowledge of ethical standards; they must have a working knowledge as well and be able to assess at what developmental level they and their colleagues are operating.

In addition, it is crucial that counselors be informed about state and national legislation and legal decisions. These will also affect the ways in which counselors work. Counselors are liable for civil and criminal malpractice suits if they violate client rights or societal rules. One way to protect themselves legally is for counselors to follow the ethical standards of the professional organizations with which they affiliate and to operate according to recognized normal practices. It is imperative that counselors be able to have a rationale to justify what they do.

Ethical standards and legal codes reflect current conditions and are ever-evolving documents. They do not cover all situations but they do offer help to counselors beyond that found in their own personal beliefs and values. As counseling continues to develop as a profession, the ethical and legal aspects of it will probably become more complicated and enforcement procedures will become more strict. Ignorance of ethics and law is no excuse for any counselor in his or her practice.

## CLASSROOM ACTIVITIES

1. Obtain copies of the ethical guidelines for specific AACD divisions. Compare these guidelines to the most recently published AACD ethical standards. What areas of conflict do you notice? How is each document unique? Discuss your observations with fellow class members.
2. In groups of four, use the ethical standards casebooks from AACD and APA as guides to enact specific ethical dilemmas before your classmates. Have the other groups of four in your class write down at least two courses of action they would pursue in solving your enacted situation. Have them justify the personal and professional reasons for their actions. Discuss each of these situations with the class as whole and your instructor.

3. Invite three or four professional counselors to your class to discuss specific ethical and legal concerns they have encountered and what areas they find the most difficult to deal with. After their presentations, question them about the role of ethics and law in the future of counseling.

4. Obtain as many copies as you can of counseling laws in states where counselors are licensed. Compare these laws for similarities and differences. What areas do you think they need to address that are not being covered?

5. Write down ways that you, as a professional counselor, can influence the development of counseling ethics and law. Be specific. Share your thoughts with fellow classmates and rank strategies for implementing this task on the basis of what you understand to be the nature of ethics and law in the regulation of a profession such as counseling.

## REFERENCES

Allen, V. B. (1981). A historical perspective of the AACD ethics committee. *Journal of Counseling and Development, 64,* 293.

American Psychological Association. (1981a). *Ethical principles of psychologists* (rev. ed.). Washington, D.C.: Author.

American Psychological Association. (1981b). *Specialty guidelines for the delivery of services by counseling psychologists.* Washington, D.C.: Author.

American Psychological Association, Committee on Professional Standards. (1982). Casebook for providers of psychological services. *American Psychologist, 37,* 698–701.

Bartlett, W. E., Lee, J. L., & Doyle, R. E. (1985). Historical development of the Association for Religious and Values Issues in Counseling. *Journal of Counseling and Development, 63,* 448–451.

Beymer, L. (1971). Who killed George Washington? *Personnel and Guidance Journal, 50,* 249–253.

Boy, A. V., & Pine, G. J. (1968). *The counselor in the schools: A reconceptualization.* Boston: Houghton Mifflin.

Brandt, R. (1959). *Ethical theory.* Englewood Cliffs, NJ: Prentice-Hall.

Burgum, T., & Anderson, S. (1975). *The counselor and the law.* Washington, D.C.: APGA Press.

Callis, R., Pope, S., & DePauw, M. (1982). *Ethical standards casebook* (3rd ed.). Falls Church, VA: American Personnel and Guidance Association.

Corey, G., Corey, M. S., & Callanan, P. (1984). *Issues & ethics in the helping professions* (2nd ed.). Monterey, CA: Brooks/ Cole.

Denkowski, K. M., & Denkowski, G. C. (1982). Client-counselor confidentiality: An update of rationale, legal status, and implications. *Personnel and Guidance Journal, 60,* 371–375.

DePauw, M. E. (1986). Avoiding ethical violations: A timeline perspective for individual counseling. *Journal of Counseling and Development, 64,* 303–305.

Fitting, M. D. (1986). Ethical dilemmas in counseling elderly adults. *Journal of Counseling and Development, 64,* 325–327.

Friedson, E. (1973). *Profession of medicine: A study of the sociology of applied knowledge.* New York: Dodd, Mead.

Gladding, S. T. (1984). Bittersweet. *Counseling and Values, 28,* 146.

Gladding, S. T., & Hood, W. D. (1974). Five cents, please. *The School Counselor, 21,* 40–43.

Gumaer, J., & Scott, L. (1985). Training group leaders in ethical decision making. *Jour-*

*nal for Specialists in Group Work, 10,* 198–204.

Hansen, J. C., Stevic, R. R., & Warner, R. W., Jr. (1986). *Counseling: Theory and process* (4th ed.). Boston: Allyn & Bacon.

Hayman, P. M., & Covert, J. A. (1986). Ethical dilemmas in college counseling centers. *Journal of Counseling and Development, 64,* 318–320

Hopkins, B. R., & Anderson, B. S. (1985). *The counselor and the law.* Alexandria, VA: AACD Press.

Huber, C. H., & Baruth, L. G. (1987). *Ethical, legal and professional issues in the practice of marriage and family therapy.* Columbus, OH: Merrill.

Huey, W. C. (1986). Ethical concerns in school counseling. *Journal of Counseling and Development, 64,* 321–322.

Humes, C. W., II. (1978). School counselors and P.L. 94-142. *The School Counselor, 25,* 192–195.

Hummel, D. L., Talbutt, L. C., & Alexander, M. D. (1985). *Law and ethics in counseling.* New York: Van Nostrand Reinhold.

Ibrahim, F. A., & Arredondo, P. M. (1986). Ethical standards for cross-cultural counseling: Counselor preparation, practice, assessment, and research. *Journal of Counseling and Development, 64,* 349–352.

Kitchener, K. S. (1986). Teaching applied ethics in counselor education: An integration of psychological processes and philosophical analysis. *Journal of Counseling and Development, 64,* 306–310.

Knapp, S., & Vandecreek, L. (1982). Tarasoff: Five years later. *Professional Psychology, 13,* 511–516.

Ladd, E. T. (1971). Counselors, confidences, and the civil liberties of clients. *Personnel and Guidance Journal, 50,* 261–268.

Levenson, J. L. (1986). When a colleague practices unethically: Guidelines for interven-

tion. *Journal of Counseling and Development, 64,* 315–317.

Locke, D. C. (1984). Counselor registration in North Carolina. *Journal of Counseling and Development, 63,* 45–46.

Mabe, A. R., & Rollin, S. A. (1986). The role of a code of ethical standards in counseling. *Journal of Counseling and Development, 64,* 294–297.

Margolin, G. (1982). Ethical and legal considerations in marital and family therapy. *American Psychologist, 37,* 788–801.

Patterson, C. H. (1971). Are ethics different in different settings? *Personnel and Guidance Journal, 50,* 254–259.

Pelsma, D. M., & Borgers, S. B. (1986). Experience-based ethics: A developmental model of learning ethical reasoning. *Journal of Counseling and Development, 64,* 311–314.

Remley, T. P., Jr. (1985). The law and ethical practices in elementary and middle schools. *Elementary School Guidance & Counseling, 19,* 181–189.

Robinson, S. E., & Gross, D. R. (1986). Counseling research: Ethics and issues. *Journal of Counseling and Development, 64,* 331–333.

Rosenbaum, M. (1982). Preface. In M. Rosenbaum (Ed.), *Ethics and values in psychotherapy.* New York: Free Press.

Shertzer, B., & Stone, S. (1980). *Fundamentals of counseling* (3rd ed.). Boston: Houghton Mifflin.

Shimberg, B. (1981). Testing for licensure and certification. *American Psychologist, 36,* 1138–1146.

Stadler, H. (1986). Preface to the special issue. *Journal of Counseling and Development, 64,* 291.

Stude, E. W., & McKelvey, J. (1979). Ethics and the law: Friend or foe? *Personnel and Guidance Journal, 57,* 453–456.

Swanson, C. D. (1983a). The law and the counselor. In J. A. Brown & R. H. Pate,

Jr. (Eds.), *Being a counselor* (pp. 26–46). Monterey, CA: Brooks/Cole.

Swanson, C. D. (1983b). Ethics and the counselor. In J. A. Brown & R. H. Pate, Jr. (Eds.), *Being a counselor* (p. 47–65). Monterey, CA: Brooks/Cole.

Talbutt, L. C. (1981). Ethical standards: Assets and limitations. *Personnel and Guidance Journal, 60,* 110–112.

Tennyson, W. W., & Strom, S. M. (1986). Beyond professional standards: Developing responsibleness. *Journal of Counseling and Development, 64,* 298–302.

Van Hoose, W. H., & Kottler, J. (1985). *Ethical and legal issues in counseling and psychotherapy* (2nd ed.). San Francisco: Jossey-Bass.

Van Hoose, W. H., & Paradise, L. V. (1979). *Ethics in counseling and psychotherapy.* Cranston, RI: Carroll Press.

Welfel, E. R., & Lipsitz, N. E. (1983a). Wanted: A comprehensive approach to ethics research and education. *Counselor Education and Supervision, 22,* 320–332.

Welfel, E. R., & Lipsitz, N. E. (1983b). Ethical orientation of counselors: Its relationship to moral reasoning and level of training. *Counselor Education and Supervision, 23,* 35–45.

Wilcoxon, S. A. (1986). Engaging non-attending family members in marital and family counseling: Ethical issues. *Journal of Counseling and Development, 64,* 323–324.

Witmer, J. M., Wedl, L., & Black, B. (1986). Genetic counseling: Ethical and professional role implications. *Journal of Counseling and Development, 64,* 337–340.

Wittmer, J. P., & Loesch, L. C. (1986). Professional orientation. In M. D. Lewis, R. L. Hayes, & J. A. Lewis (Eds.), *The counseling profession* (pp. 301–330). Itasca, IL: Peacock.

# THE COUNSELOR
# AS SPECIALIST

Photo by James S. Davidson III.

# CHAPTER 11

# *Consultation*

She went about kissing frogs
  for in her once-upon-time mind
    that's what she had learned to do.
With each kiss came expectations
  of slimy green changing to Ajax white.
With each day came realizations
  that fly-eating, quick-tongued, croaking creatures
Don't magically turn to instant princes
  from the after effects of a fast-smooching,
    smooth-talking helping beauty.
So with regret she came back from a lively lily-pond
  to the sobering stacks of the village library
To page through the well-worn stories again
  and find in print what she knew in fact
    that even loved frogs sometimes stay frogs
      no matter how pretty the damsel or how high the hope.[1]

C ounselors are constantly challenged to provide appropriate mental health services. Sometimes, they can best perform their tasks through direct counseling with individuals, groups, or families; at other times, indirect services are more effective. In this chapter, we will examine one major method by which indirect services may be offered—consultation. Some theoretical approaches, such as the Adlerian and behavioral approaches, easily encompass consultation services because they emphasize teaching and do not always require person-to-person contact in order to be applied. Other theoretical approaches, such as an existential approach and Gestalt therapy, do not as easily encompass this way of helping because of their emphasis on close personal relationships.

## CONSULTATION: AN ACTIVITY IN SEARCH OF A DEFINITION

Consultation is a function expected of all counselors and one that is receiving increased attention (Hollis & Wantz, 1986). For example, on a national level, 35 courses in consultation were added to counselor education curricula between 1984 and 1987, thus making it the sixth most rapidly increasing area in such programs. Two special issues of the *Personnel and Guidance Journal* (February and March, 1978) and a special issue of *The Counseling Psychologist* (July, 1985) are exclusively devoted to consultation. In addition, consultation training is called for by the standards of the Associa-

256

tion for Counselor Education and Supervision (ACES) as a part of counselor education. And as Splete and Bernstein (1981) reported in their survey of 144 counselor education programs, 95 percent of the programs cover the topic of consultation in some way in their course offerings. Nutt (1976) also discovered that members of APA's Division 17 (Counseling Psychology) spend approximately 15 percent of their time in this role.

Yet in spite of all the attention it has received, consultation is not well conceptualized by many counselors or educators, and they often do not understand its exact nature (Drapela, 1983). Consequently, counselors misinterpret the concept or feel uncomfortable about engaging in consultative activities or both (Goodyear, 1976). Brown (1983) relates the story of a man whose image of a consultant was "someone who blows in, blows off, and blows out" (p. 124). As inaccurate as this idea is, it may well reflect the impreciseness that the word *consultation* has.

Although consultation has "proliferated wildly" since the early 1970s, "theory and research lag far behind" actual practice (Gallessich, 1985, p. 336). The reasons for this lag, according to Gallessich, are numerous but include the following:

☐ There is an atheoretical attitude toward consultation that inhibits its development. Gallessich (1982) points out that consultation originated in many different settings with various different groups and has multiple forms, thus making it hard to organize. In addition, many counseling consultants do not conceptualize or practice consultation as a specialized professional process.

☐ Consultation is not the primary activity of most professionals or of any professional group. Therefore, it lacks "the organizational support, leadership, and resources necessary for theory-building and research" (Gallessich, 1985, p. 342).

☐ There has been a rapid change in consultation practices. Unlike most other forms of helping, consultation reacts quickly to social, political, or technical changes. For example, the consultation practices of the late 1960s, which were humanistic in nature, were not widely employed in the more conservative early 1980s.

Other factors inhibiting the growth and development of consultation are difficulties in defining variables and in obtaining permission to do specialized research in organizational settings, and the changing nature of goals in the consultation process (i.e., initial goals may change).

There is no one universally agreed-upon definition of consultation (Kurpius & Robinson, 1978), but a number of diverse definitions delineate its key components. Ohlsen (1983) defines consultation as "an activity in which a professional helps another person in regard to a third . . ." (p. 347). Kurpius (1978) says that "by definition the process . . . tends to be *triadic* (consultant, consultee, and client or client system)" (p. 335). The ethical code of the American Association for Counseling and Development (AACD) (see Appendix A), further conceptualizes this term as "a *voluntary* relationship between a professional helper and help-needing individual, group or social units in which the consultant is providing help to the client(s) in defining and solving a work-related problem or potential problem with a client or client system." The definition is adapted from Kurpius (1978).

Gallessich (1985) says that all consulting approaches have the following characteristics in common.

☐ Consultation is content based (i.e., supported by a recognized body of knowledge)
☐ Consultation is goal oriented (i.e., it has an objective)
☐ Consultation is governed by variable roles and relationship rules
☐ Consultation is process orientated (i.e., gathering data, recommending solutions, offering support)
☐ Consultation is based on ideologies or value systems

Kurpius (1986) also stresses that consultation is systems oriented. Its aim is to help change aspects of the system, such as the system's structure or people, in order to change the system itself.

### Consultation vs. Counseling

Schmidt and Osborne (1981) found that in actual practice most counselors they surveyed did not distinguish between consultation and counseling activities. They concluded that "the ultimate goals of both are so similar that it is difficult to differentiate between the two when studying them as general processes" (p. 170). Indeed, many of the principles and processes of the two are similar, yet there are distinctions.

Stum (1982) notes that consultation and counseling are both interpersonal processes but that "the content of the consulting interview, unlike counseling, is a unit external to the counselee" (p. 297). Kurpius (1986) elaborates on Stum's emphasis by noting that most consultation takes place in a natural setting (i.e., the work environment of the consultee), whereas most counseling occurs at the designated center where a counselor is employed. Nelson and

Shifron (1985) state that consultation services are usually sought when a "system is in decline or crisis" (p. 301). The same might also be said for counseling; that is, most individuals, groups, or families do not seek this activity until they are under stress or in distress. But both consultation and counseling may be offered on a primary (preventive) level, also.

Skill in communication is another area in which there are similarities and contrasts between these two activities. Communication skills employed in consultation do not differ much from the ones used in counseling (Kurpius, 1986). Both counselors and consultants listen, attend, question, clarify, confront, and summarize. But consultants initially focus more on the content than the feeling, since the process is focused primarily on problems and issues.

Another parallel between consultation and counseling is in the role of the consultant and the counselor. Professionals who operate from either of these positions function to try to initiate change in the people with whom they work. Yet the consultant plays more of a catalyst role, because the consultant does not have "direct control over the consultee or the consultee's client" (Kurpius, 1986, p. 58). A final distinction is that even though the goal of consultation and counseling is similar: "to help individuals become more efficient, effective, independent, and resourceful in their abilities to solve the problems that they face" (Nelson & Shifron, 1985, p. 298), consultation activities are conducted more on an indirect, rather than a direct, level. Often a consultant will teach a consultee a skill that can be applied to a third party, whereas counseling skills are usually focused on and directly applicable to a specific individual, group, or system, with which the counselor is working.

## CONSULTATION MODELS

### Visual Representations of Consultation

Visual representations of consultation models aid counselors in understanding the concept more thoroughly. Drapela (1983) has presented one of the best of these representations (Figure 11.1), which is based on the cube concept examined in chapter 1. Drapela, like Kurpius, emphasizes that consultation is an "indirect service to individual clients or groups for whose benefits the helping intervention is undertaken" (p. 159). The issues discussed and assistance offered focus on a third party, even though there is direct consultant/consultee contact, as Bardon (1985) suggests. It is almost inevitable that the consultee will derive some benefit from

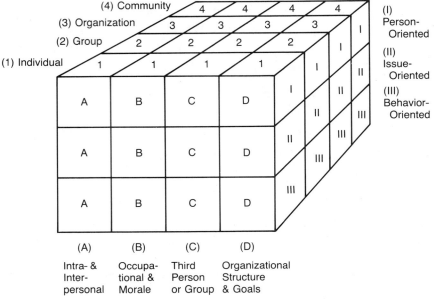

**FIGURE 11.1** Drapela's representation.

Source: From V. J. Drapela, *The Counselor as Consultant and Supervisor*, 1983. Courtesy of Charles C. Thomas, Publisher, Springfield, Illinois.

the process, but this gain is more a by-product of the process than a focus.

An interesting aspect of Drapela's model is that he defines consultation with comparisons to counseling and supervision. According to Drapela, counseling is "a direct service to individuals or groups for the purpose of stimulating self-awareness, helping to solve problems and make decisions, and promoting emotional and social growth" (p. 159). It is both interpersonal and intrapersonal. Supervision, on the other hand, is "the process of overseeing, guiding, and evaluating professional activities of counselors to ensure high quality of the counseling services delivered to clients" (p. 159). As an activity, it focuses on the outcome of counseling and is thus an indirect service to clients. Yet, it is also direct in its emphasis on the personal and professional growth of the supervised counselors. The distinctions made by Drapela of these three concepts clarify them even more.

The so-called Consulcube model (Blake & Mouton, 1976) is another visual representation of the process of consulting (Figure

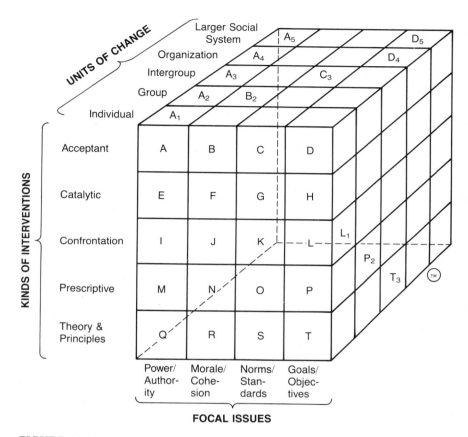

**FIGURE 11.2** Consulcube.

*Source:* From "Toward a General Theory of Consultation" by R. R. Blake and J. S. Mouton, 1978, *Personnel and Guidance Journal, 56,* p. 330. Copyright AACD. Reprinted with permission. No further reproduction authorized without further permission of AACD.

11.2). One face of the Consulcube reflects four focal issues of concern to clients—power/authority, morale/cohesion, norms/standards of conduct, and goals/objectives. Another face of the cube lists five different kinds of intervention: acceptance, catalytic, confrontation, prescriptive, and theory and principles. The final face of the cube indicates five units of change that may be addressed: individual, group, intergroup, organization, and larger social system. The focal issue that is identified suggests both the kind of intervention and the unit of change on which the client and consultant will concentrate. For instance, if the issue is morale/cohesion, a theory and principles approach on a group or organizational level might be employed. If the issue is power/authority, a confrontation intervention on an intergroup basis might be initiated.

### Four Conceptual Models

There are many different models of consultation besides the two visual representations. But only a few of them are comprehensive and useful in counseling. Among them are four comprehensive models of consultation identified by Kurpius and Brubaker (1976), Schein (1978), and Kurpius (1978):

☐ *Expert* or *Provision Model*   In this type of consultation, the consultant provides a direct service to consultees, who do not have the time, inclination, or perceived skills to deal with a particular problem area. Historically, this model of consultation was the first to develop (Kurpius & Robinson, 1978). It was used extensively in the 1940s and early 1950s. The advantage of the model is that experts can handle difficult problems and thus leave consultees free to manage their other duties without work conflicts. The major disadvantage of this model is that the consultant is blamed if a particular problem does not get better.

☐ *Doctor-Patient* or *Prescription Model*   This form of consultation does not require the consultant to bring about a change or "cure," as in the provision model. Instead, the consultant advises the consultee about what is wrong with the targeted third party and what should be done about it. A good way to conceptualize this method is to compare it to the traditional medical model, in which a patient's problem is diagnosed and a prescription to rectify the situation is given. This model is usually implemented when consultees lack confidence in their own intervention strategies.

☐ *Mediation Model*   In this model, consultants act as coordinators. Their main function is to help unify the services of a variety of people who are trying to solve a problem. They accomplish this goal in one of two ways: (1) they either coordinate the services already being provided, or (2) they create an alternative plan of services that represents a mutually acceptable synthesis of several solutions. An example of a situation where a consultant would function in this role is in a school system in which a handicapped child is receiving a variety of different services that are disrupting to both child and school. Through mediation, services are offered in a more systematic way and there is less disruption.

☐ *Process Consultation* or *Collaboration Model*   Consultants who operate from this model are facilitators of the problem-solving process. Their main task is to get their consultees actively involved in finding solutions to the present difficulties they have with clients. Thus, consultees must define their

problems clearly, analyze them thoroughly, design workable solutions, and then implement and evaluate their own plans of
action. Setting up an atmosphere in which this process can
happen is a major task for collaboration consultants. It requires the use of a number of interpersonal counseling skills,
such as empathy, active listening, and structuring. In addition,
to make the process work, consultants must be highly intelligent and analytical thinkers who are able to generate enthusiasm, optimism, and self-confidence in others. They must be
able to integrate and use affective, behavioral, and cognitive
dimensions of problem solving. Choice Awareness, as outlined
by Nelson and Shifron (1985), is a good example of collaborative
consultation. The goal of this type of consultation is to help
individuals become more aware of choices and more effective in
making them, such as in caring, enjoying, thinking, or working. Choices are defined as behaviors individuals have some
control over (Nelson, 1976). In the consultation process consultees learn that appropriate choices are usually followed by
appropriate responses.

## LEVELS OF CONSULTATION

There are several levels on which consultation services may be
delivered. Three of the most common ways to implement this process
are by working at the individual, group, and organizational/com-
munity level (Kurpius, 1985).

### Individual Consultation

One-to-one consultation is elaborated on by Kisch (1977). He
employs a role reversal process, in which a client role plays either
an active or passive consultant to the counselor who is role playing
the part of the client. The client sits in different chairs when playing
the separate roles. When passive, the client gives only familiar, safe,
and nonthreatening advice in response to the presented problem,
and there is no confrontation. When active, the client reflects
"thoughts, feelings, and strategies that are assertive, confrontive,
and may be novel and frightening" (p. 494). In each case, counselors
ask clients about the payoffs and risks of the client-consultant ideas
for change.

Another form of individual consultation is teaching self-management skills. Kahn (1976) points out that externally maintained
treatment modalities have not been very effective. In their place, he

proposes a four-part interdependent component model. The four basic components of this self-management model are:

- ☐ *Self-monitoring*   Persons observe their own behavior
- ☐ *Self-measurement*   Persons validate the degree to which the problem exists
- ☐ *Self-mediation*   Persons develop and implement strategies of change
- ☐ *Self-maintenance*   The process of continuously monitoring and measuring the desired effects of the self-management process

Kahn gives examples of excessive and deficit behaviors that can be managed through this model, including cigarette smoking, obesity, assertiveness, and depression. He points out that when individuals learn the steps of self-management, they can take preventive and remedial actions on their own.

Kurpius (1986) emphasizes that on an individual consultation level "mutual trust and respect are essential" (p. 61). For example, Fogle (1979) suggests that sometimes teaching individuals a constructive negative-thinking process can help to alleviate anxiety, restore motivation, promote risk-taking behaviors, and shift attention to the present. In this process, clients are instructed to think negatively about future-oriented events and make contingency plans if the worst possible situation occurs. Clients will only follow the instructions of the consultant if they believe what is being suggested will work. Often a consultant is required at this level to model a skill or prescribe a solution. Working on an individual level is limited if the consultee clearly has an individual problem, if a systems intervention is inappropriate or impossible, or if individual change would be more beneficial and efficient (Fuqua & Newman, 1985).

## *Group Consultation*

Group-level consultation is employed when several individuals share a similar problem, (e.g., in a work setting), or it is believed this type of consultation will be most effective, or both. On a group level, one of the most effective collaborative consultation models is the *C group* (Dinkmeyer, 1971; Dinkmeyer, 1973; Dinkmeyer & Carlson, 1973). All aspects of this approach begin with a *C*—collaboration, consultation, clarification, confrontation, concern, confidentiality, and commitment. Its primary purpose is to present new knowledge about human behavior to parents within a group setting. It encourages its members to work together as equals (collaboration), to give and receive input from each other (consultation), to understand the relationship between beliefs, feelings, and actions (clarification), to share openly with each other (confrontation), to empathize with one another (concern), to keep information within the group (confidentiality), and to make plans for specific changes (commitment). The C group has the potential to influence parent/child interactions dramatically, yet the group is always composed of adults. Further, the group is never used for counseling purposes, only for the sharing of information and for mutual support.

A program developed by Voight, Lawler, and Fulkerson (1980) that assists women in making mid-life decisions has some parallels to C groups, since it is directed toward promoting self-help and providing information in a group setting. This program makes use of women's existing social networks in order to help them become psychologically stronger and more informed about community resources and opportunities. A lasting advantage of the program is that participants not only become better educated and more self-directed but also continue to live in an environment where they can receive support and input from others who have gone through the same experience. In a similar way, a self-help center for adolescents, as described by O'Brien and Lewis (1975), functions as a form of group consultation. At the center, originally set up for substance abusers, clients are empowered with information and methods of helping themselves and each other.

Kurpius (1986) says that in work situations where group consultation is employed the group may be focused on either problem solving or persons. In a problem-solving group, the consultant will act as catalyst and facilitator. In person-focused groups, the consultant may help group members build teams in order to understand and resolve person problems.

### Organization/Community Consultation

Organization and community consultations are much larger in scope than individual or group consultations, and it is necessary for consultants to possess sophisticated knowledge of systems in order to operate effectively on this level. Unlike individual or group consultants, organization or community consultants are externally based to a project, though most of their activities involve individuals or groups. For example, counselors may function as political consultants, since they are "in a pivotal position to effectively communicate the concerns of people they serve to policy makers at local, state, and national levels of government" (Solomon, 1982, p. 580). Such activities involve lobbying with individual representatives as well as testifying before and making recommendations to special committees.

Other ways of consulting on a community or organizational level are mentioned by Conyne (1975) and Barrow and Prosen (1981).

Conyne's emphasis is on the individual within the environment, and he stresses an "environmental mapping" strategy that is people-centered. He emphasizes that when counselors find individuals who live or work in less-than-optimal mental health settings, they can work as change agents to try to improve the situation of the so-called target population. Barrow and Prosen also address the importance of counselors working as consultants on environmental factors, but they advocate a more global change process. They note that in addition to counselors' helping their clients find coping techniques to deal with stress, counselors must help clients change stress-producing environments (i.e., make the environment less stressful). This process is best achieved by working to change the structure of the system rather than the person in the system. Aplin (1985) has formulated a model that depicts the content and process areas of which a consultant should be aware in working on an organizational or community basis (Figure 11.3).

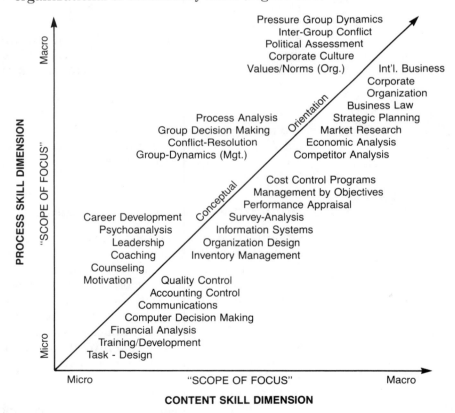

**FIGURE 11.3** Aplin's model.

*Source:* From J. C. Aplin, "Business Realities and Organizational Consultation," *The Counseling Psychologist, 13* (July 1978), p. 400. Copyright© 1978 by Sage Publications. Reprinted by permission of Sage Publications, Inc.

## STAGES AND ATTITUDES IN CONSULTATION

Developmental stages are an important part of many consultation activities. Two well-known theories propose distinct consultation stages. Splete (1982) describes a nine-stage process based on the premise that clients will collaborate with consultants to work on determined concerns. The stages are:

1. *Pre-contract*   The consultant clarifies personal skill and areas of expertise that can be used in the consultation process.

2. *Contract and exploration of relationship*   The consultant discusses a more formal arrangement between consultant and consultee. Areas that must be determined are the consultee's readiness and the consultant's ability to respond.

3. *Contracting*   A mutual agreement is set up that defines what services are to be offered and how.

4. *Problem identification*   Both the consultant and consultee determine and define the precise problem to be worked on and the desired outcome.

5. *Problem analysis*   The focus is on reviewing pertinent information and generating possible solutions.

6. *Feedback and planning*   Here the alternative solutions generated in stage 5 are evaluated and the probability of success determined. One or more solution plans are then systematically implemented.

7. *Implementation of the plan*   The consultee carries out the proposed plan with the consultant's support.

8. *Evaluation of the plan*   Both the consultant and consultee determine how well the plan worked in relationship to the desired outcome.

9. *Conclusion and termination of relationship*   Both parties in the consultation process review what has happened and plan for any follow-up, either independent of or with the consultant.

Although Splete's plan is detailed and most useful, it does not elaborate on counselor skills contained within the process. A model that does is one proposed by Dustin and Ehly (1984), which outlines a five-stage model of consultation, along with counselor techniques and behaviors that go with each. The model assumes that the consultant is working in a school setting with either a parent or teacher, but it has potential usefulness outside of that environment, such as in business, government, corrections, and rehabilitation.

1. *Phasing in*   The focus is on relationship building and can be compared to Splete's (1982) pre-contract stage. The consultant

at this juncture uses such skills as active listening, self-disclosure, and empathy and promotes a sense of trust.

2. *Problem identification*    Comparable to stages 2 through 4 in the Splete model, the focus is on determining whether a suspected third-party problem really exists. Consultants employ focusing skills as well as other counseling techniques, such as paraphrasing, restatement, genuineness, and goal setting.

3. *Implementation*    Similar to stages 5 through 7 of Splete's scheme, the focus is on defining strategies and setting up a time frame. Feedback is an important part of this process. Flexibility, dealing with resistance and negative feelings, and patience are other counselor skills involved.

4. *Follow-up and evaluation*    This stage merges with stage 3 at times, but its focus is distinct. It concentrates on the results gained from the consultation process, especially if the consultee is satisfied with the outcome of changes. Counselor skills involved in this stage are risk taking, openness, and persistence. These skills are especially important if it appears the consultee is dissatisfied or frustrated.

5. *Termination*    The consultant helps bring closure to previous activities. Some relationship skills such as empathy and genuineness are again employed. Giving and asking for feedback at this time are also important. It is vital that the consultant and consultee evaluate what was most profitable for each and what aspects of the procedure were less effective.

In addition to specific skills and abilities already covered, Splete (1982) lists four attitude areas that are generally important if one is to function as a consultant. First, consultants must display an attitude of professionalism. They must take responsibility for helping their clients deal with immediate and long-term problems. Second, consultants must be mature. They have to be willing to stand up for their own views, take risks, and deal with hostility or rejection. Third, consultants need to be open-minded and not close off ideas and input into the problem-solving process too soon. Finally, professionals who function in this capacity need to believe in the importance of individuals and place people above technology.

## SPECIFIC AREAS OF CONSULTATION

Consultation is most often thought of as occurring in schools and community agency settings, though the process may take place in almost any environment. In this section, we will examine some of the work which has been conducted in school and agency areas as an example of the kind of consultation programs that can be set up.

### School Consultation

The conceptualization of the school counselor as a consultant is one Kahnweiler (1979) has traced from its beginnings in the late 1950s. As he points out, articles and books on how the school counselor should be a consultant have evolved in theory and practice. Kahnweiler thinks more has been written about this subject than has actually been done in it. Nevertheless, he believes the difference between theory and practice can be overcome and that the counselor-as-consultant is a viable model. Podemski and Childers (1980) agree, seeing school counselors as being in the perfect position to act as consultants and change agents. They point out that in school organization charts, the counselor's position is defined as one with staff authority rather than line authority. A staff authority position is one in which the person in it is expected to have specialized knowledge and act in an advisory and supportive way to others. By functioning in this manner, school counselors help bring about environmental and systematic changes by advising those in positions of power what conditions need modifying and then supporting efforts to make those improvements.

Umansky and Holloway (1984) view the many aspects of consultation as a way of serving students and the larger population of the school community without increasing expenditures. They advocate four approaches to consultation in the schools—Adlerian-based, behavioral, mental health, and organizational development. The Adlerian-based approach is a psychological education model and assumes that individuals, groups, and communities lack information. Thus, the consultant teaches within the organizational structure of the school and emphasizes ways to promote positive behavior in children. The behavioral approach, also geared to teaching, concentrates on instructing consultees how to use behavioral principles in working with students and how to collect empirical data to validate each intervention strategy.

The mental health approach is based on the broader community mental health approach developed by Caplan (1970). Underlying mental health consultation is psychodynamic theory. The goal of this approach is to help teachers and other powerful personnel in the school gain new insight into themselves and their students. Finally, the organizational development approach emphasizes the context in which problems arise. Thus, if students and teachers have problems, the climate of the school becomes the focus of concern. To be most helpful, the consultant will have to work on changing the school's atmosphere and structure. Sometimes the task requires the support of administrators who may not favor such an objective. In other cases, it involves school counselors' setting up an environment in which other school personnel, mainly teachers, feel "that it is natural to consult and work with counselors" (Edgemon, Remley, & Snoddy, 1985, p. 298).

Brown, Wyne, Blackburn, and Powell (1979) suggest the use of group consultation sessions with teachers as an effective way of providing services to them and to schools in general. These authors also advocate and outline means of providing consultation services to exceptional children, students, parents, developers of curricula, and community organizations. They operate from three theoretical bases in the consultation process—neo-client-centered, Adlerian, and behavioral.

### Agency Consultation

Werner (1978) points out that agency consultation came about as a result of the passage of the Community Mental Health Centers Act in 1963. Implicit within the act is the philosophy that mental health is to be viewed from a local community perspective with an emphasis on prevention. The definition of prevention employed most often is a three-level one set forth by Caplan (1964).

The first level consists of *primary prevention*, that is, a reduction in the incidences of mental disorders. This goal is achieved within the general population "by actively changing environments and settings and by teaching life skills" (Goodyear, 1976, p. 513). One of the primary activities at this level of intervention is consultation. *Secondary prevention*, a reduction in the duration of mental disorders, is the next focus. This goal is achieved through working with individuals to forestall or alleviate problem areas in their lives and by attempting early detection and reversal of acute psychological crises. Finally, *tertiary prevention* is a reduction in the impairment that may result from psychological disorders. One way to conceptualize this level of prevention is as treatment. The more successful primary and secondary prevention are, the less need there will be for tertiary prevention.

There are numerous examples of primary prevention in agency settings. Werner (1978), building on Caplan's work, proposes six levels community mental health consultation may take:

*Client-centered case consultation* The goal is to enable the consultee to deal more effectively with the current situation and similar situations in the future.

*Consultee-centered case consultation* The goal is to identify collaboratively consultee difficulties in working with certain types of clients and help the consultee develop skills to deal effectively with this and future similar situations.

*Program-centered administration consultation* The goal is to help the consultee deal more effectively with specific parts of a mental health program and improve the consultee's abilities to function with future similar program problems.

*Consultee-centered administrative consultation* The goal is to identify consultee problems generated by implementing a mental health program and to develop collaboratively the consultee's skills in dealing with future similar problems.

*Community-centered ad hoc consultation* The goal is to enable an ad hoc consultee to deal more effectively with community problems encountered while developing a temporary program of mental health services.

*Consultee-centered ad hoc consultation* The goal is to identify collaboratively the ad hoc consultee's problems generated in providing temporary mental health services and to take steps to help the consultee develop skills in dealing with these problems.

In addition to specific levels of consultation intervention, Aplin (1985) points out that consultants who work with such agencies as public corporations, the government, or universities must be aware of trends that affect the process of consultation itself. He lists five trends in the 1980s that have influenced agency consultation:

☐ "Downsizing" of organizations
☐ Creation of semiautonomous work units brought about by mergers
☐ Rebirth of commitment "leadership" by managers
☐ Process-based technologies (i.e., robotics and computers) in manufacturing
☐ Egalitarian social and organizational values

Because of the rapid changes in agencies, there is a great demand for consultation skills, but "the key to successfully implementing systems change programs is to increase the basic skills the consultant brings to the change process." Aplin stresses that the demands on consultants "will grow in direct proportion to growth in organizational complexity and turbulence associated with underlying social and economic change" (p. 401).

## TRAINING IN CONSULTATION

Since the late 1970s a number of models for training individuals in consultation skills have been developed (Conoley, 1981; Kratochwill & Bergan, 1978; Randolph, 1980). Most of these models have been competency-based and have emphasized different modes of training consultants, such as didactic, laboratory, field placement, and supervision (Gallessich, 1974).

Stum's (1982) Directed Individual Response- Educational Consulting Technique (DIRECT) is an excellent example of a model that has attempted to synthesize previous knowledge and help students learn what they are supposed to do in a consulting interview and how they are supposed to do it. Stum views consulting as a systematic process with sequential steps. Thus the model is structured so that beginning students can conceptualize the consultation process developmentally; for example: (1) establish consulting relationship, (2) identify and clarify the problem situation, (3) determine desired outcome, (4) develop ideas and strategies, (5) develop a plan, (6) specify the plan, and (7) confirm consulting relationship. The DIRECT model also specifies four sequential leads for each of those seven developmental steps. These leads, based on systematic human-relations training, provide guidelines for the consultant and consultee to enter, initiate, educate, and evaluate each of the steps in the consulting process. "Cue" words are provided for the consultant trainee at each step and level of the process. An evaluation chart—the Technique and Relationship Evaluation Chart (TREC)—is available to assess the degree of competency the consultant trainee achieves (Figure 11.4).

Brown (1985) also proposes developmental stages for training consultants. He stresses didactic, laboratory, and field placement competencies that must be mastered. In addition, he elaborates on problems (e.g., resistance) and strategies to overcome these problems (e.g., ways to select proper interventions). His model requires instructors of consultant trainees to offer assistance to these individuals in mastering consultation skills through such methods as analyzing case histories, modeling cognitive strategies by "talking through" cases, and by employing a Socratic method of inquiry. Brown emphasizes that the well-trained consultant has mastered conceptual and relationship skills at each of five discernable stages of consultation: (1) relationship or entry, (2) assessment or problem identification, (3) goal setting, (4) choosing and implementing change strategies, and (5) evaluation and termination.

In the future, Gallessich (1985) advocates that consultation models and training be based on one of three not mutually exclusive models. The first is scientific-technological consultation, which focuses on knowledge deficits. In this model the consultant's primary role is that of an expert on information and technique. The second model is human-development consultation, which emphasizes that the primary role of the consultant is that of educator and facilitator in affective and cognitive processes that influence professional and personal relationships in an organization. The final model conceptualized by Gallessich is social/political consultation, in which the consultant takes a partisan role to help change organizations so they conform more with particular values, such as democracy. Methods of training consultants in these models are still being developed.

## SUMMARY

In this chapter we have examined how consultation is a systematic concept with a set of skills that is growing in importance. Ironically, consultation is still not well defined, although there are a number of unifying qualities indicative of the process. Several definitions of the term within the counseling profession emphasize that consultation is primarily an indirect service, usually triadic, voluntary in nature, based on roles, rules, and values, and goal oriented. There are distinct differences between consultation and counseling, such as the directness of the activity, the setting in which it is conducted, and the way communications are focused. Yet, as Schmidt and Osborne (1981) point out, little or no distinction is often made in consultation and counseling activities.

Visual representations of the consultation models, such as those by Drapela (1983) and Blake and Mouton (1978), help clarify ways in which consultation services may be offered. The four models of comprehensive consultation found in the literature—expert (provision), doctor-patient (prescription), mediation, and process/collaboration—go even further in emphasizing the multidimensional aspects of this concept. There are distinct consultation levels (e.g., individual, group, and organizational) and definite stages that the process goes through (e.g., phasing in, problem identification,

**Step A**—Establish Consulting Format

| *Behavior* | *Lead* |
|---|---|
| *Level 1*<br>The consultant listens, observes, repeats, and paraphrases. Attending and responding promotes understanding. | "You're saying that ______ "<br>"The problem seems to be ______ "<br>"So, the situation is ______ " |
| *Level 2*<br>The consultant uses the term *consult* or *collaborate* in regards to working together. Explaining the use of a systematic process sets the tone for the interview. | "We can consult together about ______ "<br>"In our work, we'll use a problem-solving process." |
| *Level 3*<br>The consultant briefly explains the initial steps in the problem-resolution process. This is the first "teaching" of the model and further establishes the direction for the consulting interview. | "We'll go through several steps working together."<br>"First, in clarifying the problem, we'll be ______ "<br>"Later on, we'll be trying to set some goals in regards to ______ " |
| *Level 4*<br>The consultant "checks-in" regarding this step and then suggests moving ahead to the next step. | "Can we work together along these lines?"<br>"Let's go ahead and clarify the problem further." |

**Step B**—Identify-Clarify the Problem

| *Behavior* | *Lead* |
|---|---|
| *Level 1*<br>The consultant clarifies the history, environment, causes and effects of the problem-situation. | "Tell me more about the background of ______ "<br>"What do you see as the effects of ______ "<br>"So, your position in this is that of ______ " |
| *Level 2*<br>The consultant summarizes the major factors presented in the problem-situation. A dominant "theme" is stated. | "The major factors seems to be ______ "<br>"Then to summarize, ______ " |

**FIGURE 11.4** DIRECT chart.

*Source:* From "DIRECT—A Consultation Skills Training Model" by D. Stum, 1982, *Personnel and Guidance Journal, 60,* p. 300. Copyright AACD. Reprinted with permission. No further reproduction authorized without further permission of AACD.

| *Behavior* | *Lead* |
|---|---|

**Level 3**

The consultant responds to the "feeling" of the consultee as well as the theme in the problem-situation. The consultant may have to narrow the scope of the presented problem or confront inconsistencies in the presented problem.

"You're _____ because of _____ "
    (feeling)      (theme)
"This problem seems immense. Perhaps, we can isolate part of the problem and work on that."
"You say the major problem is _____ but I also hear your concern about _____ "

**Level 4**

The consultant checks-in regarding this step and then suggests moving ahead to the next step.

"Do we have a good handle on the nature of the problem-situation?"
"Let's talk about our goals in this situation."

**Step C—Set Desired Outcomes (Goals)**

| *Behavior* | *Lead* |
|---|---|

**Level 1**

The consultant asks the consultee to discuss and list the desired outcomes and goals hoped for in this situation.

"We need to define what we want to happen. This would be the outcomes desired or goals."
"How would you like things to be?"
"Let's list the goals you have in regards to _____ "

**Level 2**

The consultant clarifies and summarizes the goals and outcomes stated.

"Your major goals seems to be _____ "
"So, the outcome desired is that _____ "
Then, to summarize _____ "

**Level 3**

The consultant asks that outcomes be stated in specific terms. The consultant may re-state the goals in objective or measureable terms.

"How would you measure progress toward your goal?"
"You could determine progress toward your goal by _____ "

**Level 4**

The consultant checks-in regarding this step and then suggests moving ahead to the next step.

"Have we set the desired outcomes/goals to work toward in this situation?"
"Let's try and develop some ideas to meet these goals."

**FIGURE 11.4** *continued*

implementation, follow-up, and termination). Important skills and attitudes make up the complete process. Consultation is implemented in school and agency settings, and training models are being used to teach consultation skills. But as Brown (1985) and Gallessich (1985) clearly imply, consultation is still developing.

## CLASSROOM ACTIVITIES

1. How do you distinguish consultation from counseling? Discuss your ideas with a fellow classmate and then with the class as a whole.
2. Which of the four comprehensive models of consultation identified in this chapter do you think is most appropriate for clients you plan to work with in the future? Why? Which of these models do you consider least appropriate for your future work? Discuss your opinions with another classmate and the class as a whole.
3. Which stage in the consultation process do you think is most important? Which one do you think is most difficult? Are they the same? Discuss in a small group setting of three other classmates what skills you possess that will enable you to be an effective consultant. Identify skills you must refine or develop within yourself to work in this capacity.
4. What theoretical approach do you find most attractive as a basis for consultation services? Divide the class into groups that are based on a similar orientation. After each group has had an opportunity to discuss their ideas, share them with fellow classmates.
5. Do you think there are other proactive activities counselors can engage in that cannot be classified as a part of counseling or consultation? What specific behaviors would you place in such a category? Discuss your ideas in groups of four and then with the class as a whole.

## REFERENCES

Aplin, J. C. (1985). Business realities and organizational consultation. *The Counseling Psychologist, 13,* 396–402.

Bardon, J. I. (1985). On the verge of a breakthrough. *The Counseling Psychologist, 13,* 355–362.

Barrow, J. C., & Prosen, S. S. (1981). A model of stress and counseling interventions. *Personnel and Guidance Journal, 60,* 5–10.

Blake, R. R., & Mouton, J. S. (1978). Toward a general theory of consultation. *Personnel and Guidance Journal, 56,* 328–330.

Brown, D. (1985). The preservice training and supervision of consultants. *The Counseling Psychologist, 13,* 410–425.

Brown, D., Wyne, M. D., Blackburn, J. E., & Powell, W. C. (1979). *Consultation: Strategy for improving education.* Boston: Allyn & Bacon.

Brown, J. A. (1983). Consultation. In J. A. Brown & R. H. Pate, Jr. (Eds.), *Being a counselor: Directions and challenges* (pp. 124–146). Monterey, CA: Brooks/ Cole.

Caplan, G. (1970). *The theory and practice of mental health consultation.* New York: Basic Books.

Conoley, J. C. (1981). Emergent training issues in consultation. In J. C. Conoley (Ed.), *Consultation in schools: Theory, research procedures* (pp. 223–263). New York: Academic Press.

Conyne, R. K. (1975). Environmental assessment: Mapping for counselor action. *Personnel and Guidance Journal, 54,* 150–154.

Dinkmeyer, D. C. (1971). The "C" group: Integrating knowledge and experience to change behavior. *The Counseling Psychologist, 3,* 63–72.

Dinkmeyer, D. C. (1973). The parent C group. *Personnel and Guidance Journal, 52,* 4.

Dinkmeyer, D., & Carlson, J. (1973). *Consulting: Facilitating human potential and processes.* Columbus, OH: Merrill.

Drapela, V. J. (1983). Counseling, consultation, and supervision: A visual clarification of their relationship. *Personnel and Guidance Journal, 62,* 158–162.

Dustin, D., & Ehly, S. (1984). Skills for effective consultation. *The School Counselor, 31,* 23–29.

Edgemon, A. W., Remley, T. P., Jr., & Snoddy, H. N. (1985). Integrating the counselor's point of view. *The School Counselor, 32,* 296–301.

Fogle, D. O. (1979). Preparing students for the worst: The power of negative thinking. *Personnel and Guidance Journal, 57,* 364–367.

Fuqua, D. R., & Newman, J. L. (1985). Individual consultation. *The Counseling Psychologist, 13,* 390–395.

Gallessich, J. (1974). Training the school psychologist for consultation. *Journal of School Psychology, 12,* 138–149.

Gallessich, J. (1982). *The profession and practice of consultation.* San Francisco: Jossey-Bass.

Gallessich, J. (1985). Toward a meta-theory of consultation. *The Counseling Psychologist, 13,* 336–354.

Gladding, S. T. (1976). Of frogs, princes and lily pond changes. In S. T. Gladding (Ed.), *Reality sits in a green-cushioned chair* (p. 17). Atlanta: Collegiate Press.

Goodyear, R. K. (1976). Counselors as community psychologists. *Personnel and Guidance Journal, 54,* 512–516.

Hollis, J. W., & Wantz, R. A. (1986). *Counselor preparation 1986–89: Programs, personnel, trends* (6th ed.). Muncie, IN: Accelerated Development.

Kahn, W. J. (1976). Self-management: Learning to be our own counselor. *Personnel and Guidance Journal, 55,* 176–180.

Kahnweiler, W. M. (1979). The school counselor as consultant: A historical review. *Personnel and Guidance Journal, 57,* 374–380.

Kisch, R. M. (1977). Client as "consultant-observer" in the role-play model. *Personnel and Guidance Journal, 55,* 494–495.

Kratochwill, T. R., & Bergan, J. R. (1978). Training school psychologists: Some perspectives on competency-based behavioral consultation models. *Professional Psychology, 9,* 71–82.

Kurpius, D. J. (1978). Consultation theory and process: An integrated model. *Personnel and Guidance Journal, 56,* 335–338.

Kurpius, D. J. (1985). Consultation interventions: Successes, failures, and proposals. *The Counseling Psychologist, 13,* 368–389.

Kurpius, D. J. (1986). Consultation: An important human and organizational intervention. *Journal of Counseling and Human Service Professions, 1,* 58–66.

Kurpius, D. J., & Brubaker, J. C. (1976). *Psycho-educational consultation: Definitions-functions-preparation.* Bloomington, IN: Indiana University Press.

Kurpius, D. J., & Robinson, S. E. (1978). An overview of consultation. *Personnel and Guidance Journal, 56,* 321–323.

Nelson, R. C. (1976). Choice awareness: An unlimited horizon. *Personnel and Guidance Journal, 54,* 463–467.

Nelson, R. C., & Shifron, R. (1985). Choice awareness in consultation. *Counselor Education and Supervision, 24,* 298–306.

Nutt, R. L. (1976). A study of consultation services provided by counseling psychologists. *Dissertation Abstracts International, 37,* 5816B. (University Microfilms No. 77-9516, 157).

O'Brien, B. A. & Lewis, M. (1975). A community adolescent self-help center. *Personnel and Guidance Journal, 54,* 212–216.

Ohlsen, M. M. (1983). *Introduction to counseling.* Itasca, IL: Peacock.

Podemski, R. S., & Childers, J. H., Jr. (1980). The counselor as change agent: An organizational analysis. *The School Counselor, 27,* 168–174.

Randolph, D. (1980). Teaching consultation for mental health and educational settings. *Counselor Education and Supervision, 33,* 117–123.

Schein, E. H. (1978). The role of the consultant: Content expert or process facilitator? *Personnel and Guidance Journal, 56,* 339–343.

Schmidt, J. J., & Osborne, W. L. (1981). Counseling and consultation: Separate processes or the same? *Personnel and Guidance Journal, 60,* 168–170.

Solomon, C. (1982). Special issue on political action: Introduction. *Personnel and Guidance Journal, 60,* 580.

Splete, H. H. (1982). Consultation by the counselor. *Counseling and Human Development, 15,* 1–7.

Splete, H., & Bernstein, B. (1981). A survey of consultation training as part of counselor education programs. *Personnel and Guidance Journal, 59,* 470–472.

Stum, D. (1982). DIRECT—A consultation skills training model. *Personnel and Guidance Journal, 60,* 296–302.

Umansky, D. L., & Holloway, E. L. (1984). The counselor as consultant: From model to practice. *The School Counselor, 31,* 329–338.

Voight, N. L., Lawler, A., & Fulkerson, K. F. (1980). Community-based guidance: A "Tupperware party" approach to mid-life decision making. *Personnel and Guidance Journal, 59,* 106–107.

Werner, J. L. (1978). Community mental health consultation with agencies. *Personnel and Guidance Journal, 56,* 364–368.

Photo by James S. Davidson III.

# CHAPTER 12

# Group Counseling

Who am I in this pilgrim group
      whose members differ so in perception?
Am I a Miles Standish man,
      with both feet on the ground,
            who lets others speak for him
                  because the fear of failure is softened somewhat
                  if a risk is never taken?
Or am I more a John Alden
      polite and proper, speaking for others
            in the courting of beauty
                  but not seeking such for self?
Perhaps I am more than either man
      or maybe I'm both!
That is what really scares me![1]

---

**O**rganized group counseling, a fairly new phenomenon, makes use of people's tendency to gather and work in groups. It was at the beginning of the twentieth century that therapeutic group work was formalized. Vander Kolk (1985) credits Joseph Hersey Pratt, a physician, for starting the first psychotherapy group in 1905. Pratt's group members were tubercular outpatients at Boston's Massachusetts General Hospital. Other pioneers in the group counseling movement were:

☐ J. L. Moreno, who introduced the term *group psychotherapy* into the counseling literature in the 1920s.

☐ Alexander Wolf and Emanuel Schwartz, who started the first certification program in group therapy at New York Medical College in the late 1940s.

☐ Kurt Lewin, whose field theory concepts in the 1930s and 1940s, became the basis for the Tavistock small study groups in Britain and the T-group movement in the United States.

☐ Fritz Perls, whose Gestalt approach to group work attracted new interest in the field.

☐ William Schutz and Jack Gibb, who emphasized a humanistic aspect to T-group work with their focus on personal growth as a legitimate goal of group work.

☐ Carl Rogers, who used the term *basic encounter group* in the 1960s to describe his humanistic and growth-oriented approach to working with people in groups. Rogers, like Perls, was a popular practitioner whose emphasis on groups encouraged other counselors to take a new look at this approach.

In this chapter we will examine the place of groups in counseling, including the types of groups most often used, the theoretical basis for group counseling, issues and stages in groups, and qualities of effective group leaders. Both national and local organizations have been established for professionals engaged primarily in the practice of leading groups. One of the most comprehensive of these, and the one to which most professional counselors belong, is the Association for Specialists in Group Work (ASGW), a national division of the American Association for Counseling and Development. This organization, which has a diverse membership of over 4,500 members, was chartered by AACD in 1974 (Carroll & Levo, 1985). It has been a leader in the establishment of educational and ethical guidelines for group leaders and publishes a quarterly journal, *The Journal for Specialists in Group Work.*

## THE PLACE OF GROUPS IN COUNSELING

Groups have a unique place in counseling. Everyone spends some time on an average day in group activities, for example, with schoolmates or business associates. Gregariousness is a part of human nature, and many personal and professional skills are learned in group interactions. It is only natural, then, for counselors to make use of this primary way of human interaction. Groups are an economical and effective means of helping individuals who share similar problems and concerns. As Corey (1983) points out, counselors who limit themselves to competency in individual counseling skills limit their options for helping.

A major decision most counselors have to make about groups involves when, where, and with whom to use them. There are some situations in which groups are not appropriate ways of helping. For instance, a counselor employed by a company would be unwise to use groups to counsel employees with personal problems who are unequal in rank and seniority in the corporate network. Likewise, a school counselor would be foolish to use a group setting as a way of working with children who are all behaviorally disruptive. But a group may be ideal when a counselor can schedule a regular time in a quiet, uninterrupted setting and has clients who can benefit from interacting with each other and who are not too disruptive or unequal. Groups differ in purpose, composition, and length, but in general they all involve *work*, which Gazda (1978) describes as "the dynamic interaction between collections of individuals for prevention or remediation of difficulties or for the enhancement of personal growth/enrichment . . ." (p. 260).

If set up properly, groups can be effective in helping individuals with a variety of problems and concerns. There are literally hundreds of studies that describe group approaches and statistically support the effectiveness of various forms of groups. Documentation of group experiences is almost occurring too fast to keep up with, though some researchers, such as Zimpfer (1981), periodically write comprehensive reviews of the field. Some of the findings reveal that:

☐ Adolescent aggression can be reduced through group assertive training (Huey, 1983).

☐ Single-parent fathers can learn more about themselves and parenting skills through group experiences (Tedder, Libbee, & Scherman, 1981).

☐ Women can be assisted in exploring and constructively dealing with anger in a group workshop setting (Hotelling & Reese, 1983).

☐ Black alcoholics, because of past socialization experiences, are especially helped in groups (Harper, 1984).

☐ Career awareness may be dealt with very effectively in groups (McWhirter, Nichols, & Banks, 1984).

☐ Perfectionist thinkers may be helped to break non-productive thought processes through group intervention (Barrow & Moore, 1983).

In addition, groups have a number of general advantages. Group members can come to realize they are not alone, unique, or abnormal in their problems and concerns. Through their interaction with one another, they may learn more about themselves in social situations. In groups, clients can try out new behaviors and ways of interacting, because the group atmosphere provides a safe environment to experiment with change and receive feedback. Members also observe how others attack and resolve problems, thus picking up skills vicariously. Finally, the group may serve as a catalyst to help a person realize a want or need for individual counseling.

Yet groups are not a panacea for all people and problems; they have definite limitations and some disadvantages. Many client concerns and personalities are not well suited for groups. The problems of individuals may not be dealt with in enough depth in a group. In addition, group pressure may force a client to take actions, such as self-disclosure, before being ready, or the group may lapse into a group think mentality, in which stereotypical and stale thought processes become the norm. Some individuals may also try to use the group for escape or for selfish purposes and thereby disrupt the group process. It may be difficult for a leader to find a suitable time to conduct a group so that all who wish to participate can. Finally, if group members do not reflect the social milieu in which clients normally operate, what they learn from the group experience may not be very relevant.

## TYPES OF GROUPS

Groups come in many forms and "there seems to be a group experience tailored to suit the interests and needs of virtually anyone who seeks psychotherapy, personal growth, or simply support and companionship from others" (Lynn & Frauman, 1985, p. 423). The following types of groups are among the most common.

***Group Guidance.*** The major purpose of group guidance is to provide information. Guidance groups are often found in educational settings, such as school classrooms, where teachers or counselors help students come to understand themselves, others, and the world better. Information is disseminated during this process, but the most important part of the process revolves around the discussion by group members of the relevance of this information for themselves (Ohlsen, 1970). Topics covered in group guidance may vary from the general to the specific. In school settings such instructional materials as unfinished stories, puppet plays, movies/films, audio interviews, and guest speakers are often employed. In adult settings, group guidance occurs in more sophisticated forms and relates to situational dilemmas, physical or mental health, motivation, and the acquiring of skills. Group guidance leaders are limited only by their imagination and available resources.

***Group Counseling.*** Group counseling has both a preventive and a remediation purpose (Gazda, 1978). The focus of the group is on the experience of its members, though some information may be imparted. Those involved in group counseling are functioning adequately in most areas of life but seek help either to resolve a situational problem or avoid anticipated developmental difficulties or both. Shertzer and Stone (1981) point out that the optimal number of individuals included in group counseling is six, though the number may vary from four to eight.

Gazda (1978) distinguishes group counseling from group guidance in the following ways:

☐ Group counseling is recommended for individuals who are having temporary or continuing problems, whereas group guidance is recommended, at least in the schools, on a regular basis as a personal educational measure.

☐ Group counseling is more direct than group guidance in attempting to modify attitudes and behaviors. For instance, group counseling stresses the affective involvement of its participants, whereas group guidance concentrates more on the cognitive and intellectual functioning of its members.

☐ Group counseling is conducted in a small, intimate setting, whereas group guidance is more applicable to classroom-size environments.

**Group Psychotherapy.**    Generally, there is some overlap in group counseling and group psychotherapy. Moreno (1962), who coined the term *group psychotherapy,* defines it as treating people in groups. It is understood from this definition that a group comprises two or more people and a therapist. The emphasis in group psychotherapy is on treatment and remediation (Gazda, 1970). There are many forms of group psychotherapy, but often the setting for this activity is in a hospital or mental health center. Yalom (1975) notes that according to studies, certain types of individuals are poor candidates for outpatient, intensive group psychotherapy. Among these are depressives, incessant talkers, paranoids, schizoid and sociopathic personalities, suicidals, and extremely narcissistic individuals. It may be easier to identify group psychotherapy candidates who should be excluded than pick those who should be included. Regardless, group psychotherapy is an American form of treatment and, as such, has provided much of the rationale for the emergence of group counseling (Gazda, 1978). Figure 12.1 shows the relationships among group guidance, group counseling, and group psychotherapy.

**T-Groups.**    The first T-group (the *T* stands for training) was conducted at the National Training Laboratories (NTL) in Bethel, Maine, in 1947. These groups appeared at a time when neither group counseling nor group psychotherapy was very popular. Kurt Lewin's ideas about group dynamics formed the basis for the original groups. Since that time, T-groups have evolved from a focus on task accomplishment to a primary emphasis on interpersonal relationships (Vander Kolk, 1985). Although it is difficult to classify T-groups in just one way, members of such groups are likely to learn

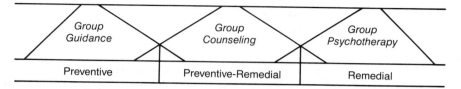

**FIGURE 12.1** Relationships among types of groups.

*Source:* From GROUP COUNSELING: A DEVELOPMENTAL APPROACH by George M. Gazda, 1970, Boston, Allyn & Bacon. Copyright 1970 by Allyn & Bacon, Inc. Reprinted by permission.

from the experience how one's behavior in a group influences others' behavior and vice versa. In this respect T-groups are similar to forms of family counseling in which the emphasis is both on how the system operates and on how an individual within such a system functions.

***Encounter Group.*** Lynn and Frauman (1985) note that encounter groups emerged from T-groups as an attempt to bring greater focus on the growth of individual members of the group instead of the group itself. Encounter groups are intended for basically "normally functioning" people who want to "grow, change, and develop" (Lieberman, 1975, p. 440). These groups take many forms, from the minimally structured groups of Carl Rogers (1970) to the highly structured, open-ended groups of William Schutz (1971). Regardless of the structure, the primary emphasis of the group is on individual expression and recognition of affect.

***Group Marathon.*** A group marathon is designed as an extended, one-session group experience that breaks down defensive barriers individuals may otherwise employ. It usually lasts for a minimum of 24 hours. The concept was pioneered by Frederick Stoller and George Bach in the 1960s (Lynn & Frauman, 1985). Group marathons have been used successfully in working with substance abusers in rehabilitation programs and with normally functioning individuals in encounter group, T-group, or group counseling settings.

***Psychodrama.*** J. L. Moreno, a Viennese psychiatrist, is credited as being the originator of psychodrama. This type of group experience, which was centered for decades at Saint Elizabeth's Hospital in Washington, D.C., was initially used only with patients in mental hospitals. In group psychodrama, which is now used in many settings, members enact unrehearsed role plays, with the leader of the group serving as the director. Other group members serve as actors in the protagonist's play, give feedback to the protagonist as members of the audience, or do both. This type of group is popular with behaviorists, Gestaltists, and encounter group leaders who have adapted it as a way of helping clients experience the emotional qualities of an event.

***Self-Help Group.*** Since the 1970s, self-help groups have grown in prominence. These groups, which are usually led by a layperson, focus on serving the needs of particular populations not serviced by mental health workers (Corey, 1985). Some examples of these groups are Alcoholics Anonymous, Weight Watchers, and Lamplighters. Lieberman (1980) mentions that there are over 200 kinds of self-help groups in the United States. They meet in churches, recreation centers, schools, and other community buildings. Occasionally, they make use of professional consultants, but the primary focus of self-help groups is to provide a supportive and accepting climate for the members themselves. Individual change within a group is the result of cognitive input, emotional support, and behavioral strategies group members receive from one another. Cole (1983) and Corey (1985) see self-help groups as healthy for the general public, and Corey thinks these groups are complementary to individual or group counseling conducted by professional counselors.

***Other Groups.*** There are also specialized groups set up for particular populations of a developmental age or stage, such as children, adolescents, adults, and the elderly. Corey (1983) offers suggestions on how to initiate such groups and what procedures work best with them. It is important to realize that the collective needs within any group are based on those of its members. No two groups or group experiences are ever the same.

Before joining a group, it is important to check first with the group organizer to make sure one receives the type of experience sought. Corey (1985) lists 12 issues that potential group participants have a right to expect clarification on before they enroll in a group. Among the most important information a potential group member should obtain are:

☐ A clear statement of the group's purpose.

☐ A description of the group format, ground rules, and basic procedures.

☐ A statement about the educational and training qualifications of the group leader(s).

☐ A pregroup interview to determine whether the potential group leader and members are suited for one's needs at the time.

☐ A disclosure about the risks involved in being in a group and the rights and responsibilities of group members.

☐ A discussion about the limitations of confidentiality and the roles group leaders and participants are expected to play within the group setting.

## THEORETICAL APPROACHES TO COUNSELING IN GROUPS

Theoretical approaches to counseling in groups vary as much as those of individual counseling do, and in many cases the theories are the same. A number of group experts (Corey, 1985; Hansen, Warner, & Smith, 1980; Vander Kolk, 1985) have written books outlining the major theories employed in group settings. Each of these authors includes chapters on psychoanalytic, Gestalt, person-centered, rational-emotive, transactional analysis, and behavioral approaches to group work. The basic positions of these theories were examined in the chapters on individual counseling; they will not be reviewed here. Yet, the implementation of any theoretical approach differs when employed with a group.

In regard to the evaluation of seven major theoretical approaches to groups, Ward (1982) has analyzed the degree to which each approach pays attention to the: (1) individual, (2) interpersonal, and (3) group levels of the process (Table 12.1). For instance, the psychoanalytic, Gestalt, and behavioral approaches to groups are strong in focusing on the individual but weak on the other two components of the group process. On the other hand, the Rogerian approach is strong on the individual level and medium on the interpersonal and group levels. Ward points out the limiting aspects of each approach and also the importance of considering other factors, such as the group task and the membership maturity, in conducting comprehensive group assignments.

In a similar way, Frey (1972) outlines how eight approaches to group work can be conceptualized on continuums of insight to action and rational to affective (Figure 12.2); while Hansen, Warner, and Smith (1980) conceptualize group approaches on continuums of process to outcome and leader centered to member centered (Figure 12.3). Group leaders and potential group members must know how theories differ in order to make wise choices.

Overall, multiple theoretical models provide richness and diversity for those involved with groups, especially for leaders. There are several factors, besides the ones already mentioned, that are

**TABLE 12.1**   Rating of theory strength at the three group levels.

| Theory | Levels | | | Limiting Factors |
| | Individual | Interpersonal | Group | |
|---|---|---|---|---|
| Freud | Strong | Weak | Weak | Task, Members, Leader |
| Perls | Strong | Weak | Weak | Task, Members, Leader |
| Behavioral | Strong | Weak | Weak | Task, Leader |
| Ellis | Strong | Medium | Weak | Task, Leader |
| Berne | Strong | Strong | Weak | Task |
| Rogers | Strong | Medium | Medium | Style |

*Source:* From "A model for the more effective use of theory in group work" by D. E. Ward, 1982, *Journal for Specialists in Group Work, 7,* p. 227. Copyright AACD. Reprinted with permission. No further reproduction authorized without further permission of AACD.

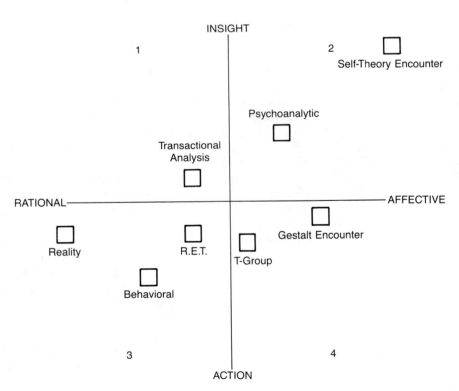

**FIGURE 12.2**   Group approaches conceptualized.

*Source:* From "Conceptualizing counseling theories" by D. H. Frey, 1972. *Counselor Education and Supervision, 11,* p. 245. Copyright AACD. Reprinted with permission. No further reproduction authorized without further permission from AACD.

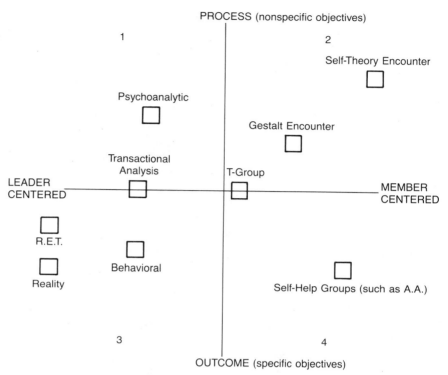

**FIGURE 12.3** Group approaches conceptualized.

*Source:* From GROUP COUNSELING: THEORY AND PROCESS, Second Edition, by James C. Hansen, Richard W. Warner, and Elsie J. Smith. Copyright © 1980, 1976 by Houghton Mifflin Company. Reprinted by permission.

useful for group leaders to consider in arriving at a decision on what approach to take. Three of the most important factors are:

1. Whether one needs a theoretical base for conducting the group.
2. What uses the theory will best serve.
3. What criteria will be employed in the selection process.

In regard to the first factor, Corey (1985) compares a theory to a map. The map "provides direction and guidance in examining one's basic assumptions about human beings, in determining one's goals for the group, in clarifying one's role and functions as a leader, in explaining the group interactions, and in evaluating the outcomes of the group" (p. 133). Corey compares trying to lead a group without an explicit theoretical rationale to attempting to fly an airplane without a map and instruments. Either procedure is foolish, dangerous, and likely to lead to injury.

Vander Kolk (1985) also says that a good theory serves many practical functions; for example, it gives meaning to and a framework for experiences and facts that occur within a setting. Good theory can help make logical sense out of what is happening and also lead to productive research. With so many theories from which to choose, the potential group leader is wise to be careful in selecting an approach.

In response to Corey's third factor, Ford and Urban (1963) contend there are four main criteria counselors can use to select a theoretical approach: personal experience, consensus of experts, prestige, or a verified body of knowledge. There are liabilities and advantages to all of these criteria. Therefore, it is crucial for beginning counselors to listen to others and to read the professional literature critically in order to evaluate the theory or theories that are most verifiable and that fit in with their personality styles.

## STAGES IN GROUPS

Groups are like other living systems in that they go through stages. If an individual or group leader is not aware of these stages, the changes that occur within the group may appear confusing rather than meaningful. On the other hand, an understanding of group stages is no guarantee that group leaders or members will make sense out of all events that happen in the group. There is debate in the professional literature about what stages groups go through and when. Developmental stages have been identified in various types of groups, such a learning groups and training groups, yet the debate about group stages mainly centers on group counseling. The most agreed-upon number of group counseling stages is four, but in this section, arguments for a three-stage process and a five-stage process will also be examined.

Tuchman (1965) was among the first to design a three-stage process. These stages are colloquially referred to as forming, storming, and norming. The forming stage lays the foundation for what is to come. In this stage, members generally express anxiety and talk about nonproblematic topics. The stage serves as a time for members to discover similarities among themselves. The storming stage, the next to develop, is characterized by conflict. Each group member seeks to find a place within the group and to deal successfully with the issues of anxiety, power, and expectations. Often the group leader is a focus of attack during this time. The final stage of norming is characterized by the development of group cohesion and task orientation. Group members become more involved with one another and individual goals. A mature group remains in this stage, with only occasional regressions, until its termination. The problem with this three-stage scheme is the absence of a time when group members consolidate gains and close off relationships with others. That lack is one reason why a four-stage conceptualization developed.

Gazda (1970) has delineated four stages of group counseling based on his own personal experience and a review of the professional literature on groups. These stages are exploration, transition, action, and termination, and they have the following characteristics. During exploration, group leaders introduce themselves, describe their goals, agree on basic ground rules for the group, talk about superficial or safe subjects, and develop a sense of mutual trust and caring. The group leader is quite active during exploration in helping members clarify goals. The leader also models facilitative behaviors such as empathy and engages in limited self-disclosure. The transition stage begins when one or more group members initiate a disclosure of information that goes beyond personal history. Other group members often display anxiety in response to such a disclosure, and the group leader must help the group move beyond anxiety and encourage action-oriented responses. If this stage is successfully negotiated, the group moves into the action stage, when its main work begins.

Definite steps are taken during the action stage to modify behaviors group members wish to change. One way this is accomplished is through interaction with others in the group. In these encounters, a member is encouraged to examine his or her actions and is often confronted about behaviors. The member is challenged by the group leader and other members to display and practice new behaviors that are more congruent with the member's goals. All of this action is completed with an emphasis on the present. The final stage, the termination stage, is characterized by a tapering off of self-disclosures and a reinforcement of group members' accomplishments. During termination, group members often express feelings about the group experience and how much the process has meant to them. The group leader is involved at this time in congratulating group members on accomplishments, in working out any differences between individuals, and in responding to the needs of any person who desires further counseling.

The five-stage model of group counseling does not differ significantly from Gazda's conceptualization, except in its detail. The model, as set forth by Hansen, Warner, and Smith (1980), distinguishes the following five stages: initiating the group, conflict and confrontation, cohesiveness, productiveness, and termination. The initiating stage is similar to the forming and exploration stages of the other two models. The conflict and confrontation stage parallels the storming and transitional stages, while the cohesiveness and productiveness stages together correspond to the norming and action stages of the other models. Finally, the termination stage is very similar to the termination stage of Gazda's. The detail in the model by Hansen et al. is excellent, and their emphasis on the fact that groups differ in the length of time and specific problems faced is also well placed. They make another good point in stressing that the "developmental stages of a group are rarely clearly differentiated. A group does not necessarily move step by step through life stages, but may move backward and forward as a part of its general development" (p. 476).

## ISSUES IN GROUP COUNSELING

There are a number of issues involved in conducting successful groups. Some deal with procedures for running groups; others deal with training and ethics.

*Selection and Preparation of Group Members.* Screening and preparation are essential for conducting a successful group. These are usually accomplished through a pre-group interview between the group leader and prospective members. ASGW's Ethical Guidelines for Group Leaders (1980) state that during a pre-group interview group members shall be selected "whose needs and goals are compatible with the established goals of the group; who will not impede the group process; and whose well-being will not be jeopardized by the group experience." (See Appendix D for ASGW Ethical Guidelines.)

In following these guidelines, certain individuals may need to be screened out or may elect to screen themselves out of the group. Corey (1983) considers screening a two-way process. Potential group members may not be appropriate for a certain group at a particular time with a designated leader. Prospective group members should be advised of their options. In selecting group members, a group leader will do well to heed Gazda's (1978) advice that individuals in the group be able to identify with other group members, at least on some issues.

Group members need to be informed as much as possible about the group process before the process begins. Veterans of group experiences will need minimal information about the procedures involved; others will require extensive preparation. Although this preparation may be time-consuming, the eventual success of the group experience depends on it. As Lynn and Frauman (1985) report, "Research evidence is beginning to converge in support of an association between time spent in preparation of group members and positive outcome" (p. 432).

***Group Size and Duration.*** The size of a group is often determined by its purpose and preference. Large groups are less likely to spotlight the needs of individual members. Therefore, outside of group guidance there is an optimal number of people that should be involved. A generally agreed-upon number of group members is 6 to 8, though Gazda (1970) notes that if groups run as long as six months that up to 10 people may productively be included. Group size and duration affect each other. Corey (1985) states: "For ongoing groups of adults, about eight members with one leader seems to be a good size. Groups with children may be as small as three or four. In general, the group should have enough people to afford ample interaction so it doesn't drag and yet be small enough to give everyone a chance to participate frequently without . . . losing the sense of 'group' " (p. 69).

***Open vs. Closed Groups.*** Open groups admit new members after they have started; closed groups do not. Lynn and Frauman (1985) point out that open groups are able to replace lost members rather quickly and thus maintain an optimal size. Thus, many long-term outpatient groups are open ended. Closed groups, though not as flexible in size, promote more cohesiveness among group members and may be very productive in helping members achieve stated goals.

***Confidentiality.*** Groups function best when members feel that what has been said within the group setting will not be revealed outside. In order to promote this sense of confidentiality and build trust, a group leader must be active. In the prescreening interview the subject of confidentiality should be raised. The importance of confidentiality needs to be stressed during the first meeting of the group and on a regular basis thereafter (Corey, 1983; Corey, Corey, & Callanan, 1984; Gazda, 1978). ASGW has published guidelines on confidentiality that emphasize the role group leaders have in protecting their members by clearly defining what confidentiality is and the importance and difficulty of enforcing it. Whenever there is any question about the betrayal of confidentiality within a group, it is best to deal with the situation immediately. Otherwise, the problem seems to grow and the cohesiveness of the group breaks down. Olsen (1971) points out that counselors must realize they can only guarantee their own adherence to the principles of confidentiality. Still, they must try to ensure the rights of all group members.

***Physical Structure.*** Where a group is conducted is either an asset or liability to the group. Terres and Larrabee (1985) emphasize the need for a physical structure within a school that assures the safety and growth of minors working in a group setting. Groups outside of a school environment also need to be conducted in places that promote the well-being of the group and its members.

***Co-leaders.*** It is not necessary for most groups to have co-leaders but co-leaders can be beneficial to the group and to each other. For example, one leader can work with the group and the other can monitor the group process. A co-leader arrangement may also be beneficial when an inexperienced leader and experienced leader are working together—the inexperienced can learn from the experienced. Many group specialists advocate that an inexperienced leader co-lead a group first before attempting this process alone (Ritter, 1982).

Dinkmeyer and Muro (1979) suggest that in order to be most successful, experienced co-leaders will: (1) possess a similar philosophical and operational style, (2) have similar experience and competence, (3) establish a model relationship for effective human interaction, (4) be aware of splitting and member loyalty ties to one leader or the other and help the group deal with this, and (5) agree on counseling goals and processes to achieve them so power struggles are avoided (p. 250).

Pietrofesa, Hoffman, and Splete (1984) recommend that co-leaders sit opposite of each other in a group so that leader responsibility and observation are maximized. They point out that it is not necessary for group co-leaders to be of the opposite sex; the skills, not the gender, matter most.

***Self-Disclosure.*** Shertzer and Stone (1981) define self-disclosure as "here and now feelings, attitudes, and beliefs . . ." (p. 206). The process of self-disclosure is highly dependent on the trust group members have for one another (Bunch, Lund, & Wiggins, 1983). If there is high trust, there will be greater self-disclosure. An interesting aspect of this phenomenon is that self-disclosure builds on itself. During the first stages of counseling, it may have to be encouraged. Morran (1982) suggests that in the beginning sessions of a group, leaders use self-disclosure often in order to serve as a model for others and promote the process. The point is well made. As Stockton, Barr, and Klein (1981) document, group members who make few verbal self-disclosures are much more likely than others to drop out of a group.

***Feedback.*** Feedback is a multidimensional process that consists of group members' responding to the verbal and nonverbal behavior of one another. It is one of the most important and abused parts of any group experience. When feedback is given honestly and with care, group members can gauge the impact of their actions on others and attempt new behavior if so desired. Corey (1985) distinguishes between group feedback given at the end of a session and that given at the termination of a group. During the latter process, Corey encourages group members to be clear, concise, and concrete with one another. He also has group members give themselves feedback about how they have changed during the group experience. After processing feedback information, Corey recommends group members record some of the things said during final feedback sessions so they will not forget and can make use of the experience in evaluating how they have progressed toward their goals.

In order to promote helpful feedback, Pietrofesa, Hoffman, and Splete (1984, p. 376) list criteria for feedback evaluation. Among the most salient of their recommendations are:

☐ Feedback should be beneficial to the receiver and not serve the needs of the giver.

☐ Feedback is more effective when it is based on describable behavior.

☐ In the early stages of group development, positive feedback is more beneficial and more readily accepted than negative feedback.

☐ Feedback is most effective when it immediately follows a stimulus behavior and is validated by others.

☐ Feedback is of greater benefit when the receiver is open and trusts the giver.

***Follow-Up.*** Gazda (1978) criticizes group leaders who conduct short-term groups but do not provide follow-up after the experience. ASGW Ethical Guidelines for Group Leaders (1980) state that leaders shall provide for follow-up of group members after termination of a group "as needed or requested." Follow-up helps group members and leaders assess what they gained in the group experience and allows the group leader to make a referral of further counseling for a group member, if appropriate (Corey, 1983, 1985; Gazda, 1978). Follow-up sessions can maximize the effects of a group experience and encourage members to keep pursuing original goals if not achieved.

Corey (1985) suggests that a follow-up session for a short-term group routinely be conducted about three months after termination of the group experience. He points out that the process of mutual feedback and support from other group members at this time can be very valuable. If group members are aware during the termination stage of their group that they will meet again for a follow-up they are more likely than not to continue pursuing their goals. In addition to a whole-group follow-up, Corey also endorses individual follow-up between leaders and group members, even if these sessions are conducted by phone.

## QUALITIES OF EFFECTIVE GROUP LEADERS

There are some qualities of group leaders that are more effective than others. For instance, group leaders who are authoritarian, aggressive, confrontational, or removed emotionally from the group are ineffective and produce group casualties (i.e., members who drop out or are worse after the group experience) (Yalom & Lieberman, 1971). On the other hand, Yalom (1975) has documented through research four leadership qualities that have a positive effect on the outcome of groups, if not used excessively. These qualities are:

☐ *Caring*  The more the better

☐ *Meaning attribution*  Includes clarifying, explaining, and providing a cognitive framework for change

☐ *Emotional stimulation*  Includes activity, challenging, risk taking, self-disclosure

☐ *Executive function*  Includes developing norms, structuring, and suggesting procedures

Finding a position between the two extremes of emotional stimulation and executive function is vital for the well-being of all. It is important that a group leader neither allows members to experience so much emotion that they are unable to process the material being discovered in the group nor structures the situation so rigidly that no emotion is expressed.

Ohlsen (1970) states that effective leaders understand the forces operating within a group, recognize whether these forces are therapeutic, and, if not, take steps to better manage the group with the assistance of its members. His assessment of leadership complements that of Yalom (1975) and Osborne (1982), who believe that good group counselors behave with intentionality because they are able to anticipate where the group process is moving and recognize when and if the group reaches a definitive stage.

In addition, Corey (1985) maintains that effective group leaders are those who are committed "to the never-ending struggle" to become effective as human beings. He lists 13 personal qualities "vitally related to effective group leadership" (p. 39). Among those qualities are: presence, personal power, courage, willingness to confront oneself, sincerity, authenticity, enthusiasm, and self-awareness/identity, inventiveness/creativity, and stamina.

Gill and Barry (1982) concentrate on group leadership skills as crucial to effectiveness (Table 12.2). They trace the evolution of the

**TABLE 12.2**  Gill and Barry's conceptualization of group-focused counseling skills.

| Stage I | Stage II | Stage III |
|---|---|---|
| *Group Formation:* Facilitating Cooperation Toward Common Goals Through Development of Group Identity | *Group Awareness:* Facilitating a Shared Understanding of the Group's Behavior | *Group Action:* Facilitating Cooperative Decision-Making and Problem-Solving |
| 1. *Norming*<br>stating explicitly the expected group behavior<br>2. *Eliciting Group Responses*<br>inquiries or invitations to members which encourage comments, questions, or observations.<br>3. *Eliciting Sympathic Reactions*<br>inquiries or invitations to members which encourage disclosure of experiences or feelings similar to those being expressed.<br>4. *Identifying Commonalities and Differences*<br>describing comparative characteristics of participants.<br>5. *Eliciting Empathic Reactions*<br>inquiries or invitations to members which encourage reflection of one member's expressed content or feeling.<br>6. *Task Focusing*<br>redirecting conversation to immediate objectives; restating themes being expressed by more than one member. | 1. *Labeling Group Behavior*<br>identifying and describing group feelings and performance.<br>2. *Implicit Norming*<br>describing behavior which has become typical of the group through common practice.<br>3. *Eliciting Group Observations*<br>inquiries or invitation to members which encourage observations about group process.<br>4. *Eliciting Mutual Feedback*<br>inquiries or invitations to members which encourage sharing of perceptions about each other's behavior.<br>5. *Identifying Conflict*<br>labeling discordant elements of communication between members.<br>6. *Identifying Non-Verbal Behavior*<br>labeling unspoken communications between members (facial expression, posture, hand gestures, voice tone and intensity, etc.)<br>7. *Validating*<br>requesting group confirmation of the accuracy of leader or members' perceptions.<br>8. *Transitioning*<br>changing the group's focus on content or feelings being expressed.<br>9. *Connecting*<br>relating material from group events at a particular time or session to what is happening currently.<br>10. *Extinguishing*<br>ignoring, cutting-off, or diverting inappropriate talk or actions of members. | 1. *Identifying Group Needs*<br>asking questions and making statements which clarify the want[s] and needs of the group.<br>2. *Identifying Group Goals*<br>asking questions and making statements which clarify group objectives.<br>3. *Attributing Meaning*<br>providing concepts for understanding group thought, feelings, and behavior.<br>4. *Eliciting Alternatives*<br>providing descriptions of possible courses of action and inviting members to contribute alternatives.<br>5. *Exploring Consequences*<br>inquiries or invitations to the group which evaluate actions and potential outcomes.<br>6. *Consensus Testing*<br>requesting group agreement on a decision or course of action. |

*Source:* From "Group-focused counseling: Classifying the essential skills" by J. G. Gill and R. A. Barry, 1982, *Personnel and Guidance Journal, 60,* 302–305. Copyright AACD. Reprinted with permission. No further reproduction authorized without further permission of AACD.

emphasis on skills in group counseling through four classification systems: Ivey (1973); Lieberman, Yalom, and Miles (1973); Dyer and Vriend (1977); and Ohlsen (1977). Their conceptualization of group-focused counseling skills is based on Egan's (1986) three-stage model of counseling. In the first stage the focus is on group formation. In the second stage it is on group awareness. In the third stage group action is highlighted.

A final quality of effective group leaders is that they are well educated in group theory and practice. In 1984, the Council for Accreditation of Counseling and Related Educational Programs (CACREP) adopted ASGW guidelines for the education of group leaders. These guidelines are too detailed to be covered in this text, but they are vital for the potential group leader to consult and follow.

## SUMMARY

As the material in this chapter shows, groups are an exciting, diversified, needed, and effective way to help people and can take an educational, preventive, or remediation form. The theories used in groups are often the same as those employed in working with individuals. There are many different issues, however, involved in group work than in individual counseling.

Group leaders must be competent in dealing with individual as well as group issues if they are to be maximally effective. Learning how to do this is a developmental process. A good group leader knows what type of group he or she is leading and shares this information with potential members. Group leaders follow ethical, legal, and procedural guidelines of professional group organizations. They are concerned with the general well-being of their groups and the people in them. They anticipate problems before they occur and take proactive steps to correct them. They also systematically follow up with group members after the group has terminated. They keep up with the professional literature about groups and are constantly striving to improve their personal and professional levels of functioning.

Overall, group counseling is an expanding area that has become a respected way of helping others. It is a stage-oriented process of counseling in which professionals acquire skills both during and after their graduate training.

## CLASSROOM ACTIVITIES

1. Reflect on the types of groups mentioned in this chapter. Then in small groups of four discuss with one another which of these groups you feel most comfortable with now.

Anticipate with your group members what types of groups you might lead in the future.

2. Divide into dyads and discuss with your partner the problems and potentials you see in leading a group. Pretend you have been asked to lead a group of your own choosing. What feelings do you have about this upcoming event? How do you see yourself behaving and thinking during each stage of the process?

3. Examine copies of professional counseling journals for the last five years. Make a report to the class on articles about groups that have a particular interest to you. Compare your findings to those of other class members.

4. Imagine that you are a counselor without any group skills. How do you see yourself functioning every day in the following settings: a school, an employee-assistance program, a mental health office, and a private practice? Discuss with the class as a whole your thoughts about counselors' engaging in various types of group work.

5. Select a topic that is of interest to a wide variety of individuals (e.g., proper diet, dealing with anger) and present a group guidance lesson to your classmates based on the information you read in this area. Process this experience directly with the class as soon as you complete it. How difficult or easy was this project?

## REFERENCES

Barrow, J. C., & Moore, C. A. (1983). Group interventions with perfectionistic thinking. *Personnel and Guidance Journal, 61*, 612–615.

Bunch, B. J., Lund, N. L., & Wiggins, F. K. (1983). Self-disclosure and perceived closeness in the development of group process. *Journal for Specialists in Group Work, 8*, 59–66.

Carroll, M. R., & Levo, L. (1985). The association for specialists in group work. *Journal for Counseling and Development, 63*, 453–454.

Cole, S. A. (1983). Self-help groups. In H. I. Kaplan & B. J. Sadock (Eds.), *Comprehensive group psychotherapy* (2nd ed.). Baltimore: Williams & Wilkins.

Corey, G. (1983). Group counseling. In J. A. Brown and R. H. Pate, Jr. (Eds.), *Being a counselor: Directions and challenges* (pp.95–123). Monterey, CA: Brooks/Cole.

Corey, G. (1985). *Theory and practice of group counseling.* Monterey, CA: Brooks/Cole.

Corey, G., Corey, M. S., & Callanan, P. (1984). *Issues & ethics in the helping profession* (2nd ed.). Monterey, CA: Brooks/Cole.

Dinkmeyer, D. C., & Muro, J. J. (1979). *Group counseling: Theory and practice* (2nd ed.). Itasca, IL: Peacock.

Dyer, W. W., & Vriend, J. (1977). *Counseling techniques that work.* New York: Funk & Wagnalls.

Egan, G. (1986). *The skilled helper* (3rd ed.). Monterey, CA: Brooks/Cole.

Ford, D., & Urban, H. (1963). *Systems of psychotherapy: A comparative study.* New York: Wiley.

Gazda, G. M. (1970). *Group counseling: A developmental approach.* Boston: Allyn & Bacon.

Gazda, G. M. (1978). *Group counseling: A developmental approach* (2nd ed.). Boston: Allyn & Bacon.

Gill, J. G., & Barry, R. A. (1982). Group-focused counseling: Classifying the essential skills. *Personnel and Guidance Journal, 60*, 302–305.

Gladding, S. T. (1979). A restless presence: Group process as a pilgrimage. *The School Counselor, 27*, 126–127.

Hansen, J. C., Warner, R. W., & Smith, E. J. (1980). *Group counseling* (2nd ed.). Chicago: Rand McNally.

Harper, F. D. (1984). Group strategies with black alcoholics. *Journal for Specialists in Group Work, 9,* 38–43.

Hotelling, K., & Reese, K. H. (1983). Women and anger: Relearning in a group context. *Journal for Specialists in Group Work, 8,* 9–16.

Huey, W. C. (1983). Reducing adolescent aggression through group assertive training. *The School Counselor, 30,* 193–203.

Ivey, A. E. (1973). Demystifying the group process: Adapting microcounseling procedures to counseling in groups. *Educational Technology, 13,* 27–31.

Lieberman, M. A. (1975). Group methods. In F. H. Kanfer & A. P. Goldstein (Eds.). *Helping people change: A textbook of methods.* New York: Pergamon.

Lieberman, M. A., Yalom, I. D., & Miles, M. B. (1973). *Encounter groups: First facts.* New York: Basic Books.

Lynn, S. J., & Frauman, D. (1985). *Group psychotherapy.* In S. J. Lynn & J. P. Garske (Eds.), *Contemporary psychotherapies: Models and methods* (pp. 419–458). Columbus, OH: Merrill.

McWhirter, J. J., Nichols, E., & Banks, N. M. (1984). Career awareness and self-exploration (CASE) groups: A self-assessment model for career decision making. *Personnel and Guidance Journal, 20,* 580–582.

Moreno, J. L. (1962). Common ground for all group psychotherapists: What is a group psychotherapist? *Group Psychotherapy, 15,* 263.

Morran, D. K. (1982). Leader and member self-disclosing behavior in counseling groups. *Journal for Specialists in Group Work, 7,* 218–223.

Ohlsen, M. M. (1970). *Group counseling.* New York: Holt, Rinehart & Winston.

Ohlsen, M. M. (1977). *Group counseling* (2nd ed.). New York: Holt, Rinehart & Winston.

Olsen, L. D. (1971). Ethical standards for group leaders. *Personnel and Guidance Journal, 50,* 288.

Osborne, W. L. (1982). Group counseling: Direction and intention. *Journal for Specialists in Group Work, 7,* 275–280.

Pietrofesa, J. J., Hoffman, A., & Splete, H. H. (1984). *Counseling: An introduction* (2nd ed.). Boston: Houghton Mifflin.

Ritter, K. Y. (1982). Training group counselors: A total curriculum perspective. *Journal for Specialists in Group Work, 7,* 266–274.

Rogers, C. R. (1970). *Carl Rogers on encounter groups.* New York: Harper & Row.

Schutz, W. (1971). *Here comes everybody: Bodymind and encounter culture.* New York: Harper & Row.

Shertzer, B., & Stone, S. C. (1981). *Fundamentals of guidance* (4th ed.). Boston: Houghton Mifflin.

Stockton, R., Barr, J. E., & Klein, R. (1981). Identifying the group dropout: A review of literature. *Journal for Specialists in Group Work, 6,* 75–82.

Tedder, S. L., Libbee, K. M., & Scherman, A. (1981). A community support group for single custodial fathers. *Personnel and Guidance Journal, 60,* 115–119.

Terres, C. K., & Larrabee, M. J. (1985). Ethical issues and group work with children. *Elementary School Guidance & Counseling, 19,* 190–197.

Tuchman, B. W. (1965). Developmental sequence in small groups. *Psychological Bulletin, 72,* 384–399.

Vander Kolk, C. J. (1985). *Introduction to group counseling and psychotherapy.* Columbus, OH: Merrill.

Ward, D. E. (1982). A model for the more effective use of theory in group work. *Journal for Specialists in Group Work, 7,* 224–230.

Yalom, I. D. (1975). *The theory and practice of group psychotherapy* (2nd ed.). New York: Basic Books.

Yalom, I. D., & Lieberman, M. (1971). A study of encounter group casualties. *Archives of General Psychiatry, 25,* 16–30.

Zimpfer, D. G. (1981). Follow-up studies of growth group outcomes: A review. *Journal for Specialists in Group Work, 6,* 195–210.

Photo by James S. Davidson III.

# CHAPTER 13

# School and College Counseling

*Just like Fall foliage*
*    we watch what you bring forth each September.*
*Your changes are not as dramatic as the red of Maples,*
*    or as warm as the orange of twilight fires;*
*But your presence, both individually and collectively,*
*    like leaves adds color to a campus*
*    that would otherwise be bland*
*    in the shades of administration grey.*
*We celebrate your coming*
*    much as we look forward to the crisp cool air*
*    at the end of a wilting Summer.*
*We welcome your spirit*
*    for it enlivens us to the metaphors and ideals*
*    that live unchanging lives. . . .* [1]

---

[1]Gladding, 1982, p. 122. Copyright AACD. No further reproduction authorized without written permission of AACD.

The field of school and college counseling involves a wide range of ages, developmental stages, and types of problems. Yet, there is a natural breakdown into specialties within this field. The professional literature reflects that counselors provide their services to four distinct populations in education: elementary school children (kindergarten through 4th grade), middle school children (5th through 8th grade), secondary school children (9th through 12th grade), and college students.

In the American Association for Counseling and Development (AACD), elementary, middle, and secondary school counselors join the American School Counselor Association (ASCA), whereas those who work with college students join the American College Personnel Association (ACPA). Both divisions publish quarterly periodicals: *Elementary School Guidance and Counseling, The School Counselor*, and the *Journal of College Student Personnel*. In this chapter, we shall examine the major emphases and roles of counselors in each of these four settings. Some of their activities overlap, such as publicizing themselves and their programs, as do some of their emphases, such as prevention.

## ELEMENTARY SCHOOL COUNSELING AND GUIDANCE

Elementary school counseling and guidance is a relatively recent development. The first book on this subject was not published until the 1950s, and for all practical purposes the discipline was virtually nonexistent prior to 1965 (Dinkmeyer, 1973). In fact, fewer than 10 universities had course work in elementary school counseling in 1964 (Muro, 1981).

The development of elementary school counseling and guidance was slow for three reasons (Nugent, 1981; Peters, 1980). First, there was a belief that elementary school teachers should serve as counselors to their students since they were with them all day and were in an ideal position to identify specific problems. Second, counseling was seen at the time as primarily concerned with vocational development, which was not a major focus of elementary school children. Finally, a need for counseling on this level was not recognized. Psychologists and social workers were employed by many secondary schools to diagnose emotional and learning problems in older children and to advise in difficult family situations, but full-time counseling on the elementary school level was not considered.

In 1964, when the National Defense Education Act (NDEA) Title V-A was passed by Congress, counseling services were extended to include elementary school children (Minkoff & Terres, 1985). Government grants to establish training institutes for elementary school counselors were authorized in 1968, and by 1972 over 10,000 elementary school counselors were employed (Dinkmeyer, 1973). The number of counselors entering this specialty leveled off temporarily in the late 1970s, but the prospect of a continued demand has been increased in states such as Maine that require elementary schools to include a counselor on the staff.

## Emphases and Roles

Muro (1981) emphasizes that elementary school counselors are a vanguard in the mental health movement. No other profession has ever been organized to work with people from a purely preventive perspective. ASCA's role statement for the practice of school counseling (ASCA Role Statement, 1981) lists five functions of elementary school counselors. They should:

☐ Provide in-service training to teachers in the hope of preventing serious problems among young children or minimizing the impact of such problems.

☐ Provide consultation to teachers in building a healthy classroom environment.

☐ Work with parents to promote understanding of childhood growth and development.

☐ Cooperate in the identification and referral of children with developmental deficiencies or handicaps.

☐ Direct older children's awareness to the relationship of school and work.

As Wilson and Rotter (1980) point out, "The elementary school counselor is charged with facilitating optimal development of the whole child" (p. 179). The task involves many preventive and proactive services, such as classroom guidance, group counseling, consultation, and special intervention strategies for high-risk children.

In a study of the perceived, actual, and ideal roles of elementary school counselors in California, it was found that the majority of counselors surveyed spent a large portion of their time in counseling, consultation, and parent help activities (Furlong, Atkinson, & Janoff, 1979). Their actual and ideal roles were nearly identical. Schmidt and Osborne (1982) found similar results in a study of North Carolina elementary school counselors. The top activities listed by the counselors were counseling with individuals and groups and consultation with teachers.

The emphases that elementary school counselors place on such services have important consequences for the children and schools they serve. In an important article on the effectiveness of elementary school counseling, Gerler (1985) reviewed research reports published in *Elementary School Guidance & Counseling* from 1974 to 1984. His focus was on studies designed to help children from behavioral, affective, social, and mental-image/sensory-awareness perspectives. He found strong evidence that elementary school counseling programs "can positively influence the affective, behavioral, and interpersonal domains of children's lives and, as a result, can affect children's achievement positively" (Gerler, 1985, p. 45). The fact that elementary school counselors can and do make a difference in the lives of the children they serve is a strong rationale for keeping and increasing their services and for seeking specialization in this field.

### Activities

Elementary school counselors engage in a number of preventive and remedial activities. A first priority is to make themselves known to the children they serve. "School personnel are not usually viewed by young children as the first source of help" (Bachman, 1975, p. 108). Thus, elementary school counselors need to promote themselves and their services through either orientation programs or a series of classroom guidance activities. Morgan and Jackson (1980) outline how one school district in Oregon has systematically made classroom guidance a part of its elementary school curriculum. The program includes an emphasis on children's awareness of different values, information, skills, and feelings. The strength of this program is that it includes a pre-test and a post-test for counselors to employ in evaluating their effectiveness in the classroom. The program is integrative in nature so that the focus is on the whole child. By participating in a systematic series of curriculum activities, counselors not only introduce guidance activities to the children in the classroom but in the process introduce themselves as well. This makes it easier for children to seek out a counselor later and to know something about counseling services.

Becoming known as a helper of children is only one task that must be accomplished by elementary school counselors. A second task is providing specific services for the children within the unique environment of the school. Thompson and Rudolph (1983) state that all major counseling theories, such as the ones discussed in this text, are applicable to elementary school children. Yet, the job of helping children at this level often requires that counselors work directly with parents and other school personnel. Elementary school children have relatively few choices in life. They are not allowed the same freedom as older children to temporarily escape an adverse home environment or classroom situation. Thus, counselors must work to "(1) try to change the child to 'fit' the environment (a favorite behaviorist strategy); (2) try and change the environment so the child will function better; or (3) some combination of one and two" (Muro & Dinkmeyer, 1977, pp. 19–20).

Deciding how to work and with whom are major tasks for elementary school counselors. They may accomplish these tasks in one of two ways. First, they may rely on established research to guide their activities. For instance, Dinkmeyer and Caldwell (1970) note that children in elementary schools generally have developmental problems in four main areas—the school, family relations and home, relationships with others, and self. This knowledge gives counselors a basis for establishing a program of services. Second, counselors can rely on the results of needs assessments conducted in a specific school environment. *Needs assessments* are structured surveys that may be purchased commercially or borrowed from other schools and modified. When the surveys are filled out by students, teachers, and parents, counselors are able to determine specific problem areas and what group is in need of what kind of services (Stiltner, 1978).

James and Kazalunas (1979) note that elementary school counselors are engaged in a variety of activities, programs, and methods that ideally are coordinated in a systematic fashion. Among these activities are: counseling with children about death (Wilder, 1980), working with young children whose parents are going through divorce (Bernard, 1978), organizing weight-control groups for overweight children (Marin, 1985), providing preservice programs for teachers on dealing effectively with child development situations (Dougherty, 1981), promoting children's self-esteem (Weinhold & Hilferty, 1983), initiating counseling services for handicapped children (DeBlassie & Lebsock, 1979), and adapting career awareness activities for elementary school pupils (Isaacson & Hayes, 1980). Many times, because of the young child's interests and short attention span, such activities are presented in the form of play techniques that require active participation by both the child and the counselor. For example, the use of art counseling (Allan & Clark, 1984) has been found to be effective in establishing a bridge between nonverbal children and other school personnel.

Child peer facilitators have also been effective in helping elementary school counselors reach more children and improve the quality of life and education within the school (Anderson, 1976; Myrick & Bowman, 1983). Training programs specifically designed to teach elementary school children to work in this way have been developed. Among such innovative programs set up by teachers and counselors to promote the mental health of students and to improve the school climate are cross-grade activities (Allan & Dyck, 1983). Younger children's anxieties are reduced in cross-grade activities because of interaction with older children, and cooperation is fostered both among children and between teachers and counselors.

## MIDDLE SCHOOL COUNSELING AND GUIDANCE

Emphasis on middle school counseling and guidance is an even more recent phenomenon than elementary school counseling. It came into prominence in the 1970s (Stamm & Nissman, 1979). The idea of a special curriculum and environment for preadolescents and early adolescents grew out of the junior high concept, which was an attempt to group younger adolescents (ages 12 through 14 and grades 7 to 9) from older adolescents. Middle schools typically enroll children between the ages of 9 and 13 and encompass grades 5 through 8. Children at this age and grade level are often referred to as "transescents" (Eichhorn, 1968) or "bubblegummers" (Thornburg, 1978). There is little homogeneity about them and their most common characteristic is "unlikeness" (Stamm & Nissman, 1979). According to Dougherty (1986), we know less about this age group than any other. Yet, as Thornburg (1986) emphasizes, there are major physical, intellectual, and social developmental tasks that middle school children must accomplish. The eight main tasks outlined by Thornburg include (pp. 170–171):

☐ Becoming aware of increased physical changes

☐ Organizing knowledge and concepts into problem-solving strategies

☐ Making the transition from concrete to abstract symbols

☐ Learning new social and sex roles

☐ Identifying with stereotypical role models

☐ Developing friendships

☐ Gaining a sense of independence

☐ Developing a sense of responsibility

Elkind (1986) notes that in addition to developmental tasks, middle graders also must deal successfully with three basic stress situations. A *Type A* stress situation is one that is foreseeable and avoidable, such as not walking in a dangerous area at night. A *Type B* stress situation is neither foreseeable nor avoidable, such as an unexpected death. A *Type C* stress situation is foreseeable but not avoidable, such as going to the dentist. It is in relation to the successful achievement and resolution of developmental tasks and other nondevelopmental situations, such as stress situations, that middle school counselors can be most helpful.

### Emphases and Roles

Often schools tend to neglect the physical and social development of the child, while stimulating intellectual growth (Thornburg, 1986). Middle school counseling and guidance, like elementary school counseling and guidance, seeks to correct such an imbalance by focusing on the total development of the child. Its emphasis is holistic, and counselors who work in this capacity stress not only the growth and development of the child but also the process of transition that these individuals make in leaving childhood and entering adolescence. Their role responsibilities include (ASCA Role Statement, 1981).

☐ Helping to smooth the transitional process for students from the more confining environment of the elementary school to the more open environment of the middle school

☐ Identifying and working with teachers to incorporate developmental units in the curriculum

☐ Organizing and implementing a career guidance program.

These roles may be fulfilled more easily if middle school counselors develop capacities and programs in certain ways. Among the capacities that middle school counselors need, according to

Thornburg (1986), are general information about developmental characteristics of middle schoolers and specific tasks students are expected to achieve. In addition, it is critical that counselors who work at this level understand the specific child with whom they are interacting and that child's perspective on a problem. Finally, counselors need to know how to assist students in making decisions, so students can help themselves in the future.

The ideal role of middle school counselors also includes providing individual counseling, teacher consultation, student assessment, parent consultation, and evaluation of guidance services (Bonebrake & Borgers, 1984). In a survey of Kansas principals and counselors, Bonebrake and Borgers found that they not only agreed on the ideal role of the middle school counselor, but were also in agreement on the lowest priorities for a middle school counselor— functioning as principal, supervision of lunchroom discipline, and teaching nonguidance classes.

The encouraging aspect of this survey is the close agreement between principals and counselors on ideal roles. Yet outside the school, various groups have different perceptions and priorities about the purpose of middle school counselors. In order to ease the tension that may arise from being evaluated by any of these groups, Bonebrake and Borgers recommend that counselors document their functions and run "a visible, well-defined, and carefully evaluated program" (p. 198). Stamm and Nissman (1979) go even further in defining how this procedure should be done.

### Activities

According to Stamm and Nissman, the activities of middle school counselors are best viewed as services that revolve around "a Human Development Center (HDC) that deals with sensitive human beings (students, teachers, parents, and the community as a whole)" (p. 52). They recommend developing a rapport with these persons and coordinating middle school counseling and guidance services with others to provide the most productive program possible. Stamm and Nissman outline eight service areas they believe are vital to a comprehensive middle school counseling and guidance program (Figure 13.1). Each of the service clusters in this model is linked with the others. However, since middle school counselors cannot perform all of the functions recommended for their programs alone, they must delegate responsibility and solicit the help of other school personnel, parents, and community volunteers. A counselor's job, then, entails coordinating service activities as well as delivering direct services when able. The functions of each service area can be briefly described as follows.

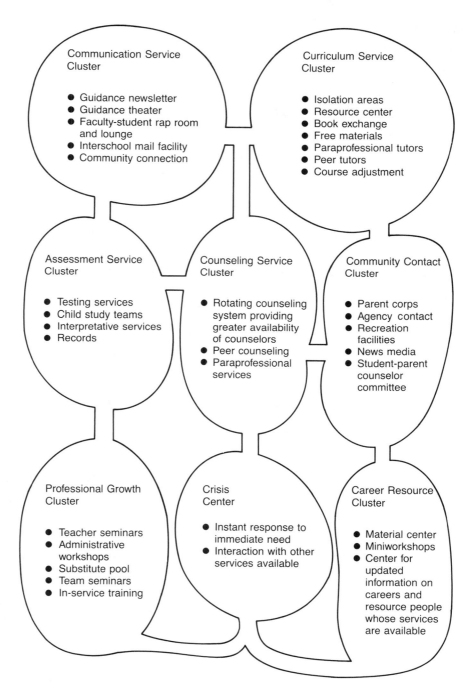

**FIGURE 13.1** Areas vital to a middle school counseling and guidance program.

*Source:* From *Improving Middle School Guidance* (p. 54) by M. L. Stamm & B. S. Nissman, 1979, Boston: Allyn and Bacon. Reprinted by permission.

The communication service cluster is primarily concerned with public relations. It is the outreach arm of the counselor and is critical for informing the general public about what the school counseling program is doing. Curriculum services, on the other hand, are concentrated on facilitating course placements and the academic adjustment of students. Beane (1986) stresses that middle school counselors need to help teachers "psychologize" the curriculum so that students can deal with significant issues in their lives, such as peer relationships and values. If the curriculum is not relevant to children at this age, they often divert their energy to nonproductive activities. The third part of the model, the assessment service cluster, provides testing and evaluation services for students and is often linked to the career resource cluster, which focuses on the student's future goals and vocation.

The fifth and sixth areas of this model are the counseling services cluster and the crisis service cluster, which are also closely connected. Counseling services are provided on an individual, peer, and group level and are offered at off-school, as well as regular school, hours. Sometimes counseling activities are aimed at self-counseling, which is "when people (including middle graders) think the ideas that they believe, then react to those ideas with logical emotional reactions and logical physical behaviors" (Maultsby, 1986, p. 207). Rational self-counseling is one research-based way to help students help themselves to deal effectively with their emotions. At other times, peer facilitators are used to help middle schoolers make friends and learn about their environments and schoolwork (Bowman, 1986). There is also someone designated in the Stamm and Nissman model as a crisis person during the school day. This individual deals with emergencies and with the help of the counselor finds an appropriate way to assist the child who is experiencing sudden distress.

The community contact cluster focuses on working with parents and other interested people to open the lines of communication between the school and other agencies. The professional growth cluster provides programs for school staff and paraprofessionals. This last task of educating other school professionals is critical to the counselor's success. If the total school environment is to be positively affected, middle school counselors must help "teachers develop skills related to enhancing the students' self-concept and self-esteem" (Beane, 1986, p. 192).

## SECONDARY SCHOOL COUNSELING AND GUIDANCE

Secondary school counseling and guidance began in the early 1900s when a primary emphasis of counseling was on guidance activities that would help build better citizens (see chapter 1). Frank Parsons influenced the early growth of the profession, though it was John Brewer who in the 1930s really pushed for the establishment of secondary school guidance (Aubrey, 1979). Brewer believed both *guidance* and *education* meant assisting the young person in living, and he thought guidance could be taught as a subject in the public schools (Shertzer & Stone, 1981). His ideas did not gain wide acceptance at the time, but they have become increasingly popular since the 1970s.

The growth of secondary school counseling was particularly dramatic during the 1960s when the employment of counselors more than tripled from about 12,000 in the school year 1958–59 to over 40,000 in 1969–70 (Shertzer & Stone, 1981). An estimated 63,000 people worked as public school counselors during 1986 according to the *Occupational Outlook Handbook*, with the ratio being about three to one in favor of secondary school counselors over elementary school counselors. Several thousand more counselors work in private schools. Though the number of secondary school counselors appears to have leveled off, job openings still result from replacement needs, especially as older counselors retire.

## Emphases and Roles

Counselors located in high school environments concentrate their attention on the following four tasks (ASCA Role Statement, 1981):

☐ Organizing and presenting classroom curricula that focus on developmental concerns of adolescents (e.g. identity, careers).

☐ Organizing and making available to students comprehensive information systems necessary for educational-vocational planning and decision making.

☐ Helping students assess their personal characteristics.

☐ Providing remedial interventions for students needing special help.

Aubrey (1979) argues that a real conflict exists for secondary school counselors faced with both the need for engaging in counseling with students and the need for doing the academic and administrative tasks, such as scheduling, often required by school administrative personnel. He contends that school counselors, especially on the high school level, frequently get bogged down in nonprofessional activities.

Peer (1985) elicited the opinions of state directors of guidance and counseling and others in regard to views about the role of secondary school counselors. He found mixed opinions on how secondary school counselors were perceived. Those who held secondary school programs in highest regard were principals, superintendents, students, college/university personnel, other secondary school counselors, and counselor educators. Teachers, parents, community leaders, and business leaders were less positive. State directors overwhelmingly reported that secondary school counselors were "probably" or "definitely" heavily involved in nonprofessional activities. If such is the case, it is understandable that secondary school counselors have come under heavy criticism from those outside the school environment.

Other negative findings from the Peer survey are that secondary school counselors are not seen as being actively involved in group counseling or group guidance, are not serving as consultants, and are not making an impact on the majority of the students. Programs at this level are not viewed as favorably overall as those in elementary schools in the same district. On a positive note, respondents perceived secondary counselors as avoiding disciplinarian roles, as being well qualified, and as being helpful to individual students, especially those who are college bound. Significantly, respondents thought that counselors could effect changes in counseling programs.

Ways of improving the perception of the secondary school counselor include an emphasis on roles that meet real needs. Jones (1977), for instance, stresses that school counselors must be facilitators of healthy learning environments. He thinks the primary functions of secondary school counselors should include: facilitating problem solving within the regular classroom, developing professional growth groups, and improving staff communications. All of these roles provide counselors with maximum exposure to groups who have traditionally held counselors in low esteem. By functioning as facilitators in student-adult interactions, as well as with adult-adult transactions, counselors provide the means for a productive exchange between divergent and often isolated groups of people.

Hargens and Gysbers (1984) suggest that an important function for any school counselor is the constant remodeling of the program of which he or she is in charge. They recommend the systematic use of evaluative instruments in guiding this task and stress that restructuring efforts always occur while the counselor is active in the system being modified. Their recommendations are similar to those of Stiltner (1978) on conducting need assessments. Secondary school counselors must be in constant touch with their constituents if they are to keep their services and roles appropriate and current.

### *Activities*

The activities of secondary school counselors can be divided into several areas. In addition to evaluation of their own activities, they are involved in prevention, remediation and intervention, and co-operation and facilitation. These categories are not mutually exclusive, and there are a multitude of issues and concerns under each of these headings.

***Prevention.*** Secondary school counselors, like elementary and middle school counselors, stress preventive services. Sprinthall (1984) notes that primary prevention is important in the secondary school because this approach creates "classroom educative experiences that affect students' intellectual and personal development simultaneously" (p. 494). Through a primary preventive approach students become more self-reliant and less dominated by their peer group. They also become less egocentric, more attuned to principles as guidelines in making decisions, and more empathic. Relationships between teacher and counselor, as well as student and counselor, are enhanced in this positive process.

Martin (1983) suggests that many of the common aims of school counseling can be addressed in the classroom through prevention-based curriculum offerings prepared by counselors. Such areas as anxieties about school and tests, study skills, interpersonal relationships, self-control, and career planning may be dealt with in this way. Two major advantages of such an approach are that less time needs to be devoted to remediation and intervention activities and the counselor maintains a positive high profile with teachers and students. Clark and Frith (1983) have described procedures for designing an effective counseling curriculum guide for meeting the needs of students from kindergarten through the twelfth grade.

***Remediation and Intervention.*** Secondary school counselors who initiate remediation and intervention programs are basically trying to help students with specific problems they are currently facing that are not amenable to prevention techniques. Two examples of problems that need counselor intervention are depression and divorce.

Forrest (1983) states that about 15 percent of all school children may be depressed because of external stressors and inadequate individual response abilities. He lists common emotional, physical, intellectual, and behavioral indicators of depression (Table 13.1).

**TABLE 13.1**   Common indicators of depression.

| Emotional (Affective) | Physical (Somatic) | Intellectual (Cognitive) | Behavioral (Doing) |
|---|---|---|---|
| Sadness | Fatigue | Negative self concept | Soft spoken, slow speech |
| Anxiety | Sleep disorders | Negative view of world | Withdrawal from normal social contact |
| Guilt | Eating disorders | Negative expectations for future | Engaging in fewer pleasurable activities |
| Anger | Dispepsia | Self-blame | Seldom smiles or laughs |
| Fear | Constipation | Self-criticism | Eats alone Studies alone |
| Unhappiness | Poorly defined plan | Loss of interest | Does not speak up in class or social encounters |
| Pessimism | Menstrual irregularity | Inability to concentrate | Avoids expressing hostile tendencies |
| Mood variation | High pulse rate with appearance apathy | Poverty of thought | Avoids groups Reduces involvement in sports and games |
| Helplessness | Headaches Stomach aches | Ambivalence | Drab dress Grades take sudden drop |
| Worthlessness | | Indecisiveness | Sighs often and cries easily Procrastinates |

*Source:* From "Depression: Information and Interventions for School Counselors" by D. V. Forrest, 1983, *The School Counselor, 30,* 269–279. Copyright AACD. Reprinted with permission. No further reproduction authorized without further permission of AACD.

Further, he emphasizes the need for school counselors to use a variety of approaches in dealing with depression. Among the most prominent of these are using Lazarus's multimodal model, teaching the student how to develop self-esteem, helping the student become aware of depression and the stress factors that influence it, teaching relaxation procedures, teaching new coping skills, and teaching the modification of negative internal self-messages. All of these approaches take a significant investment of time and energy for both the counselor and student.

Approximately one million children experience parental divorces each year. Cook & McBride (1982) point out that secondary school counselors can help children, their parents, and teachers in adjusting to this process through providing both direct and indirect services. Interventions that directly address divorce problems are individual and group counseling services within the school for the children. Structured, short-term group work can make a positive impact in helping secondary school students sort out and resolve their feelings about the divorce experience. Cook and McBride (1982) also recommend that more indirect services be implemented, such as consulting with teachers and parents about the feelings of these children. Teachers and parents need information on what to expect from children of divorce and what useful interventions they might employ in the process of helping, such as reading books on the subject that parents and children can discuss.

***Cooperation and Facilitation.*** The tasks of cooperation and facilitation involve the counselor's initiation of a variety of community and school activities besides that of care-giver. Bradley (1978) emphasizes that counselors who are not aware of or involved in community and school groups are not as effective as they could otherwise be. Jones (1977) believes that a part of the counselor's responsibility is becoming involved with others. In order to achieve this, secondary school counselors often have to take the initiative in working with teachers and other school personnel. By becoming more involved with teachers, administrators, and sponsors of extra-curricular activities, counselors integrate their views into the total life of the school and in the process help to create a more positive school environment (Edgemon, Remley, & Snoddy, 1985).

In a very practical article on the role of the school counselor as a service coordinator, DeVoe and McClam (1982) stress the importance of school counselors' being accountable for performing three roles. The first role is that of an information retriever. The counselor either collects information or works with other professionals to collect information about particularly complex situations, such as the abused and pregnant teenager who is involved with drugs. The second role is related to service coordination. The counselor determines if he or she has the expertise to meet the needs of particular students. If the counselor does not have the expertise, an appropriate referral is made. The third role is that of an information administrator. The counselor coordinates a plan for the delivery of services to a student by individuals or agencies in non-school counseling settings. This activity involves the planning and implementation of continuous communication among service providers.

A less involved but important way counselors can cooperate with others in the school and community is through participation in individualized education programs (IEPs) (Humes, 1980). Counselors engage in either direct interventions or support services with students for whom IEPs are drawn up. Humes emphasizes that counseling IEPs may be needed for some students. Regardless of special considerations, school counselors can work closely with other school and community personnel to ensure that atypical students receive appropriate educational and support services.

## COLLEGE/UNIVERSITY COUNSELING AND STUDENT AFFAIRS SERVICES

Shertzer and Stone (1980) list a number of major concerns of college students reported in the literature. Among these are future goals, dating relationships, money and jobs, health, personal appearance, social adjustment, self-concept, drugs, anxiety, and depression. The purpose of campus counseling and student affairs services (performed by student personnel professionals) is to humanize, maximize, and individualize the higher education experience and help students find meaning and enjoyment in the college experience, thus making a successful transition from community to institutional life and back again (Berdie, 1966; Brown, 1986). There are times during the college year (e.g., orientation, midterm exams, and near graduation) when student use of counseling and student affairs services peak (Houston, 1971). Although certain problems are universal, such as problems involving careers, other reasons for seeking help are unique to a particular campus, such as those involving the establishment of support networks at large, commuter universities. College and university counselors, as well as other student affairs professionals, must be aware of the nature of particular work environments and adapt services to meet the needs of a particular student population.

Counseling and working with college or university students is similar to secondary school counseling in regard to its long history and its emphasis on developmental issues (Brown & Helms, 1986;

Fitzpatrick, 1968; Johnson, 1985; Kuh & Thomas, 1983). These services have been prevalent especially since the early 1930s (Kirk, Free, Johnson, Michel, Redfield, Roston, & Warman, 1971). Among these services are those concerned with student behaviors (e.g., achievement, attrition, campus activities), student characteristics (e.g., aptitudes, aspirations, marital status), developmental growth (e.g., cognitive, moral, social/emotional), and academic performance (e.g., study skills) (Kuh, Bean, Bradley, & Coomes, 1986).

The professional organizations to which most college counselors and student personnel workers belong are the Division of Counseling Psychology of the American Psychological Association (APA), the American School Counselor Association (ASCA), and the American College Personnel Association (ACPA). The Division of Counseling Psychology and ASCA were discussed earlier so we will briefly focus on the American College Personnel Association.

ACPA, which was officially organized in 1924 and has gone through three name changes, represents the total field of college student affairs. Those who hold membership in ACPA work in a wide variety of settings providing direct and indirect services on college/university campuses, including financial aid, career planning and placement, student health, campus unions, international student activities, admissions, registration, recreation, academic advising, and residence life. The systemic interaction and integration of all of these diverse positions are important to the health and well-being of college students. Garland (1985) says that student affairs professionals must function as "institutional integrators" so that student and college/university goals may be accomplished. One way these services may be organized to benefit the entire college/university community was developed by Chandler (1973). His scheme includes the management of a number of services and personnel, which vary according to the size and mission of the college/university (see Figure 13.2).

### Emphases and Roles

Initially, the emphasis of college/university counseling and student affairs services was on helping new students adjust to campus life (Williamson, 1961). This service is still needed because of the wide variety of circumstances that entering college students face. One of the chief crises students encounter upon entering college is their own sense of identity and commitment to further study. Hayes (1981) emphasizes that graduation from high school involves a loss of identity and a need of older adolescents to re-evaluate themselves and commit to self-determined goals. They are often not helped with

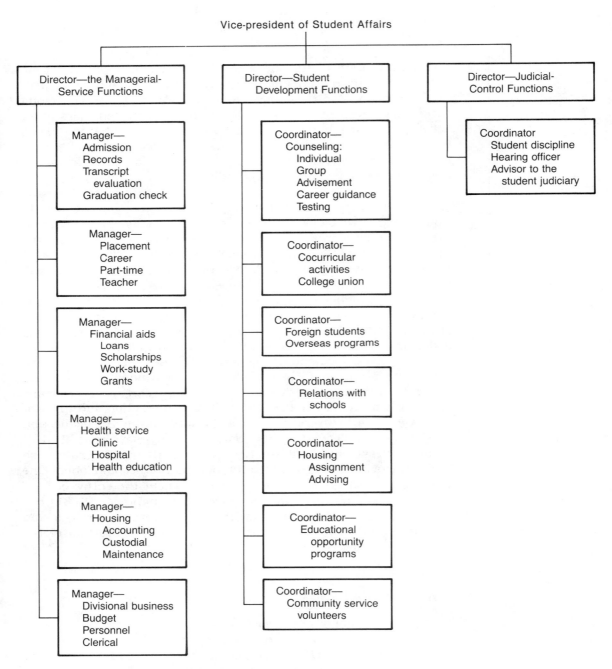

**FIGURE 13.2** A way to organize student services.

*Source:* From "Student Affairs Administration in Transition" by E. M. Chandler, 1979, in *College Student Development Revisited: Programs, Issues, and Practices,* by R. F. Giroux, D. A. Biggs, A. M. Hoffman, & J. J. Pietrofesa (Eds.). Washington, D.C.: APGA Press. Copyright AACD. Reprinted with permission. No further reproduction authorized without further permission of AACD.

this self-evaluation and goal setting in high school, and they enter college in a state of confusion and noncommitment

Grites (1979) notes that 12 of the 43 items on the Social Readjustment Rating Scale (Holmes & Rahe, 1967) almost exclusively pertain to college freshmen in their adjustment to a new environment. When translated into so-called life change units, these changes yield a score of 250, which is in the moderate life crisis category. Individuals in this category are associated with a 51 percent risk of a health change. Grites further observes that if a new student faces other changes outside the college/university environment (e.g., the death of a family member or friend) during the initial adjustment to campus life the student is likely to move into the "major life crisis" category and become more at risk for a health change. Regardless, over the traditional four years of college, approximately 10 percent of all students will encounter an emotional difficulty that is serious enough to impair academic performance (Mathiasen, 1984). In addition, other students will experience emotional, social, or academic problems to such a degree that between 40 and 60 percent of students who begin four-year institutions together will not graduate (Brown, 1986).

There are four main models of counseling services that college/university counseling centers follow and that are frequently employed in residence halls or other student services offices. These are (Utz, 1983):

☐ *Psychotherapy model*  Emphasizes long-term counseling with a small percentage of students and refers vocational/educational problems of students to academic advisers.

☐ *Vocational guidance model*  Emphasizes helping students make decisions on academic and vocational matters and refers personal/emotional problems to other agencies.

☐ *Traditional model*  Focuses on a broad range of student services, including short-term counseling, some long-term counseling, and counseling for vocational/academic problems.

☐ *Consultation model*  Emphasizes working with the entire student body to create a positive mental health atmosphere.

Few, if any, college counseling centers or student service agencies operate exclusively from any one of these four models, although some are more closely aligned to one specific model than others are.

Lewing and Cowger (1982) have identified nine counseling functions of college/university counselors. They include:

Academic and educational counseling

Vocational counseling

Personal counseling

Testing

Supervision and training

Research

Teaching

Professional development

Administration

Three of these activities—personal, vocational, and educational counseling—account for over 50 percent of the counselor's time according to these authors. Many other student personnel professionals also spend a great deal of time engaged in counseling-related services.

Most of the theories of personal counseling previously covered in this book are employed in counseling centers and student affairs offices. For instance, Thurman (1983) found that rational-emotive therapy, including the use of rational-emotive imagery, could be very effective in reducing Type A behavior (i.e., time urgency, competitiveness, and hostility) among college students and help them become healthier achievers. Watkins (1983), on the other hand, found a person-centered approach to be most effective in helping students evaluate present and future plans and decide whether or not to stay in college. Even systems theory, most often used in marriage and family counseling, has proven effective in assisting college students to understand family dynamics and interactions, and thus to make important decisions about education and the direction of personal growth (Openlander & Searight, 1983).

The ASCA role statement (1981) identifies these three main tasks of post-secondary counselors:

☐ To participate in a comprehensive program of student support services in order to assist students in meeting needs, such as financial aid.

☐ To offer students the opportunity to participate in deliberate psychological education experiences that promote interpersonal and intrapersonal growth and development.

☐ To assist students at various levels of ability and maturity identify and use school and community-based opportunities for vocational growth.

### Activities

One of the primary tasks of college/university counselors and student affairs personnel is to inform members of the campus community about the multitude of counseling services available to them. In many ways, their task is similar to that of elementary school counselors, who must make their presence known. Although students generally have a favorable attitude toward counseling and counseling-related services, only a small number of them have a basic awareness of what opportunities are offered by a college counseling center (Johnson, Nelson, & Wooden, 1985). Students turn to friends as a first source of help, then to close relatives, and finally to faculty and counseling services. Sometimes even faculty are not aware of what services are provided through the counseling center, as illustrated in Bishop's (1986) survey of faculty members at the University of Delaware. Bishop found that only 42 percent of the faculty who responded indicated having referred a student to the counseling center and that the most likely reason for referral was personal problems.

In order to increase exposure to students and faculty, counselors in campus counseling centers and other student affairs personnel have tried a number of methods. One effective way of reaching students is through peer counselors. Ragle and Krone (1985) found that freshmen who had previously undergone a summer orientation program at the University of Texas at Austin were overwhelmingly more at ease in talking with a peer advisor over the telephone about various concerns. Further, they felt such contact helpful and indicated that it made the university less impersonal

Sometimes peer counselors take the role of working as resident assistants (RAs) within residence halls (Nickerson & Harrington, 1968). In this arrangement, RAs are assigned to live in select residence halls. Their services, which include dealing with remedial, preventive, and developmental issues, are given high exposure (Schuh, Shipton, & Edman, 1986). RAs work in both a short-term counseling and an educational and referral capacity. They sponsor programs for residents on mental and physical health topics in which faculty and staff from across the campus are brought in to the dorm for presentations. Introductions of this type make it easier for students to seek out counselors or select faculty later on if the need arises. RAs usually receive ongoing training by personnel in the campus counseling center and are often supervised or work with other student affairs professionals, such as directors of residence life or deans of student affairs. This arrangement benefits the RAs, the students within the residence halls, and the campus as a whole because of its integrative nature and its emphasis on prevention and problem solving.

In addition to working with peer counselors and RAs, campus counseling staffs also provide training for potential helpers, such as bartenders, campus police, and others on and off campus who come into direct contact with students (Bernard, Roach, & Resnick, 1981). The idea behind this arrangement is that these individuals are ideally placed to serve as "gatekeepers," who function as important links between the public and college mental health providers. For instance, since many college students have acute and chronic alcohol-related difficulties (Seay & Beck, 1984), the bartender may play an important role in helping the student get needed help. The bartender is usually seen as a friend, and as Berdie & Stein (1966) note, "Having a friend who is familiar with counseling services or who recommends such services is a prime factor in service use" (p. 457).

Another major way campus counseling and student affairs services are promoted is through the direct sponsorship of educational workshops on specific topics. For example, Altmaier and McNabb (1984) describe a one-day workshop at the University of Iowa that focused on re-entry students. It included sessions on student services, study skills, admissions, career decision making, and the management of multiple roles. Workshops of this nature, which are held during the first few weeks of the academic term or even before students enroll, provide needed information on campus life and introduce students to student affairs staff members in a very positive way. However, seminars on relevant topics, such as stress management, are always popular and also help students meet real and immediate needs. Stevens (1984) notes several ways stress management can be dealt with on an individual or group basis, such as assessment of current stressors, stress information, relaxation training, and cognitive restructuring.

When students understand the reasons for campus counseling and student personnel services and know where to find those services, the students usually use them. At some colleges and universities there is the problem of a waiting list at the campus counseling center (Clack, Stone, & Thurman, 1984). Time-limited counseling, where a set number of counseling sessions is agreed upon by the counselor and client beforehand, is one way of alleviating this difficulty. Other students, whose needs involve information acquisition, can be referred to a student affairs professional outside the counseling center, such as a financial officer or a career placement specialist. This strategy of referring students to appropriate student affairs professionals works well, especially for those whose needs are more cognitively oriented or focused in a specific direction.

## SUMMARY

Counseling with students is a complex and varied professional area. Counselors who are skilled in working with one age or stage group within this domain may lack the necessary knowledge to be effective with another group. For instance, there is a vast difference between counseling elementary students and college students. Although the theories and techniques employed with these populations overlap, they also vary considerably.

Nevertheless, there are some elements in common for school and college counseling. First, counselors who work in educational settings must often make their services known to students since counselors are not high on the list of persons students normally use in time of need. Second, there is a need for counselors in all educational settings to assess the major concerns of the populations with whom they work. This type of assessment should be systematic, continuous, and representative of the population served. Third, counselors who work in education concentrate on prevention and many of their activities, therefore, take the form of classroom guidance or formal workshops. Finally, counselors who are employed within educational institutions must take an active part in helping those around them promote positive mental health and provide needed services. Counseling within education cannot be limited to one-on-one encounters within a counselor's office.

## CLASSROOM ACTIVITIES

1. Interview counselors who work in two of the four settings discussed in this chapter. Ask them to describe what they do and how they go about accomplishing it. Write up your interview and discuss the similarities and differences among counselors and settings with your classmates and instructor.

2. Review a recent edition of one of the professional journals mentioned in this chapter. What types of articles are included in the journal? What does this information tell you about present and future trends in school and college counseling?

3. As a variation on activity two, review issues of journals mentioned in this chapter that are 5, 10, and 15 years old. What problems and patterns do you detect? Are some problem areas still present?

4. Imagine that you have just been employed as a school or college counselor in a setting that has never had a counselor before. How would you go about establishing and promoting your position and program? Discuss your strategies with two other classmates and then with the class as a whole.

5. What do you see as the most pressing problems of students in schools and colleges today? Pick a specific environment, such as a middle school or a college, and describe how you might get others, especially those in the administration, to help you in working with students encountering these problems. Discuss your ideas in small groups of four and then with the class as a whole.

## REFERENCES

Allan, J., & Clark, M. (1984). Directed art counseling. *Elementary School Guidance and Counseling, 19,* 116–124.

Allan, J., & Dyck, P. (1983). Improving school climate through cross-grade interactions. *Elementary School Guidance and Counseling, 18,* 137–145.

Altmaier, E. M., & McNabb, T. F. (1984). A reentry workshop for nontraditional students. *Journal of College Student Personnel, 25,* 88–90.

Anderson, R. (1976). Peer facilitation: History and issues. *Elementary School Guidance and Counseling, 11,* 16–25.

ASCA Role Statement (1981). The practice of guidance and counseling by school counselors. *The School Counselor, 29,* 7–12.

Aubrey, R. F. (1979). Relationship of guidance and counseling to the established and emerging school curriculum. *The School Counselor, 26,* 150–162.

Bachman, R. W. (1975). Elementary school children's perceptions of helpers and their characteristics. *Elementary School Guidance and Counseling, 10,* 103–109.

Beane, J. A. (1986). The self-enhancing middle-grade school. *The School Counselor, 33,* 189–195.

Berdie, R. F. (1966). Student personnel work: Definition and redefinition. *Journal of College Student Personnel, 7,* 131–136.

Berdie, R. F., & Stein, J. (1966). A comparison of new university students who do and do not seek counseling. *Journal of Counseling Psychology, 13,* 310–317.

Bernard, H. S., Roach, A. M., & Resnick, H. (1981). Training bartenders as helpers on a college campus. *Personnel and Guidance Journal, 60,* 119–121.

Bernard, J. M. (1978). Divorce and young children: Relationships in transition. *Elementary School Guidance and Counseling, 12,* 188–198.

Bishop, J. B. (1986). A faculty review of a university counseling center: Knowledge, perceptions, and recommendations. *Journal of College Student Personnel, 27,* 413–417.

Bonebrake, C. R., & Borgers, S. B. (1984). Counselor role as perceived by counselors and principals. *Elementary School Guidance and Counseling, 18,* 194–199.

Bowman, R. P. (1986). Peer facilitator programs for middle graders: Students helping each other grow up. *The School Counselor, 33,* 221–229.

Bradley, M. K. (1978). Counseling past and present: Is there a future? *Personnel and Guidance Journal, 57,* 42–45.

Brown, R. D. (1986). Editorial. *Journal of College Student Personnel, 27,* 99.

Brown, T., & Helms, J. (1986). The relationship between psychological development issues and anticipated self-disclosure. *Journal of College Student Personnel, 27,* 136–141.

Canon, H. J. (1984). Developmental tasks for the profession: The next 25 years. *Journal of College Student Personnel, 25,* 105–111.

Chandler, E. M. (1979). Student affairs administration in transition. In R. F. Giroux, D. A. Biggs, A. M. Hoffman, & J. J. Pietrofesa (Eds.), *College student development revisited: Programs, issues and practices* (pp. 174–180). Washington, D.C.: APGA Press.

Clack, R. J., Stone, C. T., & Thurman, C. W. (1984). Waiting lists at university and college counseling centers: A national survey. *Journal of College Student Personnel, 25,* 45–49.

Clark, R., & Frith, G. H. (1983). Writing a developmental counseling curriculum: The Vestavia Hills experience. *The School Counselor, 30,* 292–298.

Cook, A. S. & McBride, J. S. (1982). Divorce: Helping children cope. *The School Counselor, 30,* 89–94.

DeBlassie, R. R., & Lebsock, M. S. (1979). Counseling with handicapped children. *Elementary School Guidance and Counseling, 13,* 199–206.

DeVoe, M. W., & McClam, T. (1982). Service coordination: The school counselor. *The School Counselor, 30,* 95–100.

Dinkmeyer, D. (1973). Elementary school counseling: Prospects and potentials. *The School Counselor, 52,* 171–174.

Dinkmeyer, D. C., & Caldwell, C. E. (1970). *Developmental counseling and guidance: A comprehensive school approach.* New York: McGraw-Hill.

Dougherty, A. M. (1981). An in-service training unit of transescence for middle school teachers. *Elementary School Guidance and Counseling, 16,* 51–53.

Dougherty, A. M. (1986). The blossoming of youth: Middle graders "on the grow." *The School Counselor, 33,* 167–169.

Edgemon, A. W., Remley, T. P., Jr., & Snoddy, H. N. (1985). Integrating the counselor's point of view. *The School Counselor, 32,* 296–301.

Eichhorn, D. H. (1968). Middle school organization: A new dimension. *Theory into Practice, 7,* 111–113.

Elkind, D. (1986). Stress and the middle grader. *The School Counselor, 33,* 196–206.

Fitzpatrick, R. (1968). The history of college counseling. In M. Siegel (Ed.), *The counseling of college students* (pp. 3–14). New York: The Free Press.

Forrest, D. V. (1983). Depression: Information and interventions for school counselors. *The School Counselor, 30,* 269–279.

Furlong, M. J., Atkinson, D. R., & Janoff, D. S. (1979). Elementary school counselors' perceptions of their actual and ideal roles. *Elementary School Guidance & Counseling, 14,* 4–11.

Garland, P. H. (1985). *Serving more than students: A critical need for college student personnel services.* Washington, D.C.: Association for the Study of Higher Education.

Gerler, E. R., Jr. (1985). Elementary school counseling research and the classroom learning environment. *Elementary School Guidance and Counseling, 20,* 39–48.

Gladding, S. T. (1982). Through the seasons to new life. *The Humanist Educator, 20,* 122.

Grites, T. J. (1979). Between high school counselor and college advisor—A void. *Personnel and Guidance Journal, 58,* 200–204.

Hargens, M., & Gysbers, N. C. (1984). How to remodel a guidance program while living in it: A case study. *The School Counselor, 32,* 119–125.

Hayes, R. L. (1981). High school graduation: The case for identity loss. *Personnel and Guidance Journal, 59,* 369–371.

Holmes, T. H., & Rahe, R. H. (1967). The social readjustment rating scale. *Journal of Psychosomatic Research, 11,* 213–218.

Houston, B. K. (1971). Sources, effects and individual vulnerability of psychological problems for college students. *Journal of Counseling Psychology, 18,* 157–161.

Humes, C. W., II (1980). Counseling IEPs. *The School Counselor, 28,* 87–91.

Isaacson, L. E., & Hayes, R. (1980). Adapting career day to the elementary school. *Elementary School Guidance and Counseling, 14,* 258–261.

James, R., & Kazalunas, J. (1979). You've come a long way, baby: Summary of the 1978 elementary guidance conference.

*Elementary School Guidance and Counseling, 13,* 279–284.

Johnson, C. S. (1985). The American College Personnel Association. *Journal of Counseling and Development, 63,* 405–410.

Johnson, D. H., Nelson, S. E., & Wooden, D. J. (1985). Faculty and student knowledge of university counseling centers services. *Journal of College Student Personnel, 26,* 27–32.

Jones, V. F. (1977). School counselors as facilitators of healthy learning environments. *The School Counselor, 24,* 157–164.

Kirk, B. A., Free, J. E., Johnson, A. P., Michel, J., Redfield, J. E., Roston, R. A., & Warman, R. E. (1971). Guidelines for university and college counseling services. *American Psychologist, 26,* 585–589.

Kuh, G., & Thomas, M. (1983). The use of adult development theory with graduate students. *Journal of College Student Personnel, 24,* 12–19.

Kuh, G. D., Bean, J. P., Bradley, R. K., & Coomes, M. D. (1986). Contributions of student affairs journals to the literature on college students. *Journal of College Student Personnel 27,* 292–304.

Lewing, R. L., Jr., & Cowger, E. L., Jr. (1982). Time spent on college counselor functions. *Journal of College Student Personnel, 23,* 41–48.

Marin, R. (1985). Lose to win: A goal oriented group for overweight children. *The School Counselor, 32,* 219–223.

Martin, J. (1983). Curriculum development in school counseling. *Personnel and Guidance Journal, 61,* 406–409.

Mathiasen, R. E. (1984). Attitudes and needs of the college student-client. *Journal of College Student Personnel, 25,* 274–275.

Maultsby, M. C., Jr. (1986). Teaching rational self-counseling to middle graders. *The School Counselor, 33,* 207–219.

Minkoff, H. B., & Terres, C. K. (1985). ASCA perspective: Past, present, and future.

*Journal of Counseling and Development, 63,* 424–427.

Morgan, C., & Jackson, W. (1980). Guidance as a curriculum. *Elementary School Guidance and Counseling, 15,* 99–103.

Muro, J. J. (1981). On target—On top. *Elementary School Guidance and Counseling, 15,* 307–314.

Muro, J. J., & Dinkmeyer, D. C. (1977). *Counseling in the elementary and middle schools.* Dubuque, IA: Brown.

Myrick, R. D., & Bowman, R. P. (1983). Peer helpers and the learning process. *Elementary School Guidance and Counseling, 80,* 111–117.

Nickerson, D. L., & Harrington, J. T. (1968). *The college student as counselor.* Moravia, NY: Chronicle Guidance Publications.

Nugent, F. A. (1981). *Professional counseling: An overview.* Monterey, CA: Brooks/Cole.

Openlander, P., & Searight, R. (1983). Family counseling perspectives in the college counseling center. *Journal of College Student Personnel, 24,* 423–427.

Peer, G. G. (1985). The status of secondary school guidance: A national survey. *The School Counselor, 32,* 181–189.

Peters, H. J. (1980). *Guidance in the elementary school.* New York: Macmillan.

Ragle, J., & Krone, K. (1985). Extending orientation: Telephone contacts by peer advisers. *Journal of College Student Personnel, 26,* 80–81.

Schmidt, J. J., & Osborne, W. L. (1982). The way we were (and are): A profile of elementary counselors in North Carolina. *Elementary School Guidance & Counseling, 16,* 163–171.

Schuh, J. J., Shipton, W. C., & Edman, N. (1986). Counseling problems encountered by resident assistants: An update. *Journal of College Student Personnel, 27,* 26–33.

Seay, T. A., & Beck, T. D. (1984). Alcoholism among college students. *Journal of College Student Personnel, 25*, 90–92.

Shertzer, B., & Stone, S. C. (1980). *Fundamentals of counseling* (3rd ed.). Boston: Houghton Mifflin.

Shertzer, B., & Stone, S. C. (1981). *Fundamentals of guidance* (4th ed.). Boston: Houghton Mifflin.

Sprinthall, N. A. (1984). Primary prevention: A road paved with a plethora of promises and procrastinations. *Personnel and Guidance Journal, 62*, 491–495.

Stamm, M. L., & Nissman, B. S. (1979). *Improving middle school guidance.* Boston: Allyn & Bacon.

Stevens, M. J. (1984). Stress management interventions. *Journal of College Student Personnel, 25*, 269–270.

Stiltner, B. (1978). Needs assessment: A first step. *Elementary School Guidance and Counseling, 12*, 239–246.

Thompson, C. L., & Rudolph, L. B. (1983). *Counseling children.* Monterey, CA: Brooks/Cole.

Thornburg, H. D. (1978). *The bubblegum years: Sticking with kids from 9 to 13.* Tucson: HELP Books.

Thornburg, H. D. (1986). The counselor's impact on middle-grade students. *The School Counselor, 33*, 170–177.

Thurman, C. (1983). Effects of a rational-emotive treatment program on Type A behavior among college students. *Journal of College Student Personnel, 24*, 417–423.

Utz, P. W. (1983). Counseling college students. In M. M. Ohlsen (Ed.), *Introduction to counseling.* Itasca, IL: Peacock.

Watkins, E. (1983). Project retain: A client centered approach to student retention. *Journal of College Student Personnel, 24*, 81.

Weinhold, B. K., & Hilferty, J. (1983). The self-esteem matrix: A tool for elementary counselors. *Elementary School Guidance and Counseling, 17*, 243–251.

Wilder, P. (1980). The role of the elementary school counselor in counseling about death. *Elementary School Guidance and Counseling, 15*, 56–65.

Williamson, E. G. (1961). *Student personnel services in colleges and universities.* New York: McGraw-Hill.

Wilson, N. H., & Rotter, J. C. (1980). Elementary school counselor enrichment and renewal. *Elementary School Guidance & Counseling, 14*, 178–187.

Photo by James S. Davidson III.

# CHAPTER 14

# *Rehabilitation and Mental Health Counseling*

*As our sessions go on you speak of your scars*
    *and show me the places where you have been burned.*
*Sadly, I hear your fiery stories*
    *reliving with you, through your memories and words,*
    *all of the tension-filled blows and events*
    *that have beaten and shaped your life.*
*"I wish I were molten steel" you say,*
*"And you were a blacksmith's hammer.*
    *Maybe then, on time's anvil, we could structure together*
    *a whole new person, with soft smooth sounds,*
    *inner strength and glowing warmth."*[1]

---

[1]Gladding, 1977, p. 246. Copyright AACD. Reprinted with permission. No further reproduction authorized without written permission of AACD.

The American Rehabilitation Counselor Association (ARCA) and the American Mental Health Counselor Association (AMHCA) are two specialty divisions of the American Association for Counseling and Development (AACD) whose activities are covered in this chapter. The history and development of these groups are strikingly similar yet distinct. Counselors in both organizations focus on the whole person, but rehabilitation counselors are more concerned with helping clients obtain or regain employment and independent living, whereas mental health counselors concentrate more on preventive services and the promotion of wellness, in addition to direct treatment services. The theories and techniques used by these two groups of counselors are basically the same, though adapted for the respective populations served.

ARCA publishes a quarterly professional journal, the *Rehabilitation Counseling Bulletin*, and cooperates with the National Rehabilitation Counseling Association (NRCA) in producing professional newsletters and in other projects that serve their common interests. Many rehabilitation professionals hold joint membership in ARCA and NRCA. AHMCA publishes the *Journal of Mental Health Counseling* (formerly *AMHCA Journal*), which is also a quarterly journal. Its members usually also belong to several professional organizations, such as other divisions of AACD or the APA. In this chapter, the focus is on these two essential areas of counseling—rehabilitation counseling and mental health counseling—and on the professional organizations that provide the structure to support their functions.

## DEVELOPMENT OF ARCA AND AMHCA:
## COMMON THREADS

The formation and development of ARCA and AMHCA parallel each other in at least three important ways. First, ARCA and AMHCA were both initially started because of the absence of counseling organizations in rehabilitation and mental health. ARCA began as an interest group of the National Vocational Guidance Association soon after World War II. Before ARCA's founding, the National Rehabilitation Association (NRA) "had no organizational membership for professional counselors, but was made up of highly diverse people from all walks of life" (DiMichael & Thomas, 1985, p. 429). Thus, ARCA filled a void for a professional counseling organization within rehabilitation. It became a part of AACD (then APGA) as the Division of Rehabilitation Counseling (DRC) in 1958 and as ARCA in 1961.

The formation of AMHCA also grew out of an unmet need. The Community Mental Health Centers Act of 1963 established over 2,000 community mental health centers nationwide that employed counselors as well as other mental health professionals, such as psychiatrists, psychologists, psychiatric nurses, and social workers. Counselors were the only group among these professionals without an organization with which to identify. The need to form a professional group was recognized by Jim Messina and Nancy Spisso at the Escambia County (Florida) Mental Health Center in 1976, and from their efforts AMHCA began. AMHCA existed for almost two years as an independent organization before officially becoming the 13th division of AACD in 1978 (Weikel, 1985).

A second area of similarity in the development of ARCA and AMHCA is the influence of federal and state legislation on the growth of each. Rehabilitation has a long history of involvement with the federal government. It began in 1920 when Congress passed the Vocational Rehabilitation Act (Schumacher, 1983). The changes that have occurred in both the role and work setting of the rehabilitation counselor since that time are described by Sinick (1973), who sees the field as being in a state of "constant flux" as the result of "societal pushes and legislative pulls, . . . out-group pressures and in-group complacencies," where "long-range goals" are "vying with short-term criteria . . ." (p. 167).

Initially, rehabilitation activities focused on the physically disabled, but now they include those with emotional, mental, and behavioral disabilities. Bitter (1979) and Porter (1981) list a number of disabilities commonly dealt with by rehabilitation counselors: alcoholism, arthritis, blindness, cardiovascular disease, deafness, developmental disabilities, cerebral palsy, epilepsy, mental retardation, drug abuse, neurological disorders, orthopedic disabilities, psychiatric disabilities, renal failure, speech impairments, and spinal cord conditions. Steps have been taken in recent years to provide services for the economically disadvantaged, public offenders, and other less obvious and often neglected groups, too. With such a heterogeneous population, rehabilitation counselors typically work with other service agencies to provide needed programs for their clients. An example of this cooperative approach is that between rehabilitation counselors and school counselors on behalf of handicapped children (DiMichael & Thomas, 1985).

Mental health counselors have also been strongly influenced by federal and state legislative acts that have set standards for the delivery of mental health services. Members of AMHCA, in turn, have been active in supporting federal and state legislation that recognizes certified clinical mental health counselors as "core practitioners" within the mental health profession. They have been involved also in defining the areas in which they work and in establishing guidelines for how to function in these areas. Seiler and Messina (1979), in keeping with these efforts, define the essence of mental health counseling as promoting healthy life-styles, identifying and eliminating stressors in individuals' life-styles, and preserving or restoring mental health. Wilmarth (1985b) notes that mental health counselors are engaged in assessing and analyzing background and current information on clients, diagnosing mental and emotional conditions, exploring possible solutions, and developing treatment plans. Preventive mental health activities and a recognition of the relationship between physical and mental health have become very prominent since the mid-1970s, when the President's Commission on Mental Health was created and initial government entitlements were directed toward prevention of mental disorders and the promotion of wellness (Fisher, 1986). Attention to these aspects of mental health counseling continues to increase.

A final similarity between the development of rehabilitation and mental health counseling is the settings in which counselors are employed. Traditionally, most rehabilitation counselors have been hired by federal, state, and local agencies. Since the late 1960s, however, more have moved into for-profit agencies and private practice (Lewin, Ramseur, & Sink, 1979). While the majority of mental health counselors in 1985 were employed in private practice, during the early years of AMHCA most worked in community mental health centers (Weikel, 1985). The movement of professionals in both disciplines from the public sector into private employment is the result of several developments, such as economic changes, new emphases by businesses and insurance companies, national professional certification requirements, and state licensure laws that have affected all counselors.

## REHABILITATION COUNSELING

*Rehabilitation* is helping "handicapped and disabled persons achieve the highest possible level of productive functioning" (Schmolling, Youkeles, & Burger, 1985, p. 9). *Rehabilitation counseling* is the professional medium for rendering this help. Specifically, it is a relationship between a counselor and a client formed to assist the client in understanding his or her problems and potentials and in learning to use personal and environmental resources to achieve the best possible vocational, personal, and social adjustment (Jaques, 1970).

Rehabilitation differs from habilitation primarily in emphasis on education. Rehabilitation stresses re-education of handicapped individuals who have previously lived independent lives; *habilitation* focuses on educating handicapped clients who have been disabled from early life and who have never been self-sufficient (Bitter, 1979). Rehabilitation counselors also distinguish between having a disability and being handicapped, and official definitions of what constitutes a disability are crucial in the work of the rehabilitation counselor (Fagan & Wallace, 1979). A person with a *disability* has either a physical or a mental condition which limits that person's activities or functioning (Department of Health, Education, and Welfare, 1974). It is estimated that 10 to 15 percent of the population of the United States is disabled (Parker & Hansen, 1981). A *handicap*, which is linked to a disability, is "an observable or discernible limitation that is made so by the presence of various barriers" (Schumacher, 1983, p. 320). An example of a disabled person with a handicap is an individual who is quadriplegic and is assigned to a third floor apartment in a building without an elevator. Rehabilitation counselors help their clients overcome handicaps and effectively cope with their disabilities.

An interesting aspect of rehabilitation counseling that distinguishes it from other forms of counseling is its historical link with the medical model of delivering services (Ehrle, 1979). The prominence of the medical model in this field is easy to understand when we recall how closely professionals in rehabilitation have been involved with the physically handicapped. Indeed, rehabilitation counselors must know medical concepts and terminology. But the dominance of the medical model appears to be giving way to more pragmatic models (Anthony, 1980; Livneh, 1984).

Stone (1978) lists three ways in which rehabilitation counseling differs from other types of counseling. First, there are differences in the nature of the clients served. Rehabilitation counselors work with a much more impaired population than do other counselors. Most rehabilitation clients have severe physical, mental, or behavioral disorders.

Second, rehabilitation counselors are responsible for providing clients with educational information and with remedial and therapeutic treatment. Unlike other counselors, rehabilitation counselors have traditionally focused their efforts and measured their success on whether a client obtains employment. Many beginning rehabilitation counseling students embrace the Protestant work ethic (Thomas, Carter, & Britton, 1982). As Sinick (1973) observes, the word "vocational" is incorporated in the name of many state agencies and job titles that relate to the field.

Third, rehabilitation counselors are expected by clients to be professionals who will provide a wide range of services, especially services connected with disabilities and employment. All clients expect much of counselors, but rehabilitation clients have more specific needs and hopes than most.

### Theories and Techniques

Rehabilitation counselors use a wide variety of counseling theories and techniques (Bitter, 1979; Schumacher, 1983). In fact they use almost all of the affective, behavioral, and cognitive theories reviewed in this text. Bitter (1979) notes that the theoretical approach employed by a rehabilitation counselor has more to do with the training, background and style of the counselor than with a psychology of the disabled. Ideally, counseling theories and the techniques that accompany them are chosen with regard for specific situations and the strengths of the client and counselor. This is in keeping with Rusalem's (1976) observation that one of the main tasks of a rehabilitation counselor is to help the client accept and adjust to his or her disability and to the attitudes and reactions of society at large.

Livneh and Evans (1984) point out that rehabilitation clients who suffer physical disabilities (e.g., blindness or spinal cord injuries) go through twelve phases of adjustment: shock, anxiety, bargaining, denial, mourning, depression, withdrawal, internalized anger, externalized aggression, acknowledgement, acceptance, and adjustment-adaptation. They believe that there are behavioral correlates that accompany each phase and intervention strategies appropriate for each phase. For example, the client who is in a state of shock may be immobilized and cognitively disorganized. Intervention strategies most helpful during this time include comforting the person (both physically and verbally), listening and attending, offering support and reassurance, allowing the person to ventilate feelings, and referring the person to institutional care, if appropriate.

Livneh and Evans think that as a general rule affective and insight strategies are more appropriate for the early phases of the adjustment process and that more action and rational orientations work best in the later phases. They also contend that disabled clients with low intelligence or low levels of energy may best be served by more direct and action-oriented counseling theories and techniques, such as Bandura's modeling, Skinner's operant conditioning, Krumboltz's behavioral counseling, and Glasser's reality therapy. On the other hand, rehabilitation clients with relatively high levels of energy and intelligence may respond better to more indirect counseling strategies, such as Rogers's person-centered approach, May's or Frankl's existential therapy, Adler's individual counseling theory, and Perl's Gestalt therapy.

Coven (1977) notes that there is little support in the research literature for the effectiveness of indirect counseling methods in rehabilitation counseling. Therefore, he also advocates that rehabilitation counselors use more action-oriented approaches, such as those generated by behavioral and Gestalt theories. Coven thinks that Gestalt psychodrama can be especially powerful in helping rehabilitation clients become more involved in the counseling process and in accepting responsibility for their lives. Techniques such as role playing, fantasy enactment, and psychodrama can be learned and used by clients to help in adjustment.

Some specific ways rehabilitation counselors provide services are best illustrated by a few examples. Hendrick (1981) points out that such physical injuries as spinal cord damage produce a major loss for an individual and consequently have a tremendous physical and emotional impact. Rehabilitation in such cases requires a concentration of effort on both the client's and the family's adjustment to the situation. Help in working through the mourning process by all involved is needed, as are the development of detailed medical, social, and psychological evaluations. A long-term commitment by the counselor is required that involves carefully timed supportive counseling, crisis intervention, confrontation, life-planning activities, sex counseling, and group counseling. In addition to the role of the counselor, a professional who works with the physically disabled must be an advocate, a consultant, and an educator. The task is comprehensive and involves a complex relationship among job functions.

When disabled children are also mentally retarded, the tasks and techniques used may be similar in some ways to those employed with a physically disabled adult or adolescent, such as supportive counseling and life-planning activities, though young clients with mental deficiencies require even more and different activities. Norton (1976) advocates that counselors who work with such populations first work through personal feelings about these children. Only then may counselors begin to be helpful. Huber (1979) asserts that in working with this population, it is crucial that counselors also help parents of such children assess feelings, ideally in a parent group setting.

Finally, Hollingsworth and Mastroberti (1983) point out that in dealing with minority groups, such as disabled women workers, counselors must be aware of the developmental processes typical in such populations, and be prepared with appropriate counseling techniques for the problems peculiar to each group. Counseling with disabled women, for examples, involves four interrelated elements: "(a) job or skill training or education; (b) family support services; (c) trait-and-factor job matching and placement services; and (d) soft counseling support services" (Hollingsworth & Mastroberti, 1983, p. 590).

It should be clear that in working with the disabled and handicapped, the rehabilitation counselor must be a "jack of all trades" (Gressard & Hume, 1983). He or she must not only provide services directly but also coordinate services with other professionals and monitor clients' progress in gaining more independence and self-control. In accomplishing this complex task for so varied a population of clients, a counselor needs skills in an array of theories and techniques and adaptability in shifting professional roles.

## Roles and Functions

There are several competing, but not necessarily mutually exclusive, ideas about what roles and functions rehabilitation counselors should assume. In the late 1960s, Muthard and Salomone conducted the first systematic investigation of rehabilitation counselors' work activities (Bolton & Jaques, 1978). They found eight major activities that characterize the rehabilitation counselor's role and noted a high degree of importance attached to affective counseling, vocational counseling, and placement duties (Muthard & Salomone, 1978). In this survey, rehabilitation counselors reported spending about 33 percent of their time in counseling activities, 25 percent of their time in clerical duties, and 7 percent of their time in placement of clients.

Twelve major functions of rehabilitation counselors listed by the U.S. Department of Labor in 1970 (Schumacher, 1983) are still relevant. They are:

☐ *Personal counseling*   This function entails working with clients individually from one or more theoretical models. It plays a vital part in helping clients make complete social and emotional adjustments to the circumstance in which they find themselves. It is an area in which rehabilitation counselors are weak, according to Plummer (1971).

☐ *Case finding*   Case finding is when rehabilitation counselors attempt to make their services known to agencies and potential clients through the use of promotional and educational materials.

☐ *Eligibility determination*   This is the process whereby rehabilitation counselors determine, through a standard set of guidelines, whether a potential client meets the criteria of an agency for funding.

☐ *Training*   The identification of client skills and the purchase of educational or training resources to help clients enhance skills are the primary aspects of training. It is necessary to provide training to some clients in order to make them eligible for employment in a specific area.

☐ *Provision of restoration*   This is the arrangement for needed devices (e.g., artificial limbs or wheelchairs) and for medical services that will make the client eligible for employment and more independent generally.

☐ *Support services*   The scope of these services ranges from the providing of medication to individual and group counseling. They are offered to help the client develop in personal and interpersonal areas while receiving training or other services.

☐ *Job placement*   This function involves directly helping the client find employment. Activities within this realm range from supporting clients who initiate a search for work to helping less-motivated clients prepare to exert more initiative.

☐ *Planning*   The planning process requires the counselor to include the client as an equal. The plan a counselor and client work out together should change the client from a recipient of services to an initiator of services.

☐ *Evaluation*   This function of the rehabilitation process is continuous and self-correcting. The counselor combines information from all aspects of the client's life in determining needs and priorities.

☐ *Agency consultation*   The rehabilitation counselor works with agencies and individuals to set up or coordinate client services, such as job placement or evaluation. Much of the counselor's work is done jointly with other professionals.

☐ *Public relations*   The counselor is an advocate for clients and executes this role by informing community leaders about the nature and scope of rehabilitation services.

☐ *Follow-along*   This function involves the counselor's constant interaction with agencies and individuals who are serving the client. It also includes maintaining contact with the clients themselves in order to assure a steady progress toward rehabilitation.

In an extensive examination of the professional duties of 1,135 Certified Rehabilitation Counselors (CRC), six major job functions were identified (Rubin, Matkin, Ashley, Beardsley, May, Onstott, & Pucket, 1984). These counselor tasks are considered essential in any work setting. First are tasks concerned with preparing and monitoring a client's progress in attaining specified rehabilitation objectives. Counselors and clients need to be sure of goals and how well those goals are being achieved. Second, counselors must make referrals of clients and coordinate services with other agencies. Rehabilitation counseling is a multidimensional task whose success is dependent on a strong system of interconnection. A third duty centers on vocational counseling, which includes such activities as the discussion of a client's assets, limitations, and possible suitable occupations.

A fourth duty of a rehabilitation counselor is focused on affective counseling. The counselor must be able to hear the feelings of a client in regard to employment or achievement of goals. A fifth duty is test interpretation and the integration of rehabilitation planning. It is essential that goals and plans be based on realistic data. Finally, counselors must continuously read the professional literature in order to keep up with current business and legal trends. This type of knowledge is essential for helping clients to the fullest.

The similarity between what rehabilitation counselors actually do and their formal job description is striking. Rehabilitation counseling has a strong and clear identity. Counselors within the profession do not engage in certain activities, such as the development and administration of tests, or the accompanying of clients to job interviews. Their roles are limited to assure functionality and efficiency.

### Certification

The pioneering spirit of rehabilitation counseling is seen in the early efforts of its members to obtain certification for the profession and credentials for its practitioners. Rehabilitation counselors were among the first to advocate and set up a system of certification for individual counselors—the Commission on Rehabilitation Counselor Certification (CRCC). A parallel move, which led to the accreditation of rehabilitation counselor training institutions, was the establishment of the Council of Rehabilitation Education (CORE). Both of these certifying agencies became firmly established in the 1970s before the first general counselor certification/licensure efforts were initiated.

Gressard and Hume (1983) predict that in the future only certified rehabilitation counselors will be employed. A clear and major trend in this field is the establishment and maintenance of standards for educational programs and for individual counselors. DiMichael and Thomas (1985) note that the majority of some 100 graduate programs in rehabilitation education are already CORE accredited and that there are over 13,000 certified rehabilitation counselors. The next step in the professionalization of rehabilitation will be licensing of rehabilitation counselors on the state level.

## MENTAL HEALTH COUNSELING

The *Occupational Outlook Handbook* (1986–1987) identifies *mental health counselors* as persons who "help individuals deal with a wide range of personal and social problems such as drug and alcohol abuse, family conflicts, including child and spouse abuse, suicide, work problems, criminal behavior, and problems of aging. They also counsel rape victims, and individuals and families trying to cope with illness and death, and people with emotional problems" (pp. 134–135). These counselors are seen as working closely with other specialists, such as psychiatrists, psychologists, clinical social workers, and psychiatric nurses.

Mental health counselors are employed in a variety of settings, including community mental health centers, community agencies, private practice counseling settings, colleges, health maintenance organizations (HMO), employee assistance programs (EAP), and health and wellness promotion programs (HWP). Many counselors employed in mental health centers initially received what Lewis and Lewis (1977) describe as a generic education in agency/community counseling. The development of the work into a speciality is attributed to the development of the community mental health center movement and the trend among all mental health service professionals to clearly define their roles and achieve licensure and certification (Jerse, 1983). That mental health practitioners with master's degrees did not have a group with which to identify professionally sparked the rapid growth of the American Mental Health Counselor Association. By 1985, it had become the largest division of AACD.

Seiler and Messina (1979) emphasize that mental health counseling includes the promotion of healthy life-styles and the identification and reduction of stressful elements that interfere with individual functioning. There are AMHCA task forces on holistic health, business and industrial mental health, aging and adult development, and mental and health-related counseling issues that involve prevention and proactive issues. This focus is very important, since the number of people who need and seek mental health services cannot adequately be dealt with by the nation's mental health providers even if the treatment of clients was the only activity in which these professionals were engaged (Lichtenberg, 1986; Meehl, 1973). An emphasis on prevention is even more essential since the number of individuals requiring mental health services is increasing (Wilmarth, 1985b).

### Theories and Functions

Mental health counselors are as diverse as rehabilitation counselors in employment of theories and techniques, in part because mental health counselors work in such varied settings and have such widely varying functions. As with rehabilitation counselors, the responsibilities of mental health counselors and the theories they choose to guide them depend on the needs of their clients.

A sense of the range of concerns of mental health counselors can be obtained by examining the types of information for which individuals in the profession have expressed a need. In a 1978 survey of all AMHCA members, Weikel and Taylor (1979) found members most preferred articles in the *AMHCA Journal* on current issues and topics, special issues on timely topics, research, applied and practice-oriented topics, and concepts and theories. Specific areas of interest to members were marriage and family counseling, licensure, substance abuse, counseling children, and divorce. In a review of the first 13 issues of the *AMHCA Journal*, Seligman and Weinstock (1984) found that the greatest number of articles published in one content area dealt with counseling models and skills. Since research indicates that mental health practitioners tend to formulate their treatment strategies from a select few possible approaches (Butcher, Scofield, & Baker, 1985), the publication of information on models and treatment modalities is of great importance to them. They need to stay abreast of proven treatment methods.

Much of the literature of mental health counseling focuses on the promotion of mental health as well as the treatment of dysfunctions. We will concentrate here on personal and environmental aspects of mental health. Hershenson (1982) suggests an approach to counseling that emphasizes healthy development. He points out that "insofar as counseling derives from a model based on healthy development, it can reasonably hope to achieve its purpose of promoting healthy development in its clients" (p. 409). He notes that Erik Erikson (1963) and Abraham Maslow (1962) offer two solid bases from which mental health counselors can work. The work of each theorist was based on observations about human development and emphasized the promotion of healthy life-styles. The integration of these two systems yields six personal development trends: survival, growth, communication, recognition, mastery, and understanding. The first two of these trends focus on the self, the middle two on interpersonal functions, and the final two on the accomplishment of tasks. Mental health counseling is geared to promoting the improvement of the self in interpersonal relationships and task performance.

In an important and related article on healthy personal development, Heath (1980) outlines a comprehensive model of healthy maturation. He points out that research demonstrates that the psychological maturity of an adolescent is a major predictor of adult mental health and vocational adaptation, and that the degree of adult maturity is related to marital sexuality adjustment and vocational adaptation. His model illustrates how the maturing of four aspects of personality—cognitive skills, self-concept, values, and personal relations—are defined by five interdependent developmental dimensions—increasing symbolization, allocentrism (i.e., other-centeredness and empathic understanding), integration, stability, and autonomy (Figure 14.1).

Heath proposes very practical general principles that counselors can apply with clients to promote their development. Four such principles are (Heath, 1980, p. 395):

☐ "Encourage the anticipatory rehearsal of new adaptations," such as those that deal with jobs and intimate relationships.

☐ "Require constant externalization of what is learned and its correction by action." In essence, Heath says practice makes perfect in the accomplishment of all human tasks.

☐ "Allow a person to experience the consequences of his or her decisions and acts." Heath is in agreement with Adler on this

Dimensions of Development

| Personality Sectors | Symbolization | Allocentrism | Integration | Stability | Autonomy |
|---|---|---|---|---|---|
| Cognitive | | | | | |
| Self-concept | | | | | |
| Values | | | | | |
| Personal Relations | | | | | |

**FIGURE 14.1**  A model for healthy development.

*Source:* From "Wanted: A comprehensive model of healthy development" by D. H. Heath, 1980, *Personnel and Guidance Journal, 58,* p. 393. Copyright AACD. Reprinted with permission. No further reproduction authorized without further permission of AACD.

idea. He notes that inappropriate or excessive rewards may have an unhealthy effect on a person's development.

☐ "Appreciate and affirm strengths." Reinforcement, according to Skinner, is crucial to new learning. Heath agrees and says that the acknowledgement and acceptance of a person's strengths can bolster self-confidence within the person and help him or her take the risks necessary for learning new behaviors.

Focusing on the person's environment is another emphasis of mental health counselors. Huber (1983) sums up much of the research in this growing area of interest and notes that environments have personalities just as people do. Some environments are controlling and rigid whereas others are more flexible and supportive. In order to make the most effective use of this "social ecological perspective," mental health counselors must do the following:

☐ Identify the problem as one essentially connected with a particular setting. Some environments elicit or encourage specific behaviors that may not be healthy.

☐ Gain the agreement of clients and significant others that the environment is the client. It is much easier for most people to see a difficulty as simply a matter related to the individual.

☐ Make an assessment of the dynamic variables within an environment. Moos (1973) has developed a number of ways to evaluate environments. Counselors can work with their clients to determine how specific environments may be functioning in favor of or counter to the client's needs.

☐ Institute social change. The counselor helps the client with specific methods for improving the present environment.

☐ Evaluate the outcome. There is no one way to do this, but the more clearly the criteria for the ideal environment are stated by the client, the better the evaluation possibility.

Marriage is an obvious example of a situation that illustrates the importance of personal, as well as environmental, factors in the well-being of individuals. Wiggins, Moody, and Lederer (1983) conducted a study on marital satisfaction and found that the most significant predictor was the compatibility of couples' tested personality typologies. They concluded, as did Holland (1978), that individuals express "satisfaction with and seek interaction in environments that meet their psychological needs" (Wiggins, et al., 1983, p. 177).

Other situations in which mental health counselors can work with clients to bring about personal and environmental changes are schools (Mayer & Butterworth, 1979) and employee assistance programs (EAPs) (Forrest, 1983). EAPs are especially likely to benefit from the work of mental health counselors. For example, Lewis and Lewis (1986) report that employees who benefit most from the short-term counseling in EAP programs are those who need help in the management of specific problem situations, those who are working to develop specific behaviors, those who are seeking support in dealing with temporary crises, and those who are hoping to improve relationships with family members. In addition to helping clients directly, mental health counselors who work in EAP programs can also train supervisors to use counseling techniques in employee/ supervisor work relationships and thus enhance work relationships, productivity, and morale. Gestalt therapy (Karp, 1985), transactional analysis (Weinrach, 1980), and rational-emotive therapy (Bennett, 1975) are especially useful theories to use in such instruction.

## Certification

AMHCA became involved in the issue of certification early in its history. Wilmarth (1985a) reports that on September 9, 1978, just two years after AMHCA's formation, the AMHCA board of directors approved a procedure for a national certification program. This procedure involved the establishment of the National Academy of Certified Clinical Mental Health Counselors (NACCMHC) as an independently incorporated certification group. Less than a year later, in July of 1979, NACCMHC came into existence and certified its first group of counselors.

**TABLE 14.1** A comparative analysis of clinical mental health service providers

| Service Provider | Minimum Educational Requirements | Clinical Experience and Supervision Requirements | National Professional Association |
|---|---|---|---|
| Certified Clinical Mental Health Counselor | Master's or doctorate degree in mental health counseling or allied mental health field from a regionally accredited institution. The degree must have been obtained from a CACREP approved program or must show a minimum of two years of graduate work of at least 45 semester hours. | Two years of post-master's experience in an applied mental health counseling setting, including a minimum of 3,000 hours of supervised clinical work over a minimum of two years and 100 hours of face-to-face supervision by qualified mental health practitioner (CCMHC preferred). | American Mental Health Counselors Association |
| Marriage and Family Counselor | Master's degree from an accredited educational institution in an appropriate behavioral science field, mental health discipline. | Either 200 hours of approved supervision of the practice of marriage and family counseling and 1,000 hours of clinical experience in the field of marriage and family counseling or 150 hours of approved supervision of the practice of psycho-therapy and 750 hours of clinical experience in the practice of psychotherapy. | American Association of Marriage and Family Therapists |
| Clinical Psychologist | Doctoral degree in clinical psychology. | Two years of supervised experience in clinical psychology. | American Psychological Association |
| Certified Clinical Social Worker | Master's degree in social work from a graduate school of social work accredited by the Council on Social Work Education. | Two years, including 3,000 hours of post-master's clinical social work practice under the supervision of a master's level social worker. | National Association of Social Workers |

*Source:* From *AMHCA News*, 8(5), 1985 Summer, p. 24. Copyright AACD. Reprinted with permission. No further reproduction authorized without further permission of AACD.

The standards that the Academy used in developing its procedures were those established by the National Commission for Health Certifying Agencies in 1977. Wilmarth (1985a) notes that AMHCA endorses the standards of NACCMHC. These standards stipulate that certified clinical mental health counselors hold a minimum of a master's degree from a regionally accredited university in either clinical mental health counseling or an allied discipline. In addition, these individuals must also have: "(1) a minimum of two years

| Code of Ethics | National Examination | National Directory/ Registry | Continuing Education Requirements for Recertification | Licensure/ Certification |
|---|---|---|---|---|
| Yes | Yes | National Academy Register of Certified Clinical Mental Health Counselors | A minimum of 100 Continuing Education Hours (CEU's) over a five-year period | 14 states |
| Yes | None | Directory of Clinical Memberships AAMFT | None | 9 states |
| Yes | Yes | National Registry for Health Services Providers in Psychology | 11 states - varying requirements | 50 states |
| Yes | Yes | NASW Register of Clinical Social Workers | None | 24 states |

post-master's experience in a mental health setting with (2) 1,500 supervised clinical hours per year with (3) a minimum of 50 hours documented face-to-face supervision per year" (Wilmarth, 1985a, p. 21). They must pass a National Certification Examination as well. The process is rigorous and requires that, once certified, a clinical mental health counselor must be recertified every five years. A comparison of the standards for four groups of clinical mental health service providers is shown in Table 14.1.

In comparing academy certification with that offered by the National Board of Certified Counselors (NBCC), AMHCA takes the position that the NBCC certification is a generic entry-level credential for professional counselors and academy (CCMHC) certification represents a specialty area in the professional counseling field (*AMHCA News*, 1984). AMHCA has proposed a special curriculum for counselor education programs to follow in educating students in mental health counseling.

## SUMMARY

The specialty areas of rehabilitation counseling and mental health counseling have much in common and yet are quite distinct. The field of rehabilitation has been a concern of the federal government since World War I, but the profession of rehabilitation counseling was established only after World War II. Despite its relatively recent inception, this profession has had a powerful influence on the lives of individuals and communities. It has helped the disabled gain employment and greater self-sufficiency and thus become productive members of society. Rehabilitation counselors have promoted the general welfare of all. In addition, they have widened the general public's perception of a disability and of the importance of eliminating artificial handicaps and barriers. Rehabilitation counselors were also among the first to stress the employment of active counseling theories and to call attention to the developmental processes involved in overcoming loss. That rehabilitation led the way in the certification of counselors and counseling programs is another positive contribution of the profession.

Although mental health counseling is among the youngest of specialties, it has made a major impact on the general public and the counseling profession in a very short time. Since the mid-1970s, mental health counseling, as embodied by AMHCA, has stressed the promotion of mental health services by influencing federal and state legislation, establishing standards for mental health counselors, and setting up certification procedures for those who wish to specialize in this area. AMHCA has helped bring a group of diversified professionals together and in the process emphasized health and preventive services, treatment procedures, and a clearer definition of the practice of mental health counseling. That AMHCA quickly became the largest division of AACD is of special significance. This movement has met a need in the counseling profession and has been blessed with strong, assertive leadership as well. The field continues to develop at a rapid pace.

## CLASSROOM ACTIVITIES

1. In groups of three, trace the impact of federal legislation on the development of rehabilitation services from the 1920s to the present. What particular pieces of legislation does your group think most important? Share your findings and opinions with the class.

2. In different small groups, examine how AMHCA has influenced the development of mental health services in the United States and in your state. What current activities of AMHCA do you think will have the greatest impact on your professional development as a counselor? Explain your opinions to the class.

3. Interview either a rehabilitation counselor or a mental health counselor about the services he or she presently provides. Ask the counselor you interview to compare his or her profession to other areas of counseling. What is unique?

4. Khan and Cross (1984) have found similarities and differences in the value systems held by three professional mental health groups—psychiatrists, psychologists, and social workers. Discuss with class members how values affect the delivery of counseling services. Be specific.

5. As a class, generate ideas of what you see as the most pressing societal needs in the next decade. Describe how the professions of rehabilitation counseling and mental health counseling can help alleviate problems associated with these needs. Apply your ideas to a specific setting in which you hope to be employed.

## REFERENCES

AMHCA Position. (1984, November/December). *AMHCA News, 8,* 1.

Anthony, W. A. (1980). A rehabilitation model for rehabilitating the psychiatrically disabled. *Rehabilitation Counseling Bulletin, 24,* 6–21.

Bennett, D. (1975). Transactional analysis in management. *Personnel, 52,* 34–44.

Bitter, J. A. (1979). *Introduction to rehabilitation.* St. Louis: Mosby.

Bolton, B., & Jaques, M. E. (1978). Rehabilitation counseling research: Editorial introduction. In B. Bolton & M. E. Jaques (Eds.), *Rehabilitation counseling: Theory and practice* (pp. 163–165). Baltimore: University Park Press.

Butcher, E., Scofield, M. E., & Baker, S. B. (1985). Clinical judgment in planning mental health treatment: An empirical investigation. *AMHCA Journal, 7,* 116–126.

Coven, A. B. (1977). Using Gestalt psychodrama experiments in rehabilitation counseling. *Personnel and Guidance Journal, 56,* 143–147.

Department of Health, Education, and Welfare. (1974). Vocational rehabilitation program: Implementation provisions, rules and regulations. *Federal Register, 39,* 42470–42507.

DiMichael, S. G., & Thomas, K. R. (1985). ARCA's journey in professionalism: A commemorative review on the 25th anniversary. *Journal of Counseling and Development, 63,* 428–435.

Ehrle, R. A. (1979). Rehabilitation counselors on the threshold of the 1980s. *Counselor Education and Supervision, 18,* 174–180.

Erikson, E. H. (1963). *Childhood and society* (2nd ed.). New York: Norton.

Fagan, T., & Wallace, A. (1979). Who are the handicapped? *Personnel and Guidance Journal, 58,* 215–220.

Fisher, K. (1986). Prevention: Here to stay. *APA Monitor, 15,* 17.

Forrest, D. V. (1983). Employee assistance programs in the 1980s: Expanding career options for counselors. *Personnel and Guidance Journal, 62,* 105–107.

Gladding, S. T. (1977). Scars. *Personnel and Guidance Journal, 56,* 246.

Gressard, C. F., & Hume, K. R. (1983). Special populations. In J. A. Brown & R. H. Pate, Jr. (Eds.), *Being a counselor* (pp. 279–304). Monterey, CA: Brooks/Cole.

Heath, D. H. (1980). Wanted: A comprehensive model of healthy development. *Personnel and Guidance Journal, 58,* 391–399.

Hendrick, S. S. (1981). Spinal cord injury: A special kind of loss. *Personnel and Guidance Journal, 59,* 355–359.

Hershenson, D. B. (1982). A formulation of counseling based on the healthy personality. *Personnel and Guidance Journal, 60,* 406–409.

Holland, J. L. (1978). *Manual for the vocational preference inventory.* Palo Alto, CA: Consulting Psychologists Press.

Hollingsworth, D. K., & Mastroberti, C. J. (1983). Women, work, and disability. *Personnel and Guidance Journal, 61,* 587–591.

Huber, C. H. (1979). Parents of the handicapped child: Facilitating acceptance through group counseling. *Personnel and Guidance Journal, 57,* 267–269.

Huber, C. H. (1983). A social-ecological approach to the counseling process. *AMHCA Journal, 5,* 4–11.

Jaques, M. E. (1970). *Rehabilitation counseling: Scope and services.* Boston: Houghton Mifflin.

Jerse, F. W. (1983). Mental health counseling. In M. M. Ohlsen (Ed.), *Introduction to counseling* (pp. 295–312). Itasca, IL: Peacock.

Karp, H. B. (1985). The ABC's (appropriate behavior changes) of effective management. *Training and Development Journal, 59,* 32–34.

Khan, J. A., & Cross, D. G. (1984). Mental health professionals: How different are their values? *AMHCA Journal, 6,* 42–51.

Lewin, S. S., Ramseur, J. H., & Sink, J. M. (1979). The role of private rehabilitation: Founder, catalyst, competitor. *Journal of Rehabilitation, 45,* 16–19.

Lewis, J. A., & Lewis, M. D. (1977). *Community counseling: A human services approach.* New York: Wiley.

Lewis, J. A., & Lewis, M. D. (1986). *Counseling programs for employees in the workplace.* Monterey, CA: Brooks/Cole.

Lichtenberg, J. W. (1986). Counseling research: Irrelevant or ignored? *Journal of Counseling and Development, 64,* 365–366.

Livneh, H. (1984). Psychiatric rehabilitation: A dialogue with Bill Anthony. *Journal of Counseling and Development, 63,* 86–90.

Livneh, H., & Evans, J. (1984). Adjusting to disability: Behavioral correlates and intervention strategies. *Personnel and Guidance Journal, 62,* 363–368.

Maslow, A. H. (1962). *Toward a psychology of being.* Princeton, NJ: Van Nostrand.

Mayer, G. R., & Butterworth, T. W. (1979). A preventive approach to school violence and vandalism: An experimental study. *Personnel and Guidance Journal, 57,* 436–441.

Meehl, P. (1973). *Psychodiagnosis: Selected papers.* New York: Norton.

Moos, R. (1973). Conceptualization of human environments. *American Psychologist, 28,* 652–665.

Muthard, J. E., & Salomone, P. R. (1978). The role and function of the rehabilitation counselor. In B. Bolton & M. E. Jaques (Eds.), *Rehabilitation counseling: The-*

*ory and practice* (pp. 166–175). Baltimore: University Park Press.

Norton, F. H. (1976). Counseling parents of the mentally retarded child. *The School Counselor, 23,* 201–205.

Parker, R. M., & Hansen, C. E. (1981). Rehabilitation service consumers—People with handicaps. In R. M. Parker & C. E. Hansen (Eds.), *Rehabilitation counseling* (pp. 103–108). Boston: Allyn & Bacon.

Porter, T. L. (1981). Extent of disabling conditions. In R. M. Parker & C. E. Hansen (Eds.), *Rehabilitation counseling* (pp. 109–142). Boston: Allyn & Bacon.

Plummer, J. M. (1971). Counseling crises in rehabilitation services. *Journal of Applied Rehabilitation Counseling, 2,* 108–112.

Rubin, S. E., Matkin, R. E., Ashley, J., Beardsley, M. M., May, V. R., Onstott, K., & Pucket, F. D. (1984). Roles and functions of certified rehabilitation counselors. *Rehabilitation Counseling Bulletin, 27,* 199–224.

Rusalem, H. (1976). Ecological approaches to counseling the physically disabled. In H. Rusalem & D. Malikin (Eds.), *Contemporary vocational rehabilitation.* New York: New York University Press.

Schmolling, P., Jr., Youkeles, M., & Burger, W. R. (1985). *Human services in contemporary America.* Monterey, CA: Brooks/Cole.

Schumacher, B. (1983). Rehabilitation counseling. In M. M. Ohlsen (Ed.), *Introduction to counseling* (pp. 313–324). Itasca, IL: Peacock.

Seiler, G., & Messina, J. J. (1979). Toward professional identity: The dimensions of mental health counseling in perspective. *AMHCA Journal, 1,* 3–8.

Seligman, L., & Weinstock, L. D. (1984). The *AMHCA Journal:* A review of the last 5 years and future possibilities. *AMHCA Journal, 6,* 106–113.

Sinick, D. (1973). Rehabilitation counselors on the move. *Personnel and Guidance Journal, 52,* 167–170.

Stone, J. B. (1978). Counseling and rehabilitation counseling: Differences in emphasis. In B. Bolton & M. E. Jaques (Eds.), *Rehabilitation counseling: Theory and practice.* Baltimore: University Park Press.

Thomas, K. R., Carter, S. A., & Britton, J. O. (1982). The Protestant work ethic, disability, and the rehabilitation student. *Counselor Education and Supervision, 21,* 269–273.

Weikel, W. J. (1985). The American Mental Health Counselors Association. *Journal of Counseling and Development, 63,* 457–460.

Weikel, W. J., & Taylor, S. S. (1979). AMHCA: Membership profile and journal preferences. *AMHCA Journal, 1,* 89–94.

Weinrach, S. G. (1980). A rational-emotive approach to occupational mental health. *Vocational Guidance Quarterly, 28,* 208–218.

Wiggins, J. D., Moody, A. D., & Lederer, D. A. (1983). Personality typologies related to marital satisfaction. *AMHCA Journal, 5,* 169–178.

Wilmarth, R. R. (1985a, Summer). Historical Perspective, Part Two. *AMHCA News, 8,* 21.

Wilmarth, R. R. (1985b, Winter). Historical Perspective, Part Three. *AMHCA News, 9,* 14–15.

Photo by James S. Davidson III.

# Marriage and Family Counseling

*At thirty-five, with wife and child*
  *a Ph.D*
    *and hopes as bright as a full moon*
      *on a warm August night,*
*He took a role as a healing man*
  *blending it with imagination,*
    *necessary change and common sense*
*To make more than an image on an eye lens*
  *of a small figure running quickly up steps;*
*Quietly he traveled*
  *like one who holds a candle to darkness*
    *and questions its power*
*So that with heavy years, long walks,*
  *shared love, and additional births*
*He became as a seasoned actor,*
  *who, forgetting his lines in the silence*
    *stepped upstage and without prompting*
      *lived them.*[1]

---

[1]Gladding, 1974, p. 586. Copyright AACD. Reprinted with permission. No further reproduction authorized without written permission of AACD.

The profession of marriage and family counseling is relatively new. Its formal beginnings are traced to the late 1940s and early 1950s, but its real growth occurred in the late 1970s (Goldenberg & Goldenberg, 1980; Okun & Rappaport, 1980; Nichols, 1984). It differs from individual and group counseling both in its emphases and clientele. Some of the theories used in marriage and family counseling are similar to those employed in other settings, but many are totally different. In this chapter, we will briefly explore the history of the rapid development of marriage and family counseling. We will also highlight some of the important similarities and differences between marriage and family counseling and individual and group counseling. Further, we will see how the family life cycle influences the perception and direction of marriage and family counselors and examine the major concepts and theories of this approach.

## THE BEGINNINGS OF MARRIAGE AND FAMILY COUNSELING

At least seven separate events influenced the formation of marital and family counseling during and after World War II. Their interaction set the stage for an entirely new way of conceptualizing and working with couples and families.

***Developments in Psychoanalysis.*** Psychoanalytic therapists began to extend their approach to include a family orientation in the late 1940s. The work of Nathan Ackerman (1958) was especially important in focusing the attention of psychoanalysis on family units. Prior to Ackerman, psychoanalytic practitioners had purposely excluded family members from the treatment of individual clients for fear that family involvement would be disruptive.

**General Systems Theory.** The originator of *general systems theory* was Ludwig von Bertalanffy (1968), a biologist. The theory views any living organism, including couples and families, as composed of interacting components that mutually affect one another. The focus is on how the interaction of parts influences the operation of the system as a whole. For example, if one person in a family system is not functioning up to capacity, the entire system has difficulty in carrying out its tasks. One of the main concepts introduced by this theory is *circular causality*, the idea that events are related through a series of interacting feedback loops. By viewing family operations in this way, the focus for family dysfunction is shifted from an individual to the family unit itself. *Scapegoating* (in which one person is singled out as the cause of the family's problems) and *linear thinking* (in which one action is seen as the cause of another) are eliminated.

**Schizophrenia and Families.** Three main teams of researchers conducted pioneer studies in the area of family dynamics and the etiology of schizophrenia: the Gregory Bateson group (Bateson, Jackson, Haley, & Weakland, 1956) at the Mental Research Institute in Palo Alto, California; the Theodore Lidz group (Lidz, Cornelison, Fleck, & Terry, 1957) at Yale; and the Murray Bowen and Lyman Wynne groups (Bowen, 1960; Wynne, Ryckoff, Day, & Hirsch, 1958) at the National Institute of Mental Health (NIMH). All observed how couples and families functioned when a family member was diagnosed as schizophrenic. Several observations and ideas were generated by these researchers, but among the most important concepts to emerge were the double bind, pseudomutuality, and marital schism and skewness. In a *double bind*, a person receives two contradictory messages at the same time and is unable to follow both. Physical and psychological symptoms (e.g., headaches, withdrawal) or even schizophrenic behavior may develop as a way to lessen tension and escape. *Pseudomutuality* is a façade of family harmony that covers underlying tension. *Marital schism* is overt marital conflict; *marital skewness* is the term for a pathological marriage in which one partner dominates the other.

**Emergence of Professional Marital Counseling.** Early pioneers in marriage counseling, such as Paul Popenoe and Emily Mudd, were instrumental in helping establish the American Association of Marriage Counselors in 1942, which is now the American Association of Marriage and Family Therapists (AAMFT), the major professional association to which most marriage and family counselors belong. The pioneers' focus on the marriage relationship, instead of just the individuals involved, was important. The new emphasis meant that three entities were considered in working with marriages—two individuals and one couple. Early marriage counseling also set a precedent for seeing couples together in conjoint sessions.

***Growth of the Child Guidance Movement*** Child guidance clinics, whose origins are based in Adlerian theory, concentrate on both the treatment and prevention of emotional disorders in children through an interdisciplinary approach. Parents, as well as children, have traditionally been worked with in such clinics by a team of specialists from the fields of psychiatry, psychology, and social work. Although early research in this area tended to focus on such parental behavior as maternal overprotectiveness (Levy, 1943), clinicians eventually began to concentrate on the family as a whole.

***Emergence of Group Counseling*** The innovative ideas in the 1940s and 1950s that emerged from small group behavior laboratories, such as the National Training Laboratory (NTL) in Bethel, Maine, and the Tavistock Institute of Human Relations in London, England, were especially important to the development of marriage and family counseling. Experiences in group settings show the powerful influence of a group on an individual and how a change in the membership or functioning of a group greatly affects its outcome. Techniques developed in psychodrama and Gestalt therapy, such as sculpting and choreography, further influenced work in marriage and family counseling. Some practitioners (e.g., Bell, 1975, 1976) even started treating families as a group and began the practice of couple/family group counseling, an approach that continues (Corey & Corey, 1987; Ohlsen, 1979, 1982).

***Postwar Changes.*** At the end of World War II, the United States experienced an unsettling readjustment from a war-time to a peacetime system that manifested itself in three trends that had an impact on the family (Walsh, 1982). Along with the "baby boom" in 1946 came a sharp upturn in the number of divorces, with about 40 percent of all couples who married eventually dissolving their marriages. Further, starting in the 1960s, more women sought employment outside the home. By the mid-1980s, almost half of the work force was comprised of women, many of them working mothers.

A third trend, the expansion of the life span, also had an impact on family life as couples found themselves living with the same partners longer than at any previous time in history. The need to work with families and individuals who were affected by these changes brought researchers, practitioners, and theorists together.

## ASSOCIATIONS, EDUCATION, AND RESEARCH

Interest in marriage and family counseling since the 1970s has grown rapidly as has the number of individuals receiving training in this specialty. Within the American Association for Counseling and Development (AACD) there are task forces on marriage and family counseling in three divisions—ACES, ASGW, and AMHCA. AACD has sponsored national professional development institutes and workshops on many different aspects of marriage and family counseling. But the majority of practitioners who identify themselves as counseling with couples and families belong to the American Association of Marriage and Family Therapy (AAMFT). Many of those counselors have received master's or doctoral degrees in marriage and family counseling/therapy based on the standards of the Commission on Accreditation for Marriage and Family Therapy (COAMFT). Approximately two-thirds of all counselor education programs, most of which are not affiliated with AAMFT or COAMFT, offer courses and/or degrees in marriage and family counseling (Peltier & Vale, 1986). There is debate among professionals about the curriculum required to work with couples and families, especially about whether its content should include courses in individual and group counseling theories.

Regardless of professional affiliation and curriculum content, the reasons marriage and family counseling has become popular are largely due to the need for it and its research base. Gurman & Kniskern (1981) report that approximately 50 percent of all problems brought to counselors are related to marriage and family issues. Unemployment, poor school performance, spouse abuse, depression, rebellion, and self-concept issues are just a few of the many situations that can be dealt with from a marriage and family counseling perspective. Okun (1984) notes that individual development dovetails with family and career issues and that each one impacts on the resolution of the other in systemic manner. Bratcher (1982) also comments on the interrelatedness of career and family development and recommends the use of family systems theory for experienced counselors in working with individuals seeking career counseling.

Further, research studies summarized by Gurman and Kniskern (1981), Haber (1983), and Wohlman and Stricker (1983) report a number of interesting findings. First, family counseling interventions are at least as effective as individual interventions for most client complaints and lead to significantly greater durability of change. Second, some forms of family counseling (such as using structural family therapy with substance abusers) are more effective in treating problems than individual counseling approaches. Third, the presence of both parents, especially noncompliant fathers, in family counseling situations greatly improves the chances for success. Similarly, the effectiveness of marriage counseling when both partners meet conjointly with the counselor is nearly twice that of counselors working with just one spouse. Finally, when marriage and family counseling services are not offered to couples conjointly or to families systemically, the results of the intervention may be negative and problems may worsen.

## THE FAMILY LIFE CYCLE

There is much diversity within the field of marriage and family counseling, though almost all theorists and practitioners view the life cycle of the family—and the marriage within it—as crucial variables influencing their work. The *family life cycle* is the name given to the stages a family goes through in its developmental history. These stages parallel and complement individual life-cycle stages, such as those proposed by Erikson (1959) and Levinson (1978). Further, most family life-cycle models include an emphasis on the marital life cycle too, such as the six-step cycle outlined by Haley (1973).

Two of the more prominent models of the family life cycle are the eight-stage concept outlined by Duvall (1977), in which each stage is defined by the age of the oldest child (Table 15.1), and the six-stage model outlined by McGoldrick and Carter (1982), which focuses primarily on necessary tasks of adults in families. Just as in individual life-cycle models, families have prescribed tasks to accomplish at certain times if the family and individuals within the cycle are to move in a healthy way from one stage to the next. The stages and tasks described by Duvall and McGoldrick and Carter overlap in many ways. McGoldrick and Carter start the family life cycle by focusing on the *unattached young adult*. The major task at this time is accepting parent-offspring separation by differentiating oneself from the family of origin, developing intimate peer relationships, and becoming established in a work environment.

**TABLE 15.1** Duvall's model of the family life cycle.

| Stage of the Family Life Cycle | Positions in the Family | Stage-Critical Family Developmental Tasks |
|---|---|---|
| 1. Married couple | Wife<br>Husband | Establish a mutually satisfying marriage<br>Adjusting to pregnancy and the promise of parenthood<br>Fitting into the kin network |
| 2. Childbearing | Wife-mother<br>Husband-father<br>Infant daughter or son or both | Having, adjusting to, and encouraging the development of infants<br>Establishing a satisfying home for both parents and infant(s) |
| 3. Preschool age | Wife-mother<br>Husband-father<br>Daughter-sister<br>Son-brother | Adapting to the critical needs and interests of preschool children in stimulating, growth-promoting ways<br>Coping with energy depletion and lack of privacy as parents |
| 4. School age | Wife-mother<br>Husband-father<br>Daughter-sister<br>Son-brother | Fitting into the community of school-age families in constructive ways<br>Encouraging children's educational achievement |
| 5. Teenage | Wife-mother<br>Husband-father<br>Daughter-sister<br>Son-brother | Balancing freedom with responsibility as teenagers mature and emancipate themselves<br>Establishing postparental interests and careers as growing parents |
| 6. Launching center | Wife-mother-grandmother<br>Husband-father-grandfather<br>Daughter-sister-aunt<br>Son-brother-uncle | Releasing young adults into work, military service, college, marriage, etc., with appropriate rituals and assistance<br>Maintaining a supportive home base |
| 7. Middle-aged parents | Wife-mother-grandmother<br>Husband-father-grandfather | Rebuilding the marriage relationship<br>Maintaining kin ties with older and younger generations |
| 8. Aging family members | Widow/widower<br>Wife-mother-grandmother<br>Husband-father-grandfather | Coping with bereavement and living alone<br>Closing the family home or adapting it to aging<br>Adjusting to retirement |

*Source:* From *Marriage and Family Development*, Fifth Edition, by Evelyn Duvall. Copyright © 1977 by J. B. Lippincott Co.

The young adult then proceeds to other life challenges connected with the family, which is where Duvall's model begins:

1.  *Married couple* (without children)   The important tasks to accomplish at this stage include breaking away from the family of origin, establishing an identity as a couple, and realigning relationships with family and friends to include one's spouse. Defining roles and making rules within the marriage is begun at this point, also.

2.  *Childbearing family* (oldest child up to 30 months old)   A realignment of family roles and duties occurs at this time. Couples become parents, as well as husbands and wives. Spouses may become jealous of the time each spends nurturing and taking care of the infant, and in the process the two may grow apart and become more distant. They are forced at this stage to deal differently with their own families, especially their parents.

3.  *Preschool-age family* (oldest child 30 months to 6 years old)   The challenge at this stage involves developing effective parenting skills to help the child learn how to interact productively with others. Parents must come to a new realization of their own development, too.

4.  *School-age family* (oldest child 6 to 13 years old)   At this stage family members must learn to renegotiate boundaries and assigned roles. The family becomes more vulnerable to outside feedback due to the child's involvement with school and community activities.

5.  *Teenage family* (oldest child 13 to 20 years old)   The family's attention at this period is usually focused on outside activities. Adolescents in the family challenge the rules and boundaries of the family system as they seek to establish their own identities. At the same time, parents confront their own mortality in the form of mid-life crises, such as dealing with their own aging parents. This is a turbulent time for many families because couples are required to deal with individual, marital, and work issues along with the developmental crises of their children and parents.

6.  *Launching-center family* (oldest child is over 20)   The primary task of the family at this point is letting go. Parents and children must separate physically and emotionally from one another, an uneven process. Haley (1980) describes this task as one of the hardest for many families to accomplish and it is where many get stuck. Other stressful family events at this time are establishing adult relationships between parents and

children, renegotiating marital systems as a dyad, and dealing with the death of parents (grandparents).

7. *Middle-aged parents family*   This stage of family life is sometimes known as the empty-nest syndrome. Many couples during this stage feel a sense of relief in having children leave the family. The couple is left with more time to themselves and the period may be one of great happiness. The main responsibilities of the couple center on dealing with any further deaths of significant others and becoming grandparents.

8. *Aging family members family*   This last stage begins at retirement and ends with the death of one of the spouses. Many couples enjoy their greater freedom at this time, but economic matters and illnesses are major concerns. The parents face physical decline but have a wealth of experience and wisdom to share with family members. The family during this stage has to prepare for and adjust to the loss of spouse, siblings, and peers.

Wilcoxon (1985) notes the importance of marriage and family counselors being aware of the different stages within the family while being concurrently attuned to developmental tasks of individuals. Through such awareness the counselors can determine whether the members of a marriage or family are stuck in a particular stage and need help in learning new skills or whether there are more serious problems. Often families, even healthy ones, seek counseling when in transition. Barnhill (1979) outlines eight interrelated dimensions of family life that identify healthy versus dysfunctional patterns of family functioning. For example, he notes that healthy families are ones in which there is clear individuation, whereas unhealthy families contain members who are "enmeshed," or overly dependent on one another in a type of symbiosis. Carter and McGoldrick (1980) have proposed sets of developmental tasks for nontraditional families as well, such as single-parent families and blended families. Thus, counselors who work with couples and families have guidelines for determining how, where, when, or whether a counselor should intervene in the family process.

## MARRIAGE/FAMILY COUNSELING VS. INDIVIDUAL/GROUP COUNSELING

There are similarities and differences in the approaches to marriage/family counseling and individual/group counseling. A major similarity between marriage/family counseling and individual/group counseling centers on theories. Some theories used in individual or group counseling (e.g., person-centered approach, Gestalt therapy, Adlerian counseling, reality therapy, and transactional analysis) are used in working with couples and families (Horne & Ohlsen, 1982). Other approaches, (e.g., structural, strategic, and communications family therapy) are unique to marriage and family counseling. Counselors must learn about additional theorists, terms, and theories, as well as learn new applications of previous theories, in order to become skilled at marriage/family counseling.

Marriage/family counseling and individual counseling share a number of assumptions. For instance, they both recognize the importance the family plays in the life of the individual. They both also focus on problem behaviors and conflicts between the individual and the environment. But a difference is that individual counseling usually treats the person outside his or her family, whereas marriage/family counseling generally includes as many family members as possible. Further, marriage/family counseling works at resolving issues within the family as a way of helping individual family members better cope with the environment (Nichols, 1984).

Marriage/family counseling sessions are similar to those in group counseling in organization, basic dynamics, and stage development. Furthermore, both types of counseling have an interpersonal emphasis. But the family is not like a typical group, though a knowledge of group process may be useful. For example, family members are not equal in status and power. In addition, families may perpetuate myths, whereas groups are more realistic in dealing with events. There is also more emotion among family members than members of another type of group, because the arrangement in a family is not limited in time and is related to sex roles and affective bonds that have a long history (Becvar, 1982). While the family may be a group, it is not well-suited to being worked with only through group theory.

Finally, the emphasis of marriage/family counseling is generally on process (dynamics) as opposed to a focus on content (linear causality) in much individual/group counseling. In other words, the dynamics behind marriage/family counseling are generally different from these other two types of counseling. In making the transition from an individual perspective to a family orientation, Resnikoff (1981) stresses specific questions that counselors should ask themselves in order to understand family functioning and dynamics. His idea is that by asking the right questions, the counselor will become more clearly attuned to the family as a client and how best to work. Among those questions are:

☐ What is the outward appearance of the family?

☐ What repetitive, nonproductive sequences are noticeable?

☐ What is the basic feeling state in the family, and who carries it?

☐ What individual roles reinforce family resistance, and what are the most prevalent family defenses?

☐ How are family members differentiated from one another, and what are the subgroup boundaries?

☐ What part of the life cycle is the family experiencing and are problem-solving methods stage appropriate?

Many of these questions could also be asked by counselors working with couples.

## MARRIAGE COUNSELING

Couples seek marriage counseling for a wide variety of reasons, including finances, children, fidelity, communication, and compatibility. Almost any situation can serve as the impetus for the couple to seek help.

Regardless of who initiates the request, it is crucial that the counselor see both members of the couple from the beginning. Whitaker (1977) notes that if a counselor is not able to structure the situation in this way, the counselor will probably not help the couple very much and possibly will do more harm than good. Trying to treat one spouse alone for even one or two sessions increases both the other spouse's resistance to counseling and his or her anxiety. Also, if one member of a couple tries to change without the knowledge or support of the other, conflict is bound to ensue. Wilcoxon and Fenell (1983) have developed a therapist-initiated letter explaining the process of marriage therapy to an absent partner. It outlines the perils of treating just one partner and is sent by counselors to the nonattending partner to help him or her see the possibilities that can accrue when working with both members of the couple.

After both partners have decided to enter marital counseling, a variety of approaches may be taken, but a number of marital approaches have weak theoretical foundations (Gurman, 1978). Three of the strongest and most widely used approaches are psychodynamic theory, social-learning theory, and systems theory.

### Psychodynamic Theory

Psychodynamic theory in marital counseling focuses on object relations. *Object relations* is concerned with the way people form attachments to others and things outside of themselves (i.e., objects). The basis of preference for certain objects as opposed to others is developed in early childhood in parent-child interactions. Individuals bring these unconscious forces with them into a marriage relationship.

In order to help the marriage, the counselor focuses with each partner on obtaining emotional insight into early parent-child relationships. The treatment process may be both individual and conjoint. In the process, the counselor serves as a transfer object while each partner restructures internally based perceptions of, expectations of, and reactions to self and others. Techniques often employed in this approach include taking individual histories of each partner and taking a history of the marriage relationship. Interpretation, dream work, and an analysis of resistance and transference are often incorporated into the treatment (Baruth & Huber, 1984).

### Social-Learning Theory

Social-learning theory is a form of behaviorism that stresses learning through modeling. The premises underlying the theory are that most behavior is learned through observing others and that marriage partners either have a deficit or excess of needed behaviors. A *deficit* may be the result of one or both partners never having witnessed a particular skill, such as how to fight fairly. An *excess* may come as a result of one or both partners thinking that just a little more of a certain behavior will solve their problems. For example, one partner tells the other everything he or she likes and does not like in the marriage in the hope that honest communication will be beneficial. While such honesty may be admired, research (Gottman, Markman, & Notarius, 1977) shows that marriages grow more through positive reciprocity than through negative feedback. Thus, select communication and interaction with one's spouse seem to work best.

The focus in social-learning marital counseling is on skill building in the present. Events that have disrupted the marriage in the past may be recognized but receive little focus. Within the treatment process, counselors may use a wide variety of behavioral strategies to help couples change, such as self-reports, observations, communication enhancement training exercises, contracting, and homework assignments (Stuart, 1980).

### Systems Theory

The focus of systems theory is on the context of the couple's interaction and how transactions in the marriage affect each partner

(Searight & Openlander, 1984). Active and reactive behaviors are considered more important than motivation or intention. The influence and power of one partner's actions on the other are emphasized. Thus, reciprocal interaction patterns are analyzed and new ways of acting initiated.

Techniques used in this approach include a focus on ways to differentiate one's self from others. A primary way of doing this is to focus on cognitively evaluating events and interactions (Bowen, 1976). Other emphases from a systems perspective center on power and control, such as who makes the rules within the system and how those rules are made (Haley, 1973).

In conclusion, the theoretical basis for most marriage counseling theories is not as strong as that for family counseling. The reasons are numerous. Many marriage counselors have been primarily practitioners and not researchers/writers. Also, marriage counseling, until recently, has been viewed as a subspecialty within family counseling, and therefore most research and theory have focused on families. Gurman (1978) suggests that marriage counseling is now becoming a stronger discipline.

## FAMILY COUNSELING

Families enter counseling for a number of reasons. Usually, though, there is an identified "patient" within the family structure that family members use as their ticket of entry. Some practitioners, such as Murray Bowen, insist on seeing entire families together, including grandparents if possible; others, such as Jay Haley, will see whomever comes.

Family counseling has expanded rapidly since the mid-1970s and encompasses many aspects of couples counseling. We will briefly examine six of its main theoretical orientations: family systems, psychodynamic family counseling, experiential family counseling, behavioral family counseling, strategic family counseling, and structural family counseling (Table 15.2).

### Family Systems Counseling

Family systems counselors operate from a general systems framework and conceptualize the family as an open system that evolves over the family life cycle in a sociocultural context. Functional families follow rules and are flexible in meeting the demands placed upon them by family members and outside agencies. Family systems counselors stress the idea of circular causality, that a change in one

**TABLE 15.2** Models of family counseling

| Model of Family Counseling | View of Normal Family Functioning | View of Dysfunction/Symptoms | Goals of Therapy |
|---|---|---|---|
| *Family systems therapy*<br>Bowen | Differentiation of self. Intellectual/emotional balance. | Functioning impaired by relationships with family of origin:<br>a. Poor differentiation.<br>b. Anxiety (reactivity).<br>c. Family projection process.<br>d. Triangulation. | 1. Differentiation.<br>2. Cognitive functioning.<br>3. Emotional reactivity.<br>4. Modification of relationships in family system:<br>  a. Detriangulation.<br>  b. Repair cutoffs. |
| *Psychodynamic*<br>Ackerman<br>Boszormenyi-Nagy<br>Framo<br>Lidz<br>Meissner<br>Paul<br>Stierlin | 1. Parental personalities and relationships well differentiated.<br>2. Relationship perceptions based on current realities, not projections from past.<br>Boszormenyi-Nagy: Relational equitability.<br>Lidz: Family task requisites:<br>  a. Parental coalition<br>  b. Generation boundaries.<br>  c. Sex-linked parental roles. | Symptoms due to family projection process stemming from unresolved conflicts and losses in family of origin. | 1. Insight and resolution of family of origin conflict and losses.<br>2. Family projection processes.<br>3. Relationship reconstruction and reunion.<br>4. Individual and family growth. |
| *Experiential*<br>Satir<br>Whitaker | Satir:<br>1. Self-worth: high.<br>2. Communication: clear, specific, honest.<br>3. Family rules: flexible, human, appropriate.<br>4. Linkage to society: open, hopeful.<br>Whitaker: Multiple aspects of family structure and shared experience. | Symptoms are nonverbal messages in reaction to current communication dysfunction in system. | 1. Direct, clear communication.<br>2. Individual and family growth through immediate shared experience. |

| Approach | Normal family functioning | Dysfunction | Goals/Interventions |
|---|---|---|---|
| *Behavioral-social exchange*<br>Liberman<br>Patterson<br>Alexander | 1. Maladaptive behavior is not reinforced.<br>2. Adaptive behavior is rewarded.<br>3. Exchange of benefits outweighs costs.<br>4. Long-term reciprocity. | Maladaptive, symptomatic behavior reinforced by<br>a. Family attention and reward.<br>b. Deficient reward exchanges (e.g., coercive).<br>c. Communication deficit. | Concrete, observable behavioral goals: change contingencies of social reinforcement (interpersonal consequences of behavior).<br>a. Rewards for adaptive behavior.<br>b. No rewards for maladaptive behavior. |
| *Structural*<br>Minuchin<br>Montalvo<br>Aponte | 1. Boundaries clear and firm.<br>2. Hierarchy with strong parental subsystem.<br>3. Flexibility of system for<br>  a. Autonomy and interdependence.<br>  b. Individual growth and system maintenance.<br>  c. Continuity, and adaptive restructuring in response to changing internal (developmental) and external (environmental) demands. | Symptoms result from current family structural imbalance:<br>a. Malfunctioning hierarchical arrangement, boundaries.<br>b. Maladaptive reaction to changing requirements (developmental, environmental). | Reorganize family structure:<br>a. Shift members' relative positions to disrupt malfunctioning pattern and strengthen parental hierarchy.<br>b. Create clear, flexible boundaries.<br>c. Mobilize more adaptive alternative patterns. |
| *Strategic*<br>Haley<br>Milan team<br>Palo Alto group | 1. Flexibility.<br>2. Large behavioral repertoire for<br>  a. Problem resolution.<br>  b. Life cycle passage.<br>3. Clear rules governing hierarchy (Haley). | Multiple origins of problems; symptoms maintained by family's<br>a. Unsuccessful problem-solving attempts.<br>b. Inability to adjust to life cycle transitions (Haley).<br>c. Malfunctioning hierarchy: triangle or coalition across hierarchy (Haley).<br>Symptom is a communicative act embedded in interaction pattern. | Resolve presenting problem only: specific behaviorally defined objectives.<br>Interrupt rigid feedback cycle: change symptom-maintaining sequence to new outcome.<br>Define clearer hierarchy (Haley). |

*Source:* From "Conceptualizations of normal family functioning" by F. Walsh, 1982, in *Normal Family Processes* (pp. 26–27), F. Walsh (Ed.). New York: Guilford Press. Copyright 1982 by Guilford Press. Reprinted by permission.

member's functioning affects all other members and the family as a whole. These counselors also emphasize the following concepts in working with families:

☐ *Nonsummativity* The family is greater than the sum of its parts. It is necessary to examine the patterns within a family rather than the actions of any specific members alone.

☐ *Equifinality* The same origin may lead to different outcomes, and the same outcome may result from different origins. Thus, the family that experiences a natural disaster may become stronger or weaker as a result. Likewise, healthy families may have quite dissimilar backgrounds. Therefore, the focus of treatment is on interactional family patterns rather than on particular conditions or events.

☐ *Communication* All behavior is seen as communicative. It is important to attend to the two functions of every interpersonal message—content (i.e., factual information) and relationship (i.e., how the message is to be understood). The what of a message is conveyed by how it is delivered.

☐ *Family rules* A family's functioning is based on both explicit and implicit rules. Family rules provide expectations about roles and other actions that govern family life. Most families operate on a small set of predictable rules—a pattern—known as the *redundancy principle*. In order to help families change dysfunctional ways of working, family counselors have to help them define and/or expand the rules under which they operate.

☐ *Morphogenesis* The ability of the family to modify its functioning to meet the changing demands of internal and external factors is known as *morphogenesis*. Morphogenesis usually requires a second order change (i.e., the ability to make an entirely new response) instead of a first order change (i.e., continuing to do more of the same things that have worked previously) (Watzlawick, Weakland, & Fisch, 1974). Thus, instead of just talking more, family members may need to try new ways of behaving.

☐ *Homeostasis* As with biological organisms, families have a tendency to remain in a steady, stable state of equilibrium unless otherwise forced to change. When a family member unbalances the family through his or her actions, other members quickly try to rectify the situation through negative feedback. The model of functioning is similar to a furnace that comes on when a house falls below a set temperature and cuts off once the temperature is reached. Sometimes homeostasis can be advantageous in helping a family achieve life-cycle goals, but often it prevents the family from moving on to another stage in its development.

Counselors who operate from a family systems approach work according to the main concepts just covered. For instance, if family rules are covert and cause confusion, the counselor will help the family clarify them. All members of the family are worked with in the systemic approach. Often, a *genogram* (a three-generational representational drawing of the family) is constructed in order to help family members and the counselor detect intergenerational patterns of family functioning. Many other theoretical orientations are built on a family systems perspective.

### Psychodynamic Family Counseling

As traditionally practiced, pschoanalysis concentrates on individuals instead of such social systems as the family. Ackerman (1966) broke with tradition by working with intact families. He saw family difficulties resulting from "interlocking pathologies" present in the couple and marriage system and projected on to children within the family. Thus, an initial major goal of psychodynamic family counseling is to change the personalities of family members so they can work with one another in a healthier and more productive way. Nichols (1984) points out that psychodynamic counselors who followed Ackerman have most often employed an "eclectic mix of psychoanalytic and systems concepts . . ." (p. 223).

A unique contribution psychodynamic practitioners have made to the field of family counseling is to utilize the concept of object relations as a primary emphasis in treatment. Object relations, as pointed out earlier, are internalized residues of early parent-child interactions, and in dysfunctional families object relations continue to exert a negative influence in present interpersonal relationships. Dysfunctional families are those with a greater degree of unconscious, unresolved conflict or loss (Paul & Paul, 1975). Three main ways of working with these families are: (1) developing a stronger parent coalition, (2) defining and maintaining generation boundaries, and (3) modeling sex-linked roles within the family (Walsh, 1982).

Overall, psychodynamic family counselors concentrate on: (1) helping family members obtain insight and resolve family of origin conflicts/losses, (2) eliminating distorted projections, (3) reconstructing relationships, and (4) promoting individual and family growth. Prominent counselors associated with this approach are James Framo, Theodore Lidz, and Norman Paul.

### *Experiential Family Counseling*

Experientialists, like psychoanalysts, are concerned as much with individuals as with family systems and consider intrapsychic problems when explaining pychopathology. Unlike most other family counselors, experientialists describe patterns of family dysfunction using the individual or a dyad as the unit of analysis. They see dysfunctional families as being made up of people who are incapable of autonomy or real intimacy, that is, people who are alienated from themselves and others. Thus, the goal of counseling is growth.

Two of the most prominent counselors in the experiential school are Virginia Satir and Carl Whitaker. Satir (1967, 1972) stresses the importance of clear communications in her approach; Whitaker (1976) is more of an existential maverick. Satir believes that when family members are under stress they may handle their communications in one of four nonproductive roles:

- ☐ *Placater*  Agrees and tries to please.
- ☐ *Blamer*  Dominates and finds fault.
- ☐ *Responsible analyzer*  Remains emotionally detached and intellectual.
- ☐ *Distractor*  Interrupts and constantly chatters about irrelevant topics.

Satir helps families by teaching members to own personal feelings and listen to one another to eliminate role playing and promote intimacy. She also stresses the importance of obtaining clarity, providing feedback, and negotiating differences when they arise. Her primary focus is on communication skills, and she uses such experiential exercises as sculpting to help family members become more aware.

Whitaker, who takes a much less structured approach to working with families, represents the extreme side of the experiential school. Basically, he advocates nonrational, creative experiences in family counseling and lets the form of his methods develop as he works. He has been known to go to sleep and share a dream with a family and has displayed other nonconventional behaviors in his efforts to be real, honest, and spontaneous.

### *Behavioral-Social Family Counseling*

Behavioral-social family counselors use learning theory techniques, originally devised for treating individuals, in their approach to working with families. They are nonsystemic in conceptualizations and in clinical interventions with families. But like the family system counselors, behaviorists emphasize the importance of family rules and patterned communication processes and take a functional approach to treatment outcome (Walsh, 1982). They believe behaviors are more determined by consequences than antecedents.

The goals are quite specific and limited. Behaviorists try to modify troublesome behavior patterns to alleviate undesirable interactions. Much of their work focuses on changing dyadic interaction and is based on operant conditioning. Behaviorists believe that change is better achieved through accelerating positive behavior than by decelerating negative behavior. Most of their work is concentrated in three main areas: (1) behavioral parent training (Patterson, 1971), (2) behavioral marriage counseling (Stuart, 1980), and (3) treatment of sexual dysfunctions (Masters & Johnson, 1970).

### Structural Family Counseling

Structural family counseling is based on systems theory. Its practitioners advocate structural changes in the organization of the family unit, with particular attention on changing interactional patterns in subsystems of the family, such as the marital dyad, and establishing clear boundaries between family members (Minuchin, Montalvo, Guerney, Rosman, & Schumer, 1967). Salvador Minuchin (1974) is often identified as the founder of this school of family counseling.

In working with families, structural family counselors join with the family in a position of leadership. They map within their minds the structure of the family and determine how it is stuck in a dysfunctional pattern. These counselors then employ a number of techniques aimed at getting the family to change the way it operates (Minuchin & Fishman, 1981). One primary technique is to work with the family's interaction. When family members repeat nonproductive sequences of behavior or demonstrate either a detached or enmeshed position in the family structure, the counselor will rearrange the physical environment so they have to act in a different way. The technique may be as simple having people face each other when they talk. Structural family counselors also often use *reframing* as a technique, which involves helping the family see its problem from a different perspective. For example, if a child is misbehaving, the behavior may be labeled "naughty" instead of "crazy." As a consequence, the child and actions will be viewed as less pathological. By helping families change their structure, reframe their problems, establish a hierarchy with the parents in charge, and create clear boundaries and appropriate ways of interacting, structuralists help families utilize the resources within themselves and function in a more productive and healthy way.

### Strategic Family Counseling

Jay Haley (1973) and the Milan Group (Selvini-Palazzoli, Boscolo, Cecchin, & Prata, 1978) are most often associated with this school of family counseling. Strategic counselors take a systemic view of problem behaviors and focus on the process rather than the content of dysfunctional interactions. They strive to resolve presenting problems and pay little attention to instilling insight. One powerful technique often used by strategic counselors is to *prescribe the symptom.* This paradoxical approach places targeted behaviors, such as family fights, under the control of the counselor by making a behavior voluntary if family members comply and eliminating a behavior if the family group resists the counselor's instructions. Strategic family counselors accept the presenting problems of families and view symptoms as serving the positive purpose of communicating.

The Milan Group often has its families go through ordeals, such as traveling or suffering, during the treatment process. The idea is that if families have to make sacrifices to get better, then the long-term improvements of treatment will be greatly enhanced. A major aspect of strategic family counseling is the assignment of original homework tasks, often given in the form of prescriptions, that are to be completed in between sessions. Many strategic counselors work in teams and limit the number of treatment sessions as a motivational factor. Overall, this treatment is short-term and very pragmatic.

## SUMMARY

The professions of marriage and family counseling have grown rapidly since the 1940s for a number of reasons, including theory development, needs within the population, and proven research effectiveness. The field of marriage counseling is sometimes incorporated into family counseling models, but since the 1970s it has become stronger as a separate entity. There are three basic approaches to marriage counseling: psychodynamic, behavioral, and systems. Family counseling has a varied range of approaches, but the dominant ones are family systems, experiential, behavioral, psychodynamic, structural, and strategic.

In working as either a marriage or a family counselor, the helping professional must be aware of the theoretical basis of the approach being employed and must consider where marriage and/ or family members are in individual and family life cycles. Counselors must also realize how individual or group theories may complement or detract from their work.

## CLASSROOM ACTIVITIES

1. Do you think the family life cycle has as much influence on a person as the individual life cycle? What conflicts might occur between these two cycles? Discuss these cycles with a group of three others.
2. Determine where you are in your own individual and family life cycles. Talk with a classmate about what changes you anticipate making in the next few years because of life-cycle demands.
3. What are the advantages and disadvantages of working with individuals who have family concerns on a one-to-one basis instead of on a family counseling basis? Do you think it is possible to work effectively with only one member of a couple or family? Divide the class up into two teams and debate the issue.
4. Which approach to marriage or family counseling do you prefer? What are the reasons behind your decision? Form groups with classmates who share your view and present your rationale to other class members.
5. Research how some of the family counseling approaches not described in this chapter (e.g., person-centered, Gestalt, and transactional analysis) work with families to bring about change. What data support the use of these theories?

## REFERENCES

Ackerman, N. W. (1958). *The psychodynamics of family life.* New York: Basic Books.

Ackerman, N. W. (1966). *Treating the troubled family.* New York: Basic Books.

Barnhill, L. R. (1979). Healthy family systems. *Family Coordinator, 28,* 94–100.

Baruth, L. G., & Huber, C. H. (1984). *An introduction to marital theory and therapy.* Monterey, CA: Brooks/Cole.

Bateson, G., Jackson, D. D., Haley, J., & Weakland, J. (1956). Toward a theory of schizophrenia. *Behavioral Science, 1,* 251–264.

Becvar, D. S. (1982). The family is not a group—or is it? *Journal for Specialists in Group Work, 7,* 88–95.

Bell, J. E. (1975). *Family therapy.* New York: Jason Aronson.

Bell, J. E. (1976). A theoretical framework for family group therapy. In P. J. Guerin (Ed.), *Family therapy: Theory and practice.* New York: Gardner Press.

Bertalanffy, L. von. (1968). *General systems theory: Foundations development, application.* New York: Brazillier.

Bowen, M. (1960). A family concept of schizophrenia. In D. D. Jackson (Ed.), *The etiology of schizophrenia.* New York: Basic Books.

Bowen, M. (1976). Theory in the practice of psychotherapy. In P. J. Guerin, Jr. (Ed.), *Family therapy: Theory and practice.* New York: Gardner Press.

Bratcher, W. E. (1982). The influence of the family on career selection: A family systems perspective. *Personnel and Guidance Journal, 61,* 87–91.

Carter, E. A., & McGoldrick, M. (1980). The family life cycle and family therapy: An overview. In E. A. Carter & M. McGoldrick (Eds.), *The family life cycle.* New York: Gardner Press.

Corey, M. S., & Corey, G. (1987). *Groups: Process and practice* (3rd ed.). Monterey, CA: Brooks/Cole.

Duvall, E. M. (1977). *Marriage and family development* (5th ed.). Philadelphia: Lippincott.

Erikson, E. H. (1959). *Identity and the life cycle: Psychological issues.* New York: International Universities Press.

Gladding, S. T. (1974). Without applause. *Personnel and Guidance Journal, 52,* 586.

Goldenberg, I., & Goldenberg, H. (1980). *Family therapy: An overview.* Monterey, CA: Brooks/Cole.

Gottman, J., Markman, H., & Notarius, C. (1977). The topography of marital conflict: A sequential analysis of verbal and nonverbal behavior. *Journal of Marriage and the Family, 39,* 461–477.

Gurman, A. S. (1978). Contemporary marital therapies: A critique and comparative analysis of psychoanalytic, behavioral and systems theory approaches. In T. J. Paolino, Jr., & B. S. McCrady (Eds.), *Marriage & marital therapy.* New York: Brunner/Mazel.

Gurman, A., & Kniskern, D. (1981). Family therapy outcome research: Knowns and unknowns. In A. Gurman & D. Kniskern (Eds.), *Handbook of family therapy* (pp. 742–775). New York: Brunner/Mazel.

Haber, R. A. (1983). The family dance around drug abuse. *Personnel and Guidance Journal, 61,* 428–430.

Haley, J. (1973). *Uncommon therapy.* New York: Norton.

Haley, J. (1976). *Problem-solving therapy.* San Francisco: Jossey-Bass.

Haley, J. (1980). *Leaving home.* New York: McGraw-Hill.

Horne, A. M., & Ohlsen, M. M. (1982). *Family counseling and therapy.* Itasca, IL: Peacock.

Levinson, D. (1978). *The seasons of a man's life.* New York: Knoft.

Levy, D. (1943). *Marital overprotection.* New York: Columbia University Press.

Lidz, T., Cornelison, A., Fleck, S., & Terry, D. (1957). Intrafamilial environment of schizophrenic patients II: Marital schism and marital skew. *American Journal of Psychiatry, 20,* 241–248.

Masters, W. H., & Johnson, V. E. (1970). *Human sexual inadequacy.* Boston: Little, Brown.

Minuchin, S. (1974). *Families and family therapy.* Cambridge, MA: Harvard University Press.

Minuchin, S., Montalvo, B., Guerney, B., Rosman, B., & Schumer, F. (1967). *Families of the slums.* New York: Basic Books.

Minuchin, S., & Fishman, H. C. (1981) *Family therapy techniques.* Cambridge, MA: Harvard University Press.

Nichols, M. P. (1984). *Family therapy: Concepts and methods.* New York: Gardner Press.

Ohlsen, M. M. (1979). *Marriage counseling in groups.* Champaign, IL: Research Press.

Ohlsen, M. M. (1982). Family therapy with the triad model. In A. M. Horne & M. M. Ohlsen (Eds.), *Family counseling and therapy* (pp. 412–434). Itasca, IL: Peacock.

Okun, B. F. (1984). *Working with adults: Individual, family, & career development.* Monterey, CA: Brooks/Cole.

Okun, B. F., & Rappaport, L. J. (1980). *Working with families: An introduction to family therapy.* Monterey, CA: Brooks/Cole.

Patterson, G. R. (1971). *Families: Applications of social learning to family life.* Champaign, IL: Research Press.

Paul, N. L., & Paul, B. B. (1975). *A marital puzzle: Transgenerational analysis in marriage.* New York: Norton.

Peltier, S. W., & Vale, S. O. (1986). A national survey of counselor education departments: Course offerings on marriage and family. *Counselor Education and Supervision, 25,* 313–319.

Resnikoff, R. D. (1981). Teaching family therapy: Ten key questions for understanding the family as patient. *Journal of Marital and Family Therapy, 7,* 135–142.

Satir, V. M. (1967). *Conjoint family therapy.* Palo Alto, CA: Science and Behavior Books.

Satir, V. M. (1972). *Peoplemaking.* Palo Alto: Science and Behavior Books.

Searight, H. R., & Openlander, P. (1984). Systemic therapy: A new brief intervention model. *Personnel and Guidance Journal, 62,* 387–391.

Selvini-Palazzoli, M., Boscolo, L., Cecchin, G., & Prata, G. (1978). *Paradox and counterparadox.* New York: Aronson.

Stuart, R. B. (1980). *Helping couples change: A social learning approach to marital therapy.* New York: Guilford Press.

Walsh, F. (1982). Conceptualizations of normal family functioning. In F. Walsh (Ed.), *Normal family processes* (pp. 3–42). New York: Guilford Press.

Watzlawick, P., Weakland, J., & Fisch, R. (1974). *Change: Principles of problem formation and problem resolution.* New York: Norton.

Whitaker, C. (1976). The hindrance of theory in clinical work. In P. J. Guerin (Ed.), *Family therapy: Theory and practice.* New York: Gardner Press.

Whitaker, C. (1977). Process techniques of family therapy. *Interaction, 1,* 4–19.

Wilcoxon, S. A. (1985). Healthy family functioning: The other side of family pathology. *Journal of Counseling and Development, 63,* 495–499.

Wilcoxon, S. A., & Fenell, D. (1983). Engaging the non-attending spouse in marital therapy through the use of therapist-initiated written communication. *Journal of Marital and Family Therapy, 9,* 199–203.

Wohlman, B., & Stricker, G. (1983). *Handbook of family and marital therapy.* New York: Plenum Press.

Wynne, L. C., Ryckoff, I., Day, J., & Hirsch, S. I. (1958). Pseudo-mutuality in the family relationships of schizophrenics. *Psychiatry, 21,* 205–220.

Photo by James S. Davidson III.

# CHAPTER 16

# Career Counseling Over the Life Span

*Far in the back of his mind he harbors thoughts*
*    like small boats in a quiet cove*
*        ready to set sail at a moment's notice.*
*I, seated on his starboard side,*
*    listen for the winds of change*
*        ready to lift anchor with him*
*        and explore the choppy waves of reality ahead.*
*Counseling requires a special patience*
*    best known to seamen and navigators'*
*        courses are only charted for times*
*        when the tide is high and breezes steady.*[1]

---

[1]Gladding, 1985, p. 68. Copyright AACD. Reprinted with permission. No further reproduction authorized without written permission of AACD.

The profession of counseling began charting its course when Frank Parsons (1909) outlined a process for choosing a career and initiated the vocational guidance movement. It was Parsons' slogan that "It is better to choose a vocation than merely to hunt a job." Since his ideas first came into prominence, a voluminous amount of research and theory has been generated in the field of career planning.

Choosing a career is more than simply deciding what one will do to earn a living. Rather, occupations influence a person's whole way of life—income, standard of living, social identity, education, clothes, hobbies, interests, friends, life-style, place of residence, and even personality characteristics (Fredrickson, 1982 p. 2). Thus, it is important for individuals to choose as wisely as possible. Herr and Cramer (1984) and Okun (1984) stress that the process of selecting a career is unique to each individual and is influenced by personality style, developmental stages, and life roles. Published studies on careers encompass a wide variety of topics, such as the relationship of a career decision to self-concept (Wellington, 1982), work values (Drummond & Barnard, 1984), happenstance (Miller, 1983), indecision (Salomone, 1982), family influences (Bratcher, 1982), gender (Wilson & Lunneborg, 1982) and race and age (Miles, 1981).

Since there is a large volume of literature on careers, a one-chapter overview will give only a brief idea of the depth of this area. We will concentrate on career development and counseling from a holistic, life-span perspective, as first proposed by Gysbers (1975). Theories and techniques of working with clients in career decisions will be examined. Specific career evaluation instruments will not be covered here but will be reviewed in chapter 19.

## CAREER COUNSELING AND THE NATURE OF CAREERS

Career counseling is a hybrid discipline, often misunderstood and not always fully appreciated by many professionals or the public. Its present status is the result of a long and varied history that has seen the field's popularity ebb and flow (Crites, 1981).

### Career Counseling Organizations

The National Career Development Association (NCDA)—formerly the National Vocational Guidance Association (NVGA)—and the National Employment Counselors Association (NECA) are the two divisions within the American Association for Counseling and Development (AACD) primarily devoted to career counseling. NCDA, the oldest division within AACD, traces its roots back to the early years of the 20th century (Sheeley, 1978). The membership of NCDA comprises professionals in business and industry, rehabilitation agencies, government, private practice, and educational settings who affiliate with NCDA's special interest groups (SIGs), such as Work and Mental Health, Substance Abuse in the Workplace, and Employee Assistance Programs (Smith, Engels, & Bonk, 1985). The membership of the National Employment Counselors Association is also diverse but more focused. Until 1966, NECA was an interest group of NCDA (Meyer, Helwig, Gjernes, & Chickering, 1985). Both divisions publish quarterly journals—*The Career Development Quarterly* (formerly *The Vocational Guidance Quarterly*) and the *Journal of Employment Counseling*, respectively.

### The Scope of Career Counseling and Careers

NCDA conceptualizes career counseling as a "one-to-one or small group relationship between a client and a counselor with the goal of helping the client(s) integrate and apply an understanding of self and the environment to make the most appropriate career decisions and adjustments" (Sears, 1982, p. 139). Herr and Cramer (1984, p. 389) elaborate further on the actual experience. They see career counseling as:

> (1) a largely verbal process in which (2) a counselor and counselee(s) are in dynamic interaction and in which (3) the counselor employs a repertoire of diverse behaviors (4) to help bring about self-under-

standing and action in the form of "good" decision-making in the counselee, who has responsibility for his or her own actions.

Brown (1985) goes a step further in stating that not only does career counseling help an individual select and prepare for an occupation, but it also assists the person in entering and functioning effectively in the type of work chosen.

Through its history, career counseling has been known by a number of different names, including vocational guidance, occupational counseling, and vocational counseling. Crites (1981) emphasizes that the word *career* is more modern and inclusive than the term *vocational*. *Career* is also much broader than the word *occupation*, which Herr and Cramer (1984) define as "a group of similar jobs found in different industries or organizations" (p. 15). Regardless of which term is used, career counselors clearly must take many factors into consideration when helping an individual make a career decision.

To understand what all of these factors are, it is important to first define a career. Super (1976, p. 4) gives an excellent definition of a career that incorporates a number of experiences. He views a career as:

> The course of events which constitutes a life; the sequence of occupations and other life roles which combine to express one's commitment to work in his or her total pattern of self-development; the series of remunerated and nonremunerated positions occupied by a person from adolescence through retirement, of which occupation is only one. [A career] includes work-related roles such as those of student, employee, and pensioner together with complementary avocational, familial, and civic roles. Careers exist only as people pursue them; they are person-centered.

While not disagreeing with Super, McDaniels (1984) broadens the definition of a career to specifically encompass leisure. He contends that leisure will occupy an increasingly important role in the lives of all individuals in the future.

All theories of counseling are potentially applicable and useful in working with individuals on career choices, but people gain understanding and insight about themselves and how they fit into the world of work through educational means as well as through counseling relationships. The well-informed may need fewer counseling services than others and respond more positively to this form of helping.

## CAREER INFORMATION

The term *career information* has been defined by NCDA (then NVGA) as "information related to the world of work that can be useful in the process of career development, including educational, occupational, and psychosocial information related to working, e.g., availability of training, the nature of work, and status of workers in different occupations" (Sears, 1982, p. 139). As discussed in a previous chapter, the word *guidance* is usually reserved for activities that are primarily educational in nature. Thus, career guidance involves all activities that seek to disseminate information about present or future vocations. These activities can take the form of career fairs, library assignments, outside interviews, computer-assisted information experiences, and shadowing (i.e., following someone around on his or her daily work routine), as well as didactic lectures and experiential exercises (e.g., role plays). Career guidance is often pictured as an activity that goes on mainly in schools. But this process is often conducted outside a classroom environment, such as at a governmental agency or with a private practitioner. Many state governments computerize information about occupations and disseminate it through public libraries. In short, the ways of becoming informed about careers are extensive.

Not all ways of learning are as effective as others, however, and those who fail to personalize career information to specific situations often have difficulty making vocational decisions and may develop unrealistic aspirations (Salomone & McKenna, 1982). Therefore, providing qualitative and quantitative occupational information to individuals who are deciding about their careers is vital. A knowledge of career information will not guarantee self-exploration in career development, but good career decisions cannot be made without such data (Fredrickson, 1982). A lack of either enough information or up-to-date information is one reason individuals fail to make decisions or make unwise choices.

Several publications are considered classic references for finding in-depth and current information on careers and trends. These include the government-published *Dictionary of Occupational Titles* and the *Occupational Outlook Handbook*. Some self-help books, such as Bolles's *What Color Is Your Parachute?* (1986) and Leape's *Harvard Guide to Careers* (1983), outline practical steps most individuals, from late adolescence on up, can follow in further defining personal values and successfully completing necessary career-seeking tasks, such as writing a résumé. These books also provide a wealth of information on how to locate positions of specific interest. A number of computer-based programs also offer career information and help individuals sort through values and interests. Among the top programs are:

☐ *SIGI-Plus*  System of Interactive Guidance and Information (*Plus* indicates a refinement of the system)

☐ *GIS*  Guidance Information System

☐ *NOICC*   National Occupational Information Coordinating Committee

☐ *DISCOVER*   A computerized career system

## CAREER DEVELOPMENT THEORIES

Career development theories try to explain the reasons why individuals choose careers. They also deal with the adjustments people make in careers over time. Modern theories, which are broad and comprehensive in regard to individual and occupational development, began appearing in the literature in the 1950s (Gysbers, 1984). Four of the most prominent ones will be dealt with here.

***Trait-and-Factor Theory.***   The origin of trait-and-factor theory can be traced back to Frank Parsons. The theory stresses matching an individual with a job that fits that person's talents. Its most widespread influence occurred during the Great Depression. It was out of favor during the 1950s and 1960s but has resurfaced in a more modern form as reflected in the work of researchers such as John Holland (1973). The trait-and-factor approach has always stressed the uniqueness of persons. Original advocates of the theory assumed that a person's abilities and traits could be measured objectively and quantified. Personal motivation was considered relatively stable. Thus, satisfaction in a particular occupation depended on a proper fit between one's abilities and the job requirements.

In its modern form, trait-and-factor theory stresses the interpersonal nature of careers and associated life-styles as well as the performance requirements of a work position. Holland (1973) identifies six categories into which both personalities and job type environments can be classified: realistic, investigative, artistic, social, enterprising, and conventional (Figure 16.1). Personal satisfaction in a work setting depends on the degree of congruence between the personality type and the work environment (Holland & Gottfredson, 1976). For example, an artistic person will probably not fit well into a conventional job, such as that of office manager. There are exceptions, of course, and as Salomone & Sheehan (1985) point out it is likely that some nonpsychological factors, such as economic, social, or cultural influences, account for many professional and nonprofessional workers accepting and maintaining their jobs. Regardless, as Holland emphasizes, it is vital for persons to have adequate knowledge of themselves and of occupational requirements in order to make informed career decisions (Herr & Cramer, 1984).

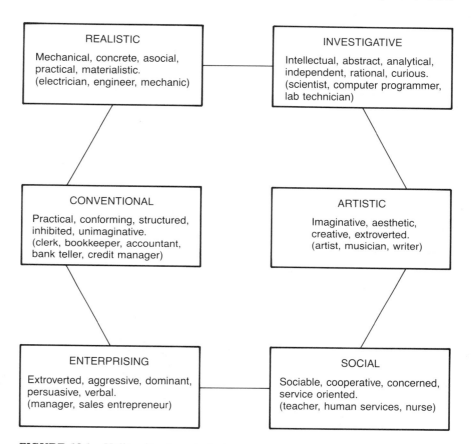

**FIGURE 16.1** Holland's six categories.

*Source:* From WORKING WITH ADULTS by Barbara F. Okun. Copyright © 1984 by Wadsworth, Inc. Reprinted by permission of Brooks/Cole Publishing Company, Monterey, California 93940.

***Psychodynamic Theory.*** This theory is best exemplified in the writings of Anne Roe (Roe, 1956; Wrenn, 1985), though in a related approach Robert Hoppock (1976) has also stressed the importance of unconscious motivation and of meeting emotional needs. Roe sees vocational interests developing as a result of the interaction between parents and their children. Career choices reflect the desire to satisfy needs not met by parents in childhood. From the psychodynamic point of view, the first few years of childhood are primarily responsible for shaping the pattern of life. Thus, Roe believes there is an unconscious motivation from this period that influences people to choose a career in which these needs can be expressed and satisfied.

Three different parent/child relationship climates are described by Roe (Figure 16.2). The first is characterized by an

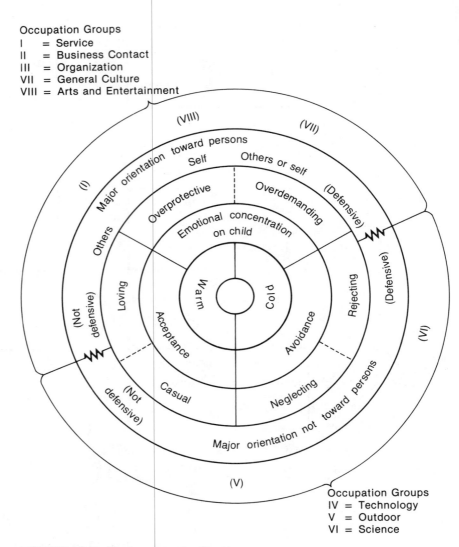

Occupation Groups
I   = Service
II  = Business Contact
III = Organization
VII = General Culture
VIII = Arts and Entertainment

Occupation Groups
IV = Technology
V  = Outdoor
VI = Science

**FIGURE 16.2**   Roe's conceptualization.

*Source:* From *The Origin of Interests* (p. 6) by Anne Roe and Marvin Siegelman, 1964, Washington, D.C.: American Personnel and Guidance Association. Copyright AACD. Reprinted with permission. No further reproduction authorized without further permission of AACD.

emotional concentration on the child. The pattern takes one of two forms. One is overprotection, in which the parents do too much for the child and thus encourage dependency. The other is an overdemanding approach, in which the parents emphasize achievement. Children who grow up in these types of environments usually develop a need for constant feedback and for rewards. They frequently choose careers that provide recognition from others, such as the performing arts.

The second childrearing pattern is avoidance of the child. There are two extremes within this pattern also. One is neglectful parenting, in which there is very little effort made to satisfy the needs of the child. The other is rejecting parenting, in which no effort is made to satisfy the child's needs. Roe speculates that children reared in such environments will concentrate on careers that involve scientific and mechanical interests as a way of finding gratification in life. They are more prone to deal with things and ideas.

The final pattern of child/parent relationships is that of an acceptance of the child. Acceptance may be casual or more actively loving; in either case, independence is encouraged. Children from these families usually seek careers that balance the personal and nonpersonal aspects of life, such as teaching or counseling.

**Developmental Theories.** The two most widely known career theories based on personal development are those associated with Donald Super and Eli Ginzberg. The original developmental theory proposed by Ginzberg and his associates has had great influence and has been revised (Ginzberg, 1972). But Super's theory will be examined in detail here because of the more extensive work that has been done with it. When compared to other approaches, developmental theories are generally "more inclusive, more concerned with longitudinal expression of career behavior, and more inclined to highlight the importance of self-concept" (Herr & Cramer, 1984, p. 122).

Super (1957) believes that career development is the process of implementing a self-concept. People's views of who they are are reflected in what they do. He suggests that vocational development unfolds in five stages, each of which contains a developmental task to be completed (Figure 16.3). The first stage is *growth* (from birth to age 14). During this stage, with its substages of fantasy (ages 4–10), interest (ages 11–12), and capacity (ages 13–14), a child forms a mental picture of the self in relationship to others. During the process of growth, the child also becomes oriented to the world of work. The second stage is *exploration* (ages 15–24). It has three substages—tentative (ages 15–17), transition (ages 18–21), and trial (ages 22–24). The major task of this stage is a general exploration of the world of work and the specification of a career preference.

Stage three is known as *establishment* (ages 25–44). Its two substages, trial (ages 25–30) and stabilization (ages 31–44), con-

| Growth (ages: birth to 14 years) | Exploration (ages: 14 to 24 years) | Establishment (ages: 24 to 44 years) | Maintenance (ages: 44 to 64 years) |
|---|---|---|---|
| *Birth* Self-concept develops through identification with key figures in family and school needs and fantasy are dominant early in this stage; interest and capacity become more important with increasing social participation and reality testing; learn behaviors associated with self-help, social interaction, self-direction, industrialness, goal setting, persistence. Substages: *Fantasy* (4–10 years) Needs are dominant; role-playing in fantasy is important. *Interest* (11–12 years) Likes are the major determinant of aspirations and activities. *Capacity* (13–14 years) Abilities are given more weight and job requirements (including training) are considered. Tasks: Developing a picture of the kind of person one is. Developing an orientation to the world of work and an understanding of the meaning of work. | *14 years* Self-examination, role try-outs and occupational exploration take place in school, leisure activities, and part-time work. Substages: *Tentative* (15–17) Needs, interests, capacities, values, and opportunities are all considered, tentative choices are made and tried out in fantasy, discussion, courses, work, etc. Possible appropriate fields and levels of work are identified. Task—Crystallizing a Vocational Preference *Transition* (18–21) Reality considerations are given more weight as the person enters the labor market or professional training and attempts to implement a self-concept. Generalized choice is converted to specific choice. Task—Specifying a Vocational Preference *Trial-Little Commitment* (22–24) A seemingly appropriate occupation having been found, a first job is located and is tried out as a potential life work. Commitment is still provisional and if the job is not appropriate, the person may reinstitute the process of crystallizing, specifying, and implementing a perference. Task—Implementing a Vocational Preference | *24 years* Having found an appropriate field, an effort is made to establish a permanent place in it. Thereafter changes which occur are changes of position, job, or employer, not of occupaiton. Substages: *Trial-Commitment and Stabilization* (25–30) Settling down. Securing a permanent place in the chosen occupation. May prove unsatisfactory resulting in one or two changes before the life work is found or before it becomes clear that the life work will be a succession of unrelated jobs. *Advancement* (31–44) Effort is put forth to stabilize, to make a secure place in the world of work. For most persons these are the creative years. Seniority is acquired; clientele are developed; superior performance is demonstrated; qualifications are improved. Tasks: Consolidation and Advancement | *44 years* Having made a place in the world of work, the concern is how to hold on to it. Little new ground is broken, continuation of established pattern. Concerned about maintaining present status while being forced by competition from younger workers in the advancement stage. Tasks: Preservation of achieved status and gains. Decline (ages: 64 years and up) *64 years* As physical and mental powers decline, work activity changes and in due course ceases. New roles must be developed: first, selective participant and then observer. Individual must find other sources of satisfaction to replace those lost through retirement. Substages: *Deceleration* (65–70) The pace of work slackens, duties are shifted, or the nature of work is changed to suit declining capacities. Many find part-time jobs to replace their full-time occupations. *Retirement* (71 on) Variation on complete cessation of work or shift to part-time, volunteer, or leisure activities. Tasks: Deceleration Disengagement, Retirement |

**FIGURE 16.3**  Super's stages.

*Source:* From *Career Guidance and Counseling Through the Life Span*, Second Edition, by E. L. Herr and S. H. Cramer. Copyright © 1984 by Little, Brown & Co.

stitute the major task of becoming established in a preferred and appropriate field of work. Once established, the person can concentrate on advancement until he or she tires or reaches the top of the profession. Then the fourth stage of *maintenance* (ages 45–65) begins, with its major task of preserving what one has already achieved. The final stage of *decline* (age 65 to death) is a time for disengagement from work and alignment with other sources of satisfaction. It includes two substages—deceleration (ages 65–70) and retirement (age 71 to death).

***Cognitive and Social-Learning Theories.*** Cognitive and social-learning theories of career development were formulated in the 1960s. Two of the most prominent cognitive models also have a developmental base (Knefelkamp & Slepitza, 1976; Tiedeman, 1961). Tiedeman and his associates rely on Erik Erikson's (1963) developmental crisis model; Knefelkamp and Slepitza have built on the work of Perry (1968), which focuses on the intellectual and ethical development of college students.

Tiedeman and O'Hara (1963) outline a seven-stage model of career decision: exploration (ages 14–18), crystallization (ages 18–21), choice (ages 18–25), clarification (ages 18–25), induction (ages 21–30), reformation (ages 21–30), and integration (ages 30–40). There is some overlap among the stages, but each requires that the individual make a decision. This emphasis on the cognitive restructuring of the person from "within to without" is Tiedeman's unique contribution to career development theory. Tiedeman and his associates view people as much more active in the formation of careers than does Super.

Knefelkamp and Slepitza (1976) also focus on a hierarchical structure of cognitive development in describing the development of career decision making in college students. They take into account nine variables that affect career planning among college students, such as locus of control, analysis, synthesis, and openness to alternative perspectives. Major weaknesses of their theory are that it does not provide for measurement of the processes on which it focuses and that it has not been studied in a noncollege population.

An equally comprehensive, but less developmental, social-learning approach is one formulated by Krumboltz (1979). He takes the position that there are four factors that influence a person's career choice: genetic endowment, conditions and events in the environment, learning experiences, and task approach skills (e.g., values, work habits). According to Krumboltz, career decisions are controlled by both internal and external processes. In other words, one has some control over the events one finds reinforcing.

## THE IMPORTANCE OF CAREER COUNSELING

Career counseling usually does not enjoy the same degree of prestige as do other forms of counseling or psychotherapy. This is unfortunate both for the counseling profession and for the many people who need these services. Surveys of high school upperclassmen and college underclassmen (e.g., Prediger, Roth, & Neoth, 1973) show that the counseling service they most prefer is career counseling. Brown (1985) also posits that career counseling may be a viable intervention for some clients who have severe emotional problems related to nonsupportive, stress-producing environments. The contribution of career counseling to personal growth and development is documented by Crites (1981, pp. 14–15). He lists five important aspects of career counseling:

☐ "The need for career counseling is greater than the need for psychotherapy." Comprehensive career counseling deals with the inner and outer world of individuals, whereas other counseling and psychotherapy approaches only deal with the inner world.

☐ "Career counseling can be therapeutic." Super (1957), Williams (1962), Williams and Hill (1962), and Crites (1969) have all found a positive correlation between career and personal adjustment. Clients who successfully cope with career decisions may also gain skill and confidence in the ability to tackle other problem areas. They may invest more of their energy in resolving noncareer problem areas because of having clarified career objectives. Brown (1985) provides a set of assessment strategies that are useful in determining whether a client needs personal or career counseling.

☐ "Career counseling should follow psychotherapy." Crites maintains that few counselors work with their clients on career problems even after clients have made some personality changes. He contends that since there is evidence to support the belief that personality is related to career choices, career counseling should follow psychotherapy in order to meet the client's needs fully. Finally, Crites believes that career counseling should be a sequential adjunct to other counseling intervention for practical and ethical reasons. Brammer and Shostrom (1982), however, argue that the stereotyped view of career counseling following personal counseling may not be appropriate.

☐ "Career counseling is more effective than psychotherapy." Direct comparisons between career counseling results and psychotherapy outcomes have not been made, but Crites maintains that the research literature (e.g., Brayfield, 1964; Garfield &

Bergin, 1978) supports his contention that the success rate for career counseling is 25 percent higher (i.e., 75 percent) than for psychotherapy (i.e., 50 percent).

☐ "Career counseling is more difficult than psychotherapy." Crites states that to be an effective career counselor a person must deal with both personal and work variables and must know how the two interface. The same is not true to the same degree for types of counseling in which the counselor mainly concentrates on the inner world of the client (Brown, 1985).

## MAJOR THEORIES OF CAREER COUNSELING

There is considerable overlap between theories of career development and those of career counseling. The Association for Counselor Education and Supervision (ACES) (1976), of the American Association for Counseling and Development, recognizes career counseling as a broad-based activity that is process oriented. Herr and Cramer (1984) stress that a career counseling viewpoint must be integrative. Crites (1981), in an overview of career counseling models and methods, examines five major approaches within this discipline that are often used in working with the whole person in a career choice setting (Figure 16.4). He assesses these approaches as follows.

***Trait-and-Factor Career Counseling.*** This type of career counseling is sometimes inappropriately caricatured as "three interviews and a cloud of dust." The first interview session is spent in getting to know a client's background and assigning tests. A client then takes a battery of tests and returns for the second interview to have the results of the tests interpreted by the counselor. In the third session, a client reviews career choices in light of the data presented and is sent out by the counselor to find further information on specific careers. Williamson (1972) originally implemented this theory to help clients learn self-management skills. But as Crites (1969, 1981) notes, trait-and-factor career counselors may ignore the psychological realities of decision making and fail to promote self-help skills in their clients. Such counselors often overemphasize test information, which clients either forget or distort.

***Client-Centered Career Counseling.*** This approach, as inspired by the writings of Carl Rogers (1942, 1951) and developed by C. H. Patterson (1964, 1974), is a synthesis of trait-and-factor components, developmental theory, and Rogerian counseling techniques.

**FIGURE 16.4** An overview of career counseling models and methods (pp. 170–173).

| | | Trait-and-Factor | Client-Centered |
|---|---|---|---|
| **M o d e l s** | **Diagnosis** | Different courses of treatment stem from a determination of what is wrong with the client | Rogers and Patterson consider diagnosis as disruptive of the client/counselor relationship; instead, they determine whether or not the client has a "vocational problem" |
| | **Process** | Involves largely the counselor in gathering and interpreting data on the client; client assists only in the actual determination of treatment or counseling to effect desired adjustment, and in follow-up | Patterson sees the process as encompassing Rogers' highest stage of personal adjustment in psychotherapy; the adjustment level of a client following psychotherapy approximates that of a vocational client before counseling when he/she is finding out who he/she is and what his/her needs are |
| | **Outcomes** | Immediate goal is to resolve the presenting problem of client; longer-term objective is to help him/her better understand and manage his/her own assets and liabilities, so s/he can solve future problems | Goal is to facilitate the clarification and implementation of the self-concept in a compatible occupational role at whatever point the client is; relates to psychotherapy's overall outcome of an individual's reorganized self that can accept and convert into reality a picture of self and role in the work world |

It deals in a complex but systematic fashion with both the emotional and cognitive aspects of making a career choise. Its major shortfalls are a failure to consider thoroughly the influence of outside phenomena on the career decisions of clients (Grummon, 1972) and an inconsistency in conveying career information to clients in a nondidactic Rogerian fashion.

***Psychodynamic Career Counseling.*** The model underlying psychodynamic career counseling was constructed primarily by Bordin (1968). It is his view, based on such psychodynamic theories as Anne Roe's, that career choices involve a client's needs and that they are developmental in nature. A major limitation of the approach is its strong emphasis on internal factors, such as motivation, and its lack of attention to external variables (Ginzberg, Ginsburg, Axelrad, & Herma, 1951). The process of career counseling from this perspective is also considered overly complex.

**FIGURE 16.4** *(continued)*

| Psychodynamic | Developmental | Behavioral |
|---|---|---|
| Bordin stipulates that diagnosis must form the basis for the choice of treatment; wants more treatment; wants more psychologcally based constructs (choice anxiety, dependence, self conflict) to be used in diagnosis | Super coins "appraisal" rather than diagnosis; delineates three types that focus on the client's potentialities and problems: (a) Problem Appraisal (b) Person Appraisal (c) Prognostic Appraisal; client is active in the appraisal process | Goodstein, in his behavioral-theoretic approach, attributes a central role to anxiety in the diagnosis of behavioral and career-choice problems; Krumboltz and Thoresen focus fully on behavioral analysis or problem identification in the specification of goals for counseling; in this behavioral-pragmatic approach, they do not focus on anxiety or diagnosis |
| Bordin defines three stages of process: (a) exploration and contract setting stage (b) critical decision stage in which client decides what facets of personal adjustment other than just vocational s/he would pursue (c) "working for change" stage in which increased understanding of self is aimed at in counseling | The immediate objective is to facilitate the client's career development; Super states that the broader goal is to bring about improvements in the individual's general personal adjustment (represents a synthesis of trait-and-factor and client-centered orientations) | According to Goodstein, process varies with the etiology of the client's problem—antecedent anxiety necessitates counter-conditioning and instrumental learning, while consequent anxiety necessitates only the latter; Krumboltz and Thoresen, on the other hand, aim at the elimination of nonadjustive behavior patterns |
| Results are twofold: (a) assist the client in career decision-making and (b) in broader terms to effect some positive change in the client's personality | The process of career development progresses from orientation and readiness for career choice to decision-making and reality testing; the counselor initiates counseling at that point in the process that the client has reached | Goodstein's theoretic outcomes are (a) elimination of antecedent and consequent anxiety and (b) acquisition of decision-making skills; Krumboltz and Thoresen's pragmatic goals involve skill acquisition—altering maladaptive behavior, learning decision-making process, and preventing problems |

***Developmental Career Counseling.*** The major contributions of developmental career counseling are its emphases on the importance of time in career decision making and on how career decisions are influenced by other decision-making processes and events in a person's life. Super (1957) has been the major advocate of this theory. The approach is descriptive and historical, which is considered both a strength and weakness. The conceptual depth of this theory is also criticized. Overall, the developmental approach is strong. With a further elaboration by Super (1981), an even more comprehensive "rainbow" theory has emerged, and criticisms of the approach as being incomplete may be less valid.

***Behavioral Career Counseling.*** The recognized advocates of the behavioral viewpoint are Goodstein (1972) for the theoretical perspective and Krumboltz and Thoresen (1976) for the pragmatic perspective. Each approach emphasizes concepts and principles of

**FIGURE 16.4** *(continued)*

|  |  | Trait-and-Factor | Client-Centered |
|---|---|---|---|
| M e t h o d s | Interview Techinque | Involves a pragmatic technological method of establishing rapport, cultivating self-understanding, advising a program of action, carrying out a plan, and referring the client to other personnel for more assistance | Counselor will make responses during the interview geared to helping the client experience and implement the self-concept in an occupational role |
|  | Test Interpretation | Involves the counselor who makes authoritative interpretations of the test results, and draws conclusions and recommendations from them for the client's deliberation | Counselor proposes that tests be used primarily for the client's edification and wants; use only as needed and requested by client; termed by Super as "precision testing" |
|  | Use of Occupational Information | Counselor provides this information to either confirm a choice already made or resolve indecision between two equally attractive options; may help a client readjust an inappropriate choice; also used to involve the client actively in the decision-making process | Introduced when there is a recognized need for it on the part of the client; counselor must recognize that such information has personal meanings to the client which must be understood and explored within the context of needs and values, and objective reality. |

learning theory to explain career behaviors. Behavioral-theoretic counseling stresses the role of anxiety and diagnosis, whereas behavioral-pragmatic emphasizes problem identification as it relates to the goals of counseling. A major problem with these two views is the importance they place on anxiety in career decision making. If anxiety must be overcome before behavioral techniques are applicable, the pragmatic viewpoint cannot be employed effectively.

***Comprehensive Career Counseling.*** In contrast to these five theories, Crites (1981) has developed his own model. His model is based on the five major approaches just discussed, the more general systems of counseling and psychotherapy, such as those described by Corsini (1984), and his own wide experience as a career counselor. He advocates that counselors make three diagnoses of a client's

**FIGURE 16.4** *(continued)*

| Psychodynamic | Developmental | Behavioral |
|---|---|---|
| Bordin enumerates three interpretive counselor response categories that can be used: (a) clarification—to focus the client's thinking and verbalizations (b) comparison and (c) the interpretation of "wish-defence" systems; *represents a synthesis of psychoanalytic practices, trait-and-factor, client-centered approaches | Super's "cyclical" approach is to respond directly to content statements by the client and nondirectly to expressions of feeling | Goodstein proposes techniques of psychotherapy for the alleviation of anxiety; he joins with Krumboltz and Thoresen in their pragmatic stance that the counselor should reinforce desired client responses, encourage social modeling, and teach discrimination learning in the acquisition of decision-making skills |
| Bordin defines three major uses: (a) that the client be an active participant in selecting the tests (as in the client-centered approach) (b) that the tests provide diagnostic information for counselor to give client and stimulate self-exploration and (c) that the counselor verbally present the test interpretation—introduce as needed rather than presenting it all at once as in trait-and-factor | The most appropriate information is the description of career patterns in different occupational pursuits; Super observes that there are approximately six types of descriptive data on career patterns that are needed for this approach | Test use, in either a theoretical or pragmatic stance, is almost negligible since they measure individual differences in behavior rather than reflect individual-environment interaction—a primary concern to a behavioral counselor; objective indices of behavior are therefore gathered |
| Information that is based upon a "need analysis" of job duties and tasks is needed; resembles the trait-and-factor approach of matching people with jobs, but differs in that variables are personality needs and gratifying work conditions, rather than static characteristics of the individual and occupation | The purpose is to maximize the value of tests in decision-making by administering them in a discriminating way, and by involving the client in each phase of the process; represents "precision" testing rather than "saturation" testing as in the trait-and-factor approach | Behavioral counselors have developed "career kits" that are more useful in stimulating further career exploration and decision-making than simply printed information |

*Source:* From *Career Counseling: Models, Methods, and Materials* (pp. 170–173) by J. O. Crites, 1981, New York: McGraw-Hill. Copyright 1981 by McGraw-Hill. Reprinted by permission.

career problems: differential (what the problems are), dynamic (why the problems have occurred), and decisional (how the problems are being dealt with). Such diagnoses result from a close working relationship between client and counselor and are facilitated by open communication. Once made, diagnoses form the basis for problem resolution strategies which can be expected to produce more fully functioning individuals intellectually, personally, socially, and vocationally.

Crites employs specific methods in his career counseling that are clearly dictated by his model. He uses client-centered and developmental counseling at the beginning in order to identify problems. The middle stage of his process is dominated by psychodynamic techniques, such as interpretation, to clarify how the problems have occurred. The final stage of the process uses trait-and-factor and behavioral approaches to help the client resolve problem areas. Comprehensive career counseling also advocates the use of tests in working with clients. The focus in test use, however, is on "interpreting the tests without the tests," that is, letting the client and counselor share responsibility for interpreting what the test results mean independently of standardized norms. Finally, this model of career counseling stresses the use of career information with clients and recommends that counselors orient clients to such information and reinforce clients when they make use of the information. Crites (1973, 1978) has developed the *Career Maturity Inventory* to help counselors determine how knowledgeable clients are of career information and of themselves. Overall, this model is most definitive and is adaptable to many counseling situations.

## CAREER COUNSELING WITH DIVERSE POPULATIONS

Career counseling and education is conducted with a wide variety of individuals in diverse settings. Brown (1985) observes that career counseling typically is offered in college counseling centers, rehabilitation facilities, employment offices, and the public schools. He thinks it could be applied with great advantage in many other places as well, including mental health centers and private practice offices. Jesser (1983) agrees and asserts there is a need to provide career information and counseling to potential users, such as the unemployed, the learning disabled, prisoners, and those released from mental hospitals who seek to reenter the job market. Since the concept of careers encompasses the life span, counselors who specialize in this area find themselves working with a full age range of clients from young children to octogenarians. Consequently, many different approaches and techniques have developed for working effectively with select groups.

### Career Counseling with Children

The process of career development begins in the preschool years and becomes more direct in elementary schools. Herr and Cramer (1984) cite numerous studies to show that during the first six years of school, many children develop a relatively stable self-perception and make a tentative commitment to a vocation. These processes are observed whether career counseling and guidance activities are offered or not. Thus, it is beneficial to children, especially those who live in areas of limited employment opportunities, to have a broad systematic program of career counseling and guidance in the school. Such a program should focus on awareness rather than firm decision making and should teach children that they have career choices. Jesser (1983) suggests that levels of career awareness in elementary school children may be raised through such activities as field trips to local industries, such as a bakery, a manufacturing plant, or a bank. When such trips are followed up with appropriate classroom learning exercises (e.g., class discussions), children become more aware of a wider spectrum of related occupations.

Splete (1982) outlines a comprehensive program for working with children that includes parent education and classroom discussions jointly planned by a teacher and counselor. He emphasizes that at the elementary school level there are three key career development areas: self-awareness, career awareness and exploration, and decision making. Well-designed career guidance and counseling programs that are implemented at an early age and coordinated with later programs throughout all levels of the educational system can go a long way in dispelling irrational and decision-hindering career development myths, such as "a career decision is an event that should occur at a specific point in time" (Lewis & Gilhousen, 1981, p. 297).

### Career Counseling with Adolescents

To meet the career needs of adolescents, ASCA (1985) developed a role statement on the expectations and responsibilities of school counselors engaged in career guidance. The five-point statement emphasizes that school counselors should involve others, both inside and outside the school environment, in the delivery of career education to students.

Cole (1982) stresses that in the middle school and junior high school, career guidance activities should include the exploration of new work areas and the evaluation by students of their own strengths and weaknesses in regard to possible future careers. Assets that students should become more aware of and begin to evaluate include talents and skills, general intelligence, motivation level, friends, family, life experience, appearance, and health (Campbell, 1974). At the senior high school, career guidance and counseling activities are related more to the maturity level of students. Herr and Cramer (1984) state that, in general, career activities with this population have three emphases: "stimulating career development, providing treatment, and aiding placement" (p. 262). More specifically, counselors provide students with reassurance, information, emotional support, reality testing, planning strategies, attitude clarification, and work experiences, depending on a student's needs and level of functioning.

Several techniques have proven quite effective in helping adolescents crystallize ideas about a career. Some of these involve the use of fantasies, such as "a typical day in the future," "an awards ceremony," "a mid-career change," and "retirement" (Morgan & Skovholt, 1977). More concrete exercises might include completing an occupational family tree (Figure 16.5) to find out how one's present interests compare with the careers of other family members (Dickson & Parmerlee, 1980).

### Career Counseling with College Students

As noted in the chapter on school and college counseling, underclassmen are most likely to visit college counseling centers for career counseling, but all college students seem to value these services. An example that illustrates this point is a study at the University of Georgia that revealed career development needs far outweighed purely personal or academic concerns of students (Weissberg, Berentsen, Cole, Cravey, & Heath, 1982). Even students who have decided on a college major and a career seek such services (Goodson, 1981).

Herr and Cramer (1984) list a number of services which a comprehensive career guidance and counseling program in an institution of higher education attempts to provide. Among them are: help with the selection of a major field of study, self-assessment and self-analysis, understanding the world of work, gaining access to employment opportunities, learning decision-making skills, and meeting the needs of special populations. Another service that Weiner and Hunt (1983) found important in college career counseling is exploring with students the role of leisure in proposed career and life-style plans. This finding supports the emphasis by McDaniels (1984) on the importance of leisure with regard to work. Anticipating problems related to work and intimate relationships, such as preparing to live in a dual-career family, have also been proposed as a career counseling service with college students (Hester & Dickerson, 1982). In a review of the published literature on career interventions with college students, Pickering and Vacc (1984) found that most approaches used are effective to some degree and that short-term behavioral interventions are most prevalent.

### Career Counseling with Adults

The two dominant ways of working with adults in regard to careers are the differential approach and the developmental approach. The differential approach stresses that "the typology of persons and

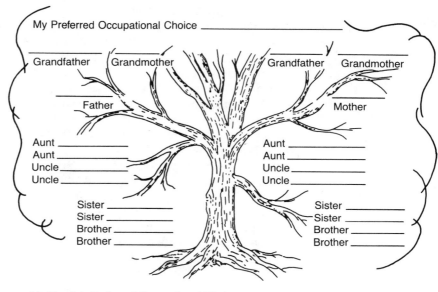

My Preferred Occupational Choice _____

Grandfather _____ Grandmother _____ | Grandfather _____ Grandmother _____

Father _____ | Mother _____

Aunt _____
Aunt _____
Uncle _____
Uncle _____

Aunt _____
Aunt _____
Uncle _____
Uncle _____

Sister _____
Sister _____
Brother _____
Brother _____

Sister _____
Sister _____
Brother _____
Brother _____

My Family's Preferred Occupational Choice _____

**FIGURE 16.5** Occupational family tree.

*Source:* From "The occupational family tree: A career counseling technique" by G. L. Dickson and J. R. Parmerlee, 1980, *The School Counselor, 28,* p. 101. Copyright AACD. Reprinted with permission. No further reproduction authorized without further permission of AACD.

environments is more useful than any life stage strategies for coping with career problems" (Holland & Gottfredson, 1976, p. 23). It avoids age-related stereotypes, gender and minority-group issues, and the scientific and practical difficulties of dealing with life-span problems. "At any age, the level and quality of a person's vocational coping is a function of the interaction of personality type and type of environment plus the consistency and differentiation of each" (Holland & Gottfredson, 1976, p. 23).

Thus, according to this view, a career counselor who is aware of typological formulations, such as those by Holland, can predict the characteristic ways a given person may cope with career problems. For example, a person with a well-defined social-artistic personality (typical of many individuals employed as counselors) would be expected to "have high educational and vocational aspirations, to have good decision-making ability, to have a strong and lifelong interest in learning, to have moderate personal competency, and to have a marked interest in creative and high level performance rather than in leadership" (Holland, 1973, p. 42). A person with such a profile also would have a tendency either to remold or to leave an environment in the face of adversity. A major advantage of working from this approach is the ease with which it explains career shifts at any age. People who become involved in shifting careers, at any point in life, are seeking to find more consistency between personality and environment.

The developmental point of view is one that examines a greater number of variables. It proposes that individuals are always undergoing change and in the process evaluating themselves in regard to their work. The theories of Super and Crites are prime examples of theories that address developmental career concerns. Okun (1984) has also emphasized incorporating individual, family, and career development issues in decisions. She contends that each of these three factors interrelates with and influences the other two. The young adult does not face the same set of developmental tasks as the person in mid or late adulthood. Those who advocate the developmental approach, therefore, assert that career counselors who work with adults are most effective when they have a knowledge of developmental issues, life tasks, and other related variables before trying to offer career assistance.

### Career Counseling with Women and Minorities

Issues related to career counseling with women and minorities have surfaced frequently in professional journals. For example, Barnhart (1983) and Hageman and Gladding (1983) found that elementary school children viewed many occupational roles as sex stereotyped and thus limited their exploration of these professions. Moses (1983) examined reasons for the differential pay scales for American women and men and, along with Wojciechowski (1982), has concentrated on evaluating the image women have of themselves in the world of work. Dillard and Campbell (1982) have focused on the subjective career values of Puerto Ricans and blacks, while McDavis and Parker (1981) have described five strategies counselors can use in helping ethnic-minority students with career development. It is impossible to discuss all of the variables and problems associated with the career counseling of women and minorities in this section. However, we will briefly touch on two groups of women where career counseling is especially needed, and highlight some particularly important issues related to career counseling with minorities.

*Displaced homemakers*, women who out of necessity enter the job market, and *late-entry women*, who decide to enter the job market after considerable time at home, pose considerable challenges for career counselors (Isaacson, 1986). The displaced homemaker often finds herself in a financial strain, uninformed about current job market trends, without a support system, and with a shaky self-concept. Career counselors must first help these individuals sort out or resolve some of these problems before dealing with major career decisions. In the process, they may assist the women in finding temporary employment, but long-term solutions to career satisfaction with these women take time. Late-entry women, because of their own motivation and status, do not face the same problems to the same degree. However, they usually need more information on careers and, like displaced homemakers, will have to tackle the issues of identifying skills, and dealing with self-concept and family responsibilities.

Minorities are so diverse that it is impossible to focus on the many factors that career counselors must deal with in working with them. That a person is culturally different from the majority of other workers is an issue counselors must help clients face. Related to this issue are others, such as discrimination, self-concept, and, in some cases, skill and language barriers. A crucial aspect of working with minorities is that the counselor keep an open attitude and help clients recognize self-potential.

In chapter 17, we will discuss many other issues associated with counseling women and minorities. Needless to say, there is a real need for career counselors to be extremely sensitive to those who have been discriminated against because of gender, age, or ethnic background. Likewise, there is a need to help individuals and society in general break down artificial barriers that in the long run hurt everyone.

## SUMMARY

The material presented in this chapter supports the view that career counseling is a very complex and rapidly developing specialty in the profession of counseling. In order to be most helpful, those who work in this area must have a vast array of knowledge and skills. The National Council for Credentialing Career Counselors (NCCCC) has set up strict guidelines for those they certify (Smith & Karpati, 1985). Minimum competencies must be demonstrated in six designated areas: general counseling, information, individual-group assessment, consultation, management-administration, and implementation. The standards set by the NCCCC further attest to Crites' contention that career counseling is more difficult than psychotherapy.

There is much debate among theorists as to the reasons behind individuals' career choices and what counseling approaches may be most useful to them. In all probability, multiple factors, including inner needs and drives and external circumstances such as the economy or social milieu, combine to influence career choice decisions. Regardless, it is crucial that career counseling services be available throughout life. Jesser (1983) notes that the average person changes jobs five times in a working life. Whether the changes are all related to a similar typology, as Holland (1973) argues, or linked to different stages in the life cycle, as Okun (1984) proposes, it is important that people have competent career counseling services to help them in these times of change.

Information on career counseling with particular populations and ages is always being gathered. There are both similarities and differences among career counselors (Cramer & Herr, 1981). However, career counseling appears to be developing rapidly in its theory and practice toward becoming a unified and stable field (Herr, 1982).

## CLASSROOM ACTIVITIES

1. Think back on your own childhood and the careers of which you were aware. How does your career dream then (before the age of 12) relate to your present professional aspirations? Discuss your memories and ideas in a general classroom discussion in relations to Holland's typology theory.
2. Pair up with another classmate and discuss with him or her the importance you see in the concept of leisure being included in the definition of career. Do you agree with McDaniels' emphasis or do you think leisure is really a separate entity? Discuss your ideas with your classmates.
3. Read about and evaluate a technique that could be used in career information guidance with an age group in which you are interested. Share your information with the class in the form of an oral report.
4. Evaluate Roe's theory of career choice in relationship to an individual you know who is established in a career. Interview the person, if possible. Discuss with your classmates how Roe's theory was verified or not verified according to the information you obtained.
5. Which of the theories of career counseling appeals to you the most? Divide the class into groups according to theory choice. In your groups discuss with one another what changes you would make in the theory of your choice to make it even stronger. Orally present your report to the class.

## REFERENCES

ACES Position Paper. (1976). *Commission on counselor preparation for career development/career education.* Washington, D.C.: Association for Counselor Education and Supervision.

ASCA Role Statement. (1985). The role of the school counselor in career guidance: Expectations and responsibilities. *The School Counselor, 32,* 164–168.

Barnhart, R. S. (1983). Children's sextyped views of traditional occupational roles. *The School Counselor, 10,* 167–170.

Bolles, R. N. (1986). *What color is your parachute?* Berkeley, CA: Ten Speed Press.

Bordin, E. S. (1968). *Psychological counseling* (2nd ed.). New York: Appleton-Century-Crofts.

Brammer, L. M., & Shostrom, E. L. (1982). *Therapeutic psychology: Fundamentals of counseling and psychotherapy* (4th ed.). Englewood Cliffs, NJ: Prentice-Hall.

Bratcher, W. E. (1982). The influence of the family on career selection: A family systems perspective. *Personnel and Guidance Journal, 61,* 87–91.

Brayfield, A. H. (1964). Research on vocational guidance: Status and prospect. In H. Borow (Ed.), *Man in a world of work* (pp. 310–323). Boston: Houghton Mifflin.

Brown, D. (1985). Career counseling: Before, after or instead of personal counseling. *Vocational Guidance Quarterly, 33,* 197–201.

Campbell, D. (1974). *If you don't know where you're going you'll probably end up somewhere else.* Niles, IL: Argus.

Cole, C. G. (1982). Career guidance for middle-junior high school students. *Vocational Guidance Quarterly, 30,* 308–314.

Corsini, R. (1984). *Current psychotherapies* (3rd ed.). Itasca, IL: Peacock.

Cramer, S. H., & Herr, E. L. (1981). A half century of similarities and differences in vocational guidance. *Vocational Guidance Quarterly, 30,* 157–166.

Crites, J. O. (1969). *Vocational psychology.* New York: McGraw-Hill.

Crites, J. O. (1973, 1978). *Theory and research handbook for the Career Maturity Inventory.* Monterey, CA: CTB/McGraw-Hill.

Crites, J. O. (1981). *Career counseling: Models, methods, and materials.* New York: McGraw-Hill.

Dickson, G. L., & Parmerlee, J. R. (1980). The occupation family tree: A career counseling technique. *The School Counselor, 28,* 99–104.

Dillard, J. M., & Campbell, N. J. (1982). Career values and aspirations of adult female and male Puerto Ricans, Blacks, and Anglos. *Journal of Employment Counseling, 19,* 163–170.

Drummond, R. J., & Barnard, L. S. (1984). Work values of employees at residential treatment centers for juvenile offenders. *Journal of Offender Counseling, 4,* 39–43.

Erikson, E. H. (1963). *Childhood and society* (2nd ed.). New York: Norton.

Fredrickson, R. H. (1982). *Career information.* Englewood Cliffs, NJ: Prentice-Hall.

Garfield, S. L., & Bergin, A. E. (1978). *Handbook of psychotherapy and behavior change* (2nd ed.). New York: Wiley.

Ginzberg, E. (1972). Toward a theory of occupational choice: A restatement. *Vocational Guidance Quarterly, 20,* 169–176.

Ginzberg, E., Ginsburg, S. W., Axelrad, S., & Herma, J. L. (1951). *Occupational choice.* New York: Columbia University Press.

Gladding, S. T. (1985). Harbor thoughts. *Journal of Humanistic Education and Development, 23,* 68.

Goodstein, L. D. (1972). Behavioral views of counseling. In B. Stefflre & W. H. Grant (Eds.), *Theories of counseling* (pp. 243–289). New York: McGraw-Hill.

Grummon, D. L. (1972). Client-centered theory. In B. Stefflre & W. H. Grant (Eds.), *Theories of counseling* (2nd ed., pp. 73–135). New York: McGraw-Hill.

Gysbers, N. C. (1975). Beyond career development—Life career development. *Personnel and Guidance Journal, 53,* 647–652.

Gysbers, N. C. (1975). Major trends in career development theory and practice. *Vocational Guidance Quarterly, 33,* 15–25.

Hageman, M. B., & Gladding, S. T. (1983). The art of career exploration: Occupational sex-role stereotyping among elementary school children. *Elementary School Guidance and Counseling, 17,* 280–287.

Herr, E. L. (1982). Comprehensive career guidance: A look to the future. *Vocational Guidance Quarterly, 30,* 367–376.

Herr, E. L., & Cramer, S. H. (1984). *Career guidance and counseling through the life span* (2nd ed.). Boston: Little, Brown.

Hester, S. B., & Dickerson, K. G. (1982). The emerging dual-career life-style—Are your students prepared for it? *Journal of College Student Personnel, 23,* 514–519.

Holland, J. L. (1973). *Making vocational choices: A theory of careers.* Englewood Cliffs, NJ: Prentice-Hall.

Holland, J. L., & Gottfredson, G. D. (1976). Using a typology of persons and environments to explain careers: Some extensions and clarifications. *The Counseling Psychologist, 6,* 20–29.

Hoppock, R. (1976). *Occupational information* (4th ed.). New York: Harper & Row.

Isaacson, L. E. (1986). *Career information in counseling and career development* (4th ed.). Boston: Allyn & Bacon.

Jesser, D. L. (1983). Career education: Challenges and issues. *Journal of Career Education, 10,* 70–79.

Knefelkamp, L. L., & Slepitza, R. (1976). A cognitive developmental model of career development—An adaptation of Perry's scheme. *The Counseling Psychologist, 6,* 53–58.

Krumboltz, J. D. (1979). *Social learning and career decision making.* New York: Carroll Press.

Krumboltz, J. D., & Thoresen, C. E. (Eds.). (1976). *Counseling methods.* New York: Holt, Rinehart & Winston.

Leape, M. P. (1983). *The Harvard guide to careers.* Cambridge, MA: Harvard University Press.

Lewis, R. A., & Gilhousen, M. R. (1981). Myths of career development: A cognitive approach to vocational counseling. *Personnel and Guidance Journal, 59,* 296–299.

McDaniels, C. (1984). The work/leisure connection. *Vocational Guidance Quarterly, 33,* 35–44.

McDavis, R. J., & Parker, W. M. (1981). Strategies for helping ethnic minorities with career development. *Journal of Non-White Concerns, 9,* 130–136.

Meyer, D., Helwig, A., Gjernes, O., & Chickering, J. (1985). The National Employment Counselors Association. *Journal of Counseling and Development, 63,* 440–443.

Miles, L. (1981). Midlife career change for blacks: Problems and issues. *Vocational Guidance Quarterly, 30,* 5–14.

Miller, M. J. (1983). The role of happenstance in career choice. *Vocational Guidance Quarterly, 32,* 16–20.

Morgan, J. I., & Skovholt, T. M. (1977). Using inner experience: Fantasy and daydreams in career counseling. *Journal of Counseling Psychology, 24,* 391–397.

Moses, B. (1983). The 59-cent dollar. *Journal of Employment Counseling, 20,* 3–11.

Okun, B. F. (1984). *Working with adults: Individual, family, and career development.* Monterey, CA: Brooks/Cole.

Parsons, F. (1909). *Choosing a vocation.* Boston: Houghton Mifflin.

Patterson, C. H. (1964). Counseling: Self-clarification and helping relationships. In H. Borow (Ed.), *Man in a world of work.* Boston: Houghton Mifflin.

Patterson, C. H. (1974). *Relationship counseling and psychotherapy.* New York: Harper & Row.

Perry, W. G. (1968). *Forms of intellectual and ethical development in the college years: A scheme.* New York: Holt, Rinehart & Winston.

Pickering, J. W., & Vacc, N. A. (1984). Effectiveness of career development interventions for college students: A review of published research. *Vocational Guidance Quarterly, 20,* 149–159.

Prediger, D. J., Roth, J. D., & Noeth, R. J. (1973). Nationwide study of career development: Summary of results. *ACT Research Report, 61.* Iowa City: American College Testing Program.

Roe, A. (1956). *The psychology of occupations.* New York: Wiley.

Rogers, C. (1942). *Counseling and psychotherapy.* Boston: Houghton Mifflin.

Rogers, C. (1951). *Client-centered therapy.* Boston: Houghton Mifflin.

Salomone, P. R. (1982). Difficult cases in career counseling: II—The indecisive client. *Personnel and Guidance Journal, 60,* 496–500.

Salomone, P. R., & McKenna, P. (1982). Difficult career counseling cases: I—Unrealistic vocational aspirations. *Personnel and Guidance Journal, 60,* 283–286.

Salomone, P. R., & Sheehan, M. C. (1985). Vocational stability and congruence: An examination of Holland's proposition. *Vocational Guidance Quarterly, 34,* 91–98.

Sears, S. (1982). A definition of career guidance terms: A National Vocational Guidance Association perspective. *Vocational Guidance Quarterly, 31,* 137–143.

Sheeley, V. L. (1978). *Career guidance leadership in America: Pioneering professionals.* Falls Church, VA: National Vocational Guidance Association.

Smith, R. L., Engels, D. W., & Bonk, E. C. (1985). The past and future: The National Vocational Guidance Association. *Journal of Counseling and Development, 63,* 420–423.

Smith, R. L., & Karpati, F. S. (1985). Credentialing career counselors. *Journal of Counseling and Development, 63,* 611.

Splete, H. H. (1982). Planning for a comprehensive career guidance program in the elementary schools. *Vocational Guidance Quarterly, 30,* 300–307.

Super, D. E. (1957). *The psychology of careers.* New York: Harpers.

Super, D. E. (1976). *Career education and the meaning of work.* Monographs of career education. Washington, D.C.: The Office of Career Education, U.S. Office of Education.

Super, D. E. (1981). The relative importance of work. *Bulletin—International Association of Educational and Vocational Guidance, 37,* 26–36.

Tiedeman, D. V. (1961). Decision and vocational development: A paradigm and its implications. *Personnel and Guidance Journal, 40,* 15–20.

Tiedeman, D. V., & O'Hara, R. P. (1963). *Career development: Choice and adjustment.* New York: College Entrance Examination Board.

Weiner, A. I., & Hunt, S. L. (1983). Work and leisure orientations among university students: Implications for college and university counselors. *Personnel and Guidance Journal, 61,* 537–542.

Weissberg, M., Berentsen, M., Cole, A., Cravey, B., & Heath, K. (1982). An assessment of the personal, career, and academic needs of undergraduate students. *Journal of College Student Personnel, 23,* 115–122.

Wellington, J. (1982). The working woman and self concept: A growing ambivalence. *Counseling and Values, 26,* 133–140.

Williams, J. E. (1962). Changes in self and other perceptions following brief educational-vocational counseling. *Journal of Counseling Psychology, 9,* 18–30.

Williams, J. E., & Hills, D. A. (1962). More on brief educational-vocational counseling. *Journal of Counseling Psychology, 9,* 366–368.

Williamson, E. G. (1972). Trait-and-factor theory and individual differences. In B. Stefflre & W. H. Grant (Eds.), *Theories of counseling* (2nd ed., pp. 136–176). New York: McGraw-Hill.

Wilson, V. M., & Lunneborg, P. W. (1982). Implications of women's changing career aspirations for college counselors. *Journal of College Student Personnel, 23,* 236–239.

Wojciechowski, D. (1982). I am a working mother . . . but who am I? *Journal of Employment Counseling, 19,* 106–112.

Wrenn, R. L. (1985). The evolution of Anne Roe. *Journal of Counseling and Development, 63,* 267–275.

Photo by James S. Davidson III.

# CHAPTER 17

# *Counseling in a Pluralistic Society*

*An old Black man in downtown Atlanta*
    *is clubfooted, blind, and bends like the willows.*
*He sits by his papers near Peachtree Street*
    *passing the time by tapping his crutches.*
*I flow by him in the five o'clock stream*
    *of white-collared, blue-suited, turbulent people*
    *rushing for MARTA trains to neighboring suburbs*
    *and the prospects of quiet in the flood-tide of life.*
*Spring rains now enrich the lands . . . but*
*Where do the willows and waters meet?*[1]

---

[1]Gladding, 1976/1986, p. 23. Copyright AACD. Reprinted with permission.
No further reproduction authorized without written permission of AACD.

*T*he effectiveness of counseling depends on many factors, but of uppermost importance is the counselor's ability to understand and relate empathetically to the client. "For effective counseling to occur, the counselor and client must be able to appropriately and accurately send and receive both verbal and nonverbal messages" (Sue & Sue, 1981, p. 420). Such a relationship is usually easier to achieve if the client and counselor are similar in cultural background, race, age, and sex (Pedersen, 1978). Since such similarity is relatively rare, it is imperative that counselors be sensitive to the backgrounds and special needs of clients and that counselors never allow differences to influence the counseling process negatively.

In this chapter, we will concentrate on counseling with three diverse populations. The first comprises such minorities as blacks, Native Americans, Asian-Americans, and Hispanics. These four groups made up 20 percent of the population of the United States in 1980—blacks (12 percent), Hispanics (6 percent), Asian-Americans (1.5 percent), and Native Americans (.5 percent) (Axelson, 1985). Their numbers and percentages are expected to increase at a faster rate than those of whites.

Researchers have consistently found that minority-group members receive unequal and poorer mental health services when compared to whites. The reason is largely due to differences in culture and values between minority clients and their counselors, the majority of whom have been white, middle-class males.

The second group is the older adult population—adults over the age of 65. In 1980, this group numbered 24 million and constituted 12 percent of the population (Myers & Rimmer, 1982). The number of older Americans and their percentage of the total population are expected to increase dramatically in the first half of the twenty-first century as the so-called baby-boomers of post-World War II mature and as improved health care continues to expand life expectancy. The aging and the aged have special needs and concerns that were not addressed by the counseling profession until the mid-1970s (Blake, 1975; Salisbury, 1975).

The final population covered includes the subgroups of women and men. As clients in counseling, members of each subgroup have distinct needs and concerns that are determined in part by the cultural climates and social groups in which they live and develop (Blimeline & Birk, 1979; Scher, 1981). Counselors who are not fully aware of the influence of stereotypes and role expectations for women and men are not likely to succeed in helping these clients in counseling (Moore & Strickler, 1980). Many theories and techniques of counseling apply to working with individuals of either gender, but because of societal discrimination, stereotyping, and insensitivity, some traditional approaches may be ineffective, limiting, or sexist in a particular case. Effective counseling with women and men requires special knowledge and insight.

## COUNSELING WITH MINORITIES

The history of counseling services for minorities is rather brief and uneven. Its focus has shifted from the client (1950s) to the counselor (1960s) to the total counseling process itself (1970s to the present). Gilbert Wrenn (1962) was one of the first professionals to call attention to the unique aspects of counseling minorities. In a landmark article, he described the "culturally encapsulated counselor" as one who disregards cultural differences and works on the mistaken notion that theories and techniques are equally applicable to all people. Such a counselor is insensitive to the actual experiences of clients from different cultures and therefore may discriminate against some clients by treating all clients the same (Sue, 1977). Despite numerous publications on the subject of counseling and culture written since that time, many counselors remain uninformed.

In AACD there is a division, the Association for Multicultural Counseling and Development (AMCD), that is dedicated primarily to defining and dealing with issues and concerns related to counseling those from minority cultures within the United States. This division, originally known as the Association for Non-White Concerns in Personnel and Guidance (ANWC), became a part of AACD in 1972 (McFadden & Lipscomb, 1985). It publishes a quarterly periodical, the *Journal of Multicultural Counseling & Development*, that addresses issues related to counseling in a culturally pluralistic society. The AMCD, in cooperation with the AACD, regularly sponsors conferences to address such issues, and the term *cross-cultural* is used frequently in reference to counseling relationships involving clients and counselors from different ethnic or cultural groups (Ahia, 1984; Axelson, 1985; Smith & Vasquez, 1985).

### Cross-Cultural Counseling

Axelson (1985) points out that there are several ways to define a culture. A broad definition is "any group of people who identify or associate with one another on the basis of some common purpose, need, or similarity of background . . ." (p. 2). The shared elements include learned experiences, beliefs, and values. Many cultures are composed of individuals from the same ethnic group, who share similar physical features, such as the Chinese, or a common history, such as the British.

A cross-cultural counseling relationship occurs when an individual from one ethnic or cultural background helps a person from a different ethnic or cultural background (Copeland, 1983). For example, a black counselor might work with an Asian-American client or a white with a Hispanic. There may be counselors from one country who work in another country or who work with foreign students who are studying in the counselor's home country. Regardless, cross-cultural counseling focuses on variables of dominant and minority cultures, ethnicity, language, values, and milieu and is applicable in individual and group settings (Ruiz, 1984).

### Problems in Cross-Cultural Counseling

Smith and Vasquez (1985) caution that it is important to distinguish differences that arise from ethnic and cultural backgrounds from those that are the result of poverty or deprived status. A failure to make this distinction can lead to *overculturalizing,* that is, "mistaking people's reactions to poverty and discrimination for their cultural pattern" (p. 533). In the United States, many members of minority groups live in poverty (Hunt & Chandler, 1983). This problem is compounded by a second—language patterns and nonverbal behaviors not accepted by the majority culture. Racism is a third problem minorities constantly face (Katz, 1985; Katz & Ivey, 1977). Each of these difficulties must be recognized, understood, and empathetically resolved if middle-class, white counselors are to be effective with minority clients.

Some 50 percent of minority-group members who begin counseling terminate after one session, as compared to only about 30 percent of whites (Sue & Sue, 1981). This significant statistic strongly suggests that as a rule minority clients have negative experiences in counseling. Indeed, Shipp (1983) holds that the tendency of black clients to drop out of counseling reflects the type of treatment they receive, a finding probably true for other minority group clients as well. The problem of understanding and working with minorities is further complicated because two groups, blacks and Hispanics, are underrepresented as students in counselor education programs, whereas three groups, Asian-Americans, blacks, and Hispanics, are underrepresented on counselor education faculties (Atkinson, 1983). This low representation of minority students and faculty in higher education makes it more difficult to learn through first-hand experiences and to encounter the knowledge and skills required for effective cross-cultural counseling.

### Issues and Theories of Cross-Cultural Counseling

A primary concern in cross-cultural counseling in the United States is the dominance of white cultural values (Katz, 1985). Because whites constitute the majority of the population in this country, the existence of a white culture is often denied (Katz & Ivey, 1977). Indeed, there are many diverse populations that make up the ethnocultural group called white, and many distinct traditions are associated with whites (Axelson, 1985). Yet, "by definition, White culture is the synthesis of ideas, values, and beliefs coalesced from descendants of White European ethnic groups in the United States" (Katz, 1985, p. 617). Some of the main beliefs and traditions of this culture are based on: the value of individualism, an action-oriented approach to problem solving, the Protestant work ethic, the scientific method, and an emphasis on rigid time schedules (Axelson, 1985; Katz, 1985). Most traditional counseling theories have been built around white, middle-class values and are not always applicable for clients from other traditions (Atkinson, Morten, & Sue, 1979; Ivey, 1980; Katz, 1985). Such popular theories as rational-emotive therapy, Gestalt therapy, transactional analysis, and realty therapy are among those whose appropriateness for multicultural populations is questioned.

Pedersen (1982) believes it is essential for counselors to be sensitive to cultural issues in three areas: knowledge, awareness, and skills. This sensitivity is derived from one's understanding of cultures. In order to help counselors achieve deeper understandings of cross-cultural issues, Pedersen (1977, 1978) has developed a triad model for helping them in four areas: "articulating the problem from the client's cultural perspective; anticipating resistance from a culturally different client; diminishing defensiveness by studying the trainee's own defensive responses; and learning recovery skills for getting out of trouble when counseling the culturally different" (Pedersen, 1978, p. 481). An "anticounselor," who functions like an alter ego in psychodrama and deliberately tries to be subversive, works in this model with a counselor and client in a videotaped session. The interaction and feedback generated through this process help break down barriers and foster greater understanding and sensitivity in the counselor.

Lee (1984) distinguishes between understanding culture from a position outside the system (an etic approach) and understanding culture from a position within the system (an emic approach). Counselors who have knowledge and awareness gained from within the cultural system are much more likely to be skilled in a culturally plural society such as the United States. Such counselors are able to share a particular world view with clients and generate appropriate microcounseling skills, and yet still maintain a sense of personal integrity (Ivey, 1977; Sue, 1978b).

Sue (1978a) gives five guidelines for effectively counseling across cultures. He believes culturally effective counselors:

☐ Recognize the values and beliefs they hold in regard to acceptable and desirable human behavior. They are then able to integrate this understanding into appropriate feelings and behaviors.

☐ Are aware of the cultural and generic qualities of counseling theories and traditions. No method of counseling is completely culture free.

☐ Understand the socio-political environment that has influenced the lives of members of minority groups. The person is a product of the milieu in which he or she has lived.

☐ Are able to share the world view of clients and in so sharing not question the legitimacy of that world view.

☐ Are truly eclectic in counseling practice. They are able to use a wide variety of counseling skills and apply particular counseling techniques to specific life-styles and experiences of clients.

Sue (1978a) further suggests a framework for cross-cultural counseling based on a two-dimensional concept with locus of control represented on the horizontal axis and locus of responsibility represented on the vertical axis (Figure 17.1). The four quadrants represent the kinds and degrees of possible interactions among these variables. The typical American is high in internal control and in internal responsibility, an outlook that underlies most

LOCUS OF CONTROL

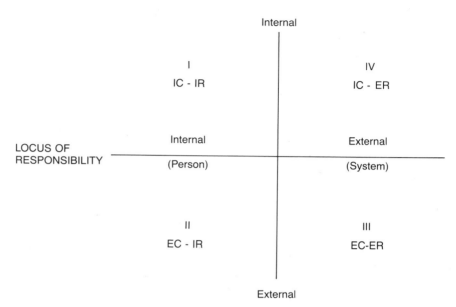

**FIGURE 17.1**  Graphic representation of world views.

*Source:* From "Counseling across cultures" by D. W. Sue, 1978, *Personnel and Guidance Journal, 56,* p. 460. Copyright AACD. Reprinted with permission. No further reproduction authorized without further permission.

counseling theories. Culturally different clients, however, usually classify themselves in one of the other three quadrants.

## Special Needs of Select Minority Populations

The four main minority groups in the United States are blacks, Hispanics, Asian-Americans, and Native Americans (Axelson, 1985). There are concerns unique to each group, and it is the counselor who must solve the problem of how to be effective with individuals from these backgrounds. Sue (1981) maintains that in dealing with multicultural populations, whites reveal biases and prejudices through theories about minorities. He mentions four stages in the development of these theories and asserts that each stage has had its own special influence on the development of counseling:

☐ *Pathological view of minorities*  This stage was characterized by the view that some minorities, such as blacks, could never be helped sufficiently to fit into white society.

☐ *Genetic deficiency model*  In this stage cultural minorities were considered to be biologically inferior.

☐ *Cultural deficiency model*  This stage focused on the environments of minority members and viewed them as deviant or inferior.

☐ *Culturally different model*  In this stage, minorities are not seen as deviant or pathological, but as living in a bicultural world in which they must function in two cultures simultaneously. Individuals are recognized as having to deal with the pressures of such a dual experience while enduring the stereotyped racial attitudes of others in regard to them.

***Blacks.***  In counseling blacks, it is crucial that counselors understand black history, cultural values, and conflicts (Smith, 1981). It is also important that counselors be aware of their own attitudes and prejudices regarding blacks. It is possible for a white counselor to be effective with a black client if the counselor has come to understand the nature of racism and stereotypical thinking and has successfully resolved these issues personally (Hunt & Chandler, 1983; Katz & Ivey, 1977). Although blacks are sometimes viewed as "deficient whites" and portrayed in other negative ways, they actually are a diverse group and should be seen as people who display a broad range of behaviors (Smith, 1977).

Hunt and Chandler (1983) note that the process of establishing rapport in counseling with some black clients may be slower because of sociocultural, political, and economic factors. Nevertheless, they assert that most blacks are knowledgeable about mental health agencies and have positive attitudes toward these agencies and their counselors. Jereb (1982) believes that a synthesis of African and Anglo-American values is the basis for the most effective theoretical framework for counseling blacks. Copeland (1977), in stressing the special problems inherent in counseling black women, sees the need for counselors to go beyond traditional counseling theories to advocacy and the emphasizing of client strengths. On the other hand, Seligman (1977) stresses that certain groups of blacks, such as Haitians, may benefit greatly from the person-centered approach in traditional counseling, and Shipp (1983) sees merit in group counseling as a treatment modality for blacks.

Wheeler (1977) suggests 10 general characteristics of many black clients and pinpoints modalities that are compatible with these. For instance, he says that many blacks are not oriented to deal with abstract approaches in counseling, such as the Gestalt empty chair technique. Therefore, he says, counselors should use more tangible approaches with these clients, such as those found in behavioral theories. Wheeler's emphasis is on fitting the approach to the client rather than the client to the approach. While some of his suggestions may not be appropriate for all black clients, his ideas serve as a base for counselor awareness.

**Hispanics.** The term *Hispanic* refers to all people of Spanish origin, replacing the term *Latino* which was formerly used as a generic label for all people of Spanish ancestry (Ruiz, 1981). There are three distinct Hispanic groups in the United States—Mexican-Americans (or Chicanos), Cubans, and Puerto Ricans. It is a mistake to assume that they are all the same (Axelson, 1985). Hispanics live mainly in urban areas but in different regions of the country. Chicanos reside primarily in the Southwest, Cubans in Florida, and Puerto Ricans in the tri-state area of New York, New Jersey, and Connecticut (Ruiz, 1981). Most Hispanics are bicultural but vary in degree of acculturation (Ruiz & Padilla, 1977).

Despite the stress they face in living in two cultures, Hispanics in general are reluctant to use counseling services. A part of this hesitancy is cultural tradition (e.g., pride) and a part is cultural heritage (e.g., reliance on extended family ties). More practical reasons are: the distance to service agencies in some areas (such as in the Southwest), inadequate transportation, and the absence of counseling professionals fluent in Spanish and familiar with Hispanic culture (Ruiz, 1981).

Many Hispanics tend to perceive psychological problems as being more similar to physical problems than do individuals from other cultures (Ruiz & Padilla, 1977). Therefore, they expect the counselor to be active, concrete, and more precisely goal directed. This perception is especially true for clients who are "very Hispanic" (Ruiz, 1981). On the other hand, Hispanics who are "very Anglo" may have more white, middle-class values and expectations. In order to help Hispanic clients derive the most from the counseling experience, Ruiz (1981) recommends they be asked to respond to an objective questionnaire to measure their degree of acculturation. This benefits both clients and counselors. Those clients most identified with the Hispanic culture can be helped through the use of experiential exercises to clarify their identity, feelings, and values more fully (Ruiz, 1975). Another recommendation, by Christensen (1977), is that counselors capitalize on the inherent strengths in the cultural backgrounds of their clients, especially in counseling Puerto Ricans. The employment of minority staff in counseling and related services (e.g., financial aid) is also endorsed in working with select Hispanic students, such as Chicanos (Casa & Ponterotto, 1984).

***Asian-Americans.*** Asian-Americans (e.g., Chinese, Japanese, Filipinos, Indochinese, and Koreans), like Hispanics, vary widely in their cultural backgrounds (Axelson, 1985). Historically, Asian-Americans have faced strong discrimination in the United States and have been the subject of many myths (Sue & Sue, 1972, 1973). A combination of factors has promoted stereotypes of Asian-Americans as hardworking, successful, and not prone to mental or emotional disturbances. As is true for all stereotyped groups, it is difficult to see Asian-Americans as individuals and to meet their mental health needs as such (Henkin, 1985).

Counselors must be aware of the subtleties of Asian-American cultures if they are to be effective helpers of the members of these populations. For instance, it is important for them to realize that Asian-Americans typically eschew occupations that call for forceful self-expression and are therefore often isolated from the mainstream of American society (Watanabe, 1973). Likewise, it is critical that counselors appreciate the history and distinct characteristics of select Asian-American groups in the United States, such as the Chinese, Japanese, and Vietnamese (Axelson, 1985; Brower, 1980; Henkin, 1985; Sue & Sue, 1972). This sensitivity often enables the counselor to facilitate the counseling process. For example, a counselor may promote self-disclosure with Chinese-Americans through educational or vocational counseling rather than through direct, confrontive psychotherapy techniques (Sue & Sue, 1972).

Henkin (1985) proposes a number of practical guidelines for counselors in interacting with Japanese-Americans, and his advice is appropriate for use with other Asian-American groups as well. Among his most helpful suggestions for counselors are:

☐ Establish a clear-cut structure for the counseling process.

☐ Explain the process to the client.

☐ Allow clients to ask questions about you as a counselor and the process itself.

☐ Refrain from making an assessment as long as possible.

☐ Educate yourself to the culture of your clients, especially to the importance of their family and community.

***Native Americans.*** Native Americans, called Indians by the first European settlers in America, comprise over 250 distinct tribes, but share many cultural traditions and problems. Axelson (1985) states that Native Americans have: strong feelings about the loss of ancestral lands, a desire for self-determination, conflicts of values with mainstream American culture, and a confused self-image resulting from past stereotyping. Native Americans also have extremely high suicide and alcoholism rates and a low life expectancy. Illiteracy and unemployment are both high (Richardson, 1981). Effective counseling approaches with them depend in part on whether or not they live on a reservation. But regardless of the physical environment, it is crucial that counselors understand the Native American culture and avoid imposing culturally inappropriate theories (Spang, 1971). Richardson (1981) stresses four ideas to be considered when counseling with Native Americans: silence, acceptance, restatement, and general lead. His vignettes illustrate each technique, and he cautions counselors above all to be real in their relationships. Joint programs between Native American tribes and universities can further help Native Americans receive appropriate counselor education (Tamminen, Smaby, Powless, & Gum, 1980). These programs give Native Americans more power and control over their own destinies as well, and benefit them personally and culturally.

***International Counseling.*** In the world at large, whites are a minority, and the cultural perspective from the United States is just one among the world's many. Super (1983) questions whether counseling, as practiced in North America, is adaptable to other countries. His earlier analysis of culture and counseling concluded that prosperous and secure countries view counseling as a way of promoting individual interests and abilities, while economically less fortunate countries and those under threat of foreign domination view counseling services as a way of channeling individuals into areas necessary for cultural survival (Super, 1954). Knowledge about such cultural differences must be considered in international counseling.

## COUNSELING WITH THE AGED

Individuals develop special needs and concerns as they age. Many of these concerns relate to economic and social factors; others are more likely to result from unique personal circumstances. Counseling did not begin addressing the problems of the elderly directly until the mid-1970s (Myers & Blake, 1984). At that time, Blake (1975) cited a lack of interest in, and consequently articles on, counseling older people. Salisbury (1975) reported that only 6 percent of counselor education programs at that time offered even an elective course on the aged and their special needs. By the mid-1980s the situation had changed dramatically. The old in America were no longer neglected by counselors. Based on a national survey, Myers (1983) reported that 36 percent of all counseling programs offered one or more courses on working with older people. The American Association for Counseling and Development (AACD) in 1987 established a Division on Adult Development and Aging.

### Old Age

The age of 65 has traditionally marked the beginning of old age, since it is the time when people have, until recently, retired from work and collected social security or pension funds. At the time of the founding of the United States, only about 2 percent of its population was 65 years old or older. By 1980, over 11 percent of the population belonged to this age group (Glass & Grant, 1983); and by the year 2000 over 13 percent of the people in the United States will be at least 65 years old. The reasons for the remarkable growth in this segment of the population include: high birthrates during the twentieth century, immigration policies that favored the admittance of individuals who are now growing older, improved health care, better nutrition, and the reduction of infectious diseases (Glass & Grant, 1983; Lefrancois, 1984).

There are several prominent theories of aging. Birren (1964) views aging from a biological, psychological, and social perspective and recognizes that the multidimensional process may be uneven. Both Erikson (1963) and Havighurst (1959) propose that aging is a natural part of development. They believe also that individuals have specific tasks to accomplish as they grow older. For example, Erikson views middle and late adulthood as a time when the individual must develop a generational sense and an ego integrity or become stagnant and despairing. Neugarten (1978), also stressing development, sees two major periods of old age. The *young-old* are those between ages 55 and 75 who are still active physically, mentally, and socially, whether they are retired or not. The *old-old* are individuals beyond age 75 whose physical activity is far more limited. The effects of decline with age are usually more apparent in the old-old population, though aging is clearly individual.

Despite an increasing understanding of aging and an ever-increasing number of older adults, the elderly have to deal with age-based expectations and prejudices concerning old age (Hitchcock, 1984; Lefrancois, 1984; Ponzo, 1978). *Ageism* is the term that refers to the negative feelings toward a group based solely on age. Even counselors are not immune to ageist attitudes (Blake, 1982).

### Needs of Older Adults

Older adults in the United States must deal with a wide variety of complex issues in their transition from mid-life to senior citizen status, including changes in physical abilities, social roles, and relationships (Buckley, 1972). Many of the changes that are a part of aging have the potential to spark an identity crisis within the person. Pulvino and Colangelo (1980) state that the developmental demands on older adults are probably second only to those on young children. According to Havighurst (1959), older adults must learn to cope successfully with (1) the death of friends and/or spouse, (2) reduced physical vigor, (3) retirement and the reduction of income, (4) more leisure time and the making of new friends, (5) the development of new social roles, (6) dealing with grown children, and (7) changing living arrangements and/or making satisfactory living arrangements.

Some of these required changes associated with aging are gradual; others are abrupt. Transitions that involve a high level of stress are those connected with major loss, such as the death of a spouse, the loss of a job, or the contraction of a major illness (Sinick, 1979a). Other transitions are less traumatic and may even involve a gain for the individual, such as becoming a grandparent. Many older adults do not successfully accomplish the necessary developmental tasks required for a smooth transition into this later stage of life. They fail to develop and maintain a stabilizing functional life perspective. (Kastenbaum, 1969).

Shanks (1982) lists five major problems of the aging—loneliness, physical illness, retirement, idleness, and bereavement. Myers (1983) estimates on the basis of studies that 25 percent of all persons over age 60 suffer some degree of depression. Members of this group also suffer more psychosis as they grow older; 30 percent of the beds in mental hospitals are occupied by the elderly. About 25 percent of all reported suicides are committed by persons over age 60, with white males being especially susceptible. Yet, despite their increased need for help, few older adults (only 1 to 4 percent of the population) are seen as outpatients in mental health clinics (Buckley, 1972; Myers, 1983). Some of the reasons for their hesitancy to seek help are: a perceived need to be self-sufficient, an inability to pay for services, and a passive acceptance of life conditions.

### Counseling Older Adults

Sinick (1979b) points out that most counselors interested in working with older adults need additional professional training in this specialty. Many simply do not understand the aging and therefore do not work with them. Another reason older people do not receive more attention from mental health specialists is the "investment syndrome" described by Colangelo and Pulvino (1980). According to these authors, many counselors feel their time and energy are better spent working with younger people "who may eventually contribute to society" (p. 69). Professionals who display this attitude are banking on future payoffs from the young and may well be misinformed as to the possibilities for change in older adults. A third reason older adults may not receive the attention of mental health specialists is the irrational fear of aging and the psychological distancing from older persons that this fear generates (Neugarten, 1971).

One broad and important approach to working successfully with the aging is to promote change in the systems in which they live (Colangelo & Pulvino, 1980; Ponzo, 1978; Sinick, 1980). The attitudes of society negatively influence older people's attitudes about themselves. Many older adults act old because their environments encourage and support such behavior. Hansen and Prather (1980) point out that American society "equates age with obsolescence and orders its priorities accordingly" (p. 74). Thus, counselors must become educators and advocates for change in societal attitudes, if destructive age restrictions and stereotypes are to be overcome. "We need to develop a society that encourages people to stop acting their age and start being themselves" (Ponzo, 1978, pp. 143–144).

In addition to working for changes in systems, counselors can help older adults deal with specific and immediate problems. Tomine (1986) asserts that counseling services to the elderly are most helpful if they are portable and practical. An educational, problem-solving model is very useful to this age group. For example, Hitchcock (1984) reviewed successful programs to help the elderly obtain employment. A particularly successful program was a job club for older job seekers, where information on obtaining employment was shared. For older adults with Alzheimer's disease, counseling based on Rogers's theories and Carkhuff's practical application is beneficial in the early stages of the disease, while group counseling, based on Yalom's existential writings, may be productive in helping family members cope as the disease progresses (LaBarge, 1981). A structured life review process has proved beneficial also in working with the elderly (Westcott, 1983). The technique helps them integrate the past and prepare themselves for the future. Short-term rational-emotive exercises have been used successfully too with some older adults in increasing rational thinking and significantly decreasing anxiety about aging (Keller, Corake, & Brooking, 1975).

In working with the elderly, the counselor often becomes the student and the older person becomes the teacher (Kemp, 1984). When this type of open attitude is achieved, the client is more likely to deal with the events in his or her life that are most important, and the counselor is more prone to learn about a different dimension of life and be helpful in the process.

## COUNSELING WITH WOMEN AND MEN

The question of whether there is a need for counselors to possess specialized knowledge and skill in counseling women and men as separate groups with specific needs is no longer debated. Both genders have much in common, but their gender-based historically and culturally determined differences prompt different counseling concerns.

### Counseling Women

Women are the primary consumers of counseling services (Greenspan, 1983; Worell, 1980). They have special needs related to biological differences and socialization patterns that make many of their concerns in counseling different from those of men (Thames & Hill, 1979). Women still lack the degree of freedom, status, access, and acceptance given men, though their social roles and career opportunities have expanded remarkably since the 1960s (Axelson, 1985; Meadow, 1982). As a group women have quite different concerns than men do about such fundamental issues as intimacy, career options, and life development. Counselors' attitudes, values, and knowledge may either facilitate or impede the potential development of women clients. There is evidence that many counselors still hold sex-role stereotypes of women (Johnson & Scarato, 1979). False assumptions, inaccurate beliefs, and a lack of understanding by counselors may also contribute to the problems of women clients (Leonard & Collins, 1979).

Committees and task forces within professional counseling organizations have been formed to address issues related to counseling women. There is a national Commission on Women within the Association for Counseling and Development (AACD), and the American Psychological Association (APA) has a division (Division 35) devoted exclusively to the psychology of women. In addition, Division 17 (Counseling Psychology) of APA sponsors a very active Committee on Women. This committee, and the APA Task Force on Sex Bias and Sex-role Stereotyping in Therapeutic Practice, have each issued ethical guidelines that address women's concerns.

**Special Problems in Counseling Women.** One of the major problems in counseling women has involved adequate information. Johnson and Scarato (1979) note that the literature in the field of women's studies and female psychology has grown from only three textbooks in the early 1970s to a plethora of texts and articles, many of which have been authored by women to correct some of the older theoretical views generated by men who lacked first-hand knowledge of women's issues (Axelson, 1985). Many early theories of the nature and development of women, especially those based on psychoanalytic principles, tended to characterize women as innately "passive, dependent, and morally inferior to men" (Hare-Mustin, 1983, p. 594). Those theories promoted the status quo in regard to women and limited the options available to them (Garfield, 1981; Hare-Mustin, 1983; Marecek & Kravetz, 1977). The general standard of healthy adult behavior came to be identified with men and a double standard of mental health evolved (Heshusius-Gilsdorf & Gilsdorf, 1975). This double standard basically depicted healthy adult female behavior as less socially desirable and healthy, a perception that lowered expectations for women's behavior and set up barriers for advancement in nontraditional roles (Broverman, Broverman, Clarkson, Rosenkrantz, & Vogel, 1970).

A second major problem in counseling women involves sexism, which Goldman (1972) describes as "more deep rooted than racism" (p. 84). *Sexism* is the belief (and behavior resulting from that belief) that females should be treated on the basis of their sex without regard to other criteria, such as interests and abilities. Such treatment is arbitrary, illogical, counterproductive, and self-serving. In the past, sexism has been blatant, such as limiting women's access to certain professions and encouraging them to pursue so-called pink collar jobs. Today, sexism is much more subtle, involving acts more of "omission rather than commission" (Leonard & Collins, 1979, p. 6). Many acts of omission result from lack of information or a failure to change beliefs in light of new facts. In either case, sexism hurts not only women but also society in general.

A survey by the task force on sex bias and sex role stereotyping of the American Psychological Association revealed four categories of sexist behavior by counselors and therapists (Brodsky, Holroyd, Payton, Rubinstein, Rosenkrantz, Sherman, & Zell, 1978). First, counselors and therapists supported traditional sex role notions, such as "a woman's place is in the home." Second, the women surveyed in this study felt they were devalued as a group and that counselors and therapists had limited expectations of them. Third, the use of psychoanalytical concepts that were sexist in nature, such as "penis envy," were employed in counseling and therapy sessions. Finally, counselors and therapists responded to women as sex objects, which included the seduction of women clients. Despite new knowledge, the demise of sexism in counselors and therapists has been slow.

**Issues and Theories of Counseling Women.** One of the main issues in counseling women involves the counselor's response to them as individuals and as a group. Women are a very diverse group, and it is important for counselors to react to women in regard to their uniqueness as well as their similarity (Blimeline & Birk, 1979). It should be recognized that specialized knowledge is required for counseling women at various stages of life, such as school-age girls (Wolleat, 1979), mid-life (Voight, Lawler, & Fulkerson, 1980), and old age (Resnick, 1979). Counselors must also understand the dynamics involved in working with females under various conditions, such as divorce (Rawlings & Carter, 1979), rape and incest (Courtois & Watts, 1982), and career development (Fitzgerald & Crites, 1979; Hanson & Keierleber, 1978).

A model that outlines the major areas of knowledge of the psychology of women has been presented by Johnson and Scarato (1979). It proposes seven areas in which counselors should increase knowledge of women and thereby decrease prejudices. These areas are: history and sociology of sex-role stereotyping, psychophysiology of women and men, theories of personality and sex-role development, life-span development, special populations, career development, and counseling/psychotherapy. In the last area, the authors focus on alternatives to traditional counseling approaches as well as on specific problems of women. Overall, the model is helpful in alerting counselors to the universal and unique aspects of women in comparison to men.

Thames and Hill (1979) assert that beyond the issue of basic knowledge, effective counselors of women need to be skilled in four basic areas of counseling: verbal, nonverbal, process, and techniques. Counselors must also be able to apply appropriate intervention skills for special populations of women, such as the depressed or the sexually dysfunctional. Finally, these counselors must be aware of personal difficulties in dealing with male and female clients. In order to achieve these objectives, Thames and Hill call for the modification of existing counselor education programs. Moore and Strickler (1980) also call for counselor education programs to concentrate more attention on women's issues and to eliminate sex-biased counseling. Worell (1980) advocates major changes in counselor education with regard to working with women. She goes a step further than Thames/Hill (1979) and Moore/Strickler (1980), however, and proposes that a whole new discipline of counseling women be established. The legitimacy of the discipline is supported by the continued development and expansion of four factors (Worell, 1980, p. 477):

> (a) A substantial and relatively new body of knowledge and theory about the biological, psychological, cultural, and political characteristics of the client population; (b) an emergent set of client populations whose nontraditional counseling needs and goals support the development of alternative intervention strategies; (c) sets of procedures specifically tailored to the unique characteristics and goals of

these new client populations; and (d) special codes of ethics and standards to monitor the implementation of counseling procedures with women.

In opposition to the specialty models for counseling women, Spiegel (1979) advocates instead a generalist model that offers broadly based training that prepares all counselors to work with a wide variety of clients. She notes that sex is only one factor that influences the relationship between counselors and clients. Other variables, such as race, age, social class, religion, an severity of psychological impairment, may have major impacts on counseling relationships. Specialized subgroups may require expert knowledge on the part of counselors, but she contends that knowledge relating to women "should be included in general counseling requirements" (p. 50). Otherwise, separate principles for counseling women may result in a new form of sexism.

### Counseling Men

An outgrowth of the focus in counseling on working with women and eliminating sexism is new attention to the unique concerns and needs of men. Collison (1981) points out that "there seem to be fewer counseling procedures tailored to men than to women, and there are no codes of ethics or standards that exist for counseling men" (p. 220). Although many counseling theories and procedures are appropriate to all populations, there are specific factors that should be taken into consideration in counseling males. In 1986, AACD set up a national committee to focus on these issues.

***Special Issues in Counseling Men.*** As a group, men are more reluctant than women to ask for counseling help (Worth, 1983). They often enter counseling only in a crisis situation, since they are generally expected to be self-sufficient and to take care of themselves (Scher, 1979, 1981). Their traditional sex-roles are more narrowly defined than those for women, and they are rewarded for being in control of themselves and their situations. Their roles are constricting and "lethal" in that they usually contribute to an insensitivity to needs and a denial of mental and physical problems and thus to a shorter life span (Jourard, 1971). Males who do seek counseling, however, are usually very hard working (Scher, 1979). They are emotionally clear, sincere, and express themselves in direct and honest ways. They also have high expectations of counseling and want productive sessions (Scher, 1979; Worth, 1983). Their high expectations stem from the ascribed masculine roles in American society that emphasize competition, power, and achievement. Males have unique concerns at different age levels (Coleman, 1981; Collison, 1981). Developmental models provided by Erikson (1968) and Levinson (1978) may prove especially helpful in working with men, since these theories specify broad tasks that most men strive to accomplish at certain times and ways.

There are other considerations besides the developmental backgrounds and stages of the male, however. One of these considerations is the way males are socialized to behave in American society. Most men operate with a cognitive orientation both outside and inside counseling situations (Scher, 1979; Washington, 1979). Affective modes are usually eschewed because of a lack of experience in dealing with them and the anxiety they create. The dominance of cognitive functioning in men creates special challenges for counselors. Marino (1979) advises counselors to stay away from the cognitive domain in working with men and explore with them the feeling tones of their voices, the inconsistencies of their behaviors and feelings, and the ambivalence they have in their lives about control and nurturance. Scher (1979) also advises moving the client from the cognitive to the affective realm and recommends that the process be started by explaining to the client the importance of owning feelings in overcoming personal difficulties and then working patiently with the man to uncover hidden affect.

Burch and Skovholt (1982) suggest that Holland's (1979) model of person-environment interaction serve as the framework for understanding and counseling men. In this model, men are most likely to operate in the realistic dimension of functioning. Such individuals usually lack social skills but possess mechanical-technical skills, therefore, the authors recommend counselors adopt a cognitive-behavioral approach to establish rapport and facilitate counseling with these men. Giles (1983) disagrees with this idea and points out that there is no conclusive research to support it. He believes that counselors are not necessarily more effective when they alter the counseling approach to fit the personal typology of clients.

Heppner (1981) states that, given the emphasis on interpersonal learning in group counseling, working with men in this way may be an effective intervention strategy. The goals of a men's group are to increase personal awareness of sex role conditioning, to practice new desired behaviors, and to promote a life-style based on the individual's needs. Yet, as potentially effective as such a group may be, it is difficult for many men to enter and participate in group counseling. The reason is the social taboo that many of them have about self-disclosure, especially before other men. To be effective, the counselor must screen potential candidates carefully, identify specific behaviors on which to focus, and develop intervention strategies aimed at deep psychological issues.

Scher (1981) provides seven guidelines to aid counselors in understanding the realities of men's situations and thereby promoting the effective working with them. These include an emphasis on: the difficulty of change for most men, the constraints imposed by sex-role stereotypes, the importance of asking for assistance, dealing with affective issues, the need to nurture oneself, the promotion of freedom in others, and the need to distinguish between differences of roles and rules in one's personal life and work life. Most men are constrained by social roles and reinforced heavily for conforming to those roles. Therefore, the counselor needs to be especially supportive in working with men who ask for help, yet not allow them to operate exclusively on a rational, logical, and intellectual level. While promoting change and an exploration of affective issues, it is crucial that the counselor be aware that rules within most men's world of work differ from those within the personal domain. Therefore, it is essential for counselors to caution men not to try to introduce newly discovered behaviors that may work in their personal lives into a hostile environment, that is, the world of work. Counseling with men, as with all groups, is a very complex phenomenon.

## SUMMARY

In this chapter we have examined counseling issues related to three special populations—minorities, the aged, and the subgroups of women and men. There is a wealth of material in the professional literature on specific concerns of each group and on counseling theories and techniques most appropriate for working with individuals from these populations. Indeed, specialty courses and counseling concentrations which focus on one or more of these groups are offered in many graduate education programs.

Although information on a special population may appear unrelated to other populations, it is not. A common theme is that counselors who work with a variety of clients must be knowledgeable about them collectively and individually in order to be able to deal effectively with their common and unique concerns. Stereotypes and prescribed roles are assigned to members of minority groups, the aged, and members of both genders. Cultural limitations on these groups as a whole, or on members from them, restrict not only the growth of the people involved but the larger society as well. Overcoming traditions, prejudices, fears, and anxieties is a major part of counseling in a pluralistic society.

In working with specific groups, counselors need to be aware of their uniqueness and common concerns. Counselors must also realize the limitations and appropriateness of counseling theories developed in the United States. Talking about problems and self-disclosure are not valued in many cultures. Likewise, many men show a hesitancy to display feelings and reveal personal weaknesses. On the other hand, the elderly may need to express emotions and resolve past conflicts if they are to benefit from counseling. Similarly, a great many women are most comfortable in counseling approaches that stress affect. Counselors must constantly ask themselves how each client is similar to and different from others. They must concentrate on increasing their sensitivity to issues and systems as well as individuals. When clients differ significantly from counselors, extra attention must be devoted to establishing and cultivating the counseling relationship.

## CLASSROOM ACTIVITIES

1. Discuss with another person of a different cultural or ethnic background the difficulties he or she faces in the United States. How many of these problems are culturally related? How many are unique to the person? Present your findings to the class. What similarities do you find in your results? Discuss your personal interviews in regard to the material presented in this chapter.

2. Research counseling approaches offered in other countries, such as Great Britain or Japan. How do you understand the theories and techniques generated in these cultures to fit the needs of individuals in these societies? How do you think the counseling approach you have researched would work in the United States?

3. Role play the following situation with another class member. Imagine that you have reached age 65. What are you doing at this

age? What are your needs and expectations? How might a counselor be of help to you? Do you find your life perspective different from your present outlook? Discuss this in relationship to Ponzo's (1978) advice that individuals need to be themselves not act their age.

4. Divide the class according to gender. Have the males in the class assume traditional female roles and vice versa in regard to making decisions about a career and marriage. Discuss what feelings each side of the class had in relation to the decision-making process.

5. Discuss the following question in groups of three. "Can a counselor ever be culturally neutral and free of bias when working with someone different from him or her?" If so, how? If not, what can he or she do to overcome this potential handicap?

## REFERENCES

Ahia, C. E. (1984). Cross-cultural counseling concerns. *Personnel and Guidance Journal, 62,* 339–341.

Atkinson, D. R. (1983). Ethnic minority representation in counselor education. *Counselor Education and Supervision, 23,* 7–19.

Atkinson, D. R., Morten, G., & Sue, D. W. (1979). *A cross cultural perspective.* Dubuque, IA: Brown.

Axelson, J. A. (1985). *Counseling and development in a multicultural society.* Monterey, CA: Brooks/Cole.

Birren, J. E. (1964). *The psychology of aging.* Englewood Cliffs, NJ: Prentice-Hall.

Blake, R. (1975). Counseling in gerontology. *Personnel and Guidance Journal, 53,* 733–737.

Blake, R. (1982). Assessing the counseling needs of older persons. *Measurement and Evaluation in Guidance, 15,* 188–193.

Blimeline, C. A., & Birk, J. M. (1979). A note of impatience. *The Counseling Psychologist, 8,* 48–49.

Brodsky, A. M., Holroyd, J., Payton, C. R., Rubinstein, E. A., Rosenkrantz, P., Sherman, J., & Zell, F. (1978). Guidelines for therapy with women: Task force on sex bias and sex role stereotyping in psychotherapeutic practice. *American Psychologist, 33,* 1112–1113.

Broverman, I., Broverman, D., Clarkson, F., Rosenkrantz, P., & Vogel, S. (1970). Sex-role stereotypes and clinical judgments of mental health. *Journal of Consulting and Clinical Psychology, 34,* 1–7.

Brower, I. C. (1980). Counseling Vietnamese. *Personnel and Guidance Journal, 58,* 646–652.

Buckley, M. (1972). Counseling the aging. *Personnel and Guidance Journal, 50,* 755–758.

Burch, M. A., & Skovholt, T. M. (1982). Counseling services and men in need: A problem in person-environment matching. *AMHCA Journal, 4,* 89–96.

Casas, J. M. & Ponterotto, J. G. (1984). Profiling an invisible minority in higher education: The Chicana. *Personnel and Guidance Journal, 62,* 349–353.

Christensen, E. W. (1977). When counseling Puerto Ricans. . . . *Personnel and Guidance Journal, 55,* 412–415.

Colangelo, N., & Pulvino, C. J. (1980). Some basic concerns in counseling the elderly. *Counseling and Values, 24,* 68–73.

Coleman, E. (1981). Counseling adolescent males. *Personnel and Guidance Journal, 60,* 215–218.

Collison, B. B. (1981). Counseling adult males. *Personnel and Guidance Journal, 60,* 219–222.

Copeland, E. J. (1977). Counseling black women with negative self-concepts. *Personnel and Guidance Journal, 55,* 397–400.

Courtois, C. A. & Watts, D. L. (1982). Counseling adult women who experienced incest in childhood or adolescence. *Personnel and Guidance Journal, 60,* 275–279.

Erikson, E. H. (1963). *Childhood and society* (2nd ed.). New York: Norton.

Erikson, E. H. (1968). *Identity, youth and crisis.* New York: Norton.

Fitzgerald, L. F., & Crites, J. O. (1979). Career counseling for women. *The Counseling Psychologist, 8,* 33–34.

Garfield, S. L. (1981). Psychotherapy: A forty year appraisal. *American Psychologist, 36,* 174–183.

Giles, T. A. (1983). Counseling services and men in need: A response to Burch and Skovholt. *AMHCA Journal, 5,* 39–43.

Gladding, S. T. (1976/1986). In passing. In S. T. Gladding (Ed.), *Reality sits in a green cushioned chair* (p. 23). Atlanta: Collegiate Press.

Glass, J. C., & Grant, K. A. (1983). Counseling in the later years: A growing need. *Personnel and Guidance Journal, 62,* 210–213.

Goldman, L. (1972). Introduction. *Personnel and Guidance Journal, 51,* 85.

Greenspan, M. (1983). *A new approach to women & therapy.* New York: McGraw-Hill.

Hansen, J. C., & Prather, F. (1980). The impact of values and attitudes in counseling the aged. *Counseling and Values, 24,* 74–85.

Hanson, L., & Keierleber, D. (1978). Born free: A collaborative consultation model for career development and sex-role stereotyping. *Personnel and Guidance Journal, 56,* 395–399.

Hare-Mustin, R. T. (1983). An appraisal of the relationship between women and psychotherapy. *American Psychologist, 38,* 593–599.

Havighurst, R. J. (1959). Social and psychological needs of the aging. In L. Gorlow & W. Katkovsky (Eds.), *Reading in the psychology of adjustment* (pp. 443–447). New York: McGraw-Hill.

Henkin, W. A. (1985). Toward counseling the Japanese in America: A cross-cultural primer. *Journal of Counseling and Development, 63,* 500–503.

Heppner, F. P. (1981). Counseling men in groups. *Personnel and Guidance Journal, 60,* 249–252.

Heshusius-Gilsdorf, L. T., & Gilsdorf, D. L. (1975). Girls are females, boys are males: A content analysis of career materials. *Personnel and Guidance Journal, 54,* 207–211.

Hitchcock, A. A. (1984). Work, aging, and counseling. *Journal of Counseling and Development, 63,* 258–259.

Holland, J. H. (1979). *The self-directed search: Professional manual.* Palo Alto, CA: Consulting Psychologists Press.

Hunt, P. L., & Chandler, M. E. (1983). Counseling blacks: Training of beginning counselors. In M. M. Ohlsen (Ed.), *Introduction to counseling* (pp. 208–240). Itasca, IL: Peacock.

Ivey, A. (1977). Toward a definition of the culturally effective counselor. *Personnel and Guidance Journal, 55,* 296–302.

Ivey, A. (1980). A person-environment view of counseling and psychotherapy: Implication for social policy. In T. Marsella & P. Pedersen (Eds.), *Cross-cultural counseling and psychotherapy.* New York: Pergamon.

Jereb, R. J. (1982). Assessing the adequacy of counseling theories for use with black clients. *Counseling and Values, 27,* 17–26.

Johnson, M., & Scarato, A. M. (1979). A knowledge base for counselors of women. *The Counseling Psychologist, 8,* 14–16.

Jourard, S. (1971). *The transparent self.* Princeton, NJ: Van Nostrand.

Kastenbaum, R. (1969). The foreshortened life perspective. *Geriatrics, 24,* 126–133.

Katz, J. H. (1985). The sociopolitical nature of counseling. *The Counseling Psychologist, 13,* 615–624.

Katz, J. H., & Ivey, A. (1977). White awareness: The frontier of racism awareness training. *Personnel and Guidance Journal, 55,* 485–489.

Keller, J. F., Corake, J. W., & Brooking, J. Y. (1975). Effects of a program in rational thinking on anxieties in older persons. *Journal of Counseling Psychology, 22,* 54–57.

Kemp, J. T. (1984). Learning from clients: Counseling the frail and dying elderly. *Personnel and Guidance Journal, 62,* 270–272.

LaBarge, E. (1981). Counseling patients with senile dementia of the Alzheimer type and their families. *Personnel and Guidance Journal, 60,* 139–142.

Lee, D. J. (1984). Counseling and culture: Some issues. *Personnel and Guidance Journal, 62,* 592–597.

Lefrancois, G. F. (1984). *The lifespan.* Belmont, CA: Wadsworth.

Leonard, M. M., & Collins, A. M. (1979). Woman as footnote. *The Counseling Psychologist, 8,* 6–7.

Levinson, D. J. (1978). *The seasons of a man's life.* New York: Knopf.

Marecek, J., & Kravetz, D. (1977). Women and mental health: A review of feminist change efforts. *Psychiatry, 40,* 323–328.

Marino, T. M. (1979). Resensitizing men: A male perspective. *Personnel and Guidance Journal, 58,* 102–105.

Meadow, M. J. (1982). Introduction. *Counseling and Values, 26,* 83.

McFadden, J., & Lipscomb, W. D. (1985). History of the Association for Non-White Concerns in Personnel and Guidance. *Journal of Counseling and Development, 63,* 444–447.

Moore, H., & Strickler, C. (1980). The counseling profession's response to sex-biased counseling: An update. *Personnel and Guidance Journal, 59,* 84–87.

Myers, J. E. (1983). A national survey of geriatric mental health services. *AMHCA Journal, 5,* 69–74.

Myers, J. E., & Blake, R. H. (1984). Employment of gerontological counseling graduates: A follow-up study. *Personnel and Guidance Journal, 62,* 333–335.

Myers, J. E., & Rimmer, S. M. (1982). Guest editorial. *Measurement and Evaluation in Guidance, 15,* 180–181.

Neugarten, B. (December, 1971). Grow old along with me! The best is yet to be. *Psychology Today,* 48–56.

Neugarten, B. L. (1978). The wise of the young-old. In R. Gross, B. Gross, & S. Seidman (Eds.), *The new old: Struggling for decent aging.* New York: Doubleday.

Pedersen, P. B. (1977). The triad model of cross-cultural counselor training. *Personnel and Guidance Journal, 56,* 94–100.

Pedersen, P. B. (1978). Four dimensions of cross-cultural skill in counselor training. *Personnel and Guidance Journal, 56,* 480–484.

Pedersen, P. B. (1978). Introduction. *Personnel and Guidance Journal, 56,* 457.

Pedersen, P. B. (1982). Cross-cultural training for counselors and therapists. In E. Marshall & D. Kurtz (Eds.), *Interpersonal helping skills: A guide to training meth-* ods, *programs, and resources.* San Francisco: Jossey-Bass.

Ponzo, Z. (1978). Age prejudice of "act your age." *Personnel and Guidance Journal, 57,* 140–144.

Pulvino, C. J., & Colangelo, N. (1980). Counseling the elderly: A developmental perspective. *Counseling and Values, 24,* 139–147.

Rawlings, E. I., & Carter, D. K. (1979). Divorced women. *The Counseling Psychologist, 8,* 27–28.

Resnick, J. L. (1979). Women and aging. *The Counseling Psychologist, 8,* 29–30.

Richardson, E. H. (1981). Cultural and historical perspectives in counseling American Indians. In D. W. Sue (Ed.), *Counseling the culturally different* (pp. 216–249). New York: Wiley.

Ruiz, A. S. (1975). Chicano group catalysts. *Personnel and Guidance Journal, 53,* 462–466.

Ruiz, A. S. (1984). Cross-cultural group counseling and the use of the sentence completion method. *Journal for Specialists in Group Work, 9,* 131–136.

Ruiz, R. A. (1981). Cultural and historical perspectives in counseling Hispanics. In D. W. Sue (Ed.), *Counseling the culturally different* (pp. 186–215). New York: Wiley.

Ruiz, R. A., & Padilla, A. M. (1977). Counseling Latinos. *Personnel and Guidance Journal, 55,* 401–408.

Salisbury, A. (1975). Counseling older persons: A neglected area in counselor education and supervision. *Counselor Education and Supervision, 4,* 237–238.

Scher, M. (1979). On counseling men. *Personnel and Guidance Journal, 57,* 252–254.

Scher, M. (1981). Men in hiding: A challenge for the counselor. *Personnel and Guidance Journal, 60,* 199–202.

Seligman, L. (1977). Haitians: A neglected minority. *Personnel and Guidance Journal, 55,* 409–411.

Shanks, J. L. (1982). Expanding treatment for the elderly: Counseling in a private medical practice. *Personnel and Guidance Journal, 61,* 553–555.

Shipp, P. L. (1983). Counseling blacks: A group approach. *Personnel and Guidance Journal, 62,* 108–111.

Sinick, D. (1979a). Adult developmental changes and counseling challenges. In M. L. Ganikos, K. A. Grady, & J. B. Olson (Eds.), *Counseling the aged, a training syllabus for educators* (pp. 31–44). Washington, D.C.: American Personnel and Guidance Association.

Sinick, D. (1979b). Professional development in counseling older persons. *Counselor Education and Supervision, 19,* 4–12.

Sinick, D. (1980). Attitudes and values in aging. *Counseling and Values, 24,* 148–154.

Smith, E. J. (1977). Counseling black individuals: Some stereotypes. *Personnel and Guidance Journal, 55,* 390–396.

Smith, E. J. (1981). Cultural and historical perspectives in counseling blacks. In D. W. Sue (Ed.), *Counseling the culturally different: Theory and practice* (pp. 141–185). New York: Wiley.

Smith, E. M. J., & Vasquez, M. J. T. (1985). Introduction. *The Counseling Psychologist, 13,* 531–536.

Spang, A. T. (1971). Understanding the Indian. *Personnel and Guidance Journal, 50,* 97–102.

Spiegel, S. B. (1979). Separate principles for counselors of women: A new form of sexism. *The Counseling Psychologist, 8,* 49–50.

Sue, D. W. (1977). Counseling the culturally different: A conceptual analysis. *Personnel and Guidance Journal, 55,* 422–425.

Sue, D. W. (1978a). Counseling across cultures. *Personnel and Guidance Journal, 56,* 451.

Sue, D. W. (1978b). World views and counseling. *Personnel and Guidance Journal, 56,* 458–462.

Sue, D. W. (1981). *Counseling the culturally different: Theory and practice.* New York: Wiley.

Sue, D. W., & Sue, S. (1972). Counseling Chinese-Americans. *Personnel and Guidance Journal, 50,* 637–644.

Sue, D. W., & Sue, D. (1973). Understanding Asian-Americans: The neglected minority—An overview. *Personnel and Guidance Journal, 51,* 387–389.

Sue, D. W., & Sue, D. (1981). Barriers to effective cross-cultural counseling. *Journal of Counseling Psychology, 24,* 420–429.

Super, D. E. (1954). Guidance: Manpower utilization or human development? *Personnel and Guidance Journal, 33,* 8–14.

Super, D. E. (1983). Synthesis: Or is it distillation? *Personnel and Guidance Journal, 61,* 511–514.

Tamminen, A. W., Smaby, M. H., Powless, R. E., & Gum, M. F. (1980). Preparing Native American counselors for the chemically dependent Native American. *Counselor Education and Supervision, 19,* 310–317.

Thames, T. B., & Hill, C. E. (1979). Are special skills necessary for counseling women? *The Counseling Psychologist, 8,* 17–18.

Tomine, S. (1986). Private practice in gerontological counseling. *Journal of Counseling and Development, 64,* 406–409.

Voight, N. L., Lawler, A., & Fulkerson, K. F. (1980). Community based guidance: "A Tupperware party" approach to mid-life decision making. *Personnel and Guidance Journal, 59,* 106–107.

Washington, C. S. (1979). Men counseling men: Redefining the male machine. *Per-*

sonnel and Guidance Journal, 57, 462–463.

Watanabe, C. (1973). Self-expression and the Asian American experience. *Personnel and Guidance Journal, 51*, 390–396.

Westcott, N. A. (1983). Application of the structured life-review technique in counseling elders. *Personnel and Guidance Journal, 62*, 180–181.

Wheeler, W. (1977). *Counseling from a cultural perspective.* Atlanta: Nellum.

Wolleat, P. L. (1979). School-age girls. *The Counseling Psychologist, 8*, 22–23.

Worell, J. (1980). New directions in counseling women. *Personnel and Guidance Journal, 58*, 477–484.

Worth, M. R. (1983). Adults. In J. A. Brown & R. H. Pate, Jr. (Eds.), *Being a counselor* (pp. 230–252). Monterey, CA: Brooks/Cole.

Wrenn, G. (1962). The culturally encapsulated counselor. *Harvard Educational Review, 32*, 444–449.

Photo by James S. Davidson III.

# CHAPTER 18

# Counseling and
# the Creative Arts

*When all my clients have left the office*
*I turn off the silent overhead lights*
*And watch a lingering afternoon sun*
*    like a patient courtsquare artist*
*        slowly spread gold-tinged hues*
*            across a wooden floor canvas*
*                and onto my cluttered desk.*
*That moment fills me with a sense of awe*
*    for quiet light and moving life.*
*Walking in twilight*
*    I picture past sessions*
*And wonder if lives I so fleetingly touched*
*    will dare envision their inner beauty*
*        painted in the colors and grace of time. . . .* [1]

Counseling is both a science and an art. It is scientific in the development of theoretical approaches to working with individuals, groups, and families. It is artistic in the methods used to implement theory into practice. Some counseling approaches, such as Gestalt and existentialism, strongly emphasize the contribution of the arts in counseling. Other theories are less sympathetic to the employment of the arts in the work of the counselor, yet most practitioners recognize that a good part of counseling involves the artistic endeavors of counselors to combine theory and methods in a creative way with a counselor's own unique personal qualities.

Cavanagh (1982) compares the practice of becoming a skilled counselor to that of becoming a competent painter. Art teachers, like counselor educators, can explain the principles involved in their profession, but they cannot teach the process itself. Individuals develop these abilities through experience in actual situations. Art students draw; counselors encounter clients. The first efforts of each are not as polished as later efforts because of increased awareness and practice. Individuals usually struggle in the beginning in attempts to form a professional identity that feels right personally.

Many counseling programs fail to impart to their graduates knowledge about the creative arts and skill in the use of them in counseling. As Mitchell and Campbell (1972) noted, those in educational fields, like counselor education, "have not shown much interest in using creative art forms in counseling students who have developmental and situational problems, or normal students who want to know themselves better, or even disturbed students who seek counseling services" (p. 691). Instead, this kind of counseling has been reserved almost exclusively for mental hospitals or psychoanalytic treatment. Two primary reasons are: (1) the systematic use of the arts in counseling is a fairly recent trend (Feder & Feder, 1981), and (2) "more value and importance has been attached to the scientific (or objective) aspects of counseling than the artistic (or subjective) ones" (Seligman, 1985, p. 2).

Yet, an overview of what artistic theories, methods, and organizations are available can be of significant importance to the growth of individual counselors and professional counseling itself in promoting new knowledge, insight, and practices. The creative arts add excitement, flexibility, and variety to the counseling process. Furthermore, art forms may lead to insight and integration, and may provide the inspiration for new scientific discoveries. The creative arts have a significant contribution to make to counseling theory and practice, but their impact will be made only if those in counseling become more knowledgeable about the arts and willing to use them with clients.

## CREATIVE ARTS IN COUNSELING

The term *creative arts* has a wide range of meanings. In its broadest sense, the designation refers to any art form, including visual art, poetry, drama, and music, that helps individuals become more in touch with the self or others. In this respect, creative arts are an independent domain. In counseling, creative arts are defined as art forms employed in therapeutic settings that help facilitate a relationship between counselors and clients (Zwerling, 1979). Naitove (1977) distinguishes between verbal and nonverbal creative arts. Music, dance, visual art, and mime are examples of nonverbal arts. Verbal art forms include drama, poetry, and bibliotherapy. All creative art forms are process oriented, tap emotional responses, promote social interaction, highlight the nature of reality, help establish a sense of inner control, and lead to a greater awareness of personal identity.

There is debate over how art forms used in therapeutic settings should be classified (Fleshman and Fryrear, 1981). Some professionals advocate a two-tier system that relegates arts and crafts used in occupational therapy to a lower level than art forms employed in other counseling settings. The suggestion is that arts and crafts are nothing more than busywork. Others see equality among all art forms. The fact is almost any art form can be employed beneficially if counselors are skilled and careful.

### Historical Overview

The use of the creative arts in mental health services has a long history. Many cultures have employed the arts to help rehabilitate disturbed persons. An early example is from ancient Egypt, where in about 500 B.C. the mentally ill were "encouraged to pursue artistic interests and attend concerts and dances" (Fleshman & Fryrear, 1981, p. 12). Other cultures, including the early Greeks, employed drama and music as a means to help the disturbed achieve catharsis, relieve themselves of pent up emotions, and return to balanced lives. The early Hebrews also used music to help calm emotions, as illustrated in the story of David's playing his harp for King Saul.

In the Middle Ages, magic and superstition replaced the arts in the treatment of the emotionally disturbed. By the eighteenth century, thanks to the reforms of Philippe Pinel in France, Benjamin Rush in the United States, and William Tuke in England, patients treated for mental illness received more rights and humane treatment. An important development at this time was the formulation of so-called moral therapy. This approach to working with mental patients included the use of occupational therapy and some art forms, such as reading and music (Fleshman & Fryrear, 1981).

Around the turn of the twentieth century, the use of the arts in the service of counseling increased even more. One reason was the influence on the public and therapeutic communities of Sigmund Freud. It was Freud who popularized systematic therapeutic approaches, including an emphasis on the unconscious and the content of dreams. His methods of free association and dream analysis opened the door for creative counselors and therapists. For example, psychodrama began when Freud's psychoanalytic treatment was the dominant therapeutic approach (Fine, 1979). The creativity and spontaneity of psychodrama's founder, J. L. Moreno, led to the acceptance and use of additional artistic treatment methods in mental hospitals and institutions. The rise in the use of such creative art forms as recreation therapy, dance, music, art, and crafts paralleled the rise in prominence of psychotherapy.

After World War II the use of the arts in counseling grew even more because of the needs of many returning soldiers and their families for mental health services. Some arts, such as music, art, and psychodrama, became adjuncts to psychiatry and clinical psychology. These arts gained acceptance in such primary treatment facilities as hospitals but were not recognized as legitimate treatment entities in which professionals could specialize outside of psychiatry and clinical psychology. To enhance the image of the arts in counseling and therapy, professional organizations were formed. These groups, like the American Dance Therapy Association, promoted and encouraged the use of the arts as a distinct discipline. Today, many art forms are used effectively in counseling by both creative counselors and registered art therapists. Four disciplines register professionals in a specific art form: music, art, dance, and poetry. These individuals are known as art therapists and must pass stringent requirements to obtain recognition in their designated specialty. Usually, they are identified by the initials that follow their names; for example, R.P.T. stands for registered poetry therapist, and A.T.R. identifies a registered art therapist.

### Artists and Art Forms in Counseling

There is considerable tension between some artists and various counselors and art therapists. On an elementary level, many artists consider the work of counselors and art therapists to be simplistic (Fleshman & Fryrear, 1981). The purposes of artists and those who use the arts therapeutically are not the same. Artists express themselves through their creations, whereas counselors and art therapists are more concerned with helping the disturbed express pent up emotions. The techniques involved differ.

Another problem is in the use of art forms with artists themselves. Fleshman and Fryrear (1981) note that "for artists, the use of the arts in therapy may be counterproductive" (p. 6). For example, many actors have difficulty engaging in psychodrama. The reason for this phenomenon may be that these professionals and other artists already support themselves psychologically through expression in the arts. Thus, engaging further in the use of art forms adds nothing new to the artist's coping skills or concept of reality.

Numerous art forms have been employed systematically in counseling; others are just beginning to emerge. The most widely used art forms in counseling are: visual art, psychodrama, poetry/bibliotherapy, and dance/music.

## VISUAL ART

Rubin (1980) has speculated that the use of visual art for healing is probably as old as humanity itself. Yet, the employment of this medium in a systematic, therapeutic way first occurred only during the last century. Initially, spontaneous drawings of institutionalized mental patients were collected and displayed (Prinzhorn, 1972). But they were viewed more as a curiosity than a therapeutic process, and little was done to promote the use of visual art in mental health settings. With the advancement of psychotherapeutic techniques, visual art was incorporated directly into diagnostic tests. Among the best known of these visual arts instruments are: the Rorschach, the Thematic Apperception Test, and the Draw-A-Person Test. The use of visual art in this way has generally been more useful for counselors and therapists than for clients and patients.

In 1969, the American Art Therapy Association was officially formed in Louisville, Kentucky (Rubin, 1979). One of the highest priorities of the association is the support of educational guidelines and standards for becoming an art therapist (Agell, 1979). Graduates of accredited institutions or programs recognized by the American Art Therapy Association may become registered art therapists (ATR). Both registered and nonregistered counselors and therapists make use of the visual arts in a number of ways, for example, drawings, photography, cartooning, and cinema.

### Drawings

Drawings have been used in counseling on both a formal and informal basis. Protinsky (1978), for instance, uses human figure drawings (HFDs) in elementary schools as a way of gaining greater knowledge about children and their families. The value of these drawings is their subtle unveiling of affective states. Children project themselves through drawings and display to others inner realities. Protinsky (1978) notes that the scientific literature on HFDs supports the drawing of certain features, such as exaggerated hands or grotesque figures, as being related to the social-emotional adjustment of the school-age child. He cautions, however, that drawings are but one indicator of the child's level of functioning and advises that a holistic approach should be taken in evaluating children. Peer interaction, family of origin, academic performance, and developmental levels also have an impact on children's drawings.

Another related approach to understanding young children through art is the family drawing/storytelling technique (Roosa, 1981). This technique retains the benefits of projective drawing and storytelling yet narrows the gap between clinical interpretation and the inner world of the child. As Roosa (1981) maintains, the technique "is used in conjunction with direct interview and more ambiguous projectives" (p. 270). It is most appropriately employed with children under 10 years old and involves a four-step process. In step one, children are instructed to draw pictures of their families, including themselves, on a piece of 8½-by-11-inch white drawing paper (horizontally oriented). In step two, they make up a story about what the family is doing in the picture. In step three, the children draw any significant members of the family left out in the original drawing, such as a divorced parent who visits regularly. This drawing is done on a separate sheet of paper. In step four, the examiner photocopies the child's completed drawings, cuts out the figures, and presents pairs and triads of cutouts to the child. The child is then asked to tell stories about each pair or triad.

Roosa (1981) explains that through the family drawing/story-telling technique, counselor examiners can formulate hypotheses about a child's family and how that family works. These hypotheses may be tested when the counselor is able to see the child's family. In such cases, it is preferable for parents to propose some possible interpretations of their child's drawing before the counselor offers explanations. A real advantage of this method is that a counselor may formulate a picture of the dynamics of a family even when the counselor does not have the opportunity to meet with the entire family.

Two other drawing techniques have been found helpful when counselors are working with entire families. One is in the symbolic drawing of the family life space (Geddes & Medway, 1977). In this exercise, family members are asked to draw their positions inside a large circle called the family life space. Family members are then queried about relationships within this social network. A similar procedure is the synallactic collective image technique (Tavantzis, 1982). This technique, which is based on psychodynamic theory, asks members of a family to draw anything they wish, separately or together, on a large (18-by-24-inch) piece of blank drawing paper. "After drawing, group members vote to decide what they want to discuss. Members are required: (a) to give the drawing a title; (b) to describe what feeling is created within them by the drawing; and (c) to relate a recent specific incident from their everyday lives that is evoked by the drawing or the feeling they have described" (Tavantzis, 1982, p. 126). In the process of doing all of this, a "collective image" (central concern) emerges (Vassiliou, 1980).

Newton (1976) and Hageman and Gladding (1983) have also found self-portraits useful in helping adults and children become more attuned with the self and personal wishes. Newton (1976) posits that the use of a visual dimension in counseling provides greater insight, clarity, and understanding into the actual depiction of a problem. His example of a sequence of eight self-portraits of a client called Billie supports his position. Hageman and Gladding (1983) also found that visual representation, in this case children's drawings of occupational choices, is most productive as a tool in helping these children come to a better understanding of what they want to be and can be vocationally. In short, drawing appears to be a frequently used and effective means for counselors and clients to understand themselves and others better. It is a nonthreatening and concrete therapeutic method.

### Photography

Another important visual art counselors use in a variety of ways is photography. Gosciewski (1975) points out that photographs are valuable in counseling to: (1) establish and build rapport, (2) help in diagnosis, and (3) increase understanding, break through resistance, and assess gains. Gosciewski describes his method of using photography as *photo counseling.* The method consists of having clients bring photographs of different situations in their lives with them to counseling. The counselor then explores with the client the meaning of certain events and relationships depicted in the pictures. Gosciewski reports that his approach is most effective with passive-resistant and dependent clients and with children (because of their limited verbal ability).

Schudson (1975), using a more varied approach than Gosciewski, has found photography a valuable aid in school counseling. Schudson cites cases within her school where the use of a camera and photography helped facilitate discussion between the counselor and a shy girl, motivated an underachiever to improve his grades, and produced greater enthusiasm while enhancing self-concept for students in group counseling. It is Schudson's contention that photography can contribute to school counseling in the following ways:

☐ Photography may personalize school life by encouraging students to share out-of-school experiences with their classmates.

☐ Photography can promote increased awareness and sensitivity and motivate students to become more self-directed as they identify important aspects of life.

☐ Photography is a potential enhancer of communication between students, between students and counselors, and between counselors and school faculties. Because of the art form's concreteness, photographs can be used in academic programs and serve as reminders of the progress and growth achieved in counseling.

☐ Photography can help bring out information that might not be revealed if a more verbal method of communication were employed. Students who are inarticulate or shy benefit most from this alternative means of expression.

☐ Photography is an activity that can be enjoyed after school graduation. Students who use this creative art form in school may engage in the activity throughout their lives and use cameras in vocational or avocational settings. Engaging in special photography programs while in school may be status enhancing, too, and promote a healthy self-concept.

Amerikaner, Schauble, and Ziller (1980) have come up with yet a third approach to using photographs. Their method employs sets of new photographs created by clients who are attempting to overcome problems. The counselor gives the client written instructions that ask the client to create a self-description using 12 photographs. The photographs can be of anything, but when the pictures are taken and developed they are ranked in order of importance by the client. A caption is mounted with each picture on a piece of white poster board. Counselors and clients then explore the photographic collage from either a content or process perspective. Blind spots or events and people not included in the pictures are observed and talked about. The emphasis of this approach is examining pictures as a set, with the photographs serving as a guide to discovering a client's strengths and weaknesses. The authors note that those who will make the best use of photography or any other visual modality are individuals who are visually oriented in processing perceptions of the world.

## Cartooning

Cartoons are a visual form of humor that entertains and also enlightens. They do not intimidate clients or make them defensive; instead, they allow clients to catch a glimpse of themselves, release tension through laughter, and promote understanding and communication. O'Brien, Johnson, and Miller (1978) have found cartoons to be especially effective in working with reluctant and resistant clients and have used cartoons in counseling children, adolescents, and married couples.

There are four main ways these authors advocate using cartoon humor. One way is within a counseling session itself. In counseling, an anthology of cartoons can be given to clients, and select cartoons related to clients' problems read and discussed. Many clients reconceptualize problems when seen in a humorous way. A second way of using cartoons is in counseling homework. Counselors may lend select groups of cartoons to clients with the understanding that the clients will study them and bring them back for discussion the next week. A third way of using cartoons is for clients to search out and select cartoons that relate to personal situations and bring this material to the next counseling session for discussion. Finally, clients can complete the ballooned parts of cartoon scenes to give themselves and their counselors a better understanding of what they are thinking.

The use of cartoons has also been fairly popular as an illustrative tool in counselor education publications and presentations. *The School Counselor*, for instance, has featured funny and informative cartoons of counseling situations in its issues. Articles punctuated with the use of cartoon humor (Gladding & Hood, 1974) and presentations featuring newspaper cartoons related to counseling (Elmore & Gladding, 1978) have also appeared in recent years.

### Cinema

The use of cinema in the therapeutic process has received increased attention over the years. Weeks (1971) proposes that commercial cinema is "a sensitive mirror of our society's values" (p. 769). As such, it can help counselors gain new insight into emerging or existing life-styles, clarify personal goals, and recognize the interaction between personal and social pathology. Weeks advocates that counselors learn from films by viewing them with a "counselor's eye."

O'Brien and Johnson (1976) agree with Weeks, but expound further on the use of cinema in counseling. They note that almost everyone sees movies, especially young people. Therefore, movies and television programs can serve as a resource for students and nonstudents to develop greater awareness of self, others, and such issues as careers. Being a viewer of select films may help:

☐ Induce catharsis.

☐ Produce a sense of empathy.

☐ Promote the formulation of goals.

☐ Increase the client's understanding of different environments and personality traits.

☐ Identify values.

☐ Examine career or academic concerns and frustrations.

In making use of films in counseling, O'Brien and Johnson (1976) recommend that the age levels and maturity of potential clients be evaluated. They also stress that interaction with a counselor is necessary for films to be truly therapeutic for clients. This interaction may occur on either an individual or group basis.

The latest use of cinema in counseling has come in marriage and family therapy, in which Frank Pittman (1985) has begun to analyze films for statements and reflections on American family life. Pittman's humor and insight provide a valuable tool in teaching counselors about developmental trends and theory simultaneously.

## DRAMATIC AND ENACTMENT ARTS

Dramatic and enactment arts have been employed in the service of counseling and the therapeutic process since the ancient Greeks. But it was not until J. L. Moreno coined the term *group psychotherapy* at a 1932 meeting of the American Psychological Association that the theory and practice of dramatic and enactment arts began to have prevalence in the United States (Blatner, 1973). Since that time various approaches have been developed in this field.

### Drama

Drama and counseling have many similarities and areas of overlap. Sylvia (1977) points out five essential elements common to both: problem, choice, crisis, climax, and resolution. It is not surprising, then, that counselors have advocated the use of drama in a variety of ways.

The use of drama in its purest form, that is, the performance of a formal play, is recommended by Wolpert (1973). He notes that "fine playwrights have the artistry to demonstrate relevant issues and themes with a multifaceted, lifelike totality and richness not found in plays produced with certain specific educational ends in mind" (pp. 30–31). In addition, plays provide concrete examples of specific issues and lend themselves to group discussions with or without the leadership of a counselor. Certain plays are especially relevant for particular issues; for example: *Antigone* (authority), *A Hatful of Rain* (the drug scene), *Splendor in the Grass* (adolescent sexuality), and *West Side Story* (racism).

There are certain cautions Wolpert recommends when using dramatic plays in a school setting. Among these cautions are: (1) keep plays to a proper length, (2) involve others outside of counseling, (3) proactively work to change restrictive schedules, if necessary, and (4) involve actors in the play as discussion leaders. Wolpert stresses that plays provide a chance for students to both model behavior and express important affect in regard to attitudes.

Sylvia (1977) and Wilson (1983) advocate the production of "counseling playlets" or "guidance plays." They report positive outcomes with students, teachers, parents, and counselors in using these specially written and focused dramas. In the articles cited, both authors provide the transcripts of the plays they have produced.

Coven (1977) also advocates the use of more informal drama techniques in counseling. Specifically, he recommends the use of gestalt psychodrama experiences with rehabilitation clients. Although his recommendations and techniques are more general than those of other authors, Coven makes an excellent point in noting that dramatic enactments can help clients feel a sense of power they may not achieve in talking about problems. Thus, dramatic techniques can enhance self-concepts as well as clarify issues.

Psychoeducational and creative dramas are also effective in helping to increase an understanding of self, others, and moral values (Urtz & Kahn, 1982; Wallin, 1980). These dramas are typically quite brief (1 to 5 minutes in length) and end with emotions heightened and unresolved situations. Group discussion, led by a trained facilitator, follows the enactments. During the discussion, which lasts from 30 minutes to 2 hours, audience members try to reach an appropriate resolution and conclusion to the drama in line with personal values, beliefs, and attitudes. In some ways, these forms of drama are similar to an incomplete form in Gestalt therapy, in that both invite individual participation and resolution.

Yager and Hector (1980) suggest that certain principles employed in the training of dramatic actors can be applied to the education of counselors. They note that "all the world is a stage, and all human beings, including counselors, are actors and actresses involved in an ongoing drama" (p. 21). Counselors play roles for one reason—to help clients solve problems. Yager and Hector note that social influence and empathy roles enacted by counselors have been empirically shown to relate to client progress. They advocate that counselors develop roles, become aware of how counselors' emotions can enhance the roles played, and then practice role strategies that are purposeful and effective with particular clients. By doing this, counselors will free themselves from the limited role of just being "authentic."

### Games

Playing games within counseling is a way of achieving greater awareness of self and others. In this respect, games are similar to drama. Crocker and Wroblewski (1975) have found recreational games to be an effective tool in group counseling. Six possible helping functions of recreational games are:

☐ Their use as a sensitizer to new behaviors.

☐ Their creation and resolution of anxiety producing feelings.

☐ Their emphasis on the rules of human behavior.

☐ The childlike playfulness they allow.

☐ The safe and permissive climate they create for new behaviors.

☐ The coping behavior they promote in both winning and losing situations.

Recreational games are not a substitute for effective counseling techniques and genuine human encounters, but they can enhance the efficacy of counseling.

Other practitioners agree with Crocker and Wroblewski on the effectiveness of games in counseling, though many articles advocate the use of counselor-made games rather than manufactured recreational games. For example, Wubbolding and Osborne (1974) have created an awareness game for elementary school children that purports "to promote self-perception, acceptance of feelings, and peer communication on an emotional level" (p. 223). Although no statistical analysis of the effects of the game have been completed, the authors report positive, informal feedback about the use of the game. Teeter, Teeter, and Papai (1976) created a group counseling game on a high school level. Their game, called Frustration, is designed to show incoming freshmen students some of the hazards of the high school experience and the effect of chance in some life experiences. The authors of the game provide directions for making the game in the cited article but provide only informal student feedback about its effectiveness.

To enhance public relations between counselors and the public, especially the local school board, Fuss, Mosher, and Rashbaum-Selig (1977) developed an educational device called The Board Game. The game, which is life-size and requires the use of a large room to play, involves demonstrating prominent counseling functions to the public, including the effects on counseling of cutting funds or providing inadequate funding. The Board Game promotes an accurate picture of counseling, while fostering local support for counseling programs.

## POETRY/METAPHOR AND BIBLIOTHERAPY

There has been increased attention to the uses of poetry/metaphor and bibliotherapy since the 1970s. Part of the interest may reflect a new emphasis on the importance of cognitive processes in counseling and psychology. Regardless, these creative art forms are enjoying renewed attention and emphasis. The National Association for Poetry Therapy has certified poetry therapists since 1981.

### *Poetry/Metaphor*

Poetic language includes the use of similes and metaphors and is a natural way of conveying feelings (Pollio, 1974). Metaphors are comparisons of two seemingly dissimilar objects, such as "I am an island." Similes are stated comparisons preceded by *as* or *like*, such as "he is standing like a wall." Both poetic metaphors and similes enhance our understanding of the objects compared. Both are useful in the counseling tasks of problem setting and problem solving by making the familiar strange and making the strange familiar (Gladding, 1979). Poetry and metaphor have also been found effective in fostering emotional insight (Berger, 1969, 1985), promoting catharsis (Luber, 1973), facilitating communication and insight (Buck and Kraemer, 1974; Matthews and Dardeck, 1985), and promoting group processes (Lessner, 1974; Gladding, 1984).

One of the more interesting aspects of poetry and metaphor in counseling is their diversity of use. Leedy (Kolodzey, 1983) notes that certain poems can be beneficial in helping clients deal with particular emotions. Thus, he may prescribe the reading of a poem such as Robert Frost's "The Road Less Traveled" for someone who is trying to cope with anxiety. The reading of the poem helps the client know that he or she is not alone in experiencing troublesome emotions. It may also lead to greater dialogue and interaction between counselor and client. Lerner (1978, 1981) conceptualizes poetry as a tool in the hands of a competent counselor. The counselor may employ the tool when and if appropriate with a wide variety of individuals and groups. He stresses that this medium can be effective for counselors from various theoretical orientations but that those who employ poetry in counseling should have a background in both literature and counseling/psychology.

In individual counseling, Gladding (1979) has found that either complete poems or poetic fragments are helpful in working with clients in a mental health setting. He notes that metaphors originated by clients may change during the course of counseling. For example, a person who describes anger as a "fire" may come to be a "firefighter" once counseling moves from the exploration stage and into the goal setting and action stages (Egan, 1986). A counselor can reinforce constructive actions of a client by employing that client's language and images. Gladding also notes that having a client complete a "poem of self" (Trotzer, 1977) or keep a poetic log (Carroll, 1970) may be beneficial. The important thing is not to force poetry or poetic exercises on clients who are not comfortable with this modality. Adams and Chadbourne (1982) have also found metaphors to be therapeutic with individuals in weight control. These authors point out that metaphors may help:

☐ Uncover underlying feelings.

☐ Reveal hidden solutions.

☐ Create an aversion to undesirable food intakes.

☐ Provide the client with a new thin self-concept.

☐ Increase compliance with a diet plan.

In group counseling, Lessner (1974) has discovered that poetry may be a catchy and stimulating catalyst. The strength of good poetry is that it is not too didactic or culturally confined and thus offers clients "hooks" (images) they can identify with in defining themselves and their emotions. Lessner finds that diverse groups of individuals, (e.g., students, housewives, policemen, and prison guards) respond positively to a poem at the beginning of a group session, especially if the presentation of the poem follows relaxation exercises. Gladding (1984) has also found the use of metaphors in group counseling to be most productive. He points out that metaphors and similes often imply what one thinks about oneself. In groups, people sometimes borrow metaphors from books, songs, or slogans; for example, "I am stronger than dirt." They may also originate descriptive metaphors within the group process itself; for example, "I'm more powerful than three acres of garlic." In either case, group leaders can help members use metaphors to determine how to fit into a group setting, to see how the group is changing, or to initiate actions. Group metaphors may also have a latent affect and evolve in a group member's mind long after the group experience has ended.

Gladding and Hanna (1982) have productively used poetry in school guidance groups as introductory devices, as ways of helping students better realize self-identity, and as a means for assisting children to concentrate and develop appropriate coping strategies through the creative combination of words and thoughts. They propose three guidelines for using poetry in schools:

☐ Make the time for using poetry brief, realistic, and relevant.

☐ Make poetic exercises clear, simple, structured, and fun.

☐ Give students as much freedom as possible in self-expression.

Metaphors and poetic devices have also been frequently used in couple and family counseling sessions. Rule (1983) says that metaphors can be employed in various stages of the family therapy process to:

☐ Explore problems.

☐ Put problems into perspective.

☐ Help reframe perceptions of situations.

☐ Reinforce what has been said.

☐ Get in touch with feelings.

☐ Deal with resistance.

☐ Encourage action.

Rule proposes that counselors consider using the pie metaphor when working with families. He reasons that everyone in a family understands what a pie is and how pies may be constructed and cut up into parts. In any case, a well-known object, such as a pie, can help family members realize both family commonality and personal distinctiveness. Other family practitioners, such as Brink (1982), Duhl (1983), Gladding, (1985), and Minuchin and Fishman (1981), advocate the use of metaphors in working with families. Poetry has been employed in couple group work (Mazza & Prescott, 1981). Overall, the use of this medium has proved flexible in helping individuals, groups, and families express themselves.

## Bibliotherapy

*Bibliotherapy* is a guided reading process that produces a dynamic interaction between the personality of the reader and a selected literature that helps individuals gain a better understanding of self, others, and problems (McKinney, 1977; Schrank & Engels, 1981). Some theorists divide bibliotherapy theory into two divisions. *Depth theory* focuses on the unconscious aspects of reading, such as emotional release and relief, whereas *surface theory* refers to what the reader reports as a response to a particular piece of literature.

Regardless of theory, three fundamental processes occur between readers and literature in this activity: identification, catharsis, and insight (Schrank & Engels, 1981; Schrank, 1982). Identification, which encompasses catharsis and insight, occurs when readers affiliate with a character or situation in a story. Catharsis takes place when readers vicariously enjoy an experience of a character or share the character's emotion in some other way. Insight occurs when readers see themselves in the behavior of a story character.

In a thorough review of the literature on counselor use of bibliotherapy, Schrank and Engels (1981) found research supporting the use of bibliotherapy as effective in modifying attitudes, promoting behavioral change, fostering self-development, and causing therapeutic gains. In a similar detailed review of the literature on bibliotherapy in elementary schools, Schrank (1982) found bibliotherapy was effective in promoting attitude change and mental health in young children, but was less effective in producing self-concept development and fear reduction. He suggests special strategies elementary school counselors might try in order to increase the effectiveness of bibliotherapy. These include summarizing the story, discussing a character's feelings, identifying with a character, exploring consequences, and drawing conclusions.

Since the landmark reviews by Schrank and Engels, articles in major counseling journals on the uses of bibliotherapy have advocated this process in multimodal projects (Bellows & Gerler, 1982), in children of divorce projects (Martin, Martin, & Porter, 1983), in promoting career awareness (Staley & Mangieri, 1984), and in preventing problems in youth of changing families (Sheridan, Baker, & deLissovoy, 1984). The last article in this group is based on research conducted by the authors and shows that combining a creative art process, that is, writing, with a troubled child may be therapeutically measurable. Art, in this case, works in the service of science. Two excellent source books on the process of bibliotherapy and its uses with diverse populations are *Using bibliotherapy* (Rubin, 1978) and *Bibliotherapy* (Hynes & Hynes-Berry, 1986).

## MUSIC AND DANCE THERAPIES

Music and dance established themselves as recognized therapeutic arts in the 1940s. Their use has varied considerably over the years, but in general they have been employed most often in such treatment centers as mental hospitals rather than in counseling offices. Few articles have appeared since 1970 in nonspecialty counseling journals, such as the *Journal for Counseling and Development,* on the use of either of these two mediums. Yet, they are important creative art therapies that have excellent potential for use with many clients traditionally seen by counselors.

### Music

Music gained status in counseling as a useful creative art during and after World War II. As a treatment modality, music therapy was developed largely by physicians in Veterans Administration hospitals rather than by music therapists. More than any of the other art therapies, music therapy follows the medical model, is less theoretically oriented, and has a strong physiological bias (Feder & Feder, 1981). On the other hand, researchers in music therapy have conducted excellent studies on the effects of music on individuals. Among the more interesting findings are that listening to music produces changes in blood flow and blood pressure, breathing rate, body posture, and mood. Listening to and playing music has also been found to be an effective antidepressant (Feder & Feder, 1981). Music is an excellent way to establish a mood, lessen anxiety, ease loneliness, and soothe irritability (Harper, 1985). Music therapy encompasses three therapeutic situations: having music in the background, actively listening to music, or making music (Fleshman & Fryrear, 1981).

As Lathom (1979) points out, music has an effect on groups as well as individuals. Those who use music in treatment and counseling employ it as a means to get clients to be more active and in touch with themselves and others on a more realistic level. White (1985) notes that people are likely to subscribe to popular-music "substreams" that advocate "their values and their perceptions about themselves, one another, other groups, society, and the world. The very choice of substream music may be an indication of apartness, alienation, or conformity . . ." (p. 68). Thus, knowing a client's musical taste can serve as a bridge in facilitating communication.

The most prevalent way music has been used in counseling is in listening to popular tunes and discussing them. Vander Kolk (1976) notes that there is a wealth of popular music that may be employed by counselors. He has used popular music in group counseling as a means of helping fatherless adolescent boys. He finds the use of selected songs helpful in increasing the boys' feelings about their present situations. After the group leader makes music selections for a couple of weeks, Vander Kolk recommends this task be at least partially turned over to the group so particularly relevant songs for individual group members will be played and discussed.

Ellis (1977) takes a more active approach in using music in the counseling process. He recommends that clients sing "rational songs" in order to help them learn to deal more effectively with irrational beliefs. The songs Ellis has written are generally humorous and help clients experience a rational thought process in an easily remembered form. Gladding and Mazza (1983) recommend a similar active technique in which clients may in fact make up songs about present feelings or possibilities. This technique enables clients to get more in touch with themselves, experience a release of emotions, and in the process plan for the future while remembering the past in an acceptable way. Active counselors may even want to model behavior by singing songs they have created or heard.

Harper (1985) finds that the use of music enhances group guidance lessons with elementary children. Songs are fun for the children, generate ideas and novel responses, and at the same time help them remember the main points of the guidance lesson. She uses songs in developmental guidance activities related to self-awareness, self-expression, social awareness, and career awareness. Harper makes several suggestions for incorporating music in guidance classes:

☐ Introduce the words of a song as a poem.

☐ Chant the words in rhythm.

☐ Practice chanting three to four minutes each class period until the words are memorized.

☐ When students know and understand the words, play the song. Cassette tapes are convenient.

☐ As the children begin to read, they benefit from looking at a copy of words already memorized. Double-space the words and number each line. Always separate the verse from the refrain with white space (p. 220).

In addition, Harper advocates that the counselor always learn the song first and that soft singing is best.

### Dance

The American Dance Therapy Association (ADTA), which was formed in 1966, defines dance therapy as a holistic psychotherapeutic approach that uses movement as a process to help individuals integrate emotional and physical aspects of themselves. ADTA recognizes that the interaction between the mind and body is complex; each influences the other (Duggan, 1981). The body is seen as the manifestation of one's personality and any spontaneous movement is viewed as an expression of personality (Bunney, 1979).

Duggan (1981) notes that there are currently two different terms used to designate the profession: dance therapy and movement therapy. The term *dance* is used by therapists who wish to stress the profession's roots in the creative arts as well as connote "expressive movement and the integrating aspects of the rhythmic use of body movement" (p. 229). Therapists who employ the term *movement* wish to avoid connotations of performance. They do not use music but focus on inner sensing by the client. Music therapy is closely associated with dance therapy, while drama and enactment techniques are closely allied with movement therapy.

Fleshman and Fryrear (1981) note that the aim of dance/ movement therapy can be classified into three general categories: physical, psychological, and social. Physical goals may include releasing physical tension through activities or broadening one's movement repertoire. Psychological goals include channeling one's self-expression in a meaningful way and helping a client adjust to reality. Social goals may include a client's joining a group interaction and a client's developing social relationships with others in movement and dance. Much of dance and movement therapy is based on psychoanalytical theory and assumes that body movements may inform the conscious part of the personality about unconscious feelings and thoughts (Feder & Feder, 1981).

Bodywork has been found to be a particularly effective approach to counseling men (Brownell, 1981). There are at least a dozen recognized forms of bodywork. Brownell takes an even broader view of this concept, defining it as any activity that is nonverbal. He uses bodywork to help men release affect, such as fear, sadness and hurt, anger and rage, and joy and pleasure. Many of the bodywork techniques Brownell advocates are related to those in Gestalt therapy and use props such as pillows to help clients experience and integrate unrealized or unexpressed emotions.

## SUMMARY

The use of the creative arts in counseling is uneven. Although some creative arts are growing in acceptance and recognition (e.g., the visual arts and drama), others are still eschewed, largely unknown, or even untried by most counselors (e.g., dance and music). Similarly, art therapy associations are growing in numbers and respectability just as they are being called into question about their theoretical bases by more established therapeutic disciplines (Feder and Feder, 1981). There is both optimism and frustration among those who advocate and employ the creative arts in counseling. Are these forms complementary adjuncts to other counseling theories or do they have the theoretical base to become counseling entities unto themselves? The question is still unsettled. One thing is certain: regardless of their status, the creative arts can make a positive contribution to both the prevention and resolution of emotional problems in individuals. As Mitchell and Campbell (1972) note, creativity, no matter what its form, can lead toward growth and liberation.

The profession of counseling is currently at a crossroads in its evolution. It may lose more than it gains if it travels on in its development without incorporating creative arts in its identity. As Seligman (1985) so insightfully points out, many of the early pioneers who influenced the formation of counseling, including Sigmund Freud, Carl Rogers, and Erik Erikson, did so initially from a nonscientific base. Their creativity was the art used to produce a healing science. Collins and Hayes (1983) observe that the use of art helps promote greater awareness and comprehension of what it is to be human. Counseling, in its best form, is concerned with the totality of human existence, encompassing affective, behavioral, and cognitive dimensions. The creative arts can contribute to a more complete understanding and treatment of emotional disorders.

Neither art nor science is superior in the service of counseling. Rather, if counseling is to be served each must balance the other. The arts promote scientific discoveries (Seligman, 1985). Science, in turn, needs to promote the arts. If counseling is to continue to advance, counselors must find ways to incorporate a blending of the art and science of helping into a single profession.

## CLASSROOM ACTIVITIES

1. Ask a counselor about the place of the arts in counseling. Find out if this person makes use of creative arts in ways not mentioned in the text. Report the results of your experience to the class.
2. Which of the creative arts appeals to you most? Divide into small groups based on similarity of appeal. Appoint a spokesperson for each group to tell the rest of the class the reasons for your choice(s).
3. Bibliotherapy is widely used in counseling. Compile a list of 10 books on a subject

relevant to counseling. Share your list with fellow classmates.
4. Divide into groups of four. As a group devise a counseling technique, based on theory, that involves the use of the creative arts. Specify the population for which this technique is suited.
5. What are some ways the effectiveness of the creative arts in counseling could be researched? In small groups of three, formulate a strategy for investigating this question.

## REFERENCES

Adams, C. H., & Chadbourne, J. (1982). Therapeutic metaphor: An approach to weight control. *Personnel and Guidance Journal, 60,* 510–512.

Agell, G. L. (1979). The history of art therapy education. In P. B. Hallen (Ed.), *The use of the creative arts in therapy* (pp. 15–17). Washington, D.C.: American Psychiatric Association.

Amerikaner, M., Schauble, P., & Ziller, R. (1980). Images: The use of photographs in personal counseling. *Personnel and Guidance Journal, 59,* 68–73.

Bellows, E., & Gerler, E. R., Jr. (1982). Helping books for children: A multimodal project for the school library. *Elementary School Guidance & Counseling, 16,* 296–303.

Berger, A. (1985, April). *The "intentional paradox": An intervention with psychiatric patients.* Paper presented at the Fifth Annual Conference of the National Association for Poetry Therapy. Evanston, IL.

Berger, A. (1969). Poetry as therapy and therapy as poetry. In J. J. Leedy (Ed.), *Poetry therapy* (pp. 75–87). Philadelphia: Lippincott.

Blatner, H. A. (1973). *Acting in: Practical applications of psychodramatic method.* New York: Springer.

Brink, N. E. (1982). Metaphor creation for use within family therapy. *American Journal of Clinical Hypnosis, 24,* 258–265.

Brownell, A. J. (1981). Counseling men through bodywork. *Personnel and Guidance Journal, 60,* 252–255.

Buck, L., & Kraemer, A. (1974). Poetry as a means of group facilitation. *Journal of Humanistic Psychology, 14,* 57–71.

Bunney, J. (1979). Dance therapy: An overview. In P. B. Hallen (Ed.), *The use of the creative arts in therapy* (pp. 24–26). Washington, D.C.: American Psychiatric Association.

Carroll, M. R. (1970). Silence is the heart's size. *Personnel and Guidance Journal, 48,* 546–551.

Cavanagh, M. E. (1982). *The counseling experience.* Monterey, CA: Brooks/Cole.

Collins, P. W., & Hayes, R. L. (1983). Education of the imagination. *Humanistic Education and Development, 22,* 2–7.

Coven, A. B. (1977). Using Gestalt psychodrama experiments in rehabilitation counseling. *Personnel and Guidance Journal, 56,* 143–147.

Crocker, J. W., & Wroblewski, M. (1975). Using recreational games in counseling. *Personnel and Guidance Journal, 53,* 453–458.

Duggan, D. (1981). Dance therapy. In R. J. Corsini (Ed.), *Handbook of innovative psychotherapies* (pp. 229–240). New York: Wiley.

Duhl, B. S. (1983). *From the inside out and other metaphors.* New York: Brunner/Mazel.

Egan, G. (1986). *The skilled helper* (3rd edition). Monterey, CA: Brooks/Cole.

Ellis, A. (1977). Fun as psychotherapy. In A. Ellis & R. Grieger (Eds.), *Handbook of rational-emotive therapy* (pp. 262–270). New York: Springer.

Elmore, T. M., & Gladding, S. T. (1978, October). *The counseling psychology of Peanuts: Illustrations of harmful and helpful helping.* Paper presented at the Southern Association for Counselor Education and Supervision Convention, Nashville, TN.

Feder, E., & Feder, B. (1981). *The expressive arts therapies.* Englewood Cliffs, NJ: Prentice-Hall.

Fine, L. J. (1979). Psychodrama. In R. J. Corsini (Ed.), *Current psychotherapies* (2nd ed., pp. 428–459). Itasca, IL: Peacock.

Fleshman, B., & Fryrear, J. L. (1981). *The arts in therapy.* Chicago: Nelson-Hall.

Fuss, C., Mosher, J. E., & Rashbaum-Selig, M. (1977). The board game. *The School Counselor, 24,* 197–199.

Geddes, M., & Medway, J. (1977). The symbolic drawing of the family life space. *Family Process, 2,* 219–228.

Gladding, S. T. (1975). Twilight. *Personnel and Guidance Journal, 54,* 230.

Gladding, S. T. (1979). The creative use of poetry in the counseling process. *Personnel and Guidance Journal, 57,* 285–287.

Gladding, S. T. (1984). The metaphor as a counseling tool in group work. *Journal for Specialists in Group Work, 9,* 151–156.

Gladding, S. T. (1985). Family poems: A way of modifying family dynamics. *Arts and Psychotherapy, 12,* 239–243.

Gladding, S. T., & Hanna, K. (1982). The use of poetic processes in school counseling. *The School Counselor, 30,* 110–114.

Gladding, S. T., & Hood, W. D. (1974). Five cents, please. *The School Counselor, 21,* 40–43.

Gladding, S. T., & Mazza, N. (1983). Uses of poetry and music in counseling. *Resources in Education,* ED 239 144, CG 017 188.

Gosciewski, F. W. (1975). Photo counseling. *Personnel and Guidance Journal, 53,* 600–604.

Hageman, M. B., & Gladding, S. T. (1983). The art of career exploration: Occupational sex-role stereotyping among elementary school children. *Elementary School Guidance & Counseling, 17,* 280–287.

Harper, B. L. (1985). Say it, review it, enhance it with a song. *Elementary School Guidance & Counseling, 19,* 218–221.

Hynes, A. M., & Hynes-Berry, M. (1986). *Bibliotherapy.* Boulder, CO: Westview Press.

Kolodzey, J. (1983). Poetry: The latest word in healing. *Prevention, 35,* 62–68.

Lathom, W. (1979). An overview of music therapy. In P. B. Hallen (Ed.), *The use of the creative arts in therapy* (pp. 36–38). Washington, D.C.: American Psychiatric Association.

Lerner, A. (Ed.). (1978). *Poetry in the therapeutic experience.* Elmsford, NY: Pergamon Press.

Lerner, A. (1981). Poetry therapy. In R. J. Corsini (Ed.), *Handbook of innovative psychotherapies* (pp. 640–649). New York: Wiley.

Lessner, J. W. (1974). The poem as a catalyst in group work. *Personnel and Guidance Journal, 53,* 33–38.

Luber, R. F. (1973). Poetry helps patients express feelings. *Hospital and Community Psychiatry, 24,* 384.

McKinney, F. (1977). Exploration in bibliotherapy. *Personnel and Guidance Journal, 55,* 550–552.

Martin, M., Martin, D., & Porter, J. (1983). Bibliotherapy: Children of divorce. *The School Counselor, 30,* 312–315.

Matthews, W. J., & Dardeck, K. L. (1985). Construction of metaphor in the counseling process. *AMHCA Journal, 7,* 11–23.

Mazza, N., & Prescott, B. (1981). Poetry: An ancillary technique in couple group work. *American Journal of Family Therapy, 9,* 53–57.

Minuchin, S., & Fishman, H. C. (1981). *Family therapy techniques.* Cambridge, MA: Harvard University Press.

Mitchell, D. W., & Campbell, J. A. (1972). Creative writing and counseling. *Personnel and Guidance Journal, 50,* 690–691.

Naitove, C. (1977). Use of the arts in therapy for creative resolution of problematic behaviors. *Congressional Record, 123,* 188.

Newton, F. B. (1976). How may I understand you? Let me count the ways. *Personnel and Guidance Journal, 54,* 257–260.

O'Brien, C. R., & Johnson, J. L. (1976). Cinema therapy. *The School Counselor, 24,* 39–42.

O'Brien, C. R., Johnson, J., & Miller, B. (1978). Cartooning in counseling. *Personnel and Guidance Journal, 57,* 55–56.

Pittman, F. (1985). Bad little boys and the mysteries of the universe. *Family Therapy Networker, 9,* 69–71.

Pollio, H. R. (1974). *The psychology of symbolic activity.* Reading, MA: Addison-Wesley.

Prinzhorn, H. (1972). *Artistry of the mentally ill.* New York: Springer-Verlag (reissue).

Protinsky, H. (1978). Children's drawings as emotional indicators. *Elementary School Guidance & Counseling, 12,* 249–255.

Roosa, L. W. (1981). The family drawing/storytelling technique: An approach to assessment of family dynamics. *Elementary School Guidance & Counseling, 15,* 269–272.

Rubin, J. A. (1979). Art therapy: An introduction. In P. B. Hallen (Ed.), *The use of the creative arts in therapy* (pp. 12–14). Washington, D.C.: American Psychiatric Association.

Rubin, J. A. (1980). Art in counseling: A new avenue. *Counseling and Human Development, 13,* 1–12.

Rubin, J. A. (1980). *Using bibliotherapy.* Phoenix, AZ: Oryx Press.

Rule, W. (1983). Family therapy and the pie metaphor. *Journal of Marital and Family Therapy, 9,* 101–103.

Schrank, F. A. (1982). Bibliotherapy as an elementary school counseling tool. *Elementary School Guidance & Counseling, 16,* 218–227.

Schrank, F. A., & Engels, D. W. (1981). Bibliotherapy as a counseling adjunct: Research findings. *Personnel and Guidance Journal, 60,* 143–147.

Schudson, K. R. (1975). The simple camera in school counseling. *Personnel and Guidance Journal, 54,* 225–226.

Seligman, L. (1985). The art and science of counseling. *AMHCA Journal, 7,* 2–3.

Sheridan, J. T., Baker, S. B., & deLissovoy, V. (1984). Structured group counseling and explicit bibliotherapy as in-school strategies for preventing problems in youth of changing families. *The School Counselor, 32,* 134–141.

Staley, N. K., & Mangieri, J. N. (1984). Using books to enhance career awareness. *Elementary School Guidance & Counseling, 18,* 200–208.

Sylvia, W. M. (1977). Setting the stage: A counseling playlet. *Elementary School Guidance & Counseling, 12,* 49–54.

Tavantzis, T. N. (1982). Family counseling, family drawings, and the initial interview. *Journal for Specialists in Group Work, 7,* 125–131.

Teeter, R., Teeter, T., & Papai, J. (1976). Frustration—A game. *The School Counselor, 23,* 264–270.

Trotzer, J. P. (1977). *The counselor and the group: Integrating theory, training, and practice.* Monterey, CA: Brooks/Cole.

Urtz, F. P., & Kahn, K. B. (1982). Using drama as an outreach and consultation tool.

*Personnel and Guidance Journal, 60,* 326–328.

Vander Kolk, C. (1976). Popular music in group counseling. *The School Counselor, 23,* 206–210.

Vassiliou, G. (1980). Overcoming barriers to communication in group therapy with total strangers. In L. Wolberg & M. Aronson (Eds.), *Group and family therapy—1980.* New York: Brunner/Mazel.

Wallin, G. J. (1980). Fostering moral development through creative dramatics. *Personnel and Guidance Journal, 58,* 630.

Weeks, J. S. (1978). Roles, goals, and values: The cinematic mirror. *Personnel and Guidance Journal, 49,* 769–774.

White, A. (1985). Meaning and effects of listening to popular music: Implications for counseling. *Journal of Counseling and Development, 64,* 65–69.

Wilson, N. S. (1983). "What can school do for me?": A guidance play. *The School Counselor, 30,* 374–380.

Wolpert, W. (1973). Theater as a guidance technique. *Personnel and Guidance Journal, 52,* 29–33.

Wubbolding, R., & Osborne, L. B. (1974). An awareness game for elementary children. *The School Counselor, 21,* 223–227.

Yager, G. G., & Hector, M. A. (1980). Acting the role of a counselor. *Personnel and Guidance Journal, 59,* 21–25.

Zwerling, I. (1979). The creative art therapies as psychotherapies: An address to the conference. In P. B. Hallen (Ed.), *The use of the creative arts in therapy* (pp. 2–10). Washington, D.C.: American Psychiatric Association.

Photo by James S. Davidson III.

# CHAPTER 19

# *Evaluation and Research in Counseling*

*There you sit Alice Average*
 *midway back in the long-windowed classroom*
 *in the middle of Wednesday's noontime blahs,*
*Adjusting yourself to the sound of a lecture*
 *and the cold of the blue plastic desk that supports you.*
*In a world full of light words, hard rock,*
 *Madonnas, long hair, confusion and change*
*Dreams fade like blue jeans*
 *and "knowing" goes beyond the books*
 *that are bound in semester days*
 *and studied until the start of Summer. . . .* [1]

---

[1]Gladding, 1980/1986, p. 203. Copyright AACD. Reprinted with permission. No further reproduction authorized without written permission of AACD.

*E*valuation and research are an essential part of counseling. It is not enough for counselors to be warm, caring, and empathetic persons trained in the theories, methods, and techniques of counseling. They must also possess the analytical and research skills required to monitor and evaluate their own work and that of others as it appears in the professional literature. Many believe that these processes constitute an ethical obligation (LaFleur, 1983; Ohlsen, 1983; Remer, 1981).

The profession of counseling has had "a long and ambivalent relationship" with evaluation and research (Sprinthall, 1981, p. 465). Many counselors feel that research studies often are poorly related to practical needs (Minor, 1981), and they perceive research and evaluation as cold and impersonal (Krauskopf, 1982). Therefore, they seldom engage in research activities after completing their academic degrees (Gelso, 1979; Stockton & Hulse, 1983; Thoresen, 1969). Counselors' reluctance to spend time and energy in these endeavors is further related to a lack of knowledge about research methods, an absence of clear goals and objectives for the programs in which they work, a lack of awareness of the importance of evaluation in planning effective treatment procedures, limited time, a fear of finding negative results, discouragement from doing research by peers or supervisors, a lack of financial support for research/evaluation projects, and low aptitudes and limited abilities for investigative and quantitative assessment (Burck & Peterson, 1975; Heppner & Anderson, 1985; Oetting, 1976; Remer, 1981; Weinrach, 1975; Wilson, 1985). In addition, some counseling theories, such as existentialism, deemphasize the importance of empirical investigations. Yet, it is generally agreed that effective counselors establish credibility and demonstrate accountability by participating in a wide variety of evaluative approaches (Humes, 1972).

In this chapter, we explore the process of evaluation and research within the counseling environment with the assumption that both kinds of skills can be cultivated.

## IMPORTANCE OF EVALUATION AND RESEARCH

Evaluation and research are important for many reasons. First, counselors need to know what effects programs and strategies are having on clients (Hill, 1975, 1982; Ohlsen, 1983). Personal observation of a client's responses is subjective and not sufficient documentation on which to base progress evaluation (Schmidt, 1974). Counselors, therefore, must be applied researchers. It is unethical and irresponsible for them to spend long periods in activities that are either nonproductive or even potentially harmful. Formally analyzing the results of counseling sessions and programs may not be easy, but such analysis helps counselors learn about themselves and their services (Remer, 1981). Another reason for analysis is that the public holds counselors accountable for what they do (Humes, 1972; Krause & Howard, 1976). As with other helping professionals, counselors are obligated to demonstrate the benefits of their work to consumers.

A further reason for the importance of evaluation and research has to do with the funding of programs (Anton, 1978; Gelso, 1979; Humes, 1972; Ohlsen, 1983). Counseling programs that demonstrate effectiveness are likely to receive financial support. According to Ohlsen (1983), "quality services, careful evaluation, and good communication of evaluation" (p. 357) are the three main components of a solid counseling program. If evaluation is not conducted or the positive results not disseminated, a counseling program will most likely suffer. Thus, besides being crucial for ethical reasons and planning purposes, evaluation and research activities are necessary for economic survival.

### A Comparison of Definitions

Evaluation and research are different and yet they have much in common. Wheeler and Loesch (1981) note that the two terms have often been paired conceptually and are frequently used interchangeably. Krauskopf (1982) asserts that there is "essentially no difference between the two. The same empirical attitude is there, and the same tools are needed" (p. 71). However, Burck and Peterson (1975) make a distinction between these concepts that is widely accepted.

*Evaluation* "is more mission-oriented, may be less subject to control, is more concerned with providing information for decision makers, tends to be less rigorous or sophisticated, and is concerned primarily with explaining events and their relationship to established goals and objectives" (Burck & Peterson, 1975, p. 564). *Research,* on the other hand, is "more theory-oriented and discipline-bound, exerts greater control over the activity, produces more results that may not be immediately applicable, is more sophisticated in terms of complexity and exactness of design, involves the use of judgment on the part of the researcher, and is more concerned with explaining and predicting phenomena" (p. 564). In the following sections, a fuller explanation is given of how these terms are commonly used in the practical world of professional counseling.

## EVALUATION

Usually, evaluation procedures involve gathering meaningful information on various aspects of a counseling program for the purpose of guiding decisions concerning the allocation of resources and assuring maximum effectiveness of the program (Burck & Peterson, 1975; Oetting, 1976; Wheeler & Loesch, 1981). There is a quality of immediate utility in evaluation. It gives counselors and administrators direct feedback on the services they are providing and insight into what new services they need to offer. It also enables clients to have a systematic and positive input into the program. Some type of evaluation should be made for every counseling program within an agency or school (Oetting, 1976; Weinrach, 1975).

### Incorrect Evaluation Methods

There are many models of evaluation from which to choose, but before elaborating on them, there is much to be learned from basically incorrect procedures often used by uninformed counselors (Daniels, Mines, & Gressard, 1981). Burck and Peterson (1975) give some examples of such procedures. They point out that among the ill-conceived methods that produce invalid and unreliable results are those that:

☐ Restrict the sampling of opinion by asking too few clients about a program.

☐ Make comparisons between nonequivalent groups.

☐ Promote services through the media rather than evaluate what is being done.

☐ Assemble a congenial group of people and have them write a committee report.

☐ Try to assess a program without any clear goals—a kind of "shot in the dark" approach.

### Steps in Evaluation

Several researchers recommend that general program evaluation be systematic and follow a sequential step-by-step process (Burck & Peterson, 1975; Oetting, 1976; Rimmer & Burt, 1980). The steps they propose differ, but all generally agree on the following procedure that Burck and Peterson have laid out.

The first step involves a *needs assessment*. If counselors are to be accountable, they must first identify problems within their programs. A *need* is "a condition among members of a specific group (students, teachers, parents, etc.) that reflects an actual lack of something or an awareness (perception) that something is lacking" (Collison, 1982, p. 115). Needs are assumed to exist based on a number of factors, such as institutional or personal philosophy, government mandate, available resources, history/tradition, and expert opinion.

The second step is "stating goals and performance objectives." Here, both terminal program outcomes (i.e., those that are most immediately recognizable) and ultimate program outcomes (i.e., those that are most enduring) are described in terms of measurable performance objectives. There are normally "several performance objectives for each goal statement" (Burck & Peterson, 1975, p. 567).

The third step is "designing the program." When programs are developed to meet stated objectives, activities that focus on the goals can be precisely designed. The fourth step in the sequence is "revising and improving the program." Both specific activities and the adequacy of communication patterns are evaluated at this point. The fifth and final step is "noting and reporting program outcome." This task is performed primarily by counselors and administrators who disseminate the findings of the program evaluation to the general public. This type of consumer information is vital for potential clients if they are to make informed decisions. Counselors within a program need this kind of feedback in order to improve their skills and services.

Oetting (1976) and Rimmer and Burt (1980) stress that evaluators must get others involved in the evaluation process in order for the results of a study to have any direct impact on a program. If other individuals invest in conducting a needs assessment, for example, they are more likely to help counselors in meeting identified needs and establishing program goals.

### Selecting an Evaluation Model

Because evaluation is continuous, counselors must prepare accordingly (Wheeler & Loesch, 1981). Part of this preparation includes setting aside time to conduct evaluation studies. Equally important is educating themselves and others about the different models of evaluation available. Frey, Raming, and Frey (1978) advocate a qualitative approach to evaluating counseling practices and programs. Their model emphasizes "a thick description" of the phenomena being studied. They compare the counselor to a "connoisseur" who looks at entire episodes experientially as well as from a data base, thus incorporating both subjective and objective approaches.

A more exclusively quantitative approach is provided by House (1978), who has compiled a list of evaluation models and the critical dimensions of each (Table 19.1). The models are: systems analysis, behavioral objectives, decision making, goal free, art criticism, accreditation, adversary, and transaction. Daniels, Mines, and Gressard (1981) have studied the dimensions along which these major models are judged and have offered some very practical ways of comparing them to determine which is most appropriate for a specific situation. They note that both internal and external restrictions "define the limits to which each model may be effectively applied" (p. 580), and they provide a framework to further help counselors judge which model to employ in specific situations (Figure 19.1).

Since questions raised prior to an evaluation procedure are more likely to be answered satisfactorily than those brought up after the evaluation is complete, evaluators must ask themselves at the outset what it is they wish to evaluate and how they are going to do it (Davidson, 1986). Two models that incorporate these concerns are the planning, programming, budgeting systems (PPBS) and the context-input-process-product (CIPP) models (Humes, 1972; Stufflebeam, Foley, Gephart, Guba, Hammond, Merriman, & Provus, 1971).

In the PPBS model, there is an emphasis on planning programs with specifically stated goals, objectives, and evaluation criteria. The situation, population, and treatment involved are all major concerns in this process. Humes (1972) emphasizes that information derived from a PPBS system is *criterion-referenced* (related directly to the dimension being measured) rather than *normative-*

**TABLE 19.1** Major evaluation models compared.

| Classes of Models | Major Audiences | Outcome | Consensual Assumption(s) | Methodology | Typical Questions |
|---|---|---|---|---|---|
| Systems analysis | Economists, managers | Program efficiency | Goals, known cause and effects, quantified variables | PPBS, cost benefit analysis | Are the expected effects achieved? What are the most efficient programs? |
| Behavioral objectives | Managers, psychologists | Productivity, accountability | Prespecified objectives, quantified variables | Behavioral objectives, achievement tests | Are the students achieving the objectives? Is the teacher producing? |
| Decision-making | Administrators | Effectiveness, quality control | General goals, evaluation criteria | Surveys, questionnaires, interviews, natural variation | Is the program effective? What parts are effective? |
| Goal free | Consumers | Consumer choices, social utility | Consequences, evaluation criteria | Bias control, logical analysis | What are *all* of the effects of the program? |
| Art criticism | Connoisseurs, consumers | Improved standards | Critics, standards of criticism | Critical review | Would a critic approve this program? |
| Accreditation | Professional peers, public | Professional acceptance | Panel of peers, procedures & criteria for evaluation | Review by panel, self-study | How would professionals rate this program? |
| Adversary | Jury, public | Resolution | Procedures, judges | Quasi-legal procedures | What are the arguments for and against the program? |
| Transaction | Client practitioners | Understanding | Negotiations, activities | Case studies, interviews, observations | What does the program look like to different people? |

*Source:* From "A meta-model for evaluating counseling programs" by M. H. Daniels. R. Mines. and C. Gressard. 1981. *Personnel and Guidance Journal, 59,* p. 579. Copyright AACD. Reprinted with permission. No further reproduction authorized without further permission of AACD.

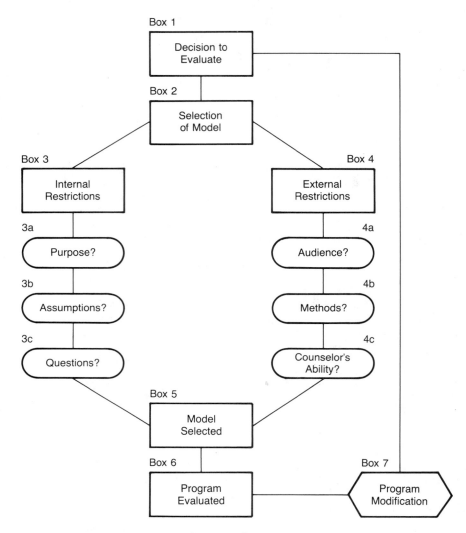

**FIGURE 19.1**  An evaluation framework.

*Source:* From "A meta-model for evaluating counseling programs" by M. H. Daniels, R. Mines, and C. Gressard, 1981, *Personnel and Guidance Journal, 59*, p. 581. Copyright AACD. Reprinted with permission. No further reproduction authorized without further permission of AACD.

*referenced* (related to other members of a group, as is the case when standardized tests are used). Therefore, if proper planning and programming are carried out, the counselor will be able to demonstrate that effective counseling is an important variable in a client's progress. Also, when budget decisions are being made, the impact of counseling and its cost efficiency can be clearly shown and program strengths and weaknesses can be documented. Those in charge of counseling services are in a better position at such times to justify requests for funds for developing and delivering services not being provided. This aspect of program analysis is vital.

In the CIPP model, there are four types of evaluation. In the first, *context evaluation,* a comparison is made between what the program set out to do and what it actually accomplished. In the second, *input evaluation,* information is gathered on what resources are needed and which are available to meet program objectives. This part of the evaluation can be used to demonstrate cost effectiveness as well as to point out the need for additional resources. The third type of evaluation in this model involves process and basically focuses on the strengths and weaknesses of the program's design. If there are weaknesses in the design, such as those involving communication, corrective measures may be taken. The fourth type of evaluation focuses on the final outcome of the entire program. Evaluators ask at this time how effective the program really was. Plans can be made to continue, reuse, expand, or eliminate the program. Most evaluation processes will involve the use of research design and statistics.

## *RESEARCH*

There are many definitions of research, but Barkley (1982) gives one of the best: "Research is the systematic collection, organization, and interpretation of observations in order to answer questions as unambiguously as possible" (p. 329). The challenge of research is to answer questions that do not yield truths easily. The quality of research depends on the degree to which one can overcome resistances and devise ways to answer questions with a maximum of confidence by minimizing contaminating influences. In addition to the usual difficulties associated with all types of research, counseling research has some problems peculiar to it. According to Gelso (1979), it is in a state of "chaos." There is no one unified and agreed-upon way to conduct and report counseling research (Forsyth & Strong, 1986). Rather, many differing views exist on how counseling should be conceptualized and studied. The lack of a shared set of fundamental beliefs and goals makes counselor researchers vulnerable to periodic influences about where their efforts should be focused (Frey, 1978) and makes it extremely difficult to establish universally accepted investigative practices.

### Reasons for Research

Despite the many barriers to conducting research in counseling, there are three main reasons for continuing the effort. The first relates to the counselor's decision-making process. Counseling is a decision-making profession, and research provides counselors with factual information on which to make decisions. Those who lack solid research knowledge will have only inadequate and unreliable information based on trial-and-error methods, biases, prior experience, or authority figures (LeFleur, 1983; Pietrofesa, Hoffman, & Splete, 1984). Such information may work on occasions, but in the long run it is ineffective, harmful, or both. Thus, counselors must know how to conduct research and draw inferences from the results of well-designed research in order to be most effective. Studies that answer the questions of practitioners are especially important, but research is also vital to clients.

Some research methods, especially those that are behaviorally based, may be used by clients outside of counseling sessions to help them monitor, understand, and manage their situations more effectively (Goldman, 1978; Thoresen, 1978). For example, it has been demonstrated that the process of observing behavior is a factor in changing it. Clients can be taught what to look for and when to look for it and thus improve the quality of their lives and extend the benefits of counseling beyond formal sessions.

Finally, research is important for the continuation of the profession of counseling itself (Lewis & Hutson, 1983). Federal agencies, insurance health providers, and consumer advocacy groups have all shown increased interest in the efficacy of counseling since the late 1970s. Counselors are now called upon to prove the cost effectiveness of their skills. Research on intervention approaches as well as preventive approaches have shown that positive differences are made in the lives of those the approaches are intended to help. Such demonstrations of usefulness must continue if counseling is to survive and grow as a profession (Heppner & Anderson, 1985; Wilson & Yager, 1981).

### Steps in the Research Process

Good research is scientific in the broadest definition of that word. It begins with systematic observations that concentrate on a particular population, variable, or question (Marken, 1981). Such complete and systematic observation is aimed at an explanation of relations among variables and why certain events happen. Explanation leads to understanding and finally some degree of prediction and control of events. There are some guidelines for conducting such investigations. Campbell and Katona (1953), for instance, have developed a flow chart to indicate the sequence of steps involved in carrying out survey research. Ary, Jacobs, and Razavich (1979) have devised this eight-step process ideally suited for clinical work but applicable to other areas of counseling research:

1. *Statement of the problem*   The researcher must be sure the statement is clear and concise. If there is confusion at this step, the investigative endeavor will probably produce little of value. An example of a clear problem statement is: "The purpose of this research is to test the hypothesis that eye contact between counselor and client is related to the effectiveness of the counseling process."

2. *Identification of information needed to solve the problem*   This step may include a variety of information derived from such sources as psychological or educational tests or from systematic observations, including experiments. Some data that investigators need may be impossible to collect. They must then decide whether to modify the question or end the research.

3. *Selection or development of measures for gathering data* Common measures for gathering data are surveys, tests, and observational report sheets. If researchers cannot find an existing appropriate measure, they must develop one and test its reliability and validity.

4. *Identification of the target population and sampling procedures*   If a group is small enough, an entire population may be studied. Otherwise, a sample is selected by careful standard sampling procedures.

5. *Design of the procedure for data collection*   This part of research basically involves determining how, when, where, and by whom information will be collected.

6. *Collection of data*   A systematic procedure is implemented to obtain the desired information. Usually this process involves careful monitoring and a substantial investment of time.

7. *Analysis of data*   Select procedures are employed at this step to organize the data in a meaningful fashion and determine whether the data provide an answer to the problem being investigated.

8. *Preparation of a report*   Research results should be made available to others in some meaningful form, such as a journal article or a professional presentation.

### The Relevance of Research

One of the primary questions raised by readers of counseling research focuses on the relevance of a study's results for practitioners. Goldman (1976, 1977, 1978, 1979, 1986) asserts that much of the research in counseling does not produce results relevant to practical issues and is therefore not very useful. Many research efforts lack a broad vision and instead concentrate on small details. Goldman thinks that researchers have too readily accepted the experimental research designs of the physical and biological sciences and in the process have failed to develop research methods appropriate for counseling. Thus, what passes as research in the field, and is published in the journals, is often sterile and trivial.

The argument for relevancy centers on the fact that not all knowledge is equally useful for counselors (Krumboltz & Mitchell, 1979). Therefore, limited funds and energy should be directed toward studies that are likely to make a difference in the way counselors function. One way to define relevance in research is to emphasize studies that focus on the reasons individuals seek counseling, such as their goals, intentions, and purposes (Howard, 1985). Another very important way to assess the relevance of research is to determine "how closely the research approximates what is done in the counseling office" (Gelso, 1985, p. 552). "Experience-near" research of this type is much more applicable to counselors and much more likely to be read and used. But such research is likely to be less controlled and not as easily generalized as more rigorous research. To help solve the problem of relevancy in research, Gelso (1985) suggests reading all research studies with certain questions in mind, such as "How will this research influence the way I practice counseling?"

### Choosing a Research Method

Despite the chaos, controversy, and problems in counseling research, there are a number of investigative methodologies that counselors regularly employ. Kaplan (1964) defines a *method* as a procedure that is applicable to many disciplines. In contrast, a *technique* is a discipline-specific procedure. Most counseling research uses procedures, such as controlled observations, that are common to other disciplines. Therefore, the term *method*, rather than *technique*, is appropriate when referring to ways of doing counseling research. None of these methods is considered "best to test the counseling process" (Hill, 1982, p. 16), although they do provide answers to research questions and do make possible the control of variables (Kerlinger, 1973).

All research methods have what Gelso (1979) describes as "bubbles," or flaws. Gelso says that selecting research methods is like putting a sticker on a car windshield. Bubbles always appear, and though one may try to eliminate as many bubbles as possible, some remain. The only way to eliminate the bubbles totally is to remove the sticker. In research, the only way to avoid all flaws is not to do research. Thus, as imperfect as research methods are, they are necessary for professional edification and development. The alternative is to remain uninformed about the effects of counseling and to forgo the development of newer methods and techniques.

### *Emphases of Research*

There are many different counseling research emphases. Four of the most prominent can be represented as contrasts (Baruth & Huber, 1985; Gelso, 1979; Hill, 1982; Neimeyer & Resnikoff, 1982):

☐ Laboratory versus field research.
☐ Basic versus applied research.
☐ Process versus outcome research.
☐ Quantitative (group) versus qualitative (individual) research.

Each of these emphases is concerned with the contrast between two investigative dimensions. The various dimensions are not mutually exclusive, and many research studies will include more than one of them, such as studies that quantitatively report the outcome of counseling techniques in a laboratory setting.

The first emphasis is on laboratory research versus field research. Laboratory research concentrates on conducting the investigation within a situation, such as a counseling lab, where as many extraneous variables as possible may be controlled (e.g., Dobson & Campbell, 1986). It is in such conditions that some researchers think they can obtain the most reliable information. Practitioners of field research, on the other hand, see laboratory investigations as artificial and believe that counseling theories and techniques are best observed and recorded in actual counseling situations, such as counseling centers and clinics. They argue that these settings are realistic and that the results are more likely to be applicable by other practitioners.

The second emphasis is basic research versus applied research. Basic research is oriented to theory, and those who practice it are "interested in investigating some puzzle or problem that is suggested by theory" (Forsyth & Strong, 1986, p. 113). An example is the work by Wilder Penfield in probing select parts of the brain to verify Eric Berne's theory of distinct ego states within the person. In contrast, applied researchers focus on examining practical problems and applying their findings to existing problems. An example of applied research is that by Jesness (1975), which compared the effectiveness of transactional analysis and behavior modification in counseling delinquents.

The third emphasis is process research versus outcome research. Hill (1982) observes that process research, which assesses the ongoing change occurring in counseling, "can be quite overwhelming and frustrating" (p. 7). It demands a concentrated amount of time and energy focused on a few variables, such as the reactions of the counselor to the client. The burnout rate among process-oriented researchers is high. Yet, such research is indispensable in enlightening counselors about dynamics within the counseling relationship itself. An example of process research is the work of Allen Ivey (1980) in assessing the importance of counselor skills in select stages of counseling. Outcome research, on the other hand, is "typified by measurement before and after treatment on specified dependent variables" (Hill, 1982, p. 7). An example of outcome research would be the effect of person-centered counseling with depressed persons. The emphasis of outcome research is on results rather than on the factors producing them.

The fourth emphasis is quantitative research versus qualitative research. Neimeyer and Resnikoff (1982) describe a quantitative approach as "deductive and objective, usually subordinating subjective understanding to clarity, precision, and reproducibility of objective phenomena," whereas a qualitative approach is "inductive and phenomenological, placing primary emphasis on understanding the unique frameworks within which persons make sense of their feelings, thoughts, and behaviors" (p. 84). The major strength of quantitative research is its emphasis on analyzing large amounts of data in a clear, mathematical fashion. The major strength of qualitative research is in picking up on subtle, individually focused, and experientially reported aspects of counseling.

Counseling is moving in the direction of espousing research that is more qualitative (versus quantitative), and more field oriented (versus laboratory). Clients are seen as active, as opposed to passive, in the counseling process (Gelso, 1985; Howard, 1985). Overall, a more holistic emphasis within counseling research emphases and methods is being proposed (Froehle, 1985).

## MAJOR RESEARCH METHODS

The research methods chosen by counselors are determined by the question(s) they are trying to answer, their special interests, and the amount of time and resources they have available for the study. Smith (1981) points out that methods should be the slaves not the masters of research. No method is suitable for all research attempts. Ohlsen (1983) says that "developing and clarifying a research question is a slow, painstaking process" (p. 361). A research question provides the context in which one begins to consider a research method. There are so many quantitative and qualitative research methods and designs available that deciding on one can take considerable time.

Research methods and ways of obtaining data may differ for research into individual, group, and family counseling. Yet the primary methods can be broadly classified as historical, descriptive, and experimental (Galfo & Miller, 1970). The procedures used in these methods are not mutually exclusive. For example, Tracey (1983) reports that *N* of 1 research, which focuses on the study of a single entity (e.g., a person) and has become increasingly popular in counseling since the 1970s, may be employed in historical studies, case studies, and intensive design studies. It may also be either associational or experimental in nature. That this and other research methods are so flexible gives investigators more latitude in planning and carrying out studies.

### Historical Methods

Historical research has been largely neglected in counseling (Goldman, 1977). The reasons are numerous, but among the most salient are the association of historical research with psychohistory (Frey, 1978). Psychohistory has been closely linked to the theory of psychoanalysis, and its usefulness as a way of understanding persons and events has been questioned (Thoresen, 1978). Yet, as Frey (1978) reports, psychohistory, as practiced by Erik Erikson (1958) and the "Wellfleet group," including Kenneth Keniston and Robert Coles, involves not only the experiencing and reporting of events and procedures from earlier times that have influenced the development of the counseling profession but also the embellishment of current theories and the generation of new research hypotheses.

The closest most counseling journals come to dealing with historical research is the reporting of obituaries of prominent counselors and the featuring of interview articles with pioneers in the profession. Although the methods used in historical research are usually less rigorous and more qualitative than those employed in other research, they produce both interesting and enlightening results. They also have an important place in the understanding of persons as exemplified in the idiographic studies of traits and personality by Gordon Allport. This approach to research is clearly open for further development.

### Descriptive Methods

Descriptive research concentrates on depicting present factors in a profession. There are three subcategories into which these studies fit: surveys, case studies, and comparative studies.

***Surveys.*** Surveys are one of the most popular and widely used methods for gathering information. They are similar to other methods of research in that they begin with the formation of a research question, which is followed by the generation of hypotheses, the selection of a research design, and the collection and analysis of data (Kerlinger, 1973). Survey data can be collected in any one of four ways: through personal interviews, mailed questionnaires, telephone interviews, and nonreactive measures, such as existing records or archives (Hackett, 1981; Marken, 1981; Moser & Kalton, 1972). Survey data are gathered in either a structured or a nonstructured way and with either a cross-section of people at one point in time or longitudinally with the same people at two or more points in time (Hackett, 1981).

If conducted properly, survey research can provide counselors with a great deal of information about how they and their programs are perceived by clients and about their clients' needs. Four major problems often plague survey research, however. First, survey instruments may be poorly constructed. Second, they may not generate a very high rate of return. Third, the sample surveyed is sometimes nonrandom and unrepresentative of the population (Hackett, 1981; Marken, 1981). Finally, such research can be expensive. The impact on society of well-conceived and well-conducted survey research is seen in the work of Kinsey on the sexual practices of men and women. An example of the usefulness of the method for counseling is the Hollis and Wantz (1986) survey that is employed to gather information for the publication of their directory of counselor education programs every few years. This survey is quantitative in emphasis and yields relevant data about program trends in counseling on a national level.

***Case Studies.*** A *case study* is an attempt to understand one unit, such as a person, group, or program, through an intense and systematic investigation of that unit longitudinally. Some case studies rely on self-report methods that are not very reliable, while others involve the use of *naturalistic inquiry,* in which the study extends over a period of time (Smith, 1981). The difficulties involved in naturalistic research are many and include such issues as what constitutes good research, the high cost in labor, the problems of establishing causality, and restrictions on generalizing results. In addition to these, the ever-present problem of observer bias and the *halo effect* (i.e., a favorable observation generalized to a person or situation as a whole) can be especially troublesome (Goldman, 1977). To help minimize such problems, Anton, (1978) and Huber (1980) describe several intensive experimental designs suitable for case studies. Counselors with limited time and resources may find them useful in tracing changes over time. We will discuss these designs in the current chapter section on experimental methods.

***Comparative Studies.*** Comparative research studies (also called correlational studies) form a link between historical/case study methods and experimental and quasi-experimental designs. They make directional and quantitative comparisons between sets of data. Such studies are nonmanipulative in nature (Cozby, 1981) and simply note similarities in variations among factors with no effort to discern cause-and-effect relationships. An example of such a study is the relationship of scores on a test of religiosity with scores on instruments measuring various aspects of mental health (Gladding, Lewis, & Adkins, 1981). A major finding of this study was that those people who scored high on the test of religiosity also scored high on the mental health instruments. The results do not suggest that religiosity causes a person to have better mental health; rather, the study simply compares the direction of the scores. Any study that compares measures in this manner is an example of comparative research.

### Experimental Methods

Experimental research methods are those employed to describe, compare, and analyze data under controlled conditions (Galfo & Miller, 1970; Marken, 1981). Experimental methods used in counseling research have their origin in the natural sciences. The purpose of using these methods is to determine the effect of one variable on another by controlling for other factors that might explain the effect. In other words, researchers who use this method are seeking to determine causation. In order to do this, independent and dependent variables are defined. The *independent variable* is the one manipulated by the researcher. The *dependent variable* is the one in which the potential effect is recorded. It is assumed that if the effect of other factors is eliminated then any change in the dependent variable will be a result of the independent variable. Examples of independent variables in counseling might be the age, sex, personal attractiveness, or physical appearance of the counselor. Examples of dependent variables are client's reactions to these counselor traits, such as degree of relaxation, cooperation, and overall responsiveness in the counseling setting. The reactions could be measured by a variety of procedures, including an analysis of an audio/video tape or a post-counseling interview or questionnaire.

The most common way of controlling for potentially contaminating variables is through the establishment of equivalent experimental and control groups. When the independent variable is manipulated for the experimental group while being held constant for the control group, the effect of the independent variable can be determined by comparing the post-experimental data for the two groups. Campbell and Stanley (1963) describe in detail the problems involved in experimental and quasi-experimental research. Their work is recommended for those who wish to pursue the issue further.

Traditional experimental research has involved group comparison studies. However, since the 1970s, single-subject research, commonly known as *N* of 1 research, has become increasingly popular as a way to conduct experimental research in counseling. Miller (1985, p. 491) summarizes six major advantages, derived from Hill, Carter, and O'Farrell (1983) and Sue (1978), that single-subject research has over traditional group studies:

1. It allows more adequate description of what happens between a counselor and client.
2. Positive and negative outcomes can be understood in terms of process data.
3. Outcome measures can be tailored to the specific problems of the client.
4. It allows one to study a rare or unusual phenomenon.
5. It is flexible enough to allow for novel procedures in diagnosis and treatment.
6. It can be used in evaluating the effectiveness of an intervention strategy on a single client.

Anton (1978) and Huber (1980) describe three intense experimental designs that focus on individuals.

☐ *Simple Time Series* This, the most common of these methods, is referred to as an *AB* design. First, a baseline (*A*) is established by having the client observe and record the occurence of the targeted behavior every day. Then, an intervention strategy (*B*) is introduced. The client continues to record the targeted behavior in the same way as before. The manifestation of the targeted behavior is compared during these two periods and trends are noted. From comparing graphed results during these times, counselors can determine what, if any, effect the intervention strategy had.

☐ *Reversal Design* This method is more complex and involves a reversal, an *ABAB* design. The first part of the design is executed as in the simple time series, but the intervention strategy (*B*) is discontinued after a time and a second baseline and intervention follow. "If the second intervention period produces proportionately the same results as the first intervention period, then it can be safely assumed that it is the strategy itself that is causing the changes in the level of interactions made" (Huber, 1980, p. 212).

☐ *Multiple Baseline Design* This is the most complex of these designs, and it permits a greater generalization of the results. There are three types of multiple baseline research designs: across individuals, across situations, and across behaviors (Schmidt, 1974). Each emphasizes a different focus. The common trait of all three is that intervention is employed with a select individual, situation, or behavior initially, while the researcher continues to gather baseline data on other persons, situations, or behaviors. When intervention strategies are extended to the baseline populations, counselors are able to see more clearly the power of the intervention. As with other designs, it is important to graph the results.

Overall, there are five steps involved in intensive experimental designs on individuals. They are: (1) identify an observable problem that can be monitored for change, (2) gather baseline data, (3) decide on the intervention to be studied, (4) carry out the intervention strategy within one of the three research designs, and (5) evaluate the changes, if any, in the targeted behavior.

## STATISTICS

In concluding this chapter on evaluation and research, it is important to mention the use of statistics in these processes. Statistics are not a fixed part of evaluation and research. Instead, they are tools for researchers to use in analyzing and interpreting findings and in communicating findings to others (Wilson & Yager, 1981). As Barkley (1982) emphasizes: "It is possible to be a good researcher and know nothing about sophisticated statistical techniques. It is also possible to know a great deal about statistics and be a mediocre or poor researcher" (p. 327). The distinction between the two is important.

### Statistical Concepts

There are some statistical concepts that every counselor must know in order to read and evaluate research reports intelligently. A few of them will be listed here. One is the concept of *central tendency,* that is, the median, the mean, and the mode. All of these measures encompass different meanings of the term "average" (Galfo & Miller, 1970). The *median* is the midpoint of a distribution of scores ranked highest to lowest. The *mean* is the arithmetic average of scores. The *mode* is the score or measure that occurs most often in a distribution. In a true normally distributed population the median, mean, and mode are the same; this rarely occurs.

Two other statistical concepts counselors need to be aware of are standard deviation and sampling procedure. A *standard deviation* is "a measure of the dispersion of scores about their mean" (Marken, 1981, p. 42). It is important because it indicates how much response variability there is in a set of scores; that is, it is a measure of how homogeneous a group is. *Sampling* is important because it determines how applicable research findings are. When a sample does not adequately represent the population on which it is based the results cannot be considered applicable to the population. When samples are chosen in a representative random way, however, results can be generalized to the population with confidence.

### Statistical Methods

Descriptive and inferential statistics are the two most widely used statistical methods in research. *Descriptive statistics* are simply devices used to organize, summarize, and describe data. They are most appropriately used in analyzing single-subject research (Miller, 1985). They are also used in simply describing populations. The mean and standard deviation are examples of descriptive statistics. In contrast, *inferential statistics* are methods used to make predictions about an entire population from a sample. They determine whether research results are due to chance or to the treatment of variables in a study (Cozby, 1981; Marken, 1981). A number of statistical tests have been devised to measure the probability of change occurring by chance in an experimental research design.

In addition to being used to describe and make inferences about the data collected in one study, statistics can be used to compare research findings across studies. One of the most prominent ways this procedure is done is through an empirically based method known as meta-analysis (Glass, 1976; Willson, 1981). Before the conceptualization of meta-analysis, researchers were forced to compare studies through a narrative method that was often filled with errors. Now with meta-analysis, large amounts of data can be compared and contrasted (Baker, Swisher, Nadenichek, & Popowicz, 1984). Statistics are invaluable to the counselor in understanding, organizing, communicating, and evaluating data (Remer, 1981).

## SUMMARY

This chapter has focused on the relationship between evaluation and research. Although the two are sometimes identical, many times they are not. Evaluation is aimed mainly at helping counselors as decision makers to determine how programs are meeting the goals and objectives of staffs and clients. A major first step in conducting an evaluation is to do a needs assessment. The process is continuous, but there are several excellent models counselors can use in completing this task.

Research scares many counselors (Remer, 1981; Stockton & Hulse, 1983). Yet, the fear of research may be diminished as counselors become more aware that there are many ways to conduct investigative studies. Three of the main research methods are historical, descriptive, and experimental. For years, experimental research has been valued most highly, but now this emphasis is changing. Case studies and intensive experimental designs are gaining in popularity. In addition, the difference between understanding research methods and statistics is growing. Both are important, but it is possible for researchers to be stronger in one than the other. Overall, counselors must continuously strive to update skills in these areas and stay current. The life span of knowledge is brief, and counselors who do not exercise their minds and find areas of needed change will become a statistic instead of an influence.

## CLASSROOM ACTIVITIES

1. In dyads, visit a mental health agency or school and find out what procedures are used to evaluate services and personnel. Read the institution's annual reports and assess how uniformly an evaluative method is employed in describing the institution's activities. Report your field study findings back to the class. Discuss what recommendations you would make to the agency or school visited.

2. As a class, gather examples of needs assessments from community schools and agencies. Evaluate the instruments according to the step-by-step procedure outlined in this chapter. What are the strengths and weaknesses of these assessments? What improvements would you make if you were to be put in charge of the procedure? Have select members of the class role play the steps they would take at select sites in conducting a needs assessment.

3. As a class, choose two 3-person teams to debate the pros and cons of this statement: "Counseling research must be relevant." What definition of *relevant* does each side advocate? How does an interpretation of the term influence the type of research recommended? After the debate, discuss as a class the merits of doing basic and applied research.

4. From the three major types of research described in this chapter (historical, descriptive, and experimental), decide which one you would be most comfortable in conducting. Divide the class according to these research interests and discuss with your fellow classmates the reasons behind your choice. Report back to the class your combined rationale for choosing a particular research approach.

5. What are your feelings about statistics? In triads, discuss how feelings can either promote or interfere with the learning of statistical procedures. Practice taking a thinking approach to the learning of statistics. Does thinking, instead of feeling, about statistics affect your attitude and approach to learning these procedures? Discuss your impressions with the class. As a class, do you think there are any counseling approaches that would be useful in helping a person overcome anxiety related to the learning of statistics? Which ones?

## REFERENCES

Anton, J. L. (1978). Intensive experimental designs: A model for the counselor/researcher. *Personnel and Guidance Journal, 56*, 273–278.

Ary, D., Jacobs, L. C., & Razavich, A. (1979). *Introduction to research in education* (2nd ed.). New York: Holt, Rinehart & Winston.

Baker, S. B., Swisher, J. D., Nadenichek, P. E., & Popowicz, C. L. (1984). Measured effects of primary prevention strategies. *Personnel and Guidance Journal, 62*, 459–464.

Barkley, W. M. (1982). Introducing research to graduate students in the helping professions. *Counselor Education and Supervision, 21*, 327–331.

Burck, H. D., & Petersen, G. W. (1975). Needed: More evaluation, not research. *Personnel and Guidance Journal, 53*, 563–569.

Campbell, A., & Katona, G. (1953). The sample survey: A technique for social science research. In L. Festinger & D. Katz (Eds.), *Research methods in the behavioral sciences.* New York: Dryden Press.

Campbell, D. T., & Stanley, J. C. (1963). *Experimental and quasi-experimental designs for research.* Chicago: Rand McNally.

Collison, B. B. (1982). Needs assessment for guidance program planning: A procedure. *The School Counselor, 30,* 115–121.

Cozby, P. C. (1981). *Methods in behavioral research* (2nd ed.). Palo Alto, CA: Mayfield.

Daniels, M. H., Mines, R., & Gressard, C. (1981). A meta-model for evaluating counseling programs. *Personnel and Guidance Journal, 59,* 578–582.

Davidson, J. P., III. (1986, March). Developing an effective evaluation plan. Paper presented at the Jefferson County (Alabama) Model School Program. Birmingham, AL.

Dobson, J. E., & Campbell, N. J. (1986). Laboratory outcomes of personal growth groups. *Journal for Specialists in Group Work, 11,* 9–15.

Erikson, E. H. (1958). *Young man Luther.* New York: Norton.

Forsyth, D. R., & Strong, S. R. (1986). The scientific study of counseling and psychotherapy. *American Psychologist, 41,* 113–119.

Frey, D. H. (1978). Science and the single case in counseling research. *Personnel and Guidance Journal, 56,* 263–268.

Frey, D. H., Raming, H. E., & Frey, F. M. (1978). The qualitative description, interpretation, and evaluation of counseling. *Personnel and Guidance Journal, 56,* 621–625.

Froehle, T. C. (1985). Guest editorial. *Counselor Education and Supervision, 24,* 323–324.

Galfo, A. J., & Miller, E. (1970). *Interpreting educational research* (2nd ed.). Dubuque, IA: Brown.

Gelso, C. J. (1979). Research in counseling: Methodological and professional issues. *The Counseling Psychologist, 8,* 7–36.

Gelso, C. J. (1985). Rigor, relevance, and counseling research: On the need to maintain our course between Scylla and Charybodis. *Journal of Counseling and Development, 63,* 551–553.

Gladding, S. T. (1980/1986). Thoughts on Alice Average midway through the mid-day class on Wednesday. *Humanist Educator, 18,* 203–204.

Gladding, S. T., Lewis, E. L., & Adkins, L. (1981). Religious beliefs and positive mental health: The GLA scale and counseling. *Counseling and Values, 25,* 206–215.

Glass, G. V. (1976). Primary, secondary, and meta-analyses of research. *Educational Researcher, 5,* 3–8.

Goldman, L. G. (1976). A revolution in counseling research. *Journal of Counseling Psychology, 23,* 543–552.

Goldman, L. G. (1977). Toward more meaningful research. *Personnel and Guidance Journal, 55,* 363–368.

Goldman, L. G. (1978). Science, research, and practice: Confusing the issues. *Personnel and Guidance Journal, 56,* 641–642.

Goldman, L. G. (1979). Research is more than technology. *The Counseling Psychologist, 8,* 41–44.

Goldman, L. G. (1986). Research and evaluation. In M. E. Lewis, R. L. Hayes, & J. A. Lewis (Eds.), *The counseling profession* (pp. 278–300). Itasca, IL: Peacock.

Hackett, G. (1981). Survey research methods. *Personnel and Guidance Journal, 59,* 599–604.

Heppner, P. P., & Anderson, W. P. (1985). On the perceived non-utility of research in counseling. *Journal of Counseling and Development, 63,* 545–547.

Hill, C. A. (1975). A process approach for establishing counseling goals and outcomes. *Personnel and Guidance Journal, 53,* 571–573.

Hill, C. A. (1982). Counseling process research: Philosophical and methodological dilemmas. *The Counseling Psychologist, 10* 7–19.

Hill, C. E., Carter, J. A., & O'Farrell, M. K. (1983). A case study of the process and outcomes of time-limited counseling. *Journal of Counseling Psychology, 30,* 3–18.

Hollis, J. W., & Wantz, R. A. (1986). *Counselor preparation 1986–1989: Programs, personnel, trends* (6th ed.). Muncie, IN: Accelerated Development.

House, E. R. (1978). Assumptions underlying evaluation models. *Educational Researcher, 7,* 4–12.

Howard, G. S. (1985). Can research in the human sciences become more relevant to practice? *Journal of Counseling and Development, 63,* 539–544.

Huber, C. H. (1980). Research and the school counselor. *The School Counselor, 27,* 210–216.

Humes, C. W., II. (1972). Accountability: A boon to guidance. *Personnel and Guidance Journal, 51,* 21–26.

Ivey, A. E. (1980). *Counseling and psychotherapy: Skills, theories, and practice.* Englewood Cliffs, NJ: Prentice-Hall.

Jesness, C. (1975). Comparative effectiveness of behavior modification and transactional analysis programs for delinquents. *Journal of Consulting and Clinical Psychology, 43,* 759–779.

Kaplan, A. (1964). *The conduct of inquiry.* San Francisco, CA: Chandler.

Kerlinger, F. N. (1973). *Foundations of behavioral research* (2nd ed.). New York: Holt, Rinehart, & Winston.

Krause, M. S., & Howard, K. I. (1976). Program evaluation in public interest: A new research methodology. *Community Mental Health Journal, 12,* 291–300.

Krauskopf, C. J. (1982). Science and evaluation research. *The Counseling Psychologist, 10,* 71–72.

Krumboltz, J. D., & Mitchell, L. K. (1979). Relevant rigorous research. *The Counseling Psychologist, 8,* 50–52.

LaFleur, N. K. (1983). Research and evaluation. In J. A. Brown & R. H. Pate, Jr. (Eds.), *Being a counselor* (pp. 173–190). Monterey, CA: Brooks/Cole.

Lewis, W. A., & Hutson, S. P. (1983). The gap between research and practice on the question of counseling effectiveness. *Personnel and Guidance Journal, 61,* 532–535.

Marken, R. (1981). *Methods in experimental psychology.* Monterey, CA: Brooks/Cole.

Miller, M. J. (1985). Analyzing client change graphically. *Journal of Counseling and Development, 63,* 491–494.

Minor, B. J. (1981). Bridging the gap between research and practice: An introduction. *Personnel and Guidance Journal, 59,* 485–486.

Moser, C. A., & Kalton, G. (Eds.). (1972). *Survey methods in social investigation* (2nd ed.). New York: Basic Books.

Neimeyer, G., & Resnikoff, A. (1982). Qualitative strategies in counseling research. *The Counseling Psychologist, 10,* 75–85.

Oetting, E. R. (1976). Planning and reporting evaluative research: Part II. *Personnel and Guidance Journal, 55,* 60–64.

Ohlsen, M. M. (1983). Evaluation of the counselor's services. In M. M. Ohlsen (Ed.) *Introduction to counseling* (pp. 357–372). Itasca, IL: Peacock.

Pietrofesa, J. J., Hoffman, A., & Splete, H. H. (1984). *Counseling: An introduction* (2nd ed.). Boston: Houghton Mifflin.

Remer, R. (1981). The counselor and research: An introduction. *Personnel and Guidance Journal, 59,* 567–571.

Rimmer, S. M., & Burt, M. A. (1980). Need assessment: A step-by-step approach. *The School Counselor, 28,* 59–62.

Schmidt, J. A. (1974). Research techniques for counselors: The multiple baseline. *Personnel and Guidance Journal, 53,* 200–206.

Smith, M. L. (1981). Naturalistic research. *Personnel and Guidance Journal, 59,* 585–589.

Sprinthall, N. A. (1981). A new model for research in service of guidance and counseling. *Personnel and Guidance Journal, 59,* 487–496.

Stockton, R., & Hulse, D. (1983). The use of research teams to enhance competence in counseling research. *Counselor Education and Supervision, 22,* 303–310.

Stufflebeam, D. L., Foley, W. J., Gephart, W. J., Guba, E. G., Hammond, R. L., Merriman, H. D., & Provus, M. M. (1971). *Educational evaluation and decision-making.* Bloomington, IN: Phi Delta Kappa.

Sue, D. W. (1978). Editorial. *Personnel and Guidance Journal, 56,* 260.

Thoresen, C. E. (1969). Relevance and research in counseling. *Review of Educational Research, 39,* 264–282.

Thoresen, C. E. (1978). Making better science, intensively. *Personnel and Guidance Journal, 56,* 279–282.

Tracey, T. J. (1983). Single case research: An added tool for counselors and supervisors. *Counselor Education and Supervision, 22,* 185–196.

Weinrach, S. G. (1975). How effective am I? Five easy steps to self-evaluation. *The School Counselor, 22,* 202–205.

Wheeler, P. T., & Loesch, L. (1981). Program evaluation and counseling: Yesterday, today, and tomorrow. *Personnel and Guidance Journal, 59,* 573–578.

Willson, V. L. (1981). An introduction to the theory and conduct of meta-analysis. *Personnel and Guidance Journal, 59,* 582–584.

Wilson, F. R., & Yager, G. G. (1981). A process model for prevention program research. *Personnel and Guidance Journal, 59,* 590–595.

Wilson, N. S. (1985). School counselors and research: Obstacles and opportunities. *The School Counselor, 33,* 111–119.

Photo by James S. Davidson III.

# CHAPTER 20

# Use of Psychological Tests in Counseling

*I read the test data like a ticker tape*
*of the New York Stock Exchange.*
*The "neurotic" scales of the MMPI are slightly higher*
*but there is less discrepancy*
*between verbal and performance WAIS-R scores.*
*Intuition and extroversion are in the moderate range*
*with a high need for achievement. . . .*
*At first, like a Wall Street wizard, I*
*try to predict your next quarter's performance,*
*After all, my future depends on it.*
*But in talking about expected dividends*
*I find the unexpected . . .*
*Alone and longing for the warmth of relationships*
*a fellow human being emerges*
*Much like me, except for test results.*
*Behind what is revealed on paper is a person. . . .* [1]

---

[1]Gladding, 1986, p. 176. Copyright AACD. Reprinted with permission. No further reproduction authorized without written permission of AACD.

The use of psychological tests in counseling has a long, paradoxical, and controversial history. Zytowski (1982) notes that counselors have been a part of the testing movement since the time of Frank Parsons (1909), who believed that vocational guidance should be based on formal assessment. The initial "tests" he used were work samples and guided self-estimates. Opposite this tradition are many of the most respected theorists associated with counseling, such as Carl Rogers, Rollo May, and William Glasser. These professionals do not advocate formal testing procedures except on rare occasions. Whether a counselor is involved in directly administering tests depends on his or her theoretical background, education, and values. But it is helpful for almost all counselors to have a knowledge of test theory, construction, and practice.

Within AACD, counselors who are involved in activities that require the use of tests usually belong to the Association for Measurement and Evaluation in Counseling and Development (AMECD). This division, originally named the Association for Measurement and Evaluation in Guidance (AMEG), was charted as the seventh division of AACD in 1965 (Sheeley & Eberly, 1985). It publishes a quarterly journal, *Measurement and Evaluation in Counseling and Development*, that includes critiques of tests used in counseling and articles on current issues and trends in the field of measurement. In APA, several divisions are involved with the use of tests and other assessment instruments. Clinical Psychology (Division 12), School Psychology (Division 16), and Counseling

Psychology (Division 17) are among the most prominent. Both AACD and APA have clearly established standards for psychological and educational tests (American Association of Counseling and Development, 1980; American Psychological Association, 1974).

In this chapter, we will explore the nature of tests and how they fit into the profession of counseling. We will also examine basic concepts associated with testing, such as validity, reliability, and standardization. In addition, we will briefly review some of the major tests that counselors use and are expected to understand.

## TESTS AND TEST SCORES

Anastasi (1982) defines a *psychological test* as "essentially an objective and standardized measure of behavior" (p. 22). Most often test results are reported as test scores—a statistic that has meaning only in relationship to a person. A score is thus a reflection of a particular behavior at a moment in time. Test scores are important in counseling, despite their limitations. They provide information that might not be obtained in any other way, and they do so with comparatively small investments of time and effort. Though tests and test scores have been criticized for a number of reasons, they appear entrenched as an indispensable part of the assessment and evaluation process in counseling. As Loesch (1977) observes, "We usually don't have a choice about whether we will be involved with testing" (p. 74). It is therefore crucial that counselors, regardless of their work settings and theoretical orientation, be knowledgeable about the administration and interpretation of frequently used tests (Chew, 1984).

To understand a test fully, a counselor must know "(1) the characteristics of its standardization sample, (2) the types and degree of its reliability and validity, (3) the reliability and validity of comparable tests, (4) the scoring procedures, (5) the method of administration, (6) the limitations, and (7) the strengths" (Kaplan & Saccuzzo, 1982, p. 192). Much of this information is contained in the test manual that accompanies each standardized test, but to gain a thorough knowledge of a test takes years of study and practice.

### Assessment and Professional Identity

Many individuals in counseling identify themselves with the administration and interpretation of tests. Those who are employed as specialists in the area of testing and appraisal are known as *psychometrists* (Harper, 1981). Most professionals who deal with tests, however, are not full-time psychometrists. They are counselors, counseling psychologists, and other helping professionals who are sometimes uncomfortable with these instruments and the association that goes with the word *test*. A test is often linked to "a heavy emphasis on objectivity" (Loesch, 1977, p. 74) and the process of testing is considered a mechanical one that creates psychological distance between examiner and client. For that reason the word is often avoided and in its place are substituted a number of suggested terms.

Loesch (1977) and Pate (1983), respectively, recommend that the terms *psychological assessment* or *assessment* be used in place of the word *test*. Both authors believe that *assessment* is more descriptive of what counselors actually do. It emphasizes the humanness of counseling and the relationship of test results with other information counselors may obtain on clients. Indeed, *assessment*, according to Shertzer and Linden (1982), refers "to those procedures and processes used in collecting measures of human behavior. Specific measures are obtained by using educational and psychological tests and inventories, observations, interview data, and other non-test-data-gathering techniques" (p. 10). The goal of the assessment process is a comprehensive evaluation of individuals in the present and a prediction of outcomes (Kaplan & Saccuzzo, 1982).

Tests, one part of the assessment process, are emphasized in this chapter because of their widespread use and importance. Almost all counselors have to deal with tests as a part of evaluating clients and making decisions concerning them. Therefore, it behooves counselors to be well-informed about as many of these instruments as possible. Understanding the nature of tests is crucial to a counselor's ability to conduct a thorough assessment of a client in an enlightened and productive way. These data, combined with additional information gathered from other sources, can inform counselors about how to work best with select individuals. It is also vital that counselors be informed about frequently used tests so they may converse in a knowledgeable manner with other helping professionals.

Many periodicals in counseling and psychology regularly review standardized tests. Included in this group are the *Journal of Counseling Psychology, Journal of Counseling and Development, Journal of Consulting Psychology,* and the *Review of Educational Research*. There are also a number of authoritative reference books on tests. A series of such books was started by O. K. Buros on personality tests, vocational tests, and tests in print. His best work, however, was the editing of eight editions of the *Mental Measurement*

*Yearbook* (e.g., Buros, 1978). The publication of the yearbook continues and provides a wealth of information on the background of various tests.

## A History of Tests in Counseling

Counselors first became involved with psychological tests during World War I when the army hired a group of psychologists to construct paper-and-pencil intelligence tests to be used to screen its inductees (Aiken, 1979). These test pioneers, led by Arthur Otis and Robert Yerkes, built on the work of Alfred Binet (an originator of an early intelligence test), Charles Spearman (an important contributor in the area of test theory), Sir Francis Galton (an inventor of early techniques for measuring abilities),and James M. Cattell (an early researcher into the relationship of scores to achievement)(Anastasi, 1982). The testing movement, which gained impetus in the 1920s, gave counselors an identity and respectability they had not previously had. It linked them closely to the psychometric dimension of psychology and provided them with an expanded theoretical rationale on which to base their job descriptions, especially in schools.

As a group, counselors have varied from time to time in their degree of involvement with tests. Two distinct periods of high counselor involvement with assessment and testing are noteworthy—the 1930s and the 1960s. Vocational testing was emphasized in the 1930s because of the Great Depression. The University of Minnesota's Employment Stabilization Research Institute was the leader in this movement. Its personnel assembled and administered batteries of tests in an effort to help the unemployed find suitable work. Paterson and Darley (1936) estimated that up to 30 percent of the unemployed were mismatched in regard to their jobs in the 1930s. The launching of the satellite *Sputnik* by the Soviet Union in 1957 was the impetus for a high interest and involvement in assessment and testing during the 1960s. Congress passed the National Defense Education Act, which contained a provision, Title V, for the funding of testing in the secondary schools to identify students with outstanding talents and encourage them to continue their education, especially in the sciences.

The period of greatest criticism of testing came in the 1970s and 1980s. Goldman (1972) set the tone for the criticism in an article which declared that the marriage between counseling and testing had failed. The National Education Association (NEA) in the same year passed resolution 72-44, which called for a moratorium on the use of standardized tests of intelligence, aptitude, and achievement (Engen, Lamb, & Prediger, 1982; Zytowski, 1982). Since that time, many court suits have been filed to challenge the use of tests and many bills introduced in state legislatures to prohibit the administration of certain tests. Jepsen (1982) observes that the trends of the 1970s have made it more challenging than ever before for counselors to select tests and interpret scores in career counseling. His observation on testing can be generalized to other areas of counseling too. As Tyler (1984) notes, "The antitesting movement has become a force to be reckoned with" (p. 48). Ironically, the use of tests in schools is more popular now than ever (Engen, Lamb, & Prediger, 1982).

Many of the problems with tests in the schools and in other settings have been and are being addressed by revising problematic instruments (Cronback, 1979). Indeed, Anastasi (1982) observes that "psychological testing today does not stand still long enough to have its picture taken" (p. *v*). In comparing the fourth (1976) and fifth (1982) editions of Anastasi's classic *Psychological Testing*, more than a third of the tests included in the revised text were either new or "substantially revised." In addition to the emphasis on test development and revision, renewed attention is also being paid to the education of counseling students in the use and abuse of psychoeducational tests (Chew, 1984).

### Problems and Potential of Using Tests

The way tests are used is crucial for their success in serving the welfare of clients and the public in general. Tests may be used singly or as part of a group or battery. Cronbach (1970) asserts that a battery of tests is of little value unless there are competent, well-educated counselors available to interpret them. The same is true for an individual test. Many of the problems associated with testing are usually the result of the way instruments are used or interpreted rather than with the tests themselves. Nevertheless, there are serious criticisms of both (Talbutt, 1983).

Shertzer and Stone (1980, p. 311) maintain that opponents of testing generally object to the use of tests for the following reasons:

1. testing encourages client dependency on the counselor and an external source for problem resolution,

2. test data prejudice the counselor's picture of an individual, and

3. test data are invalid and unreliable enough so that their value is severely limited.

Other serious criticisms of tests are they may: be biased and discriminatory, measure irrelevant skills, obscure talent, be mechanically used, invade privacy, be subject to fakability, and foster undesirable competition (Prescott, Cavatta, & Rollins, 1977; Shertzer & Linden, 1979; Talbutt, 1983). Oakland (1982) notes that the use of tests with minorities has been an especially controversial area and one in which abuse is demonstrable. He lists 10 major concerns of using tests when assessing minority students. Among these are the unfairness of testing pupils in a language not native to them and the unfairness of testing for white, middle-class abilities. He also points out that testing can be a dehumanizing experience and that minority students may be placed in ineffective or inappropriate programs for years as a result of test scores.

Part of the problem with tests used in counseling is related to the degree of sensitivity and ability of counselors who select, administer, and interpret these instruments. As a result of such criticism, Glaser (1981) believes professionals have become more sensitive about the profession's image. Counselors are more accountable than ever in making sure test instruments are used correctly. Many even include clients in the selection of tests.

Learner (1981) and Oakland (1982) report that the general public's attitude toward testing is positive, even among minorities. The public may have this attitude perhaps because tests are seen as serving many useful purposes. The primary function tests serve is in helping clients reach better decisions in planning the future. Tests may also help in the following ways (Shertzer & Stone, 1980):

☐ Assist clients in gaining self-understanding.

☐ Assist counselors in deciding whether clients' needs are within their range of expertise.

☐ Assist counselors in better understanding clients.

☐ Assist counselors in determining which counseling methods might be most appropriately employed.

☐ Assist counselors in predicting the future performance of clients in select areas, such as mechanics, art, or graduate school.

☐ Assist counselors in stimulating new interests within their clients.

☐ Assist counselors in evaluating the outcome of their counseling efforts.

## QUALITIES OF GOOD TESTS

All tests are not created equal, but those that do the job best have certain qualities in common. Among the most important of these are validity, reliability, standardization and norms to facilitate the interpretation of scores (Aiken, 1979; Anastasi, 1982).

### Validity

*Validity*, unquestionably the most important test quality, is "the degree to which a test actually measures what it purports to measure" (Anastasi, 1982, p. 27). If a test does not fulfill this function, it is basically useless. The validity of a test is determined by comparing its results with measures of a separate and independent criterion. Thus, if a test purports to measure an individual's probability of succeeding in a professional field, such as medicine, law, or counseling, the scores of the test are correlated with measures of success, such as grades and ratings of instructors, once the person completes his or her education. If scores on the testing instrument correlate highly and positively with these independent measures of success, then the instrument is said to possess a high degree of validity.

There are three types of validity—content, construct, and criterion-based (Anastasi, 1982; Kaplan & Saccuzzo, 1982). *Content validity* is also referred to as face validity because it is an indication of the degree to which a test appears to measure what it is supposed to (Aiken, 1979). More importantly, content validity is concerned with whether the test includes a fair sample of the universe of factors it is supposed to assess. As a general rule, content validity is associated with achievement, aptitude, and ability tests.

*Construct validity*, the most general type of validity, is "the extent to which the test may be said to measure the theoretical construct or trait" it purports to measure, such as empathy or intelligence (Anastasi, 1982, p. 144). Much depends on the test maker's definition of the construct, but generally construct validity is applied to personality and interest inventories.

*Criterion-based validity* refers to the comparison of scores on a test with a person's performance on given criterion measures across time and situations, such as the fine motor skills needed in typing. When the criterion is available at the time of testing, then the *concurrent validity* of the test is being measured. When the criterion is not available until after the test is administered, then the *predictive validity* of the test is being measured (Aiken, 1979). Two of the best known criterion-based instruments frequently used in counseling are the Minnesota Multiphasic Personality Inventory (MMPI)—a test with concurrent validity—and the Strong-Campbell Interest Inventory (SCII)—a test with predictive validity (Borgen & Bernard, 1982).

### Reliability

*Reliability* is a measure of the degree to which a test produces consistency of test scores when people are retested with the same or an equivalent instrument (Anastasi, 1982). It is related to validity, though a test may be reliable but not valid. Three traditional ways of determining reliability are (Aiken, 1979):

☐ *Test-retest*   The same test is given again after a period of time.

☐ *Parallel forms*   Two equivalent forms of the same test are administered.

☐ *Internal consistency analysis*   The scores of two arbitrarily selected halves of a test are compared.

### Standardization and Norms

*Standardization* refers to the uniform conditions under which a test is administered and scored (Aiken, 1979; Anastasi, 1982). Standardization makes possible the comparison of successive scores of an individual over time and the comparison of scores of different individuals. *Norms,* or average performance scores for specified groups, make possible meaningful comparisons among people in regard to what can be expected (Kaplan & Saccuzzo, 1982). Test norms have their limitations and may be misused. For example, a major criticism of some tests is that their norms were established on members of the majority population and that they therefore discriminate against such subgroups as minorities and the disadvantaged (Talbutt, 1983). Counselors must carefully examine the norming procedures of tests, and they should also establish their own local norms. In this way prejudice and the inappropriate use of tests can be minimized.

## CLASSIFICATION OF TESTS

There are many ways in which tests can be classified. Shertzer and Stone (1981) list seven:

☐ *Standardized versus nonstandardized*   Tests that are administered and scored according to specific directions, such as the Self-Directed Search, as opposed to those that are not, such as an experimental projective test.

☐ *Individual versus group*   Tests, such as the Kaufman Assessment Battery for Children (Hopkins & Hodge, 1984), that are designed to be given to one person at a time as opposed to those instruments that are given to groups, such as the Minnesota School Attitude Survey (Callis, 1985).

☐ *Speed versus power*   Tests that must be completed within a specified period of time, such as most achievement tests, as opposed to tests that allow for the demonstration of knowledge with generous time boundaries, such as many individually administered intelligence tests.

☐ *Performance versus paper and pencil*   Tests that require the manipulation of objects, such as the Object Assembly subtest of the Wechsler Intelligence Scale for Children-Revised (WISC-R), as opposed to tests where subjects mark answers or give written responses, such as on the Adjective Check List.

☐ *Objective versus subjective*   Tests that require the scorer not to make a judgment, such as those that involve short answer, true-false, matching, and multiple choice (Aiken, 1979), as opposed to those that require the scorer to exercise a judgment, such as the vocabulary subtest of the Wechsler Adult Intelligence Scale-Revised (WAIS-R).

☐ *Maximum versus typical performance*   Tests that require the examinees to do their best, such as tests of intelligence and special abilities, as opposed to tests that measure what a person most likes to do or usually does, such as tests that indicate interests or attitudes.

☐ *Norm versus criterion-based*   Tests that compare an individual's score to scores within a group, such as intelligence or achievement test scores, as opposed to tests that measure a person's score compared to a desirable level or standard, such as a reading test (Aiken, 1979).

Another way tests may be classified—one that is even more important for counselors—is "by the purpose for which they are designed or by the aspects of behavior they sample . . ." (Shertzer & Stone, 1981, p. 242). In this classification, Shertzer and Stone list six categories of tests: mental ability, aptitude, achievement, interests, career development, and personality. Another system of classification includes these categories: educational, vocational, or personal aspects of counseling (Elmore & Roberge, 1982). A third classification scheme, originated by Sylvania (1956), groups tests according to the frequency of their use under three main headings: intelligence/scholastic aptitude, vocational (and other aptitude), and achievement/diagnostic. All of these classification systems have their merits and limitations. Counselors, however, are usually involved in dealing with four distinct but sometimes overlapping categories of tests: intelligence/aptitude; interest/career; personality; and achievement. It is on these four categories that we will briefly focus our attention.

### *Intelligence/Aptitude*

Among the most controversial but popular types of tests are those that attempt to measure general intelligence and special aptitude. The term *intelligence* is defined in many different ways and there is no absolute meaning associated with the word (Karmel, 1970, p. 169). Indeed, Anastasi (1982) reports that most intelligence tests "are usually overloaded with certain functions, such as verbal ability, and completely omit others" (p. 228). She notes that many intelligence tests are "validated against measures of academic achievement" and "are often designated as tests of scholastic aptitude" (Anastasi, 1982, p. 228). In line with her observation is Aiken's (1979) definition of an intelligence test which states that these instruments are "designed to measure an individual's aptitude for scholastic work or other kinds of occupations requiring reasoning and verbal ability" (p. 307). Many intelligence tests are used primarily as screening devices in counseling and are followed up with more specialized aptitude tests that assess aptitude in particular areas, such as music or mechanics.

Most intelligence tests today are descendants of the original scales developed in France by Alfred Binet in the early 1900s. The Stanford-Binet Intelligence Scale, which was a revision of the Binet-Simon scales was prepared by L. M. Terman and published in 1916, and is the "grandfather" of American intelligence tests. It is individually administered and has traditionally been used with children more than adults. In 1986 it underwent a fourth revision to include more material appropriate for adults.

Another popular series of individually administered intelligence tests are those originated by David Wechsler: the Wechsler Preschool and Primary Scale of Intelligence (WPPSI), designed for ages 4 years, 0 months, to 6 years, 6 months; the Wechsler Intelligence Scale for Children-Revised (WISC-R), designed for ages 6 years, 0 months, to 16 years, 11 months; and the Wechsler Adult Intelligence Scale-Revised (WAIS-R), designed for ages 16 years and older. The Wechsler intelligence tests are noteworthy in providing a verbal IQ, performance IQ, and full scale IQ score. There has been extensive research on all of the Wechsler scales, and they are often the instruments of choice in the evaluation of intelligence (Zytowski & Warman, 1982).

In addition to the Stanford-Binet and Wechsler intelligence tests, there are a number of other widely respected individually administered intelligence tests. Among them are the Bayley Scales of Infant Development, the Vineland Social Maturity Scale, the Kaufman Assessment Battery for Children (K-ABC), the McCarthy Scales of Children's Abilities, and the Peabody Picture Vocabulary Test (revised).

There are also numerous intelligence scales intended to be administered to groups. These instruments were first developed during World War I. The army Alpha and Beta tests are the best-known forerunners of today's group intelligence instruments. They were initially employed to screen army inductees and to classify them for training according to ability level. Among the most widely used and respected group intelligence tests today are the Otis-Lennon School Ability Test, the College Board Scholastic Aptitude Test (SAT), the American College Testing (ACT) Assessment, and the Miller Analogies Test (MAT).

Aptitude tests are similar in many ways to intelligence tests, but they are designed to tap a narrower range of ability. Aiken (1979) defines an *aptitude* as a "capability for a task or type of skill," and an aptitude test as one that measures "a person's ability to profit from further training or experience in an occupation or skill" (p. 302). Aptitude tests are usually divided into two categories: (1) multi-aptitude batteries, which test a number of skills by administering a variety of tests, and (2) component ability tests, which assess a single ability or skill, such as music or mechanical ability (Bradley, 1984). Some of the best-known multi-aptitude batteries are the General Aptitude Test Battery (GATB), the Differential Aptitude Test (DAT) and the Armed Services Vocational Aptitude Battery (ASVAB) (Anastasi, 1982; Bradley, 1984; Zytowski & Warman, 1982).

### Interest/Career

While there is an expected relationship between ability and interest in exercising that ability, the tests that best measure interests are those designed specifically for the purpose. Aiken (1979) defines an interest inventory as "a test or checklist, such as the Strong-Campbell Interest Inventory and the Kuder General Interest Survey, which assesses a person's preferences for activities and topics" (p. 307). Responses derived from such tests are compared to the scores of others at either a similar developmental level, such as in an educational setting, or with people already working in a particular area, such as in a vocational setting. Anastasi (1982) notes that "the study of interests has probably received its strongest impetus from educational and career counseling" (p. 534). This is because of the value of interest inventories in these particular areas of counseling. A person's achievement in a learning situation or in a career is greatly influenced by his or her interests.

Instruments that measure career interests originated in a systematic and standardized way with the publication in 1927 of the Strong Vocational Interest Blank (SVIB). The revised edition of the original test, the Strong-Campbell Interest Inventory (SCII), is one of the most widely used and researched tests in existence (Borgen & Bernard, 1982; Campbell & Hansen, 1981; Zytowski & Warman, 1982). It is notable and highly respected for its empirical and theoretical base. It is linked to John Holland's theory of career development, which proposes six major types of people and environments: realistic (R), investigative (I), artistic (A), social (S), enterprising (E), and conventional (C) (Holland, 1973). The closer the link between the person and the environment, the more satisfying the relationship. Another popular career inventory, also based on Holland's six personality/environmental types, is the Self-Directed Search (SDS) (Holland, 1979a). This instrument is untimed (as is the SCII) and is self-scoring. After scoring, the client is given the Occupations Finder (Holland, 1979b), which allows him or her to compare the three-letter occupational code derived from the test (e.g., SAE or RIC) with a list of 495 occupations that are similarly coded. An important aspect about any of the career interest tests based on Holland's theory is the Compatibility Index, which allows for the comparison of any two three-letter Holland codes on a nine-point scale (Moody, 1983). The more compatibility between the scores, the more likely the person and environment will match harmoniously.

A third popular interest/career inventory is the Kuder Occupational Interest Survey (Kuder, 1966). There are several forms of this instrument, but each has a forced-choice, triad-response format and is untimed. Some forms of the test are computer scored; others are self-scored. Clients respond to each triad item by selecting the activity that is the most preferred and the one that is the least preferred for them. Scores on the Kuder correlate highly with commonly expressed interests of those in select career groups. The 10 broad career areas for which the Kuder yields scores are: social service, persuasive, clerical, computational, musical, artistic, literary, mechanical, outdoor, and scientific.

Other well-known interest/career tests include the California Occupational Preference System, the Jackson Vocational Interest Survey, the Ohio Vocational Interest Survey, and the Vocational Preference Inventory. For noncollege-bound students, Bradley (1984) reports three interest inventories designed to "measure interests in occupations that do not require college training" (p. 7). These are the Minnesota Vocational Interest Inventory, the Career Assessment

Inventory, and the Career Guidance Inventory in Trades, Services, and Technologies. Interest tests designed for more specialized use are the Bem Sex-Role Inventory, the Jenkins Activity Survey, the Personal Orientation Inventory, the Survey of Values, and the Survey of School Attitudes.

### Personality

Aiken (1979) defines a *personality test* as "any one of several methods of analyzing personality, such as checklists, personality inventories, and projective techniques" (p. 311). Such tests may be divided into two main categories—objective and projective. The best-known and most widely used of the objective tests are the Minnesota Multiphasic Personality Inventory (MMPI), the Myers-Briggs Type Indicator (MBTI), and the Edwards Personal Preference Schedule (EPPS). These tests yield a score that is independent of any opinion or judgment of the scorer, as do all objective tests. Projective tests include the Rorschach, the Thematic Apperception Test (TAT), and the House-Tree-Person (HTP) Test. This type of test yields measures that in varying degrees depend on judgments and interpretations of the scorer.

The prototype of the personality test was a self-report inventory developed during World War I by R. S. Woodworth and known as the Personal Data Sheet (Anastasi, 1982; Kaplan & Saccuzzo, 1982). The first of the significant projective tests was the Rorschach Inkblot Test, published in 1921 (Erdberg, 1985). The objectively scored personality tests are more widely used in counseling, and we will begin our discussion with a review of these tests.

The Minnesota Multiphasic Personality Inventory (MMPI) is the most popular of all the many personality tests (Anastasi, 1982). It has several forms, but the original form consists of 550 affirmative statements, to which a client responds in reference to him- or herself in one of three ways: true, false, or cannot say. There are ten clinical scales and four validity scales on the MMPI that distinguish between people who are experiencing psychiatric problems and those who are not (Aiken, 1982). Extensive training and experience are necessary for one to use this instrument accurately and appropriately.

The Myers-Briggs Type Indicator (MBTI) is a test that was designed to reflect Carl Jung's theory of personality types (Myers, 1962, 1980). The inventory contains 166 two-choice items "concerning preferences or inclinations in feelings and behaviors" (Aiken, 1979, p. 248). It yields four indexes: extroversion versus introversion (EI), sensing versus intuition (SN), thinking versus feeling (TF), and judgment versus perception (JP). Combinations of these four indexes result in 16 possible personality types. A clear understanding of personality types provides counselors with constructive information on how clients perceive and interact with their environments (Lynch, 1985). Research indicates that different MBTI types appear to be attracted to certain occupations and life-styles. For example, 76 percent of tested counseling students score high on the intuitive/feeling scales of the MBTI and are described as insightful, enthusiastic, and able to handle challenging situations with personal warmth. By contrast, 77 percent of tested research scientists are classified as intuitive thinkers and are able to handle challenging situations with impersonal analysis and logic (Myers, 1980).

The Edwards Personal Preference Schedule (EPPS) is based on the need-press theory of personality developed by Henry Murray (1938) and consists of 225 forced-choice questions, which examine the strength of 15 individual needs identified by Murray in relationship to a person's other needs (Anastasi, 1982). The scores are plotted on a percentile chart based on group norms, for college students or for adults in general. Other objectively scored, self-report personality tests whose titles suggest the intended use are the California Psychological Inventory (CPI), the Guilford-Zimmerman Temperament Survey, the Mooney Problem Check List, the Sixteen Personality Factor Questionnaire (16 PF), and the State-Trait Anxiety Inventory (STAI).

Projective personality tests are much less structured and far more difficult to score. But they are harder for the client to fake, and advocates claim that these tests measure deeper aspects of a client's personality than do other instruments. In recent years, some research/clinicians, such as Exner (1974), have tried to standardize the methods by which projectives, such as the Rorschach Inkblot Test, are administered and scored. While there has been some success in this area for some instruments, the scoring of many other projectives, such as the Thematic Apperception Test, is still questionable. Besides the three tests already mentioned, projective tests include the Holtzman Inkblot Technique, the Bender Gestalt, the Draw-a-Person Test, the Children's Apperception Test, and the Rotter Incomplete Sentences Blank.

### Achievement

An *achievement test* is "a measure of an individual's degree of accomplishment or learning in a subject or task" (Aiken, 1979, p. 301). They are much more direct as measurement instruments than any other type of tests. The results of such tests give clients a good idea of what they have learned in a certain area as compared to what others have learned and provide them with the type of information they need to make sound educational and career decisions (Bradley, 1984). If a client has aptitudes, interests, or personality dispositions suitable for given select career areas but has little knowledge or skill in these areas, the client can take positive steps to correct those deficiencies.

Both Aiken (1979) and Karmel (1970) point out that achievement tests may be either teacher-made or standardized. The advantages of a teacher-made test are: they measure specific units of study emphasized in an educational setting, they are easy to keep up-to-date, and they reflect current emphases and information. Standardized tests, on the other hand, measure more general educational objectives, are usually more carefully constructed, and give the client a good idea about how he or she compares to a wider sample of others in a particular subject. Actually, teacher-made and standardized tests complement each other, and both may be used profitably in the helping process.

Different achievement tests are employed for distinct purposes. In a school setting, a combination of teacher-made and standardized tests are linked to age and grade levels. General achievement batteries used in elementary and secondary schools that measure basic skills include the California Achievement Tests, the Iowa Tests of Basic Skills, the SRA Achievement Series, the Metropolitan Achievement Tests, the Wide Range Achievement Test, and the Stanford Achievement Test (Anastasi, 1982; Bradley, 1984). School counselors must become especially knowledgeable about these instruments in order to converse intelligently and efficiently with teachers, parents, administrators, students, and educational specialists.

In addition to elementary and secondary school achievement tests, there are instruments that measure achievement for adults. Such tests as the National Teacher Examination, Law School Admissions Tests, and the National Board of Certified Counselors Examination are examples of these professionally oriented achievement tests. They help to protect the public and the professions they represent by ensuring that individuals who pass them achieve a minimum level of informational competence.

## ADMINISTRATION OF TESTS AND INTERPRETATION OF TEST RESULTS

A major criticism of the use of tests in counseling focuses on the administration of these instruments and the interpretation of scores. The process of administration of a test is described in the test manual that accompanies each test, and most tests specify uniform procedures to be followed at each step, from preparing the room to giving instructions. Some tests have specialized instructions unique to them, and counselors must follow these procedures if they expect to obtain valid test results. One question that is not usually addressed by test manuals is whether or how much a client should be involved in the selection of the instrument to be used. There are some cases, such as the administration of achievement tests in elementary schools, where it is inappropriate for clients to be involved in the test selection. But there are other occasions where it is beneficial for this to occur. Goldman (1971) lists advantages of involving the client in the process of test selection. Among these are the willingness of the client to accept test results more readily, the promotion of independence from the counselor, the value to the client of the decision-making experience that might generalize to other decisions, the opportunity for diagnosis by the counselor based on the client's reactions to various tests, and the selection of tests that best fit the needs of the client.

After tests are selected, administered, and scored, there is a need to interpret the results in an understandable way. Tinsley and Bradley (1986) note that "most counselors may never have learned how to go about interpreting tests to clients" (p. 462). Thus, clients may not understand the meaning of "the numbers, charts, graphs or diagrams presented to them" (Miller, 1982, p. 87), and they may leave counseling as uninformed and unenlightened as when they began. Several ways have been suggested to correct this deficiency. First, counselors should be well-educated in the use of test theory and construction. Counselors cannot explain test results unless they are first informed about the instruments with which they are dealing.

Second, Tyler (1984) points out that in test interpretation scores are only "clues" and should be seen as such. Scores must be considered in the light of what else is known about a client. The total combination of information can form the basis for a more meaningful and productive dialogue between the counselor and the client. Goldman (1971) points out that if a test is given on an individual basis, counselors will notice many things about clients that otherwise would be missed. This extra information, when combined with the test scores themselves, often allows for a more nearly complete assessment of the client as recommended by Loesch (1977) and Pate (1983).

Third, Tinsley and Bradley (1986) and Miller (1982) advocate concrete ways of dealing with test results. Tinsley and Bradley believe that before meeting with a client, the counselor must be prepared to make a clear and accurate interpretation of test results for the client. They advise against interpreting "off the cuff." A reasonable plan is to begin the interpretation with more concrete information, such as interest or achievement test scores, and then move to more abstract information, such as personality or ability test results. If the interpretation of information is to be meaningful, the emotional needs of the client must be considered and the information must be fresh in the counselor's mind. One way to achieve both goals is to interpret test results on an as-needed basis (Goldman, 1971). There is less information to deal with when this approach is followed, and both counselor and client are likely to remember results better. The major disadvantage of this approach is that it may become fragmented.

Tinsley and Bradley (1986) propose that when interpretation of test results occurs, a client should be prepared by the establishment of rapport between counselor and client. Test information can then be delivered in a way that focuses on what the client wants to know. Client feedback is promoted and dialogue is encouraged. Miller (1982) makes similar remarks in his five-point plan for interpreting test results to clients. First, he has his client remember feelings on the test day and give impressions of the test or tests. He then explains to the client again the purpose of testing and how test scores are presented, for example by percentiles. Next, he and the client actually examine the test results together and discuss what these scores mean to the client. Meaning is elicited by asking the client open-ended questions. Then the client is helped to integrate scores with other aspects of self-knowledge. The final stage involves incorporating all such knowledge into a client-originated plan for continuing self-study. Counselors can help clients formulate a plan, but the plan itself should come from the client. Test interpretation is perhaps the most sensitive part of any assessment process, but clients benefit greatly from it when it is done properly (Miller, 1977).

## SUMMARY

The use of tests in counseling is almost as old as the profession itself. The popularity of test use has varied over the years, but it appears tests will remain as an essential part of most assessments. Therefore, counselors must be well-versed in the types of tests available and their appropriate use in counseling in order to help themselves attain more professional competence and to assist clients in living more healthy and productive life-styles. A part of being well-informed is that counselors are aware of the validity, reliability, standardization, and norms of the instruments they use. A test that is reliable but not valid is inappropriate. Similarly, an instrument that discriminates against minorities because it has been normed only on the majority population is of no value and in fact can be quite harmful.

Four main types of tests are most frequently encountered by counselors. They are intelligence/aptitude tests, interest/career tests, personality tests, and achievement tests. Counselors who work with tests must constantly examine the current research results to assure that various instruments are appropriate. They also need to consult with clients to be certain that the tests used will provide clients with the type of information wanted. Finally, counselors must be sensitively involved with the interpretation of test data. It is of little benefit for a client to take a test if the client does not ultimately understand what the results mean. Counselors who are well-prepared and who prepare their clients well are likely to be most helpful.

## CLASSROOM ACTIVITIES

1. Send away for educational and psychological test catalogs from major test publishers. Examine the variety of tests available and the information the publisher gives you about each. Individually, try to group these tests under the four categories outlined in this chapter. What tests are easy to classify? Which ones are most difficult? Report your results to the class.
2. In dyads, do an in-depth report on one of the tests mentioned in this chapter or one recommended to you by your instructor. Be sure to notice the validity, reliability, standardization, and norms of the instrument you investigate. Report your results to the class and explain to them when you think the instrument you have studied could be appropriately used in counseling.
3. Some counselors do not think that tests should be used in counseling. Divide the class into two debate teams of four members each. One side should take the posi-

tion that counseling and testing are not compatible (see Goldman, 1972). The other side should advocate the use of tests in counseling (see Tinsley & Bradley, 1986). What conclusions do you as members of the class reach from listening to this debate?
4. In triads, discuss your previous experiences in having a test interpreted to you. What did you think when the test interpreter explained your results? What do you remember feeling at the time and how did you behave? How does this experience still affect your reaction to psychological tests and test interpretations?
5. Discuss in groups of four the ethical and legal considerations of using tests in counseling. What issues does your group think are most sensitive to ethical and legal questions? Cousult the ethical codes and guidelines of AACD and APA on the use of tests. Share your group opinions with the class as a whole.

## REFERENCES

Aiken, L. R., Jr. (1979). *Psychological testing and assessment* (3rd ed.). Boston: Allyn & Bacon.

American Association for Counseling and Development. (1980). *Responsibilities of users of standardized tests.* Alexandria, VA: AACD Press.

American Psychological Association. (1974). *Standards for educational and psychological tests.* Washington, D.C.: American Psychological Association.

Anastasi, A. (1982). *Psychological testing* (5th ed.). New York: Macmillan.

Borgen, F. H., & Bernard, C. B. (1982). Test review: Strong-Campbell Interest Inventory, third edition. *Measurement and Evaluation in Guidance, 14*, 208–212.

Bradley, L. J. (1984). Lifespan career assessment for counselors and educators. *Counseling and Human Development, 16*, 1–16.

Buros, O. K. (Ed.). (1978). *The eighth mental measurements yearbook.* Lincoln, NE: University of Nebraska, Buros Institute of Mental Measurement.

Callis, R. (1985). Minnesota School Attitude Survey, Lower and Upper Forms. *Journal of Counseling and Development, 63*, 382.

Campbell, D. P., & Hansen, J. C. (1981). *Manual for the SVIB-SCII* (3rd ed.). Stanford, CA: Stanford University Press.

Chew, A. L. (1984). Training counselors to interpret psychoeducational evaluations: A course model. *Counselor Education and Supervision, 24*, 114–119.

Cronbach, L. J. (1979). The Armed Services Vocational Aptitude Battery—A test battery in transition. *Personnel and Guidance Journal, 57*, 232–237.

Elmore, T. M., & Roberge, L. P. (1982). Assessment and experiencing: On measuring the marigolds. *Measurement and Evaluation in Guidance, 15*, 95–102.

Engen, H. B., Lamb, R. R., & Prediger, D. J. (1982). Are secondary schools still using standardized tests? *Personnel and Guidance Journal, 60*, 287–290.

Erdberg, P. (1985). The Rorschach. In C. S. Newmark (Ed.), *Major psychological assessment instruments* (pp. 65–88). Boston: Allyn & Bacon.

Exner, J. E. (1974). *The Rorschach: A comprehensive system.* New York: Wiley.

Gladding, S. T. (1986). Thoughts of a Wall Street counselor. *Journal of Humanistic Education and Development, 24*, 176.

Glaser, R. (1981). The future of testing: A research agenda for cognitive psychology and psychometrics. *American Psychologist, 36*, 923–935.

Goldman, L. (1971). *Using tests in counseling* (2nd ed.). New York: Appleton Century Crofts.

Goldman, L. (1972). Tests and counseling: The marriage that failed. *Measurement and Evaluation in Guidance, 4*, 213–220.

Harper, F. D. (1981). *Dictionary of counseling techniques and terms.* Alexandria, VA: Douglass.

Holland, J. L. (1973). *Making vocational choices: A theory of careers.* Englewood Cliffs, NJ: Prentice-Hall.

Holland, J. L. (1979a). *Self-directed search: A guide to educational and vocational planning.* Palo Alto, CA: Consulting Psychologists Press.

Holland, J. L. (1979b). *The occupational finder.* Palo Alto, CA: Consulting Psychologists Press.

Hopkins, K. D., & Hodge, S. E. (1984). Review of the Kaufman Assessment Battery for Children (K-ABC). *Journal of Counseling and Development, 63*, 105–107.

Jepsen, D. A. (192). Test usage in the 1970s: A summary and interpretation. *Measurement and Evaluation in Guidance, 15*, 164–168.

Kaplan, R. M., & Saccuzzo, D. P. (1982). *Psychological testing.* Monterey, CA: Brooks/Cole.

Karmel, L. J. (1970). *Measurement and evaluation in the schools.* New York: Macmillan.

Kuder, G. (1966). *Kuder Occupational Interest Survey: General manual.* Chicago: Science Research Associates.

Learner, B. (1981). Representative democracy, "men of zeal," and testing legislation. *American Psychologist, 36*, 270–275.

Loesch, L. (1977). Guest editorial. *Elementary School Guidance and Counseling, 12*, 74–75.

Lynch, A. Q. (1985). The Myers-Briggs Type Indicator: A tool for appreciating employee and client diversity. *Journal of Employment Counseling, 22,* 104–109.

Miller, G. M. (1977). After the testing is over. *Elementary School Guidance and Counseling, 12,* 139–143.

Miller, G. M. (1982). Deriving meaning from standardized tests: Interpreting test results to clients. *Measurement and Evaluation in Guidance, 15,* 87–94.

Moody, A. (1983). The compatibility index: Beyond high point codes. *AHMCA Journal, 5,* 85–89.

Murray, H. A. (1938). *Explorations in personality.* New York: Oxford University Press.

Myers, I. B. (1962). Manual for the Myers-Briggs Type Indicator. Palo Alto, CA: Consulting Psychologists Press.

Myers, I. B. (1980). *Gifts differing.* Palo Alto, CA: Consulting Psychologists Press.

Oakland, T. (1982). Nonbiased assessment in counseling: Issues and guidelines. *Measurement and Evaluation in Guidance, 15,* 107–116.

Parsons, F. (1909). *Choosing a vocation.* Boston: Houghton Mifflin.

Pate, R. H., Jr. (1983). Assessment and information giving. In J. A. Brown & R. H. Pate, Jr. (Eds.), *Being a counselor* (pp. 147–172). Monterey, CA: Brooks/Cole.

Paterson, D. J., & Darley, J. (1936). *Men, women, and jobs.* Minneapolis: University of Minnesota Press.

Prescott, M. R., Cavatta, J. C., & Rollins, K. D. (1977). The fakability of the Personality Orientation Inventory. *Counselor Education and Supervision, 17,* 116–120.

Sheeley, V. L., & Eberly, C. G. (1985). Two decades of leadership in measurement and evaluation. *Journal of Counseling and Development, 63,* 436–439.

Shertzer, B., & Linden, J. D. (1979). *Fundamentals of individual appraisal, assessment techniques for counselors.* Boston: Houghton Mifflin.

Shertzer, B., & Linden, J. D. (1982). Persistent issues in counselor assessment and appraisal. *Measurement and Evaluation in Guidance, 15,* 9–14.

Shertzer, B., & Stone, S. C. (1980). *Fundamentals of counseling* (3rd ed.). Boston: Houghton Mifflin.

Shertzer, B., & Stone, S. C. (1981). *Fundamentals of guidance* (4th ed.). Boston: Houghton Mifflin.

Sylvania, K. C. (1956). Test usage in counseling centers. *Personnel and Guidance Journal, 34,* 559–564.

Talbutt, L. C. (1983). The counselor and testing: Some legal concerns. *The School Counselor, 30,* 245–250.

Tinsley, H. E. A., & Bradley, R. W. (1986). Test interpretation. *Journal of Counseling and Development, 64,* 462–466.

Tyler, L. E. (1984). What tests don't measure. *Journal of Counseling and Development, 63,* 48–50.

Zytowski, D. G. (1982). Assessment in the counseling process for the 1980s. *Measurement and Evaluation in Guidance, 15,* 15–21.

Zytowski, D. G., & Warman, R. E. (1982). The changing use of tests in counseling. *Measurement and Evaluation in Guidance, 15,* 146–152.

# *Ethical Standards of the American Association for Counseling and Development*

## PREAMBLE

The Association is an educational, scientific, and professional organization whose members are dedicated to the enhancement of the worth, dignity, potential, and uniqueness of each individual and thus to the service of society.

The Association recognizes that the role definitions and work settings of its members include a wide variety of academic disciplines, levels of academic preparation and agency services. This diversity reflects the breadth of the Association's interest and influence. It also poses challenging complexities in efforts to set standards for the performance of members, desired requisite preparation or practice, and supporting social, legal, and ethical controls.

The specification of ethical standards enables the Association to clarify to present and future members and to those served by members, the nature of ethical responsibilities held in common by its members.

The existence of such standards serves to stimulate greater concern by members for their own professional functioning and for the conduct of fellow professionals such as counselors, guidance and student personnel workers, and others in the helping professions. As the ethical code of the Association, this document establishes principles that define the ethical behavior of Association members.

SOURCE: Copyright AACD. Reprinted with permission. No further reproduction authorized without further permission of AACD.

Approved by Executive Committee upon referral of the Board of Directors, January 17, 1981.

## SECTION A: GENERAL

1. The member influences the development of the profession by continuous efforts to improve professional practices, teaching, services, and research. Professional growth is continuous throughout the member's career and is exemplified by the development of a philosophy that explains why and how a member functions in the helping relationship. Members must gather data on their effectiveness and be guided by the findings.

2. The member has a responsibility both to the individual who is served and to the institution within which the service is performed to maintain high standards of professional conduct. The member strives to maintain the highest levels of professional services offered to the individuals to be served. The member also strives to assist the agency, organization, or institution in providing the highest caliber of professional services. The acceptance of employment in an institution implies that the member is in agreement with the general policies and principles of the institution. Therefore the professional activities of the member are also in accord with the objectives of the institution. If, despite concerted efforts, the member cannot reach agreement with the employer as to acceptable standards of conduct that allow for changes in institutional policy conducive to the positive growth and development of clients, then terminating the affiliation should be seriously considered.

3. Ethical behavior among professional associates, both members and nonmembers, must be expected at all times. When information is possessed that raises doubt as to the ethical behavior of professional colleagues, whether Association members or not, the member must take action to attempt to rectify such a condition. Such action shall use the institution's channels first and then use procedures established by the state Branch, Division, or Association.

4. The member neither claims nor implies professional qualifications exceeding those possessed and is responsible for correcting any misrepresentations of these qualifications by others.

5. In establishing fees for professional counseling services,

members must consider the financial status of clients and locality. In the event that the established fee structure is inappropriate for a client, assistance must be provided in finding comparable services of acceptable cost.

6. When members provide information to the public or to subordinates, peers or supervisors, they have a responsibility to ensure that the content is general, unidentified client information that is accurate, unbiased, and consists of objective, factual data.

7. With regard to the delivery of professional services, members should accept only those positions for which they are professionally qualified.

8. In the counseling relationship the counselor is aware of the intimacy of the relationship and maintains respect for the client and avoids engaging in activities that seek to meet the counselor's personal needs at the expense of that client. Through awareness of the negative impact of both racial and sexual stereotyping and discrimination, the counselor guards the individual rights and personal dignity of the client in the counseling relationship.

## SECTION B: COUNSELING RELATIONSHIP

This section refers to practices and procedures of individual and/or group counseling relationships.

The member must recognize the need for client freedom of choice. Under those circumstances where this is not possible, the member must apprise clients of restrictions that may limit their freedom of choice.

1. The member's *primary* obligation is to respect the integrity and promote the welfare of the client(s), whether the client(s) is (are) assisted individually or in a group relationship. In a group setting, the member is also responsible for taking reasonable precautions to protect individuals from physical and/or psychological trauma resulting from interaction within the group.

2. The counseling relationship and information resulting therefrom be kept confidential, consistent with the obligations of the member as a professional person. In a group counseling setting, the counselor must set a norm

of confidentiality regarding all group participants' disclosures.

3. If an individual is already in a counseling relationship with another professional person, the member does not enter into a counseling relationship without first contacting and receiving the approval of that other professional. If the member discovers that the client is in another counseling relationship after the counseling relationship begins, the member must gain the consent of the other professional or terminate the relationship, unless the client elects to terminate the other relationship.

4. When the client's condition indicates that there is clear and imminent danger to the client or others, the member must take reasonable personal action or inform responsible authorities. Consultation with other professionals must be used where possible. The assumption of responsibility for the client(s) behavior must be taken only after careful deliberation. The client must be involved in the resumption of responsibility as quickly as possible.

5. Records of the counseling relationship, including interview notes, test data, correspondence, tape recordings, and other documents, are to be considered professional information for use in counseling and they should not be considered a part of the records of the institution or agency in which the counselor is employed unless specified by state statute or regulation. Revelation to others of counseling material must occur only upon the expressed consent of the client.

6. Use of data derived from a counseling relationship for purposes of counselor training or research shall be confined to content that can be disguised to ensure full protection of the identity of the subject client.

7. The member must inform the client of the purposes, goals, techniques, rules of procedure and limitations that may affect the relationship at or before the time that the counseling relationship is entered.

8. The member must screen prospective group participants, especially when the emphasis is on self-understanding and growth through self-disclosure. The member must maintain an awareness of the group participants' compatibility throughout the life of the group.

9. The member may choose to consult with any other professionally competent person about a client. In choosing a consultant, the member must avoid placing the consultant in a conflict of interest situation that would preclude the consultant's being a proper party to the member's efforts to help the client.

10. If the member determines an inability to be of professional assistance to the client, the member must either avoid initiating the counseling relationship or immediately terminate that relationship. In either event, the member must suggest appropriate alternatives. (The member must be knowledgeable about referral resources so that a satisfactory referral can be initiated). In the event the client declines the suggested referral, the member is not obligated to continue the relationship.

11. When the member has other relationships, particularly of an administrative, supervisory and/or evaluative nature with an individual seeking counseling services, the member must not serve as the counselor but should refer the individual to another professional. Only in instances where such an alternative is unavailable and where the individual's situation warrants counseling intervention should the member enter into and/or maintain a counseling relationship. Dual relationships with clients that might impair the member's objectivity and professional judgment (e.g., as with close friends or relatives, sexual intimacies with any client) must be avoided and/or the counseling relationship terminated through referral to another competent professional.

12. All experimental methods of treatment must be clearly indicated to prospective recipients and safety precautions are to be adhered to by the member.

13. When the member is engaged in short-term group treatment/training programs (e.g., marathons and other encounter-type or growth groups), the member ensures that there is professional assistance available during and following the group experience.

14. Should the member be engaged in a work setting that calls for any variation from the above statements, the member is obligated to consult with other professionals whenever possible to consider justifiable alternatives.

## SECTION C: MEASUREMENT AND EVALUATION

The primary purpose of educational and psychological testing is to provide descriptive measures that are objective and interpretable in either comparative or absolute terms. The member must recognize the need to interpret the statements that follow as applying to the whole range of appraisal techniques including test and nontest data. Test results constitute only one of a variety of pertinent sources of information for personnel, guidance, and counseling decisions.

1. The member must provide specific orientation or information to the examinee(s) prior to and following the test administration so that the results of testing may be placed in proper perspective with other relevant factors. In so doing, the member must recognize the effects of socio-economic, ethnic and cultural factors on test scores. It is the member's professional responsibility to use additional unvalidated information carefully in modifying interpretation of the test results.

2. In selecting tests for use in a given situation or with a particular client, the member must consider carefully the specific validity, reliability and appropriateness of the test(s). *General* validity, reliability and the like may be questioned legally as well as ethically when tests are used for vocational and educational selection, placement, or counseling.

3. When making any statements to the public about tests and testing, the member must give accurate information and avoid false claims or misconceptions. Special efforts are often required to avoid unwarranted connotations of such terms as *IQ* and *grade equivalent scores*.

4. Different tests demand different levels of competence for administration, scoring, and interpretation. Members must recognize the limits of their competence and perform only those functions for which they are prepared.

5. Tests must be administered under the same conditions that were established in their standardization. When tests are not administered under standard conditions or when unusual behavior or irregularities occur during the testing session, those conditions must be noted and the results

designated as invalid or of questionable validity. Unsupervised or inadequately supervised test-taking, such as the use of tests through the mails, is considered unethical. On the other hand, the use of instruments that are so designed or standardized to be self-administered and self-scored, such as interest inventories, is to be encouraged.

6. The meaningfulness of test results used in personnel, guidance, and counseling functions generally depends on the examinee's unfamiliarity with the specific items on the test. Any prior coaching or dissemination of the test materials can invalidate test results. Therefore, test security is one of the professional obligations of the member. Conditions that produce most favorable test results must be made known to the examinee.

7. The purpose of testing and the explicit use of the results must be made known to the examinee prior to testing. The counselor must ensure that instrument limitations are not exceeded and that periodic review and/or retesting are made to prevent client stereotyping.

8. The examinee's welfare and explicit prior understanding must be the criteria for determining the recipients of the test results. The member must see that specific interpretation accompanies any release of individual or group test data. The interpretation of test data must be related to the examinee's particular concerns.

9. The member must be cautious when interpreting the results of research instruments possessing insufficient technical data. The specific purposes for the use of such instruments must be stated explicitly to examinees.

10. The member must proceed with caution when attempting to evaluate and interpret the performance of minority group members or other persons who are not represented in the norm group on which the instrument was standardized.

11. The member must guard against the appropriation, reproduction, or modifications of the published tests or parts thereof without acknowledgment and permission from the previous publisher.

12. Regarding the preparation, publication and distribution of tests, reference should be made to:

a. *Standards for Educational and Psychological Tests and Manuals,* revised edition, 1974, published by the American Psychological Association on behalf of itself, the American Educational Research Association and the National Council on Measurement in Education.

b. The responsible use of tests: A position paper of AMEG, APGA, and NCME, *Measurement and Evaluation in Guidance,* 1972, 5, 385-388.

c. "Responsibilities of Users of Standardized Tests," APGA, *Guidepost,* October 5, 1978, pp. 5-8.

## SECTION D: RESEARCH AND PUBLICATION

1. Guidelines on research with human subjects shall be adhered to, such as:
   a. *Ethical Principles in the Conduct of Research with Human Participants,* Washington, D.C.: American Psychological Association, Inc., 1973.
   b. Code of Federal Regulations, Title 45, Subtitle A, Part 46, as currently issued.

2. In planning any research activity dealing with human subjects, the member must be aware of and responsive to all pertinent ethical principles and ensure that the research problem, design, and execution are in full compliance with them.

3. Responsibility for ethical research practice lies with the principal researcher, while others involved in the research activities share ethical obligation and full responsibility for their own actions.

4. In research with human subjects, researchers are responsible for the subjects' welfare throughout the experiment and they must take all reasonable precautions to avoid causing injurious psychological, physical, or social effects on their subjects.

5. All research subjects must be informed of the purpose of the study except when withholding information or providing misinformation to them is essential to the investigation. In such research the member must be responsible for corrective action as soon as possible following completion of the research.

6. Participation in research must be voluntary. Involuntary participation is appropriate only when it can be demon-

strated that participation will have no harmful effects on subjects and is essential to the investigation.

7. When reporting research results, explicit mention must be made of all variables and conditions known to the investigator that might affect the outcome of the investigation or the interpretation of the data.

8. The member must be responsible for conducting and reporting investigations in a manner that minimizes the possibility that results will be misleading.

9. The member has an obligation to make available sufficient original research data to qualified others who may wish to replicate the study.

10. When supplying data, aiding in the research of another person, reporting research results, or in making original data available, due care must be taken to disguise the identity of the subjects in the absence of specific authorization from such subjects to do otherwise.

11. When conducting and reporting research, the member must be familiar with, and give recognition to, previous work on the topic, as well as to observe all copyright laws and follow the principles of giving full credit to all to whom credit is due.

12. The member must give due credit through joint authorship, acknowledgment, footnote statements, or other appropriate means to those who have contributed significantly to the research and/or publication, in accordance with such contributions.

13. The member must communicate to other members the results of any research judged to be of professional or scientific value. Results reflecting unfavorably on institutions, programs, services, or vested interests must not be withheld for such reasons.

14. If members agree to cooperate with another individual in research and/or publication, they incur an obligation to cooperate as promised in terms of punctuality of performance and with full regard to the completeness and accuracy of the information required.

15. Ethical practice requires that authors not submit the same manuscript or one essentially similar in content, for simultaneous publication consideration by two or more journals. In addition, manuscripts published in whole or in substantial part, in another journal or published work

should not be submitted for publication without acknowledgment and permission from the previous publication.

## SECTION E: CONSULTING

*Consultation* refers to a voluntary relationship between a professional helper and help-needing individual, group or social unit in which the consultant is providing help to the client(s) in defining and solving a work-related problem or potential problem with a client or client system. (This definition is adapted from Kurpius, DeWayne. Consultation theory and process: An integrated model. *Personnel and Guidance Journal,* 1978, 56.

1. The member acting as consultant must have a high degree of self-awareness of his-her own values, knowledge, skills, limitations, and needs in entering a helping relationship that involves human and-or organizational change and that the focus of the relationship be on the issues to be resolved and not on the person(s) presenting the problem.
2. There must be understanding and agreement between member and client for the problem definition, change goals, and predicated consequences of interventions selected.
3. The member must be reasonably certain that she/he or the organization represented has the necessary competencies and resources for giving the kind of help that is needed now or may develop later and that appropriate referral resources are available to the consultant.
4. The consulting relationship must be one in which client adaptability and growth toward self-direction are encouraged and cultivated. The member must maintain this role consistently and not become a decision maker for the client or create a future dependency on the consultant.
5. When announcing consultant availability for services, the member conscientiously adheres to the Association's *Ethical Standards.*
6. The member must refuse a private fee or other remuneration for consultation with persons who are entitled to these services through the member's employing institu-

tion or agency. The policies of a particular agency may make explicit provisions for private practice with agency clients by members of its staff. In such instances, the clients must be apprised of other options open to them should they seek private counseling services.

## SECTION F: PRIVATE PRACTICE

1. The member should assist the profession by facilitating the availability of counseling services in private as well as public settings.

2. In advertising services as a private practitioner, the member must advertise the services in such a manner so as to accurately inform the public as to services, expertise, profession, and techniques of counseling in a professional manner. A member who assumes an executive leadership role in the organization shall not permit his/her name to be used in professional notices during periods when not actively engaged in the private practice of counseling.

    The member may list the following: highest relevant degree, type and level of certification or license, type and/or description of services, and other relevant information. Such information must not contain false, inaccurate, misleading, partial, out-of-context, or deceptive material or statements.

3. Members may join in partnership/corporation with other members and-or other professionals provided that each member of the partnership or corporation makes clear the separate specialties by name in compliance with the regulations of the locality.

4. A member has an obligation to withdraw from a counseling relationship if it is believed that employment will result in violation of the *Ethical Standards*. If the mental or physical condition of the member renders it difficult to carry out an effective professional relationship or if the member is discharged by the client because the counseling relationship is no longer productive for the client, then the member is obligated to terminate the counseling relationship.

5. A member must adhere to the regulations for private practice of the locality where the services are offered.

6. It is unethical to use one's institutional affiliation to recruit clients for one's private practice.

## SECTION G: PERSONNEL ADMINISTRATION

It is recognized that most members are employed in public or quasi-public institutions. The functioning of a member within an institution must contribute to the goals of the institution and vice versa if either is to accomplish their respective goals or objectives. It is therefore essential that the member and the institution function in ways to (a) make the institution's goals explicit and public; (b) make the member's contribution to institutional goals specific; and (c) foster mutual accountability for goal achievement.

To accomplish these objectives, it is recognized that the member and the employer must share responsibilities in the formulation and implementation of personnel policies.

1. Members must define and describe the parameters and levels of their professional competency.
2. Members must establish interpersonal relations and working agreements with supervisors and subordinates regarding counseling or clinical relationships, confidentiality, distinction between public and private material, maintenance, and dissemination of recorded information, work load and accountability. Working agreements in each instance must be specified and made known to those concerned.
3. Members must alert their employers to conditions that may be potentially disruptive or damaging.
4. Members must inform employers of conditions that may limit their effectiveness.
5. Members must submit regularly to professional review and evaluation.
6. Members must be responsible for inservice development of self and-or staff.
7. Members must inform their staff of goals and programs.
8. Members must provide personnel practices that guarantee and enhance the rights and welfare of each recipient of their service.
9. Members must select competent persons and assign

responsibilities compatible with their skills and experiences.

## SECTION H: PREPARATION STANDARDS

Members who are responsible for training others must be guided by the preparation standards of the Association and relevant Division (s). The member who functions in the capacity of trainer assumes unique ethical responsibilities that frequently go beyond that of the member who does not function in a training capacity. These ethical responsibilities are outlined as follows:

1. Members must orient students to program expectations, basic skills development, and employment prospects prior to admission to the program.
2. Members in charge of learning experiences must establish programs that integrate academic study and supervised practice.
3. Members must establish a program directed toward developing students' skills, knowledge, and self-understanding, stated whenever possible in competency or performance terms.
4. Members must identify the levels of competencies of their students in compliance with relevant Division standards. These competencies must accommodate the para-professional as well as the professional.
5. Members, through continual student evaluation and appraisal, must be aware of the personal limitations of the learner that might impede future performance. The instructor must not only assist the learner in securing remedial assistance but also screen from the program those individuals who are unable to provide competent services.
6. Members must provide a program that includes training in research commensurate with levels of role functioning. Para-professional and technician-level personnel must be trained as consumers of research. In addition, these personnel must learn how to evaluate their own and their program's effectiveness. Graduate training, espe-

cially at the doctoral level, would include preparation for original research by the member.

7. Members must make students aware of the ethical responsibilities and standards of the profession.

8. Preparatory programs must encourage students to value the ideals of service to individuals and to society. In this regard, direct financial remuneration or lack thereof must not influence the quality of service rendered. Monetary considerations must not be allowed to overshadow professional and humanitarian needs.

9. Members responsible for educational programs must be skilled as teachers and practitioners.

10. Members must present thoroughly varied theoretical positions so that students may make comparisons and have the opportunity to select a position.

11. Members must develop clear policies within their educational institutions regarding field placement and the roles of the student and the instructor in such placements.

12. Members must ensure that forms of learning focusing on self-understanding or growth are voluntary, or if required as part of the education program, are made known to prospective students prior to entering the program. When the education program offers a growth experience with an emphasis on self-disclosure or other relatively intimate or personal involvement, the member must have no administrative, supervisory, or evaluating authority regarding the participant.

13. Members must conduct an educational program in keeping with the current relevant guidelines of the Association and its Divisions.

# Code of Ethics of the American Psychological Association

## Principle 1: Responsibility

*In providing services, psychologists maintain the highest standards of their profession. They accept responsibility for the consequences of their acts and make every effort to ensure that their services are used appropriately.*

a. As scientists, psychologists accept responsibility for the selection of their research topics and the methods used in investigation, analysis, and reporting. They plan their research in ways to minimize the possibility that their findings will be misleading. They provide thorough discussion of the limitations of their data, especially where their work touches on social policy or might be construed to the detriment of persons in specific age, sex, ethnic, socioeconomic, or other social groups. In publishing reports of their work, they never suppress disconfirming data, and they acknowledge the existence of alternative hypotheses and explanations of their findings. Psychologists take credit only for work they have actually done.

b. Psychologists clarify in advance with all appropriate persons and agencies the expectations for sharing and utilizing research data. They avoid relationships that may limit their objectivity or create a conflict of interest. Interference with the milieu in which data are collected is kept to a minimum.

c. Psychologists have the responsibility to attempt to prevent distortion, misuse, or suppression of psychological findings by the institution or agency of which they are employees.

d. As members of governmental or other organizational bodies, psychologists remain accountable as individuals to the highest standards of their profession.

e. As teachers, psychologists recognize their primary obligation to help others acquire knowledge and skill. They maintain high standards of scholarship by presenting psychological information objectively, fully, and accurately.

f. As practitioners, psychologists know that they bear a heavy social responsibility because their recommendations and professional actions may alter the lives of others. They are alert to personal, social, organizational, financial, or political situations and pressures that might lead to misuse of their influence.

## Principle 2: Competence

*The maintenance of high standards of competence is a responsibility shared by all psychologists in the interest of the public and the profession as a whole. Psychologists recognize the boundaries of their competence and the limitations of their techniques. They only provide services and only use techniques for which they are qualified by training and experience. In those areas in which recognized standards do not yet exist, psychologists take whatever precautions are necessary to protect the welfare of their clients.*

*They maintain knowledge of current scientific and professional information related to the services they render.*

a. Psychologists accurately represent their competence, education, training, and experience. They claim as evidence of educational qualifications only those degrees obtained from institutions acceptable under the Bylaws and Rules of Council of the American Psychological Association.

b. As teachers, psychologists perform their duties on the basis of careful preparation so that their instruction is accurate, current, and scholarly.

c. Psychologists recognize the need for continuing education and are open to new procedures and changes in expectations and values over time.

d. Psychologists recognize differences among people, such as those that may be associated with age, sex, socioeconomic, and ethnic backgrounds. When necessary, they obtain training, experience, or counsel to assure competent service or research relating to such persons.

e. Psychologists responsible for decisions involving individuals or policies based on test results have an understanding of psychological or educational measurement, validation problems, and test research.

f. Psychologists recognize that personal problems and conflicts may interfere with professional effectiveness. Accordingly, they refrain from undertaking any activity in which their personal problems are likely to lead to inadequate performance or harm to a client, colleague, student, or research participant. If engaged in such activity when they become aware of their personal problems they seek competent professional assistance to determine whether they should suspend, terminate, or limit the scope of their professional and/or scientific activities.

## Principle 3: Moral and Legal Standards

*Psychologists' moral and ethical standards of behavior are a personal matter to the same degree as they are for any other citizen, except as these may compromise the fulfillment of their professional responsibilities or reduce the public trust in psychology and psychologists. Regarding their own behavior, psychologists are sensitive to prevailing community standards and to the possible impact that conformity to or deviation from these standards may have upon the quality of their performance as psychologists. Psychologists are also aware of the possible impact of their public behavior upon the ability of colleagues to perform their professional duties.*

a. As teachers, psychologists are aware of the fact that their personal values may affect the selection and presentation of instructional materials. When dealing with topics that may give offense, they recognize and respect the diverse attitudes that students may have toward such materials.

*Source:* From *Ethical Principles of Psychologists*, June 1981. Copyright 1981 by the American Psychological Association. Reprinted by permission of the publisher.

b. As employees or employers, psychologists do not engage in or condone practices that are inhumane or that result in illegal or unjustifiable actions. Such practices include, but are not limited to, those based on considerations of race, handicap, age, gender, sexual preference, religion, or national origin in hiring, promotion, or training.

c. In their professional roles, psychologists avoid any action that will violate or diminish the legal and civil rights of clients or of others who may be affected by their actions.

d. As practitioners and researchers, psychologists act in accord with Association standards and guidelines related to practice and to the conduct of research with human beings and animals. In the ordinary course of events, psychologists adhere to relevant governmental laws and institutional regulations. When federal, state, provincial, organizational, or institutional laws, regulations, or practices are in conflict with Association standards and guidelines, psychologists make known their commitment to Association standards and guidelines and, wherever possible, work toward a resolution of the conflict. Both practitioners and researchers are concerned with the development of such legal and quasi-legal regulations as best serve the public interest, and they work toward changing existing regulations that are not beneficial to the public interest.

## Principle 4: Public Statements

*Public statements, announcements of services, advertising, and promotional activities of psychologists serve the purpose of helping the public make informed judgments and choices. Psychologists represent accurately and objectively their professional qualifications, affiliations, and functions, as well as those of the institutions or organizations with which they or the statements may be associated. In public statements providing psychological information or professional opinions or providing information about the availability of psychological products, publications, and services, psychologists base their statements on scientifically acceptable psychological findings and techniques with full recognition of the limits and uncertainties of such evidence.*

a. When announcing or advertising professional services, psychologists may list the following information to describe the provider and services provided: name, highest relevant academic degree earned from a regionally accredited institution, date, type, and level of certification or licensure, diplomate status, APA membership status, address, telephone number, office hours, a brief listing of the type of psychological services offered, an appropriate presentation of fee information, foreign languages spoken, and policy with regard to third-party payments. Additional relevant or important consumer information may be included if not prohibited by other sections of these Ethical Principles.

b. In announcing or advertising the availability of psychological products, publications, or services, psychologists do not present their affiliation with any organization in a manner that falsely implies sponsorship or certification by that organization. In particular and for example, psychologists do not state APA membership or fellow status in a way to suggest that such status implies specialized professional competence or qualifications. Public statements include, but are not limited to, communication by means of periodical, book, list, directory, television, radio, or motion picture. They do not contain (i) a false, fraudulent, misleading, deceptive, or unfair statement; (ii) a misinterpretation of fact or a statement likely to mislead or deceive because in context it makes only a partial disclosure of relevant facts; (iii) a testimonial from a patient regarding the quality of a psychologist's services or products; (iv) a statement intended or likely to create false or unjustified expectations of favorable results; (v) a statement implying unusual, unique, or one-of-a-kind abilities; (vi) a statement intended or likely to appeal to a client's fears, anxieties, or emotions concerning the possible results of failure to obtain the offered services; (vii) a statement concerning the comparative desirability of offered services; (viii) a statement of direct solicitation of individual clients.

c. Psychologists do not compensate or give anything of value to a representative of the press, radio, television, or other communication medium in anticipation of or in return for professional publicity in a news item. A paid advertisement must be identified as such, unless it is apparent from the context that it is a paid advertisement. If communicated to the public by use of radio or television, an advertisement is prerecorded and approved for broadcast by the psychologist, and a recording of the actual transmission is retained by the psychologist.

d. Announcements or advertisements of "personal growth groups," clinics, and agencies give a clear statement of purpose and a clear description of the experiences to be provided. The education, training, and experience of the staff members are appropriately specified.

e. Psychologists associated with the development or promotion of psychological devices, books, or other products offered for commercial sale make reasonable efforts to ensure that announcements and advertisements are presented in a professional, scientifically acceptable, and factually informative manner.

f. Psychologists do not participate for personal gain in commercial announcements or advertisements recommending to the public the purchase or use of proprietary or single-source products or services when that participation is based solely upon their identification as psychologists.

g. Psychologists present the science of psychology and offer their services, products, and publications fairly and accurately, avoiding misrepresentation through sensationalism, exaggeration, or superficiality. Psychologists are guided by the primary obligation to aid the public in developing informed judgments, opinions, and choices.

h. As teachers, psychologists ensure that statements in catalogs and course outlines are accurate and not misleading, particularly in terms of subject matter to be covered, bases for evaluating progress, and the nature of course experiences. Announcements, brochures, or advertisements describing workshops, seminars, or other educational programs accurately describe the audience for which the program is intended as well as eligibility requirements, educational objectives, and nature of the materials to be covered. These announcements also accurately represent the education, training, and experience of the psychologists presenting the programs and any fees involved.

i. Public announcements or advertisements soliciting research participants in which clinical services or other professional services are offered as an inducement make clear the nature of the services as well as the costs and other obligations to be accepted by participants in the research.

j. A psychologist accepts the obligation to correct others who represent the psychologist's professional qualifications, or associations with products or services, in a manner incompatible with these guidelines.

k. Individual diagnostic and therapeutic services are provided only in the context of a professional psychological relationship. When personal advice is given by means of public lectures or demonstrations, newspaper or magazine articles, radio or television programs, mail, or similar media, the psychologist utilizes the most current relevant data and exercises the highest level of professional judgment.

l. Products that are described or presented by means of public lectures or demonstrations, newspaper or magazine articles, radio or television programs, or similar media meet the same recognized standards as exist for products used in the context of a professional relationship.

## Principle 5: Confidentiality

*Psychologists have a primary obligation to respect the confidentiality of information obtained from persons in the course of their work as psychologists. They reveal such information to others only with the consent of the person or the person's legal representative, except in those unusual circumstances in which not to do so would result in clear danger to the person or to others. Where appropriate, psychologists inform their clients of the legal limits of confidentiality.*

a. Information obtained in clinical or consulting relationships, or evaluative data concerning children, students, employees, and others, is discussed only for professional purposes and only with persons clearly concerned with the case. Written and oral reports present only data germane to the purposes of the evaluation, and every effort is made to avoid undue invasion of privacy.

b. Psychologists who present personal information obtained during the course of professional work in writings, lectures, or other public forums either obtain adequate prior consent to do so or adequately disguise all identifying information.

c. Psychologists make provisions for maintaining confidentiality in the storage and disposal of records.

d. When working with minors or other persons who are unable to give voluntary, informed consent, psychologists take special care to protect these persons' best interests.

## Principle 6: Welfare of the Consumer

*Psychologists respect the integrity and protect the welfare of the people and groups with whom they work. When conflicts of interest arise between clients and psychologists' employing institutions, psychologists clarify the nature and direction of their loyalties and responsibilities and keep all parties informed of their commitments. Psychologists fully inform consumers as to the purpose and nature of an evaluative, treatment, educational, or training procedure, and they freely acknowledge that clients, students, or participants in research have freedom of choice with regard to participation.*

a. Psychologists are continually cognizant of their own needs and of their potentially influential position vis-à-vis persons such as clients, students, and subordinates. They avoid exploiting the trust and dependency of such persons. Psychologists make every effort to avoid dual relationships that could impair their professional judgment or increase the risk of exploitation. Examples of such dual relationships include, but are not limited to, research with and treatment of employees, students, supervisees, close friends, or relatives. Sexual intimacies with clients are unethical.

b. When a psychologist agrees to provide services to a client at the request of a third party, the psychologist assumes the responsibility of clarifying the nature of the relationships to all parties concerned.

c. Where the demands of an organization require psychologists to violate these Ethical Principles, psychologists clarify the nature of the conflict between the demands and these principles. They inform all parties of psychologists' ethical responsibilities and take appropriate action.

d. Psychologists make advance financial arrangements that safeguard the best interests of and are clearly understood by their clients. They neither give nor receive any remuneration for referring clients for professional services. They contribute a portion of their services to work for which they receive little or no financial return.

e. Psychologists terminate a clinical or consulting relationship when it is reasonably clear that the consumer is not benefiting from it. They offer to help the consumer locate alternative sources of assistance.

## Principle 7: Professional Relationships

*Psychologists act with due regard for the needs, special competencies, and obligations of their colleagues in psychology and other professions. They respect the prerogatives and obligations of the institutions or organizations with which these other colleagues are associated.*

a. Psychologists understand the areas of competence of related professions. They make full use of all the professional, technical, and administrative resources that serve the best interests of consumers. The absence of formal relationships with other professional workers does not relieve psychologists of the responsibility of securing for their clients the best possible professional service, nor does it relieve them of the obligation to exercise foresight, diligence, and tact in obtaining the complementary or alternative assistance needed by clients.

b.  Psychologists know and take into account the traditions and practices of other professional groups with whom they work and cooperate fully with such groups. If a person is receiving similar services from another professional, psychologists do not offer their own services directly to such a person. If a psychologist is contacted by a person who is already receiving similar services from another professional, the psychologist carefully considers that professional relationship and proceeds with caution and sensitivity to the therapeutic issues as well as the client's welfare. The psychologist discusses these issues with the client so as to minimize the risk of confusion and conflict.

c.  Psychologists who employ or supervise other professionals or professionals in training accept the obligation to facilitate the further professional development of these individuals. They provide appropriate working conditions, timely evaluations, constructive consultation, and experience opportunities.

d.  Psychologists do not exploit their professional relationships with clients, supervisees, students, employees, or research participants sexually or otherwise. Psychologists do not condone or engage in sexual harassment. Sexual harassment is defined as deliberate or repeated comments, gestures, or physical contacts of a sexual nature that are unwanted by the recipient.

e.  In conducting research in institutions or organizations, psychologists secure appropriate authorization to conduct such research. They are aware of their obligations to future research workers and ensure that host institutions receive adequate information about the research and proper acknowledgment of their contributions.

f.  Publication credit is assigned to those who have contributed to a publication in proportion to their professional contributions. Major contributions of a professional character made by several persons to a common project are recognized by joint authorship, with the individual who made the principal contribution listed first. Minor contributions of a professional character and extensive clerical or similar nonprofessional assistance may be acknowledged in footnotes or in an introductory statement. Acknowledgment through specific citations is made for unpublished as well as published material that has directly influenced the research or writing. Psychologists who compile and edit material of others for publication publish the material in the name of the originating group, if appropriate, with their own name appearing as chairperson or editor. All contributors are to be acknowledged and named.

g.  When psychologists know of an ethical violation by another psychologist, and it seems appropriate, they informally attempt to resolve the issue by bringing the behavior to the attention of the psychologist. If the misconduct is of a minor nature and/or appears to be due to lack of sensitivity, knowledge, or experience, such an informal solution is usually appropriate. Such informal corrective efforts are made with sensitivity to any rights to confidentiality involved. If the violation does not seem amenable to an informal solution, or is of a more serious nature, psychologists bring it to the attention of the appropriate local, state, and/or national committee on professional ethics and conduct.

## Principle 8: Assessment Techniques

*In the development, publication, and utilization of psychological assessment techniques, psychologists make every effort to promote the welfare and best interests of the client. They guard against the misuse of assessment results. They respect the client's right to know the results, the interpretations made, and the bases for their conclusions and recommendations. Psychologists make every effort to maintain the security of tests and other assessment techniques within limits of legal mandates. They strive to ensure the appropriate use of assessment techniques by others.*

a.  In using assessment techniques, psychologists respect the right of clients to have full explanations of the nature and purpose of the techniques in language the clients can understand, unless an explicit exception to this right has been agreed upon in advance. When the explanations are to be provided by others, psychologists establish procedures for ensuring the adequacy of these explanations.

b.  Psychologists responsible for the development and standardization of psychological tests and other assessment techniques utilize established scientific procedures and observe the relevant APA standards.

c.  In reporting assessment results, psychologists indicate any reservations that exist regarding validity or reliability because of the circumstances of the assessment or the inappropriateness of the norms for the person tested. Psychologists strive to ensure that the results of assessments and their interpretations are not misused by others.

d.  Psychologists recognize that assessment results may become obsolete. They make every effort to avoid and prevent the misuse of obsolete measures.

e.  Psychologists offering scoring and interpretation services are able to produce appropriate evidence for the validity of the programs and procedures used in arriving at interpretations. The public offering of an automated interpretation service is considered a professional-to-professional consultation. Psychologists make every effort to avoid misuse of assessment reports.

f.  Psychologists do not encourage or promote the use of psychological assessment techniques by inappropriately trained or otherwise unqualified persons through teaching, sponsorship, or supervision.

## Principle 9: Research with Human Participants

*The decision to undertake research rests upon a considered judgment by the individual psychologist about how best to contribute to psychological science and human welfare. Having made the decision to conduct research, the psychologist considers alternative directions in which research energies and resources might be invested. On the basis of this consideration, the psychologist carries out the investigation with respect and concern for the dignity and welfare of the people who participate and with cognizance of federal and state regulations and professional standards governing the conduct of research with human participants.*

a. In planning a study, the investigator has the responsibility to make a careful evaluation of its ethical acceptability. To the extent that the weighing of scientific and human values suggests a compromise of any principle, the investigator incurs a correspondingly serious obligation to seek ethical advice and to observe stringent safeguards to protect the rights of human participants.

b. Considering whether a participant in a planned study will be a "subject at risk" or a "subject at minimal risk," according to recognized standards, is of primary ethical concern to the investigator.

c. The investigator always retains the responsibility for ensuring ethical practice in research. The investigator is also responsible for the ethical treatment of research participants by collaborators, assistants, students, and employees, all of whom, however, incur similar obligations.

d. Except in minimal-risk research, the investigator establishes a clear and fair agreement with research participants, prior to their participation, that clarifies the obligations and responsibilities of each. The investigator has the obligation to honor all promises and commitments included in that agreement. The investigator informs the participants of all aspects of the research that might reasonably be expected to influence willingness to participate and explains all other aspects of the research about which the participants inquire. Failure to make full disclosure prior to obtaining informed consent requires additional safeguards to protect the welfare and dignity of the research participants. Research with children or with participants who have impairments that would limit understanding and/or communication requires special safeguarding procedures.

e. Methodological requirements of a study may make the use of concealment or deception necessary. Before conducting such a study, the investigator has a special responsibility to (i) determine whether the use of such techniques is justified by the study's prospective scientific, educational, or applied value; (ii) determine whether alternative procedures are available that do not use concealment or deception; and (iii) ensure that the participants are provided with sufficient explanation as soon as possible.

f. The investigator respects the individual's freedom to decline to participate in or to withdraw from the research at any time. The obligation to protect this freedom requires careful thought and consideration when the investigator is in a position of authority or influence over the participant. Such positions of authority include, but are not limited to, situations in which research participation is required as part of employment or in which the participant is a student, client, or employee of the investigator.

g. The investigator protects the participant from physical and mental discomfort, harm, and danger that may arise from research procedures. If risks of such consequences exist, the investigator informs the participant of that fact. Research procedures likely to cause serious or lasting harm to a participant are not used unless the failure to use these procedures might expose the participant to risk of greater harm, or unless the research has great potential benefit and fully informed and voluntary consent is obtained from each participant. The participant should be informed of procedures for contacting the investigator within a reasonable time period following participation should stress, potential harm, or related questions or concerns arise.

h. After the data are collected, the investigator provides the participant with information about the nature of the study and attempts to remove any misconceptions that may have arisen. Where scientific or humane values justify delaying or withholding this information, the investigator incurs a special responsibility to monitor the research and to ensure that there are no damaging consequences for the participant.

i. Where research procedures result in undesirable consequences for the individual participant, the investigator has the responsibility to detect and remove or correct these consequences, including long-term effects.

j. Information obtained about a research participant during the course of an investigation is confidential unless otherwise agreed upon in advance. When the possibility exists that others may obtain access to such information, this possibility, together with the plans for protecting confidentiality, is explained to the participant as part of the procedure for obtaining informed consent.

## Principle 10: Care and Use of Animals

*An investigator of animal behavior strives to advance understanding of basic behavioral principles and/or to contribute to the improvement of human health and welfare. In seeking these ends, the investigator ensures the welfare of animals and treats them humanely. Laws and regulations notwithstanding, an animal's immediate protection depends upon the scientist's own conscience.*

a. The acquisition, care, use, and disposal of all animals are in compliance with current federal, state or provincial, and local laws and regulations.

b. A psychologist trained in research methods and experienced in the care of laboratory animals closely supervises all procedures involving animals and is responsible for ensuring appropriate consideration of their comfort, health, and humane treatment.

c. Psychologists ensure that all individuals using animals under their supervision have received explicit instruction in experimental methods and in the care, maintenance, and handling of the species being used. Responsibilities and activities of individuals participating in a research project are consistent with their respective competencies.

d. Psychologists make every effort to minimize discomfort, illness, and pain of animals. A procedure subjecting animals to pain, stress, or privation is used only when an alternative procedure is unavailable and the goal is justified by its prospective scientific, educational, or applied value. Surgical procedures are performed under appropriate anesthesia; techniques to avoid infection and minimize pain are followed during and after surgery.

e. When it is appropriate that the animal's life be terminated, it is done rapidly and painlessly.

# AAMFT Code of Principles for Marriage and Family Therapists

## AAMFT Code of Ethical Principles for Marriage and Family Therapists

The Board of Directors of AAMFT hereby promulgate, pursuant to Article II, Section (1)(C) of the Association's Bylaws, a Revised Code of Ethical Principles for Marriage and Family Therapists.

## 1. Responsibility to Clients

**Marriage and family therapists are dedicated to advancing the welfare of families and individuals, including respecting the rights of those persons seeking their assistance, and making reasonable efforts to ensure that their services are used appropriately.**

1.1 Marriage and family therapists do not discriminate against or refuse professional service to anyone on the basis of race, sex, religion, or national origin.

1.2 Marriage and family therapists are cognizant of their potentially influential position with respect to clients, and they avoid exploiting the trust and dependency of such persons. Marriage and family therapists therefore make every effort to avoid dual relationships with clients that could impair their professional judgement or increase the risk of exploitation. Examples of such dual relationships include, but are not limited to, business or close personal relationships with clients. Sexual intimacy with clients is prohibited.

1.3 Marriage and family therapists do not use their professional relationship with clients to further their own interests.

1.4 Marriage and family therapists respect the right of clients to make decisions and help them to understand the consequences of these decisions. Marriage and family therapists clearly advise a client that a decision on marital status is the responsibility of the client.

1.5 Marriage and family therapists continue thera-peutic relationships only so long as it is reasonably clear that clients are benefiting from the relationship.

1.6 Marriage and family therapists assist persons in obtaining other therapeutic services if a marriage and family therapist is unable or unwilling, for appropriate reasons, to see a person who has requested professional help.

1.7 Marriage and family therapists do not abandon or neglect clients in treatment without making reasonable arrangements for the continuation of such treatment.

## 2. Confidentiality

**Marriage and family therapists have unique confidentiality problems because the "client" in a therapeutic relationship may be more than one person. The overriding principle is that marriage and family therapists respect the confidences of their client(s).**

2.1 Marriage and family therapists cannot disclose client confidences to anyone, except: (1) as mandated by law; (2) to prevent a clear and immediate danger to a person or persons; (3) where the marriage and family therapist is a defendant in a civil, criminal or disciplinary action arising from the therapy (in which case client confidences may only be disclosed in the course of that action); or (4) if there is a waiver previously obtained in writing, and then such information may only be revealed in accordance with the terms of the waiver. In circumstances where more than one person in a family is receiving therapy, each such family member who is legally competent to execute a waiver must agree to the waiver required by sub-paragraph (4). Absent such a waiver from each family member legally competent to execute a waiver, a marriage and family therapist cannot disclose information received from any family member.

2.2 Marriage and family therapists use clinical materials in teaching, writing, and public presentations only if a written waiver has been received

*Source:* From *AAMFT Code of Ethical Principles for Marriage and Family Therapists.* Reprinted by permission of American Association for Marriage and Family Therapy. This revised code was approved in September 1985. AAMFT can make further revisions of the code at any time, as the Association deems necessary.

in accordance with sub-principle 2.1(4), or when appropriate steps have been taken to protect client identity.

2.3 Marriage and family therapists store or dispose of client records in ways that maintain confidentiality.

## 3. Professional Competence and Integrity

**Marriage and family therapists are dedicated to maintaining high standards of professional competence and integrity.**

3.1 Marriage and family therapists who (a) are convicted of felonies, (b) are convicted of misdemeanors (related to their qualifications or functions), (c) engage in conduct which could lead to conviction of felonies, or misdemeanors related to their qualifications or functions, (d) are expelled from other professional organizations, or (e) have their licenses or certificates suspended or revoked, are subject to termination of membership or other appropriate action.

3.2 Marriage and family therapists seek appropriate professional assistance for their own personal problems or conflicts that are likely to impair their work performance and their clinical judgement.

3.3 Marriage and family therapists, as teachers, are dedicated to maintaining high standards of scholarship and presenting information that is accurate.

3.4 Marriage and family therapists seek to remain abreast of new developments in family therapy knowledge and practice through both educational activities and clinical experiences.

3.5 Marriage and family therapists do not engage in sexual or other harassment of clients, students, trainees, or colleagues.

3.6 Marriage and family therapists do not attempt to diagnose, treat, or advise on problems outside the recognized boundaries of their competence.

3.7 Marriage and family therapists attempt to prevent the distortion or misuse of their clinical and research findings.

3.8 Marriage and family therapists are aware that, because of their ability to influence and alter the lives of others, they must exercise special care when making public their professional recommendations and opinions through testimony or other public statements.

## 4. Responsibility to Students, Employees and Supervisees

**Marriage and family therapists do not exploit the trust and dependency of students and supervisees.**

4.1 Marriage and family therapists are cognizant of their potentially influential position with respect to students, employees and supervisees, and they avoid exploiting the trust and dependency of such persons. Marriage and family therapists therefore make every effort to avoid dual relationships that could impair their professional judgement or increase the risk of exploitation. Sexual harassment or exploitation of students, employees, or supervisees is prohibited.

4.2 Marriage and family therapists do not permit students, employees or supervisees to perform or to hold themselves out as competent to perform professional services beyond their training, level of experience, and competence.

## 5. Responsibility to the Profession

**Marriage and family therapists respect the rights and responsibilities of professional colleagues; carry out research in an ethical manner; and participate in activities which advance the goals of the profession.**

5.1 Marriage and family therapists remain accountable to the standards of the profession when acting as members or employees of organizations.

5.2 Marriage and family therapists assign publication credit to those who have contributed to a publication in proportion to their contributions and in accordance with customary professional publication practices.

5.3 Marriage and family therapists who are the authors of books or other materials that are published or distributed should cite appropriately persons to whom credit for original ideas is due.

5.4 Marriage and family therapists who are the authors of books or other materials published or distributed by an organization take reasonable precautions to ensure that the organization promotes and advertises the materials accurately and factually.

5.5 Marriage and family therapists, as researchers, must be adequately informed of and abide by relevant laws and regulations regarding the conduct of research with human participants.

5.6 Marriage and family therapists recognize a responsibility to participate in activities that contribute to a better community and society, including devoting a portion of their professional activity to services for which there is little or no financial return.

5.7 Marriage and family therapists are concerned with developing laws and regulations pertaining to marriage and family therapy that serve the public interest, and with altering such laws and regulations that are not in the public interest.

5.8 Marriage and family therapists encourage public participation in the designing and delivery of services and in the regulation of practitioners.

# 6. Fees

**Marriage and family therapists make financial arrangements with clients that conform to accepted professional practices and that are reasonably understandable.**

6.1 Marriage and family therapists do not offer or accept payment for referrals.

6.2 Marriage and family therapists do not charge excessive fees for services.

6.3 Marriage and family therapists disclose their fee structure to clients at the onset of treatment.

# 7. Advertising

**Marriage and family therapists engage in appropriate informational activities, including those that enable laypersons to choose marriage and family services on an informed basis.**

7.1 Marriage and family therapists accurately represent their competence, education, training, and experience relevant to their practice of marriage and family therapy.

7.2 Marriage and family therapists claim as evidence of educational qualifications only those degrees (a) from regionally-accredited institutions or (b) from institutions accredited by states which license or certify marriage and family therapists, but only if such regulation is recognized by AAMFT.

7.3 Marriage and family therapists assure that advertisements and publications, whether in directories, announcement cards, newspapers, or on radio or television, are formulated to convey information that is necessary for the public to make an appropriate selection. Information could include:

1. office information, such as name, address, telephone number, credit card acceptability, fee structure, languages spoken, and office hours;

2. appropriate degrees, state licensure and/or certification, and AAMFT Clinical Member status; and

3. description of practice.

7.4 Marriage and family therapists do not use a name which could mislead the public concerning the identity, responsibility, source, and status of those practicing under that name and do not hold themselves out as being partners or associates of a firm if they are not.

7.5 Marriage and family therapists do not use any professional identification (such as a professional card, office sign, letterhead, or telephone or association directory listing), if it includes a statement or claim that is false, fraudulent, misleading, or deceptive. A statement is false, fraudulent, misleading, or deceptive if it (a) contains a material misrepresentation of fact; (b) fails to state any material fact necessary to make the statement, in light of all circumstances, not misleading; or (c) is intended to or is likely to create an unjustified expectation.

7.6 Marriage and family therapists correct, wherever possible, false, misleading, or inaccurate information and representations made by others concerning the marriage and family therapist's qualifications, services, or products.

7.7 Marriage and family therapists make certain that the qualifications of persons in their employ are represented in a manner that is not false, misleading, or deceptive.

7.8 Marriage and family therapists may represent themselves as specializing within a limited area of marriage and family therapy, but may not hold themselves out as specialists without being able to provide evidence of training, education, and supervised experience in settings which meet recognized professional standards.

7.9 Marriage and family therapist Clinical Members—not associates, students or organizations—may identify their membership in AAMFT in public information or advertising materials.

7.10 Marriage and family therapists may not use the initials AAMFT following their name in the manner of an academic degree.

7.11 Marriage and family therapists may not use the AAMFT logo. The Association (which is the sole owner of its name, logo, and the abbreviated initials AAMFT) and its committees and regional divisions, operating as such, may use the logo. A regional division of AAMFT may use the AAMFT insignia to list its individual members as a group (e.g., in the Yellow Pages), when all Clinical Members practicing within a directory district have been invited to list themselves in the directory, any one or more members may do so.

7.12 Marriage and family therapists use their membership in AAFMT only in connection with their clinical and professional activities.

Violations of this Code should be brought to the attention of the AAMFT Committee on Ethics and Professional Practices, in writing, at the central office of AAMFT, 1717 K Street, N.W., Suite 407, Washington, D.C. 20006.

# Ethical Guidelines for Group Leaders of the Association for Specialists in Group Work

## PREAMBLE

One characteristic of any professional group is the possession of a body of knowledge and skills and mutually acceptable ethical standards for putting them into practice. Ethical standards consist of those principles which have been formally and publicly acknowledged by the membership of a profession to serve as guidelines governing professional conduct, discharge of duties, and resolution of moral dilemmas. In this document, the Association for Specialists in Group Work has identified the standards of conduct necessary to maintain and regulate the high standards of integrity and leadership among its members.

The Association for Specialists in Group Work recognizes the basic commitment of its members to the Ethical Standards of its parent organization, the American Personnel & Guidance Association and nothing in this document shall be construed to supplant that code. These standards are intended to complement the APGA standards in the area of group work by clarifying the nature of ethical responsibility of the counselor in the group setting and by stimulating a greater concern for competent group leadership.

The following ethical guidelines have been organized under three categories: the leader's responsibility for providing information about group work to clients, the group leader's responsibility for providing group counseling services to clients, and the group leader's responsibility for safeguarding the standards of ethical practice.

Approved by the ASGW Executive Board, November 11, 1980.

## A. RESPONSIBILITY FOR PROVIDING INFORMATION ABOUT GROUP WORK AND GROUP SERVICES

A-1.   Group leaders shall fully inform group members, in advance and preferably in writing, of the goals in the group, qualifications of the leader, and procedures to be employed.

A-2.   The group leader shall conduct a pre-group interview with each prospective member for purposes of screening, orientation, and insofar as possible, shall select group members whose needs and goals are compatible with the established goals of the group; who will not impede the group process; and whose well-being will not be jeopardized by the group experience.

A-3.   Group leaders shall protect members by defining clearly what confidentiality means, why it is important, and the difficulties involved in enforcement.

A-4.   Group leaders shall explain, as realistically as possible, exactly what services can and cannot be provided within the particular group structure offered.

A-5.   Group leaders shall provide prospective clients with specific information about any specialized or experimental activities in which they may be expected to participate.

A-6.   Group leaders shall stress the personal risks involved in any group, especially regarding potential life-changes, and help group members explore their readiness to face these risks.

A-7.   Group leaders shall inform members that participation is voluntary and that they may exit from the group at any time.

A-8.   Group leaders shall inform members about recording of sessions and how tapes will be used.

## B. RESPONSIBILITY FOR PROVIDING GROUP SERVICES TO CLIENTS

B-1.   Group leaders shall protect member rights against physical threats, intimidation, coercion, and undue peer pressure insofar as is reasonably possible.

B-2.   Group leaders shall refrain from imposing their own agendas, needs, and values on group members.

B-3. Group leaders shall insure to the extent that it is reasonably possible that each member has the opportunity to utilize group resources and interact within the group by minimizing barriers such as rambling and monopolizing time.

B-4. Group leaders shall make every reasonable effort to treat each member individually and equally.

B-5. Group leaders shall abstain from inappropriate personal relationships with members throughout the duration of the group and any subsequent professional involvement.

B-6. Group leaders shall help promote independence of members from the group in the most efficient period of time.

B-7. Group leaders shall not attempt any technique unless thoroughly trained in its use or under supervision by an expert familiar with the intervention.

B-8. Group leaders shall not condone the use of alcohol or drugs directly prior to or during group sessions.

B-9. Group leaders shall make every effort to assist clients in developing their personal goals.

B-10. Group leaders shall provide between-session consultation to group members and follow-up after termination of the group, as needed or requested.

## C. RESPONSIBILITY FOR SAFEGUARDING ETHICAL PRACTICE

C-1. Group leaders shall display these standards or make them available to group members.

C-2. Group leaders have the right to expect ethical behavior from colleagues and are obligated to rectify or disclose incompetent, unethical behavior demonstrated by a colleague by taking the following actions:

(a) To confront the individual with the apparent violation of ethical guidelines for the purposes of protecting the safety of any clients and to help the group leader correct any inappropriate behaviors.

(b) Such a complaint should be made in writing including the specific facts and dates of the alleged violation and all relevant supporting data. The complaint should be forwarded to:

The Ethics Committee,
c/o The President
Association for Specialists in Group Work
5999 Stevenson Avenue
Alexandria, Virginia 22304

The envelope must be marked "CONFIDENTIAL" in order to assure confidentiality for both the accuser(s) and the alleged violator(s). Upon receipt, the President shall (a) check on membership status of the charged member(s), (b) confer with legal counsel, and (c) send the case with all pertinent documents to the chairperson of the ASGW Ethics Committee within ten (10) working days after the receipt of the complaint.

(c) If it is determined by the Ethics and Professional Standards Committee that the alleged breach of ethical conduct constitutes a violation of the "Ethical Guidelines," then an investigation will be started within ten (10) days by at least one member of the Committee plus two additional ASGW members in the locality of the alleged violation. The investigating committee chairperson shall: (a) acknowledge receipt of the complaint, (b) review the complaint and supporting data, (c) send a letter of acknowledgment to the member(s) of the complaint regarding alleged violations along with a request for a response and relevant information related to the complaint and (d) inform members of the Ethics Committee by letter of the case and present a plan of action for investigation.

(d) All information, correspondence, and activities of the Ethics Committee will remain confidential. It shall be determined that no person serving as an investigator on a case have any disqualifying relationship with the alleged violator(s).

(e) The charged party(ies) will have not more than 30 days in which to answer the charges in writing. The charged party(ies) will have free access to all cited evidence from which to make a defense, including the right to legal counsel and a formal hearing before the ASGW Ethics Committee.

*(f)* Based upon the investigation of the Committee and any designated local ASGW members one of the following recommendations may be made to the Executive Board for appropriate action:

1. Advise that the charges be dropped.

2. Reprimand and admonishment against repetition of the charged conduct.

3. Notify the charged member(s) of his/her right to a formal hearing before the ASGW Ethics Committee, and request a response be made to the Ethics Chairperson as to his/her decision on the matter. Such hearing would be conducted in accordance with the APGA Policy and Procedures for Processing Complaints of Ethical Violations, "Procedures for Hearings," and would be scheduled for a time coinciding with the annual APGA convention. Conditions for such hearing shall also be in accordance with the APGA Policy and Procedures document, "Options Available to the Ethics Committee, item 3."

4. Suspension of membership for a specified period from ASGW.

5. Dismissal from membership in ASGW.

# Code of Ethics for Certified Clinical Mental Health Counselors of the National Academy of Certified Clinical Mental Health Counselors

## PREAMBLE

Certified Clinical Mental Health Counselors believe in the dignity and worth of the individual. They are committed to increasing knowledge of human behavior and understanding of themselves and others. While pursuing these endeavors, they make every reasonable effort to protect the welfare of those who seek their services or of any subject that may be the object of study. They use their skills only for purposes consistent with these values and do not knowingly permit their misuse by others. While demanding for themselves freedom of inquiry and communication, certified clinical mental health counselors accept the responsibility this freedom confers: competence, objectivity in the application of skills and concern for the best interests of clients, colleagues, and society in general. In the pursuit of these ideals, clinical mental health counselors subscribe to the following principles:

## PRINCIPLE 1. RESPONSIBILITY

In their commitment to the understanding of human behavior, clinical mental health counselors value objectivity and integrity, and in providing services they maintain the highest standards. They accept responsibility for the consequences of their work and make every effort to insure that their services are used appropriately.

a. Clinical mental health counselors accept ultimate responsibility for selecting appropriate areas for investigation and the methods relevant to minimize the possibility that their finding will be misleading. They provide thorough discussion of the limitations of their data and alternative hypotheses, especially where their work touches on social policy or might be misconstrued to the detriment of specific age, sex, ethnic, socioeconomic, or other social categories. In publishing reports of their work, they never discard observations that may modify the interpretation of results. Clinical mental health counselors take credit only for the work they have actually done. In pursuing research, clinical mental health counselors ascertain that their efforts will not lead to changes in individuals or organizations unless such changes are part of the agreement at the time of obtaining informed consent. Clinical mental health counselors clarify in advance the expectations for sharing and utilizing research data. They avoid dual relationships which may limit objectivity, whether theoretical, political, or monetary, so that interference with data, subjects, and milieu is kept to a minimum.

b. As employees of an institution or agency, clinical mental health counselors have the responsibility of remaining alert to institutional pressures which may distort reports of counseling findings or use them in ways counter to the promotion of human welfare.

c. When serving as members of governmental or other organizational bodies, clinical mental health counselors remain accountable as individuals to the Code of Ethics of the National Academy of Certified Mental Health Counselors.

d. As teachers, clinical mental health counselors recognize their primary obligation to help others acquire knowledge and skill. They maintain high standards of scholarship and objectivity by presenting counseling information fully and accurately, and by giving appropriate recognition to alternative viewpoints.

e. As practitioners, clinical mental health counselors know that they bear a heavy social responsibility because their recommendations and professional actions may alter the lives of others. They, therefore remain fully cognizant of their impact and alert to personal, social, organizational, financial or political situations or pressures which might lead to misuse of their influence.

f. Clinical mental health counselors provide reasonable and timely feedback to employees, trainees, supervisors, students and others whose work they may evaluate.

## PRINCIPLE 2. COMPETENCE

The maintenance of high standards of professional competence is a responsibility shared by all clinical mental health counselors in the interest of the public and the profession as a whole. Clinical mental health counselors recognize the boundaries of their competence and the limitations of their techniques and only provide services, use techniques, or offer opinions as professionals that meet recognized standards. Throughout their careers, clinical mental health counselors maintain knowledge of professional information related to the services they render.

a. Clinical mental health counselors accurately represent their competence, education, training and experience.

b. As teachers, clinical mental health counselors perform their duties based on careful preparation so that their instruction is accurate, up-to-date and scholarly.

c. Clinical mental health counselors recognize the need for continuing training to prepare themselves to serve persons of all ages and cultural backgrounds. They are open to new procedures and sensitive to differences between groups of people and changes in expectations and values over time.

d. Clinical mental health counselors with the responsibility for decisions involving individuals or policies based on test results should know and understand literature relevant to the tests used and testing problems with which they deal.

e. Clinical mental health counselors/practitioners recognize that their effectiveness depends in part upon their ability to maintain sound interpersonal relations, that temporary or more enduring aberrations on their part may interfere with their abilities or distort their appraisals of others. Therefore, they refrain from undertaking any activity in which their personal problems are likely to lead to inadequate professional services or harm to a client, or, if they are already engaged in such activity when they become aware of their personal problems, they would seek competent professional assistance to determine whether they should suspend or terminate services to one or all of their clients.

## PRINCIPLE 3. MORAL AND LEGAL STANDARDS

Clinical mental health counselors' moral, ethical and legal standards of behavior are a personal matter to the same degree as they are for any other citizen, except as these may compromise the fulfillment of their professional responsibilities, or reduce the trust in counseling or counselors held by the general public. Regarding their own behavior, clinical mental health counselors should be aware of the prevailing community standards and of the possible impact upon the quality of professional services provided by their conformance to or deviation from these standards. Clinical mental health counselors should also be aware of the possible impact of their public behavior upon the ability of colleagues to perform their professional duties.

a. To protect public confidence in the profession of counseling, clinical mental health counselors will avoid public behavior that is clearly in violation of accepted moral and legal standards.
b. To protect students, counselors/teachers will be aware of the diverse backgrounds of students and, when dealing with topics that may give offense, will see that the material is treated objectively, that it is clearly relevant to the course, and that it is treated in a manner for which the student is prepared.
c. Providers of counseling services conform to the statutes relating to such services as established by their state and its regulating professional board(s).
d. As employees, clinical mental health counselors refuse to participate in employer's practices which are inconsistent with the moral and legal standards established by federal or state legislation regarding the treatment of employees or of the public. In particular and for example, clinical mental

health counselors will not condone practices which result in illegal or otherwise unjustifiable discrimination on the basis of race, sex, religion or national origin in hiring, promotion or training.

e. In providing counseling services to clients clinical mental health counselors avoid any action that will violate or diminish the legal and civil rights of clients or of others who may be affected by the action.

f. Sexual conduct, not limited to sexual intercourse, between clinical mental health counselors and clients is specifically in violation of this code of ethics. This does not, however, prohibit the use of explicit instructional aids including films and video tapes. Such use is within accepted practices of trained and competent sex therapists.

## PRINCIPLE 4. PUBLIC STATEMENTS

Clinical mental health counselors in their professional roles may be expected or required to make public statements providing counseling information, professional opinions, or supply information about the availability of counseling products and services. In making such statements, clinical mental health counselors take full account of the limits and uncertainties of present counseling knowledge and techniques. They represent, as objectively as possible, their professional qualifications, affiliations, and functions, as well as those of the institutions or organizations with which the statements may be associated. All public statements, announcements of services, and promotional activities should serve the purpose of providing sufficient information to aid the consumer public in making informed judgments and choices on matters that concern it.

a. When announcing professional services, clinical mental health counselors limit the information to: name, highest relevant degree conferred, certification or licensure, address, telephone number, office hours, cost of services, and a brief explanation of the types of services offered but not evaluative as to their quality of uniqueness. They will not contain testimonials by implication. They will not claim uniqueness of skill or methods beyond those available to others in the profession unless determined by acceptable and public scientific evidence.

b. In announcing the availability of counseling services or products, clinical mental health counselors will not display their affiliations with organizations or agencies in a manner that implies the sponsorship or certification of the organization or agency. They will not name their employer or professional associations unless the services are in fact to be provided by or under the responsible, direct supervision and continuing control of such organizations or agencies.

c. Clinical mental health counselors associated with the development or promotion of counseling devices, books, or other products offered for commercial sale will make every effort to insure that announcements and advertisement are presented in a professional and factually informative manner without unsupported claims of superiority. Such claims must be supported by scientifically acceptable evidence or by willingness to aid and encourage independent professional scrutiny or scientific test.

d. Clinical mental health counselors engaged in radio, television or other public media activities will not participate in commercial announcements recommending to the general public the purchase or use of any proprietary or single-source product or service.

e. Clinical mental health counselors who describe counseling or the services of professional counselors to the general public accept the obligation to present the material fairly and accurately, avoiding misrepresentation through sensationalism, exaggeration or superficiality. Clinical mental health counselors will be guided by the primary obligation to aid the public in forming their own informed judgments, opinions and choices.

f. As teachers, clinical mental health counselors ensure that statements in catalogs and course outlines are accurate, particularly in terms of subject matter to be covered, bases for grading, and nature of classroom experiences. As practitioners providing private services, CMH counselors avoid improper, direct solicitation of clients and the conflict of interest inherent therein.

g. Clinical mental health counselors accept the obligation to correct others who may represent their professional qualifications or associations with products or services in a manner incompatible with these guidelines.

## PRINCIPLE 5. CONFIDENTIALITY

Clinical mental health counselors have a primary obligation to safeguard information about individuals obtained in the course of teaching, practice, or research. Personal information if communicated to others only with the person's written consent or in those circumstances where there is clear and imminent danger to the client, to others or to society. Disclosures of counseling information are restricted to what is necessary, relevant, and verifiable.

a. All materials in the official record shall be shared with the client who shall have the right to decide what information may be shared with anyone beyond the immediate provider of service and to be informed of the implications of the materials to be shared.

b. The anonymity of clients served in public and other agencies is preserved, if at all possible, by withholding names and personal identifying data. If external conditions require reporting such information, the client shall be so informed.

c. Information received in confidence by one agency or person shall not be forwarded to another person or agency without the client's written permission.

d. Service providers have a responsibility to insure the accuracy and to indicate the validity of data shared with their parties.

e. Case reports presented in classes, professional meetings, or in publications shall be so disguised that no identification is possible unless the client or responsible authority has read the report and agreed in writing to its presentation or publication.

f. Counseling reports and records are maintained under conditions of security and provisions are made for their destruction when they have outlived their usefulness. Clinical mental health counselors insure that privacy and confidentiality are maintained by all persons in the employ or volunteers, and community aides.

g. Clinical mental health counselors who ask that an individual reveal personal information in the course of interviewing, testing or evaluation, or who allow such information to be divulged, do so only after making certain that the person or authorized representative is fully aware of the purposes of the interview, testing or evaluation and of the ways in which the information will be used.

h. Sessions with clients are taped or otherwise recorded only with their written permission or the written permission of a responsible guardian. Even with guardian written consent one should not record a session against the expressed wishes of a client.

i. Where a child or adolescent is the primary client, the interests of the minor shall be paramount.

j. In work with families, the rights of each family member should be safeguarded. The provider of service also has the responsibility to discuss the contents of the record with the parent and/or child, as appropriate, and to keep separate those parts which should remain the property of each family member.

## PRINCIPLE 6. WELFARE OF THE CONSUMER

Clinical mental health counselors respect the integrity and protect the welfare of the people and groups with whom they work. When there is a conflict of interest between the client and the clinical mental health counselor employing institution, the clinical mental health counselors clarify the nature and direction of their loyalties and responsibilities and keep all parties informed of their commitments. Clinical mental health counselors fully inform consumers as to the purpose and nature of any evaluative treatment, educational or training procedure, and they freely acknowledge that clients, students, or subjects have freedom of choice with regard to participation.

a. Clinical mental health counselors are continually cognizant both of their own needs and of their inherently powerful position vis-à-vis clients, in order to avoid exploiting the client's trust and dependency. Clinical mental health counselors make every effort to avoid dual relationships with clients and/or relationships which might impair their professional judgment or increase the risk of client exploitation. Examples of such dual relationships include treating an employee or supervisor, treating a close friend or family relative and sexual relationships with clients.

b. Where clinical mental health counselors' work with members of an organization goes beyond reasonable conditions of employment, clinical mental health counselors recognize possible conflicts of interests that may arise. When such conflicts occur, clinical mental health counselors clarify the nature of the conflict and inform all parties of the nature and directions of the loyalties and responsibilities involved.

c. When acting as supervisors, trainers, or employers, clinical mental health counselors accord recipients informed choice, confidentiality, and protection from physical and mental harm.

d. Financial arrangements in professional practice are in accord with professional standards that safeguard the best interests of the client and that are clearly understood by the client in advance of billing. This may best be done by the use of a contract. Clinical mental health counselors are responsible for assisting clients in finding needed services in those instances where payment of the usual fee would be a hardship. No commission or rebate or other form of remuneration may be given or received for referral of clients for professional services, whether by an individual or by an agency.

e. Clinical mental health counselors are responsible for making their services readily accessible to clients in a manner that facilitates the client's ability to make an informed choice when selecting a service provider. This responsibility includes a clear written description of what the client may expect in the way of tests, reports, billing, therapeutic regime and schedules.

f. Clinical mental health counselors who find that their services are not beneficial to the client have the responsibility to make this known to the responsible persons.

g. Clinical mental health counselors are accountable to the parties who refer and support counseling services and to the general public and are cognizant of the indirect or long-range effects of their intervention.

h. The clinical mental health counselor attempts to terminate a private service or consulting relationship when it is reasonably clear to the clinical mental health counselor that the consumer is not benefiting from it. If a consumer is receiving services from another mental health professional, clinical mental health counselors do not offer their services directly to the consumer without informing the professional persons already involved in order to avoid confusion and conflict for the consumer.

## PRINCIPLE 7. PROFESSIONAL RELATIONSHIP

Clinical mental health counselors act with due regard to the needs and feelings of their colleagues in counseling and other professions. Clinical mental health counselors respect the prerogatives and obligations of the institutions or organizations with which they are associated.

a. Clinical mental health counselors understand the areas of competence of related professions and make full use of other professional, technical, and administrative resources which best serve the interests of consumers. The absence of formal relationships with other professional workers does not relieve clinical mental health counselors from the responsibility of securing for their clients the best possible professional service; indeed, this circumstance presents a challenge to the professional competence of clinical mental health counselors, requiring special sensitivity to problems outside their areas of training, and foresight, diligence, and tact in obtaining the professional assistance needed by clients.

b. Clinical mental health counselors know and take into account the traditions and practices of other professional groups with which they work and cooperate fully with members of such groups when research, services, and other functions are shared or in working for the benefit of public welfare.

c. Clinical mental health counselors strive to provide positive conditions for those they employ and that they spell out clearly the conditions of such employment. They encourage their employees to engage in activities that facilitate their further professional development.

d. Clinical mental health counselors respect the viability, reputation, and the proprietary right of organizations which they serve. Clinical mental health counselors show due regard for the interest of their present or prospective employers. In those instances where they are critical of policies, they attempt to effect change by constructive action within the organization.

e. In the pursuit of research, clinical mental health counselors give sponsoring agencies, host institutions, and publication channels the same respect and opportunity for giving informed consent that they accord to individual research participants. They are aware of their obligation to future research workers and insure that host institutions are given feedback information and proper acknowledgment.

f. Credit is assigned to those who have contributed to a publication, in proportion to their contribution.

g. When a clinical mental health counselor violates ethical standards, clinical mental health counselors who know firsthand of such activities should, if possible, attempt to rectify the situation. Failing an informal solution, clinical mental health counselors should bring such unethical activities to the National Academy of Certified Clinical Mental Health Counselors.

## PRINCIPLE 8. UTILIZATION OF ASSESSMENT TECHNIQUES

In the development, publication, and utilization of counseling assessment techniques, clinical mental health counselors follow relevant standards. Individuals examined, or their legal guardians, have the right to know the results, the interpretations made, and where appropriate, the particulars on which final judgment was based. Test users should take precautions to protect test security but not at the expense of an individual's right to understand the basis for decisions that adversely affect that individual or that individual's dependents.

a. The client has the right to have and the provider has the responsibility to give explanations of test results in language the client can understand.

b. When a test is published or otherwise made available for operational use, it should be accompanied by a manual (or other published or readily available information) that makes every reasonable effort to describe fully the development of the test, the rationale, specifications followed in writing items, analysis or other research. The test, the manual, the record forms and other accompanying material should help users make correct interpretations of the test results and should warn against common misuses. The test manual should state explicitly the purposes and applications for which the test is recommended and identify any special qualifications required to administer the test and to interpret it properly. Evidence of validity and reliability, along with other relevant research data, should be presented in support of any claims made.

c. Norms presented in test manuals should refer to defined and clearly described populations. These populations should be the groups with whom users of the test will ordinarily wish to compare the persons tested. Test users should consider the possibility of bias in tests or in test items. When indicated, there should be an investigation of possible differences in validity for ethnic, sex, or other subsamples that can be identified when the test is given.

d. Clinical mental health counselors who have the responsibility for decisions about individuals or policies that are based on test results should have a thorough understanding of counseling or educational measurement and of validation and other test research.

e. Clinical mental health counselors should develop procedures for systematically eliminating from data files test score information that has, because of the lapse of time, become obsolete.

f. Any individual or organization offering test scoring and interpretation services must be able to demonstrate that their programs are based on appropriate research to establish the validity of the programs and procedures used in arriving at interpretations. The public offering of an automated test interpretation service will be considered as a professional-to-professional consultation. In this the formal responsibility of the consultant is to the consultee but his/her ultimate and overriding responsibility is to the client.

g. Counseling services for the purpose of diagnosis, treatment, or personalized advice are provided only in the context of a professional relationship, and are not given by means of public lectures or demonstrations, newspapers or magazine articles, radio or television programs, mail or similar media. The preparation of personnel reports and recommendations based on test data secured solely by mail is unethical unless such appraisals are an integral part of a continuing client relationship with a company, as a result of which the consulting clinical mental health counselor has intimate knowledge of the client's personal situation and can be assured thereby that his written appraisals will be adequate to the purpose and will be properly interpreted by the client. These reports must not be embellished with such detailed analyses of the subject's personality traits as would be appropriate only for intensive interviews with the subjects.

## PRINCIPLE 9. PURSUIT OF RESEARCH ACTIVITIES

The decision to undertake research should rest upon a considered judgment by the individual clinical mental health counselor about how best to contribute to counseling and to human welfare. Clinical mental health counselors carry out their investigations with respect for the people who participate and with concern for their dignity and welfare.

a. In planning a study the investigator has the personal responsibility to make a careful evaluation of its ethical acceptability, taking into account the following principles for research with human beings. To the extent that this appraisal, weighing scientific and humane values, suggest a deviation from any principle, the investigator incurs an increasingly serious obligation to seek ethical advice and to observe more stringent safeguards to protect the rights of the human research participants.

b. Clinical mental health counselors know and take into account the traditions and practices of other professional groups with members of such groups when research, services, and other functions are shared or in working for the benefit of public welfare.

c. Ethical practice requires the investigator to inform the participant of all features of the research that reasonably might be expected to influence willingness to participate, and to explain all other aspects of the research about which the participant inquires. Failure to make full disclosure gives added emphasis to the investigator's abiding responsibility to protect the welfare and dignity of the research participant.

d. Openness and honesty are essential characteristics of the relationship between investigator and research participant. When the methodological requirements of a study necessitate concealment or deception, the investigator is required to insure as soon as possible the participant's understanding of the reasons for this action and to restore the quality of the relationship with the investigator.

e. In the pursuit of research, clinical mental health counselors give sponsoring agencies, host institutions, and publication channels the same respect and opportunity for giving informed consent that they accord to individual research participants. They are aware of their obligation to future research workers and insure that host institutions are given feedback information and proper acknowledgment.

f. Credit is assigned to those who have contributed to a publication, in proportion to their contribution.

g. The ethical investigator protects participants from physical and mental discomfort, harm and danger. If the risk of such consequences exists, the investigator is required to inform the participant of that fact, secure consent before proceeding, and take all possible measures to minimize distress. A research procedure may not be used if it is likely to cause serious and lasting harm to participants.

h. After the data are collected, ethical practice requires the investigator to provide the participant with a full clarification of the nature of the study and to remove any misconceptions that may have arisen. Where scientific or humane values justify delaying or withholding information, the investigator acquires a special responsibility to assure that there are no damaging consequences for the participants.

i. Where research procedures may result in undesirable consequences for the participant, the investigator has the responsibility to detect and remove or correct these consequences, including, where relevant, long-term after effects.

j. Information obtained about the research participants during the course of an investigation is confidential. When the possibility exists that others may obtain access to such information, ethical research practice requires that the possibility, together with the plans for protecting confidentiality, be explained to the participants as a part of the procedure for obtaining informed consent.

# *Credentialing Information*

Information on counselor certifications can be obtained from:

American Art Therapy Association
5999 Stevenson Avenue
Alexandria, VA 22304

American Association for Marriage and Family Therapy
1717 K Street, N.W.
Suite 407
Washington, DC 20006

American Dance Therapy Association
Suite 230, 2000 Century Plaza
Columbia, MD 21044

Commission on Rehabilitation Counselor Certification
162 North State Street
Suite 317
Chicago, IL 60601

National Academy for Certified Clinical Mental Health Counselors
5999 Stevenson Avenue
Alexandria, VA 22304

National Association for Music Therapy
P.O. Box 610
Lawrence, KS 66044

National Association for Poetry Therapy
225 Williams Street
Huron, OH 44839

National Board for Certified Counselors, Inc.
5999 Stevenson Avenue
Alexandria, VA 22304

National Council for Credentialing of Career Counselors
c/o NBCC
5999 Stevenson Avenue
Alexandria, VA 22304

Information on program accreditations and licensures for
counselors and psychologists, respectively, can be obtained from:

American Association for Counseling and Development
5999 Stevenson Avenue
Alexandria, VA 22304

American Psychological Association
1200 Seventeenth Street, N.W.
Washington, DC 20036

# Counseling-Related Organizations

American Association for Counseling and Development
5999 Stevenson Avenue
Alexandria, VA 22304

*Divisions:*

Association for Adult Development and Aging

American College Personnel Association

Association for Counselor Education and Supervision

National Career Development Association

Association for Humanistic Education and Development

American School Counselor Association

American Rehabilitation Counseling Association

Association for Measurement and Evaluation in Counseling and Development

National Employment Counselors Association

Association for Multicultural Counseling and Development

Association for Religious and Value Issues in Counseling

Association for Specialists in Group Work

American Mental Health Counselors Association

Public Offender Counselor Association

Military Educators and Counselors Association

American Psychological Association
Division 17/Counseling Psychology
1200 Seventeenth Street, N.W.
Washington, DC 20036

American Association for Marriage and Family Therapy
1717 K Street, N.W.
Suite 407
Washington, DC 20006

# NAME INDEX

# SUBJECT INDEX